KNOW YOUR

FASHION ACCESSORIES

KNOW YOUR

FASHION ACCESSORIES

Celia Stall-Meadows

Northeastern State University

FAIRCHILD PUBLICATIONS INC. ▪ NEW YORK

Executive Editor: Olga T. Kontzias
Assistant Acquisitions Editor: Carolyn Purcell
Development Editor: Sylvia L. Weber
Production Editor: Amy Zarkos
Art Director: Adam B. Bohannon
Director of Production: Priscilla Taguer
Editorial Assistant: Suzette Lam
Copy Editor: Words & Numbers
Interior Design: Carla Bolte
Cover Design: Adam B. Bohannon
Cover Illustrations: Julie Johnson

Library of Congress Catalog Card Number: 2002105407
ISBN: 1–56367–245–6
GST R 133004424
Printed in the United States of America

CONTENTS IN BRIEF

Preface xxi
Acknowledgments xxii

PART ONE ▪ AN OVERVIEW OF FASHION ACCESSORIES

Chapter 1. The Fashion Accessories Industry ▪ 3

Chapter 2. Product Development ▪ 28

PART TWO ▪ THE MATERIALS OF FASHION ACCESSORIES

Chapter 3. Textiles and Trims ▪ 45

Chapter 4. Leather ▪ 67

Chapter 5. Fur ▪ 92

Chapter 6. Metals and Stones ▪ 117

PART THREE ▪ THE CATEGORIES OF FASHION ACCESSORIES

Chapter 7. Footwear ▪ 147

Chapter 8. Handbags, Small Personal Goods, Luggage, and Belts ▪ 179

Chapter 9. Socks and Hosiery ▪ 215

Chapter 10. Scarfs, Ties, and Handkerchiefs ▪ 239

Chapter 11. Hats, Hair Accessories, Wigs, and Hairpieces ▪ 259

Chapter 12. Gloves, Umbrellas, and Eyewear ▪ 287

Chapter 13. Fine Jewelry ▪ 327

Chapter 14. Costume Jewelry ▪ 360

Chapter 15. Watches ▪ 380

Bibliography ▪ 403

Index ▪ 416

EXTENDED TABLE OF CONTENTS

PREFACE ▪ xxi

ACKNOWLEDGMENTS ▪ xxii

Part One ▪ An Overview of Fashion Accessories

CHAPTER 1. THE FASHION ACCESSORIES INDUSTRY ▪ 3

What IS the Accessories Industry? ▪ 3
The Fashion Accessories Business 4
Categories of Accessories 5
Why Study Accessories? 5

What Influences Accessories ▪ 6
BOX: TECH TALK: SILICON VALLEY WEDS SEVENTH AVENUE 7

The Fashion Life Cycle ▪ 8
Introduction 8
Rise 9
Culmination 9
Decline 9
Obsolescence 9

Accessories and Apparel ▪ 10

Marketing and Merchandising Accessories ▪ 11
BOX: PROFILE: ACCESSORIESTHESHOW 15

Creating and Selling Accessories ▪ 15
Designing 15
Manufacturing 16
Wholesaling 17
Retailing 17

Career Opportunities ▪ 17

    Assistant Designer 18

    Production Specialist 19

    Junior Sales Representative 19

    Department Manager 19

    Area Sales Manager 20

    Assistant Accessory Buyer 20

    Copywriter 21

    Visual Merchandiser 21

    Store Planner 21

Salaries for Fashion Accessories Careers ▪ 22

Trade Organizations, Publications, and Shows ▪ 22

Summary ▪ 25

CHAPTER 2. PRODUCT DEVELOPMENT ▪ 28

Line and Collection Design ▪ 28

    Styling Versus Designing 29

    The Line Plan 30

    Selecting Colors 30

    BOX: PROFILE: COLOR ASSOCIATION OF THE UNITED STATES 32

    Selecting Materials 33

    Choosing Shapes 33

The Manufacturing Process ▪ 34

    Prototypes and Line Sheets 34

    Precosting 35

    Specifications 36

    Production 36

    Production Schedules 37

    Final Costing 37

    Pricing 37

Manufacturing Considerations ▪ 38

    Internal Manufacturing 38

    External Manufacturing 39

    Domestic Production 39

    Offshore Production 39

Summary ▪ 40

Part Two • The Materials of Fashion Accessories

CHAPTER 3. TEXTILES AND TRIMS • 45

A Brief History of Textiles and Trims • 45

An Introduction to Textiles • 46
Cellulose Fibers 46
PROFILE: THE HEMP CONTROVERSY 47
Protein Fibers 47
Manufactured Fibers 48

The Textile Manufacturing Process • 49
Yarns 49
Fabrications 50

An Introduction to Notions and Trims • 54
Zippers and Pulls 54
Buttons 54
Snaps, Grommets, Velcro®, and Buckles 54
Braid 54
Threads, Lacing, Ribbons, and Bows 54
Artificial Flowers 57
Feathers 57
Shells and Stones 58

Textiles in the Fashion Accessories Industries • 58
How Designers Use Textures 59
Trends in Fabrics, Colors, and Prints 59

The Global Textiles, Notions, and Trims Industry • 60
Trade Organizations, Publications, and Shows 60

Merchandising Trends and Techniques • 63

Summary • 63

CHAPTER 4. LEATHER • 67

A Brief History of Leather • 67

The Leather Industry • 69
The Leather Manufacturing Process 70
Leather Treatments 73

Classifications of Leather 73

Imitation Leather 73

High-Performance Leather 77

Leather Industry Regulations 77

The Leather Fashion Industry ▪ 78

Design of Leather Products 78

BOX: PROFILE: COACH 79

Care of Leather Products 80

BOX: TECH TALK: PRICEY, BUT PRACTICAL 81

The Global Leather Industry ▪ 83

Trade Organizations, Publications, and Shows 85

Merchandising Trends and Techniques ▪ 85

Summary ▪ 89

CHAPTER 5. FUR ▪ 92

A Brief History of Fur ▪ 92

An Introduction to Fur ▪ 94

Fur Dressing and Processing 95

Fur Treatments 95

Fur Product Construction 96

Classifications of Fur ▪ 97

Durability 97

Fur Industry Regulations ▪ 97

Fur Products Labeling Act 97

Endangered Species Act 100

Fur Farming Regulations 100

BOX: FUR CONTROVERSY 101

The Fur Fashion Industry ▪ 101

Design of Fur Products 102

BOX: THE MEDIA AND FURS 103

Faux Fur 104

Care of Fur Products 104

The Global Fur Industry ▪ 105

Fur Auctions 106

Trade Organizations, Publications, and Shows 107

Merchandising Trends and Techniques ▪ 109
    Leased Departments 109
    Home Fashion Accessories 109
    BOX: PROFILE: THE FENDI SISTERS 110
    Internet Retailing 110
    Previously Owned Furs 111

Selling Furs ▪ 112
    Restyling Furs 113
    Price and Value 113

Summary ▪ 114

CHAPTER 6. METALS AND STONES ▪ 117

A Brief History of Metals and Stones ▪ 117

An Introduction to Metals and Stones ▪ 119
    Precious Metals 119
    Plated and Filled Metals 123

Gemstones ▪ 124
    Precious Stones 125
    BOX: THE WORLD'S MOST FAMOUS DIAMONDS 129
    Semi-precious Stones 130
    Other Gems 131
    BOX: RIVALING REAL REARLS 133
    Faux Stones and Gems 133
    Birthstones 134

Care of Metals and Stones ▪ 134
    BOX: OTHER ACCESSORIES MATERIALS 135

Gemstone Industry Regulations ▪ 136

The Global Metals and Stones Industries ▪ 136

Trade Organizations, Publications, and Shows ▪ 137

Merchandising Trends ▪ 137
    BOX: PROFILE: DEBEERS CONSOLIDATED MINES 140

Summary ▪ 141

Part Three · The Categories of Fashion Accessories

CHAPTER 7. FOOTWEAR · 147

A Brief History of Footwear · 147

An Introduction to Footwear · 151
Parts of Footwear 151
Footwear Manufacturing 153

Classifications of Footwear · 155

Design · 155
BOX: IF THE SHOE FITS 157
BOX: TECH TALK: SMART SHOES 159

Care of Footwear · 160

The Global Footwear Industry · 161
The Global Scope of Footwear Production 161
Trade Organizations, Publications, and Shows 163

Merchandising Trends and Techniques · 165
In-Store Retailing 165
BOX: TECH TALK: POI (POINT OF INFORMATION) SYSTEMS 167
Internet Retailing 167
Catalog Retailing 168
Merchandising Techniques 168

Selling Footwear · 168
Price and Value 171
Sizing and Fitting 171
Meeting Customer Needs 173

Summary · 173
Box: FITTING CHILDREN'S SHOES 174
Box: PROFILE: MANOLO BLAHNIK 175

CHAPTER 8. HANDBAGS, SMALL PERSONAL GOODS, LUGGAGE, AND BELTS · 179

A Brief History of Handbags, Small Personal Goods, Luggage, and Belts · 180

Handbags · 182
Parts of a Handbag 183

Handbag Manufacturing 183

BOX: PROFILE: KATE SPADE 186

Basic Styles of Handbags 187

Care of Handbags 187

The Global Handbag, Small Personal Goods, Luggage, and Belts Industries ▪ 189

Manufacturing 189

Trade Organizations, Publications, and Shows 190

Merchandising Trends and Techniques for Handbags ▪ 190

Department Stores 190

Travel Retail Stores 193

Internet Retailing 193

BOX: TECH TALK: TASS CUSTOMIZATION FOR CYBERSHOPPERS 194

Catalog Retailing 194

Selling Handbags ▪ 195

Price and Value 195

Meeting Customer Needs 195

Small Personal Goods ▪ 196

Basic Styles of Small Personal Goods 197

Merchandising Trends and Techniques for Small Personal Goods ▪ 198

Selling Small Personal Goods ▪ 198

Luggage ▪ 199

Luggage Manufacturing 199

BOX: TECH TALK: RIGOROUS TESTING: AMERICAN TOURISTER 200

Design 200

Production 201

Materials 201

Classifications of Luggage ▪ 201

Basic Styles of Luggage 202

Merchandising Trends and Techniques for Luggage ▪ 203

BOX: AIRLINE CARRY-ON REGULATIONS 204

In-Store Retailing 204

Internet Retailing 204

Selling Luggage ▪ 205

Belts ▪ 205

Belt Manufacturing 206

Basic Styles of Belts 206

Belt Sizes 208

Care of Belts 209

Merchandising Trends and Techniques for Belts ▪ 209

Selling Belts 210

Price and Value 210

Summary ▪ 210

CHAPTER 9. SOCKS AND HOSIERY ▪ 215

A Brief History of Socks and Hosiery ▪ 215

An Introduction to Socks and Hosiery ▪ 217

Socks and Hosiery Manufacturing 218

Materials 221

Classifications of Socks and Hosiery 222

Basic Terminology of Socks and Hosiery 222

Care of Socks and Hosiery 224

The Global Socks and Hosiery Industries ▪ 225

Merchandising Trends and Techniques ▪ 228

Store Retailing 228

Internet Retailing 229

Catalog Retailing 230

Selling Socks and Hosiery ▪ 230

Price and Value 230

Sizing and Fitting 231

Meeting Customer Needs 232

BOX: RULES ARE MADE TO BE BROKEN 234

Summary ▪ 235

CHAPTER 10. SCARFS, TIES, AND HANDKERCHIEFS ▪ 239

A Brief History of Scarfs, Ties, and Handkerchiefs ▪ 239

An Introduction to Scarfs, Ties, and Handkerchiefs ▪ 242

Scarfs, Ties, and Handkerchiefs Manufacturing 242

Materials 244

Traditional Tie Patterns 245

BOX: THE FOUR-IN-HAND KNOT AND THE BOW TIE KNOT 246

Tying a Tie 246

Care of Scarfs, Ties, and Handkerchiefs 247

The Global Scarfs, Ties, and Handkerchiefs Industry ▪ 247

Merchandising Trends and Techniques ▪ 249

Store Retailing 250

Internet Retailing 252

Catalog Retailing 253

Selling Scarfs, Ties, and Handkerchiefs ▪ 253

Price and Value 253

BOX: PROFILE: HERMÈS TIES 254

BOX: FOLDING A POCKET SQUARE 255

Meeting Customer Needs 256

Summary ▪ 256

CHAPTER 11. HATS, HAIR ACCESSORIES, WIGS, AND HAIRPIECES ▪ 259

A Brief History of Hats and Hair Accessories ▪ 259

An Introduction to Hats and Hair Accessories ▪ 261

Parts of a Hat 262

Hats and Hair Accessories Manufacturing 262

BOX: PROFILE: PHILIP TREACY 265

Materials 266

BOX: TECH TALK: TURNING HEADS 267

Basic Styles of Hats 267

Basic Styles of Hair Accessories 270

Hat Sizing and Fitting 272

The Global Hat Industry ▪ 273

Merchandising Trends and Techniques ▪ 275

Store Retailing 275

Internet Retailing 276

Catalog Retailing 276

Selling Hats and Hair Accessories ▪ 277

Price and Value 277

Care of Hats 278

Meeting Customer Needs 278

A Brief History of Wigs and Hairpieces ▪ 279

Wigs, Hairpieces, and Toupees ▪ 280
    Merchandising Trends 280
    Price and Value 281
    Care of Wigs and Hairpieces 282
    Meeting Customer Needs 282

Summary ▪ 283

CHAPTER 12. GLOVES, UMBRELLAS, AND EYEWEAR ▪ 287

A Brief History of Gloves ▪ 287

An Introduction to Gloves ▪ 290
    Parts of Gloves 291
    Glove Manufacturing 291
    BOX: TECH TALK: GORE-TEX: GUARANTEED TO KEEP YOU DRY 293
    Basic Styles of Gloves 294
    Glove Fitting and Sizes 295

Care of Gloves ▪ 296

The Global Glove Industry ▪ 297
    Trade Organizations, Publications, and Shows 298

Merchandising Trends and Techniques ▪ 299

Store Retailing ▪ 299
    BOX: PROFILE: TOTES>>ISOTONER 300
    Internet Retailing 300
    Catalog Retailing 301

Selling Gloves ▪ 301
    Price and Value 301
    Meeting Customer Needs 301

A Brief History of Umbrellas ▪ 302

Umbrella Manufacturing ▪ 303
    Design 303
    Parts of the Umbrella 304
    Production 305
    Materials 305
    Basic Styles of Umbrellas 305

The Global Umbrella Industry ▪ 306

Merchandising Trends and Techniques ▪ 307
 Store Retailing 308
 Internet Retailing 308
 Catalog Retailing 308

Selling Umbrellas ▪ 309
 Price and Value 309
 Meeting Customer Needs 309
 Care of Umbrellas 310

A Brief History of Eyewear ▪ 310

An Introduction to Eyewear ▪ 311
 Parts of Eyewear 312
 Styles of Eyewear 312
 Eyewear Manufacturing 313

The Global Eyewear Industry ▪ 315

Merchandising Trends and Techniques ▪ 317
 Store Retailing 318
 Internet Retailing 320
 Catalog Retailing 320

Selling Eyewear ▪ 320
 Price and Value 321
 Meeting Customer Needs 321
 Basic Facial Shapes for Eyewear 321
 Eyewear Do's and Don'ts 321

Summary ▪ 321

CHAPTER 13. FINE JEWELRY ▪ 327

A Brief History of Fine Jewelry ▪ 327

An Introduction to Fine Jewelry ▪ 330
 Vintage and Estate Jewelry 331

Manufacturing Fine Jewelry ▪ 333
 Design 333
 Materials 334
 Production 334

Preparing Stone Settings 335
Metals for Fine Jewelry 336

Jewelry Styles ▪ 336
Necklaces 336
Necklace Lengths 337
Necklace Styles 337
Earrings 337
Earring Fastenings 339
Earring Styles 339
Bracelets 340
Brooches, Pins, and Clips 342
Rings 343
Headpieces 344

The Global Fine Jewelry Industry ▪ 344
Trade Organizations, Publications, and Shows 345

Merchandising Trends and Techniques ▪ 345
Store Retailing 349
Internet Retailing 350
Catalog Retailing 350

Selling Fine Jewelry ▪ 351
BOX: TECH TALK: GEMSTONE ENHANCEMENTS *352*
Price and Value 352
Care of Fine Jewelry 353
Meeting Customer Needs 353
BOX: PROFILE: TIFFANY & COMPANY *354*

Summary ▪ 355

CHAPTER 14. COSTUME JEWELRY ▪ 360

A Brief History of Costume Jewelry ▪ 360

An Introduction to Costume and Bridge Jewelry ▪ 363
Manufacturing Costume Jewelry 363
BOX: PROFILE: THE BLACK CAMEO *367*

Men's Jewelry Styles ▪ 369

The Global Costume Jewelry Industry ▪ 369

Merchandising Trends and Techniques ▪ 372

    Store Retailing 373

    Internet and Television Retailing 374

    Catalog Retailing 375

Selling Costume and Bridge Jewelry ▪ 375

    Price and Value 375

    Sizing 376

    Care of Costume and Bridge Jewelry 376

    Meeting Customer Needs 377

Summary ▪ 377

CHAPTER 15. WATCHES ▪ 380

A Brief History of Watches ▪ 380

An Introduction to Watches ▪ 382

    Parts of a Watch 384

    Functions of a Watch 385

    Watch Manufacturing 386

    BOX: PROFILE: FOSSIL® 387

    BOX: TECH TALK: WRIST TECHNOLOGY: GPS, EDI, PC, TV, AND VCR 389

    Styles of Watches 391

    Shapes of Watchcases 391

The Global Watch Industry ▪ 391

    Trade Organizations, Publications, and Shows 393

Merchandising Trends and Techniques ▪ 393

    Store Retailing 394

    Internet Retailing 396

    Catalog Retailing 397

Selling Watches ▪ 397

    Price and Value 397

    Care of Watches 398

    Meeting Customer Needs 399

Summary ▪ 400

BIBLIOGRAPHY ▪ 403

INDEX ▪ 417

PREFACE

BEYOND THE OBVIOUS ASSUMPTION THAT THE PRODUCTS DESCRIBED IN THIS BOOK ARE ALL fashion accessories, what is the similarity between a pair of dress shoes and an umbrella? Or a leather belt and a diamond ring? They are made of many different materials—some are cut and sewn, while others are molded. Some have life cycles that last for decades, while others last only for a season. Yet they are similar because all are shaped by the same social, economic, political, and environmental influences. These influences, spun together, create the red thread that ties all the accessories categories together in the textbook.

Target Readers

This textbook provides college-level apparel merchandising and marketing students a detailed study of important accessories categories in the women's, men's, and children's fashion industry. It is appropriate for students who have completed the introductory fashion-merchandising course. This includes second-year community college students and third- or fourth-year university students. This book may be useful in a historic costume class or in a current trends and issues class. Finally, this textbook may be helpful as a reference or training book used by retail stores selling any of the products mentioned in the chapters.

Objectives

The objectives of this book are:

- To instill an excitement for the fashion accessories industry and present career opportunities
- To challenge students to be actively engaged in their learning
- To provide parallel coverage of the important fashion accessories categories
- To demonstrate how each unit of the industry affects the other units
- To provide an overview of the historic and contemporary components of accessories so students will be more able to predict the future fashion trends
- To ensure product knowledge competency in graduates of fashion-related programs

Components

The book is divided into three major parts covering an overview, the materials, and the categories of accessories. Part One, An Overview of Fashion Accessories (Chapters 1 and 2), introduces the industries as well as career opportunities. In addition, it summarizes the key stages of product development, regardless of the type of accessory. In Part Two, The Materials of Fashion Accessories (Chapters 3–6), the focus is on the variety of materials used in the manufacture of fashion accessories. These include textiles, notions, trims, leather, fur, metals, and stones. Part Three, The Categories of Fashion Accessories (Chapters 7–15), provides a comprehensive study of the major types of wearable (or carried) fashion accessories. These are:

Chapter 7: Footwear

Chapter 8: Handbags, Small Personal Goods, and Belts

Chapter 9: Socks and Hosiery

Chapter 10: Scarfs, Ties, and Handkerchiefs

Chapter 11: Hats, Hair Accessories, Wigs, and Hairpieces

Chapter 12: Gloves, Umbrellas, and Eyewear

Chapter 13: Fine Jewelry

Chapter 14: Costume Jewelry

Chapter 15: Watches

Careers

One fascinating part of the fashion accessories industries is the diversity of opportunities for students of fashion. This book provides an overview of the fashion accessories business so that students can grasp the basics of this complex mesh of industries. Competent employees are in greater demand, and expectations of college graduates are greater than ever before. In every accessories industry numerous jobs are available to competent college graduates—textiles, notions, and trim manufacturers and sourcing agents, designers and stylists, production supervisors, marketers, store planners, advertisers and promoters, merchandisers, buyers, fashion coordinators, display designers, and the most important of personnel, salespeople. The bottom line is: we manufacture clothing and accessories, but we must sell fashion.

Acknowledgments

The development of this book occurred because of the encouragement and support from family and friends. To my family—Kendall, Faye, Kendra, and Elaine—I owe a special debt of gratitude. To our parents and siblings—thank you for your support and love.

To my college students, both former and present, your interest in learning motivated me to put my teaching into print. To see you as successful professionals in the fashion industry and life in general is a great pleasure and the reason I teach.

My colleagues and other educators in the Family and Consumer Sciences field have been influential in the development of this book. Some of these I studied under, while others I studied with. Particular thanks go to my colleagues and friends at NSU.

Several people have played a very special role in the preparation of this book. My sincere appreciation is extended to the Fairchild editors and staff for this enriching experience. I appreciate the vital role Sylvia Weber played in launching this book; Roberta Moore's meticulous and helpful editing; and help during the critical stages of the book's development from Olga Kontzias, Mary McGarry, Beth Applebome, Amy Zarkos, Suzette Lam, Priscilla Taguer, and Adam Bohannon. A special thanks goes to the talented illustrator of this book, Bina Abling, whose drawings are a perfect fit, and Tana Stufflebean, my mentor and friend.

I also wish to thank the following reviewers, selected by the publisher, for their helpful suggestions: Leo Archambault, Mount Ida College; Martha Baker, University of Massachusetts-Amhearst; Betsey Davis, Florida Community College; Virginia H. Elsasser, Centenary College; Ellen Goldstein, Fashion Institute of Technology; Debra McDowell, Southern Missouri State University; Sarah Moore, Eastern Michigan University; Patricia Morrison, Berkeley College; Karen Schaeffer, University of Delaware; Sue Sharp, University of Southern Mississippi; Tana Stufflebean, University of Central Oklahoma; Phyllis Tortora, Queens College (emerita); Marilayn Van Court, Mississippi Gulf Coast Community College; and Lauretta Welch, Florida State University.

To all these and to any others who may see their influence in this book, I extend my heartfelt thanks.

—C.S.M.

PART ONE

AN OVERVIEW
OF FASHION
ACCESSORIES

CHAPTER 1

✦

THE FASHION ACCESSORIES INDUSTRY

"If you want to dress well, it takes time to look as if it took no time at all."
—American actor, Douglas Fairbanks

"The fickle junior customer may change her mind every week about her favorite outfit and place to shop, but one category is staying at the top of her shopping list: accessories."
—Melanie Kletter *(Feb. 14, 2000), WWDMagic/Junior Accessories,* p. 26

WHAT IS THE ACCESSORIES INDUSTRY?

THE ACCESSORIES INDUSTRY INCLUDES FASHION ITEMS THAT ARE UTILITARIAN AND/OR decorative and complement wearing apparel. For example, an umbrella serves primarily as protection against the elements, but umbrella designers look to the fashion industry to determine the style and colors of umbrellas to produce to create a *total look* for consumers. The accessories industry is comprised of a network of designers, materials and component producers, product manufacturers, retailers, and promoters of fashion accessories.

The fashion accessories industry is a worldwide industry producing products ranging in price from less than one dollar to hundreds of thousand dollars. In the United States alone, the industry is worth more than $25 billion. Whether referring to a plain pair of knee-high hosiery or a bejeweled, handcrafted watch, the accessories industry is keenly tied to current apparel fashions.

The international scope of the industry is evident throughout production. Creative inspirations and design ideas are often developed by U.S. companies. However, because of the labor-intensive production required for the manufacture of accessories components and products, production often occurs in developing countries where the labor costs are lower. Competition from imports is a never-ending and increasing concern for domestic manufacturers of accessories, but for many retailers, lower-priced, imported accessories allow for greater profits. To consumers who demand frequent accessories changes and prefer accessories as an inexpensive way to update their wardrobe, imported goods have price appeal. Although the United States continually loses industry shares in terms of exported goods, the consumption of accessories in the United States continues to grow.

The Fashion Accessories Business

Accessories are available through almost every soft-goods (apparel) distribution channel, including brick-and-mortar stores (department, specialty, discount, etc.), direct mail catalogs, and Internet Web sites. Accessories are available at all price zones, including budget, moderate, better, and designer. Data compiled by the NPD American Shoppers Panel (October 1998-September 1999) from more than 1,400 participating stores are presented in Figure 1.1. The chart shows that department stores sell the greatest amount of accessories.

The high visibility and accessibility of fashion accessories in department stores may account for their significant contribution to store profits. Much of the success of the fashion accessories business is built on the concept of impulse buying at the retail level. Customers may pass an attractive merchandise display, rack, or outpost at a store and impulsively select a reasonably priced accessories item to complement their wardrobe. Businesses at all levels of the industry work together to provide consumers with attractively packaged, priced, and displayed accessories to stimulate unplanned purchases.

Retailers are not the only businesses that benefit from higher profits due to fashion accessories. The sale of accessories has become a major source of revenue for companies that once primarily sold apparel. Today, the designer-level or top-tier clothing collections are frequently financial drains for fashion houses. Accessories lines are used to offset the lagging profits of soft

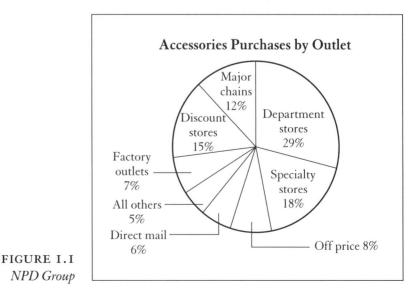

FIGURE 1.1
NPD Group

goods manufacturers. Perfumes have been profitable products sold to support runway fashion shows, but now accessories are helping pay the bills.

In recent years, fashion businesses have relied on computers to more effectively manage inventories. Special tracking systems help reduce the guesswork of ordering what business owners *think* will sell. Computer programs generate relevant data for analysts to track sales trends. An understanding of the direction in which fashions are moving provides companies with greater opportunities to maintain ideal merchandise assortments. That is, they can have the right merchandise, at the right time, in the right places, in the right quantities, at prices their customers are willing to pay.

Categories of Accessories

Fashion accessories include functional and decorative products that extend wardrobes and complement fashion looks. Fashion accessories are available in a variety of materials, textures, colors, shapes, and sizes. This textbook is divided into three sections—an overview of the accessories industry, the materials used in the manufacture of accessories, and the more important accessories categories. Accessories categories discussed in this textbook are footwear, handbags, small personal goods, luggage, belts, socks, hosiery, scarfs, ties, handkerchiefs, hats, hair accessories, gloves, umbrellas, eyewear, fine jewelry, costume jewelry, and watches.

Why Study Accessories?

The question *Why study accessories?* has numerous viable answers. First, apparel and accessories are worn together, so one should not be considered independent of the other—as one changes, the other must also change to complement it. Consumers buy a *total look,* and successful merchandisers must understand how to create this look.

Second, to understand the direction of fashion, students must study the history of fashion. When dealing with personnel in the workplace, it is often said that past performance is a good predictor of future behavior. This is true in the life cycle of fashion goods as well. This textbook provides a look at past fashion accessories and discusses historical events that led to the adoption of these accessories fashions. Once a fashion has been adopted, business representatives must be educated to reasonably predict the fashion life cycle and to identify upcoming trends. For example, the adoption of neckties by women has been a part of accessories fashions several times during the 20th century. Typically considered a male fashion with no functional purpose, one might wonder why the necktie fashion recurs periodically in the women's sector. Does it signal the beginning of a larger social trend—women's assertiveness? Can fashion marketers predict that other masculine accessories will soon follow in popularity for women when neckties appear in fashion? How long will the trend last? These questions aren't easily answered, particularly when a trend is current. However, studying the duration of the trend and the length of time the style was popular in the past helps to draw parallels to contemporary fashions.

Profit is the third reason students should study fashion accessories. Knowledgeable and well-trained salespeople are more likely to be successful in sales. With sales of fashion accessories amounting to billions of dollars in the United States, the accessories business is lucrative for graduates with a detailed understanding of accessories categories.

A fourth reason for students to study fashion accessories is because there are no geographical boundaries limiting this industry. Opportunities are available in major market centers in the United States and in most corners of the world. To students unable to relocate, accessories departments are a part of virtually every fashion store. Cottage industries are common in the accessories industry as well. Enterprising graduates can begin their own fashion accessories collection using the Internet as a retailing channel.

Challenging, exciting, fast paced, and *rewarding* are key words used to describe the unlimited possibilities in the fashion industry. Creative individuals can choose to design or promote accessories. Students skilled in construction or manufacturing methods can pursue a career in production. Students with a talent for verbal or written communication may prefer working as a fashion writer or enjoy the challenge of personal sales.

Regardless of which level of the industry students choose for employment, they will ultimately be business representatives marketing products or services to other consumers (either trade or ultimate). A basic knowledge of the industry will help fashion students identify and understand the needs of others in the industry, making them more marketable to their employers.

WHAT INFLUENCES ACCESSORIES?

Upscale retail stores that buy from designers and vendors launch trends in the accessories industry. Designers struggle with identifying major market trends and creating new ones. Those designers who follow trends, rather than set them, translate others' original ideas into workable designs with a more widespread appeal. Frequently, apparel designers inspire accessories fashion ideas. Ready-to-wear apparel themes including patriotism, orientalism, minimalism, hippie chic, and glam, provide inspiration for fashion-forward accessories designs. These "spin-off" looks work their way from high fashion down to the popular-priced retail departments and fashion stores. This concept is often referred to as the **trickle-down theory.**

When fashion trends in accessories are started by young people—particularly those in low-income families or by youth that adopt low-income lifestyles—it is called the **trickle-up theory.** It is more common in the fashion accessories industry for trends to trickle across from innovative teen buyers at all income levels. Mass production allows for simultaneous introduction of new styles at all price ranges. This **trickle-across theory** was proposed by Charles W. King in 1963. Teenagers at all income levels are the heaviest purchasers of fashion accessories, especially those inspired by their favorite celebrities. Musicians and Hollywood personalities are fashion trendsetters, and teens are often the first to adopt an interesting style featured in a television show, music video, or movie.

Tech Talk: Silicon Valley Weds Seventh Avenue

Technological innovations have a surprising influence on accessories. From eyewear to shoes and jewelry, the marriage of fashion and technology is unusual, yet complementary. Imagine wearing eyeglasses that improve your night vision and can act as a miniature computer screen, or a digital necklace that allows you to send and receive e-mail. Have you considered flashing earrings that actually signal an incoming call? How about a wrist-sized personal digital assistant (PDA) or wristwatch that provides global positioning information (exact earth coordinates) and takes video footage that can be downloaded onto your PC? For your active feet, you can purchase computerized athletic shoes that conform the cushioning to your sports activity or a pair that records your stride length, heart rate, or jump height.

Techno-fashion companies offer these wearable computing products, some of which can be customized to fit the consumers' needs. One company, Thinking Materials, headquartered in Stockholm, Sweden, creates wearable communicators (such as cell phones) out of soft materials. The image on the right shows a handbag embedded with technology. Another innovative company, inViso, in Sunnyvale, California, offers e-shades that resemble popular sunglasses and provide a "big screen" computer viewing experience virtually anywhere.

Trade shows are organized to bring about business partnerships in the wearable computer industry. In October 2001, the Tech-U-Wear conference and exhibition was held in Madison Square Garden in New York City. At the conference, state-of-the-art companies participated in panel discussions and interactive demonstrations of wearable computer applications.

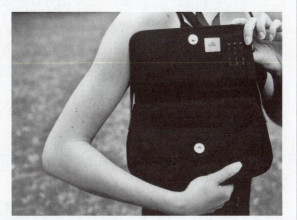

Wearable technology.
Courtesy of Thinking Materials.

The shrinking size and decreasing component costs of wearable computers have contributed to the increasing consumer demand. All of these bells and whistles are great, you say, but only if the *customer* gets to choose the color!

Sources:

Company Information. (n.d.). Retrieved Oct 5, 2001, from http://www.inviso.com; http://www.thinkingmaterials.com, and http://www.tech-u-wear.com

Meyer, M. (Oct. 7, 2000). Wearable Technology is the Latest Fashion Revolution. *St. Louis Post-Dispatch*, p. 32.

Yaukey, J. (Nov. 14, 2000). Computers to Wear. *Muskogee Daily Phoenix*, p. 1–2C.

The economy has a direct effect on the popularity of accessories in general, as well as certain categories of accessories. During periods when the economy is soft, consumers cut back on purchases of trendy designs; however, accessories remain an inexpensive way to update a wardrobe. When the economy is strong, there is increased demand for more fashion looks and trendy merchandise. This relationship has often been discussed, but lacks adequate research testing, although some might refer to it as a **pragmatic fashion accessories theory.**

If an economy is suddenly weakened, as in the extreme case of the catastrophic terrorist attacks in September 2001, the industry is plagued with heavy markdowns and clearance merchandise. Although a weakened economy is one result of a catastrophic event, the same event can inspire designers when creating accessories fashions. For example, the tragic terrorist attacks on the United States in September 2001 created a demand for American-themed merchandise in apparel and accessories. The various U.S. logos and symbols became a popular, genderless, and ageless fashion statement showing national pride.

The rising price of petroleum affects the retail prices of many accessories categories. Oil-based fabrics, such as nylon and polyvinyl chloride (PVC), are commonly used in accessories including hosiery, handbags, backpacks, and luggage.

THE FASHION LIFE CYCLE

As with all fashions, accessories evolve over time and have a complete life cycle. Many categories of accessories, such as fashion jewelry, hair accessories, hosiery, and sunglasses, have a shorter life cycle than ready-to-wear apparel. Classic accessories, including loafers, basic leather handbags, and driving gloves, have a longer life cycle than apparel. The length of time may range from one season to several seasons, yet all accessories ultimately complete the fashion cycle.

There are five stages in the **fashion product life cycle:** introduction, rise, culmination, decline, and obsolescence. Figure 1.2 depicts a product life cycle curve, with the vertical axis representing the level of acceptance and the horizontal axis representing the length of time.

Introduction

New designs are presented to consumers during the **introductory stage** of the fashion cycle. Often, higher-priced accessories created by high-fashion designers offer consumers their first glimpse of a new style. Consumers may see celebrities or public personalities on television or in photographs wearing a specific accessory. For example, actress Sarah Jessica Parker, portraying Carrie Bradshaw on HBO's *Sex and the City,* wore several trendsetting accessories. Her

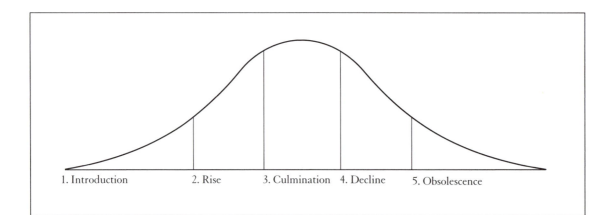

1. Introduction   2. Rise   3. Culmination   4. Decline   5. Obsolescence

FIGURE I.2
A fashion product life cycle curve.

wardrobe, costumed by designers Patricia Field and Rebecca Field, included silk flowers, nameplate necklaces, and fur-trimmed clothing. As a result of the show's promotional power in fashion, Patricia Field and Rebecca Field received a special recognition award for "The Best Accessorized Television Program" presented by the Accessories Council in 2000.

Sometimes new accessories designs are introduced by **street fashions,** which come from groups other than the rich and famous. Examples include ball caps, tattoo-like jewelry, bandana headscarves, denim bags, and some of the hip-hop look accessories.

Rise

The **rise stage** of the fashion life cycle represents the acceptance of a fashion by a limited group of early adopters and a larger group of late adopters. Teenagers are frequently the power-wielding consumers during the early rise stage. The accessories may be more limited and expensive during this stage because the risk of rejection is significant. Assortments are usually complete when an accessory is in the later rise stage and stores advertise complete selections in a variety of colors and sizes at regular prices.

Culmination

The **culmination,** or **peak stage,** of the fashion life cycle occurs when acceptance by fashion followers is widespread. By this time, prices have dropped, and store sales are advertised. Retailers obtain their greatest sales volume during this stage. Everyone that wants the accessory will now have it; however, trendsetters will discard the fashion and introduce a new fashion. Sometimes the culmination stage is extended when a manufacturer introduces a new color or fabrication of an existing style. For example, Keds white canvas tennis shoes were popular in the late 1980s and early 1990s. As the fashion waned, the company introduced colored canvas, then printed canvas, and eventually leather material. By continually introducing a new twist to the existing style, Keds extended the fashion life cycle by several seasons.

Decline

During the **decline stage,** the fashion is still being worn, but stores are closing out inventory and advertising clearance of the few remaining items. The fashion may still be available in some discount and off-price stores.

Obsolescence

By the **obsolescence stage,** only a few fashion laggards continue to wear the accessories fashion. Most people have discarded the style in favor of a current fashion. Closeout outlets may carry the odd-lot assortments.

ACCESSORIES AND APPAREL

The relationship between fashion accessories and apparel is usually complementary. The obvious connection is they are worn together and should complement each other. When clothing is highly ornamented, accessories are more conservative; during fashion seasons in which apparel is tailored or conservative, accessories are more decorative and embellished (see Figure 1.3).

Both fashion categories are influenced by the same environmental factors, such as political, social, and economic climates. Producers of apparel and accessories subscribe to the same color forecasting services, such as the Color Association of the United States. Many times designers produce both apparel and accessories, and often, similar materials and trim are used for both categories.

Major fashion trends cross many product category boundaries, challenging apparel and accessories designers to translate a pervasive trend into saleable products. One of the best examples of a boundless fashion trend in the late 1990s and the early 2000s was animal prints. These prints were available in virtually every apparel and accessories fashion, as well as home fashions.

It is common for an apparel designer to create matching accessories for a collection or to contract with specialty designers like shoe guru Manolo Blahnik or millinery designer Philip Treacy. Apparel manufacturing companies also diversify into related product areas that include accessories, while accessories manufacturing companies get involved in the production of apparel.

FIGURE 1.3
Fashion accessories complement apparel.
Courtesy of Fairchild Publications, Inc.

MARKETING AND MERCHANDISING ACCESSORIES

The ability to adapt to quickly changing accessories trends is important to the success of marketing accessories. Retailers may have difficulty predicting which trends will become important, so flexibility and the ability to adjust to changes are critical. Vendors and retailers are reporting that customers are demanding more rapid fashion changes by quickly adopting and discarding trends. Vendors are forced to develop new products or discover innovative display and packaging concepts to maintain a competitive edge and remain forefront in consumers' minds. Rapidly changing consumer preferences may be because of an increased availability of accessories at lower price points and an increase in discretionary income among teenagers. Companies targeting the teen market understand that this group gets tired of trends more quickly than more mature customers.

Another merchandising challenge is that retailers must maintain an assortment balance between trendier fashion lines and basic core categories (staple goods). Fashion lines should complement the core categories without overpowering the selection. During some seasons, fads outperform basics; at other times core categories, such as brown and black leather goods, can keep an accessories departments afloat.

The concept of **cross-merchandising,** also called cross-pollination or one-stop shopping, refers to offering a related-products presentation to customers. Products may be related by color, texture, lifestyle, function, or gift-giving ideas. For example, the concept of cross-merchandising could be demonstrated in a store with an accessories outpost containing impulse items useful on a summer outing, such as sunglasses, sun visors, plastic sandals, hair clasps, and handbags with cell phone compartments. This presentation would give the customer a powerful merchandising message about complete fashion looks. This type of merchandising is more effective than separating the goods into individual departments and merchandising them with competing products.

Another in-store merchandising technique is to create destination points. A **destination point** is an in-store location that becomes heavily traveled by targeted consumers because of unique merchandise, ideal assortments, cross-merchandised displays, or one-stop shopping. This is particularly appealing to the teen market, which has disposable personal income and is prone to impulse purchasing of accessories. A destination point might be centrally located on the end of a main aisle to draw attention to related items, regardless of their original location in the store. For example, a destination point might be located near the main entrance of the junior department containing cross-merchandised items often found in a teen's bedroom, such as hair accessories, costume jewelry, sleep masks, and makeup accessories. This display would entice shoppers to take notice as they entered the department. The result would be increased sales of profitable accessories.

The junior market, which includes tweens (girls aged 8 to 12) and teens, has become an important market for accessories firms because of its purchasing power and its sheer size. For merchandisers, the junior market can include consumers of any age, from young girls to their mothers who desire a youthful image. In response to this growing market segment, retailers are expanding merchandise lines and developing junior accessories departments containing quick-moving, novel merchandise. The key phrase for retail marketers is *quick-moving*. Teens let trends go as quickly as they adopt them; therefore, overmarketing an accessories trend is especially unsuccessful in the junior accessories market.

An emphasis on housekeeping is a key merchandising tactic used in accessories departments. The physical nature of many accessories does not lend itself to neatness in merchandising—customers typically will not reclose packages, refold, or rehang the merchandise once it has been examined and a decision is made *not* to buy. Therefore, the study of accessories is more than just a product analysis. It includes the study of consumer buying and shopping habits and how merchandisers can best maintain attractive, well-kept displays. Customers are more likely to treat merchandise respectfully if the display is neat and organized. A neat and attractive selling floor leads to increased sales and decreased merchandise theft or damage. Because retailers want to increase sales, students of fashion accessories must also learn about the retail environment.

Some stores contract with outside service companies to maintain the departments, while others rely on sales associates to maintain the departments. These stores that utilize service companies argue that the 15 to 18 percent increase in costs can be built into the retail price of items, and the store can hire fewer full-time salespeople. Other stores prefer to give responsibility to one or two permanent full-time employees who can learn the layout of the merchandise on the selling floor and reshelve and restock merchandise daily.

Packaging has become an important marketing and merchandising partnership opportunity for fashion accessories manufacturers and retailers. Manufacturers attempt to create durable packaging that is unique, unobtrusive, and pilfer-proof. Less-obtrusive packaging has been designed so that it doesn't obscure the view of the merchandise. Customers don't have to open plastic containers or remove large labels to look closely at the merchandise. Durable packaging includes hangers and containers that won't break if dropped or tear when consumers pull items off fixtures.

A key channel for marketing accessories is the trade show. In New York two important general trade shows are the Accessorie Circuit and AccessoriesTheShow, both held during the accessories market weeks. They offer a designated time when retail store buyers visit the market center and make selections for their stores (see Figure 1.4).

Numerous other New York City trade shows, such as the Fashion Avenue Market Expo (FAME), the Atelier, Nouveau Collection, and Femme, feature apparel and general accessories to retail store buyers. Other major cities throughout the United States also have market weeks and host accessories trade shows. Accessories shows are held at the Chicago Apparel Center and Merchandise Mart (see Figure 1.5), the Dallas Market Center (see Figure 1.6), the Denver Merchandise Mart, Atlanta's AmericasMart, and the California Mart in Los Angeles. Category-specific trade shows are listed in Parts Two and Three of this book.

Trade associations abound; each category of accessories has one or more specialized trade associations for industry members. The National Fashion Accessories Association (NFAA) and

FIGURE 1.4
Accessories TheShow in New York City.
Courtesy of Fairchild Publications, Inc.

the Fashion Accessories Shippers Association (FASA) represent several accessories product areas.

Another trade organization is the Accessories Council, established in 1995 to serve accessories businesses in the United States. Their Web site provides accessories fashion forecasts and news, a calendar of events, an online forum, and a career information exchange. It also links consumers to other Web sites of name brand accessories products.

FIGURE 1.5
The Chicago Apparel Center.
Courtesy of Fairchild Publications, Inc.

FIGURE I.6
The Dallas Market Center. Courtesy of Fairchild Publications, Inc.

Profile: AccessoriesTheShow

In the fashion accessories industry, the largest and longest running show featuring all types of accessories is AccessoriesTheShow. It is held three times annually at the Jacob Javits Convention Center in New York City. Prior to 2000, the trade show was known as the Fashion Accessories Expo.

More than 7,500 buyers from nearly all 50 states and 40 foreign countries attend each show. They represent specialty stores, boutiques, museum shops, craft shops, department stores, jewelry stores, and catalog companies. About 85 **percent** of the attendees are shopping for mid- to high-price points. Buyers are encouraged to attend with promises of personal amenities, such as free fashion totes or complimentary beverages and daily prize drawings.

Vendors are wooed to exhibit at the show because of the visual display opportunities and national brand awareness exposure at the event. The show organizers even maintain a year-round Web site featuring exhibitor information. The trade magazine, *Accessories,* obtains information that may be published in an upcoming issue, and editors from consumer magazines attend the show looking for accessories to feature in their magazines.

Both new and established designers are featured at the trade show. Packaging, marketing, and private label ideas are also publicized. An "Emerging Labels in Accessory Design" section is subsidized by the show sponsors. A "Foreign Pavilion" section features European exhibitors offering American buyers fashion jewelry, luxury gifts, and souvenir collections.

CREATING AND SELLING ACCESSORIES

The four major channels of distribution in the fashion accessories industry are designing, manufacturing, wholesaling, and retailing. At each stage, the accessories are "sold" to the following stage, with consumers ultimately purchasing the finished goods from retailers. The designer creates ideas for the manufacturer to mass-produce. The wholesaler purchases quantities of goods from manufacturers located all over the world and makes the selections available to retailers. Retailers provide ways for consumers to buy individual quantities at convenient locations. A sample channel of the distribution flowchart is shown below:

Designing → Manufacturing → Wholesaling → Retailing

Designing

There is a close interface in designing between apparel and accessories products because the two categories are worn together. Apparel designers have begun to see the profit potential in designing accessories to match the clothing. To further blur industry lines, popular accessories designers are branching into apparel and home fashions where name recognition is valued.

Designers gain inspiration and formulate new ideas from a variety of sources including historic fashions; new fiber developments; the film industry; ethnic cultures; social, economic, and political climates; and specific worldwide events. Successful designers have an aptitude for blending these inspirational sources with an original idea to create a saleable product.

When creating an accessories design, the amount of designer input varies from complete control to a legal agreement in which a well-known designer licenses the use of his or her name to an approved company. The company produces accessories that meet established guidelines, and the designer usually receives royalties on sales.

Top contributing designers are recognized each fall with the Accessories Council Excellence Award. The Best New Accessory Designer award is given to a nominee who has just entered the accessories field and has made an important contribution during the year. In addition, five other awards are given by the Accessories Council: Best Accessories Licensed Program, Best Accessorized Television Program, Best Coverage of Accessories by a Consumer Fashion Magazine, Best Accessories Ad Campaign, and Best Accessories Visual Merchandising by a Retailer. A final award, the ACE Hall of Fame Award, goes to a designer who is recognized for an outstanding contribution to the field.

Manufacturing

Accessories manufacturers transform an accessories design into a mass-produced item. **Manufacturing** includes pattern making, cutting, sewing and assembling, inspecting, and packaging. All manufacturing steps may be performed under one roof (inside shops), or the work may be contracted out to specialized shops (outside shops) (see Figure 1.7).

The original pattern may be created by the designer or the designer's assistant, either by hand or via computer aided design (CAD). Once it is judged suitable for mass production, the pattern may be graded to all of the needed size offerings. With increasing frequency, computers are

FIGURE 1.7
Licensed products from Nine West.
Courtesy of Fairchild Publications, Inc.

used to grade the patterns and create layout sheets indicating proper placement of pattern pieces for the greatest materials savings. Cutting may be performed on a single layer with a pair of shears, or multiple layers may be spread on a cutting table, and a knife blade or laser can be used to cut the layers. Sewing and assembling are usually the most expensive manufacturing steps, so offshore production is a likely part of labor-intensive accessories production. Once assembled, fashion accessories products may be returned to the U.S. company for inspection and packaging.

Wholesaling

Wholesalers act as selling middlemen for one or more lines of accessories. A wholesaler may buy from an overseas manufacturer and resell the goods to retailers in the United States. This type of middleman, called an importer, can take advantage of inexpensively produced goods and pass the cost savings on to retail stores. Wholesalers can be independent representatives of several manufacturers' lines.

Retailing

A **retailer** buys products from a wholesaler and sells them to the ultimate consumer. Retailers hire buyers who purchase goods at **wholesale prices** in large quantities, and then resell smaller or single items to consumers at **retail prices** (typically about double the wholesale price). Buyers attend collection openings and line releases at markets all over the world to select wholesalers' accessories for the store's target customers.

A retail store may be a brick-and-mortar building or a virtual site on the Internet. Retailing on the Internet is referred to as e-tailing or e-commerce. Regardless of the selling channel, the retailing function is the final market for fashion goods.

CAREER OPPORTUNITIES

The fashion accessories industry abounds with career opportunities for college graduates. Retail work experience in accessories while in college is useful to gain an understanding of the fundamentals of the accessories industry. The retailing adage, "Nothing happens until the sale is made," is best experienced working at the retail end of the fashion business.

Upon graduation, the fashion accessories student should be armed with a college degree, some retail work experience, knowledge of the computer programs used in the industry, and a goal-oriented résumé and portfolio. Bilingual ability in English and Spanish is especially helpful. Graduates can expect to start as an assistant or intern with a company. These entry-level jobs provide the opportunity to learn about the business under the guidance of knowledgeable professionals. Excitement, travel, and performance-based monetary rewards can be expected in many fashion accessories careers. Several common entry-level careers are described in the following sections.

Assistant Designer

This position may also be called a pattern maker. Courses in fashion sketching, computer aided design (CAD), pattern making, pattern grading, art, textiles, and basic construction are necessary to be successful in this field. Prior experience with software packages used by assistant designers is often required, including Excel®, Colour Matters, Photoshop®, and Illustrator®. Important personal qualities include creativity, drawing ability, and organizational skills. One men's accessories company advertised the need for a belt designer able to gather, interpret, and communicate fashion trends. Relocation to major market centers on the East Coast and West Coast provides graduates with the greatest number of assistant designer opportunities, although manufacturing firms hiring assistant designers are located throughout the United States in other market centers like Chicago and Dallas.

An assistant designer works closely with the head designer to create a workable pattern from a designer's sketch. Knowledge of CAD systems and computer graphic skills are frequently requirements for assistant designers and pattern makers. From the pattern, a prototype will be manufactured. The assistant designer, designer, and production specialist will "cost out" the product to determine the profitability of the design and ultimately if the design will go to production. **Costing** refers to assigning dollar amounts to every production detail including materials, trims, linings, notions, labor, and profit. Assistant designers may be required to keep the sample fabric and trim room stocked with yardage and notions. They may have the responsibility of developing trend, design, or storyboards, which are flat visual presentations covered with fabric swatches, photos, and fashion sketches. Figure 1.8 shows an advertisement for an accessories designer with Brighton. Brighton accessories include belts, handbags, jewelry, small leather goods, sunglasses, and watches.

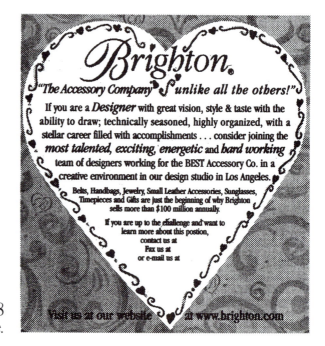

FIGURE 1.8
Brighton classified advertisement.

Production Specialist

Accessories production specialists work for manufacturing companies and oversee an accessory's production from start to finish. To become a successful production specialist, a graduate should be willing to accept an entry-level position as a production assistant, gaining exposure to career options. Students should take classes in construction and have experience operating sewing machinery. Knowledge of Microsoft Word® and Excel software systems is important. In addition, retailing experience selling the specific fashion accessory provides students with training to differentiate quality among similar accessories.

Production specialists and their assistants must be highly organized and schedule all phases of production in the most efficient manner. Production specialists evaluate costs for each stage of production. To determine the most efficient use of resources, they must have knowledge of textiles and trims, the technical cutting and sewing operations, and the quality standards of the company. Job responsibilities of production assistants include following up on deliveries, communicating with overseas suppliers, monitoring quality control, and approving samples.

Junior Sales Representative

Junior sales representatives work for manufacturers, both in market showrooms and on the road, and sell products to retail store buyers. They may be assigned a territory with existing accounts to call on, as well as be expected to develop new clients. Relocation depends on the assigned geographic territory and can be a single market center, a state, or several states. Although many companies advertise for experienced sales representatives or representatives with a "following," some companies are willing to train enthusiastic and energetic college graduates as entry-level sales representatives. During market weeks, college students have opportunities to work as temporary showroom help, which may lead to job offers upon graduation. Any previous sales experience, regardless of the types of merchandise and services, is beneficial. Many of these positions are partially or wholly commission-based incomes, so an understanding of sales is vital. Business and marketing classes are helpful for this career. Figures 1.9 and 1.10 are examples of classified advertisements for accessories companies in the *Women's Wear Daily* classified advertisements.

Department Manager

An accessories department manager is often an attainable position for recent college graduates. This position requires previous experience on the selling floor that may be acquired prior to graduation. This manager is responsible for training employees as well as ensuring that the department is adequately staffed. In addition, he or she must oversee the general merchandising of the department, record markdowns, replenish stock, and handle other merchandising

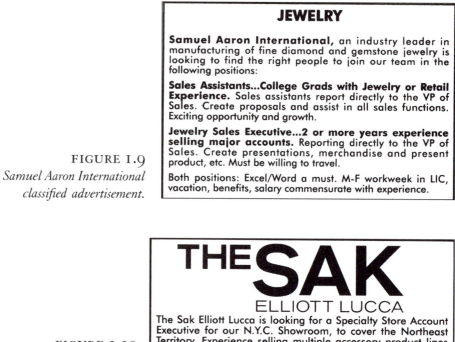

FIGURE 1.9
Samuel Aaron International classified advertisement.

FIGURE 1.10
The SAK, Elliott Lucca classified advertisement.

duties. The department manager has a departmental sales quota to meet—and must encourage employees to sell, sell, sell!

Area Sales Manager

This person reports to the store manager and is in charge of several departments and department managers. Prior retailing experience is a must. The most marketable of graduates are those with directly related work experience.

The area sales manager may organize special events to promote the departments and work with department managers to ensure that all departments are working toward a common goal. In a midsize department store, there may be three to four area sales managers, each assigned to a set of related departments. For example, the women's area sales manager may be responsible for the accessories department and the cosmetics, junior, missy, and children's departments.

Assistant Accessories Buyer

This position may also be called associate or junior buyer. The assistant usually reports directly to an accessories buyer and is responsible for order follow-up with vendors. Negotiating abilities, basic merchandising mathematics, computer knowledge, and verbal and written skills are important to job success. The assistant buyer may travel to different markets to help select merchandise as well as spend considerable time on the telephone locating potential resources. After gaining experience, the assistant buyer may be given the responsibility for prescreening vendors or buying certain accessories lines.

Copywriter

Copywriting for fashion accessories requires education in both journalism and fashion, although some copywriters have English majors. Most copywriting jobs require relocating to the company headquarters or company buying offices. Excellent grammar and creative writing skills are vital to copywriting careers. Experience with college newspapers is a benefit to students who are interested in this career. Advertising, catalogs, trade and consumer fashion publications, and other types of promotional literature are written by copywriters. For example, at the J.C. Penney company home office in Plano, Texas, copywriters are employed in the catalog division. The copywriters work closely with the vendors and buyers to develop merchandise descriptions for J.C. Penney's various catalog issues.

Visual Merchandiser

This creative career involves coordinating the store interior across all departments. Exterior and interior displays, signage, store decor, floor plans, and lighting are responsibilities of visual merchandisers. Most department stores have at least one visual merchandiser, while larger stores may have a team of visual merchandisers reporting to a visual manager. College students may work as trimmers under the supervision of a visual merchandiser. Trimmers are especially needed prior to the Christmas holiday season when decorations must be set up throughout the store and taken down after the holiday. Many regional malls hire college students as trimmers to hang Christmas decorations on a temporary basis. Other stores hire a team of part-time help to completely remerchandise the floor and walls on a periodic basis, such as once a month, often after the store closes. Visual merchandising and art are important courses for students preparing for a career in visual merchandising.

Store Planner

A career as a store planner involves determining the best placement of merchandise and fixtures to maximize sales. Store planners work closely with visual merchandisers. Store planners create planograms, or floor sets and wall elevations, on CAD. This shows retail store merchandisers the correct placement of merchandise. Store planners may send photographs suggesting (or mandating) in-store merchandise looks.

College graduates should spend time working in the retail stores before moving to company headquarters. A student interested in a position as a store planner can get a jump start on his or her career by working part-time as a trimmer, visual merchandiser, or salesperson in the store.

Most store planning positions are located at company headquarters and involve designing on computers. A prototype store may be used to test, evaluate, and refine floor layouts and wall elevations. The goal of a store planner is to maintain the company-wide image projected to all store customers, regardless of their location in the store.

SALARIES FOR FASHION ACCESSORIES CAREERS

Exciting and diverse career opportunities await college graduates interested in careers in fashion accessories. Salaries are competitive with those received by other college graduates with degrees in business. The salary is dependent upon the geographic location, sales volume, and level of responsibility. Graduates with direct work experience can negotiate for higher salaries and are the most sought after by employers. Graduates may attain some positions with higher levels of responsibility after only a few years experience at one of the lower positions. Students should attempt to get as much salary information as possible while still in school, so they will be able to obtain the best possible salaries upon graduation. Table 1.1 lists median salaries for a variety of fashion careers. The careers are categorized by trade and ranked from lowest to highest responsibility.

TRADE ORGANIZATIONS, PUBLICATIONS, AND SHOWS

For each accessories category listed in Part Three of the text, various trade organizations, publications, and shows are discussed. The diverse nature of accessories products often lends itself to specialized trade organizations. For example, the Fur Information Council and the Fashion Footwear Association of New York were created to promote these specific and large accessories industries. By contrast, the Accessories Council, the National Fashion Accessory Association, and the Fashion Accessory Shippers Association promote the use of most fashion accessories products and provide support for the trade (see Table 1.2).

Graduates should join the relevant trade associations for their industries because the associations provide support for businesses. Types of support include government lobbies, publications and publicity releases, advertising campaigns, employment contacts and networking, trade shows, and educational opportunities.

Trade publications are available to industry personnel. Business people can stay abreast of industry changes, new legislation affecting the trade, and other important market issues. Trade advertisements provide businesses with exposure to new products and services that may be beneficial (see Table 1.3).

TABLE I.I

Salaries for Fashion Careers

Career	Salary Range
Designing Careers	
Assistant Designer/Pattern Maker	$32,000–$50,000
Manufacturing Careers	
Production Assistant	$36,000
Production Specialist	$58,000
Wholesale Careers	
Junior Sales Representative	$36,000
Account Executive (Sales)	$80,000
Retail Careers	
Retail Sales Associate	$15,800–$19,500
Merchandising Assistant	$22,000
Assistant Department Manager	$22,500
Retail Management Trainee	$34,000
Department Manager	$39,000
Area Sales Manager	$36,000–$44,000
Selling Supervisor	$46,135
Store Manager	$65,200
Retail Support Careers	
Assistant Accessories Buyer	$31,500–$45,000
Buyer	$42,600–$60,000
Copywriter	$32,000
Trimmer	$22,900
Visual Merchandiser	$28,900–$35,000
Store Planner	$55,000

Sources:
California Employment Development Department. Labor Market Information.
    Available at http://www.calmis.cahwnet.gov/file/occguide/Buyer.htm
Median Salaries for Retail Careers.
    Available at http://www.retail.monster.com/archives/salaryguide/
Retail Career Opportunities, October 2001.
    Available at http://www.retailrecruitersusa.com/career.html
Women's Wear Daily classified advertisements.

Trade shows should be attended to gain a feel for market conditions. Trade shows may be centrally located in various regions of the continent, or they may be located in a major world-wide market center. New products and services are featured first at trade shows, and those attending the shows can gain a competitive edge. In addition, helpful industry contacts and career information can always be found at trade shows (see Table 1.4).

TABLE 1.2

Trade Organizations for the Fashion Accessories Industry

Organization	URL	Objectives
The Accessories Council	www.accessoriescouncil.org	Provides industry news, fashion forecasts, events calendar, press releases, accessories company links, and allows individuals to post resumes free of charge.
National Fashion Accessory Association (NFAA) and the Fashion Accessory Shippers Association (FASA)	www.accessoryweb.com	Represents all accessories categories; publishes retail guide, *How to Sell Accessories;* disseminates information to importers and manufacturers; and fosters labor relations.

TABLE 1.3

Trade Publications for the Fashion Accessories Industry

Trade Publication Name	Description
Accessories Magazine	Monthly trade publication; covers most accessories classifications, including bridge and costume jewelry.
Women's Wear Daily – Monday	Weekly issue of a trade newspaper, published by Fairchild; features business and fashion information on fine jewelry, as well as other accessories.
WWD Accessory Supplement	Fairchild special edition featuring fashion information on all accessories, including fine jewelry.

TABLE 1.4

Trade Shows for the Fashion Accessories Industry

Trade Show	Location	Sponsor
AccessorieCircuit	New York, NY	ENK International
AccessoriesTheShow	New York, NY	Business Journals, Inc.
Fashion Coterie	New York, NY	ENK International
Intermezzo Collection	New York, NY	ENK International
WWD/MAGIC Show	Las Vegas, NV	*Women's Wear Daily* and Men's Apparel Guild in California

SUMMARY

- Fashion accessories have higher profit margins than most other fashion merchandise because of better inventory management systems. These include ordering closer to the selling season and balancing assortments of fashion and classic goods.

- Other key elements of accessories merchandising include acting on trends, providing impulse item merchandise, creating lifestyle brands, targeting teens, featuring related merchandise from a variety of departments in unifying displays, and implementing destination points in departments.

- Accessories are influenced by designer and higher-price ready-to-wear trends; accessories designers translate these important trends to suit the needs of their target customers.

- The teen market has a major influence on fashion accessories because teens are often the first to adopt new fashions.

- Fashion accessories follow the trickle-down, trickle-up, and trickle-across adoption theories.

- Accessories are a reflection of the economic, political, and social mood of the people. In a soft economy, accessories are more conservative; in a strong economy, they are more fashion-forward. Technological innovations and political, social, and economic events also create fashion trends.

- Accessories follow the same fashion life cycle as other fashion and consumer products. The five stages are introduction, rise, culmination, decline, and obsolescence.

- Fashion accessories and fashion apparel are complementary and follow the same trends. Both are influenced by the same environmental factors and forecasting information. Apparel and accessories may be created by the same design teams.

- Accessories marketers respond quickly to fashion while the trend is still hot. *Flexibility* and *newness* are key merchandising terms.

- Accessories assortments should be balanced between fashion and core lines to ensure all target customers have adequate selections.

- Cross-merchandising, also called one-stop shopping, refers to featuring several related products in a single display area called a destination point. These strategic, high-traffic destinations attract the teen market, which has enormous size and purchasing power.

- In accessories departments, housekeeping is required. These duties are handled by in-store or outside service companies. Prepackaged accessories in pilfer-proof, less obtrusive, and stronger packages help with department maintenance.

- Trade shows are a key method of disseminating new accessories product information. Each major market center hosts accessories trade shows during market weeks. Some feature a variety of categories, while others are specific, such as fine jewelry trade shows.

- Trade associations are organized by accessories classifications. Associations may disseminate information to ultimate consumers or foster business-to-business relationships.

General accessories trade associations include the National Fashion Accessories Association, the Fashion Accessories Shippers Association, and the Accessories Council.

■ The fashion accessories industry is divided into four major channels: designing, manufacturing, wholesaling, and retailing. Selling occurs at each stage until the products reach the ultimate consumers.

■ Career opportunities in fashion accessories are available in manufacturing, wholesaling, retailing, and store support. College students with related work experience will have marketable skills and knowledge upon graduation.

TERMS FOR REVIEW

costing	manufacturing	street fashions
cross-merchandising	obsolescence stage	trickle-across theory
culmination (peak) stage	pragmatic fashion accessories	trickle-down theory
decline stage	theory	trickle-up theory
destination point	retail price	wholesale price
fashion product life cycle	retailer	wholesaler
introductory stage	rise stage	

REVIEW QUESTIONS

1. Why do fashion accessories typically have a higher profit potential than other segments of the fashion industry?
2. How has technology affected the accessories industry?
3. What are the five life cycle stages of an accessories product? Describe each one.
4. How are accessories and apparel closely related?
5. How do fashion accessories trends differ from fashion apparel trends?
6. What are some trends that influence fashion accessories?
7. What is meant by cross-merchandising and destination-point merchandising?
8. Why are the junior and teen markets important to the fashion accessories industry?
9. How has accessories packaging improved, and why?
10. What types of entry-level positions exist for students of fashion accessories?

KNOWLEDGE APPLICATIONS

1. Visit a drug store, mass merchandise store, or a discount store. Identify an accessories destination point or cross-merchandised display in the store. List the types of merchandise featured and evaluate your findings. Type a one-page analysis of your opinion on the success of the area. Include topics such as neatness, variety, theme, location, packaging, price points, and likelihood of success.
2. Visit an accessories department in a store of your choice. Evaluate the neatness of the area and make suggestions for improvement in a typed critique.

3. In small groups, peruse a fashion magazine. Discuss what constitutes a trend and identify major trends in apparel and accessories. Explain the relationship between the two and orally present findings to the class.

4. Draw the five stages of the fashion life cycle. Locate ten accessories pictures from magazine or catalog advertisements, two representing each of the five stages in the life cycle.

5. Visit a techno-fashion company's Web site. Make a comprehensive list of wearable computing products. Share your findings with the class and create a master list.

6. Perform some career research on the Internet or at your library. Locate posted salaries for fashion accessories jobs and compare these with the average salaries listed in Table 1.1 in this chapter. Share your findings with the class.

CHAPTER 9

❦

PRODUCT DEVELOPMENT

Dozens of fashion and interior design students compete each spring in a trend board competition as a part of Career Day at the Market Center in Dallas, Texas. The annual Career Day hosted by the Dallas Chapter of The Fashion Group International attracts over a thousand students from colleges and universities in the United States each spring. The trend board competition features natural fibers grown in Texas. The competitive event allows college students to gain practical experience in a creative area of the product development process and showcase their talents to prospective employers.

THE FASHION ACCESSORIES INDUSTRY INCLUDES MANY DIVERSE CATEGORIES, AND THE steps involved in manufacturing accessories vary widely. However, most of the categories do follow similar product development stages, even if the process within each stage is quite different.

The process begins when a designer provides the initial ideas and sketches with the goal of creating an entire seasonal line or collection. Colors, materials, and shapes are selected. Prices are estimated and later finalized. Samples are created, tested, revised, and produced, so sales representatives can show them to potential retail buyers. In the final stage, the product is manufactured in large quantities. Profit margins are the driving force throughout production, and at every stage, costs are of utmost concern.

LINE AND COLLECTION DESIGN

Designers get their inspiration from a variety of sources including ready-to-wear fashions, trade shows, and fashion services. The Première Classe accessories show, held semiannually in

FIGURE 2.1
*Examples from the Kate Spade
Spring 2003 collection.*
Courtesy of Fairchild Publications, Inc.

Paris, is one of the important trade shows where accessories designers learn about new trends. Accessories fashions are also influenced by the apparel collections. The sheer size and number of designer collections presented each season may be too large for any one accessories designer to make an accurate interpretation of major trends. Fashion services offer reports summarizing and detailing the apparel collections with videos, print stories, sketches, slides, photographs, and swatches. By subscribing to these services, designers can create a line that includes only those major trend components that best suit their particular target market.

A **product line** (or simply **line**) is the production of one type of item, such as a line of handbags, developed by a single manufacturer and presented to retail store buyers for delivery at a specific time. A **collection** is a group of related items, such as handbags, planners, attaché cases, and portfolios. A collection also refers to designer and higher-priced merchandise (see Figure 2.1). Manufacturers hope the buyers will purchase all the merchandise in the collection, creating a maximum visual impact in the stores.

Lines and collections originate with a designer's series of sketches or illustrations on a drawing board. The most saleable products will be selected for production from a large number of illustrations and later, samples. Manufacturers of accessories may update colors and fabrications, rather than producing a completely new line each season. In apparel, lines are produced four to six times yearly, while in accessories, lines are produced from one to five times per year, depending on the accessories category.

Styling Versus Designing

Styling refers to taking existing fashions and changing the details. For example, a popular wallet may be produced in several types of leathers, from ostrich to bullhide. Styling involves far less risk, but has the potential to become stagnant for lack of "new" merchandise. A stylist has less creativity than a designer, who actually creates unique merchandise. **Designing** refers to the actual creation of new ideas, either drawing by hand or using computer aided design (CAD).

FIGURE 2.2
Via Spiga help wanted advertisement

Courtesy of Fairchild Publications, Inc.

Manipulation of existing styles is simplified with CAD, so designers and stylists can inexpensively generate modified looks with a minimum of effort. Figure 2.2 is an example of a help wanted advertisement for an accessories designer. One of the requirements is a working knowledge of CAD.

Product developers are stylists that wait until the selling season begins to see what styles are performing the best at retail. They may purchase several popular items from a fashion-forward retailer to use for styling inspiration. The product developers try to match (to varying degrees) the fabric, design, trim, or color. In other words, they "borrow" from well-known designer brands to create customized looks for their own line.

The Line Plan

A **line plan** is a rough estimation of the styles needed to fill out the line. Is there an adequate representation of key looks? In large manufacturing firms, a team of **merchandisers** works with the design staff to create a line plan that meets the needs of the target customer. The merchandisers are attuned with those styles most likely to sell, based on sales data and market research. In smaller firms, the owner and/or designer may determine the line plan. As the line evolves from research, the designer places selected sketches on a **style** or **trend board** that becomes a master working plan. By creating a visual "story," the decision makers can add and subtract styles until the line is complete. Previous successes or failures should be considered during the development of the line plan (see Figure 2.3).

Selecting Colors

Selecting color in fashion accessories is usually one of the first decisions made by designers when creating a line. The cyclical popularity of colors in fashion is influenced by social, economic, political, and cultural factors. Major color forecasting services available to designers include the Color Association of the United States (CAUS), Worldwide Intercolor, and the International

FIGURE 2.3
Student trend board competition at the annual Career Day in Dallas, Texas, hosted by the Fashion Group International.
Courtesy of Kate Widener.

Color Authority (ICA). Other color consulting services, such as PANTONE®, D3 Doneger, Color Box, Huepoint, and Design Intelligence, provide designers and manufacturers with trend "reports" outlining important seasonal colors. The popular Pantone Color System provides thousands of color chips for computerized exact matches and swatches for designers' creative palettes. In addition, Pantone, Munsell, and similar color systems are numerically based ensuring a common matching system regardless of national language barriers that may exist. The information is presented using **trend books, yarn cards,** and **color stories.** Trend books offer insight into pervasive fashion themes or the direction in which fashion is moving. For example, if nostalgia is the trend in accessories, denim and other cotton fabrics, laces, and natural colors may be featured across accessories and apparel lines. Yarn cards provide samples of dyed yarns for each of the popular colors of the upcoming season. The colors are often categorized by themes, such as sherbet pastels or jewel tones. A color story focuses on a key fashion color featured in a variety of apparel and accessories.

Accessories designers may subscribe to multiple consulting services to determine color commonalities across the services. Annual fees range from $600 to $1,500.

Once designers have selected the line colors, they prepare **storyboards,** also called **colorways, presentation boards, mood boards,** or **work boards,** to project specific color themes and schemes, or "color feelings." The storyboards feature silhouette line drawings, street photographs or swipes (clippings from magazines or catalogs), paint cards, sample trims and notions, and fabric swatches representing important colors and patterns. Storyboards inspire and assist designers and manufacturers in keeping track of dominant themes. As the design season progresses, these storyboards evolve from creative work boards into saleable product line boards. Companies such as Gerber Technology offer a storyboard publisher software that allows designers to insert photos, fabrics, line sketches, and text into a template to create storyboards.

When discussing colors, designers refer to three components: hue, value, and chroma. **Hue** is the specific color family, for example red. **Value** is the darkness or lightness of a color, such as

ᶜᴬᵁˢ

Profile: Color Association of the United States

Can you predict what colors people will be wearing in two years? The Color Association of the United States (CAUS) can—and with amazing success! A volunteer committee of professionals and experts forecast colors, using them grouped into four categories: interiors, women, men, and children. In addition to forecasting the color climate, the CAUS supports color research in other product areas, such as desktop accessories.

Prior to 1915, no professional organization existed to set color for the upcoming seasons. Milliners, or hat makers, took cues from industry leaders: Germany for dyestuffs and Paris for fashions. When World War I restricted communication with these foreign fashion markets, textile producers in the United States joined with related industries to form the Textile Color Card Association (TCCA). The purpose was to prepare a semiannual color card featuring standardized colors for a variety of market segments, from thread and button producers to apparel manufacturers. The hat and hosiery manufacturers were also prominent users of the services. An information clearinghouse, the Manhattan-based TCCA boasted 117 members and 110 standardized colors the first year! Even the U.S. military enlisted the services of the TCCA to standardize colors for military uniforms, flags, ribbons, and other decorations.

Other developments included international memberships in the 1940s and expansion into home fashions in the 1950s, men's wear in the 1960s, and children's wear in the 1980s. By 1955, the TCCA had changed its name to the Color Association of the United States (CAUS). Current membership in CAUS is more than 1,000 and includes design companies, textile mills, and paint manufacturers.

CAUS offers several services, including a bimonthly newsletter called *CAUS News*, color archives dating back to 1915, an informative Web site, workshops, a color hotline to answer any color-related question, and individualized consultations for members.

CAUS offers internships to interested students worldwide. Interns may conduct original research in an area of interest. Interns also learn to interpret color forecasts and create marketing campaigns; they visit museums weekly and communicate with and assist CAUS members.

Sources:

Color information (n.d.) Color Association of the United States. Retrieved Sept. 19, 2001 from the World Wide Web at http://www.colorassociation.com /docs/copy2a.html

Jarnow, J. and Dickerson, K. (1997). *Inside the Fashion Business*. Upper Saddle River, NJ: Merrill, an imprint of Prentice Hall.

brick red or baby pink. **Chroma** (or intensity) refers to the brightness or dullness of a color, such as shocking pink or dull blue gray.

The Munsell Color Theory is a more complex color system. A single color is represented by a three-dimensional figure that allows for independent adjustments to the color's hue, value, or chroma.

The use of specific color terminology promotes accurate communication among all people involved in production. Designers may need to communicate with manufacturers, even in other countries, to increase or decrease one of the components of a color. For example, a value may need to be darker by 20 percent, or a chroma may need to be brighter (increased) by 10 percent. The terms *tint* and *shade* are also descriptors of specific colors. A **tint** or **pastel** refers to the hue with white added. A **shade** refers to the hue with black added. For example, baby blue is a tint of blue, and navy blue is a shade of blue.

Designers don't necessarily change colors in every new line. Colors that sell well one season may prove to be successful the following season as well. Wise designers stay with what is proven. They pay attention to the trends and stay up-to-date, but not at the expense of what works.

Selecting Materials

Materials for fashion accessories include fabrics, plastics, leather, straw, stones, metals, and other materials such as wood. These are selected according to the end use, price point, styling, and the material's availability. In the fashion industry, fabrics are called **piece goods** because they are goods sold by linear measurements or fixed portions. When selecting fabric, several factors must be considered: fiber content and appearance, yardage requirements, price per yard, textile mill location, delivery time and reliability, import and export quotas, and costs associated with offshore production of goods. Simply put, materials are **sourced,** or ordered, from the resource offering the best overall package.

Considerations for other accessories materials include price per unit (such as zippers), price per pound (such as feathers and leathers), durability requirements, materials availability, and transportation or import costs. Table 2.1 shows materials costs for a cotton-lined nylon tote with plastic handles.

Materials alone can be used to achieve variation in a product line. Some companies produce several versions of just a few styles or designs. The materials or fashion fabric may be the only real difference among the versions. A change in materials can create a completely different-looking product style. Designers and manufacturers of moderate- and lower-priced accessories can achieve the look of a more expensive accessory by using comparable but less costly materials. For example, a vinyl, line-for-line copy of a costly top-grain leather status handbag will sell for considerably less than the prestigious original. Fashion and price-conscious consumers can purchase a look-alike bag for about one third of the price of the leather bag.

Choosing Shapes

Shape is an important design consideration for some accessories categories such as handbags and shoes (see Figure 2.4). When creating shapes, designers consider past sales history, current fashions, functional needs, upcoming fashion trends, and target customer preferences. For example, a handbag designer might develop a purse shape similar to a best-seller from a previous season. A look at past sales data will give clues to the fashion life cycle of a particular shape.

TABLE 2.1

Materials Costs Analysis for a Cotton and Nylon Tote

Rectangular metal frame	$4.00
3/8 yard nylon fabric @ $5.00/yard	1.88
3/8 yard cotton batiste @ $4.25/yard	1.59
2 plastic handles @ .95 each	1.90
Total materials cost	$9.37

FIGURE 2.4
The shapes of handbags can have significant effects on their sales.
Courtesy of Fairchild Publications, Inc.

Designers conduct what is called **style out analysis** of popular shapes. This study provides clues to specific details that seem to have widespread customer appeal regardless of the brand.

The functional components of handbags include handles, pockets, and pouches. Each component adds to the manufacturing costs and can alter the final shape of the handbag. If the trend is toward larger accessories, the designer may increase the scale without changing the basic shape. If the target customer is junior or preteen, the designer may downscale the handbag to complement smaller body frames. Designers of trendy or cutting-edge fashions exhibit a greater willingness to introduce new shapes. By contrast, designers catering to more conservative customers make slight seasonal modifications to proven shapes.

THE MANUFACTURING PROCESS

Accessories manufacturers cannot afford to produce products that don't sell. While this sometimes happens despite everything they do, there are preproduction steps in the manufacturing process that guard against product failure and low-profit margins. These steps include methods used to give buyers a preview of products and the opportunity to place orders before production begins. Companies also calculate their costs and pricing of products to ensure profitability of the new lines.

Prototypes and Line Sheets

Once a new product design has been selected from the sketches, a **prototype** or first sample accessory is produced to determine its costs and salability. Numerous decisions must be made before the accessory is mass-produced. A prototype helps the manufacturer answer production questions. Is the design workable? What are the needs in terms of materials, trim, and labor? Is the assembly method efficient? How is the fit?

After adjustments are made on the prototype and the decision makers are satisfied, samples are manufactured for the sales representatives to show to retail store buyers as part of the seasonal line. Technology allows for three-dimensional (3-D), rotating computer image samples to be used in place of physical samples for some sales presentations.

When 3-D samples of products are not necessary, designs may be shown on **line sheets.** These sheets contain simple line drawings or glossy photographs of each style offered by a manufacturer for the selling season. Beside the illustration of each style are the style number and name, a brief description, color lots, sizes available, and wholesale cost (unless this is provided on a separate sheet). Some line sheets are simply information for potential buyers, while others may be combined with the buyers' order form. Figure 2.5 is a simplified example of a line sheet and order form for a fashion ball cap.

Once buyers have made the selections, only those styles that receive adequate interest from retail buyers will be mass-produced. Styles for which there are only a few orders are usually dropped from the line. This is referred to as **editing the line.** Sales representatives contact the buyers who ordered the dropped or cancelled styles and ask them to redirect their purchases to more successful styles.

Precosting

Before production begins, a **precosting** procedure involves a meeting between the designer, the sample maker, and the production specialist or engineer. They calculate approximate costs

Style #4317 Fashion Ball Cap in Denim-100% Cotton Twill Fabric #18862

Color Number	Color Name	Size Scale	Wholesale $	Retail $	Total Quantity	Total Value Wholesale/Retail	
1A	Light denim	One Size (O/S)	$12.00	$25.00			
2A	Medium denim	O/S	$12.00	$25.00			
3A	Dark denim	O/S	$12.00	$25.00			

FIGURE 2.5
Example of a line sheet and order form.

based on the sample or model. During this meeting the group makes educated guesses about yardage, trim, and notions estimates. These are not exact figures, but they are helpful in the decision to produce or not to market a design.

Specifications

Specifications or "specs" are critical statistics that define exactly how to produce a design. Some accessories, such as footwear, require exacting details while others have a tolerance for measurement deviations (+ or −), as might be the case in knitted accessories such as winter scarves. Specifications or spec sheets provide detailed sketches or visual references of the accessories, along with detailed measurements at every strategic point. It is especially important to have an accurate and understandable visual representation of the item, because many of the accessories are produced overseas, in countries where an understanding of the English language can be problematic.

Production

Production methods for each fashion accessories category are discussed in Part Three. However, there are some general stages that take place across the board. In general, labor costs are calculated at each stage. Following is a brief overview of each stage:

- *Pattern making* The pattern maker translates the visual design into flat pattern pieces. This process may be performed by hand or on a computer.
- *Grading* Grading refers to converting a single-sized pattern into all the required sizes. What was once an exacting manual process performed by skilled workers can now be accomplished by CAD programs in a fraction of the time (see Figure 2.6).

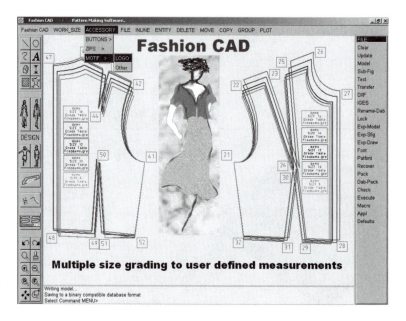

FIGURE 2.6

Pattern grading done on a computer.

Courtesy of Fashion Cad.

- *Marking* This refers to the placement of the pattern pieces with the most efficient layout on the fabric. This procedure can now be generated with CAD. A cutting guide showing all pieces can be directly printed from a plotter.
- *Cutting* The price or type of material affects the cutting stage. For example, with leather handbags, the leather is cut in single layers to work around skin imperfections, while multiple layers of woven fabric can be cut to make fabric totes.
- *Assembling* The sewing, gluing, molding, or other construction methods used in assembly are often labor intense and likely to be performed outside the United States in developing countries. The country in which the assembly takes place is the country of origin. Production workers may be paid by the number of items produced or tasks performed each hour. Called **piecework,** this procedure encourages efficiency and speed, but is less intrinsically rewarding than assembling an entire product from start to finish. Other production workers, such as pattern makers, graders, and markers, are paid a set hourly wage or a salary.

Production Schedules

Each phase of production works under deadlines. A production schedule is a detailed timetable outlining the time frame and deadline date for each stage. Availability of accessories should coincide with the introduction of related apparel. Because of the perishable nature of fashion, a delay at any stage of manufacturing can make the difference in **full-price sell-throughs** or **discounted prices.** These terms refer to the selling performance success at retail. If the accessory can be sold with the maximum amount of profit, the item is considered a full-price sell-through. If the retailer must reduce the price before the sale is made, it is called a discounted price. Retailers expect adherence to delivery dates and may cancel orders if they are not met.

Final Costing

The **final costing** process is a precise dollar calculation of all production expenses and profit. Specific factors contributing to the cost include materials, notions, labor, packaging, administrative expenses, trade discount, taxes, and profit. The cost of every component must be calculated, from the smallest button or length of piping used, to the yardage for lining or fashion fabric. This amount is the **wholesale price,** the cost that will be charged to retailers. Table 2.2 shows an example of a detailed breakdown of a costing sheet for a silk necktie.

Pricing

Even best-selling accessories should not be mass-produced unless they can be produced within the manufacturing company's wholesale price zones and sold at a profit. And just as manufacturers are concerned with the **bottom line profit margin,** retailers have similar concerns. A store

TABLE 2.2
Final Costing Sheet: Silk Necktie

Materials	$5.38
Notions: thread/lining	.70
Labor	5.18
Packaging	.72
Administrative expenses	4.19
Trade discount (for prompt payment)	1.17
Taxes	.81
Profit	1.35
Total wholesale cost	$19.50

TABLE 2.3
Retail Price Analysis: Silk Necktie

Wholesale cost	$19.50
Less 6% cash discount (for early payment)	1.17
Markdown allowance (assuming the item doesn't sell at full price)	4.65
Store expenses (rent, salaries, advertising, etc.)	14.70
Taxes	.97
Profit	1.35
Total retail price	$40.00

buyer cannot purchase the minimum for a line of accessories unless the overall sell-through of the line is profitable to the store. Table 2.3 details a store's costs, cash discounts (for early payment of the invoice), markdown allowances (assuming the item does not sell at full price), expenses (such as rent, salaries, and advertising expenses), tax, and profit requirements for the same silk necktie discussed in Table 2.2. At full-price, the retail price of an accessories item is approximately double the wholesale price.

MANUFACTURING CONSIDERATIONS

The entire production process rarely occurs under one roof. Any production stage (often cutting and/or assembly) may be performed by an outside shop, either domestic or foreign. In fact, the production of a single line of accessories may be quite global in scope. For example, it would be possible for a product to be designed in the United States, cut from fabric woven in India, sewn in Bangladesh, sent to Mexico for embroidery, and returned to the United States for sale in a retail store. At all stages of production, quality control should be ensured, although this becomes increasingly difficult when production is global.

Internal Manufacturing

Internal manufacturing means the styles are produced in-house or in an inside shop. The manufacturing company owns the production equipment and has greater quality control over the assembly of the accessories. A disadvantage of internal manufacturing is the large capital investment that must be made in machinery. Smaller firms do not produce the volume that would keep their expensive equipment in use on a continuous basis. In some very small firms, the designer may create the accessory from start to finish, as in the case of a milliner's shop. However, this type of work is made-to-order on an individual basis or for one-of-a-kind designs rather than mass-produced styles.

External Manufacturing

External manufacturing refers to sending the styles to outside shops or outside contractors for mass-production. If orders are particularly heavy or sporadic, a company may contract to have several outside shops assemble products. The shelf life of some fashion accessories is relatively short, which may require selecting the fastest production method available. A disadvantage of external manufacturing is the limited quality control. If the assembly is performed off the premises of the contracting company, scrutinizing quality standards becomes difficult. Quality problems, such as trim substitutions or slight color adjustments are more likely to occur.

Outside shops may be located within the country or abroad. Because the sewing and assembly stages of manufacturing are usually the most labor intensive, frequently outside shops are located in developing countries, where labor costs are lower.

Domestic Production

Domestic production refers to the manufacture of accessories in facilities located in the United States. Domestic companies are not usually price-competitive with foreign producers, but they compete based on availability and a quick turnaround time. Many domestic manufacturers employ a concept called supply chain management. This marketing strategy was originally promoted by the Crafted with Pride in the USA Council for staple goods, such as hosiery or socks. Supply chain management involves a coordinated effort among textile mills, manufacturers, and retailers. Domestic textile mills aim to provide prompt order fulfillment to domestic accessories manufacturers, who, in turn, provide prompt order fulfillment to domestic retail stores. As sales are made, the data are transmitted to the textile mills and manufacturers, so inventory can be quickly replenished.

Offshore Production

Offshore production refers to the manufacture of accessories at plants located in foreign countries. Usually, offshore production is performed in developing countries that have large supplies of workers willing to work for very low wages. Domestic companies either own the facilities or have contracts to import goods made by these manufacturing facilities. Mexico is becoming increasingly appealing for offshore production because shipping costs are less and Mexico is a part of the **North American Free Trade Agreement** (NAFTA), ratified in January 1994. NAFTA is a preferential trade program that facilitates trade across the three North American Continent countries—Mexico, the United States, and Canada. The purpose of NAFTA was to eliminate quota limits and tariffs on goods traded between the United State and Mexico and the United States and Canada.

Both tariffs and quotas are legislative methods to limit the importing of certain goods. An **import tariff** or **duty** refers to extra taxes charged to the importing company because the imported product may compete with a domestically produced product. These tariffs help equalize the playing field for domestic producers, who are required to pay U.S. workers higher salaries, and to support unions not present in some foreign countries. Some countries operate under a duty-free status as a form of assistance from the United States. For example, the Caribbean Basin Initiative (CBI) eliminates tariffs on goods imported from Caribbean countries, such as Jamaica, Haiti, and Barbados.

Quotas are limits on quantities of certain foreign-made goods allowed to be shipped to the United States. Once the limit has been reached, the goods are embargoed for a specified time period. **Embargoed** means the goods are prevented from reaching the trade customer, even if the shipment is sitting in a warehouse within the borders of the United States.

Other disadvantages of offshore production are the difficulty of getting reorders and the longer lead time required between the time the order is placed and the receipt of the completed order. In addition, language and cultural barriers can cause production problems or delays. In spite of these disadvantages, the singular advantage of low labor costs in foreign countries often outweighs the disadvantages.

SUMMARY

- Stages of product development across accessories categories are line and collection design; color, material, and shape choices; prototype development; production methods and specifications; and cost analysis.
- Designers get their inspiration from ready-to-wear, trade shows, and fashion services, as well as their own understanding of the target customers' wants and needs.
- A new product line or collection is produced one to five times per year. The line plan is a rough draft of styles that fill out the line. It is evaluated, and the decision is made to proceed with production or drop some styles.
- Manufacturers produce only the most profitable and saleable new designs. They may also choose to update colors and fabrics of current best sellers.
- Styling is changing details of an existing design; designing is creating completely new looks. A visual story of sketches or CAD drawings forms a master plan, and designers add or subtract styles as needed.
- Color is one of the first decisions made by designers. To accurately assess trends, designers subscribe to multiple color forecasting services.
- Storyboards, colorways, and presentation boards, mood boards, or work boards are terms for a visual depiction of color themes. Boards contain colors, pictures, and items that illustrate colors, provide inspiration, and suggest dominant themes.
- Color is comprised of three components: hue, value, and chroma. Use of numeric color systems helps ensure accurate colors during production.
- Materials for fashion accessories include fabrics, plastics, leather, straws, and metals. Materials used depend on the end use, price, styling, and availability. Other factors are durability, fiber content, fabric appearance, yardage requirements, price, mill location, availability, delivery time and reliability, quotas, and transportation costs.

- Different shapes of new accessories are heavily influenced by previous sales history, current and upcoming fashions, function, and customer preferences.
- Prototypes and line sheets provide manufacturers with important feedback on the workability and sales potential of designs. Only products that receive adequate buyer orders will be mass-produced.
- Production schedules are timetables for each stage of production. The relatively short life cycle of accessories means any manufacturing delays can result in unsold inventory.
- Production stages include pattern making, grading, marking, cutting, and assembling. Methods of compensation are based on the number of items produced, hourly wages, or salaries.
- Precosting is a calculation of approximate costs based on estimates of fabric, trim, notions, and labor to determine how the product can be produced profitably.
- Specifications are a detailed visual representation of written instructions for cutting and assembling a product.
- The sum total of all materials, notions, labor, packaging, administrative expenses, discounts, taxes, and profit is the cost or wholesale price. This amount will be charged to retail buyers.
- The price the store charges for the product is the retail price and is approximately double the wholesale price. The manufacturer and retailer incorporate profit into the selling price.
- Production performed under one roof is called internal manufacturing. Production performed by specialized, outside companies is external manufacturing.
- Domestic and offshore production refers to the location of the manufacturing facilities. Low labor costs in developing countries are incentives to produce offshore; tariffs and quotas are hindrances. Other disadvantages of offshore production include difficulty of reorders, longer lead times, and language and cultural barriers.

TERMS FOR REVIEW

bottom line profit margin
chroma
collection
color stories
designing
domestic production
editing the line
embargo
external manufacturing
final costing
full-price sell-through
hue
import tariff (duty)
internal manufacturing

line plan
line sheets
merchandiser
North American Free Trade
    Agreement
offshore production
piece goods
piecework
precosting
product developer
product line (line)
prototype
quota
shade

sourced
specifications
storyboards (colorways,
    presentation boards, mood
    boards, work boards)
style (trend board)
style out analysis
styling
tint (pastel)
trend books
value
wholesale price
yarn cards

REVIEW QUESTIONS

1. What sources of inspiration do designers consider when creating lines or collections?
2. How do styling and product development differ from designing?
3. What is the purpose of color storyboards?
4. What terms are used to describe color components?
5. What is a production schedule, and why is it important?
6. Why are prototypes valuable to the manufacturer?
7. What are the advantages of internal and external manufacturing?
8. What are advantages and disadvantages of offshore production?
9. How do specification sheets facilitate manufacturing?
10. What is the relationship between wholesale cost and retail price?

KNOWLEDGE APPLICATIONS

1. Work with a small group to develop a storyboard around a current fashion theme. Attach sketches, color and fabric swatches, street photographs, swipes, paint samples, and sample trims and notions to a foam core board.
2. Test for accuracy in visual color discrimination by practicing with the school's set of the Farnsworth-Munsell 100 Hue Test.
3. Visit an accessories manufacturing facility and develop a chronological list of production stages.
4. Visit a retail store to observe a sizable selection of accessories in one category. Devise a tally system to record the number of featured colors for each unique item or stock-keeping unit (SKU). Compile class findings to locate emerging color themes.
5. Develop a list of ten production questions about a particular category of accessories of interest to you. Locate one or two Web sites for specific brands. E-mail your list of questions to the company's inquiry URL. Report on your findings to the class.

PART TWO

THE
MATERIALS
OF ACCESSORIES

CHAPTER 3

❦

TEXTILES
AND TRIMS

Of all the textiles available for fashion accessories, none is more precious than silk. The value of silk can be traced to the Silk Road trade route, so called because as much as 30 percent of the commodities transported across the trade route was silk. The trade route spanned the continent from the Mediterranean Sea, across the Gobi Desert, and into China. The Silk Road lasted for centuries, and its most famous trader was Marco Polo of Venice (1254–1324). Inheritance records indicated Marco Polo's estate contained a large quantity of valuable cloth covering, including brocades of silk and gold. In his later years, Polo published an exaggerated account of his travels called A Description of the World. *On his deathbed, he made the often-quoted statement to a priest, "I have only told the half of what I saw!"*

A BRIEF HISTORY OF TEXTILES AND TRIMS

THE TEXTILE AND TRIM INDUSTRY EVOLVED WITH AGRICULTURAL SOCIETIES THAT settled for extended periods of time and cultivated land and raised livestock. Linen (flax), cotton, and wool are the three textile fibers that are known to have been in use almost 5,000 years ago. According to historic information, myth, and fact, a Chinese empress discovered silk fibers sometime between 2700 and 2600 B.C. Tales of espionage surrounded the closely guarded secret of silk production or **sericulture.**

Archeological finds indicate that the first textile construction process was probably the weaving or interlacing of branches, leaves, and grasses to form shelters. Later, indigenous fibers, such as cotton or linen, were woven into cloth for protection and adornment.

Fiber processing and cloth weaving were home-based industries until the 18th and 19th centuries. The rise of the Industrial Revolution moved the limited production from home or cottage industries to factories.

Two inventors played pivotal roles in the mass production of textiles. Samuel Slater, a textile machinist, memorized the plans for a cotton mill while living in England. Disguising himself as a farmer, he immigrated illegally to Providence, Rhode Island. There he recreated a spinning mill, from memory, in 1791 in spite of the English laws forbidding it. Slater has been dubbed the Father of the Industrial Revolution for his pioneering of the factory system. Eli Whitney is credited with the development of the saw-type cotton gin that separated cottonseeds from the lint (fibers) in 1793. As a result of these inventions, the production of domestic cotton jumped from a mere 3,000 bales per year in 1790 to over one million bales by 1835.

Hand knitting first appeared in the third century and continued as a handicraft until 1589 when William Lee invented a mechanical knitting machine. The popularity of knits was partly due to increased production speed compared to woven fabrics and the resulting lower costs.

The 16th century marked the introduction to the art of lace making, pillow lace, and needle-point, although braids and some narrow laces were manufactured before this time. Nuns often fostered the lace-making industry by providing workrooms in the convents so peasant women could be commissioned to create laces for the church and children could be trained in the art. In 1837, John Leavers created lace-making machinery, paving the way for mass-produced laces.

Historically, the U.S. textile industry was built on the labor of young women and ethnic minorities. The textile industry in the colonial United States grew as immigrants skilled in weaving and lace-making trades entered the country. Immigrants with skills in the needles trade readily found work, although in some instances the wages were low and working conditions were substandard. Southern slaves who were skilled in sewing were selected to work in the plantation houses, rather than performing the grueling fieldwork. With the abolition of slavery in 1865, some former household slaves found employment in northern textile factories and dressmaking and millinery shops.

AN INTRODUCTION TO TEXTILES

The development of textile mills is tied to the historical fashion accessories industry. Cotton, wool, linen, and silk were used extensively and often exclusively for fashion accessories products. For example, stockings and socks were necessities for all colonists; silk was used for the wealthy and cotton or wool for all others. Hats were also indispensable, from cotton calico bonnets to silk hats trimmed with ribbons, netting, and feathers. The demand for other accessories, such as gloves, shawls, purses, and travel bags, commonly made of textile fabrics had implications for the development of the textile industry in the United States.

Cellulose Fibers

Cellulose fibers used for fashion accessories include cotton, linen (flax), hemp, and jute. These common accessories fibers are grown naturally in plant sources. **Cotton** fibers grow out of seeds; while linen, hemp, and jute are fibers that grow inside the stalk of the plants. Cotton is used for

The Hemp Controversy

The first use of hemp, a tough fiber from Asia, can be dated to 2300 B.C. in China. Hemp uniquely adapts to diverse climates ranging from altitudes of 8,000 feet above sea level to extremely hot climates. Hemp is a dark tan, reedy or straw-like fiber that grows in bundles inside the stem of the plant. Hemp fibers resemble coarse flax and are one of the strongest of the natural fibers. In accessories, hemp is artistically knotted, as in macramé, and used for fashion jewelry (necklaces, bracelets, and anklets). Hemp is braided into casual shoe soles, handbags, belts, hats, and even cosmetics (from hemp seed oil).

In the United States, industrial hemp cultivation is illegal and has been outlawed since 1937, except for the years between 1942 and 1945. During World War II, the government encouraged farmers to grow the plants for rope and parachute cords to offset war shortages caused by the country's inability to obtain Japanese hemp. The government produced a film called *Hemp for Victory* selling farmers on the benefits of raising hemp.

Legislators argue that hemp is too close a cousin to marijuana and fear that pot growers would raise their crops alongside hemp, making the illegal weed harder to spot. However, U.S. farmers are lobbying Congress to make hemp cultivation legal, as Canada did in 1998.

In spite of government restrictions, some companies are still creating hemp products. One ecological shoe company, Deep E, offers casual men's and women's shoes made of environmentally friendly and non-toxic materials, including hemp. "Hemp," explained company founder, Julie Lewis, "is three times stronger than cotton, has twice the abrasion resistance, and is naturally resistant to mold and bacteria. Plus, hemp is a renewable resource that doesn't need toxic agri-chemicals for cultivation."

In the late 1990s, Adidas used hemp as a component in some 30,000 pairs of athletic shoes.

Hemp for socks, developed by the E.G. Smith Company was touted as a wonder fiber. Laurie Mallet, company president in 1999, explained, "Hemp is ecologically healthy, doesn't require pesticides, has the natural quality of resistance to mildew and sweat, and also takes color very well."

The popularity of imported hemp for fashion accessories continues despite the U.S. government ban on growing the fiber. Some well-known designers, including Calvin Klein and Giorgio Armani, have recently offered hemp designs in their collections. These designers have increased their use of hemp because of technological changes that have made the hemp fabrics softer with more of a linen look. Fashion jewelry bracelets and necklaces continue to sell in stores and make-your-own jewelry with beads and braided hemp are popular with teens and young adults. But unless hemp cultivation is legalized in the United States, the supply for hemp will remain limited. In the past, hemp fiber accessories have tended to appeal to a niche of ecology-aware consumers, but the recent spotlight focus on hemp as a fashion material has created a widespread demand for hemp fashions.

Sources:

Deep E's Hemp–Environmentally Correct. (Oct. 28, 1996). *Footwear News*, 52(47), p. 4.

Hessen, W. (Feb. 1999). Keeping It Simple and Stylish. *Women's Wear Daily Magic International Supplement*, p. 28.

all kinds of fashion accessories, from cotton canvas satchels and tapestry luggage to sports socks, bandanas, handkerchiefs, scarfs, hats, and caps. To a lesser extent, **linen** is used for accessories–including summer shoes and handbags. **Hemp** and **jute** are rope-like fibers, more coarse than linen, and are used in items such as summer sandals and fashion jewelry.

Protein Fibers

Protein fibers are from animal sources, like wool from sheep or silk from silkworm cocoons. Protein fibers used in accessories include pashmina (cashmere or cashmere/silk blend), wool, silk, leather, and fur. **Pashmina** comes from the underbelly of the Capras goat that lives in the

Himalayan Mountains in India. The most recognizable pashmina accessory is the elegant, higher-priced shawl. Chapter 10 provides additional information on the origins of pashmina. **Wool** fibers can be used in the manufacture of all kinds of accessories. Wool winter hats, scarfs, and mittens come in many varieties and fringed, plaid, worsted woolen scarfs have long been staples in winter accessories wardrobes.

Silk fibers were used in the past for many fashion accessories, from elegant top hats to stockings and gloves. Today, moderate- and lower-priced accessories use fibers and fabrics that resemble silk, such as polyester and nylon microfibers. These have the look and feel of silk, but are sold at lower costs. Silk is still used in some accessories offered at higher price points, such as pashmina wraps, women's fashion scarves, and men's ties. **Leather** and **suede leather,** although not usually considered fibers, are natural protein textiles used for many fashion accessories, including handbags, luggage, gloves, footwear, belts, and many small personal goods. Chapter 4 is devoted entirely to the leather goods industry. Leather scraps can be shredded and reconstituted to create an inexpensive leather textile, but it lacks the durability associated with leather. Products made from it may be labeled *ground leather, pulverized leather, shredded leather, reconstituted leather,* or *bonded leather.* **Fur** used to make accessories may be left on the animal skin or the **fur fibers** may be removed and spun into yarns. Usually fur fibers are used for aesthetic enhancement in textiles, such as five percent Angora rabbit hair in a knitted winter scarf. A current fashion emphasis on fur trims and accessories has resulted in creative fur fabrications. Additional information can be found in Chapter 5, which focuses on the fur industry.

Manufactured Fibers

The history of manufactured fibers begins with the invention of artificial silk in the late 19th century. Later named **rayon,** it was manufactured from cotton linters and wood pulp. The success of rayon paved the way for subsequent generations of manufactured fibers, including **acetate** and **triacetate.**

Nylon was the first truly synthetic fiber. It was considered a synthetic fiber because it was derived from petroleum, rather than regenerated cellulose fibers. Its enormously successful introduction at the 1939 World's Fair came in the form of nylon stockings. Nylon was soon followed by the development of other synthetic fibers including "wash and wear" **polyester** and "warmth without weight" **acrylic.** Acrylic is frequently used as a substitute for wool in winter accessories because many consumers can develop skin irritations when sensitive skin is exposed to wool.

Spandex, a synthetic substitute for rubber, has important applications in the accessories industry. The comfort and action stretch obtained with small amounts of spandex are desirable in hair accessories, elastic-fabric shoes, socks, and hosiery. Usually spandex is found in small percentages in accessories and apparel, and is combined with other fibers like cotton or nylon.

Microfibers are very fine (diameter) manufactured fibers with the feel of pure silk. The Japanese were the first to develop polyester microfibers under the trade name **Ultrasuede®.** Today, many manufactured fibers are spun as microfibers. Men's ties and women's scarfs may be polyester microfibers that are often difficult to distinguish from pure silk items. Women's hosiery and tights may be nylon microfibers with a silk-like hand. Even fashion shoes for women may have microfiber uppers. The popularity and application of microfibers continue to increase in accessories.

Currently the accessories industry uses many techno-fabrics for fashion accessories materials, including fabrics with breathable synthetic fibers, waterproof Teflon® coatings, and climate-adjusting or color-changing abilities. Some fabrics even contain tiny embedded microchips to allow for adaptation to their environments. Hats, socks, neckties, and pocket squares are a few of the fashion accessories than have been made from techno-fabrics. These fabrics will be discussed in detail in each accessories chapter.

THE TEXTILE MANUFACTURING PROCESS

Yarn manufacturing is the next step in textile production. Fibers are twisted together to create yarns suitable for weaving, knitting, or other fabrications, such as nonwovens, lace, macramé, and crochet. In addition to traditional fibers, straw and bamboo can be used in the creation of yarns and fabrics for accessories.

Yarns

Yarns can create an attractive appearance and desirable hand for accessories fabrics. Smooth, flat fabrics are created from **simple yarns,** which are characterized by even amounts of twist throughout the length of the yarn. Men's ties, women's scarfs, and hosiery are examples of fashion accessories manufactured in simple yarns. **Complex** or **novelty yarns** can have varying amounts of twist throughout the length of the yarns and usually create bulk to increase warmth. Complex yarns are characterized by a general lack of uniformity, an uneven appearance, or loops and curls. Winter scarves and mittens in **chenille** (fuzzy caterpillar) fabrics are examples of complex yarns in fashion accessories.

Another type of complex yarn used in manufacturing winter scarves, hats, and mittens is **bouclé,** the French word for buckle. These complex yarns are characterized by loops projecting from the axis of the yarns. Both types of complex yarns create dead air spaces near the skin to hold body heat (see Figure 3.1).

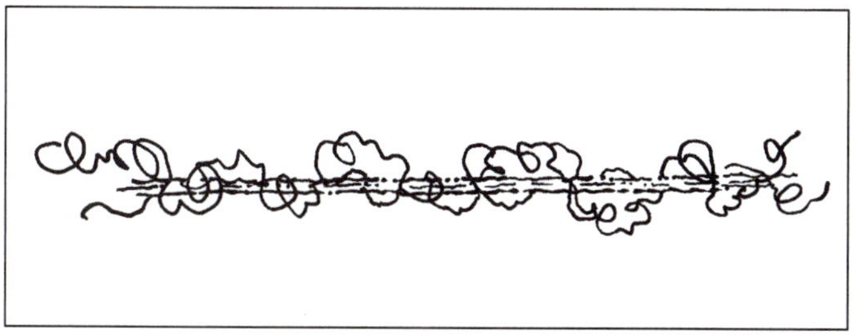

FIGURE 3.1
Bouclé yarn.

Fabrications

Fabrication refers to the manufacture of fabric from yarns or fibers. Wovens, knits, nonwovens, and other decorative construction processes create attractive fabrics for fashion accessories. Durability, price, appearance, and end use are selection factors for choosing particular fabrication methods. In some cases, fabric is used as an inexpensive substitute for leather.

Wovens

Weaving is the process of interlacing two sets of yarns at right angles to create a textile fabric. Woven fabrics generally have a slight amount of stretch on the bias (the fabric diagonal), but do not possess stretch lengthwise or crosswise. **Stretch wovens** (possessing lengthwise and crosswise stretch) have become popular because of the inclusion of spandex fibers in the woven fabric.

Durability (long life) and dimensional stability (the ability not to stretch) are benefits of many woven fabrics. These qualities are important for accessories that are frequently machine laundered. Handbags, backpacks, and luggage are usually woven from strong fibers, such as nylon, which can support excessive weight. Smaller accessories, such as silk scarfs and ties, and narrow items, such as belts, watchbands, and ribbons, benefit from the strength and durability of woven fabrics (see Figure 3.2).

Knits

Knitting is a process of interlocking yarn loops to create a textile fabric. Knitted fabrics provide comfort and action stretch, allowing for ease of movement and a conforming fit. Spandex fibers

FIGURE 3.2
Denim watchband by Movado.
Courtesy of Fairchild Publications, Inc.

may be added for superior **elasticity,** or holding power. In general, knits are less expensive to produce than wovens.

Many wearable accessories use knitted fabrics. Shoes can be designed with nylon and spandex to provide an additional degree of comfort stretch not available in leather shoes. Usually, accessories comprised of knitted fabrics are priced much lower than comparable items in leather. Other examples of knitted accessories include handbags (made of knitted fabric stretched over a support frame), knitted gloves and hosiery that ensure a close fit with no bagging, and fuzzy winter hats and scarfs that are bulky and warm because of dead air spaces that hold body heat and retain warmth.

Nonwovens

Nonwoven textiles vary from a mass of randomly arranged fibers to a film-coated fabric producing leather-like materials. The nonwoven category includes interfacings, felt, vinyl, and suede cloth, which are important to the fashion accessories industry.

Felt originally referred to the process by which randomly arranged wool fibers become sufficiently entangled from the application of heat, moisture, and agitation and to the resulting textile. Felt hats are worn in cool weather and may be made of wool, fur fibers (such as beaver), or modacrylic (synthetic fur) fibers. Modacrylic fiber felts have been popular in shoes and handbags for recent fall/winter seasons. Felt fabric is best for accessories that are not subjected to laundering, pulling, or stretching, for example hats, because of the low dimensional stability (see Figure 3.3).

Vinyl is made by applying a polyvinyl chloride (PVC) or polyurethane film to a base fabric. Called **coated fabrics,** vinyls may resemble a patent leather or be embossed with a grain to imitate the skin patterns of certain animals.

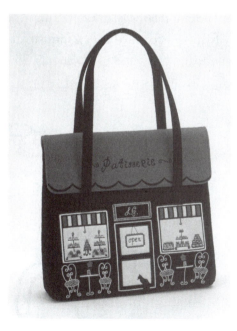

FIGURE 3.3
Felt fabric handbag by Lulu Guinness.
Courtesy of Lulu Guiness.

Suede cloth is created with randomly arranged microfibers spun into a nonwoven web with the feel of real suede. Ultrasuede® is a sophisticated brand of suede-like fabric distributed in the United States by the Skinner Division of Spring Mills. Fashion accessories made of suede cloth include fall and winter fashion footwear, handbags, and some hair accessories.

Lace

Historically lace was a highly prized textile as it was handmade and exquisite. Machine-made lace was developed around 1815 on equipment designed by Englishman John Levers (pronounced leevers). The two major categories of lace were needlepoint lace and bobbin lace. **Needlepoint lace** may have originated in Venice, Italy, in the 1400s. Elaborate patterns were drawn on parchment, and threads were basted on the pattern lines. Decorative stitches were embroidered over the threads to connect them, and the basting stitches were removed. To manufacture **bobbin** or **pillow lace,** a pattern is drawn onto paper that is then stretched over a pillow. Pins, spaced close together, are inserted through the pattern into the pillow. Yarn is wound onto bobbins and interlaced around the pins, forming open and closed patterns. **Netting** is formed by decorative yarn knots at regular intervals and is often used as trim for hats. **Bobbinet lace** has hexagonal-shaped openings and includes traditional nylon netting. Most laces are subject to snagging and are usually used for special-occasion hosiery, bridal dresses and gloves, shawls, and hats.

Macramé

Macramé lace may have originated in Arabic countries. The term comes from the Turkish word, *makrama* or *mahrama,* meaning napkin or towel. Sailors may have brought the craft to Italy. It is similar to the geometric weaving process used to make nets. Cords are looped and knotted, and beads may be inserted to create patterned designs interspersed with ornamental knots. Macramé enjoyed brief periods of popularity prior to the 1900s, but became relatively unimportant until the late 1960s and early 1970s. A macramé explosion heavily influenced the fashion industry, as macramé found its way into hair ornaments, necklaces, handbags, belts, and even sandals. The recent 1960s and 1970s retro fashions reintroduced the art of macramé (see Figure 3.4).

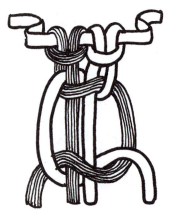

FIGURE 3.4
Macramé accessory.

Crochet

Crochet is an open-worked fabric or lace made with a single-hooked needle that loops and interlocks the yarn. Ireland has been credited with promoting the craft of crochet when, during the 1840s potato famine, convent nuns taught poor women how to crochet to produce additional income for their needy families. Irish immigrants brought the craft to the United States where it became popular as scalloped edging on many household items. As a fashion accessory, it may be used to edge decorative handkerchiefs, or it may be the base fabric of a handbag or a shawl (see Figure 3.5).

Straws and Bamboo

Straw comes from numerous plant sources, including several palm varieties, wheat stalks, grasses, sisal hemp, and rice paper (toyo). Hats and handbags for the summer season are the most common fashion accessories made from straw and similar natural materials, including thin strips of bamboo, woven like straw. **Bamboo** is a wood-like tropical grass that is somewhat pliable. Bamboo canes may also be used as sturdy handles for handbags. The durability and flex-abrasion resistance of most straws is poor. Repeated bending in one location can cause the natural plant fibers to break. Although aesthetically attractive, delicate straw accessories have a relatively short product life cycle, usually only a single season (see Figure 3.6).

FIGURE 3.5
Cotton crochet bag by Liz Claiborne.
Courtesy of Fairchild Publications, Inc.

FIGURE 3.6
Straw handbag by Tote Le Monde.
Courtesy of Fairchild Publications, Inc.

AN INTRODUCTION TO NOTIONS AND TRIMS

Notions are small, useful items, such as zippers, buttons, snaps, and buckles, which may or may not be decorative. Trims are usually applied decorations and include artificial flowers, feathers, shells, and stones.

Zippers and Pulls

The common zipper is often taken for granted, but it is only slightly over 100 years old. Also called slide fasteners, zippers were invented in the early 1890s and sold by the Talon Company (still making zippers) in 1917. The B.F. Goodrich Company secured a patent on the name *zipper* in 1923. In addition to standard zippers, accessories manufacturers make use of **invisible zippers,** with the nylon teeth completely covered by the fabric tape, and **industrial zippers** with large heavy-duty brass teeth. Both have applications in fashion accessories.

Many types of accessories that require a secure closure to prevent loss of items and a close fit are fastened with zippers. Handbags, soft-sided luggage, and most money belts and change purses close with slide fasteners to prevent valuables from being lost. Another advantage of zippers is their ability to widely open a seam. Form-fitting knee boots are often designed with slide fasteners the length of the inside leg seam.

Zippers have become something of a fashion item in and of themselves. Designers have made zippers with rhinestone teeth, a shoe designed from a zipper, and "zipper necklaces" that have adjustable slide fasteners in gold and silver.

Buttons

A button, derived from the French word *bouton,* is a disk, knob, or ball used as a closure or an ornament. Most buttons are attached via a shank to a base layer and inserted through a slip or loop on a top layer. Button materials include wood, shell, horn, plastic, glass, stone, metal, and leather. Some may be fabric covered.

The closure method of buttons into buttonholes may have originated in the early 1300s. Prior to that time, **fibulae** (sharp pins), belts, and drawstrings were used to hold items closed. Tiny buttons were used to secure over-the-ankle shoes (called high-button shoes) in the late 19th century and early 20th century. In the late 1990s, a popular accessory was decorative button covers made to slide over women's plain shirt buttons. Buttons in today's fashion accessories can be functional or only decorative. For example, bangle bracelets and crocheted purses covered entirely with antique or colorful buttons have been recent fashion accessories.

Snaps, Grommets, Velcro®, and Buckles

Fashion accessories closures protect belongings, provide support, allow for size adjustments, and generally increase the function of the accessory. **Snaps,** inexpensive substitutes for zippers

FIGURE 3.7
Grommets reinforce eyelets on this handbag.
Courtesy of Fairchild Publications, Inc.

or buttons, may be decorative or hidden from view. Normally they do not have the holding power of buttons or zippers, but they do allow for quick opening and closing. Snaps may be found on handbags, small leather goods, and casual hats.

Grommets are metal eyelets for lacing reinforcements. They are tightly inserted in a hole in the fabric to protect it from tearing when laces or other types of fasteners are inserted and tightened (see Figure 3.7). Grommets have been added to the crowns of soft-structured hats, like fishermen hats, to allow for heat and air transfer to keep the wearer cooler.

Velcro is a tape-like fastener made of two pieces of nylon tape with raised pile surfaces. One side of the tape has nylon-hooked bristles that mesh with nylon loops on the opposite tape. When compressed together, the piles interlock and provide moderate holding power. Children's shoes are designed with Velcro rather than laces or buckles because small children can manage Velcro even if they are not skilled at tying shoelaces. Velcro is also used on the expanders of ball caps and the wristbands of watches, eliminating the need for buckles or snaps.

Buckles, like buttons, are both functional and decorative and undergo periods of popularity in accessories. Sometimes buckles are large and ornate, even gem studded, while another season's fashions may feature inconspicuous gold or silver-toned buckles. Buckle materials include plastic, wood, metal, tortoise shell, mother-of-pearl, and rhinestones. Buckles can be found on handbags, luggage, shoes, belts, and watchbands.

Braid

Braids are narrow woven trims used as finishes on raw edges of accessories. Straw hat brims often are edged in narrow braids, as are the exposed seam edges of some straw handbags. Braids may also be stitched onto the accessories fabric in a decorative pattern. **Soutache** or **Russian braid** was popular during the mid-1990s as a looped decorative trim on apparel and accessories.

Threads, Lacing, Ribbons, and Bows

Colorful threads, ribbons, and bows remain consistently popular. Threads vary from fuzzy, to matte, to shiny and may be simple or complex yarns. Decorative threads are often used as embroidery or topstitching on accessories (see Figure 3.8).

FIGURE 3.8
Embroidery and mink trim on a cashmere wrap by Josie Natori. Courtesy of Fairchild Publications, Inc.

FIGURE 3.9
Metallic yarns. Courtesy of Fairchild Publications, Inc.

Crewel thread consists of matte, colored, heavy woolen yarns embroidered on the surface of the accessory. Accessories such as pashmina shawls or handbags can be personalized with unique embroidered patterns. **Metallic threads** are colorful aluminum yarns coated with plastic to improve durability. **Lurex**® is a popular brand of metallic threads used in many fashion accessories to add sparkle and visual interest (see Figure 3.9).

Lacing from leather is a decorative or functional treatment used on accessories, such as handbags and footwear. Figure 3.10 shows accessories creations by Shannon Diego that feature leather laces.

Ribbon is usually classified as grosgrain or satin and is manufactured in a variety of widths. **Grosgrain ribbon** has a distinct ribbed appearance, while **satin ribbon** is smooth and shiny. Both are frequently used as trim and knotted into bows for girls' accessories, but may also be creatively designed into other unique items. Figure 3.11 shows designer Felix Rey's creations from grosgrain ribbon.

FIGURE 3.10
Laced leather handbag and shoe by Shannon Diego.
Courtesy of Fairchild Publications, Inc.

FIGURE 3.11
Grosgrain ribbon handbag by Felix Rey.
Courtesy of Fairchild Publications, Inc.

FIGURE 3.12
Artificial flower hat. Courtesy of Fairchild Publications, Inc.

Artificial Flowers

Artificial or silk flowers recently experienced a surge in popularity as hat, hair, and handbag ornaments and fashion pins (see Figure 3.12). When silk flowers become popular, feminine floral prints and fragrances may also have a surge in popularity. Couture designer Coco Chanel became known for her beautiful feather camellia flowers created by a French company, Le Marier, known for its feather applications and handmade flowers.

Feathers

Feathers are produced as a by-product of the meat industry or shed naturally (during August and September) from many different birds. Popular feathers are chicken and rooster, goose, turkey, ostrich, pheasant, pigeon, peacock, and rhea (similar to, but smaller than, ostrich feathers). On any type of bird, the feathers appear different, depending on the part of the body from which they are taken. For example, soft, fuzzy **marabou feathers** come from turkey hips, while other parts of the turkey have coarse feathers with stiff quills (feather spines). **Coquille** are small and delicate goose neck feathers between 1 1/2 and 5 inches in length, while the flight or spike wing feathers, called pointers, may be 7 to 14 inches in length. Small feathers are usually sold by the pound, with several hundred to several thousand feathers per pound. Exotic feathers and many kinds of tail feathers may be sold individually or by the dozen or strung together and sold by the yard (as are marabou feathers). Many feather suppliers market their products to retail or wholesale buyers on extensive Web sites that feature color images of the different types of feathers. Figure 3.13 shows a unique feather hat by famed milliner Philip Treacy.

FIGURE 3.13 *Feather hat by Philip Treacy.*

FIGURE 3.14 *Decorative belt.*

Shells and Stones

The popular **au natural look** (use of natural materials) in fashion accessories includes ornamenting with shells and semiprecious stones. Some shells, such as cowrie shells from the Indian Ocean, were used as currency in ancient China and Africa. Cowrie shells have become one of the symbols of the African continent and multicultural fashion.

Seashell or iridescent mother-of-pearl attachments or inlays add a natural beauty to accessories. Designers creatively use semiprecious stones, like turquoise and lapis lazuli, to ornament more than just jewelry. Figure 3.14 shows creative uses for these materials.

TEXTILES IN THE FASHION ACCESSORIES INDUSTRY

The textile of a product can be described in terms of its texture, fabric, color, or print. Each of these elements gives a textile a particular appearance that designers use to project a certain product image when designing accessories. Usually accessories textiles follow ready-to-wear trends so consumers can readily purchase accessories that complement their clothing purchases.

How Designers Use Textile Textures

The **texture** of an accessory can be determined by the look and feel of the component materials. The term, **hand,** describes the tactile qualities of a material as experienced through the sense of touch. Texture terms include *smooth, abrasive, rough, crisp, soft, silky, firm, fuzzy, furry, pebbly,* and *hard.* A mix of textures creates a greater contrast between the different textures, making each more distinctive. Using this knowledge, designers may combine two or more textures in an accessories item, manufacturers may produce lines that have complementary pieces in contrasting textures, or visual merchandisers may display accessories of one texture against a prop of a contrasting texture. Some examples are seed pearls sewn on an angora winter hat to provide a tactile and visual contrast of textures, a line of straw handbags featuring a different weaving style for each purse in the line, and the shine of sterling silver bracelets displayed on pieces of rough driftwood.

Repetition of a texture among accessories pieces is used to reinforce the texture's visual impact. For example, if mother-of-pearl is the season's popular accessories material, stores will carry the look in items from watch faces and bands to hair accessories, handbags, and eyeglass frames. A cross-merchandise display of all in-store accessories containing mother-of-pearl (along with a few natural mollusk shells) creates a greater visual impact and informs customers of the pervasive shell trend for that season.

Trends in Fabrics, Colors, and Prints

Accessories fabrics often follow ready-to-wear trends. If shine, glitter, and glam are key trends in ready-to-wear, they will likely be a part of the accessories trend. Accessories trends change more quickly than clothing—every three months or sooner. Conservative accessories designers may introduce new fabrics for accessories shapes that were selling well the previous season. This philosophy minimizes risks but provides customers with the newness they desire. Changes in seasons require a change in materials, but the basic popular shapes may make the weather transition. For example, if totes are selling well as canvas or straw bags for spring and summer, manufacturers understand the fashion life cycle of the style has not yet run its course. They will introduce winter tote looks in leather, fur, herringbone, tweed, or felt to capitalize on the best-selling style during cool weather.

Colors and prints of fabrics also undergo periods of popularity. Changing the color of print is an inexpensive way for manufacturers to update their existing lines. For example, if a staple accessory like cowboy hats have a good sell-through (selling well at full prices), the manufacturer can update the existing style with new fabrics, such as python and camouflage prints, sequins, or unusual colors. This concept keeps the merchandise new looking and fresh, with a minimum investment of the designer's time.

THE GLOBAL TEXTILES, NOTIONS, AND TRIMS INDUSTRY

The textile and trims industry is centered mostly outside of the United States. Staple goods, such as buttons, snaps, grommets, zippers, and other small piece goods, are produced in developing countries in Asia. Textile machinery plants are often one of the first types of domestic manufacturing facilities to locate in developing countries. Labor is cheaper in these countries than in the United States, and staple products with a relatively consistent demand can be ordered far enough in advance to meet production schedules.

A few fashion products require a short lead time, and their vendors choose to locate in the United States. For example, Rainbow Feather Dyeing Company, a feather supplier, is strategically located in Las Vegas, Nevada, a city renowned for its elaborate, feathered costumes (see Figure 3.15).

Trade Organizations, Publications, and Shows

Trade organizations serve a variety of purposes, but usually they support those holding membership in the organization. Support takes the form of lobbying and legislative actions, research, continuing education, information dissemination, public relations, publications, trade show sponsorship, and employment assistance. The number and types of trade organizations

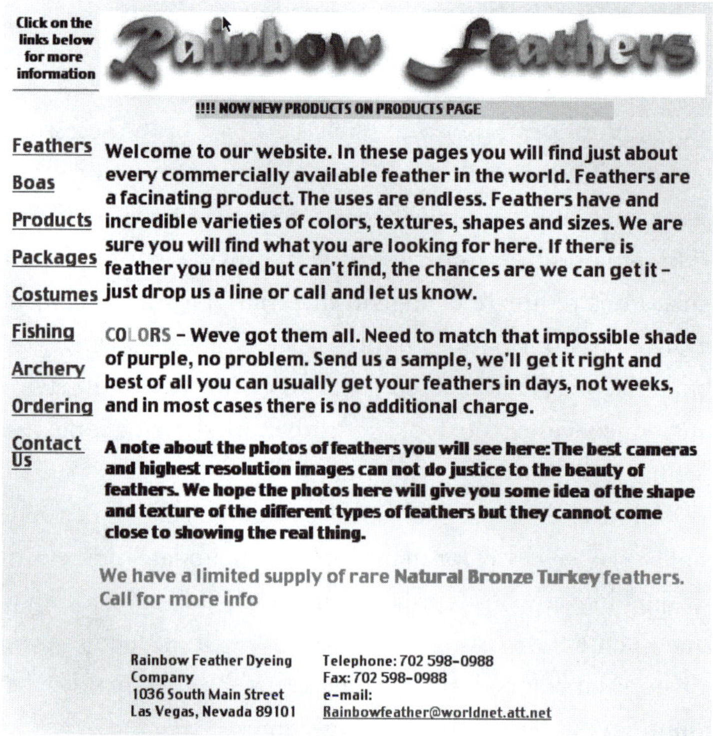

FIGURE 3.15
Rainbow Feather Dyeing Company.

Courtesy of Rainbow Feather Dyeing Company.

continues to fluctuate, as new organizations are formed, names are changed, and complementary organizations merge to form strategic alliances. Trade organizations in the apparel and accessories supplier sectors can be aimed at very specific business markets, and almost every area of apparel and accessories production offers at least one trade organization. Specific trade organizations for textiles include those for fibers, textile production, textile machinery, accessories notions and components, and decorative treatments. These numerous groups typically publish electronic and/or print trade journals. Table 3.1 lists important trade organizations for the textiles, notions, and trims industries. Table 3.2 lists the related trade publications.

TABLE 3.I

Trade Organizations for the Textile, Notions, and Trims Industries

Organization	Location	Objectives
Sewn Products Equipment & Suppliers of the Americas (SPESA) www.spesa.org	Raleigh, NC	To promote and protect the interests and images of suppliers for the global sewn products industry.
American Apparel & Footwear Association/The Fashion Association (AAFA/TFA) www.americanapparel.org	Washington, DC	To promote and enhance U.S. apparel, footwear, and other sewn products companies and their suppliers, and to keep abreast of legislative activities affecting the domestic industry.
Cotton Board www.cottonboard.org	Memphis, TN	To serve cotton producers and importers by promoting demand and research in the industry.
Cotton Council International/ National Cotton Council of America www.cottonusa.org www.cotton.org	Washington, DC	To sponsor trade shows, conferences, and programs promoting cotton fibers and manufactured cotton products in markets around the world.
Cotton, Incorporated www.cottoninc.com	Carey, NC	To sponsor trade shows and conferences promoting cotton fibers, and to increase the demand for and profitability of cotton through research and promotion.
The Bobbin Group www.bobbin.com	Columbia, SC	To sponsor a triennial, worldwide trade show and annual trade shows for the global apparel and sewn products manufacturing industries, and to organize educational courses, conferences, and seminars.
National Network of Embroidery Professionals www.nnep.net	Stow, OH	To represent professionals and companies in the embroidery industry, and to host a conference and trade show.
Embroidery Trade Association www.embroiderytrade.org	Dallas, TX	To strengthen the commercial embroidery business through member education, representation, networking, research, and consumer outreach.

TABLE 3.2

Trade Publications for the Textiles, Notions, and Trims Industries

Trade Publication Name	Description
Global Sources	An online global trade catalog offering volume buyers access to vendors of all types of general merchandise, including accessories components.
Behind the Seams	Published by Sewn Products Equipment & Suppliers of the Americas (SPESA). An electronic trade journal that includes a comprehensive list of trade show sponsors and the event dates.
Apparel Magazine	Published by the Bobbin Group both in print and electronically. Monthly articles on all types of sewn products, including apparel and accessories.
Apparel Buyers Guide	Published by the Bobbin Group. An online guide provides B2B (business to business) services including company listings by product and name.

The number of trade shows in the accessories supply industry appears to be increasing and is not limited to any geographic location. Companies in North and South America, Europe, and Asia heavily promote the accessories supply industry by sponsoring trade shows. Other trade shows promoting specific products, such as jewelry or leather, are described in each chapter. Important trade shows are listed in Table 3.3.

TABLE 3.3

Trade Shows for the Textiles, Notions, and Trims Industries

Trade Show	Location	Sponsors
Bobbin World	Orlando, FL	Bobbin Group, Sewn Products Equipment and Suppliers of the Americas, American Apparel and Footwear Association, and Embroidery Trade Association
Bobbin Mexico	Ciudad de México, México	Bobbin Group
Material World Miami Beach	Miami Beach, FL	Urban Expositions
Network	Cleveland, OH	National Network of Embroidery Professionals
International Fashion Fabric Exhibition	New York, NY	MAGIC International
International Textile Manufacturers Association Exhibition	Birmingham, England, and western Europe	International Textile Manufacturers Association
Intertextile	Sophia, Bulgaria	Bulgarian Chamber of Commerce and Industry
International Sewn Products Expo and Bobbin World	North America	Sewn Products Equipment and Suppliers of the Americas and American Apparel and Footwear Association
World Footwear Materials Exposition	Taichung, Taiwan	Footwear Industries of America and American Apparel and Footwear Association

MERCHANDISING TRENDS AND TECHNIQUES

The merchandising of textiles, notions, and trims is primarily conducted business-to-business. Most manufacturing companies rely on trade shows to introduce new products and make important business contacts. A recent trade show trend has been educating business customers by offering informational activities. These activities include current event seminars, academic facilitators sponsoring research forums, presentations of technical papers, and innovative products and services presentations.

The Internet affords businesses many opportunities to reach trade customers, but a certain degree of difficulty exists when buying fashion textiles from a remote location. The inability to touch and visually inspect the fabric must be considered. However, swatches may be sent through the mail, the customer may reorder on existing yardage, or the customer may be familiar with the merchandise and need not actually see it before ordering. Purchasing staple goods, such as notions and trims, through the Internet offers significant time-saving opportunities for businesses.

Electronic Data Interchange (EDI) is another method for buying or reordering staple (consistently used) textiles and trims. With an EDI system, the businesses (supplier, manufacturer, and retailer) are connected via an electronic networking system. As stock-keeping units (SKUs) from inventory are sold, all partners in the EDI system receive the information and make plans for replenishment. Integrated technology, such as EDI, will be used increasingly in the future.

SUMMARY

- Cotton, linen, hemp, and jute are natural cellulosic fibers; wool, silk, pashmina, leather, and fur are natural protein fibers; rayon, acetate, polyester, nylon, acrylic, and spandex are common manufactured fibers that are often used as less expensive substitutes for natural fibers.
- Simple yarns produce smooth, flat fabrics, while complex yarns produce textured and napped fabrics. Chenille and bouclé are two complex yarns used for fashion accessories.
- Fabrication is the manufacture of fabric from yarns or fibers into wovens, knits, and nonwovens.
- Microfibers are very fine manufactured fibers used in place of silk fibers.
- Fabrications create decorative elements of fashion accessories. Lace, macramé, and crochet produce an openwork design in fabric.
- Straws come from plants and have limited durability. Common uses for straws include sandal soles, handbags, and summer hats.
- Bamboo has a stiffer texture, similar to wood and is most often used for handbag handles.
- Zippers, also known as slide fasteners, are only about 100 years old. They are used to prevent the loss of small items and to allow an accessory to form-fit the body. Zippers are usually functional, but may also be used to enhance the aesthetics of accessories.

- Buttons are a functional closing device made of such materials as wood, shell, horn, plastic, glass, stones, metal, and leather or fashion fabric.
- Snaps, grommets, Velcro, and buckles are used for fastening many types of accessories and may be substituted for one another depending on the end use.
- Braids are narrow, woven fabrics used as finishings on edgings and as ornamental trims.
- Threads, lacing, ribbons, and bows may be used in topstitching or embroidery applications or as decorative narrow wovens. Leather lacings are used to close two parts of an accessory.
- Artificial silk flowers are used on women's and children's accessories, especially headwear. Feathers, from chickens and turkeys to peacocks, are attractive embellishments lacking durability.
- Seashells, such as iridescent mother-of-pearl and semiprecious stones, are popular natural ornamentation on fashion accessories.
- A textile can be described in terms of its texture, fiber content, fabrication, color, or print. Textile trends in ready-to-wear are usually interpreted into fashion accessories products. Often, designers introduce new textile components into best-selling shapes to minimize risks.
- Much of the manufacturing of components occurs in Asian countries. Component parts, such as snaps and grommets, remain consistent in appearance over seasons, so orders can be placed well in advance of the manufacturing.
- Trade shows are located throughout the world, with key shows being held in cities important to global commerce.
- The textiles, notions, and trims industry promotes to other businesses to a greater extent than to the general public. Business-to-business trade shows are important information exchange opportunities. Web sites are used for business-to-business commerce, and electronic data interchange (EDI) is a cost-saving networking system between the supplier, manufacturer, and retailer in which partners receive sales data and make replenishment plans.

TERMS FOR REVIEW

acetate	chenille	fibulae
acrylic	coated fabrics	fur
au natural look	complex (novelty) yarns	fur fibers
bamboo	coquille	grommets
bobbin (pillow) lace	cotton	grosgrain ribbon
bobbinet lace	crewel thread	hand
bouclé	crochet	hemp
braids	elasticity	industrial zippers
buckles	fabrication	invisible zippers
cellulose fibers	felt	jute

knitting	notions	spandex
lacing	nylon	straw
leather	pashmina	stretch wovens
linen	polyester	suede cloth
Lurex	protein fibers	suede leather
macramé lace	rayon	texture
marabou feathers	satin ribbon	triacetate
metallic thread	sericulture	Ultrasuede
microfibers	silk	Velcro
needlepoint lace	simple yarns	vinyl
netting	snaps	weaving
nonwovens	soutache (Russian braid)	wool

REVIEW QUESTIONS

1. What are some of the important natural and manufactured fibers used in fashion accessories?

2. What are some basic differences in accessories manufactured with simple yarns compared to those manufactured with complex yarns?

3. What are the major fabrication methods used for fashion accessories?

4. What are some similarities among lace, macramé, and crochet, and what are some accessories applications for these specialty textiles?

5. What is meant by narrow, woven fabrics?

6. In what ways have zippers become fashion items, rather than strictly functional notions?

7. What are some ways texture in accessories can be visually enhanced?

8. How might a designer use colors and prints to update an existing line?

9. What are some important trade organizations, publications, and shows for the textiles and trims industry?

10. How is computer technology used as a marketing tool in the textiles and trims industry?

KNOWLEDGE APPLICATIONS

1. Visit a department store (or Web site) carrying straw accessories, such as hats or handbags. Record the types of straw used for all available accessories. Research each type of straw and explain plant and fiber characteristics.

2. Visit a store carrying a wide selection of one type of accessory, such as wallets, handbags, belts, scarfs, or ties. Create a chart and record the fiber content or materials used and the price points. Evaluate the relationship between materials and price point. Compare findings with others in the class.

3. Interview a person employed in the textiles and trims industry, such as a fabric store, manufacturing facility, or design firm. Develop a list of important questions in advance of the meeting.

4. Visit a fabric store or notions department and locate examples of at least ten textiles and trims discussed in this chapter. On a chart, record the name, description, price, quantity and packaging information where applicable. Optional: Provide a detailed sketch of each product.

5. Visit your school library to select an article in a textiles or trims trade journal or an issue of *Women's Wear Daily*. Type a one-page report summarizing and critiquing the article. Include bibliographic information and attach a copy of the article.

CHAPTER 4

LEATHER

An ancient eastern king enjoyed touring his kingdom but was frustrated by the rocky and uneven surface of the landscape. He found walking difficult for bare feet, so ordered his servants to lay animal skins over the path, covering the ground on which he walked. This tedious process was much too time consuming for the impatient king. In a rage, he demanded his prime minister to devise a way to cover all the earth of his kingdom with animal skins — or face certain death.

Believing there was no way to fulfill the demand, the prime minister resigned himself to an untimely demise. He refused to see anyone, giving up hope for a solution. An inventive young man heard of the demand and tried to arrange an appointment with the prime minister. Distraught, the prime minister refused to grant him an audience.

The determined boy sneaked into the king's palace and managed to enter the king's chambers. Before the king could ring for a guard, the boy hurriedly uncovered a pair of leather sandals.

"As far as you are concerned, Your Highness, the earth will forever more be covered in leather!" quickly exclaimed the boy.

The inventive young man was appointed the new prime minister, and leather became a valuable commodity.

—author unknown

A BRIEF HISTORY OF LEATHER

THE BEAUTY AND DURABILITY OF LEATHER HAS MADE IT AN IDEAL TEXTILE FOR APPAREL AND accessories, dating back to prehistoric times. Some scientists claim leather making is the oldest trade in the world, even predating farming. World-renowned anthropologist L.S.B. Leaky discovered tools in Africa that were used for leather making about 600,000 years ago. The

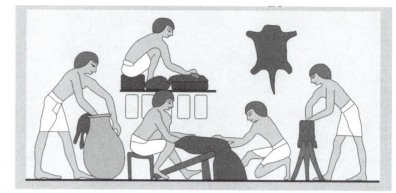

FIGURE 4.1
Ancient Egyptians tanning leather.

development of **tanning,** a preservation process that prevents animal skins and hides from decomposing, is credited to the ancient Hebrews and Egyptians who left written records of their tanning methods. The fundamentals of this ancient tanning process are still used in many regions of the world (see Figure 4.1).

Over the ages, leather became an extremely important textile as civilizations developed. In addition to apparel and accessories, leather was used for writing materials (a paper-like form called *vellum*), water flasks, furniture, saddles, body armor, and tents or nomadic houses. At times, leather was so valued it was placed among gold, silver, ivory, and gems in importance. Elaborately gilded and jewel-encrusted leather capes, furniture, and chests offer evidence of the historic status of leather.

In North America, Native Americans developed their own process for tanning hides and skins. Their buckskin was one of the most prized leathers. The broader commercial leather industry began in North America when tanneries were established in Massachusetts after the first Pilgrims landed at Plymouth Rock (see Figure 4.2).

Vegetable tanning was most common until the 1800s when a New England tanner discovered the use of chromium salts as a tanning agent. The method used by early American tanners was lengthy and unorthodox by today's standards, requiring at least a year. During the Civil War, the need for speedy footwear production led to several mechanical inventions and chemical discoveries. These, in turn, contributed to processing speed and improved leather goods during the 19th century. Among the improvements were Samuel Parker's splitting machine (1809), which could split 100 steer hides per day, and the discovery that chromium mineral salts could replace ground vegetable matter (bark) as the tanning agent.

During the peak of U.S. leather production in the 19th century, South Street in Boston was considered the hub of the leather industry and controlled much of the trading. Tanneries became cornerstones of the most sizable New England towns and moved westward to cities such as Milwaukee, Chicago, and St. Louis. Hides were shipped from the western cattle states and imported from Argentina and Mexico to meet demands.

During the last century, the once-prosperous leather industry was plagued with significant problems. Mechanization, while improving efficiency, created overproduction problems, caus-

FIGURE 4.2
Early American tanners.
Painting by Mort Kunstler.

From the original painting, *First Tanner in America,*
by Mort Kunstler. © Mort Kunstler, Inc.

ing many small tanneries to close or be forced into mergers with larger companies. A boom in the beef cattle industry glutted the hide market, requiring hides to be exported to Japan, Hong Kong, Korea, and Taiwan. The introduction of and demand for man-made leather materials for shoes further harmed the domestic leather industry. Finally, the stringent pollution control standards enforced in the United States have further caused a dwindling of U.S. tanneries.

THE LEATHER INDUSTRY

While leather production in the United States has declined, the global market for leather has been improving. Many developing countries engage in leather production, either by raising their own animals or by processing U.S. skins and hides. Many accessories use leather, including footwear, headwear, gloves, belts, handbags, personal (small) leather goods, and luggage. Its widespread use and special care requirements make leather an important topic in the study of fashion accessories.

Leather encompasses all of the processed skins and hides (fur removed) from land animals, reptiles, fish, and birds (feathers removed). In the leather industry, the animal skin is referred to as a **hide** when it comes from large animals, such as cattle and horses, and a **skin** when it comes from smaller animals, such as calves, sheep, and goats.

The **grain** of the skin or hide is the uppermost skin surface from which the hair grows. Layers beneath it, called **splits,** are also turned into leather. The **full** or **top grain** is the layer of the skin with characteristic markings (only the hair has been removed) and is the most attractive and durable. The **markings** in the top grain, irregularities that give skins their distinctive appearances, make it more expensive than splits.

The Leather Manufacturing Process

Leather, like most natural textiles, undergoes many cost-increasing changes before being manufactured into products. The sources of leather vary significantly, from meat industry by-products, to animals farmed specifically for their skins, to animals that are trapped in the wild. Once the hides are removed from the slaughtered animal, decomposition begins to occur immediately. A temporary preservation process, called **curing,** must take place within a few hours after the carcass flesh is removed. Curing involves either controlled drying of the skins, or more commonly, the application of sodium chloride (salt) to the skins. The curing process is not a part of tanning, but it is a necessary prerequisite.

Tanning is the preservation process used to create breathable, supple skins, and to prevent putrefaction, the decomposition of organic matter. Agents used for tanning include minerals such as alum, chrome, and zircon; vegetable tannins, such as extracts from oak, hemlock, chestnut, and mimosa barks, fruits, and leaves; oil tannins, such as fish oils; and chemical tannins, such as formaldehyde.

Numerous interrelated steps are involved in the processing of hides and skins into leather for the manufacture of products. Although each step can be tailored for specific end uses, the effects of each step have a bearing on subsequent steps. The leather-making operations can be divided into two major categories—wet operations and dry operations.

Wet Operations

The five basic steps in **wet operations** are as follows:

1. Preparatory cleaning
2. Wet chemical treatments to ready the hides for tanning
3. Tanning
4. Splitting to reduce the thickness of hides
5. Enhancing the visual and tactile appearances

These steps can be further broken down as follows:

1. **Receiving and Storage**—Before raw hides can be processed, they are placed in a **hide house** where sorting, weighing, and batching occurs. Some raw hides are received as cured (salted) hides, while others may be fresh hides, very recently removed from carcasses.
2. **Soaking**—Because the sodium chloride used in the curing process draws out much of the moisture, hides and skins are placed in detergent and disinfectant-filled vats for softening and cleaning.
3. **Unhairing**—Alkaline chemical depilatories dissolve the hair fibers. If the hair fibers are to be salvaged and sold for felt products, weaker depilatories are used, or the hair is mechanically removed.

4. **Bating**—The alkaline solution is neutralized and washed from the hides during the first stage of bating, called **deliming.** The second stage is the addition of an enzymatic bate, which dissolves the remaining surface contaminants.

5. **Pickling**—Salt or brine and an acid (such as sulfuric acid) ready the hides for tanning. This reverses the alkaline solution of the bating process, so the hides and skins are ready to accept the chrome tanning agents.

6. **Tanning**—The skins and hides are converted to a **nonputrescible** (does not rot) material, with improvements in dimensional stability, moisture and abrasion resistance, heat and chemical resistance, and flex-abrasion resistance. The earliest commercial method was vegetable tanning using ground tree bark. The most popular and least time-consuming tanning method, **chrome tanning,** involves penetrating the hides in rotating vessels with basic chromium sulfate or chrome (chromium salts, sugar-like substances, and sulfuric acid). Once adequate levels of chrome have penetrated the hides, they have a bluish-green tint, called "in the blue" or "wet blue" state. The tanner gradually increases the pH conditions by adding a mild alkaline (such as baking soda) to permanently set the chrome agents. The tanning process takes between four and six hours to complete.

7. **Wringing and Sorting**—The tanned skins and hides are run between two rollers to squeeze the excess chemical moisture from them, and then sorted for thickness.

8. **Trimming and Siding**—A flat conveyor belt carries the hides to a trimmer who slices off the undesirable perimeter areas, such as the head and shanks (legs) of the hides. A circular saw cuts the hide lengthwise down the center back, making two half sides.

9. **Splitting and Shaving**—Uniform thicknesses are created on the hide to ensure ease of product manufacturing.
   a. *Splitting*—With the grain side up, the skins are fed through a splitting machine, which cuts off the too-thick sections of the flesh side. These are called splits and can be used for suede and other less expensive products.
   b. *Shaving*—Machines further level the thickness of the skins. Usually, the center back is the thickest section of the hide, gradually thinning as it approaches the belly. Figure 4.3 shows the shape of a full hide and its designated subdivisions. Figure 4.4 is an illustration of designated splits on a hide.

10. **Retanning, Coloring, and Fatliquoring**—These three steps, although very different in nature, occur in one drum.

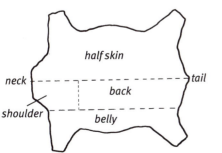

FIGURE 4.3
Subdivisions of a full hide.

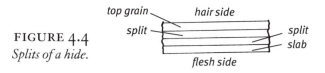

FIGURE 4.4
Splits of a hide.

a. *Retanning* is the application of additional chemicals, such as vegetable extracts or minerals.

b. *Coloring* adds penetrating **aniline dye,** a synthetic organic dye, usually from petroleum sources.

c. *Fatliquoring* creates soft, supple leather with increased **tensile strength** (stretching). Oily substances are added to a rotating drum containing the skins and hides.

11. **Setting Out**—Rollers compress the skins and hides, squeezing out the excess moisture and smoothing and stretching the skins to ready them for the drying operations.

Dry Operations

Dry operations include the following four basic steps:

1. Removing excess moisture
2. Softening and smoothing treatments
3. Applying special topical finishes
4. Readying the finished products for shipment to product manufacturers

These steps can be described in more detail as follows:

1. **Drying**—All but the normal 10 to 12 percent of moisture contained in leather is removed in low-heat ovens or in vacuums.

2. **Conditioning**—Water is sprayed over the stacked hides and left for several hours to allow for uniform moisture absorption.

3. **Staking and Dry Milling**—The skins are passed between hundreds of oscillating pins that stretch the leather in every direction creating pliable and soft leather. Dry milling requires tumbling the skins into rotating drums until soft.

4. **Buffing**—Abrasive cylinders smooth the surface grain and minimize grain imperfections. Full grains are not usually buffed.

5. **Finishing**—Full-grain hides receive a minimal finishing to ensure visibility of the attractive grain. Opaque or pigment finishes with heavier coverage may be applied to upgrade less attractive leathers.

6. **Plating**—Steam and pressure smoothes the surface of the leather. Engraved plates can emboss grain patterns on the surface. Split leathers are often embossed because they have no grain pattern.

7. **Grading**—Leather is graded based on the softness, degree of uniformity in color and thickness, and the extent of imperfections. Pricing is based on the grade it receives during this process.

8. **Measuring**—Hides are measured in square feet, and the size is stamped on the flesh side.

Leather Treatments

To create versatile and useful leathers, a variety of finishing treatments can be applied to the skins, altering the appearance or hand. The treatments or treated leathers listed below provide manufacturers and designers ways to create the appearance of expensive, exotic leathers from plentiful and lower-priced skins, such as cattle hide. These include:

Aniline Finish Application of a transparent finish, allowing the top grain to be visible; protective coating with protein, resin, lacquer, or wax

Bleaching Application of chemicals to lighten the color of the leather

Boarding A mechanical process of folding a skin, natural grain side in, and imprinting or embossing a grained effect on the flesh side—also called **box** or **willow finish**

Dyeing An aniline dye used to alter the natural color of a hide in two ways:

    Dip-dyeing Submerging leather to ensure color penetration throughout the skin

    Brush-dyeing Color applied only to the surface of the skin

Embossing Using an engraved plate, pressure, and heat to permanently imprint the unique grain of an expensive leather onto another, less expensive leather surface. (For example, crocodile-embossed split cattle hide is a split layer of cattle hide imprinted with the unique top grain appearance of a crocodile.)

Glazing Running the grain leather under a high-speed, pressurized roller to create a high gloss

Napping Creating suede by placing the flesh side of the skin against an emery wheel

Nubuck or **Rybuck** Light buffing of the top grain of cattle hide to a very fine nap, smoother than suede; creates buck sides, resembling buckskin

Patent Applying a glossy polyurethane finish over the grain side of leather to create a nonporous, lustrous, "plasticized" appearance

Pigment or **Paint** An opaque color that covers the surface of the leather

Sueding Flesh side (usually) of the skin napped on an emery wheel to create a velvety surface

Classifications of Leather

Leather comes from a wide range of animals. It is usually a by-product of the meat, milk, and wool industries, but some leathers come from animals that are slaughtered specifically for their skins, such as alligators. These types of leathers are much more costly.

The most common of all leathers is **bovine leather,** a by-product of the cattle industry. The supply of cattle leather is primarily dependent upon the demand for beef. A decline in the demand for red meat has caused an increase in the cost of hides. In addition, the increasing prices of cattle feed and hay have discouraged the rebuilding of herds.

Only about five percent of leather hides obtained from the beef industry are usable as "naked" top-grain, aniline-finished leather products. About 20 percent are usable as smooth-finished leathers, needing an application of pigment with additional covering power. About 75 percent require embossing, filling, buffing, and stuffing to camouflage barbed wire scars, insect bites, skin folds, seared brand marks, scratches, and other blemishes.

Although bovine leather is not the only classification used for the various accessories, it does have the lion's share of the market. In addition to bovine leather, several other land and water animal skins are used for fashion accessories. The end use is determined by the thickness of the skin, durability, leather processing, and rarity. The following tables classify leathers according to the animals from which the skin originates, the leather name, and common accessories uses. These classifications of leather provide the automobile, home, apparel, and accessories industries with a wide variety of products.

Table 4.1 lists the land animal, leather name, and some common accessories products. Table 4.2 lists the water animal, leather name, and related accessories products.

Each animal has a distinct marking pattern on the top grain. Figure 4.5 illustrates a close-up view of several leather textures from a variety of animals.

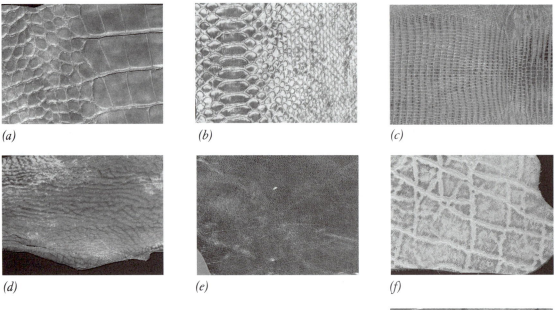

(a) (b) (c)

(d) (e) (f)

FIGURE 4.5 *Closeup view of various topgrain leathers: (a) alligator skin, (b) snake skin, (c) lizard skin, (d) shark skin, (e) goat skin, (f) elephant skin, and (g) ostrich skin.*

Skin samples provided by Independence Leather, L.L.C. (www.independenceleather.com).

(g)

TABLE 4.1

Land Animals Used for Leather

Animal	Type of Leather	Typical Products
Cow, Bull, Steer	Cattle hide, Cowhide, Bullhide, Steerhide	Shoes, boots, patent leather, apparel, handbags, belts, luggage, upholstery
	Rawhide (undergoes many preparatory processes, but left in an untanned state)	
	Saddle leather (vegetable tanned, left "naked" with only an aniline finish)	
Calf	Calf leather	Shoe uppers, slippers, handbags, small leather goods, hat sweatbands
	Vellum (similar to parchment)	Lamp shades
Horse	Cordovan or Shell (tanning process developed in Cordova, Spain)	Men's shoe uppers
Goat, Kid	Glazed or Glace (chrome tanned, highly polished)	Gloves
	Levant (shrunken grain pattern; also from sheep or seal)	Gloves, shoes, small leather goods
	Morocco	Gloves, shoes
	Cabretta	Gloves, apparel
Sheep, Lamb	Chamois or Chamoise (soft, sueded); also from antelope	Gloves, apparel
	Mocha suede or leather	Gloves
	Capeskin or Cape leather	Gloves, apparel
	Napa or Nappa (chrome or alum tanning)	Gloves
	Sheepskin or Shearling (wool left on skin during tanning)	Slippers, apparel
	Skiver (grain-split of a sheepskin)	Handbags, hat sweatbands, small leather goods
Pig, Hog, Peccary (wild boar), Carpincho (water rodent)	Pigskin (chrome tanned; may be sueded)	Shoes, dress and sport gloves, small leather goods
Deer, Elk, Antelope	Deerskin (grain surface intact)	Shoes, gloves, apparel
	Buckskin (grain surface removed)	Shoes, gloves, apparel
Water Buffalo (not American Bison)	Buffalo (from Far East)	Shoes, work gloves, handbags, luggage
Kangaroo, Wallaby	Kangaroo (resembles glazed kid; very strong)	Men's shoes, small leather goods, luggage
Ostrich	Ostrich (very expensive)	Western boots, small leather goods
Lizard	Teju or Alligator Lizard	Western boots, handbags, small leather goods
Snake	Anaconda (water snake), Cobra, Python	Shoes, apparel
Miscellaneous Land Animals	Camel, Elephant, Anteater (Pangolin)	Small leather goods

TABLE 4.2

Water Animals Used for Leather

Animal	Type of Leather	Typical Products
Alligator	Alligator (farm raised for characteristic glossy squares called "scoots" or "tiles")	Shoe uppers, handbags, small leather goods
Crocodile	Crocodile	Shoe uppers, handbags, small leather goods, watchbands, apparel
Eel	Eelskin (from Sea of Japan)	Small leather goods
Seal, Walrus	Pin Seal (attractive grain, often imitated by embossing other leathers)	Shoes, belts, luggage watchbands, small leather goods
Shark	Sharkskin (smooth, mesh-like grain, similar to pin seal)	Watchbands, wallets
Miscellaneous Aquatic Animals	Frogskin, turtleskin	Watchbands, wallets

Imitation Leather

Imitation or **simulated leather** is becoming increasingly difficult to distinguish from real leather. Technology enables the textile industry to create simulated leather that resembles real leather in almost every way except, perhaps, the smell. Terms, such as *leatherette, Naugahyde*®, *vinyl, pleather, Liquid Leather*®, *Belleseime*®, *Super-suede*®, *Facile*®, *and Ultrasuede*® connote images of simulated leather and suede, sometimes possessing qualities, such as washability, better than real leather.

Some of the simulated leather textiles are a base fabric coated with a plasticized, waterproof coating such as polyvinyl chloride (PVC) or polyurethane. The woven or knitted base fabric provides stabilization, while the coating or film offers protection from moisture, dirt, chemicals, and abrasion. Suede-like material may be made of needlepunched fabrics, often a combination of polyester and polyurethane foam. Synthetic accessories manufacturers are developing lines that simulate the softer and more expensive leathers, such as suede and kidskin.

Liz Claiborne, in an effort to reach the fashion-forward, yet price-conscious consumer, offered PVC handbags retailing for approximately $60. These fashionably styled, fake leather bags bore a strong resemblance to genuine leather. Her version of the popular python pattern featured a metal and leather mixture, for example, a shiny silver python print on a narrow, suede belt. Several other designers foiled and bronzed leather accessories, including a holographic leather shoe by Calvin Klein.

High-Performance Leather

In the late 1990s, scientists engineered a special tanning process in which chemicals permeate the leather to create washable, stain-resistant, and waterproof leather garments and shoes while retaining their softness and breathability. This high-performance leather, called Lezanova®, was developed by a Japanese manufacturer, Daikin Industries. In addition to improving existing tanning methods, the leather industry is working to develop additional high-performance leathers.

Leather Industry Regulations

Federal regulations affect the leather industry in several ways. Tanneries are regulated to protect the environment, and there are laws to protect animals whose skins are used for leather products. Other laws and regulations ensure accurate labeling and advertising of leather goods.

The Environment

The Environmental Protection Agency (EPA) is the federal agency that issues and administers regulations governing the tanning industry, including waste treatment standards. Under the Resource Conservation and Recovery Act and the Clean Water Act, hazardous chemical effluents used in tanning, such as sulfides, chromium, and acidity, must be pretreated before being released into waste treatment facilities. U.S. tanneries are adopting tanning procedures that meet federal, state, and local standards and are producing less chemical waste. In some parts of the country, state and local laws are more restrictive than federal regulations.

Concern exists regarding chromium pollutants in landfills from waste scrap leather, wet-blue trimmings, shavings, and tannery sludge. Efforts are being made to reduce or eliminate the chromium salts used to tan hides. Tanneries are adopting methods such as recycling chromium or replacing it with nontoxic metal salts or other organic tanning materials like vegetable or synthetic resins. According to the U.S. Trade and Industry Outlook 2000, the industry has developed and is adopting new tanning systems that will use nontoxic metal salts to replace some or all of the chromium currently used.

Three important factors are credited with reducing environmental impact and lowering tanning costs: recycling chromium during tanning, new processes producing fewer chemicals, and the installation of technologically advanced equipment.

Animal Preservation

Congress passed the Endangered Species Act in 1973 and reauthorized it in 1988. The Act prohibits the importing, exporting, possession, sale or use of fish, animals, and plants that are endangered or threatened with extinction. The Fish and Wildlife Service and the National Marine Fisheries Service are responsible for the administration of the Act.

Among the North American leather-bearing animals listed as endangered or threatened are the American Crocodile, the American Alligator, the Stellar Sea Lion, some lizards, and a few snakes. International agreements also exist to protect species on other continents. A complete copy of the Endangered Species Act may be obtained from the U.S. Fish and Wildlife Service and is accessible through its Web site.

The leather industry has been challenged by animal rights activists such as People for the Ethical Treatment of Animals (PETA), although to a lesser degree than the fur industry (see Chapter 5). In June 2000, PETA spokesperson RaeLeann Smith explained the animal rights group's protests against the wearing of leather. "Where animals are being slaughtered for their meat and leather, you can find cruelty and abuse."

Content, Labeling, and Advertising

Leather industry regulations pertaining to content, labeling, and advertising are closely tied to the standards of shoe production and merchandising. The list below contains excerpts from the shoe regulations that pertain to the leather industry in general:

1. Trade names that suggest *leather* are prohibited unless the product is actually leather.
2. The label *genuine leather* can only be used on top grain leather.
3. Products must be labeled as to the exact finishes used, such as embossing or dyeing, when the product appearance simulates another animal skin. For example, "Simulated alligator made of split cowhide."
4. Man-made materials simulating leather must be identified.
5. Advertising must indicate if leather appearance is actually split leather or imitation leather.

THE LEATHER FASHION INDUSTRY

Leather is frequently the textile of choice for fashion accessories because of its beauty and durability. Many of the accessories categories are dominated by leather or simulated leather products. The heavy demand for leather has shifted in product emphasis over time, moving away from footwear and toward automobile upholstery and home fashions. However, leather has always been an integral part of quality accessories and apparel, and the global, long-term outlook remains strong.

Design of Leather Products

A creative designer treating leather like fabric may be inspired to create beautiful apparel and accessories. However, it takes a highly skilled craftsperson to sort through bundles of leathers, matching colors and textures, and exactly cutting the pattern pieces (see Figure 4.6).

Today's designers are changing the hard-edge image of leather accessories and apparel by offering supple skins enhanced with pearlized luster looks; shiny, bronzed, or foiled finishes; and studding or embroidery. Durable leather appears delicate and feminine when shaved to a thin layer and dyed in pastel colors. Buttery soft kidskins are especially suitable for the softer designs.

Profile: Coach

Like Ralph Lauren or Eddie Bauer, Coach Leather is an American icon. It arose from the love of an American tradition — baseball. Inspired by the beauty and suppleness of a patinaed leather baseball glove, the founder of Coach applied the same principle to the creation of a woman's handbag. Coach uses the vegetable tanning process to produce their superior top-grain, glove-tanned leathers. A transparent aniline dye finish enhances the beautiful grains selected from the best 10 percent of available skins.

The Manhattan-based company began in 1941, with its first collection consisting of 12 classic handbag styles. Today, Coach is still famous for supple, glove-leather handbags, but the company has expanded offerings to include backpacks, shoes, sunglasses, straw and cotton handbags, personal leather goods, pet collars and leashes, and home fashions from pillows to furniture and leather privacy screens. The high-profile Manhattan flagship store is located on 57th Street and Madison Avenue.

Coach began in the women's accessories industry, but now offers Travel and Business Collections for women and men. A need for lightweight luggage inspired the Travel Collection made of cotton twill fabrics. The Business Collection consists of briefcases, organizers and planners, notepads, computer cases, and cell phone cases. Now, as in the past, Coach is committed to designing classic, but not static, well-proportioned leather products that reflect the American style.

"People want fashion," said Reed Krakoff, executive creative director at Coach. "So we have fabric travel bags and paisley bags with leather trim and animal prints on raffia. Coach never had anything non-leather until a year and a half ago," Krakoff explained in 1999. "We're not doing a ready-to-wear collection, but . . . we'll do the perfect leather peacoat, the perfect trench, the perfect leather pants, the perfect T. And there'll be a suede poncho and suede shirt, and it will all relate to the handbags." (Schiro, July 27, 1999, p. 9). By 2000, the newly introduced fashion products accounted for about half of total Coach sales.

Coach uses traditional retailing channels — brick-and-mortar stores, mail-order catalogs, and factory outlet stores — and a Web site to merchandise their products. The Web site includes sections on gifts, ordering, repairs, cleaning, services, and links to each accessories category. So fine-tuned are Coach services, that customers can

Hampton handbags by Coach.
Courtesy of Fairchild Publications, Inc.

even order replacement straps for their handbags! U.S. customers can go to one of the 106 physical stores or 63 outlet locations or order directly from the Internet site. Coach will open an additional 56 full-price stores by 2003.

Licensing and cooperative ventures are important parts of the Coach strategy. Baker Furniture's John Black and Reed Krakoff have teamed up to create sleek, modern Coach leather furniture. Signature Eyewear licenses Coach sun and optical eyewear, and Movado has the licensing rights to the Coach watch collection, some of which have stainless steel bracelet bands without leather trim.

Advertising budgets of $14 million in the United States and $1.5 million in Japan (whose per capita expenditures on handbags is higher) are being channeled into print media, reinforced by window displays, postcards, phone kiosks, and city panels. Advertising copy has taken on a lighter tone. A recent print advertising campaign featured portraits of actresses Candice Bergen and Julianne Moore.

The words *forward thinking* and *fashion focused* describe the company whose handbags became synonymous with luxurious leather in the last part of the 20th century. The Coach name will be expanding to many other fashion goods during the next decade, and consumers can expect the same superb craftsmanship and high-quality leathers that created the icon.

FIGURE 4.6
John Galliano's couture crocodile hat and dress.
Courtesy of Fairchild Publications, Inc.

The application of specific leather treatments, such as dyeing, embossing, and sueding, affects the appearance of the material. Designers work closely with tanning researchers, chemists, and engineers to create novel surface appearances desired by customers.

Care of Leather Products

Most leather products can be attractively maintained for several seasons if proper care procedures are followed. The rich appearance of fine leather products as they are worn, chafed, or scratched over the life of the product is known as **patina.** This natural aging enhances the character and beauty of the leather. Manufacturers even produce **distressed leather,** a new leather that has a weathered appearance achieved by tanning unevenly.

Because of the extensive tanning and processing the raw material undergoes, finished garments require little more than an occasional dry cleaning. Unless a leather garment is specifically marked "washable," it must be dry-cleaned. Dry-clean-only leathers that are subjected to wet cleaning can become stiff and brittle because of a loss of oils in the leather. Water-tolerant leathers do exist, and more are on the horizon in the apparel and footwear leather industries.

The type of care required depends on the type of leather. Customers should be informed of the requirements by hangtags and knowledgeable salespeople. Following are rules guiding the care of different types of leather.

Tech Talk

Pricey, But Practical

"$358 for a pair of five-pocket jeans?!"

"Ah, but they're machine washable… and leather."

Is there a market for high-end fashions in washable leather? Daikin Industries thinks so. And so do Bloomingdale's, Macy's, Burdine's, and Dillard's, all of which recently ordered a holiday line of washable leathers from Calvin Klein.

A special chemical process, more penetrating than a Gore-Tex® Teflon® membrane or Scotchguard®, permeates suedes and leathers rather than simply coating the surface. According to Daiken Industries, the developer of Lezanova®, the waterproof and washable leathers and suedes are made with a patented tanning process that completely and evenly permeates and cross-links the collagen molecules with fluoro-chemicals, forming a kind of molecular latticework. Water droplets are repelled, but air can still pass through Lezanova® leather so that it breathes as well as untreated leather.

The result is leather that can be made into shoes, handbags, gloves, luggage, belts, hats, caps, sofas, chairs, and apparel that possess easy wear and care characteristics. Lezanova® leathers are waterproof, stain-resistant, machine washable with minimal shrinkage, wrinkle-resistant, dry-cleanable, odor and rot repellent, and breathable. All this, yet the leathers are still buttery soft. Stringent, yet successful tests for Lezanova® leather products include a two-hour submersion in water with no water spotting; oil-based paint droplets that wipe off with no effect on the leather; and complete repellence of wine, mustard, ketchup, soy sauce, cooking oil, and salad dressing.

During the introductory stages of Lezanova®, the company was willing to send trade consumers a tester kit, complete with Lezanova®-treated and untreated leather samples, and a packet of soy sauce!

Patent Leathers Usually a damp cloth and a small amount of soap (if needed) will wipe away any spots on patent leather, and the leather can be dried and polished with a soft dry cloth. A greater problem with patent leather is a concern about cracking and splitting due to very cold temperatures. Perhaps this problem gave birth to the old fashion rule that patent leather accessories were spring and summer fashions. Although much of the patent leather today is synthetic, it can also be damaged by extreme cold and should not be exposed to inclement weather.

Smooth-Surfaced Leathers A wide range of leather care products exists for leathers with a smooth finish. Most of these products are in a creamy foundation, designed to be gently rubbed into the leather. Saddle soap, leather balm, wax polish, and leather conditioner clean and restore moisture (suppleness) to the leather. Consumers should spot test the item in an inconspicuous location to check for colorfastness before applying the cleaner to the rest of the accessory or garment.

Suede-Finished Leathers The napped finish of suede requires careful brushing with a soft nylon-bristled brush or a dry terrycloth towel. Stiff or metal bristles can damage the suede surface, leaving scrape marks on the skin. Shiny spots can develop on suede products in areas of abrasion. The nap can be roughened by gently brushing an emery cloth or emery nail board over the shiny patches. To prevent color loss, spots should not be rubbed too forcefully.

Water-Repellent and Waterproof Leathers Shoe oils, waxes, and silicon sprays are moisture-repellent finishes that consumers can apply to make leather products water and stain resistant.

Shoe oils and waxes are thick, penetrating substances that waterproof most smooth leathers and can be used on a variety of leather products, such as hiking boots, luggage, and handbags. In addition to waterproofing the leathers, many oils preserve the life of the product by preventing the drying out of leather. Oils should be rubbed into the leather and allowed to dry for several hours before reapplying a second coat. Oils remain in the leather even after exposure to rain, sleet, or snow and create a supple feel. Silicon sprays are applied from an aerosol can and create a much lighter coating than rubbed-in oils. Silicons bond to leathers to create a water barrier. These sprays still allow the leather to breathe, but they should be reapplied after soaking rains. Some brands of silicon sprays may be applied to suede or napped leathers, while other brands specifically recommend against suede or napped applications. Consumers should read product labels carefully to determine the types of leathers on which to use the products. There are many water-repellent products on the market, and brands include Scotchguard® by 3M, Kiwi, and Meltonian.

Whereas shoe oils, waxes, and silicon sprays are applied by consumers, Teflon® is applied to leather products during the manufacturing stages. Its molecules are affixed to the surface of the leather with relative permanence. More lasting finishes may permeate the entire thickness of the leather. Consumers who are willing to pay the higher prices for manufacturers' waterproof finishes, such as Gore-tex® and Lezanova®, benefit from simplified leather care (see Figure 4.7).

Washable Leathers Customers should adhere closely to the care instructions provided with leather products. Usually a small degree of shrinkage occurs with washable leathers. According to an August 2000 study by Daikin Industries, shrinkage percentages were between 3.6 and 5.6 percent for suede leathers and between 4.0 and 8.0 percent for gain leathers. Leathers treated with flouro-chemicals for waterproofing have the least amount of shrinkage.

FIGURE 4.7
Waterproof Lezanova leather shoe.
Courtesy of Lezanova®.

If a leather item is labeled washable, customers will get the best results by following these basic steps:

1. Initially test for colorfastness, by rubbing a damp swab in an inconspicuous area of the leather product. Multicolored items should be tested to ensure colors do not bleed.
2. Once colorfastness has been determined, the item can be hand washed in warm water, with a minimum of soap, and then rinsed completely to remove soap residue.
3. To prevent stretching, carry the item away from the sink on a towel.
4. Transfer the item to another towel and spread it flat to air dry away from heat sources and the sun. (It may be necessary to change towels periodically as the excess moisture is absorbed).
5. Once dry, the leather may feel slightly stiff to the touch. If so, apply a leather balm to soften it.

THE GLOBAL LEATHER INDUSTRY

The United States imports 44 percent of the tanned leather used to produce products domestically, and almost 80 percent of leather products sold in the United States are imported. Table 4.3 lists the import percentage of major categories of leather goods consumed in the United States.

Most of the processing of leather and the production of leather goods occur in China and developing countries because of their low labor costs. Although China is important for its leather products production, the country is not among the important suppliers of leather cattle hides. China alone manufactures more than one half (51 percent) of leather product imports worldwide, particularly leather footwear. China ranks first in the production of sheepskins and goatskins; developing countries in Africa and Asia also produce significant quantities of goatskin. Of the approximately 72 countries supplying the United States with leather skins and hides, Mexico is the chief supplier. Table 4.4 ranks the countries that supply leather hides to the United States.

TABLE 4.3
U.S. Leather Goods Imports

Category	Percentage Imported
Tanned Leather	44%
Handbags	88%
Leather Apparel	86%
Footwear	82%
Luggage	82%
Gloves	73%
Personal Leather Goods	62%
Product Average	79%

Source: U.S. Industry and Trade Outlook 2000: Footwear, Leather, and Leather Products

TABLE 4.4

Foreign Suppliers of Leather to the United States

Country	Percentages
Mexico	43%
Italy	16%
Argentina	16%
Brazil	4%
Germany	3%
Uruguay	3%

Source: U.S. Industry and Trade Outlook 2000: Footwear, Leather, and Leather Products

The United States imports a variety of leather types, but bovine leather (cattle hide and calf-skin) is the dominant category. Table 4.5 ranks U.S. imports by country according to leather types.

Although the United States ranks lower than many developing countries in the manufacture of leather goods, domestic production of good quality and large-size cattle hides is strong. The United States produces the greatest number (37 million) and heaviest weight of usable cattle hides due to better feedlot practices, including animal husbandry and nutrition, slaughter, preservation, and transportation practices. Table 4.6 shows the United States' relative position in bovine (cattle, calf, and buffalo) population. It is important to note that the United States ranks first in recovered cattle hides, although the country has a smaller cattle population.

Because the United States produces heavy hides and good quality bovine leather, the export market is important for supplying leather to high-priced foreign footwear manufacturers and furniture and automotive upholstery manufacturers. The United States supplies about 61 countries with leather, with about 43 percent of the supply being used for automobile seats. An increasing amount of the supply (17 percent in 1999) is **wet-blue leathers** (tanned, but not yet processed). Table 4.7 shows the ranking of countries that receive the largest percentages of U.S. exports. Most

TABLE 4.5

U.S. Leather Imports by Type and Country of Origin

Leather Type	Country	Percentages
Cattle hide, calfskin, buffalo, & equine	Mexico	90%
Sheepskin leather	Italy	3%
Goatskin & kidskin	China	1%
Other		6%

Source: U.S. Industry and Trade Outlook 1999: Footwear, Leather, and Leather Products.

TABLE 4.6

Ranking of Top Four Countries by Bovine Population

Country	Bovine Population
India	301.3 million head
Brazil	162.7 million head
China	147 million head
United States	99.5 million head

Source: U.S. Industry and Trade Outlook 2000: Footwear, Leather, and Leather Products.

of the countries to which the United States exports are considered developing countries. They have the low labor costs needed by manufacturers of labor-intensive footwear products.

Trade Organizations, Publications, and Shows

Tables 4.8, 4.9, and 4.10 represent the leather trade organizations, leather trade publications, and leather trade shows available to businesses. Many countries involved in leather trade support the leather industry with their own promotional organizations, publications, and major leather trade fairs.

MERCHANDISING TRENDS AND TECHNIQUES

The merchandising of leather products varies within specific product categories. The type of accessory rather than the material is the driving factor. Leather accessories are promoted, displayed, and sold along with their nonleather or simulated leather counterparts. Leather accessories tend to be at higher price points than nonleather accessories. Top grain leather is more expensive than split leather. Many of the top-of-the-line brands have separate counters or boutiques in department stores.

TABLE 4.7

U.S. Leather Exports

Country	Percentages of Exports
Mexico	28% (upholstery leathers)
China/Hong Kong	16%
Japan	11%
Canada	10%
South Korea	7% (wet-blue leathers)

Source: U.S. Industry and Trade Outlook 2000: Footwear, Leather, and Leather Products.

TABLE 4.8

Trade Organizations for the Leather Industry

Organization	Location	Objectives
Council for Leather Exports	Tamilnada, India	Promote India's leather industry
Export Promotion Council for Finished Leather and Leather Manufacturers	Kanpur, India	Promote finished leather products
Indian Leather Technologists' Association www.leatherindia.com	West Bengal, India	Improve leather technologies
Japanese Association of Leather Technology	Tokyo, Japan	Improve leather technologies
Leather Apparel Association www.leatherassociation.com	New York, NY	Monitor and improve the health and future of the leather apparel industry
Leather Industries of America www.leatherusa.com		Research tanning methods and promote a global awareness of American leather
Pakistan Society of Leather Technologists		Improve leather technologies
Society of Leather Technologists and Chemists www.sltc.org		Improve leather technologies

Leather products such as handbags are usually grouped by size, style, and color. In better department and specialty stores, larger leather accessories are often grouped first by brand, then subgrouped by style, color, or both. More expensive leather goods are arranged by color and brand in glass cases, accessible only with a salesperson's assistance, while less expensive products are displayed on racks or as countertop displays.

Men's small accessories, such as leather belts, are often grouped by color rather than by brand. Merchandisers have determined that men are generally more interested in finding the correct color, with brand or price points being secondary factors.

Two of the fastest growing segments of leather consumption are automobile interiors and upholstered furniture. Currently, about 43 percent of U.S. exported leather is used for manufacturing these upholstery products.

Smaller leather accessories for the home are a natural outgrowth of the increased popularity of leather furniture. Coach, a company famous for high-end handbags, now offers suede sofa and throw pillows on their Web site. Prices range from $125 to $195 per pillow. As the demand for leather continues to be strong, an increasing number of home accessories categories will offer leather as a "fabric" option.

TABLE 4.9
Trade Publications for the Leather Industry

Publication Name	Purpose
American Leather Chemists Association Journal	Reports on technological advancements in the tanning and leather industry
BLC Journal	Provides leather technology research
Business Ration Plus: Leather Manufacturers & Processors	Provides charts and statistics from the manufacturing industry
Chicago Daily Hide and Tallow Bulletin	Offers price guides, trade charts, statistics
Hide and Leather Bulletin	Provides the shoe industry with daily reports on hide trading
Hong Kong Leather Goods and Bags	Provides up-to-date product information
Indian Leather	Contains leather trade news
International Leather Guide	Contains data for the leather goods tanners and manufacturers
Key Note Market Report: Hand Luggage and Leather Goods	Provides trade news on luggage and leather goods
Leather	An online trade journal offering book reviews, illustrations, and market reports
Leather Conservation News	Provides scientific research on historical leather items' conservation, preservation, and restoration
Leather, Hides, Skins, Footwear Report	Covers the India leather industry
Leather Industries of America Membership Directory and Buyer's Guide	Lists member companies and their products
Leather Industries of America Technical Bulletin	Contains environmental and technical newsletter articles
Leather Manufacturer	Established for the shoe trade
Leather Markets	Surveys the international markets for leather goods
Leathers	Focuses on the India leather industry
Luggage, Leather Goods, and Accessories	Focuses on the Canadian leather industry
U.S. Leather Industries Statistics	Contains annual domestic and foreign data
World Leather	Provides tanning news and technical information

Internet retailing of leather products is a well-established trade. Consumers can locate a variety of products, from leather bow ties to exotic western boots. International vendors from India, Pakistan, Turkey, Mexico, and Canada have Web sites offering ready-to-wear or custom-made apparel and accessories. Unusual leathers, such as frog skin, water snake, deep-sea snake, teju lizard, iguana, anaconda, python, and cobra are available in accessories, such as briefcases, handbags, wallets and small leather goods, boots, and shoes. Internet retail prices for exotic accessories can be quite steep, with a python briefcase retailing for $589 and a frog skin purse selling for $389.

Many of the Internet sites feature merchandise identical to what can be found at brick-and-mortar stores or in direct-mail catalogs. On better sites, shoppers can click on small photo-

TABLE 4.10

Trade Shows for the Leather Industry

Name	Location	Focus
All China Leather Exhibition	Shanghai Mart, China	Features a wide range of exhibitors, including raw materials producers, chemical and dye companies, machinery manufacturers, and accessories, garment, and finished product suppliers. Also offers professional seminars on technological developments and industry updates.
Asia Pacific Leather Fair	Hong Kong	Raw materials and manufacturing show featuring more than 3,000 exhibitors from 65 countries. Attracts more than 14,000 buyers from 94 countries.
Panamerican Leather Fair	Miami, FL	A global trade fair with 1,400 exhibitors, including raw hide producers, leather dyers and finishers, and chemical companies. Attracts more than 6,200 buyers from 77 countries.
Semaine du Cuir	Paris, France	The largest global trade fair featuring exhibitors from leather associations as well as leather product vendors.

graphs and enlarge them to see details. Accurate colors are most difficult to view, but some retailers offer enhanced color-viewing capabilities. Customers may be able to narrow selection searches by category, occasion, or style. Well-designed Web sites offer related items to increase multiple sales. Merchandise returns are often made more convenient by allowing customers to return the unwanted items to the nearest brick-and-mortar store (see Figure 4.8).

FIGURE 4.8

Web sites may refer customers to brick-and-mortar store locations to provide more extensive customer service.

Courtesy of Fairchild Publications, Inc.

SUMMARY

- The beauty and durability of leather has made it an ideal textile for apparel and accessories, dating back to prehistoric times.

- The basic chemistry of the leather preserving and tanning processes has not changed much over the centuries. Vegetable and mineral tanning are the two most common tanning methods. A decrease in the length of time it takes to tan a skin or hide is an important advancement, as is the mechanization of many steps in the process.

- The domestic leather industry experienced a peak in the 19th century and then declined due to a number of factors, including mechanization, overproduction, the popularity of man-made leather materials, and strict governmental pollution controls.

- While U.S. leather production has declined, the global market has been improving. Many developing countries engage in leather production.

- The two major categories of leather processing are wet operations, involving the addition of chemicals to the skins and tanning, and dry operations, involving the removal of processing chemicals from the skins.

- Depending on the quality of the skin or hide, the resulting top grain or split leather may be colored with an opaque or transparent finish. The flesh side of the skin may be sueded with a nap. The original appearance may be altered to resemble an exotic animal through the process of embossing.

- The majority of leather is a by-product of the meat industry. In some instances, animals are raised specifically for their leather, but leather goods from these animals are quite costly.

- The Environmental Protection Agency issues and administers regulations controlling the leather industry. The Endangered Species Act, the Resource Conservation and Recovery Act, and the Clean Water Act regulate the actions of the leather industry.

- Animal preservation legislation and standards pertaining to content, labeling, and advertising are also a part of the regulations that govern the leather industry.

- Leather is an extremely popular textile among designers of accessories and is growing in use as softer and more durable leathers are enabling designers to produce even more desirable products. Simulated leathers and high-performance, including washable leathers, are also having a major impact on the design and production of accessories.

- Most leather products can be cleaned by wiping with a damp cloth and using a leather cream. Leather apparel requires special dry cleaning unless it is chemically treated to make it machine washable.

- Low labor costs in developing nations make them attractive for the processing of leather and the production of leather goods. The United States produces excellent quality hides that are exported to other countries for processing, tanning, and manufacturing.

- Leather products are merchandised with similar, nonleather fashion accessories. The primary difference between the two is price point, with leather goods being more expensive than nonleather goods.

- Growing industry segments for leather are home furnishings and automobile interiors.
- Internet retailing is popular for personal and home leather accessories, as well as many exotic leathers sold by domestic and international companies.

TERMS FOR REVIEW

aniline dye	fatliquoring	pigment (paint)
aniline finish	finishing	plating
bating	full (top) grain	receiving and storage
bleaching	genuine leather	retanning
boarding	glazing	setting out
bovine leather	grading	skin
box (willow) finish	grain	soaking
brush-dyeing	hide	splits
buffing	hide house	splitting and shaving
chrome tanning	imitation (simulated)	staking and dry milling
coloring	leather	sueding
conditioning	leather	tanning
curing	markings	tensile strength
deliming	measuring	trimming and siding
dip-dyeing	napping	unhairing
distressed leather	nonputrescible	wet operations
dry operations	nubuck (rybuck)	wet-blue leather
drying	patent	wringing and sorting
dyeing	patina	
embossing	pickling	

REVIEW QUESTIONS

1. What historical event in the United States caused major changes in the leather manufacturing process and amount of time it takes? Why did this occur?
2. What are three reasons for the decline of leather manufacturing in the United States?
3. What are the major wet operations and dry operations in the processing of hides or skins into leather?
4. What leather treatments are available, and when might they be used?
5. Give several reasons that fashion designers choose to produce simulated leather products.
6. Name and describe three kinds of leather industry regulations. In what ways do legislative acts affect the leather industry?
7. What special care requirements are needed for leather accessories?
8. In reference to global leather production, how does the United States compare to other countries? Why?
9. How do price points affect the merchandising of leather goods in a retail store?
10. How is the Internet being used to sell leather accessories?

KNOWLEDGE APPLICATIONS

1. Peruse fashion magazines or visit numerous Internet sites selling leather goods. Find and print close-up images of grain illustrations for each of the leathers listed in this chapter, as well as other exotic leathers. Create a file on leather grain characteristics by mounting pictures on note cards with descriptions.

2. Visit a retail store that specializes in leather products. Discuss with the manager how selling leather goods differs from selling similar, nonleather goods.

3. Select any leather accessories category, such as western boots or wallets, and evaluate a store's offerings of 5 to 10 products within the category. Make a chart and include item description, price, country of origin, animal source, top grain or split, and other special finishes noted. Be prepared to report on your findings to the class.

4. Tour a tannery, leather goods manufacturer, or farm that raises leather-bearing animals.

5. Research and write a report on a leather goods company of your choice. Use Web sites, periodicals, books and personal interviews with company representatives as resources. Include visual aids in your presentation.

6. Watch the movie *Erin Brockovich* to gain a greater understanding of the importance of responsible waste disposal by chrome-use industries, such as tanneries.

7. Gather information on a leather trade association or a trade fair. Compile the information into a short report.

CHAPTER 5

FUR

The elegant and beautifully bedecked model glides down the runway, cameras flashing, as photographers try to capture the best angle. She wears a full-length fur coat, a dozen silver foxtails dangling from the hem. As she nears the front of the runway, she turns, swinging the foxtails. She slips the fur from her shoulders like a cape and allows the foxtails to drag behind. As she returns to center stage, the foxtails leave a sickening trail of blood on the runway.

Real-life video? No. A reenactment sponsored by animal-rights activists. Furs have been one of the greatest ongoing fashion controversies in recent decades. Although the vast majority (96 percent) of American women oppose the tactics used by animal-rights activists, the fur industry has been plagued by activists' demonstrations and boycotts by sympathizers. To these groups, the wearing of furs should be publicized as inhumane and, at the very least, politically incorrect.

—Celia Stall-Meadows

A BRIEF HISTORY OF FUR

PREHISTORIC CAVE PAINTINGS DATING FROM 30,000 YEARS AGO CRUDELY DEPICT EARLY humans in various forms of clothing that resemble capes, skirts, and trousers. These garments may have been fashioned from untreated bear skins held together with bone fasteners. Archaeologists have discovered sewing needles and bone scrapers used for manufacturing clothing, although the articles of clothing themselves no longer exist.

Historians believe Eskimos and North American Indians may have been the first civilizations to dress in furs and tailor skins to fit closely to their bodies. Close-fitting layers of fur provided a layer of air next to the body, insulating and protecting the wearer from the cold. The fur side was often worn next to the body for maximum comfort and warmth.

During the Middle Ages, people living in northern climates found they had no adequate heating systems—not even in the most lavish of castles, with fireplaces and window coverings. Fur was needed on all garments during the cold winter months and usually was sewn to the inside of the clothing. Fur was used for many home furnishings as well, because of its insulating properties. Fur bedspreads, fur throws, and fur window coverings were found in most households, although the type of fur differed according to economic class and rank in society.

In European countries, the wearing of fur became a social hierarchy distinction and an outward symbol of prestige. Luxury furs were worn by the wealthy, while sheepskin was deemed appropriate for commoners. High-ranking clergy in the church wore special fur-lined robes, which evolved into ceremonial button-front, short capes. Snowy white ermine fur garments were depicted in many paintings of aristocratic ladies and gentlemen (see Figure 5.1).

By the 16th century, furs had reached an all-time importance in Europe. European fur trappers and traders moved north and west, gradually inhabiting the interior of the North American continent. They established trading posts to buy furs from the Native Americans, which they sold to Europeans for food and provisions. These trading posts stretched from Nova Scotia in Canada and throughout what would later become the United States. Cities such as New

FIGURE 5.1
White ermine fur interspersed with tiny black spots was decreed a royal fur by England's King Edward III.
© Bettman/CORBIS

York, New Orleans, St. Louis, Chicago, Detroit, St. Paul, and Spokane developed as early fur trading posts. New York City has become the heart of the fur industry in the United States. Today, the several city blocks that make up the fur district in New York City are contained within the larger garment district.

The Victorian Era of the 19th century heralded the fur coat as a part of every fashionable woman's wardrobe. By presenting a major fur exhibition in France in 1900, the fur industry paved the way for French fashion houses to show fur coats and accessories in their fall collections. The 1920s and 1930s continued the success and status of fur in fashion. The long fur boas and excessive fur trim of the 1920s gave way more subdued fox, mink, sable, and shearling collars, cuffs, and hemlines of the 1930s and 1940s. Since the 1960s, designers have continued to broaden the range of fur products in the marketplace and have introduced all kinds of novelty fur garments and accessories, using innovative treatments, techniques, and coloring.

AN INTRODUCTION TO FUR

Fur-bearing animals are trapped in the wild during the cold season or raised on fur farms. Although fur trapping has been an industry in the United States for several hundred years, fur farming did not begin until about 100 years ago. Farmed furs account for about 80 percent of the fur garments sold in the United States, while trapped furs account for around 20 percent.

Because animals raised in colder climates have thicker fur, most North American fur farms are located in the upper United States and in Canada. In the United States, Wisconsin is the largest pelt-producing state. Harvesting takes place during late November and December. Table 5.1 ranks the most productive states for domestic fur farming.

Most fur farms allow for controlled and cross breeding, which have produced many unique colors. A **ranched fur** refers to fur-bearing animals bred in captivity for special colors and quality. Most of these pelts are mink and fox.

TABLE 5.1
Top 10 U.S. Fur Farming States

1. Wisconsin
2. Utah
3. Minnesota
4. Washington
5. Idaho
6. Oregon
7. Illinois
8. Pennsylvania
9. Michigan
10. Iowa

Source: Fur Farming in North America. Fur Farm Animal Welfare Coalition.

Fur Dressing and Processing

In the fur industry, the term *fur* means any animal skin or part thereof with hair, fleece, or fur fibers attached. It does not include skins that are to be converted into leather or those that will have the hair, fleece, or fur fiber completely removed. Furs are comprised of the outer **guard hairs,** which are often coarse, long, and lustrous; and the **underfur,** which is beneath the guard hair. Underfur is soft, downy, and provides the majority of the warmth.

An animal skin with the fur attached is called a **pelt.** The steps in transforming a raw pelt into wearable furs are highly specialized, requiring up to several months and as many as 100 steps, depending upon the size and type of the accessory or garment. In the first step, the skins are **dressed** at a dressing plant. Dressing is the fur equivalent of tanning leather, done to prevent the skins from putrefying. The skins are washed in salt water to remove the dirt, scraped to remove the flesh or fat, and then washed again in a chemical bath for preservation. Several skins are placed in a **tramping machine** with **kickers,** or mechanical mallets. A tramping machine beats the pelt fibers until they are broken down, making pliant skins. Oils are reapplied and worked into the skins. Then excess oils are removed by tumbling the skins in a sawdust-filled drum that resembles a Laundromat dryer. The dressing process creates supple, long-lasting, and well-preserved pelts.

Fur Treatments

Fur garments and accessories are made in an amazing array of styles and colors. This is due to innovative treatments, especially colorizing and reducing the weight of pelts that give designers the range of furs they need to be creative. **Natural pelts** are those that have received no dyeing or bleaching. Natural variation or unusual color also comes about through genetic **mutation,** usually due to crossbreeding or inbreeding on farms. Selective breeding encourages mutations of desirable qualities and colors. Forward thinking on the part of the fur suppliers has led to many new and creative fur treatments being added to the numerous tried and true treatments. Several popular fur treatments include:

Bleaching   Often performed on furs with a yellowish tinge. Furs may be bleached before being redyed a darker color.

Corduroy-Grooved   Soft, downy underfur is unevenly sheared (see Shearing), creating an appearance of corduroy fabric (see Figure 5.2).

Double Face or **Reversible**   Pelts are dressed and processed on both sides; the leather side may be stenciled, sueded, dyed, or embossed.

Dyeing   The entire pelt is immersed in a dye bath. Dyeing does not damage the fur.

Fur on Fur   Two distinct fur types are combined into one accessory, such as a hat with a fox brim and a mink crown.

Knitting   Fur pelt is split into thin strips, then knitted into fabric.

FIGURE 5.2
Corduroy-grooved fur.
Courtesy of J. Mendel.

Plucking   More coarse guard hairs are removed from the pelt, leaving the soft downy under-fur and a much lighter coat that resembles velvet.

Pointing   Color is applied to the tips of the guard hairs.

Shearing   The underfur is sheared to a uniform length, leaving a lightweight, soft, and velvet-like pile to the fur, with the same insulating qualities as unsheared fur.

Stenciling   Dye is applied in patterns on the fur. Stencil-dyed furs resemble other animals, such as the spotted leopard.

Tip Dyeing   Only the fur fibers are dyed; the skin is not affected.

Tipping   Only the lighter colored skin is dyed so it will not show under the hair fibers.

Fur Product Construction

Once the dressing process is completed, skins are sent to manufacturers who work closely with designers to create accessories from the pelts. Pelts are matched, sorted, and bundled into the correct quantities needed to make the fur product. A **cutter** may **let out** smaller pelts by intricately slicing the skins into narrow (1/8″) diagonal strips, then resewing them with hundreds of seams to create a long, narrow section reaching from neckline to hemline. The letting-out process creates a supple, flowing fur piece.

Because of the expense involved in making fur accessories and garments, pelts may also be **semi let out,** which involves fewer cuts. **Leathering** is another cost-cutting measure in which narrow strips of leather are sewn as expansions between strips of fur. This decreases the amount of fur needed for the item and can decrease the bulky appearance of some furs.

Letting out of small skins is a costly process and may be eliminated for lower-priced furs. **Skin-on-skin construction** is used on small pelts. Pelts are sewn together, creating a patchwork effect, without changing the length or width of the pelts. It may also be a cost-cutting measure in mink or rabbit accessories. Lower-priced furs may be made of plates or small pieces that are matched and pieced together for fur garments. Some costly furs do not lend themselves to the letting-out process. Chinchilla, a perishable and expensive fur, is not usually let out; instead, a skin-on-skin construction process is used.

For shaping and softening, skins are wetted and tacked, fur side down, to a blocking table. Pelts are cut according to the pattern, and special sewing machines are used to sew the pelts together. For fur coats, a dress form is used to ensure a proper fit and hang. Many fur accessories are lined in satin fabrics so they are easy to slip on. Other furs are reversible to suede leather.

The hours of handiwork throughout the numerous stages, from pelt production to designing and manufacturing, affect the final cost of fur accessories. About one year lapses from the time the farmers or trappers harvest their pelts to the time the accessory reaches the retail stores. All of this time and work must be accounted for in the cost of a fur accessory.

CLASSIFICATIONS OF FUR

Furs are classified by animal families and characteristics, such as bear, dog, cat, pouched, rodent, hoofed, and weasel. Within each classification, the fur-bearing animals have unique characteristics, such as hair length, warmth, durability, and rarity. The more common fur-bearing animals are discussed in Table 5.2.

Durability

Durability refers to the degree of continuous shedding or hair loss of these pelts once they are made into garments. Furs vary in their ability to withstand shedding and are classified between very durable and perishable. Table 5.3 shows the durability range of selected furs.

FUR INDUSTRY REGULATIONS

The Environmental Protection Agency (EPA) and the Occupational Safety and Health Administration (OSHA) regulate the fur-dressing industry. These U.S. agencies protect the environment and the more than 4,000 fur-industry workers. More than 85 percent of the workers are employed by family-owned and -operated fur businesses. The fur industry has imposed its own set of regulations to ensure animal welfare in farming and trapping. Standards reflect the most humane care procedures based on consultations with veterinarians and animal scientists. Two significant federal laws that directly affect the fur industry are the Fur Products Labeling Act (FPLA) and the Endangered Species Act.

Fur Products Labeling Act

In 1952, the government passed the Fur Products Labeling Act, which was later amended in 1980. This act protects consumers and reputable fur businesses from false or misleading

TABLE 5.2
Fur-Bearing Animals

Family	Animal	Characteristics
Bear	**Raccoon**	Long and medium-length guard hairs in brownish gray/black with silvery tips. Woolly underfur. May be plucked and sheared to resemble beaver or nutria. Moderately priced.
	Finn Raccoon	Tan guard hairs with black tips.
	Tanuki (Japanese Raccoon)	Light amber color with dark, distinctive markings. Longer guard hairs and dense underfur. More expensive than other raccoon furs.
Canine (Dog)	**Coyote**	Gray to tan color, long guard hairs and thick, soft underfur.
	Fox	Second only to mink in wide natural color range. May be dyed. Long, lustrous guard hairs; lush underfur creates bulky appearance. Best sources are Alaska, Canada, and Russia.
	Red Fox	Wild variety, usually used for trim, but not for coats.
	Silver Fox	Ranched fur. Silver guard hairs and blue-black fur fibers.
	Platinum Fox	Mutation of silver fox with more silver.
	White Fox	From northern United States and Canada. Dramatic in appearance.
	Blue Fox	Brown fur, with a bluish tinge.
	Norwegian Blue Fox	A mutation from fur farming; bluish in color.
	Gray Fox	Less desirable than other varieties. Often dyed to resemble silver fox.
	Wolf	Colors vary from northern climate whites to southern climate tans.
	Arctic Timber Wolf	Whitish, soft underfur and long guard hairs.
	Prairie Wolf	White or black markings on yellowish-gray and brown to tan pelts, with coarser guard hairs.
Feline (Cat)	**Leopard**	Currently considered an endangered species and not for sale in the United States. Characterized by black rosettes against creamy yellow background. Leopard pattern may be used in faux (fake) furs.
	Lynx	Creamy white tones with beige to darker markings. Dense, fluffy fur with long silky guard hairs. Increased white coloring is desirable.
	Canadian Lynx	Darker markings.
	Russian Lynx	Longer hair and subtle beige markings.
	Lynx Cat	Similar to lynx, but smaller markings and less expensive.
	Ocelot	Tan-colored fur with black or brown rings or markings. Distinctive markings are more valuable.
Marsupialia (Pouched Animal)	*American Opossum*	Coarse, grayish-white guard hairs with silver to black tips. May be plucked and sheared to reveal soft, dense underfur. Often dyed.
	Australian Opossum	Best color is bluish-gray with black-tipped guard hairs. Also, yellow-gray to brown colors. Wool-like, plush underfur.
Rodentia (Gnawing Animal)	**Beaver**	Rare colors, such as blonde, may be left intact, but usually beaver is plucked of coarse guard hairs. Underfur is usually sheared for a soft, velvety texture, and often colorfully dyed.
	Chinchilla	Expensive and silky. Dense, short fur. Colors range in grays. Best color is slate blue guard hairs and dark underfur.
	Marmot	Short, yet warm fur fibers; coarse and lustrous guard hairs. Often dyed to resemble mink.
	Muskrat	Dense fur. Black stripe and pale beige sides.
	New Jersey Muskrat	Lighter weight than other types of muskrats.
	Northern Muskrat	Best quality of muskrats, with long guard hairs and dense underfur.
	Southern Muskrat	Less underfur and duller color than other muskrats. Used as imitation for more expensive furs, such as mink or sheared beaver.
	Nutria	Short, downy underfur. Often sheared and designed in sporty apparel. Frequently dyed. Used for linings and trim.
	Rabbit	Shearing and grooving imitate more expensive furs. Colors may be natural or dyed. Less expensive due to abundance and continuous shedding.

(continued on page 99)

TABLE 5.2 *(continued)*
Fur-Bearing Animals

Family	Animal	Characteristics
	Squirrel	Lightweight. Shorter and flatter hair; dense underfur. Natural colors range in gray tones.
Ungulata (Hoofed Animal)	**Calf**	Short, flat, semishiny hair with swirled patterns. May be dyed.
	Kid	Young, short-haired goat. Lustrous, moiré pattern. Relatively inexpensive.
	Pony	Actually calfskin (a misnomer from the 1960s). Flat, shiny fur, relatively inexpensive. Currently very trendy, but expensive due to limited designer use.
	Sheep	Most pelts are taken from lambs, in order to get the tightly curled fur fibers. Most are raised in Central Asia or Southwest Africa.
	Broadtail Lamb	Brown, black, and gray colors. Flat fur with moiré pattern (water-marked appearance). Often dyed.
	Mongolian Lamb	Off-white color naturally, but often dyed. Very long, silky, and wavy guard hairs.
	Mouton Lamb	Sheared lamb with straightened hairs. Thick, soft, flat fur. Often dyed. Sheep from South America.
	Persian Lamb	Mostly black, also brown and gray colors of flat curls with a high luster. From farm-raised karakul sheep in Africa or Asia. Requires expert craftsmanship to "match" the curls in the pelts to ensure a flowing pattern to the garment.
	Shearling Lamb	Reversible lambskin, with suede or bronze-leather side worn on the outside and fur worn on the inside.
Mustelidae (Weasel)	**Ermine**	Brown in warmer climates; in cold climates (Siberia, Russia) ermine pelts are lustrous and pure white (black-tipped tails), with dense and very long underfur, almost as long as guard hairs. From Russia and Canada. Longstanding association with royal garb.
	Fisher	Black-tipped, silky guard hairs. Colors from medium brown to dark blue-brown and blackish. Thick underfur. From Canada.
	Fitch	Black-tipped, long guard hairs. Underfur ranges from beige to yellowish-orange. Brighteners may be used to colorize.
	Siberian Fitch	White underfur.
	Kolinsky	Long hair, dyed in dark colors to resemble mink. Considered an *Asian mink*, with best quality from Siberia.
	Marten	Similar in appearance to sable, yet less expensive.
	American Sable Marten	Blue-brown to dark brown colors. Long, silky guard hairs with dense underfur. From Alaska and Canada.
	Baum Marten	Yellow-brown color, resembles sable. Softer and silkier than *American Sable Marten*. Shiny and dense fur.
	Japanese Marten	Yellowish color. Usually dyed to resemble sable.
	Stone Marten	Finest of all martens. Bluish-brown, thick guard hairs. Whitish-gray underfur.
	Mink	Dark stripe running down the back (or grotzen) of the pelt. Most popular fur farmed (ranched) animal in North America. Guard hairs may be plucked or sheared for lighter weight and velvet-like appearance. Many colors of ranched minks and mutations, including ranch wild, mahogany, gunmetal, and sapphire.
	Sable	One of the most luxurious of furs. Medium to long guard hairs and dense underfur, but lightweight.
	Russian Sable (Barguzin Sable)	Best color and most expensive fur. Dark blueish-brown with a silvery cast. Increased silver guard hairs are most desirable.
	Canadian Golden Sable	Amber-colored, enhanced with darker golden grotzen.
	Skunk	Glossy fur, black background with white stripe running down the back. White fur may be cut out because of coarseness and dyeing difficulty.
	Weasel	Yellowish or light brown color; similar to mink or ermine in appearance, but shorter guard hairs and underfur.
Miscellaneous	**Mole**	Dyed in many colors. Straight guard hair that grows in swirls. Obtained from Scotland and Holland.
	Seal	Dyed in many colors. Guard hairs may be plucked. Best quality from Alaska.

TABLE 5.3

Most Popular Fur-Bearing Animals by Relative Durability

Very Durable	Durable	Semidurable	Semiperishable	Perishable
Otter	Fitch	Fox	Ermine	Mole
Skunk	Opossum	Weasel	Kid	Chinchilla
Raccoon	Sable	Marten	Squirrel	Broadtail Lamb
Mouton Lamb	Muskrat	Marmot	Leopard	
Mink	Alaska Seal		Rabbit	
Beaver	Coyote		Lynx	
Persian Lamb	Wolf			
Nutria				

branding or advertising. The law requires furs to be labeled, in English, with the following information: the country of origin; a disclosure of any artificial treatments to the fur or pelt that alter the appearance or color; and a disclosure of used, damaged, secondhand, rebuilt or scrap fur, if applicable. In addition, the animal must be identified with its true English name.

Prior to this law, furs could be deceptively sold under a name other than the English name, or an English or foreign name that resembled the names of more expensive furs. For example, a rabbit fur coat might be labeled beaverette, marmink, northern seal, or *lapin,* the French word for rabbit. Notable examples of blatantly false labeling included a spotted skunk coat labeled civet cat, a weasel coat falsely labeled summer ermine, and a plucked and dyed muskrat coat labeled Hudson seal. Although the labeling has been beneficial to consumers, it does not address the variances in quality among pelts of the same species. Consumer education and topnotch showroom furriers and salespersons are essential to quality discernment.

Endangered Species Act

The Federal Endangered Species Act (1973, 1988) regulates the use of animals considered endangered or threatened with extinction. Certain fur-bearing animals are listed in the Federal Register and are protected by the provisions of the act. Penalties for violators include up to one-year imprisonment and up to a $100,000 fine. To protect against creating more endangered species, the fur trade only uses species that are abundant and are capable of sustaining a harvest.

Fur Farming Regulations

In the United States, the Fur Farm Animal Welfare Coalition provides fur farmers with humane care guidelines outlining best practices for raising healthy animals. These codes of practice include industry standards for nutrition, housing, veterinary care, and euthanasia methods.

Fur Controversy

Anti-fur activists only make up a small percentage of the population, but in recent years they have gained much media attention because of their vocal and graphic techniques and celebrity endorsers. Many consumers prefer not to wear furs because of the humanitarian issues, but these consumers may not agree with radical activists.

In May 1999, the voters of Beverly Hills, California, defeated a proposed, single-issue measure to require a credit card-sized hangtag be attached to all furs sold in the city. The hang tag was to read: "Consumer notice: This product is made with fur from animals that may have been killed by electrocution, gassing, neck breaking, poisoning, clubbing, stomping, or drowning and may have been trapped in steel-jaw leg-hold traps." Many of the voters believed the proposal was initiated by the animal rights activists' anti-fur agenda.

One organization, called People for the Ethical Treatment of Animals (PETA), endorses the abolition of animal testing for any scientific research, including AIDS, cancer, and Alzheimer's disease. They have claimed to oppose the eating of meat, killing of insects, and owning of pets. PETA boasts a publicity-generating group of celebrities and loyalists who picket retailers and verbally attack fur wearers.

Extreme activists, such as the Animal Liberation Front (ALF) have bombed, destroyed, and sabotaged industry facilities. Most of these extremists work alone or in small groups to engage in criminal acts, and few get caught. These crimes have included firebombing a feed producer that manufactured feed for fur farms, and etching anti-fur graffiti on the windows of a fur retailer in Washington, D.C. ALF activists feel their crimes are justified because the legal and political processes are too slow. A future concern of the fur industry may be Internet hackers, affiliated with the ALF, who break into a company's computer system to sabotage data or deluge the company's e-mail system.

Putting People First (P.P.F.) is a counter group opposing the viewpoints of animal rights activists. In a 1998 Internet letter addressed to "Fellow Americans," P.P.F. Chairman Kathleen Marquardt, Chairman of P.P.F. explained, "Common sense shows it's people who have rights, not animals. We must all be very conscientious about animal welfare, but there's a big difference between animal 'welfare' and animal 'rights'."

The controversy becomes more heated as furs increase in popularity. Activists who oppose the wearing of fur may try more extreme tactics to discourage the wearing of fur in the name of fashion. In contrast, once a trend begins, it is difficult to change the direction in which fashion is moving.

Source: Marquardt, K. (April 2, 1998). Putting People First. Internet correspondence. Retrieved April 2, 1998, from the World Wide Web at http://www.thewild.com/ppf

Fur farmers are encouraged to follow these guidelines because their livelihood and financial success depends on producing high-quality furs. The Canada Mink Breeders and Fox Breeders Associations publish similar guidelines.

Most animals harvested in the United States are euthanized with practices recognized by the American Veterinary Medical Association and recommended by the Fur Farm Animal Welfare Coalition. Mink are euthanized with pure carbon monoxide gas or lethal injections, and fox are euthanized with a lethal injection. However, other countries have their own standards for harvesting pelts.

THE FUR FASHION INDUSTRY

A fur garment begins with a sketched fur design that is translated into a cloth "canvas." A mock-up is created and carefully fit to a dress form before the fur pelts are ever cut. Once the canvas is complete, it is converted to a flat pattern that can be used as a guide to cut the pelts.

The recent popularity of furs has caused more designers than ever before to begin or resume featuring fur in their lines. In 1985, only 42 designers used fur in their lines. By the 1999–2000 season, almost 200 designers featured fur in what the industry called a designer-led fur renaissance.

Design of Fur Products

Designing trends include visible logos, sportswear looks, lightweight coats for a more casual lifestyle, and colorfully dyed furs (see Figure 5.3). Most appreciated by designers are the technological advancements in fur processing that can create unique fur appearances in beautiful colors and light weights. However, some designers prefer the rich, natural colors of the furs and limit dyeing of furs to the colors found in nature.

FIGURE 5.3
Zuki's swing coat with reversible, dyed, sheared beaver.
Courtesy of Fairchild Publications, Inc.

The Media and Furs

Even before the sixth annual Fur Fashion Week held in New York in June 2000, industry personnel suspected the show and the season would be successful. A day before the scheduled event, Sarah Jessica Parker and other *Sex and the City* cast members were featured wearing an abundant wardrobe of sheared mink, silver fox, and chinchilla coats on the season premiere. Industry personnel were thrilled with the exposure on the popular HBO program. According to Anne Dee Goldin, a fur manufacturer, "It's the best thing that can happen to us as an industry. That show is the epitome of what's hip and what's cool. People all over the country watch it to see what people in New York are wearing."[1] Fur designers hope to target the young viewers of *Sex and the City* by offering lightweight and sporty fur garments in sleek styles.

In addition to television, fashion magazines have renewed their interest in photographing furs. Supermodels and celebrities are often photographed in beautiful fur coats. Supermodels who once supported the animals rights groups and spoke out against the killing of animals for luxury garments were later photographed modeling fur coats on the runways and in advertisements and wearing fur coats to social functions. "Once Fendi draped sable on former 'I'd-rather-go-naked-than-wear-fur' (PETA slogan) supermodel Naomi Campbell the fashion world took notice."[2]

Actresses and celebrities have always worn furs. To many Americans, furs represent opulence, luxury, status, and wealth. Sharon Stone, Madonna, and Gwyneth Paltrow have contributed to the increase in fur sales by endorsing the wearing of furs. As an extra boost to the industry, rap singers, such as Lil' Kim and Sean (P. Diddy) Combs, have publicly been seen wearing furs.

Naomi Campbell was photographed for Vogue *magazine wearing a chinchilla stole after posing nude for the "I'd rather go naked than wear fur"* PETA Campaign. AP/Worldwide Photos.

Sources:

[1] McCants, L. (June 13, 2000). "Fur Week's Sex Appeal." *Women's Wear Daily*, 179(114), p. 8.

[2] North American Fur and Fashion Exposition (NAFFEM). (July 6, 2000). Press Release. Retrieved from the World Wide Web at www.naffem.com

In 1999, the fur industry engaged in the promotion of "fake cloth," a new category for furs. Fake cloth designers attempt to minimize the formal image of furs and emphasize a more casual look. Designers such as Oscar De La Renta and Givenchy began featuring brightly dyed and floral printed furs in sportswear and accessories. Products included ski vests; reversible fur raincoats; and fur-lined collars, cuffs, and hemlines. Sheared mink, lamb, and sable have been top choices for these products because the furs resemble a pile-like fabric. The heavy, bulky mink that conjures images of grandmother's fur coat is not part of contemporary fashions.

Faux Fur

An alternative to real fur is **faux fur** (pronounced "fō") or fake fur. This fabric is usually made of acrylic and modacrylic or polyester to simulate the guard hairs and underfur. Many of the fake furs appear quite similar to natural furs (see Figure 5.4).

Care of Fur Products

Customers should be encouraged to wear their furs often, but they should be instructed to follow proper procedures for wearing and care. Some shedding is normal in new furs, particularly the more perishable furs, and an occasional healthy shake outdoors will reduce the shedding during wearing. In addition, customers should be advised to follow these care tips:

- Store on a wide plastic hanger or a cloth-covered hanger.
- Provide ample closet space to avoid crushing fur fibers.
- Hang fur in a cool and dark location.

FIGURE 5.4
*Giacca has capitalized on the popularity of
furs and offer their own faux fur jackets.*

Courtesy of Fairchild Publications, Inc.

- Never use plastic bags or dry-cleaner film for storing furs.
- Fur pelts "breathe" and should be left uncovered or draped with a muslin sheet.
- Mild rain will not harm furs. Hang to dry in a well-ventilated room, and then gently shake. Avoid rubbing, brushing, or combing.
- Soaking rains require professional furrier services.
- Avoid sliding into cars; the friction causes excessive wear.
- Immediately repair tears or rips to avoid further damage.
- Apply hair sprays and spray colognes before donning furs; they may discolor furs.
- Avoid wearing brooches and other jewelry on furs. They detract from the appearance of the fur, and the pinholes may damage the pelts.
- Avoid continuous use of shoulder strap handbags.
- Have furs professionally cleaned and glazed annually.
- Use services of a professional furrier, not a dry cleaner.
- Never mothproof a fur.
- During warm months, place furs in cold storage, not a household closet.

Professional care of fur is essential and involves the following three steps:

- *Cleaning*   The process of working coarse grains, saturated with oil into the pelt and fur. This oil treatment prevents the pelt from drying out and becoming brittle. The excess oils are cleaned from the coat by tumbling the fur garment in a large, sawdust-filled drum.
- *Glazing*   A sheen created on the fur fibers by applying either a water spray or chemicals, then gently pressing the fur.
- *Storage*   During warm months, furs are placed in cold storage in a professional fur vault that maintains a 50 degree Fahrenheit temperature and has a 50 percent controlled humidity.

THE GLOBAL FUR INDUSTRY

Fur is truly a global commodity, and the prices of furs are affected by worldwide supply and demand. The United States produces about 10 percent of the worldwide supply of mink pelts, while Canada produces about 4 percent. Much of the production from the approximately 2,000 North American farms is exported to other countries. Figure 5.5 represents the world pelt production of the top producing countries.

The United States spends more money on fur garments than any other country in the world. One in five women owns a fur, with the greatest sales occurring in the 24 to 44 age group. Their fur purchases are predominantly mink, with fox a distant second, and beaver an even more distant third. Sales of men's fur garments represent less than 5 percent of U.S. sales. Table 5.4

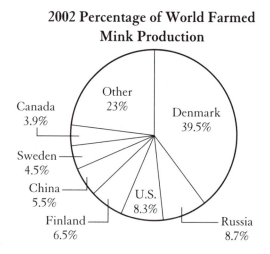

2002 Percentage of World Farmed Mink Production

FIGURE 5.5

The world's top producing countries for fur pelts.

Courtesy of The Fur Farm Animal Welfare Coalition.

TABLE 5.4

Annual U.S. Fur Sales in Dollars

1999	$1.40 billion
1998	$1.21 billion
1997	$1.27 billion
1996	$1.25 billion
1995	$1.20 billion
1994	$1.10 billion
1993	$1.20 billion
1992	$1.10 billion
1991	$1.00 billion

Source: Fur Information Council of America, Feb. 25, 2000.

shows sales in the United States from 1991 to 1999, with the most sizable increase (15 percent) from 1998 to 1999.

Although cold weather is an important factor in the decision to purchase a fur garment, some major cities with warm climates rank in the list of top retail fur sales in the United States. Table 5.5 shows a ranking of the U.S. cities with the highest fur sales.

Fur Auctions

Fur buyers purchase pelts for manufacturers. Buyers visit several international fur auction houses to bid on batches of fur pelts. Important fur auctions take place in Copenhagen, New York, Seattle, Toronto, and North Bay. These auction houses may be cooperative ventures

TABLE 5.5

U.S. Markets with the Highest Retail Fur Sales

1. New York, NY
2. Chicago, IL
3. Philadelphia, PA
4. Los Angeles, CA
5. Washington D.C./Baltimore, MD
6. Boston, MA
7. Detroit, MI
8. Cleveland, OH
9. Dallas/Ft. Worth, TX
10. San Francisco, CA
11. Milwaukee, WI
12. Seattle, WA

Source: Fur Information Council of America, Feb. 25, 2000.

among fur trappers and farmers and offer services, such as grading and handling furs. Technicians grade, inspect, and classify the pelts by color, size, primeness, and gender. Fur buyers are given the opportunity to inspect samples from each lot or grouping of similar furs in order to determine the value and price they are willing to pay. Fees are paid to the auction houses through the deduction of commissions from producers' fur sales. Buyers from all over the world attend these fur auctions. Each buyer must have a great deal of experience and a sharp eye for identifying grades and types of pelts.

Trade Organizations, Publications, and Shows

The fur industry supports promotional and lobbying organizations. The organizations promote wildlife management, regulate standards of animal welfare for fur businesses, and promote a consumer's freedom to choose to wear or not wear a fur. Table 5.6 shows top fur organizations that provide information to consumers and assistance to fur industry employees.

Many trade organizations publish a periodical, although the circulation may be limited to the organization members. Some of these trade publications are reproduced in part on the organization's website. A list of important trade publications is shown in Table 5.7.

The marketing of fur fashions occurs at fur and outerwear fashion fairs in various countries throughout the world. One of the largest trade fairs in the world is the North American Fur and Fashion Exposition in Montreal, Canada, (NAFFEM) featuring fur outerwear. The trade show's "FurWorks Canada" was introduced as an innovative concept of sportswear and fun furs by leading manufacturers and designers. The FurWorks project was a collaboration of the Fur Council of Canada and the North American Fur Association.

TABLE 5.6

Trade Organizations for the Fur Industry

Organization	Location	Objectives
British Fur Trade Association www.britishfur.co.uk/	London, England	To build awareness of fur issues and dispel fur production myths and to create a greater understanding and appreciation of fur.
Fur Commission USA (FCUSA) www.furcommission.com	Coronado, CA	To promote the fur industry through educational information and press kits, as well as downloadable videos, and to provide career information.
Fur Council of Canada www.furcouncil.com	Montreal, Quebec	To sponsor design competitions and to provide information about the Canadian fur trade to consumers, educators, and the public.
Fur Information Council of America (FICA) www.fur.org	West Hollywood, CA	To provide information on industry developments; to engage in consumer research; to report on sales and pricing; to represent the fur industry to the press, the public and trade sectors, and the government; and to monitor legislation.
Fur Institute of Canada www.fur.ca	Ottowa, Ontario	To promote the conservation and sustainable development of Canada's fur resources and to emphasize education and communications.
International Fur Trade Federation www.iftf.com	London, England	To promote a factual and fashion image of today's fur trade and to maintain a close relationship with government.
National Trappers Association www.nationaltrappers.com	Bloomington, IL	Provides lists of related organization Web site links.
U.S. Fish and Wildlife Service http://endangered.fws.gov/wildlife.html	Washington, D.C.	Provides a list of endangered species.

TABLE 5.7

Trade Publications for the Fur Industry

Publication Name	Purpose
American Trapper	Published by the National Trappers Association.
Fur Age	Fashion emphasis. Available as a monthly subscription and at www.furs.com.
Fur Information Council Newsletter	Promotes fur and the conservation of fur-bearing animals.
Fur Taker Magazine	Educates trappers on humane trapping techniques.
National Chinchilla Breeders of Canada Bulletin	Provides technical education for the chinchilla rancher.
Sandy Parker's Fur World	Lists auction prices, fur fair news, fashion, storage, and cleaning.
Sandy Parker Reports	Contains international fur trade news: Pricing, supply and demand, and government actions.
Trapper and Predator Caller	Focus on trapping.
Weekly International Fur News	Considers the worldwide fur market.
Blue Book of Farming	Focus on fur farming.

MERCHANDISING TRENDS AND TECHNIQUES

Consumers may choose faux furs or real furs, but marketers of fur fashions should be attentive to their target customers' wants and needs. Marketers must fine-tune their ability to interpret social, economic, and political happenings and provide products that will closely parallel these trends.

Although many antifur activists would disagree, the wearing of furs holds prestige in the fashion industry. Many women and men purchase fur clothing for the luxury, beauty, and warmth they perceive can only be obtained with genuine fur. Other consumers may opt for faux furs because of budget constraints, moral beliefs, or personal preferences.

Larger fur accessories are often located in the outerwear department of many large retail stores, while smaller fur items are located in the accessories department. Some designers are avoiding the trap of having their line merchandised (mixed in) with other lines in a traditional outerwear department. They are offering luxury sportswear collections, in which the fur pieces are only a part of the total collection. Fur outerwear, related accessories, sportswear, and knits are grouped together to encourage multiple sales.

Leased Departments

Exclusive specialty and department stores may merchandise fur products in a fur salon, but increasingly these salons are being leased to a fur company. The high cost and difficult management of inventory and the lack of knowledgeable management have encouraged the leasing of selling space by fur companies, such as Birger Christensen. This enormous fur company now operates most of the department store salons in the Midwest and Northeast. Birger Christensen operates the fur salons in Macy's, Saks Fifth Avenue, Carson Pirie Scott, Bloomingdale's, Dayton's, Hudson's, Marshall Field's, Rich's, Goldsmith's, Lazarus, and Filene's Basement. Although leased by the same fur company, the fur fashions within each store may differ, depending on the price points and target customers of each retailer. For example, Macy's carries mid-priced and popular-priced clothing and its furs are lower-priced, affordable, and more conservative. By contrast, Bloomingdale's caters to more upscale and designer-savvy crowds.

Consignment agreements provide the retailer with inventory to sell, but the manufacturer retains ownership of the goods. The store is allowed to return any unsold inventory to the manufacturer. In order to be considered a full-service salon, the salons may offer specialized services, such as storage, cleaning, and alterations, but these services may be outsourced to a service company.

Home Fashion Accessories

When a fashion like fur becomes popular in ready-to-wear, the fashion often trickles into home-furnishing accessories. Not only do consumers desire fur coats, hats, handbags, shoes, and knitted sweatshirts, but home fashions as well. At the 2000 NAFFEM in Montreal, Canada, bolsters, pillows, cushions, plaids, throws, bedspreads, and rugs were shown repeatedly in a variety

Profile: The Fendi Sisters

"Fur was never out. We never stopped using it and have always treated fur like the most luxurious fabric. People now say fur is back because women want the freedom to wear whatever they want." -Carla Fendi[1]

The Italian House of Fendi is synonymous with the most beautiful furs in the world, with Karl Lagerfeld holding the honor of head designer. After more than 30 years with the 5 Fendi sisters, he has the distinction of being dubbed the "sixth Fendi child." Karl Lagerfeld has designed for Fendi since 1962 and has earned recognition for his nontraditional fur garments. Lagerfeld's innovative fur designs have been given credit for bringing the House of Fendi to the fashion press forefront. During his early designing years at Fendi, he created the recognizable double FF griffe.

The business began as a leather and fur workshop by the Fendi sisters' maternal grandparents and was expanded by their parents until their father's death in 1954. Because there was no male heir, principal ownership fell to the five daughters: Paola (born 1931), Anna (1933), Franca (1935), Carla (1937), and Alda (1940), under the encouragement and watchful eye of their mother, Adele. With President Paola at the helm in 1955, the first Fendi high fashion collection was produced. The Fendi sisters opened several successful Italian boutiques selling bags and furs in the 1960s. The first couture fur collection was presented in 1966 and was received with immediate success, and the first ready-to-wear collection was presented three years later. Under the direction of Karl Lagerfeld, the House of Fendi has created many unique real fur designs, some resembling fake fur and fabrics.

A Lagerfeld fur design for Fendi.
Courtesy of Fairchild Publications, Inc.

Fendi furs have been sheared and printed to look like damask; pelts have been perforated with thousands of tiny holes to create a fur coat that is lighter in weight; fur strips have been knitted; and denim coats have been lined with mink. "More recently, Lagerfeld has covered an entire fur coat with woven mesh and created completely reversible fur coats as his stand against the anti-fur movement that has created great problems for the trade"[2]

of furs. Often these accessories combine fur with other natural materials, such as leather and linen.

Fur lends itself well to the modernity of at-home "cocooning." The Fur Council's slogan, "You'll Feel Comfortable in Fur," can easily be translated into home fashions. Promotion emphasize the key directions of "sophistication" and "nature,"—a kind of rustic chic. Additionally, department merchandisers should embrace the related-accessories concept to sell the customer multiple fur products.

Internet Retailing

Furs are considered luxury goods, and the high prices for traditional fur coats do not lend themselves to Internet shopping. Most Web sites encourage shoppers to visit a nearby store to meet

Profile: The Fendi Sisters *(continued)*

Karl Lagerfeld and Silvia Fendi.

Courtesy of Fairchild Publications, Inc.

The Fendis revived fashion interest in nontraditional furs, such as mole and unshaved beaver, and nontraditional colors. Historically, the Fendis have selected un pedigreed furs, making them fashionable. The Fendis today still use squirrel, badger, Persian lamb, and fox, often combining several in one garment.

The children of the Fendi sisters launched (in 1987) the Fendissime collection of accessories and sportswear fashions that combine fur with luxurious fabrics, like cashmere. Fendissime shearling is Fendi's combination of luxury fiber and fur trim designed to appeal to the younger markets.

Although Fendi merchandise has been in major United States department stores like Bloomingdale's since the late 1960s, it wasn't until 1989 that Fendi opened its first boutique in the United States. The flagship store, located on Fifth Avenue, carries a large variety of Fendi products in a 22,000 square foot store.

The 1990s was a time of change for the Fendis. The sisters launched a complete men's wear product line, Uomo, in 1990, achieving noteworthy success at correctly interpreting men's needs. In 1994, Carla Fendi succeeded Paola as the president of the board of directors. Most recently, the team of sisters and Lagerfeld, in 1999, agreed to a 51 percent takeover of the Rome-based house of Fendi by an alliance between Italian businessmen, Patrizio Bertelli and Bernard Arnault.

Despite the changes in the Fendi company structure, the designs have continued to shape the future of the fur industry. The most recent collection of Fendi furs reflected a colorful 1970s theme. "Seldom left in its virgin state, Fendi furs were dyed, beaded, and shaved; embroidered with silver threads and encrusted with sequins. Sliced and diced, fur pieces were sewn together patchwork style to form skirts and coats."[3] The Fendis' continuous research to find revolutionary fur treatments provides Lagerfeld with the tools to create some of the world's most unusual and elegant furs.

Sources:

[1] Sherwood, James. (Oct. 23, 1999). "How to Spend It: Wild Things." *The Financial Times Weekend*, p. 10.

[2] Woram, Catherine. (1998). "Fendi." In *Contemporary Fashion*. New York: St. James Press.

[3] Young, Clara. (July 8, 2000). "Lagerfeld Funks Up Fendi." Retrieved: July 8, 2000, from http://www.worldmedia.fr/fashion/catwalk/PAPOOha/MIL/couturier/FEN-nav.html

with knowledgeable salespeople. However, some fur accessories such as ponyskin shoes and handbags, fur home accessories, and other low-ticket items are for sale on the Internet.

Previously Owned Furs

Another option for a consumer is to purchase a previously owned fur. Consumers who purchase these furs may not have the resources to purchase a new fur garment, or they may not be willing to contribute to the deaths of more fur-bearing animals.

Some fur salons have a section or room that contains fur garments that have been "traded in" on more expensive coats and may also contain unclaimed stored furs. The customer must pay an annual storage fee when fur is not removed from storage. The salon owner will make every effort to collect the fee, but if unsuccessful, may sell the coat to recoup the storage costs.

FIGURE 5.6 *Home page of efurs.com.*
Used with permission from efurs.com.

Consignment selling is another service retailers may want to offer. Under a consignment arrangement, the actual ownership of the fur garment remains with the customer until the garment is sold. For a commission, the retailer furnishes the selling space and offers assistance to interested customers.

Web sites are available for customers to locate and purchase previously owned fur garments. However, the Web sites are only as reputable as the people that develop them. A brick-and-mortar store with a longstanding reputation is probably a better resource for buying and selling used furs. The Web site efurs.com is devoted to selling many types of fur products, such as accessories and blankets. Scrap furs, fur yarn, and previously owned fur garments are also available for sale. Because there is no product guarantee for buying a used fur over the Internet, efurs.com explicitly reminds resale shoppers to remember the caveat emptor, "let the buyer beware" (see Figure 5.6).

SELLING FURS

Selling furs is a specialty that requires sufficient training and product knowledge. Salespeople need to be able to evaluate and compare the variety of furs offered in a fur department, boutique, or salon. The salesperson should know how to present product information in the form of customer benefits and refrain from overwhelming the purchaser with too much technical information. In addition to the quality considerations, the salesperson should offer a few key points customers should know when buying a fur, such as the following:

- Fur warmth is determined by the underfur.
- Shorthaired furs may be as warm longhaired furs.
- Furs may be restyled after a few years, if they have been cared for properly (professional storage and cleaning annually).
- Fur selection should match the wearer's lifestyle.

A good salesperson listens carefully to customer comments and objections and interprets nonverbal communications. Salespeople should stress the importance of buying the best quality the customer can afford. In the majority of cases, a customer will be happier if she buys a nice-quality raccoon coat, rather than an inferior-quality mink coat. In a few years, when the customer can afford to pay more for a coat, she will still be pleased with her original purchase and the store will enjoy the customer's loyalty.

Restyling Furs

Fur clothing, like all fashion goods, is perishable. Fashionable fur stylings change over a period of seasons. If properly cleaned, glazed, and stored each year, the fur pelts may outlast the fashion of the style. Fur manufacturers and designers discourage the "heirloom" concept of furs, instead encouraging the restyling of furs, so they can be continuously worn and enjoyed.

For retailers, the restyling service can be a significant part of the store's income. Customers may be reluctant to purchase another fur if they still have a fur that contains well-preserved pelts. A customer may feel justified in purchasing a second fur garment if the first one can be restyled.

Restyling may take the form of narrowing the lapels, shoulders or silhouette, or shortening the length of the item. Some larger fur garments may be transformed into the linings of jackets, collars and cuffs, or even pillows. The type of restyling depends on the condition of the pelts. Restyling typically reduces the size of the original garment, and customers should be thoroughly informed before the item is restyled.

Price and Value

Many factors affect the price of a fur coat or accessory. These include fur pelt quality (luxurious look and feel), rarity, fur origin, craftsmanship, and design. However, durability may not be a pricing factor. For example, the costly chinchilla fur and an inexpensive rabbit fur are both fragile and perishable. Consumers should spend a significant amount of time comparison shopping so they will become familiar with the differences in the look and hand (feel) of similar furs. The appearance of the pelts should be lustrous, with glossy guard hairs, if present, and the skins should be well matched. The hand of the fur should be supple, with dense, soft underfur. Female pelts are often softer and lighter in weight than the more coarse and heavy male pelts.

In addition to the look and feel of the coat, the cost is affected by the type or rarity of the fur, fur origin, and craftsmanship. Mink furs dominate the market share of fur coats sold. Mink's durability, softness, beauty, and minor amount of shedding are qualities that make these furs, more than any other, desirable to customers. There are differences that occur within the same fur category. For example, the American Legend mink is one of the finest minks available. The fur origin is frequently a factor in determining quality and price. Sable furs from Russia have long been associated with luxury and high prices. Typically, animals raised farther north and in colder climates grow thicker (hence, better quality) furs. Craftsmanship is often reflected in the price of the fur. One way to evaluate craftsmanship is to try on the fur and inspect it in a full-length mirror. A well-balanced fur coat will fall evenly from the wearer's shoulders. The hem-line circumference should be equidistant from the floor. A lining should be secured to the coat hem, but not completely sewn down. Buyers should be able to lift the lining and inspect the backs of the pelts and the seams. Quality furs have tight, secure stitching. In some expensive fur coats the pockets may not be cut into the coat until the customer selects the coat. This ensures the pockets are customized at exactly the right level for the wearer. The same principle may apply to the front clasp.

A final factor in determining the quality of a fur garment is the designer. The elevated taste level of top designer's fur fashions can affect the price of the fur. Designer names, like Karl Lagerfeld, Roy Halston, and Oscar de la Renta, are associated with exclusive and expensive furs.

Times have changed since the husband or father deigned to purchase a prestigious fur for his wife or daughter. Women now purchase the majority of furs with money they have earned. Many styles and fur types are tried on before the buyer makes a final decision. By giving a fur the proper care, the owner can frequently wear it for several years.

SUMMARY

- Fur has been used for warmth and comfort since prehistoric times. As with all other fashion items, furs tend to increase or wane in popularity, reflecting the mood of the people in society, but throughout history fur has been used to produce luxury garments and household items.

- Fur comes from animals that are trapped in the wild or raised on fur farms. North American fur farms are located in the northern United States and Canada because cold climates produce animals with thicker fur.

- The production of fur garments is a labor-intensive business. Furs are dressed to prevent deterioration, then enhanced with special treatments. Fur is used in its natural color or dyed to resemble another animal or fashion color. It may be sculptured, plucked, or sheared to provide consumers with a variety of fashion looks and to encourage the purchase of second and third fur garments.

- Depending on the fur classification and price point, furs may be leathered, let-out, or sewn skin-on-skin.

- A fur is classified according to its family. The main classifications are bear, canine, feline, marsupial, rodent, ungulate, and weasel.

- The Fur Products Labeling Act and the Endangered Species Act are two important pieces of legislation that directly affect the fur industry. The fur industry also has imposed many stringent self-regulations.

- Animal rights groups oppose the wearing of furs and use a variety of tactics, from publicity stunts and criminal activities to celebrity spokespersons, to publicize their point of view.

- Fur is increasing in popularity, and some designers who shunned fur are now featuring it in their collections, because of greater consumer acceptance. Faux fur is a fashionable alternative to real fur.

- Consumers who do purchase fur apparel should follow proper and professional care procedures. By buying the best quality of whatever fur classification they can afford, consumers will get years of wearing pleasure from their furs.

- The United States is a large consumer of fur, and industry sales are affected by the mood of the people, economy, and climate.

- More than 75 percent of the world's fur comes from Scandinavia and Russia.

- In the world market, fur pelts are sold at auctions.

- Fur salons and departments in large retail stores offer many services that help support the business during off-seasons. Cleaning, cold storage, repairs, alterations, restyling, and consignment selling provide steady sources of income to the fur retailer.

- The fur theme has become popular in home fashions, as well as ready-to-wear. Its luxurious feel has been promoted by the industry through its campaign, "You'll feel comfortable in fur."

- Internet retailing is predominantly used for small ticket fur items, such as accessories and trim. Although not widespread, Web sites do exist for selling furs, but many of these are either direct buyers to brick-and-mortar stores or sell previously owned furs.

- The high cost of purchasing a fur garment creates an expectation of personalized customer service. The infrequent purchasing of furs requires customer reliance on knowledgeable salespeople.

- The durability of a fur is the degree to which it sheds during the life of the garment. The price of a fur is not necessarily tied to the durability. For example, chinchilla is very fragile, yet very expensive.

TERMS FOR REVIEW

bleaching	dressed	fur on fur
consignment selling	durability	guard hair
corduroy-grooved	dyeing	kickers
cutter	faux fur	knitting
double face (reversible)	fur	leathering

let out	pointing	stenciling
mutation	ranched fur	tip dyeing
natural pelts	semi let out	tipping
pelt	shearing	tramping machine
plucking	skin-on-skin construction	underfur

REVIEW QUESTIONS

1. How and why have furs evolved from a functional item to a fashion item?
2. Describe the basic steps involved in preparing a fur pelt for use.
3. How does the letting-out process differ from the skin-on-skin process?
4. What are some of the major fur classifications and their advantages and disadvantages?
5. What legal actions might a person who is opposed to the wearing of furs employ?
6. What techniques is the fur industry using to counteract the negative publicity generated by the antifur organizations?
7. What is the difference between animal welfare and animal rights?
8. How does the Fur Products Labeling Act protect manufacturers, retailers, and consumers?
9. What features and benefits might a fur salesperson highlight when speaking to a potential customer?
10. What special care requirements are needed for a fur garment?

KNOWLEDGE APPLICATIONS

1. Visit a fur salon and talk to a knowledgeable salesperson or manager. Look carefully at the variety of construction processes used and compare price points. Write a summary of your findings.
2. Obtain promotional literature from high-end fur retailers and the color photographs of designers' furs and compare the descriptions in this chapter with the featured furs. Develop a pictorial glossary of types of furs, such as mink, sable, or chinchilla.
3. Write an essay supporting your views on the fur controversy and the future of the fur industry. Include information from credible resources that reflect your position. Be prepared to orally present your paper.
4. Research the Internet to find various retailing methods used. Identify brick-and-mortar retailers' Web sites, and sites that offer fur services. Write an evaluation of your findings.
5. Contact a large furrier and arrange to take a tour of the cleaning, glazing, and cold storage facilities.
6. If possible, take a field trip to a nearby fur farm or a fur dressing facility. Prepare a list of questions in advance to ask the spokesperson.
7. Visit the U.S. Fish and Wildlife Service Web site and read about the Endangered Species Act. Make a list of fur-bearing endangered species that are similar to the animals legally used for fur accessories.

CHAPTER 6

METALS AND STONES

"Driven by a compulsion to possess tiny bits of shiny stone that were (at least until the advent of technology) utterly useless in themselves, men have crossed oceans and deserts, scaled mountains and dived beneath the surface of the sea; they have schemed and plotted, lied and stolen, fought wars and suffered agonies of torture; they have killed and they have been killed."

—O'Neil, Paul. (1983). *Planet Earth Gemstones.* Chicago: Time Life Books. pp. 21–22.

A BRIEF HISTORY OF METALS AND STONES

NATURE HAS GIFTED GEMSTONES AND PRECIOUS METALS WITH RADIANCE, COLOR, AND A HIGH SHEEN. Even in the rough, metals and stones seem to be more esteemed than other natural creations. Whether believed to be supernatural or simply beautiful, metals and stones have always been highly valued.

A study of the metals and stones, the basic materials of fashion accessories, logically begins with the most desirable of all materials, diamonds. The Greek word, *adamas* (meaning "unconquerable") gives origin to the word, ***diamond.*** From earliest times diamonds have been the material of myth and fantasy. Greek myths told of diamonds as splinters of fallen stars and tears of the gods. An ancient legend describes an inaccessible central Asian valley carpeted with diamonds and patrolled by birds of prey and snakes with deadly gazes.

Diamonds evolved from being a symbol of status and wealth to a symbol of love. Cupid's arrows have been said to be diamond tipped. Early evidence of diamond engagement rings can be traced to 1477, when Austrian Archduke Maximilian presented Mary of Burgundy with a diamond ring. The tradition of wearing a diamond on the third finger of the left hand stems from an ancient Egyptian belief that the *vena amoris* (vein of love) ran from that finger straight to the heart.

The scientific origins of diamonds are considerably less glamorous than the myths and legends. Diamonds are common carbon—the same composition as a lump of coal or the graphite in a pencil. Formations of diamond crystals require volcanic heat (2,200 degrees Fahrenheit) and intense pressure (from rocks) more than 93 miles beneath the earth's surface. The crystals grow for a few billion years, probably making diamonds the oldest of gemstones. Volcanic eruptions gradually forced a type of rock called Kimberlite to the earth's surface. These rocks, or pipes, contain the crystals from which most diamonds, the hardest known substance, are mined. An average of 250 tons of Kimberlite must be crushed and processed to produce a one-carat diamond.

India was originally the world's main source of diamonds. In the early 1700s, diamond pipes were discovered in Brazil. In the middle 1800s, a huge diamond pipe was discovered in South Africa, and enterprising men began buying diamond mine claims in South Africa. By 1888, a landowner named Cecil Rhodes managed to buy a great number of small, privately owned diamond claims, creating the giant DeBeers Diamond Company. In addition to South African mines, Russia and Australia have also unearthed diamond sites.

Diamonds were not the only legendary gemstones. Many ancient cultures regarded other gemstones as supernatural in origin and capable of warding off many ills. The ancient Greeks believed that drinking wine from an amethyst goblet prevented drunkenness. The south Asian Burmese people believed a ruby embedded in the skin would make a warrior invincible. Burmese rubies have an incandescent red color, likened to pigeon blood, and are reputed to be the finest in the world.

The ancient Persians believed that the earth rested on a giant sapphire, its reflection making the sky blue. Sapphires were also thought to have powerful rays that could kill a poisonous snake or work as an antidote to venom. The star sapphire was reputed to ward off witchcraft. Emeralds were dedicated to Venus, the goddess of love. It was believed that finely ground emeralds and topazes could improve the mind or body if ingested. Later, scientists, such as physicist Robert Boyle, simply regarded gemstones as "rare and noble productions of nature."

The belief that gemstones possessed magical properties eventually gave way to the capitalistic notion that gemstones are valuable commodities and a declaration of the owner's wealth. However, love and luck are still associated with gemstones.

Gold- and silver-toned metals have been used as an adornment metal since the beginning of recorded history. Jewelry, sculptures, beads, and threads beautified many ancient and modern civilizations. The ancient Egyptians did not have a coinage system until the last of the major dynasties, but their elaborate uses of gold for decoration can still be appreciated in museums today. Like gemstones, these metals have been symbols of divinity, wealth, and royalty. For those unable to afford the more expensive metals, inexpensive alternatives were developed. Although the ancient Egyptians are credited with creating alloys, in the early eighteenth century a modern chemist Christopher Pinchbeck introduced Pinchbeck Gold, a fake gold created from an alloy of zinc and copper.

Many powerful civilizations, including ancient Rome and the United States, built their currency on the values of gold and silver. In the United States, the discovery of gold in California set off the 1849 Gold Rush that sped the settlement of the western United States with one of the largest and fastest human migrations in world history.

Metals and stones are the most appealing material for fashion accessories. Used for adornment or currency, precious metal and gemstone accessories have universal appeal. Many of these accessories are purchased for their heirloom quality, to be passed down for generations and worn as a symbol of wealth.

AN INTRODUCTION TO METALS AND STONES

In the accessories industry, metals, stones, and other materials discussed in this chapter are used mainly in the manufacture of jewelry. Other accessories, such as belts, trims, and notions, can also be made from these materials. This chapter's focus will be mainly the precious metals and precious and semiprecious stones used in jewelry production. The jewelry industry is covered in depth in three chapters in Part Two: Chapter 13, "Fine Jewelry"; Chapter 14, "Costume Jewelry"; and Chapter 15, "Watches."

Precious Metals

The important metals in jewelry production, gold, silver, platinum, and palladium, are classified as **precious metals.** Although the precious metals are rare and valuable, the price each commands is quite different. In the fashion accessories industry, price points determine which metals are used. In most instances, the degree of rarity is a key pricing factor. Table 6.1 shows a comparison of the average annual prices of gold, silver, platinum, and palladium in May 2003.

Gold

The price of an ounce of **gold** has equaled the price of a good quality man's suit for hundreds of years. In Shakespeare's time, Beethoven and Jefferson's time, during the 1930s depression, and through the 1980s, an ounce of gold could be exchanged for a fine suit. But in the 1990s that ex-

TABLE 6.1

Precious Metals Per Ounce Price Comparison

Precious Metal	Price Per Ounce
Gold	$366.00
Silver	$ 4.74
Platinum	$662.00
Palladium	$169.00

Source: Kitco. Retrieved May 20, 2003, from www.kitco.com

change could no longer be made. Several hundred, even a thousand dollars, are needed to buy a good suit. The price of an ounce of gold still hovers near $300—no longer enough to purchase the clothes.

From 1934 to 1972, gold was a price-controlled metal and sold for $35 per ounce. The United States and seven other nations agreed to buy and sell gold to support the $35 per troy ounce price until the price was increased in 1972 to $38 and in 1973 to $44.22 per ounce. When the United States Department of the Treasury began publicly selling gold stocks in 1975, gold prices began to fluctuate, reflecting economic and political activities. The cost of gold skyrocketed in 1980, selling for as much as $850 per ounce. In the late 1970s, Middle East oil-producing countries increased their investments in the gold market. High gold prices in January 1980 were attributed to a worldwide recession as well as negative political events in the Middle East, including Iran's capture of U.S. citizens.

After 1980, gold prices continued to descend gradually through the remainder of the century. In March 2002, gold sold for $298 per ounce. Figure 6.1 shows the annual average gold price per ounce from 1968 to 1998.

Today, South Africa and Ghana in West Africa mine the largest quantities of gold, followed by the United States (chiefly in Alaska) and Australia.

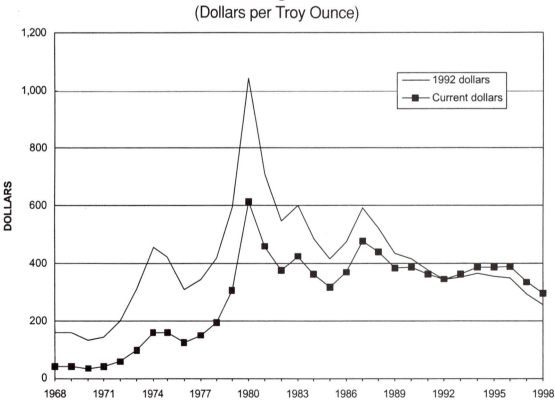

FIGURE 6.1 *Average annual gold prices from 1968 to 1998.*

When jewelry is manufactured, pure gold is usually mixed with stronger base metals to become **karat gold.** Pure gold is 24 karats, or 24/24 parts gold. When pure gold is **alloyed** (combined) with a base metal, the ratio of gold is decreased. Alloyed with copper, gold becomes a reddish-yellow gold; alloyed with silver, it becomes a greenish-yellow gold; and alloyed with palladium or nickel, it becomes white gold.

Gold that is 24k (karat) is soft and malleable. The benefits of lesser amounts of karat gold are increased durability and, of course, lower costs. Karat gold with 22 parts pure gold and 2 parts base metal is 22 karat gold. Similarly, karat gold can decrease in gold content down to 10 karat gold, the least amount of gold that can still be called karat gold. Any number below 10k is not karat gold. Gold karat items produced after June 1962 must have the karat mark and the manufacturer's name or trademark imprinted on the item.

Silver

One of the more inexpensive precious metals, pure **silver** has the whitest color and is the shiniest metal. Pure silver is 1000/1000 parts silver. **Sterling silver** has at least 925 parts silver (for luster) and 75 parts copper (for strength). It will tarnish over time. Sterling silver items are marked on the product for authenticity.

For thousands of years, silver has been used as a basis for coin currency, for example, in the powerful Roman Empire. Large silver deposit discoveries in the New World during the 18th and 19th centuries resulted in the conversion of most countries' monetary systems to the gold standard. In 1968, the United States Department of the Treasury ceased the use of silver in its currency. The average price of silver in 1998 was $5.10 per ounce. Figure 6.2 shows the price of silver from 1959 to 1998. The radical increase in 1980 was attributed to political strife in the Middle East and a worldwide recession.

Silver is mined in North and South America, chiefly in Mexico, the United States, and Peru. Much of the silver is a by-product of other mining operations, such as copper, gold, lead, and zinc.

Platinum

Platinum is a luminescent, silvery-white, dense metal that is more expensive and 60 percent heavier than white gold. Platinum is tarnish resistant and chemical resistant. The name is derived from a Spanish word, *platina,* which means "little silver." Originally, the Spaniards viewed platinum as an impurity when mining for silver.

Since its temporary rationing as a "strategic metal" during World War II," platinum has become increasingly popular for jewelry and nonfashion products, such as automobile engine parts.

The average price per ounce of platinum in 2000 was $544.45 per ounce. That was a 45 percent increase over the per-ounce price in 1999. Part of the reason for the high cost of platinum-group metals is the rarity of the metal. South Africa is the chief source of platinum metals. Figure 6.3 shows the annual average platinum price from 1959 to 1998. As with other precious metals, platinum reached a peak price in 1980, selling for $677 per ounce.

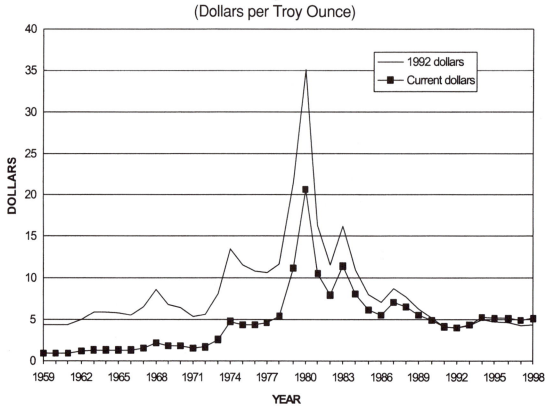

FIGURE 6.2 *Average annual silver prices from 1959 to 1998.*

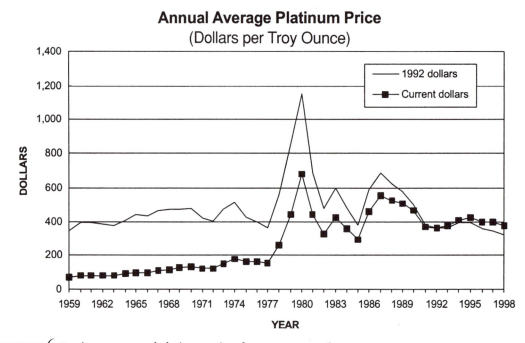

FIGURE 6.3 *Average annual platinum prices from 1959 to 1998.*

Platinum is frequently combined with five to ten percent other platinum-group metals to increase its durability. These other metals include palladium, iridium, rhodium, osmium, and ruthenium. Platinum is very popular for wedding and engagement rings.

Like silver, the platinum standard is parts per thousand. For example, a ring that is 95 percent platinum would be 950/1000 parts platinum. It would bear one of the following stamps: Pt 950, 950 Pt, 950 Plat, Plat 950, Pt, Plat, or Platinum.

Palladium

Palladium is a rare metallic element of the platinum group; it is silver-white in color. South Africa and Russia rank first and second in palladium metal production.

Figure 6.4 shows the price-per-ounce fluctuations from 1959 to 1998. Although the 1980 price for palladium was extremely high, at $201 per ounce, the 1998 price at $290 per ounce was the record high price.

Plated and Filled Metals

While consumers prefer the look of gold, many are unwilling or unable to the pay the high prices commanded by the gold market. Several lower-priced options are available, but they lack the durability of karat gold.

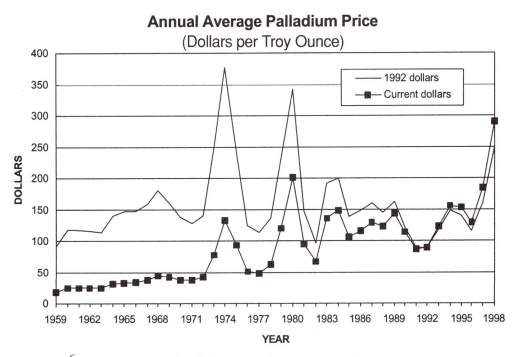

FIGURE 6.4 *Average annual palladium prices from 1959 to 1998.*

Gold Filled

Metal that is **gold filled** consists of thin sheets of gold (10 karat minimum) adhered to a grooved base metal, such as nickel. The karat gold is melted, rolled, and pressed onto the base metal. The amount of gold is 1/20 of the total weight of the item.

Gold Plate

Gold is dissolved and using an electrical current is attracted to a base metal, such as copper, to make metal that is **gold plate.** This procedure is called **electroplating** and results in a very thin layer of at least 10-karat gold deposited on a base metal. The terms **gold flashed** or **gold washed** describe products with a very thin electroplating of gold (less than .175 microns thick) that will wear away more quickly than the other methods. **Gold vermeil** consists of a sterling-silver base coated, or plated, with a minimum of 10 karat gold.

Other Metals

Other plated and filled metals are called **rolled gold, gold overlay**, and **rolled gold plate.** They are similar to gold filled, except the gold content is less. The amount of gold must be 1/40 of the total weight.

GEMSTONES

Gemstones are minerals that have been cut and polished to make them sparkle. Polishing stones is sometimes done by tumbling the stones in barrels filled with abrasive substances. The effect is similar to the natural process that polishes rocks in riverbeds as they continuously roll downstream over other rocks. The colors of gemstones are created by the elements found in each gem, and the degree to which light travels through the gem affects the sparkle. Three terms, *transparent, translucent,* and *opaque,* refer to the degree to which light passes through the stone.

Transparent   Clear; allows light to pass through

Translucent   Milky appearance that prevents visibility through the stone but allows light to pass through, like a frosted glass

Opaque   Does not allow light to pass through the object

In 1812 German scientist Frederick Mohs devised a numeric scale system that gauged the hardness (ability to resist scratching) of minerals. The minerals were ranked from one to ten. The hardest substance, the diamond, was ranked a ten, while the softest substance, talc, was ranked a one. Substances with higher numbers scratched substances with lower numbers. Gemstones rated less than seven are not durable and should be cautiously used in jewelry that is frequently bumped or scratched, such as rings. Table 6.2 shows the **Mohs scale** of hardness for minerals.

TABLE 6.2

Mohs Scale

Mineral	Ranking (Hardest=10, Softest=1)
Diamond	10
Corundum (Ruby and Sapphire)	9
Topaz	8
Emerald	7.5
Quartz (Amethyst)	7
Orthoclase	6
Opal	5.5_5.6
Turquoise	5_6
Apatite	5
Fluorite	4
Calcite	3
Gypsum	2
Talc	1

Source: Clark, D. *Hardness and Wearability.* International Gem Society.

Precious Stones

The category of **precious stones** includes diamonds, rubies, sapphires, emeralds, and real pearls (which are not actually a stone). They are classified as *precious* because of their rarity and beauty. Some gemologists discourage the classification of gems into precious and semiprecious categories because some rare "semiprecious" stones, such as alexandrite, are of greater value than lesser quality "precious stones," like a poor quality diamond. However, for simplification, this textbook will continue to use these two classifications.

Diamond

The hardest of all stones, diamonds range in grade from near perfect to poor quality, industrial-use-only diamonds. Eighty percent of mined diamonds are not suitable for jewelry. They are used for industrial purposes, such as cutting tools and drill bits. Diamonds are mined all over the world, but the largest percent of the world's production of gemstone diamonds come from Australia, Botswana, Russia, and South Africa.

Gem-quality diamonds (and other gems as well) are rated on 4 Cs: carat, cut, clarity, and color. The combination of these four qualities determines the price of a diamond.

Carat Originally, a carat was the weight of a uniform carob seed that was used as a standard of measurement for diamonds. A **carat** is equal in weight to 1/5 gram, 1/142 ounce, and is subdivided into 100 equal parts called **points.** The purpose of classifying a carat using points is to ensure accuracy in weighing, which may significantly affect the price. For example, a 50-point diamond equals one-half carat. A 25-point diamond equals one-quarter carat. The term *total carat weight* refers to the total points of all the stones in the item.

Cut Most precious stones have 58 symmetrical **facets,** or flat-surfaced **cuts.** Several special cuts are used for gemstones to create a vibrant sparkle, called **light refraction.** This process was discovered in 1666 by Sir Isaac Newton. He determined that when he aimed a narrow beam of white light at a specially cut prism, the light bent and separated into all the colors of the rainbow.

One who specializes in the art of cutting stones is called a **lapidary** and must undergo intense training for precision and skill. There are many different cuts for gemstones, depending on the type of stone.

An **ideal cut** shows the stones to their best advantage; however, this cut is used on less than one percent of all diamonds. With an ideal cut, the diamond is shaped to optimum proportions for maximum brilliance. Much of the rough diamond is cut away. In some instances, a well-cut stone can minimize the appearance of imperfections in a gem.

The **round ideal** or **brilliant cut** is the most popular of all cuts. Mathematician Marcel Tolkowsky developed the round ideal cut as part of a doctoral dissertation in 1919 (see Figure 6.5). Subsequent round cuts were the Hearts on Fire, 58 facets (1996); Eternal, 81 facets (1999); Escada, 97 facets (2000); and Leo, 66 facets (2000). Some of the other popular cuts and shapes for diamonds and other gemstones are illustrated in Figure 6.6. A cabochon cut is used on polished opaque stones, such as turquoise or lapis. Other cuts include barion, oval, heart, navette (similar to marquis), cushion (similar to sofa cushions), shield, rhomboid, parallelogram, triangle, hexagon, and octagon. Table 6.3 describes several popular gemstone cuts.

FIGURE 6.5 *Brilliant Cut.*   Top view   Side view

    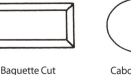

Emerald Cut   Marquis Cut   Pear Cut   Baguette Cut   Cabochon Cut

FIGURE 6.6 *Other popular gemstone cuts.*

TABLE 6.3
Popular Gemstone Cuts

Round Ideal and Brilliant Cut	Round shape; 58 facets at specific angles to ensure maximum light refraction.
Emerald Cut	Rectangular shape with cutaway corners; 58 facets. This cut is most often used for transparent, colored gemstones. Also known as a *step cut.*
Marquis Cut	Elliptical shape; 58 facets.
Pear Cut	Rounded bottom with tapered top.
Baguette	Long and rectangular-shaped cut.
En Cabochon	Also known as *cutting cabs.* A flat-bottomed stone with a polished dome top, without facets.
Melee	Cut stones of less than a carat weight.
Carved	Raised surface figures, such as *cameo,* or lowered figures, such as *intaglio.*

Clarity **Clarity** refers to the presence or absence of diamond flaws, known as **inclusions** or "birthmarks of nature." The fewer the inclusions, the more desirable the diamond. These flaws range from those visible to the naked eye, to minute-sized inclusions, which require the use of a magnification device, such as a jeweler's **loupe** (a gem microscope) to view them. A handheld loupe allows the jeweler to see the diamond under 10X magnification. Inclusions may take the form of feathering, cloudy areas, black spots, or cracks. Diamonds are graded for any departure from flawless–the complete absence of external or internal blemish under 10X magnification.

Diamonds are assigned descriptors ranging from *flawless* to *imperfect.* Table 6.4 describes each of the clarity terms used in grading diamonds. See Figure 6.7 for variations in the clarity of diamonds.

TABLE 6.4
Clarity Grading Scale

Term	Definition
Flawless	No external blemishes or internal inclusions visible under 10X magnification.
IF	Internally flawless; external blemishes but no internal inclusions.
VVS1, VVS2	Very, very slight inclusions.
VS1, VS2	Very slight inclusions.
SI1, SI2	Slight inclusions.
I1, I2, I3	Imperfect; inclusions visible under 10X magnification as well as to the human eye.

Source: Mondera. Retrieved May 10, 2001, from mondera.com

Clarity Grading Scale

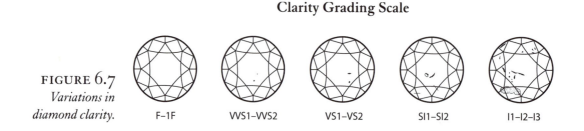

FIGURE 6.7
*Variations in
diamond clarity.*

F–1F   VVS1–VVS2   VS1–VS2   SI1–SI2   I1–I2–I3

Color A diamonds' **color** is graded from D to Z. The logic is that there can be no A grade of diamonds, because perfection is not consistent with the natural world. Undiscovered diamonds may one day have a B or C ranking on the grading scale. Diamonds near the front of the alphabet are nearly colorless. As the ranking falls further down, the diamonds take on a yellowish tinge and ultimately, a brownish tinge. Ideal cutting measures can be taken by jewelers to disguise the lower grades of diamonds.

A master grading set of diamonds is available to jewelers. This set displays uniform-sized stones in predetermined colors (from colorless to faintly yellowed to strong yellow) matched to specific alphabet letters. Real diamonds should be viewed from the side to determine color and compared to the master stone grading set.

The price of precious stones depends on these factors as well as size, which is usually measured in carats. Like precious metals, they are considered investments and appreciate in value over time.

Ruby

Rubies are formed in limestone within a mineral called corundum and are extremely rare. The best quality is found in Burma (Myanmar). The stone gets its red color from the trace element chromium. Red corundum is called ruby, and all other colors are called sapphire. Some gemologists disagree over the point at which a ruby becomes a pink or plum sapphire. Dealers want the gems they sell to be classified as rubies because the name alone increases its value.

Sapphire

The name **sapphire** is derived from the Greek word *sappeiros,* meaning blue. Also from the mineral corundum, sapphires contain a few trace elements not found in rubies. The best sapphires are a velvety, cornflower blue color attributable to the trace elements iron and titanium. The velvety appearance is because of tiny, needle-like inclusions in the gem. An excess of inclusions creates a translucent or opaque stone. When the inclusions are oriented properly, light is reflected as a floating star. This is called a **star sapphire. (Star rubies** are similar in appearance.) Sapphires can also be green, orange, and yellow-colored stones.

Emerald

A transparent greenish stone from the mineral beryl, the **emerald** derives its color from traces of chromium. The finest emeralds have been found in Columbia, South America. The clear green color is the most important aspect of emeralds. The emerald cut shows off this feature to its best

The World's Most Famous Diamonds

The Hope Diamond

Few gemstones boast a history as colorful and legendary as the Hope Diamond. Perhaps the major reason why the Hope Diamond is one of the world's most famous gems is its more than three-century history of mystery and intrigue, one that includes kings, a revolution, a daring theft, and perhaps even a curse. It is not known exactly when and where the Hope Diamond was discovered, but it was prior to 1668 and most likely in the Golconda area of India. In 1668 Jean-Baptiste Tavernier, a French gem merchant, sold a 112 3/16-carat blue diamond from India to King Louis XIV of France, who had the stone recut to about 67 carats. In 1749 Louis XV had the diamond, now known as the French Blue, set into a piece of ceremonial jewelry. The royal treasury was looted in September 1792, and the Crown Jewels, including the French Blue, disappeared. In 1830 the diamond was recut to 45.52 carats and was purchased by London banker and gem collector Henry Philip Hope, whose name it bears today. Pierre Cartier purchased the stone in 1909 and placed it in a platinum setting, surrounded by sixteen white pear-shaped and cushion-cut diamonds,

suspended from a chain containing forty-five diamonds, and sold it to Washington socialite Evalyn Walsh McLean. Upon her death in 1947, the diamond was sold to New York Jeweler Harry Winston. In 1958, he presented it to the Smithsonian Institution, where it is the foundation piece in of the National Gem Collection in the National Museum of Natural History.

The Koh-i-noor Diamond

Another of the world's most famous diamonds was once owned by an Afghan prince, and was owned (and occasionally worn in a brooch) by England's Queen Mother before she died in 2002. Similar to the Hope Diamond because of its tempestuous history, the lackluster 108.93 carat Koh-i-noor Diamond has been associated with sealing the fate of its many owners. Some authorities believe the bloody history of this diamond can be traced back 5,000 years to references in an ancient Sanskrit epic. The story is that a greedy Persian invader, Nadir Shah, plotted to steal the stone from an acquaintance, Muhammad Shah Rangila, who secretly kept the stone in his turban. Upon discovering the hiding place, Nadir arranged a celebration banquet for Muhammad Shah Rangila. During the banquet, Nadir Shah proposed a "gesture of good will and mutual respect" which included trading turbans. Good breeding made a refusal by Muhammad Shah Rangila unthinkable. The exchange was made and when Nadir Shah unwound Muhammad's turban, out tumbled the diamond. Nadir Shah exclaimed, "Koh-i-noor!" (mountain of light). And Koh-i-noor is the name by which the diamond has been known ever since.

Sources:

Information about the Hope Diamond from Jeffrey E. Post of the Smithsonian Institution.

O'Neil, P. (1983). *Planet Earth Gemstones*. Chicago: Time Life Books.

---

advantage. The rich color can be distinctly seen, even in unpolished and uncut stones. Inclusions in the gems do not hinder the value unless they appear cloudy. Some emeralds have a branching, graceful inclusion called a *jardin* (French for "garden").

Real Pearls

These fall under the category of a precious gem, but they are not really a stone. Real pearls are a natural secretion from oysters. Real and cultured pearls are covered in detail in the section of this chapter entitled "Other Gems."

Semiprecious Stones

Semiprecious stones are often as beautiful as precious stones, and may even be more costly if the semiprecious stone ranks higher on the four Cs (carat, cut, clarity, and color). Usually, semiprecious gemstones are more plentiful than precious gemstones. Their abundance contributes to their lower prices. Table 6.5 describes several popular semiprecious stones. Figure 6.8 shows an example of jewelry made from turquoise.

TABLE 6.5
Semiprecious Stones

Alexandrite	A green-tinged transparent stone; may change to a reddish color under artificial lighting. Moderately priced, except when found in the rare, large size.
Amethyst	A valuable, but modestly priced, quartz crystal; purple color is derived from traces of iron. Found in many regions of the world, including Arizona, Brazil, and Zambia.
Aquamarine	A sister to the emerald and the tougher of the two. Transparent blue to blue-green stone from the mineral beryl. Mainly found in South America and Africa.
Cat's Eye	From a mineral called chrysoberyl; the band of light that cuts across the diameter of the greenish to yellowish stone is caused by thousands of parallel impurities or inclusions that enhance the light reflection. Name derived from a combination of French words, *chat* (cat) and *oeil* (eye).
Garnet	Colors range from violet or ruby red to rich green, although garnets are usually associated with a deep red color. Historically, large ruby gemstones have been confused with garnets and some garnets are referred to as *Cape rubies* or *Arizona rubies.*
Jade	Usually found in irregular chunks, from jadeite (better quality) and nephrite (lesser quality). Occurs in several colors, but the most common is green. Better quality jade is found in China.
Lapis Lazuli	Literally translated, "blue stone," lapis is an opaque royal-blue stone with a mineral-flecked or solid appearance. Usually, cut lapis gems have few facets.
Malachite	An opaque green gemstone with a polished surface that reflects light.
Moonstone	From the feldspar family; milky and translucent.
Onyx	A semitranslucent to opaque quartz stone, polished to a high luster. Colors range from light oranges and reds to white. Often used for the carved figure in cameos. Black onyx is actually dyed quartz.
Opal	Found in host rocks, opals are very delicate, ranging from transparent to opaque stones. Opals have irregularities and tiny cracks that hold moisture and light, creating an optical, iridescent effect.
Peridot	Pronounced "pear-uh-doe." A soft, transparent, yellowish-green stone that ranges from a bright grass green to a dark olive green. Originally mined off the coast of Egypt, the peridot was a prized gem.
Spinel	An inexpensive stone, often mistaken for rubies. The British Crown of State bears the *Black Prince's Ruby,* a two-inch long spinel gem, which for centuries was believed to be a ruby.
Topaz	Usually a sherry-yellow-colored or colorless stone, shaped with an emerald cut. Other topaz colors include transparent pink, red, and brown.
Turquoise	A soft, opaque stone, shaped and polished to a waxy luster. Blue-green color is a result of traces of copper. Found as veins in host stones (see Figure 6.8).
Zircon	A warm-colored or colorless, transparent quartz, sometimes with less sparkle or refractive index than a diamond (a plain cousin to diamonds), but often used as a substitute for diamonds. Zircons are natural gemstones and should not be confused with the synthetic stone, cubic zirconia.

FIGURE 6.8 *Turquoise jewelry.* Courtesy of Montana Denim by Barse.

Other Gems

Additional information about the gems listed in this chapter and information regarding many that are not listed are described on the International Gem Society Web site. Some gems are not actually stones at all, but originate from living things (organic) or chemical elements. A few of these important gems are discussed below.

Amber

Amber is fossilized resin, a natural substance found in pine and other resin-bearing trees. Most amber deposits are found along the beaches of the Baltic Sea, which was once a forest of resinous trees. The discovery of organisms trapped in amber for millions of years was the story-line behind the science fiction novel and movie *Jurassic Park.*

FIGURE 6.9
Real pearl.
Courtesy of Fairchild Publications, Inc.

Coral

Coral is harvested from millions of skeletons of tiny sea creatures that grow in the ocean's coastal regions. Its semitransparent to opaque colors include white, pink, dark red, and black. The most common is the orange-red coral.

Jet

Jet is a dense, hard, black coal that can be polished to a high sheen.

Real Pearls

Real pearls are considered a precious gem, but they are not a stone. They are actually a natural secretion of oysters. Pearls form when a foreign particle, such as a grain of sand, becomes lodged in the soft tissue of the oyster. To lessen the irritation, the oyster begins to coat the particle with layers of calcium carbonate, or **nacre,** creating a pearl. Unlike stones that are measured in carats, pearls are measured in millimeters. Pearl colors range from creamy white to shades of gray and black (see Figure 6.9).

Pearl surfaces are evaluated on a scale from clean to heavily blemished. Clean pearls have virtually no spots, bumps, pits, cracks, circles, or wrinkles on them. These types of imperfections dominate heavily blemished pearls. However, irregular shapes are characteristics of baroque pearls. *Baroque pearl* is the term used to describe any variety of pearl with an unusual shape.

Cultured pearls are made in the same fashion as real pearls, except the tiny irritants are artificially inserted into the mollusk tissue to encourage the development of a pearl. The process may take up to three years before a cultured pearl is sufficiently coated with nacre.

Cultured pearls may be created in freshwater or saltwater. One of the rarest and most expensive varieties of cultured saltwater pearls is called **South Sea pearls.** They are cultivated over a two- to three-year period and develop a thick coating of nacre. Fine South Sea cultured pearls look like natural pearls. The difference can be identified only when examining them by X-ray. Another costly cultured pearl is the large **Tahitian pearl** grown in French Polynesia. Its colors range from light gray to black, and green to purple, and the pearls can be grown to large sizes.

The Rivaling Real Pearls

For centuries, Japan has been the leading producer of expensive **Akoya saltwater cultured pearls** that are found individually in oysters. The Chinese are credited with the development of the less expensive freshwater cultured pearls from mussels. As early as 800 A.D. the Chinese were implanting tiny lead Buddhas in mussels until the talisman became coated with nacre, making a lucky pearlized Buddha. Now the Chinese have developed the art of creating cultured freshwater pearls that rival the size, round shape, and glow of real pearls.

The process involves implanting multiple pieces of mollusk tissue into a one-year-old triangular-shaped mussel rather than the traditional process of implanting a bead into a two-year-old mussel. The result is a cluster (10-30) of irregular- and round-shaped cultured pearls inside a single mussel.

In 2001, the world's supply of more than 1500 tons of freshwater pearls were cultivated in China. During the same year, only 60 tons of saltwater pearls were produced. As a result, cultured pearls are available at a fraction of the cost of real pearls. A nine-millimeter real pearl might wholesale at $350 while a cultured pearl of similar size and appearance costs $125.

Even fine jewelry retailers have found the market for cultured pearls too lucrative to resist. Tiffany & Company featured a $250 cultured rice pearl bracelet on page two of their catalog that has traditionally been reserved for costly diamond jewelry. Experts estimated the company's investment in the materials (cultured pearls and silver clasp) to be less than $35.

Irregular-shaped rice pearls (similar to puffed rice cereal) cost much less and are popular with the under-25 set, more casual consumers who are just beginning to purchase fine jewelry. They are a casual fashion statement, frequently worn with jeans as a symbol of **affordable luxury,** which means that customers have the means to purchase merchandise that offers them status or prestige. Jewelry marketers consider this concept to be a psychological lift for consumers and a key selling strategy for retailers at any price point.

Faux Stones and Gems

Faux (fake) stones and gems are all manufactured, but differ in chemical composition. Faux stones and gems are classified as synthetic or simulated.

Synthetic stones are man-made stones that are chemically and atomically identical to real stones. They closely resemble the real stones, but are available at a fraction of the cost. Because of the similar components, an untrained eye can easily mistake synthetic stones for real stones. An expert can identify physical differences, but may need magnification to do so.

The first truly synthetic stone was a ruby. In 1837 French chemist Marc Gaudin melted the same elements found in a ruby and produced a few flecks of colored stone. In 1902 a French chemist named Auguste Verneuil improved on Gaudin's success with the first commercially successful process, creating hundreds of carats of rubies in just a few hours. The success of synthesizing rubies soon expanded to sapphires. The Verneuil process has been adapted to modern-day synthetic stone production.

Cubic zirconia is a sophisticated diamond substitute that can be produced in batches of 100 pounds. At wholesale, it costs a few dollars per carat. Cubic zirconia properties make it almost impossible to distinguish the synthetic from a real diamond, and it can be manufactured with realistic inclusions or flaws. It can have the same fire (sparkle) as a diamond and is extremely durable.

Simulated stone, imitation stone, rhinestone, and **brilliant** are stones made out of glass or a similar substance. They are not chemically and atomically identical to the stones they imitate.

TABLE 6.6

Birthstones of Modern and Ancient Times

Month	Modern Stone	Ancient Stone
January	Garnet	Garnet
February	Amethyst	Amethyst
March	Aquamarine	Bloodstone
April	Diamond	Diamond
May	Emerald	Emerald
June	Alexandrite	Pearl or Moonstone
July	Ruby	Ruby
August	Peridot	Sardonyx
September	Sapphire	Sapphire
October	Rose zircon	Opal or Pink tourmaline
November	Golden topaz or Citrine quartz	Topaz
December	Blue zircon	Turquoise or Lapis lazuli

Source: Birthstone List. International Gem Society.

A common simulant or imitation stone is a faceted paste or glass stone backed with foil to look like a diamond. **Doublets** are slices of real gems cemented to a paste base or less expensive stone base. The term *rhinestone* is of French origin, where stones of this type were made in factories along the Rhine River. Rhinestone glass is derived from a heated mixture of quartz, red lead, potassium carbonate, borax, and white arsenic. Common simulants include YAG (yttrium aluminum garnet) and GGG (gadolinium gallium garnet). Other materials, such as ceramic and plastic, have been used to create simulated turquoise, pearls, and ivory. Imitation pearls, sometimes called Mallorca or Majorica pearls, may be made of beads coated with lacquer and ground fish scales to simulate the iridescence and color of real pearls.

Birthstones

Birthstone rings, necklaces, and other birthstone jewelry are among the most popular accessories. Several cultures offer their own version of monthly birthstones, so there is some variance among published lists. Table 6.6 represents commonly recognized birthstones for each of the 12 months. Early 20th century jewelers selected a modern list of birthstones including only transparent gems so that mothers' rings would be more uniform and attractive. Jewelers and customers are encouraged to mix the two lists. The modern list was intended to supplement, not replace, the ancient list.

CARE OF METALS AND STONES

Special care requirements for precious metals accessories include checking for loose settings or prongs, removing rings when hand washing, and avoiding contact with harsh chemicals. Avoid

Other Accessories Materials

Several other materials may be used in fashion accessories. These range from minerals to organic or synthetic substances. The following list includes the more popular materials:

Horn Translucent, hard, and smooth material from mammal horns. Colors include ivory to mottled brown. The term may be used to describe simulated as well as real horn.

Ivory A hard, creamy-white material that comes from the tusks of the walrus, whale, or elephant—can be carved into intricate designs. **Scrimshaw** is ivory carved into fine details. Asian elephants are an endangered species and ivory from these animals is outlawed in the United States.

Tortoiseshell Translucent, brownish-black mottled shell of certain sea turtles. Also any plastic or substitute material that resembles natural tortoise shell. Used for making combs, jewelry, and eyeglass frames.

Mother-of-pearl Also called nacre, the iridescent and lustrous inside of certain mollusk shells. Similar to **abalone,** from a pearly and colorful ear-shaped marine shellfish. Both are used for jewelry inlay, buttons, and other adornments.

Glass Colored glass is a frequent substitute for gems. It is resistant to most household chemicals, but it may scratch or break if abraded by other (harder) surfaces.

Aluminum, steel, and **titanium** Used for accessories, such as watches and eyeglass frames.

Plastic A popular and inexpensive natural materials substitute; may simulate real pearls, wood, tortoise shell, horn, and some metals.

Clay An inexpensive and colorful alternative to glass beads. Clay beads can be painted, glazed, and fired and used for bead necklaces, bracelets, and earrings. Clay is breakable and should be used in accessories worn in protected areas, like necklaces and earrings.

Wood Wooden accessories include costume jewelry, such as carved bracelets, earrings, pins, and necklaces; some purse handles, and some shoe soles. Cork, either natural or synthetic, may also be used for shoe soles.

Stringing materials May be natural or man-made. Materials include natural hemp for necklaces, bracelets, and anklets; synthetic ropes, such as strong nylon filament, used to suspend beads and pendants. Illusion necklaces were so-called because transparent nylon filament was used to suspend a gemstone setting or similar pendant, creating a floating illusion. Pearls are usually suspended on a strong multifilament rope (traditionally silk) with knots between each pearl. This method prevents the expensive gems from scattering if the rope breaks.

pressing against the raised areas of the metal, such as prongs. Regular pressure may cause the metals to bend or break, particularly softer metals, such as 18 karat gold.

Jewelers advise against reusing (melting down) gold accessories and casting the gold into new jewelry items. Tiny pockmarks and imperfections mar the recast gold.

Gemstones need regular cleaning to ensure maximum light reflection and sparkle. Diluted ammonia or soap and water on a soft-bristled toothbrush tends to be the best remedies for dingy gems, although commercial cleaners are available. All stones are subject to breakage, especially in the area of inclusions. Hard blows may cause the gem to chip, split, or shatter. **Ultrasonic cleaners** may not harm a durable stone, like diamonds, rubies, and sapphires, but they have been known to cause breakage in opaque gems, like opals or turquoise. Opaque stones should simply be wiped clean with a dry polishing cloth. The porous nature of these stones can cause absorption of damaging chemicals, including soap or ammonia. Opals are especially delicate stones, containing water. They will not withstand cleaning chemicals, extreme temperature changes, and strong lights.

Organic gems, like pearls, should be worn regularly to maintain a high luster. Body oils are absorbed into the stones, creating a sheen. They can be cleaned with a clean, damp cloth. Perfumes and hair sprays should never be sprayed on pearls because of the likelihood of discoloration over time.

The Mohs scale should be considered when storing gems. Some gems are harder than others and may scratch softer stones. Most gems are harder than precious metals and will scratch the settings of jewelry if heaped in jewelry boxes.

GEMSTONE INDUSTRY REGULATIONS

The Federal Trade Commission (FTC) requires that all synthetic and imitation gem materials be identified as such to the buyer at the time of the sale. In addition, any treatment significantly affecting the gemstone's value must be disclosed. The purpose of the FTC regulations is to protect buyers against unfair or deceptive trade practices. The FTC publishes informational literature about color and clarity-enhancing treatments for gemstones, and the increasing use of laser drilling on diamonds. **Laser drilling** refers to the removal of black spots or inclusions by aiming a laser beam at the spot, creating a tiny tunnel through which acid is forced to remove the inclusion. The FTC offers a consumer Web site with jewelry purchasing guidelines.

The United Nations Security Council has passed regulations to embargo what it calls "blood" or "conflict" diamonds. Some African countries, like Liberia, use the sale of illegally mined diamonds to fund their wars and purchase weapons. The United Nations, hoping to halt the rebel conflicts, imposed sanctions against the Liberian government and president.

THE GLOBAL METALS
AND STONES INDUSTRIES

The United States is a chief importer of gems and precious metals for jewelry and for many years has been the major buyer with a share of more than 38 percent. The slowdown in the U.S. economy in 2001 had an impact on imports, particularly on diamond demand, which accounts for as much as 50 percent of the worldwide diamond jewelry demand. Major diamond centers worldwide include Mumbai (Bombay), India; Tel Aviv, Israel; Antwerp, Belgium; Johannesburg, South Africa; Tokyo, Japan; and New York City.

"The Diamond Industry is Shedding Its Mystery," read an April 2001 headline in *The New York Times*. After centuries of trading diamonds in secrecy, and on little more than a handshake, diamond companies are changing the way they do business. Many companies feel forced to open up to the public to dispel threats of a diamond boycott (similar to fur boycotts) because of the politics of countries that sell diamonds. African nations have been accused of using "conflict diamonds" to finance civil wars. Some diamond companies feel low-priced competitors (discount stores, like Wal-Mart, expanding its line of fine jewelry) have forced changes in the diamond market.

A "diamond pipeline" exists from mine to market. The New York City diamond market is centrally located along 47th Street, between Fifth Avenue and the Avenue of the Americas. Diamonds pass through diamond brokers up and down the block, sometimes changing hands several times in one day.

Diamond business practices have been changing all over the world. These changes involve marketing tactics, company restructuring, and transaction policy changes. Most notable is the attempt at diamond branding to differentiate commodity products. De Beers has pressured its **sightholders** (a group of its key diamond cutters and brokers) into marketing and promotions. Sightholders are expected to allot advertising budgets of ten percent of their sales, compared to the one percent of sales that it has traditionally allotted. De Beers also began asking sightholders to enter into written contracts, replacing the oral agreements that had been satisfactory in the past. Restructuring by companies in the industry includes acquisitions, mergers, vertical integration, and other methods developed to improve profit margins.

Gold is the most important precious metal in the world and is traded extensively around the globe. A rise in gold demand is often tied to increases in political and financial uncertainties worldwide as a hedge against risk. By contrast, the demand for precious metal jewelry may decrease during uncertain times. In 2001 the world gold demand ended slightly below 2000 prices. The year began strongly, but in the aftermath of the September 11, 2001, terrorist attacks on U.S. soil, economic growth faded. However, plain-gold jewelry sales set a record in 2001, in part due to significant quantities of jewelry purchased as keepsakes or symbols of relationships in connection with the months following the terrorist attacks.

TRADE ORGANIZATIONS, PUBLICATIONS, AND SHOWS

The gemstone and metals industry has several trade organizations in the world, many of which are similar in name and objectives. Most organizations provide educational training or licensing and promote the wearing of jewelry made from precious metals and gemstones. Table 6.7 represents several important trade organizations representing the gemstone and precious metals industries. Table 6.8 represents trade publications, and Table 6.9 represent trade shows associated with these industries.

MERCHANDISING TRENDS

Both the gem and precious metal industries have struggled with creating brand-name appeal for commodity goods. Especially in the diamond trade, adding value to a generic product requires marketing, advertising, and promotion. The fashion house Escada teamed up with the Pluczenik Group to produce an Escada diamond. These 12-sided, 97-faceted diamonds may still be classified according to the 4 Cs, but company officials hope the brand-name presence will create a competitive edge. Most customers lack confidence in their own knowledge to accu-

TABLE 6.7

Trade Organizations for the Gemstone and Precious Metals Industries

Organization	Location	Objectives
American Gem Society www.ags.org	Las Vegas, NV	Ensures consumer protection when purchasing gems; disseminates knowledge
American Gem Trade Association www.atga.com	Dallas, TX	Promotes the natural-colored gemstone, pearl, and cultured pearl industries; sponsors trade shows
Cultured Pearl Information Center www.pearlinfo.com	Online	Educates consumers and the trade with information on varieties, farming, fashion, and buying guides
Gemological Institute of America (GIA) www.gia.edu	Los Angeles, CA	Provides gem information; offers on-site or correspondence courses; provides a Web site with links to related sites
Japan Pearl Exporters Association www.japan-pearl.com	Japan	Promotes Japanese Akoya cultured pearls
International Colored Gemstone Association www.gemstone.org	Hornbrook, CA	Increases consumer appreciation and sale of colored gemstones
International Gem Society www.gemsociety.org	Redding, CA	Offers educational services; certifications
International Gemological Institute www.igiworldwide.com	New York, NY	Offers diamond and colored gem appraisals and courses; gem appraisals
World Diamond Council www.worlddiamondcouncil.com	New York, NY	Monitors the export and import of rough diamonds to prevent funding of illicit purposes, such as war and inhumane acts
World Gold Council www.gold.org	New York, NY	Represents gold mines worldwide; promotes the use of gold
Platinum Guild International www.preciousplatinum.com	Newport Beach, CA	Promotes the use of platinum as an alternative to white gold
Diamond Trade and Precious Stone Association of America, Inc.	New York, NY	U.S. member of the World Federation of Diamond Bourses; provides membership directory of diamond dealers in good standing with the bourse

TABLE 6.8

Trade Publications for the Gemstones and Precious Metals Industries

Trade Publication Name	Description
Gems and Gemology	News articles, laboratory reports, scientific research abstracts, and book reviews.
Gold	Published by the World Gold Council; provides online commentaries, press releases, reports, and bulletins.
New York Diamonds	Closely monitors the New York City diamond market.

TABLE 6.9

Trade Shows for the Gemstone and Precious Metals Industries

Trade Show	Location	Sponsor
Week of Gold Technology	Vincenza, Italy	World Gold Council; Vincenza Fair
Tucson Gem Show	Tucson, AZ	Gem and Lapidary Dealers Association
World Diamond Congress	Antwerp, Belgium	World Federation of Diamond Bourses; International Diamond Manufacturer's Association
AGS International Conclave	Vancouver, British Columbia	American Gem Society

rately assess the value of a diamond. Brand names are one way to help customers feel confident about what they are purchasing.

De Beers has successfully marketed diamonds generically. Several years ago, the company launched an advertising campaign that encouraged males "to spend two months' salary on an engagement ring." "A Diamond Is Forever" and "A Girl's Best Friend" were also successful marketing campaigns of the De Beers Company. To ensure a premium price for diamonds, the De Beers Company traditionally stockpiled diamonds, creating a false supply scarcity. Taking a different marketing approach, the company is now aggressively marketing diamonds, in hopes of generating a greater demand.

The Platinum Guild International, Kwiat Diamonds, and Stuart Weitzman, a celebrity shoe designer, created a one-million-dollar pair of stiletto shoes worn at the 2002 Oscar Awards. Specially spun platinum threads hold 64 carats of diamonds, including two five-carat pear shaped diamonds over the insteps. For added appeal, the shoes can be disassembled and worn as a necklace and bracelet.

The World Gold Council has begun a repositioning campaign for gold metals, especially in jewelry. The campaign draws on gold's historical association with the sun. Gold, with its warm properties, is positioned as bridging the gap between fashion and the desire for a more positive way of life, summed up by the slogans, "Glow with gold" and "Warm is the new kind of cool."

Profile Box: De Beers Consolidated Mines

The De Beers brothers never realized the profit potential of the little farm they owned in South Africa. Overwhelmed and annoyed with swarming diamond prospectors, brothers Johannes and Diedrich sold their farm to a mining syndicate for a small profit over their original investment from eleven years prior. The site of their farm became the famous Kimberley Diamond Mine. Many small claims were established but were eventually bought out by Cecil Rhodes, who described the claims as "an immense number of ant heaps covered with black ants, as thick as can be, the latter represented by human beings."[1]

Since the company's founding in 1888 by Cecil Rhodes, De Beers has been the dominant marketer and miner of diamonds in the world. They have less tactfully been referred to as a monopoly on uncut diamonds. In fact, in the United States, an outstanding indictment against De Beers for violating anti-trust laws prevents De Beers' senior executives from entering the country.

In January 2001, De Beers entered into a licensing agreement with LVMH Moet Hennessy Louis Vuitton. The two firms planned to create a brand of jewelry called De Beers to be sold in freestanding stores in cities such as London, New York, Paris, and Tokyo. By using the recognizable name of De Beers for jewelry, Nicky Oppenheimer, chairman of De Beers, hoped to increase demand for branded diamond jewelry. Cautious industry officials questioned the success of the branding venture. John Wakely, a luxury goods analyst, explained, "The success of turning a commodity 'diamond' into a brand is not promising."

Claire Kent, also a luxury goods analyst said, "At the moment, De Beers does not have an identity. It's not known for any particular style and that will be the main challenge."[2] However, LVMH Moet Hennessy Louis Vuitton had expertise in luxury goods. In fact, the LVMH is one of the world's largest luxury goods companies. According to Myron Ullman of LVMH, "Diamonds are the ultimate luxury product and, as the world's leading luxury goods group, LVMH is the ideal partner to develop the great potential of the De Beers names among consumers."[3]

The joint venture requires an increase in marketing expenditures. The proposed global promotions budget is $180 million, almost three times larger than the 1998 budget of $68 million. However, the strength of De Beers has been waning for two decades, dropping market shares from 80 percent to 65 percent in 2000. In spite of a loss of market shares, "De Beers' net earnings rose 84 percent in 2000, to $1.29 billion. This may be due to the fact that De Beers spends significant amounts of money on institutional advertising."

The 2000 holiday season was the focus of a $15 million advertising blitz by De Beers. From buying up significant advertising space, to Internet contests followed by romantic television advertisements, De Beers used the tagline, "A diamond is forever." Clever one-liners in print advertisements included, "Only her eyes need enhancing," and "Of course there's a return on your investment. We just can't print it here," and "Not to pressure you, but there's a poster like this outside her office too." Advertising expenditures have been on the increase at De Beers. In 1999, the company spent $67 million and during 2001, De Beers spent $180 million in advertising.

Recent developments at De Beers centered on the sale of the company. The Oppenheimer family, which was already part owner and controller of De Beers, was attempting to privatize the company, eliminating much of the shareholdings.

Masters at appealing to love and emotion, DeBeers hopes to strengthen its image among consumers. Through an intense advertising campaign aimed at creating a greater demand for diamonds, the company's success rests on marketing not just diamonds, but De Beers diamonds.

Sources:

[1] O'Neil, Paul. (1983). *Planet Earth: Gemstones.* Chicago: Time Life Books.

[2] Fallon, James. (Jan. 17, 2001). Diamonds: LVMH's New Best Friend. *Women's Wear Daily,* 181(11), p 14.

[3] "De Beers Triples Spend to UKPd110m." (Jan. 18, 2001). *Marketing Week,* p 8.

SUMMARY

- Most gems and all precious metals are inorganic substances, mined from the earth. A few "gems" are organic substances, from living creatures. These include pearls, amber, and coral.

- The precious metals are gold, silver, and the platinum family, which includes platinum and palladium. Gold is measured in karats, with pure gold consisting of 24 karats. It may be alloyed with other metals to alter the color or improve the strength.

- Silver and platinum are measured in parts per 1000. Platinum is a heavy and silvery-white metal, more expensive (and rarer) than gold. Palladium is silvery-white and a less expensive platinum.

- To reduce costs, gold jewelry is often given a light coating of karat gold over a base metal. These processes may be called gold filled, rolled gold, gold plate, or gold vermeil.

- Gemstones are minerals that have been cut and polished; they may be transparent, translucent, or opaque. The Mohs scale measures the hardness (scratch resistance) of minerals on a scale of ten to one. Diamonds are the hardest substance, with a ranking of ten.

- Diamonds and other gems are graded on the four Cs: carat, cut, clarity, and color. Carat refers to the weight of a diamond, with one carat equaling 100 points. Cut refers to the faceting or carving process of gems. Clarity refers to the amount and type of flaws or inclusions; rankings range from flawless to inclusions visible to the naked eye. Gemstone quality diamond colors range from D to Z, from colorless to yellowish.

- Other precious gems include rubies, sapphires, emeralds, and real pearls. Semiprecious gems include alexandrite, amethyst, aquamarine, cat's eye, garnet, jade, lapis lazuli, malachite, moonstone, onyx, opal, peridot, spinel, topaz, turquoise, zircon, amber, coral, cultured pearls, and jet.

- Faux, or fake, stones may be synthetic or simulated. Synthetic stones are chemically identical to the real stones, but are available at a fraction of the cost. Simulated stones may also be referred to as imitation stones, rhinestones, or brilliant stones (not to be confused with the brilliant cut). They may be made of glass or plastic.

- Other materials used in fashion accessories include horn, ivory, tortoiseshell, mother-of-pearl, glass, other metals, plastic, clay, wood, and stringing materials.

- Gemstones may scratch or fracture if hit against a solid surface. Regular cleaning ensures maximum light reflection and enhanced sparkle. Caution should be taken with chemicals and ultrasonic cleaners.

- Gemstones and precious metals are mined all over the world. Major diamond centers are headquartered in India, Israel, Belgium, South Africa, Japan, and the United States. New York City is the major market center in the United States. Diamond companies are beginning to uncloak some of the mystery surrounding the industry.

- De Beers Mining Company has been a leader in marketing commodity diamonds and is currently focusing on generating a greater demand for diamonds.
- The Federal Trade Commission regulates the precious gems and metals industry. Current concerns are invisible gemstone treatments (enhancements), such as laser drilling or any unfair or deceptive trade practices. Diamonds mined in regions of conflict are a concern to the gemstone industry.

TERMS FOR REVIEW

abalone	gold flashed	precious stones
affordable luxury	gold overlay	real pearls
Akoya saltwater cultured pearls	gold plate	rhinestone
	gold vermeil	rolled gold
alloyed	gold washed	rolled gold plate
aluminum	Hope diamond	round ideal (brilliant cut)
amber	horn	ruby
baroque pearl	ideal cut	sapphire
brilliant	imitation stone	scrimshaw
carat	inclusions	semiprecious stones
clarity	ivory	sightholders
clay	jardin	silver
color	jet	simulated stone
coral	karat gold	South Sea pearls
cubic zirconia	Koh-i-noor diamond	star ruby
cultured pearls	lapidary	star sapphire
cut	laser drilling	steel
De Beers Consolidated Mines	light refraction	sterling silver
diamond	loupe	stringing materials
doublet	Mohs scale	synthetic stones
electroplating	mother-of-pearl	Tahitian pearls
emerald	nacre	titanium
facets	opaque	tortoiseshell
faux	palladium	total carat weight
gemstones	plastic	translucent
glass	platinum	transparent
gold	points	ultrasonic cleaner
gold filled	precious metals	wood

REVIEW QUESTIONS

1. What is karat gold and what are some look-alike alternatives?
2. What are the 4 Cs of a diamond, and how are they interrelated?

3. What is an alloy, and why are metals alloyed?
4. Which gems are not geological stones?
5. How does the Mohs scale classify minerals?
6. How do synthetic stones differ from simulated stones?
7. Name and describe some of the more important gemstones.
8. What are some of the more popular gem cuts, and why is each used?
9. Compare the terms *transparent, translucent,* and *opaque.*
10. What are some of the changes occurring in the diamond industry? What are some factors causing these changes?

KNOWLEDGE APPLICATIONS

1. Visit a precious metals Web site, such as Kitco.com, and study the information provided. Research terms and concepts and follow related links for a more complete understanding of the precious metals market.
2. Perform a fashion count of jewelry materials featured in a fashion magazine. Develop a tally sheet recording all the identified materials for each jewelry advertisement in the magazine. Combine class members' findings and create a class master list. Evaluate for major trends.
3. Visit a jewelry store and speak to the manager. View examples of a loupe, a master diamond set, and compare a cubic zirconia to a real diamond under a 10X magnification.
4. Perform an Internet subject search for a specific precious or semiprecious gemstone (such as a birthstone), or a precious metal. Write a current events paper about the mineral, how it is mined or obtained, important geographic locations, prices, and legislation.
5. Locate a trade journal article on one of the materials discussed in this chapter. Write a summary/critique and attach a copy of the article. Learn how to access the library databases from a remote location.
6. Visit the Federal Trade Commission Web site. Follow the links to legislation affecting the gemstone or precious metals industry. Summarize the legislation in brief bulleted points. Present your findings to the class via a PowerPoint presentation.

PART THREE

THE CATEGORIES OF FASHION ACCESSORIES

CHAPTER 7

❦

FOOTWEAR

Two salesmen traveled to remote corners of the world. Each was sent with a truckload of shoes to sell. After one week they reported back to their sales manager at company headquarters. The first salesman lamented, "None of the natives wear shoes here. I'll never be able to sell any!" The second salesman found a similar situation. "None of the natives wear shoes here," he reported excitedly. "How soon can you ship me another truckload?"

A BRIEF HISTORY OF FOOTWEAR

SHOES WERE INVENTED TO PROTECT THE FEET FROM THE ELEMENTS AND TERRAIN. JUST AS they are today, sandals were worn in hot weather to protect the soles of the feet from the hot ground, while the open upper portion allowed for air circulation. Lace-up leather boots and ankle-high slippers were made for wear during cold seasons and for hunting and traveling.

Economics has also long been a factor in footwear. When weather conditions were warm, most ancient civilizations went barefoot. Before mass production of goods was widespread, working-class people often swathed their feet in skins or cloth for protection from the elements.

In history and in modern times, the fashion aspects of footwear reflect the lines of fashionable apparel of the day. During the 14th and 15th centuries, the fashion emphasis on Gothic and narrow silhouettes extended from the high pointed "hennin" hat, to the extended toes of poulaine shoes (see Figure 7.1). In the late 15th and 16th centuries shoes were excessively wide, paralleling the drum-shaped skirts, wide-ruffled collars, and bloated "leg-o-mutton" sleeves that were in fashion (see Figure 7.2).

In an effort to create the illusion of smaller, daintier, and narrower feet, women have chosen high heels and tight shoes. These shoes place the foot in a more vertical position in a narrow

FIGURE 7.1
The pointed-toe shoe, called the poulaine *(pronounced poo-layne) in France and the* crackowe *in England, reached exaggerated proportions and was eventually outlawed after the Church of England declared it to be a phallic symbol and denounced it as "licentious."*

shoe. Extremely high-heeled shoes or improperly fitting shoes have been known to cause foot deformities and back problems in women.

Raised heels first appeared on clog-like wooden platforms called **pattens** in the 15th century. The patten may have been the first high-heeled shoe for men. **Chopines** (pronounced show-peens) were among of the first high-heeled shoes for women. Introduced in Venice in the 16th century, they ranged in height from 6 to 24 inches. Ladies wearing the higher platforms required assistance for walking (see Figure 7.3).

In the 17th century, men's boots and women's shoes were low-heeled but elaborately decorated with rosettes, buckles, and bows. In the 18th century men's shoe fashions were simpler, with a square-toe and heel and large square tongues. Women's shoes also had blocky heels and square toes.

Boots became popular with 19th-century men. They were named for military leaders or army groups—Jeffersons (brogans), Hessians, Wellingtons, Napoleons, and Cossacks were a few of these namesakes. At the same time, the American cowboy boot was designed for utility and function (see Figure 7.4). Native-American moccasins were another important utilitarian style, for both the Native Americans and settlers.

High-heeled, laced or buttoned shoes, and dainty satin or kidskin slippers became a vital part of every fashionable lady's wardrobe in the 19th century. The hoop skirts of the period required frequent lifting and swayed when the wearer walked, thus making the shoe a fashion focal point (see Figure 7.5).

FIGURE 7.2
Two popular wide-toe styles were the duckbill (not shown) and bear's paw.

©Marc Carlson

FIGURE 7.3
Extremely high shoes, such as chopines, reinforced the notion that women were dependent and frail.

FIGURE 7.4
The cowboy boot's pointed toe slips easily into a saddle stirrup, and the wide high heel prevents the foot from sliding through. The heel also provides traction when walking. The high leather boot top provides protection from abrasion and the elements.

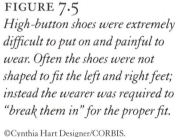

FIGURE 7.5
High-button shoes were extremely difficult to put on and painful to wear. Often the shoes were not shaped to fit the left and right feet; instead the wearer was required to "break them in" for the proper fit.

©Cynthia Hart Designer/CORBIS.

Technological innovations and raised hemlines prompted 20th-century women's shoe fashions to change more rapidly than in previous eras. Because of the visibility of the feet, manufacturers increased their design offerings, and shoes and stockings became key fashion items. Heels reached an all-time high for modern American women in the late 1950s, with the stiletto. Named after a dagger-like weapon, the heels were very narrow, with a steel spike inside for reinforcement.

Shoe styles reappear periodically in fashion. Some features or details, such as spectators, appeal to consumers year after year. The only things really "new" in fashion are the consumers wearing the fashion (see Figures 7.6a–c).

There are numerous historic examples of the parallels between shoe styles and period clothing. Shoe styles have progressed from wide to narrow, flat to high-heeled, and squared to pointed toes. Footwear fashions are a reflection of the mood of the people. Therefore, they are perfectly suited to the apparel fashions of that same time period.

FIGURE 7.6

Platform shoes, popularized by Carmen Miranda, a 1940s Latin American dancer/singer, were taken to extreme heights by the 1980s rock group KISS and the 1990s pop singers the Spice Girls. KISS performers often appeared on stage in platform shoes well over a foot high. (a) Kobal Collection (b) and (c) AP/Worldwide Photos

(a)

(b)

(c)

AN INTRODUCTION TO FOOTWEAR

As with other accessories, shoe fashions have evolved with ready-to-wear. Shoes are an affordable status symbol. While most consumers may not be able to wear **haute couture** or high fashion clothing, or drive a luxury car, they can afford a popular brand or style of shoes.

Footwear fashions are a reflection of the mood of the people, and shoe designs parallel apparel fashions. Athletic shoes, casual shoes, dress shoes, and boots are all influenced by fashion. Like all fashion products, shoe brands and styles follow the stages of consumer acceptance, beginning with the introductory stage and ending with the obsolescence stage. Styles and brands that have enjoyed widespread consumer acceptance in the United States in recent decades include T-straps; spectators; platforms; huarache sandals; go-go boots; cowboy boots; hiking boots; casual shoes and boots such as Dr. ("Doc") Martens; and athletic shoes such as Keds, Nike, and Adidas.

The increasing age of baby boomers—a large segment of footwear consumers in the United States—has caused footwear manufacturers to improve product comfort. Over a lifetime, the wearer has been subjected to hereditary foot problems, improperly fitting shoes, 200 billion steps, and possibly foot neglect or abuse. Because of the emphasis on comfort, important features of shoe production now include padding, cushioning, and shock dispersion. **Orthotics,** support devices for feet and ankles, are frequently used to reduce the stress on aging feet. Shock-diffusion inserts may be added to absorb impact and evenly disperse weight pressure on the bottom of the feet. **Heel pads, cushioned insoles,** and **arch supports** are relatively inexpensive methods for relieving everyday stress on the feet.

Parts of Footwear

The parts that make up an item of footwear are categorized into two major subgroups—the *lowers* and the *uppers.* The lower includes the heel and sole. The upper is comprised of the components covering and supporting the top of the foot. Figure 7.7 provides detailed drawings of men's and women's basic shoes.

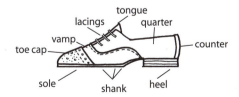

FIGURE 7.7a
Anatomy of a man's shoe.

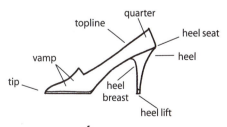

FIGURE 7.7 b
Anatomy of a woman's shoe.

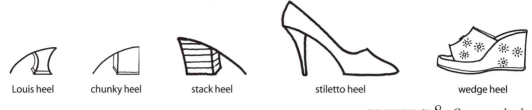

FIGURE 7.8 *Common heels.*

Lowers

The following parts comprise the lowers:

Heel Measured in 1/8-inch increments. For example, a one-inch heel height is classified as an 8/8 heel. A high heel is classified as a 22/8, which translates to 2 3/4 inches. Heels may be manufactured from a variety of materials. Stacked leather (which looks like wood), plastic, and cork are frequently used. Heels may be covered with rope, suede, leather, fabric, and other glued materials. Figure 7.8 identifies five common heel styles.

Heel lift The replaceable plastic piece that protects the bottom of the heel.

Base sole Attaches the upper to the lower. Manufactured in rubber, man-made materials, and leather, depending on the end use. End use considerations include cushion, comfort, flexibility, reduced weight, shock absorption, traction, water and oil resistance, and durability.

Insole Covers the inner construction and is the part on which the foot rests, often padded.

Outsole Outside sole of the shoe that touches the terrain.

Welt Narrow strip of material stitched or cemented just above the sole.

Shank Between the heel and the ball of the foot.

Uppers

A variety of materials is used in the manufacture of shoe uppers. Leather is the most common at higher price points. Synthetic materials, such as polyurethane, are considered leather substitutes for footwear at lower price points. Fabrics may be used in dressier shoes but do not have the durability associated with leather.

Uppers include the following parts:

Sock lining Covers the rough edges on the inside of the shoe upper. In better-quality shoes the sock lining is leather. Nylon tricot may be used in less expensive shoes.

Counter Decorative trim that hides the center back seam.

Quarter Back portion of the shoe upper.

Saddle Separate piece of upper material that crosses the foot over the instep.

Vamp Forward section of the shoe upper, covering the top of the foot.

Tongue Extension of the vamp or separate piece that protects the top of the foot.

Toe Cap An extra covering over the toe section of the vamp.

Footwear Manufacturing

The tools used in manufacturing footwear remained basically the same from ancient Egyptian times until the 1850s. American shoemakers have been credited with successfully inventing machinery for mass-producing shoes. The rolling machine, invented in 1845, compactly pounded the shoe leather fibers, thereby increasing the wearability of the shoe soles. Elias Howe's sewing machine revolutionized the shoe industry in 1846, paving the way for other mechanical devices that simplified shoe manufacture. Manufacturing steps were no longer performed by hand; instead machines created more uniform shoes and production increased significantly.

Shoes are produced to the specifications of a last. A **last** is a plastic (or wooden) form, resembling a foot, over which a shoe is manufactured and shaped (see Figure 7.9).

Most shoes undergo a series of seven routine steps during manufacturing, many of which may be performed on computerized equipment. These steps are designing, pattern making, cutting, fitting, lasting, bottoming, and finishing.

1. **Designing** Footwear designers create the season's collections. Their ideas come from numerous sources, including market research, historic collections, current fashion trends, and market trips. The designer's imagination is limited by textile requirements, construction problems, and production economics. The phrase "form follows function" is more applicable to shoe designers than to most other accessories designers. Utility and comfort characteristics are vital to shoe designs, particularly in athletic shoes. After conferring with fashion merchandisers and trend forecasters, the designer sketches many shoe styles. Designers work with production engineers to determine which styles will be made up in model sizes.

2. **Pattern making** The shoe design is translated into components that can be cut and assembled in the most economical manner. Patterns must be made for uppers, linings, insoles, soles, heels, and all other shoe parts. The pattern maker must make parts that will smoothly cover a three-dimensional last. A sample pattern may be graded into smaller and larger sizes using a computerized program.

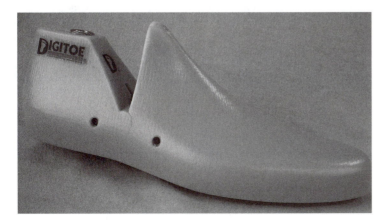

FIGURE 7.9 *Shoe last.*

Courtsey of ShoeSchool.com.

3. **Cutting** The uppers are cut from man-made or natural materials. Man-made materials may be cut several layers thick, while natural materials, such as leather, must be cut in single layers so the cutters are able to observe imperfections. Steel dies, similar to sharp-edged cookie cutters, are used to cut the pattern shapes in the material.

4. **Fitting** The parts of the upper are joined by stitching, gluing, or heat welding during this stage. Production details that are necessary for comfort and durability are completed. Seams are finished, and eyelets for laces are added.

5. **Lasting** The assembled upper components are tightly shaped over the last and fastened to the insole. Synthetic materials may be heat set into the desired shape; leather is stretched to conform to the shape of the last. Leather is allowed to remain on the last for several days to relieve the tendency to return to its original shape.

6. **Bottoming** The sole is attached to the upper. In more expensive shoes, the upper is stitched to the sole. In less expensive shoes, cement is used, or the whole shoe may be molded with the upper and sole as one.

7. **Finishing** Footwear with leather soles and heels usually receives several finishing operations—the heels are attached with nails or glue; the shoe is buffed and polished; a sock lining is added; decorations are attached; and laces are inserted.

Standard Footwear Measurement

A separate last is needed for each size/width combination for each style. According to "The Standard Measurement of Lasts," a norm for shoemakers, the difference between sizes such as size 6 1/2 to size 7 is about 1/3 inch in length. Widths vary 1/4 inch between sizes, such as A to AA. The standard width for men's shoes is a D, and women's shoes are manufactured in a standard B width. Children's shoes usually are simply described as narrow, medium, or wide. Table 7.1 describes shoe widths for men, women, and children.

TABLE 7.1
Shoe Widths and Descriptions

Description	Men's Shoes	Women's Shoes	Children's Shoes
Extra Narrow	AAAA (4A) AAA (3A) A (1A)	AAA (3A) AA (2A) AA (2A)	
Narrow (N)	B (or C)	A	A
Standard, Regular, Average, or Medium	D	B	B
Wide	E (W) EE (WW, XW, or 2E)	D or C (C less commonly used than D)	C or D
Extra Wide or Doublewide	EEE (3E) EEEE (4E) EEEEE (5E)	EE (2E, WW) EEE (3E)	

Materials

Leather is considered the ideal material for shoes and shoe linings. It has the ability to conform to the shape of the foot, and it "breathes" (allows for air and moisture transfer). Breathable materials provide comfort to the wearer by keeping air circulating to ensure perspiration evaporation.

Because many consumers want fashionable footwear at inexpensive prices, synthetic materials such as polyurethane and PVC have supplanted leather's domination of the budget footwear market. Synthetic materials may closely resemble leather, but styles that do not disguise the plastic or other nonleather materials are also popular.

Textile fabrics are increasingly used as footwear uppers. For decades, only bridal and formal shoes were made in satin or dress fashion fabrics, often dyed to match a gown. Today, in spring and summer, linen-look fabrics and ribbed-weave fabrics may be used for dressy and casual shoes. Stretch microfiber textile shoes are shown for every season. Wool and flannel fabrics are popular for winter shoes. Stretch fabrics for shoe uppers may add fashion elements and improve fit and comfort. Athletic and casual shoes are often canvas or nylon fabrics, or a combination of leather and fabric materials.

Outdoor footwear, such as snow, ski, and hiking boots, are manufactured in moisture-repellent fabrics. Nylon fabric is frequently chosen because of its inherent moisture resistance, strength, light weight, and tight weave. Gore-Tex, created by W.L. Gore, is a Teflon laminate that can be applied to a base fabric, such as nylon or polyester. This coating allows for perspiration vapor transfer through the fabric and away from the foot. The laminate has pores too small for water droplets or wind to permeate.

Lining fabrics may be designed to keep moisture away from the foot or keep the feet warmer. A recent textile development, Thinsulate®, has thermal footwear applications. The lightweight fabric is used in boot linings and is considerably warmer than down feathers.

CLASSIFICATIONS OF FOOTWEAR

Most footwear may be classified as shoes, boots, or house slippers. **Shoes** are street wearable or performance-oriented footwear that do not extend above the ankles. **Boots** are high-top footwear that rise above the ankle, ending at some point between the lower calf and the thigh. **House slippers** may be soft- or hard-soled footwear, but are not usually designed to be street wearable.

Although the number of footwear styles is extensive, most can be generally categorized, with few gender exceptions. General categories for footwear are athletic, boot, clog, loafer, moccasin, mule, oxford, pump, and sandal. Figure 7.10 shows selected styles of footwear.

DESIGN

Shoes are often designed more for fashion than utility. Manufacturers are striving to design attractive and comfortable shoes that reduce the incidence of foot ailments associated with im-

basketball shoe

ankle or chukka boot

platform clog

penny loafer

moccasin

mule

wingtip oxford

espadrille

open-toe slingback pump

spectator pump

T-strap pump

D'Orsay pump

thong sandal

FIGURE 7.10 *Popular footwear style lariations.*

properly fitting footwear. Fit and comfort are increasing in importance in all areas of footwear. Historically, comfortable dress shoes were viewed as unfashionable or ugly and usually associated with elderly customers.

The popularity of athletic shoes has created a $12 billion market for the footwear industry. In 2000, the big market players in the United States were Nike, Reebok, and Adidas. Figure 7.11 shows a graph of these companies and the relationship among their respective market shares between 1983 and 1998.

During the 1960s, consumers had one choice for athletic or sport shoes—sneakers. By the turn of the 21st century, consumers were offered hundreds of brands and styles of fashion-

If the Shoe fits. . .

When it comes to shoes, the phrase "fashion victim" can be interpreted both figuratively and literally! Many people, and especially women, have suffered great pain and developed chronic foot and back problems from wearing ill-fitting shoes and shoes that placed fashion over comfort.

One extreme example was the painful custom of foot binding for young girls, an old custom of some wealthy Mainland Chinese families. The **Chinese lily foot** required tiny, highly arched shoes with virtually no space for toes. From infancy, girls' toes were folded under their feet and bound tightly to their heels, making their feet highly arched and approximately half their normal size. This caused great pain and made walking unassisted difficult. A three-inch "golden lotus" foot was the ideal, while a four-inch "silver lotus" was somewhat less desirable. The purposes of the lily foot fashion were to restrict the mobility of Chinese royal women, to prevent them from engaging in physical labor, to promote the notion of the husband's wealth and the wife's economic uselessness, and to provide an additional female erogenous zone.

Whereas the Chinese lily foot custom of foot binding caused deformity in just a few years, the high heels and tight shoes worn by emancipated women cause foot deformities over a period of decades. Claw toes, mallet toes, hammertoes, bunions, bunionettes, corns, and neuromas (painful nerves) have all been blamed on women's shoes. These physical deformities cause pain, difficulty with walking, inflammation, and infection. The American Orthopaedic Foot and Ankle Society published research blaming fashion footwear for many foot ailments, especially in women.

Research findings concluded that wearing high heels can almost double the pressure across the ball of the foot. Heels less than one inch in height caused a 22 percent increase in pressure on the ball of the foot. Heels measuring 3 1/4 inches in height caused a 76 percent increase in pressure (Rossi & Tennant, 1993).

Fashion critics must understand the conditions under which women adopt footwear that causes such maladies. To simply blame women for choosing to wear such ridiculous fashions is to ignore social pressures that demand conformity and limit the shoe style offerings. The lily foot is an extreme and obvious example of how young girls were forced to succumb to fashion. More subtle, yet still coercive, are contemporary cultural norms that dictate footwear fashions. Increased physical height is a desirable quality in many societies because longer, shapelier legs are considered more attractive. In addition, increased height is associated with increased power.

Tokyo, Japan, faced an orthopedic crisis in 1999, due to a 20 percent increase in women wearing thick soledshoes that inhibited walking and caused serious and fatal accidents. The Japan Consumer Information Center warned the public of the dangers of wearing platform shoes. Japanese women believed the shoes made their legs look long and shapely and the additional height gave them a power advantage over men. One young Japanese woman explained, "In the commuter train, the level of my eyes is higher than middle-aged men, who are so arrogant in the office."[1]

Source:

[1] Sims, C. (Nov. 26, 1999). Be Tall and Chic as You Wobble to the Orthopedist. *The New York Times International*, p. A4.

A woman's feet deformed from Chinese foot binding.

©Bettmann/CORBIS.

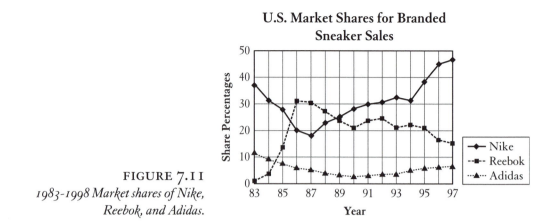

FIGURE 7.11
1983-1998 Market shares of Nike, Reebok, and Adidas.

forward athletic shoes designed for most any sport or activity. Running, walking, aerobic, tennis, and basketball shoes became available and were designed to prevent injuries and provide comfort.

Consumers who participate in multiple sports often select cross trainer shoes because these shoes combine many outstanding features. **Cross trainer athletic shoes** offer many of the technologies designed for specific sports, from motion control to shock absorption. One brand of athletic cross trainer shoes, New Balance, offers 11 distinctive components in its cross training athletic shoe. These lightweight components provide breathability, cushioning, foot stability and control, heel cushioning, compression resistance, and shock absorbency.

The production of casual fitness shoes that incorporate comfort technology is an important trend in the footwear industry. **Casual fitness** means consumers may not actually engage in athletics or sports, but they like the look and comfort of casual and sports shoes. **Comfort technologies** include in-sole cushioning, molded and contoured footbeds, padding, shock dispersion, reinforced uppers, and air ventilation. Most of the comfort shoes are lighter in weight and tend to be designed as shock absorbers that prevent standing and walking fatigue.

Many shoe companies, including the luxury brand Cole-Haan, have claimed the inclusion of comfort technologies. Cole-Haan and its parent company, Nike, developed a line of lifestyle footwear targeted to affluent, entrepreneurial men and women between the ages of 30 and 40. The collection, although upscale in appearance and price, boasts polyurethane capsules filled with a pressurized gas in the insoles, much like Nike's walking shoes.

The ready-to-wear trends of **corporate casual** (dressing down at work) and **khaki casual** (the acceptance of casual khaki slacks in professional offices) have offered shoe manufacturers additional design opportunities. Shoe lines designed specifically to be worn with khakis and casual slacks are important growth segments in the footwear industry.

Western, work, and hiking boots—traditionally functional—evolved into ornamented fashion accessories. Rain and snow boots fundamentally must keep the wearer's feet dry, but by increasing the fashion appeal, manufacturers can increase sales.

Knee-high and ankle-high boots for women undergo periods of popularity, primarily from a fashion perspective (see Figure 7.12).

Tech Talk: Smart Shoes

Computer chips in shoes to measure athletic performance? Reebok's Traxtar (track star) for children ages 6–11 (about $65-$75 retail) combines fashion and a motion-detecting microprocessor chip. The oval pod containing the chip is located on the tongue of the shoe. Children are able to see lights and hear music as performance is measured with a gold, silver, or bronze rating. The Traxtar is able to measure with at least 90 percent accuracy on the high jump, sprint, and running long jump. Reebok hopes to increase its share of the athletic footwear market by marketing interactive shoes with computer technology and an accompanying CD-Rom containing nutrition and performance information. As a technological innovation, the primary benefit is the athlete's ability to keep track of mileage and know when to purchase a new pair of shoes.

FIGURE 7.12 *Knee-high boots were extremely popular in the 1960's.* AP/Worldwide Photos.

Today, the use of stretch microfibers in boots allows manufacturers to create tight-fitting boots with increased comfort. Previously, zippers were required to run the length of the tight-fitting boot in order to obtain a close fit.

The ultimate comfort shoes, casual house slippers, have become more popular due to the increased consumer interest in at-home ready-to-wear. Slip-on styles with contoured footbeds and molded soles are popular types of adult leisure footwear for both genders. Ambitious retailers find that footwear fashion accessories are excellent opportunities for add-on sales. At-home or leisurewear departments feature coordinating house slippers to increase profits.

CARE OF FOOTWEAR

Consumers should be encouraged to regularly clean and care for their footwear. The care of shoes includes wearing, cleaning, polishing, and storing. Shoe experts recommend a person own several pairs of shoes so they can be worn in rotation.

The many footwear care products available on the market can produce add-on sales for a shoe retailer. Customers should be encouraged to purchase **shoehorns** (a curved tool, originally made of real horn, that is inserted in the back of the shoe to allow the heel to slide in easily), brushes, and polishes. Aromatic cedar **shoe trees** or cedar-filled **shoe pouches** absorb acid and salt from foot perspiration and retain the shape of the shoes. Saddle soaps and leather balm should be used to clean and preserve the suppleness of leather shoes and boots. Foam cleansers, creams, and odor-reducing agents are needed to clean fabric and synthetic materials. Store sales associates should assume that a customer buying new footwear will be receptive to products that enhance or preserve their shoes or boots.

Sales associates should advise customers to follow these steps to lengthen the life of their footwear:

- Give shoes "time off" between wearings. One-fourth cup of foot perspiration is absorbed into shoes daily.
- Wet shoes should be dried at room temperature, away from direct heat sources, such as sunlight, radiators, or in dryers.
- Stuff dry newspapers into the shoes to absorb the excess moisture. Periodically remove wet newspaper and replace with fresh, dry newspaper.
- Rub a soft cloth soaked in diluted vinegar and water solution over stains to remove damaging salt residue.
- Allow mud or wet spots to dry thoroughly before brushing.
- Brush to remove all dirt particles before applying shoe cream or polish.
- Apply leather balm to replenish the natural oil and prevent leather from drying or cracking.
- Regularly clean leather or synthetic leather-like materials with a nylon-bristled brush or damp cloth.

- Brush dry suede shoes with a terry cloth or stiff, plastic-bristled suede brush. Re-nap bald patches on suede shoes with an emery board.
- Remove scuffs on patent leather by rubbing the mark with old nylon hosiery.
- Use a shoehorn to prevent crushing the heel counter.
- Clean canvas shoes with a foam cleanser made especially for shoes. The foam chemicals work to loosen the dirt on the canvas and can be wiped clean with a damp cloth. Some canvas shoes, such as gym shoes, sneakers, or soft running shoes, can be washed in the washing machine on gentle cycle with detergent.
- Clean regularly to reduce bacteria and fungi growth inside the shoes and control footwear odors.
- Polish shoes regularly. Carefully match the original polish color to avoid undesirable discoloring.

THE GLOBAL FOOTWEAR INDUSTRY

In 1997, the U.S. consumption of footwear was 14.7 percent of the world total. China consumed 21 percent of the world total, but per capita consumption was larger in the United States. American consumers purchased an average of 6.2 pairs of footwear in 1997 (up from 5.9 pairs in 1996). By contrast, Chinese consumers purchased 1.8 pairs per capita. Per capita consumption worldwide was 1.91 pairs.

Forty-six percent of footwear consumed worldwide is leather. Shoes with leather uppers use approximately 2.3 square feet of leather per pair.

Footwear production is a global industry. For every footwear dollar the United States exports to other countries, it imports in excess of $20 of footwear, according to 1999 Census data.

Figure 7.13 represents the United States' involvement in the production, export, import, and consumption of pairs of shoes from 1967 through 1998. Based on figures compiled by Footwear Industries of America in 1999, production has decreased, exports have remained stable and low, and imports and consumption have both increased.

The Global Scope of Footwear Production

Most of the world's footwear production occurs in Asia. Computerized equipment can perform most shoe-manufacturing operations. This equipment is easily transportable to Far Eastern countries in which labor costs are lowest and unit production is high. The high cost of labor in developed countries has discouraged domestic shoe production. In 2000, the average U.S. production cost for a pair of shoes was $20.18, while the average production cost worldwide was $8.66.

In 2001, China, Brazil, Indonesia, Italy, and Thailand were ranked as top shoe-producing

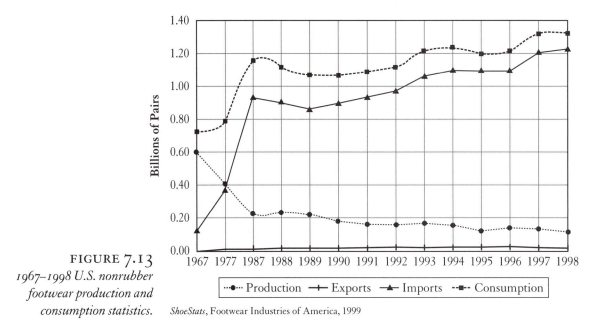

FIGURE 7.13
1967–1998 U.S. nonrubber footwear production and consumption statistics.

ShoeStats, Footwear Industries of America, 1999

countries. Seventy-eight percent of nonrubber footwear and 80 percent of rubber footwear originates in China. The average price per shoe was lowest for Asian countries due to their relatively low labor costs. Italy dominates the $20-and-above price range because the country has concentrated on the higher-priced fashion footwear and has developed high-quality standards to ensure continued exports to the U.S. and other markets. Table 7.2 shows the ranking of world footwear production by top producing countries and the average price per shoe in 2001.

Although as much as 85 percent of all shoes worn in the United States are imports, U. S. manufacturers have opportunities to compete with low-priced imports because imported footwear requires longer lead times for production. Domestic manufacturers can compete on

TABLE 7.2

Top Footwear-Producing Countries in 2001

Country	Percentage of World Production	Average Price per Shoe
China	78.3%	$7.06
Brazil	6.58%	$12.05
Indonesia	3.93%	$9.40
Italy	3.28%	$25.98
Thailand	1.26%	$12.05

Source: U.S. Nonrubber Footwear. (Jan–Dec 2001). Retrieved July 2, 2003, from the World Wide Web at http://www.apparelandfootwear.org/data/Trends 2001Q4Revised 030129.pdf

TABLE 7.3

The Ten Largest Distributors of Footwear in the United States and Annual Sales

Company	Annual Sales
Adidas America, Inc	$1,043,035,000
Sperry Top-Sider, Inc	$500,000,000
Skechers USA, Inc.	$473,680,000
Dr. Martens Airwair USA LLC	$261,604,558
Cole Haan Holdings, Inc.	$250,000,000
Cole Haan, Inc.	$225,000,000
Kinney Service Corporation	$214,600,000
Keds Corporation	$200,000,000
Schwartz, Jack Shoes, Inc.	$190,000,000
Stride Rite Children's Group I	$189,000,000

Source: Dun's Market Identifiers, SIC 5139, Dun and Bradstreet, Dec. 27, 1999.

better quality, excellent service, expanded computer-aided design, shortened production times and delivery schedules, controlled inventories, and computerized technology.

Although much of the footwear production has moved overseas, U.S. companies own many of the most popular name brands. Table 7.3 shows a ranking of the 10 largest wholesale distributors of footwear in the United States, based on annual sales.

Trade Organizations, Publications, and Shows

Footwear is a multibillion dollar industry in the United States, and it supports several trade organizations, publications, and shows for footwear manufacturers and retailers worldwide. Trade organizations exist to serve the domestic and international markets. Table 7.4 lists several important footwear trade organizations.

Some trade organizations publish statistical data and sales and service information, such as style and merchandising trend advice, methods to increase profits, and promotional strategies. In addition, they offer membership directories and newsletters. Table 7.5 lists important trade publications in the footwear industry.

State, national, and international footwear associations provide opportunities for trade shows and fairs where representatives from all marketing levels of the footwear industry can meet. Many foreign countries hold footwear trade shows. These countries include Brazil, Canada, China, Columbia, Croatia, Czech Republic, Germany, Hungary, India, Indonesia, Italy, Mexico, Russia, South Africa, Spain, Turkey, and Vietnam. Footwear trade shows exist in regions throughout the United States. Table 7.6 lists some of the more important trade shows scheduled at least once a year in the United States.

TABLE 7.4

Trade Organizations for the Footwear Industry

Organization	Location	Objectives
Fashion Footwear Association of New York www.ffany.org	New York, NY	Sponsor the annual New York Shoe Expo
Footwear Distributors and Retailers of America www.fdra.org	Washington, D.C.	Represent retail firms, distributors, and affiliates
American Apparel and Footwear Association www.thefashion.org	Washington, D.C.	Promote and enhance its members' competitiveness, productivity, and profitability; minimize trade restraints; summarize trade data
National Shoe Retailer Association www.nsra.org	Columbia, MD	Represent and support independent shoe retailers, promote the industry, and lobby legislators
Pedorthic Footwear Association www.pedorthics.org	Columbia, MD	Represent the prescription and comfort footwear industry
Shoe and Allied Trade Research Association (SATRA) www.satra.co.uk	United Kingdom	Offer technology and research services to members

TABLE 7.5

Trade Publications for the Footwear Industry

Trade Publication Name	Description
The Art and Science of Footwear Manufacturing	Illustrated handbook of the shoe-manufacturing process. Available from the American Apparel and Footwear Association (AAFA).
FOCUS: An Economic Impact Profile of the Apparel and Footwear Industries	A statistical compendium. Available from the AAFA.
Footwear Market Monitor	Quarterly analysis on U.S. retail sales of footwear. Offered by the AAFA.
Footwear News	Provides current events, statistical data, and fashion information. Published weekly by Fairchild.
Shoe Stats	Shortened version of FOCUS. Published by the FIA.
Shoesonthenet.com	Internet subscription resource.
Shoeworld.com	Connects the European shoe industry via the Internet assisting businesses creating tailor-made Web sites linked to the broad umbrella of Shoe World.
Sole Source	Contains trade associations, footwear resources, and retailers. Published by Footwear Industries of America (FIA).
Women's Wear Daily (Monday)	Provides current trade and fashion information on many accessories, including footwear. Published by Fairchild.
World Footwear Markets	Provides industry statistics published by SATRA.

TABLE 7.6
Trade Shows for the Footwear Industry

Trade Show	Location	Sponsor
Boston Shoe Travelers Trade Show	Marlborough, MA	Boston Shoe Travelers
Empire State Footwear Show	Syracuse, NY	Empire State Footwear Association
EShoeShow.com and Shoeinfonet.com	Internet sites	List names and dates of many major footwear trade shows
New York Shoe Expo	New York, NY	Fashion Footwear Association of New York
North American Shoe and Accessory Market	Atlanta, GA	Southeastern Shoe Travelers
Southwestern Shoe Travelers Show	Dallas, TX	Southwestern Shoe Travelers
The Shoe Show	Las Vegas, NV	World Shoe Association

MERCHANDISING TRENDS AND TECHNIQUES

Shoe merchandising has taken on a lifestyle orientation. This means cross merchandising or offering related items for sale. Instead of a single pair of shoes in a display, customers can see a head-to-toe outfit, of which the shoes are just one component.

Selling related products means increased multiple sales and, ultimately, increased profits. For example, a manufacturer of athletic shoes may also offer cushioned removable insole inserts, heel cushions, decorative laces, and athletic tote bags. The merchandising concept is to provide an array of products that can be mixed and matched to create a total look.

Customers do not heed seasonal fashion rules the way they once did. Many manufacturers are blurring the seasonal distinction with footwear that is casual and seasonless, made with materials that easily make the transition from warm to cool weather, regardless of the calendar dates.

In-Store Retailing

Cutting-edge footwear fashions may be initially introduced in a specialty boutique. These stores play a significant role in fashion acceptance. Small shoe retailers who create awareness and credibility for the line also build a brand's identity. Prices are usually higher when styles are in the introductory stage. Department, chain, or big **box stores** (such as Foot Locker or Athlete's Foot) subsequently offer those styles once an image has been established.

Shoes are typically merchandised by brand, category, function, size, and color. The type of store, such as department, specialty, or discount, affects the merchandising method. For example, in athletic shoe stores, all brands of shoes may be grouped according to the activity, such as basketball, running, or aerobic activities. In discount stores, lower-priced footwear may be grouped according to category, size, and color, with little or no emphasis on brand names.

Footwear store planners work to create an environment that is comfortable, with an appealing ambience of calm energy. Ample seating is an important requirement for all types of footwear stores. Adequate lighting levels should illuminate the darker silhouettes of displayed footwear, as well as entice the customers to shop throughout the entire department, including on the back wall.

Many retail stores are featuring *shoppertainment* (shopping and entertainment) services that create an image of the store as a social gathering place for the shoppers and their friends. A big screen television, café, shoe shine and foot massage booths, pool tables, and music may be tools that create a leisure atmosphere. In self-selection and quick-service stores, these services may be replaced by accessible understock and convenient check out counters.

Leased Departments

In department and specialty stores, **leased shoe departments** are common because sales require a substantial inventory investment. Numerous size/width combinations for each style must be stocked. In a lease agreement, footwear-specialist companies stock the footwear department with merchandise supplied by several manufacturers. These specialists retain inventory ownership but operate within the store and abide by store policies. Most customers are unaware that the shoe department is leased.

Stock Control

Retailers are relying heavily on inventory-management software for stock control, a critical element in managing extensive footwear inventories. Technology tools, such as electronic bar codes, scanners, and magnetic-strip readers, assist shoe retailers in carrying the right quantities of styles with the best sell-throughs and profits. Distribution centers serving several chain store units enable large companies to take advantage of economies of scale. They can buy large quantities of shoes from low-cost foreign suppliers. From distribution centers, retailers can quickly obtain fast-selling styles and reduce the incidence of lost sales.

The communication system using electronic data interchange (EDI) and universal product codes (UPC) is becoming increasingly important in the shoe industry. A computer linkage between shoe retailers and manufacturers encourages rapid vendor responses to store orders and inventory replenishments. This partnership is referred to as **Quick Response.** Some vendors are offering stores discounts for using EDI technology. Domestic shoe manufacturers may improve their market standing and more successfully compete with imports by using EDI.

Shoe & Sport Talk (SST) is one example of an electronic communication service between retailers and suppliers. The SST software package focuses on electronic-data interchange using universal product codes and e-mail.

Tech Talk: POI Systems: Customers in the Stockroom?

"Excuse me, do you have this in a size nine?"

"Um, I'm not sure. Let me just finish helping this other customer first, then I'll go check our stockroom to see if we have your size."

"No, that's okay, I'm just browsing anyway."

Lost sale. Unimpressed customer. Decrease to the lifetime value of that customer. Reduced profits.

Shoppers are time poor and may not have time to wait for the harried salesperson to check the stockroom for the right size and color. Retail technology company Gemmar Systems International (GSI) offers interactive software that allows customers to access a user-friendly terminal and scanner in the store. Customers follow on-screen prompts to scan the sample product bar code and determine whether their size and color choices are available in the stockroom or at another company store location. If the shoes are available in the store, a request is sent to the stockroom and the shoes are pulled from the shelf and delivered to the selling floor. If the item is not available, it may be special ordered.

In addition to increasing customer satisfaction and generating immediate sales, the GSI point of information software allows for market research, such as online customer surveys and feedback, and customer evaluation of new products. GSI offers similar point of information systems to multiple-unit apparel, home furnishings, and jewelry stores.

Vertical Marketing

Shoe manufacturers and shoe retailers sometimes disagree on methods for reaching the ultimate consumers. A number of manufacturer-owned shoe stores have opened in recent years, causing some dissatisfaction among department store retailers. The term **vertical marketing** refers to a process of manufacturing and retailing by a single company. The rise of vertical marketing may be attributed to a perceived risk reduction and a company's attempt to elicit more control over its destiny. Department store merchandisers may feel threatened by vendors who open competing manufacturer-owned stores and attempt to sell the same brands in a department store. Likewise, manufacturers are frustrated with department stores offering private-label shoes, which compete with the national brands. Each feels the other is infringing on an area of expertise.

Internet Retailing

E-commerce sites include shoe malls, online stores, and Web sites that specialize in uncommon sizes. Selling footwear on the Internet has been slower to advance than other fashion industries because fitting is complex and risky, unless the consumer is familiar with the brand. Rather than selling the actual shoes, many of the Internet sites provide product information, promotional advertising, store locators, and coupons redeemable at stores.

Shoe retailers are using the Internet to expand their reach, while shoe manufacturers have limited direct sales efforts in order to avoid alienating shoe retailers. Manufacturers are, however, using the Internet for **cyberbranding,** which means creating brand awareness and product demand. Their Web sites, especially those devoted to younger customers, are cleverly crafted, forward-thinking marketing tools.

Catalog Retailing

Shoes have long been sold in most fashion catalogs as complementary accessories to apparel, but some limited-line specialty catalogs feature exclusive offerings of footwear and related accessories. Usually the catalog is viewed as supplementary to the physical store sales. Catalog merchandise offerings may be similar to those found in the store with convenience as the primary driver behind the success. Other catalog retailers, such as JCPenney, may offer merchandise in direct competition to in-store offerings. Companies view catalog sales as a supplementary (and complementary) way to reach both existing and new customers.

Merchandising Techniques

Many retailers have shifted their selling strategy to a degree of self-selection. Although customers may easily be able to locate a style and size, they are not responsible for restocking unwanted merchandise after trying it on. An increase in self-selection requires constant merchandising to ensure styles and sizes are replaced and refilled so subsequent customers can be serviced.

Regardless of the methods used, proper merchandising should include the following:

- Display in an attractive and accessible presentation
- Offer complete size assortments
- Provide sufficient product information or sales assistance
- Simplify fitting and purchasing procedures

Figures 7.14 and 7.15 are selling floor and stockroom planograms from a large, moderately priced department store. A **planogram** is a merchandise blueprint developed to maximize sales by placing merchandise in logical zones. In the stockroom and on the selling floor, the retailers and manufacturers must work together to ensure the most efficient use of selling floor and stockroom spaces.

SELLING FOOTWEAR

Footwear salespeople require special training and knowledge to be employed in a full-service shoe salon. The technical information regarding shoe sizing, style, and proper fitting is more comprehensive than the information needed to sell most fashion apparel and accessories. Footwear salespeople should stress the value received from the merchandise in relation to the price. Customers must perceive that they are getting the best possible product and services for the money spent.

Footwear manufacturers offer product information to store buyers and department managers to disseminate to salespeople. But, in spite of most retailers' awareness of the need for professionally trained shoes salespersons, only about five percent of shoe salespersons have received

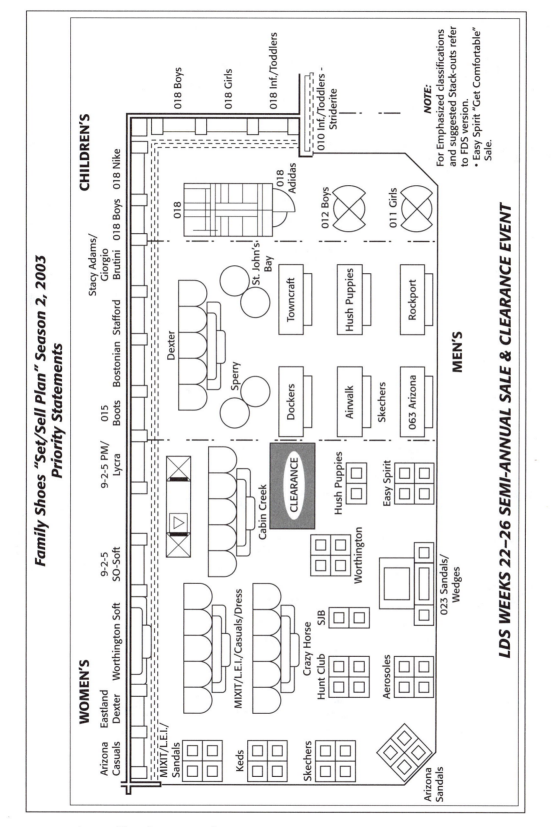

FIGURE 7.14 *Shoe department planogram.*

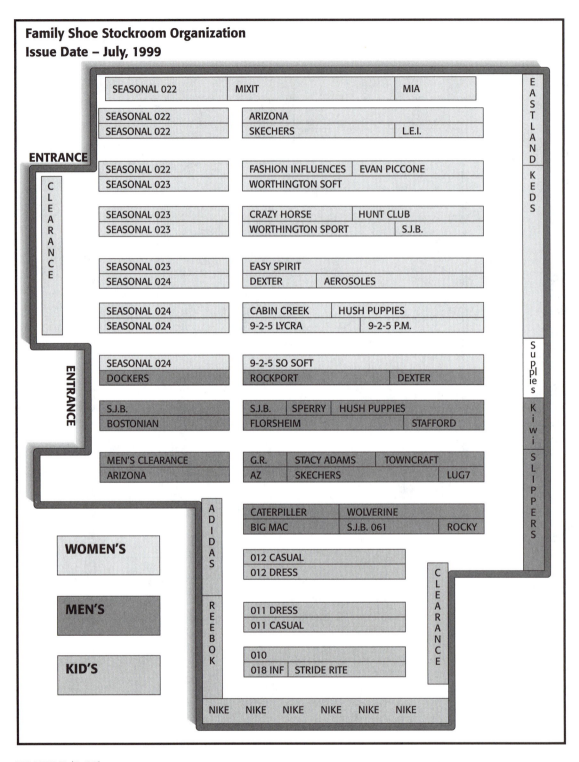

FIGURE 7.15
Shoe stockroom planogram.

formal training in fitting. Because of the expertise required and the insufficient number of professionally trained salespeople, many retailers offer commissions as an incentive to encourage and keep productive employees.

Not all retail stores necessarily need training for salespeople. Self-service shoe departments and stores hire merchandisers and cashiers rather than salespeople. These employees may offer suggestions to customers when asked, but generally they replenish stock and operate the cash registers.

Price and Value

Some consumers may be willing to pay more for footwear if they believe the footwear is of value. Value characteristics include comfort, construction, materials, fashionability, manufacturer or name brand, and store image. Consumers tend to believe that leather footwear is of greater value than synthetic materials, but many consumers desire a certain fashion "look," with less interest in the materials used.

Fashion footwear often commands a higher markup than nonfashion (or staple) footwear, such as work boots. Shoe manufacturers may create fashion among basic products in order to achieve additional markup. In the 1980s and 1990s, Keds basic canvas sneakers evolved from a single white color into a variety of fashion colors. Keds continued to extend the fashion cycle of the basic sneaker by introducing patterns, such as plaids and holiday prints. Leather was also introduced in the basic shoe. The fashionable image of Keds afforded retailers extra markup.

The manufacturer or name brand of footwear affects consumers' perceptions of price and value. In the case of athletic footwear, consumers frequently associate better quality with higher prices. Many times, celebrity endorsements create an image of value. Consumers may be willing to pay more for the shoes if the endorser is credible. In the 1990s, Nike athletic shoes achieved enormous success by hiring professional basketball athlete Michael Jordan as a celebrity endorser. Young male consumers perceived they might achieve a similar athletic prowess by purchasing athletic shoes endorsed by Michael Jordan. A brand that began its popular appeal in athletics soon permeated the fashion market. Females and males, athletes and nonathletes, babies, and the elderly all adopted Nike footwear and other Nike fashion products.

Successful promotional campaigns by retail companies create an image of high value in the minds of their target customer. However, a high value does not necessarily correspond to a high price. Payless Shoe Source is a successful footwear retail chain offering fashionable footwear at budget prices. Customers perceive they are getting a fair value, which means the relationship between price and quality is what the target customers expect.

Sizing and Fitting

Although the making and wearing of shoes is several thousand years old, the sizing of shoes is relatively recent. In the fourteenth century, English King Edward II decreed that one barleycorn (approximately one-third inch) was the increment between shoe sizes. Until 1880, sizing was loosely standardized, often depending on the shoemaker. Better shoes came in two widths, fat and slim, while all other shoes were made in one width, "to be broken in."

In New York, in 1880, Edwin B. Simpson introduced a sizing system for shoe lasts. The lasts were proportioned by length and width measurements and included half sizes as well as whole sizes. The U.S. and British footwear industries eventually adopted this system. It required a significant increase in shoe inventories, because there are almost 300 length/width combinations possible for any one style.

Properly fitting shoes can greatly reduce the incidence of foot problems. The foremost shoe fitting criteria is comfort. Does the shoe feel comfortable to the wearer? Shoes should not need "breaking in." The size is not as important as proper fit, so a customer should not be concerned if the size is not what she or he is accustomed to wearing.

Shoe retailers that specialize in fitting customers with foot problems are sometimes frustrated that manufacturers don't offer multiple-size widths. Concern exists over manufacturers who tend to limit size runs available to retailers. Retailers understand that customers expect a range of widths from which to choose and that each width represents a sizable market segment.

A problem with fitting shoes is that, among different shoe brands, identical size/width combinations may not have the same measurements or fit. Differences in styles, heel heights, materials, patterns, lasts, construction, and manufacturers can cause a difference in shoe fit. Support Plus, a catalog mail-order company, offers a fit solution service to its customers. Each shoe featured in the catalog provides the last number, which identifies the form used to make the shoe. Customers may purchase other styles of well-fitting shoes that were produced using the same last.

Initially, the shoe fitter should measure the length and widest part of the foot while the customer is standing. The amount of space needed at the toe varies, depending on the heel height and the angle of the toes. The shoe should be fit to the longer foot. The width of the foot across the ball will determine the shoe width, such as AA or B. The heel should fit snugly and should not slip when walking.

Both mechanical and electronic devices are available for measuring the feet. The **Brannock Device**® is commonly used to measure the length, ball width, and heel-to-ball length. All three of the dimensions are important for proper shoe fit. The device should be used while the customer is standing and the larger of the feet should be used in determining which shoe size to purchase (see Figure 7.16).

Another device, the **Ritz Stick**® looks like a yardstick with a sliding device that will measure length or width, depending on how the foot is placed on the measuring stick. This is less accurate than the Brannock Device and should be evaluated against the comfort experienced by the wearer. Another method that may be used for fitting shoes is the presence of a floor mat with gradations of footprints on which customers can stand to measure foot length. This footprint method is less accurate and may be found in discount and self-service retail stores.

Computer imaging is the most accurate method for determining footwear needs. At the store level, it helps salespeople to select the correct size for the customer, regardless of the perceived

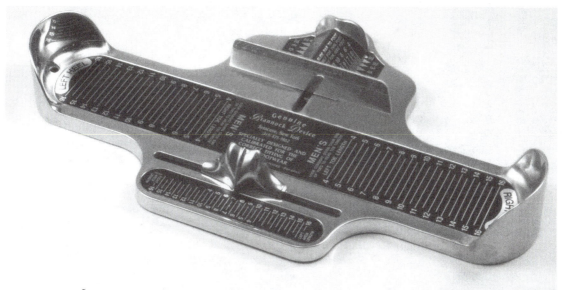

FIGURE 7.16
Brannock Device®. Photograph provided by The Brannock Device Company, Inc.

size. Customers may be able to special-order every pair of shoes. At the manufacturing level, footwear can be mass customized, possibly eliminating the production of unwanted sizes.

Meeting Customer Needs

To sell shoes, a salesperson should determine the customer's needs in five areas—fit, color, style, price, and comfort (end use). Any one of these factors may take precedence during the sale. For example, a young woman choosing a pair of shoes for a formal occasion may be most concerned with color and price. A female executive may be primarily concerned with style, while a nurse or doctor may select a pair of shoes based on fit and comfort.

Shoe gurus Drs. William Rossi and Ross Tennant (1993) agree that shoe fit and comfort are the shoe characteristics most sought by adult buyers. They explain, "Even the most fashionable or expensive shoe will be denied much of its esthetic value if it soon loses shape and quality functional performance as a result of shortcomings in fit." (p. v).

SUMMARY

- *Function* and *fashion* are the threads that run through the footwear industry, historically and today.
- The large baby boomer market has currently caused comfort and casual trends in shoe designs to dominate the market.

ᴐⱴᴐ

Fitting Children's Shoes?

Adult foot problems may be reduced if shoe-fitting care is taken during the developmental years. Properly fitting footwear is critical for infants, because their feet are rapidly growing and changing. Infants' shoes should be broad across the toes to allow for the necessary physiological action of toe wiggling. Until a child begins to walk, toe wiggling is the exercise used to develop foot strength.

Many shoe retailers express concern over the amount of support needed by toddlers. Authors Rossi and Tennant in their publication, *Professional Shoe Fitting* (p. 111) recommend, "The less the shoe does to the foot, the better." They suggest that traditional concerns over ankle and arch support are unfounded. They recommend the shoe need only to protect the wearer from outside elements. At all stages of a child's development, shoe flexi-

bility and adequate sizing are keys to the elimination of shoe-related foot problems.

As a child experiences rapid growth spurts, each foot may grow at a different rate. Shoe fitters must always measure both feet and fit to the larger foot. Shoes with excessive grow room allowances may be as harmful to feet as too-tight shoes. Feet that slide toward the toe of the shoes are compressed, just as feet that have insufficient room are compressed. Hand-me-down shoes are not suitable for children. The authors recommend that parents buy inexpensive new shoes rather than have children wear hand-me-down worn shoes. Parental neglect of replacing their children's outgrown shoes with correctly sized shoes has caused children to grow into adults with unnecessary foot ailments. Pedorthists or shoe therapists may recommend prescription footwear.

- Footwear is comprised of many parts, which can be classified as uppers and lowers. Materials used in manufacturing include leather, synthetic leathers, and fabrics for shoe uppers, while almost all shoe lowers are manufactured using man-made materials.

- Shoes may be categorized by style or classification. There are nine footwear categories for females and males—moccasin, boot, mule, oxford, loafer, pump, sandal, athletic, and clog. Footwear classifications are shoes, boots, and house slippers.

- Many occupations require specialized footwear. These include cushioned shoes for employees who stand several hours per day, pointes for ballet dancers, functional boots for firefighters, and work boots for laborers. Athletic shoes may be preferred by employees in some of these employment areas, due to the high degree of cushioning engineered in athletic shoes.

- Eighty-five percent of the footwear consumed in the United States is produced overseas—primarily in Asian countries. This is due to low labor costs in Asian countries. Most manufacturing steps are computerized, and parts are produced on equipment that can be set up in developing countries with low labor costs.

- U.S. consumers purchase approximately 25 percent of the world footwear produced.

- Shoes require a minimum of care, but should be properly maintained to increase longevity. Materials that "breathe" are desirable for comfort. Comfort technologies are some of the most important criteria in the manufacture of all shoes being produced today.

Profile Box: Manolo Blahnik

Londoner Manolo Blahnik (Ma-NO-lo BLAH-nik) has been designing theatrical shoes "for the moment" for thirty years. He has that uncanny gift of interpreting the female mind. Like Christian Dior before him, Blahnik is attuned to the mood of his customers and can design fashionable shoes that express his customers' attitudes. So adept is Manolo Blahnik at capturing a woman's innermost feeling, that at a Los Angeles trunk show, an enthusiastic customer ordered 50 pairs!

Considering that the retail prices range from $425 to $2,400, any customer could be considered a shoe fanatic. In 1999, the $425 Manolo designed three-inch halter-back heels in black were a best seller on the Neiman-Marcus Web site. Plans are underway to make limited-edition shoes, retailing for around $15,000 per pair. Proud owners of "Blahniks" include Cher, Sarah Ferguson (Fergie), Jerry Hall, Bianca Jagger, Madonna, Kate Moss, Sarah Jessica Parker, Joan Rivers, Winona Ryder, Donatella Versace, and Elle MacPherson.

Manolo Blahnik is a fashion designer, not just a shoe designer. Timeless, elegant, feminine, and fantastic are terms used to describe Blahnik's shoes. Says Blahnik, "My shoes don't have fashion. I do not do shoes that next season you're going to throw them away."[1] He further explains, "I don't do things because they're fashionable. In fact, my shoes are absolutely out of fashion, out of context of fashion. Of course they're fashion in that people buy them and wear them, but I don't do things because of what will be fashionable. I think my trick is I have managed to create a product that is timeless."[2] When chunky heels are in fashion, Blahnik still features stiletto heels, elegantly curved. The shoes' toes are usually pointed, creating a delicate appearance. He's not a fashion follower. Instead he creates his own fashion—and names each one, too!

Blahnik's designs are graceful and often whimsical art forms. Color and texture are important design elements, which he mixes like an artist with a palette. Gunmetal gray, burgundy, turquoise, black, and other exotic colors are texturized into flannel, brocade, embroidery, lamé, satin, velvet, suede, leather, rawhide, snake and alligator skins, and fur. Ornamentation for these exotic shoes includes feathers, beads, crystals, buckles, sequins, rhinestones, pearls, and, for the wealthiest of customers, diamonds, emeralds, and rubies.

Blahnik designs shoes for couture and fashion designer showings, as well as for private customers. Designers John Galliano, Marc Jacobs, Michael Kors, Carolina Herrera, and Badgley Mischka have used Blahniks in their shows. Commercial production is of less interest to Blahnik than creating original works. Blahnik personally draws every shoe. Once the design is drawn, he whittles and sculpts a wooden last and shapes a heel that will function with the shoe. States Blahnik, "The most difficult part is creating the last and the heel. If the heel technically doesn't work, you don't sell shoes because

- Some shoe manufacturers are becoming increasingly involved in retailing. Other manufacturers prefer to promote footwear products without actually engaging in the retailing function.

- Technological innovations, such as Internet retailing, are increasing in popularity. Inventories are being managed and closely monitored with software designed for footwear companies.

- The process of retailing has evolved into customer-friendly sites, either physical or virtual, with a focus on convenience and/or entertainment.

- Shoes may be merchandised by brand, category, or color. Self-selection retailers should provide easy access to well-kept inventories, while full-service retailers should provide adequate and knowledgeable sales associates.

- Regardless of the level of service, proper fit and sizing are keys to comfort, perceived value, and increased sales.

Profile Box: Manolo Blahnik *(continued)*

people will fall off."[3] The carved wooden last is recreated as a plastic mold encased in a plastic drawing sheet, eventually becoming the prototype shoe. Blahnik experiments and determines colors and textures, then sends the sample to Italy for production. The entire process takes about six months to complete a pair of hand-made shoes.

The creation of a shoe evolves from fantasy ideal to technical object. "It's a cross between carpenter work and creating an object. The things that I do are borderline of difficulty of execution," says Blahnik.[4] One such design was a shoe with narrow ties up the legs, adorned with satin leaves and rosebuds. Although Blahnik did not anticipate the style's popularity, it became a top seller.

While Manolo is the creative genius behind his shoe successes, he credits his sister, Evangeline, with the business acumen. Evangeline manages the flagship London shop, European business operations, and the special order business. Both siblings attribute distinctive parts of their success to their mother and father—from their Spanish mother, discipline and style; from their Czech father, business sense. The company president, American businessman George Malkemus III, holds the North and South American licenses.

Manolo Blahnik shoes can be purchased all over the world, at Neiman Marcus stores and Blahnik's store on West 55th Street in New York City, as well as stores in Washington, D.C., Paris, London, and Los Angeles. Although the high prices prevent most consumers from purchasing his shoes, Blahnik shoes are not unheard of in the average household. The word "Blahniks" became known to the popular culture in recent years when they were periodically mentioned in HBO's Sex and the City.

Shoes: Beautiful, sexy, graceful, but not practical. All hand-crafted. These are the Manolo Blahnik creations offered by the finest stores in the world.

Sources:

[1] Cowie, Denise. (March 14, 1996). Designer Manolo Blahnik is the High Priest of Sexy Shoes. *Philadelphia Inquirer.* Knight-Ridder/Tribune News Service, p. 314.

[2] Sole Trained: A Passion for Italy. (1997). Hearst Corp. Available: wysiwyg://11/http://homearts.com/depts/style/47manb3.htm

[3] Inspiration and Artistry. (Nov. 22, 1999). Sole Trained, World of Style, Hearst Corporation. Available: http://homearts.com/depts/style/47manbl.htm

[4] Ibid.

- Brand name, fashionability, celebrity endorsers, promotional campaigns, and price affect the perceived value of footwear.
- A single shoe style can have up to 300 length/width combinations.
- Five selling criteria are fit, color, style, price, and comfort (end use).

TERMS FOR REVIEW

arch supports	casual fitness	cross trainer athletic shoe
base sole	Chinese lily foot	cushioned insoles
boots	chopines	cutting
bottoming	comfort technologies	cyberbranding
box stores	corporate casual	designing
Brannock Device	counter	fashion footwear

fitting	lower	tongue
finishing	outsole	vamp
haute couture	orthotics	vertical marketing
heel	pattern making	welt
heel lift	pattens	shank
heel pads	planogram	shoehorns
house slippers	quarter	shoe pouches
insole	Quick Response	shoe trees
khaki casual	Ritz Stick	shoes
last	saddle	sock lining
lasting	stock control	upper
leased shoe departments	toe cap	

REVIEW QUESTIONS

1. What are the basic parts of a shoe?

2. What are the basic heel styles?

3. How are the seven routine steps of shoe manufacturing related to quality and cost?

4. What might the feminist perspective be on why the wearers of extreme shoe fashions are willing to follow such difficult-to-manage fashions?

5. Are there other accessories or fashionable items that are worn by people today that cause physical restrictions? Why do these become fashions?

6. What are some basic care requirements for footwear in a variety of climatic conditions?

7. Describe three technological innovations that have had an impact upon the footwear industry?

8. How does the shift of shoe production overseas affect U.S. shoe companies?

9. What are some ways in which domestic shoe manufacturers can compete with lower-cost overseas manufacturers?

10. Explain why proper fit is so important to buying and selling shoes.

KNOWLEDGE APPLICATIONS

1. Visit an historic costume museum and view the shoe collection or visit one of these on-line museum sites: The Bata Shoe Museum at bata.com or Solemates: The Century in Shoes at http://www.centuryinshoes.com/intro.html

2. Participate in a field trip to a local shoe store and talk to the store manager about merchandising trends. Compile an expanded bulleted list of merchandising techniques in addition to those listed in the chapter.

3. Visit a footwear-manufacturing company, or teleconference with a footwear designer. Develop a list of ten questions related to design inspirations or steps in production, and compare to the methods discussed in the chapter.

4. Visit a store with a shoe department and randomly evaluate several pairs of shoes on the following criteria: price point, construction methods, merchandising techniques (materi-

als, colors, categories, and/or brands), country of origin, sizing, and inventory supply. Develop a form for recording the information before visiting the store.

5. Evaluate your most recent shoe purchase. Describe the criteria on which you based your purchase decision.

6. Choose a single shoe criterion, such as color, style, brand, heel heights, toe shape, and so on. Develop a recording sheet and count at least 50 pairs of shoes with the selected criteria. Calculate percents and analyze the findings.

7. Visit two Internet sites selling the same brand and style of shoe. Compare their promotional approaches, ease of negotiating the Web site, prices, availability, and services.

8. Locate numerous shoe brands' Internet sites. What percentage of sites offer consumers the option of purchasing from the Web site? What percentage of Web sites refers customers to stores where they may purchase the shoes?

9. Using several mail-order catalogs or fashion magazines, cut and paste fashionable women's shoe styles. Identify the heel and vamp styles for each pair of shoes.

CHAPTER 8

‖‖

HANDBAGS, SMALL PERSONAL GOODS, LUGGAGE, AND BELTS

IT'S IN THE BAG!

The typical handbag of the average woman in 1945 contained:

One or two lipsticks

A compact (that wouldn't close)

1 fresh handkerchief

2 or 3 crumpled handkerchiefs

A package of letters

The laundry bill

3 tickets from the cleaner

1 nylon stocking to be repaired

1 address book

1 pack of cigarettes

3 packs of matches

1 leather picture folder

All ration books (including expired ones)

Several cards with addresses of a furrier, a wholesale place for children's coats, a beauty parlor, etc.

2 scraps of paper with telephone numbers and no names

1 hairnet

1 bottle of vitamins

3 samples of slipcovers

1 fountain pen

2 pencils

1 parcel of V-mail letters covering several months held by a rubber band.

The typical handbag of the average woman in 1998 contained:

Banking card

Beeper

Breath mints

Cell phone

Change purse

Checkbook

Crumpled tissues

Electronic organizer

Hand cream

Hairbrush

Keys

Lip balm

Makeup case filled to capacity

Pens

Wallet filled with cash and credit cards

One bag is not enough: Contents spill over into our tote bags, which contain:

Agenda	Newspaper
Packed lunch	Shoes to change at work
Paperback book/magazine	Umbrella

NFAA accessoryweb.com, 1998.

A BRIEF HISTORY OF HANDBAGS, SMALL PERSONAL GOODS, LUGGAGE, AND BELTS

Sacks, packs, pouches, purses, bags, and belts have always been practical ways to carry items of necessity and value when people leave their homes. These "carriers" were crafted from available materials, such as straw, rope, skins, or fabrics, and were slung across the back, draped across the shoulders, worn at the waist, or balanced on the head, freeing the travelers' hands.

The Middle Ages, or medieval times, gave rise to a number of accessories items and names that are recognizable today. During those times, the craft of leather-bag making became more specialized, as did the assortment of styles available for both the elite and working classes. Fashionable gentlemen and ladies carried little bags, called **pockets,** suspended from a leather **girdle,** or belt.

Bags and travel boxes were developed and named for specialized functions. **Budget bags** were used to carry bookkeeping accounts, while travelers used **male bags** to carry letters. Both have retained their names in modern society, although the latter's spelling was changed to *mail bags*. Sturdy **document** and **deed boxes** were useful during colonial times when travelers carried locking, narrow boxes for their valuables.

A great deal of European lore contains stories about medieval chastity belts, usually made of iron or bronze, and occasionally, of precious metals studded with gemstones. These locking belts were developed to ensure the chastity of a crusading knight's woman while he was away for extended periods of time. A religious parallel was offered by 14th-century historian Règine Pernoud, a contemporary scholar living in France, who explained that the simple cord worn around a monk's waist was symbolic of his religious vows of purity and chastity.

Up through the 16th century, the level of a man or woman's wealth was often evidenced by the degree of ornamentation and size of his or her purse. Drawstrings and tassel ornamentation were typical details for purses that were hand carried, attached to a girdle, or worn under the clothing (see Figure 8.1).

During the 17th century, men's wear began to feature sewn-in pockets, and purses for men disappeared. Briefcases and attaché cases became acceptable totes for men. For a period in the early 19th century, women also converted to carrying their belongings in generous pockets sewn into side seams of their full skirts. But by the end of the 19th century, dress fashions had

FIGURE 8.1
A purse from the 16th century.
®Museum of Bags and Purses, Amstelveen, the Netherlands.

become too narrow to allow for side-seam pockets, and detached handbags became fashionable again.

Prior to industrialization, traveling was reserved primarily for society's upper echelons. Trunks were the most common form of luggage and were made sturdy enough to withstand steamer ship and carriage trips. Rectangular and flat topped, trunks were easily packed and stacked in cargo holds. It wasn't long before creative designers determined that by making the tops of the more expensive trunks softly rounded, wealthy customers' trunks would have to be stacked on top of all the others. Thus, their clients' **barrel-top trunks** would be the first unloaded upon arrival at the destination!

Although belts have been in existence as a complement to clothing for centuries, the 20th century heralded the introduction of belt loops on trousers, thus increasing the popularity of belts. Prior to this time, fashionable men wore custom-made silk braces or suspenders as part of their undergarment wardrobe, not to be seen in public. The popularity of three-piece suits with vests added an extra layer of material around a man's waist, so belts became less important, while braces were more suited to the style. Two-piece suits, left open at the jacket, revealed the suspender undergarments, a fashion faux pas. Consequently, belts served the function of holding up trousers without being unseemly and in poor taste.

Early 20th-century handbags were small and mainly used to conceal cosmetics and cigarettes. A woman's handbag became the ultimate catchall, and was used to carry car keys, cigarette holders, and other symbols of women's increasing freedoms.

Thousands of troops in World War II followed strict dress code regulations and dressed in belted military attire. Those same young men, the workforce of the 1950s, were ingrained with the notion of the indispensable belt—if trousers had belt loops, a belt must be worn.

The 1950s began an era of status handbags. Famous designers created a demand for affordable status symbols that has continued to the present day. Coco Chanel, the couture fashion designer, created a sensation called the 2.55 Chanel Bag. The diamond-quilted bag, suspended on golden shoulder strap chains, is probably the most copied handbag of the 20th century. It was named for the month and year of its inception—February 1955.

Glamorous personalities have influenced 20th-century handbag fashions. Hollywood actress-turned-princess, Grace Kelly (Princess Grace of Monaco), was featured on the cover of a 1950s *Life Magazine* concealing her pregnancy with a large crocodile Hermès bag, later dubbed the "Kelly Bag" in her honor. Princess Diana, the late Princess of Wales, helped popularize the Ferragamo clutch purse and the Lady Dior bag, which became a worldwide sellout. Movie stars Cameron Diaz and Gwyneth Paltrow set fashion trends today.

The mid-1960s and early 1970s, called the **Peacock Era** because of the flamboyant men's wear fashions, sparked a decline in the need for suspenders and dress belts. Men's slacks often had waistband tabs with adjustable button spacings. When belt loops were provided, the pants were often hip-hugger styles that created a market for wider, decorative belts or loose chain belts. In the 1970s, belts narrowed, and "the skinny belt" became a fashion item for women. More for fashion than function, skinny belts were worn on the outside of many ensembles regardless of the presence of belt loops.

In the 1980s, men's wear returned to fuller-cut clothes, with trousers at the natural waistline. Braces briefly reappeared, but belts dominated the men's wear fashions of the latter 20th century.

HANDBAGS

Although a desire for fashion or status influences the selection of a handbag, the suitability and fit with a person's lifestyle is just as important. Today, handbags have evolved into sturdy and functional pieces of "equipment" necessary to support the busy and diverse lifestyles of those who carry them. Wilsons Leather company offered a line of handbags named the Wilsons for Women Executive Collection. Features included the following items, all of which were removable: cosmetic case, business card holder, eyeglass/utility case, key ring holder, mirror and lipstick holder, phone bag, pen loops, and credit card holders. The advertising copy essentially summed up the handbag needs of the contemporary businesswoman, who is time-starved and shopping on the Internet:

> Efficiency. Strength. Flexibility. Style. That's what working women want. And we responded with the Wilsons for Women Executive Collection. Designed by women, for women, these exclusive leather bags work hard to make your life easier. Bags with laptop compartments. Bags that organize. Bags that travel from office to gym. Bags that simplify

your life. Rich and lasting cowhide. All value priced. Just choose the bag that works for you and click. Simple.

More than fashion, handbags are essential support devices and often, *one is not enough.* Backpacks, briefcases, portfolios and agendas, tote bags, sport bags, and handbags are basic parts of men's and women's everyday wardrobes.

Parts of a Handbag

Handbag construction varies depending on the style of the bag. Sturdier handbags have a longer intended life. The minimum required component of a handbag is the outer covering, with the other features, such as the frame, lining, handle, closure, gussets, and trimmings, considered options.

- **Outer covering** Comprised of fashion fabric, straw, leather, or other attractive, yet durable materials. May cover the frame or be used without a frame for support.
- **Frame** A heavy-gauge steel or brass structure giving the handbag its shape.
- **Padding** Foam or other material. May be used to cover the hard edges of the frame and protect the outer covering from the metal frame.
- **Lining** Covers construction details, such as seams and frame. Leather linings are most durable and usually found at higher price points, while fabric linings are most common. Some handbags are unlined.
- **Underlining** Cardboard or heavy paper placed between the outer covering and the lining for additional support.
- **Handle** May be the same fabrication as the outer covering or may be a hard material, such as plastic or chain. Attached to the top or sides of the bag, the handle should adequately support the weight of the contents. Figure 8.2 shows some of the more popular handle styles.
- **Fastener** or **closure** A decorative or hidden closing device, such as a flap, snap, drawstring, lock, or zipper. Must be sturdy enough to protect the contents of the purse. With the profusion of copycat designs, status bag manufacturers often create logo-type hardware to provide status-conscious consumers with unique copyrighted identifications.
- **Gusset** Expansion gores or panels on the sides of the handbags to make it larger.
- **Trimmings** All decorative features that adorn the handbag. May be hidden, such as inside pockets or mirrors; or visible, such as brand labels and seam pipings (which adorn and protect from abrasion). Outer trimmings should be smooth, so as not to snag apparel.

Handbag Manufacturing

A handbag is an important part of the total image a person projects. Handbag designs are created either as a separate line or as part of a total-look concept. Samples are created to determine

bracelet

chain

shoulder strap

FIGURE 8.2

Handle styles. Courtesy of Fairchild Publications, Inc.

the feasibility of production. If the style is approved, pattern pieces are created and cut from leather or fabric. In the case of straw or knitted handbags, the materials are often fashioned into a style.

Design

Whether they are inspired by vintage styles, new technology, ready-to-wear fashions, or nature, handbag designers are masters of creating something for everyone. The entry of ready-to-wear designers into the handbag market is on the upswing. Designers are discovering that a related line of handbags enhances their ready-to-wear line. The amount of designer input into the actual design of the handbags varies. Some designers exercise control over the product, but others may depend on licensing departments to monitor the product appearance and image.

The famous couture name Chanel is widely known for its signature bag, but other designers are finding the potential for accessories-generated profits appealing. Italian luxury designer,

Miuccia Prada found that her fake Chanel bags of the 1980s and her $350 black nylon backpack of the early 1990s fostered the growth of the Prada Group apparel business. Michael Kors, modern American ready-to-wear designer, launched a collection of handbags in spring 2001. He believed in totally committing to the line rather than gradually introducing the collection, in hopes that it would become a signature line.

As with other accessories products, apparel designers license their names to handbag manufacturers. Unity across product lines is an important part of creating a successful brand image. Many designers offer collections of complimentary footwear, handbags, and small leather goods, creating a total look among licensed products.

In the United States, the concept of **knockoff** or **copycat designing,** which means copying originals line for line, is an irritant to creative, original designers. Of continual concern are the persons who hover around original design companies and their suppliers to steal ideas and copy them, often even before the original designs are on the market. In spite of the frustration, knockoffs are a legal and natural part of the trickle-down fashion business in the United States. What is illegal, however, is the copying of registered trademarks on knockoff designs. For example, the duck emblem on Dooney and Burke handbags and accessories has often been illegally pirated, as has the LV symbol on Louis Vuitton bags. It is not uncommon to read in *Women's Wear Daily* of trademark infringement legal battles and lawsuits between fashion businesses.

The United Kingdom and France have some stringent laws and organizations that protect creative designs. One organization, Anti-Copying in Design (ACID), achieved a victory in a 2000 lawsuit on behalf of Vexed Generation, a U.K.-based company. Vexed Generation designed a courier-style bag, with a unique Velcro® closure on the strap, which was replicated by the defendant, Badge Sales. A compensation settlement was reached after ACID and Vexed Generation proved that "having similar styles out in the marketplace was commercially damaging to the business" ("Vexed Generation Bags Victory," 2000)

Production

Once a handbag design has been approved, a muslin or felt sample is created. Special fittings or closures are also attached to ensure a proper match with the design. Before the design goes to production, a pattern is created for each part of the handbag. Fabric outer coverings can be blade or laser cut as multiple layers of fabric. Leather outer coverings require die cutting one thickness at a time to avoid scars or imperfections on the leather.

Assembly involves dozens of steps and may be a combination of hand and machine piecework. Handbag parts are stitched together, and underlinings of filler (stiffening materials and padding), and linings are sewn or glued to the frame and outer covering.

Materials

Many retailers credit the boom in handbag sales to the variety of nonleather materials available, including canvas, wool flannel, corduroy, silk shantung, sweater knits, and animal prints in

Profile Box: Kate Spade

Both a designer and an astute businesswoman, with target customers who are "savvy working women who happen to be handbag fanatics,"[1] Kate Spade has managed to build a successful empire in just a few short years. With annual sales of approximately $70 million, Kate Spade LLC, part of the Neiman-Marcus Group, is the United States' top-producing handbag company, with wholesale sales and retail stores as part of the empire.

Kate Spade began designing handbags in 1993 with a collection of six classic shapes that are still in the line. However, the line has taken on a broader appeal with the inclusion of other accessories like stationary, shoes, luggage, scarves, gloves, and beauty products licensed to Estée Lauder.

According to Andy Spade, the company's chief executive officer and husband to Kate, opening stores is a top priority for the company. "As we expand our retail presence we are focused on finding unique spaces in the heart of areas where our best customers live."[2] Beverly Hills, Boston, San Francisco, and Manhattan are a few of the cities in which the exclusive boutiques have opened.

A designer's name is only as good as the reputation of the manufacturers producing the product. Kate Spade has been plagued with indirect negative publicity from two of her handbag manufacturers. In 1998, a leather goods factory, VG Leather, dismissed several factory workers, allegedly for trying to establish a union. Because Kate Spade contracted with VG Leather to produce merchandise, union activists also targeted her company name. VG Leather is now unionized and continues to produce merchandise for the Kate Spade lines. A similar situation arose in 2000, when union members picketed the SoHo Kate Spade store, accusing the company of supporting a manufacturer that temporarily closed its doors rather than recognizing union efforts. KC Accessories, which almost exclusively produced Kate Spade handbags, "stayed closed for about a week and then began hiring back a few people at a time, but only those who had not signed on to join the union."[3]

Kate Spade partner and spokesperson, Elyce Cox, played down Kate Spade's dealings with KC Accessories, describing KC's merchandise production as a small percentage of Kate Spade's total goods. "We do manufacture at other shops. KC is a private business, and whatever difficulties there are have to do with KC Accessories' president and his workers. We're not privy to anything."[4]

Most recently in Kate Spade history, Andy and Kate Spade hired former Donna Karan executive, Robin Marino, as president. Ms. Marino "understands both sides—the product and the numbers,"[5] said Andy Spade. The Spades were impressed by Marino's passion for merchandise and innovative designs.

With profits firmly in the black, the Spades anticipate sales reaching as high as $200 million in the next few years. Under the leadership of Marino, licensing ventures into women's shoes and men's bags may easily propel the company toward this goal.

Sources:

[1] Curan, Catherine. (July 19, 1999). Shouldering Expansion. *Crains New York Business*, p. 41.

[2] Moin, David. (2000). Spade's on a Roll, Expands Its Plan. *Women's Wear Daily*, 179(96), p. 12.

[3] UNITE Protesters Picket at Kate Spade SoHo Store. (Aug. 4, 2000). *Women's Wear Daily*, 180(23), p. 17.

[4] Ibid.

[5] Curan, p. 41.

faux fur. Many of these nonleather materials can be pleated, shirred, and quilted. Straw, usually a summer outer covering, may be natural, such as willow and wicker, or synthetic, called **Pontova,** and **Toyo,** a crocheted paper straw.

NPD Accessory Watch, a marketing agency that tracks point-of-sale consumer purchases at department stores, credited the consumer's desire for nylon and microfibers, in part, for the recent growth of the handbag market. These materials accounted for about one quarter of department store handbag sales in 1999, a 50-percent increase over 1998. Of the top-selling handbag styles, sixteen were leather and nine were nylon microfibers. Table 8.1 shows a

TABLE 8.1

Top Materials Used for Women's Handbags and Average Price Per Handbag

Material	Percent of Total Handbags	Average Price Per Handbag
Nylon/Microfiber	23.6%	$40.72
Leather	33.2%	$81.27
Vinyl	6.3%	$27.91
Straw	2.2%	$24.90
Silk/Satin/Velvet	1.0%	$24.91
Canvas	1.0%	$34.90
Suede/Nubuck	1.3%	$60.61
Exotic	.3%	$56.31
Unspecified/Other	31.1%	$37.69–$41.49

Source: Retail Sales Hit New Highs. (Apr. 24, 2000). Advertising Supplement, *Women's Wear Daily,* p. 12. Courtesy of Fairchild Publications, Inc.

ranking of women's handbags sales by materials used and the average retail price for a handbag of that material.

Basic Styles of Handbags

Handbags are manufactured in many styles, with variations in handles and materials. Figure 8.3 shows several popular handbag styles.

Care of Handbags

Handbags may be manufactured in the same materials as shoes, but they do not get the same degree of wear and tear. It is easier for customers to maintain an attractive appearance with minimal effort. Retailers may offer cleaning products on display near the handbag racks and cases to increase add-on sales and suggestive selling. Some handbag companies offer their own cleaning products, which are mentioned on purse hangtags. Customers who purchase **investment handbags** (more expensive handbags with fashion appeal over several seasons) are receptive to products that prolong the life of their expensive purchase.

Customer Care Tips

Retail sales associates should offer customers the following advice about the care of handbags:

- Remove dirt by wiping with a slightly damp, clean cloth
- Avoid saddle soaps on leather handbags to protect the natural oils
- Rub new suede bags with dry terrycloth to remove excess dyes

box and halfmoon handbags

cell phone bag

Chanel signature bag

framed clutch handbag

drawstring, feedbag, or bucket

hobo or slouch handbag

minaudière handbag

satchel handbag

FIGURE 8.3
Basic Styles of Handbags.
Courtesy of Fairchild Publications, Inc.

tote bag

top flap handbag

THE GLOBAL HANDBAG, SMALL PERSONAL GOODS, LUGGAGE, AND BELTS INDUSTRIES

The handbag, small personal goods, luggage, and belt industries are closely related in the manufacturing and marketing of products and in the trade organizations, publications, and shows that producers and other participants in these industries support.

Manufacturing

Like footwear, handbag production is labor intensive and most manufacturing is performed overseas, although company headquarters tend to be domestically stationed. The lure of offshore, low labor costs is too attractive for many domestic companies to resist. China is the largest producer of handbags consumed in the United States. In 1997, the United States census counted 136 domestic women's handbags and purse manufacturers, employing about 3,520 people. As with other domestic manufacturing industries, the number of manufacturers has gradually decreased during the last several years.

In spite of the loss of manufacturing jobs, many domestic designing jobs exist because of the relatively small start-up capital required. One new designer, Sarah Shaw, began manufacturing handbags in her garage, with as little as $5,000. By 2000, the company showed annual sales of almost one million dollars.

Not all manufacturing is done overseas, however. Because accessories usually have a shorter life cycle than ready-to-wear—only about three months—time is critical and often problematic with overseas production. The convenience and faster turnaround time of domestic production appeals to companies selling faddish accessories.

The handbag industry is comprised of both large and small manufacturers, accounting for over one billion dollars in handbags sales in 1999. Table 8.2 shows a ranking of the ten largest producers of handbags in the United States based on annual sales (in millions).

Two-thirds of the consumption of small personal, or flat, leather goods are imported into the United States from countries in which labor costs are low. China supplies over one half of the total imports, while India and Italy supply less than ten percent each.

The United States does produce some small personal goods, that are exported primarily to Japan and China. The Japanese market has been considered a good one for expansion of higher-priced handbags and small personal leather goods designed by American companies. Innovative and aggressive domestic producers may be able to expand exports, even though the labor costs in the United States are cost prohibitive.

Like other leather goods, the majority of belts are manufactured overseas. Many companies that produce handbags and small personal leather goods also produce belts. Designers frequently include matching belts in their ready-to-wear line, although the production of the belts may be licensed to another company.

TABLE 8.2

The Ten Largest Producers of Handbags in the United States

Company	Annual Sales (in Millions)
Kate Spade LLC	70.0
Jaclyn, Inc.	58.77
Dooney & Bourke PR, Inc.	35.29
Sara Lee Corp. (Coach) (Miami, FL)	32.2
Sara Lee Corp. (New York, NY)	16.3
Excel Handbags Co., Inc.	15.0
The Monet Group, Inc.	13.7
J.L.N., Inc.	9.2
Terners of Miami Corp.	8.0
Time Products	7.7

Source: Duns Market Identifiers, SIC 3171, Dun and Bradstreet, Aug. 18, 2000.

Trade Organizations, Publications, and Shows

The handbag, small personal goods, luggage, and belts industries support trade organizations, publications, and shows that often represent accessories in general, rather than just a single product area, like handbags. However, a few exclusive associations do exist. Table 8.3 shows trade organizations for handbags, small personal goods, luggage, and belts. Table 8.4 lists and describes trade publications for these accessories and Table 8.5 lists some of the more important trade shows for these industries.

MERCHANDISING TRENDS
AND TECHNIQUES FOR HANDBAGS

The sale of handbags dominates the accessories market, totaling 50 percent of all accessories sales. Key brands accounting for the sales increase included Kate Spade, Guess?, and Ralph Lauren/Polo Sport. Best-selling styles have recently included top flaps, top zips, and satchels. Handbags are most likely to be purchased at a department store, perhaps because of the large selection of styles, brands, colors, and price points. Table 8.6 shows a sales distribution of all handbag sales by store classification in 1999.

Department Stores

According to the National Fashion Accessories Association, handbags are not usually purchased on impulse. Instead they are considered **planned purchases,** which means the shopper had predetermined a need for the item. Female shoppers are typically looking to replace a

TABLE 8.3

Trade Organizations for the Handbags, Small Personal Goods, Luggage, and Belts Industries

Organization	Location	Objectives
American Luggage Dealers Association (ALDA) **www.luggagedealers.com**	Santa Barbara, CA	To represent luggage retailers
British Luggage and Leathergoods Association (BLLA) **www.blla.org.uk**	Birmingham, UK	To promote the growth and image of the luggage and leathergoods industries
Fashion Accessories Shippers Association (FASA) **www.accessoryweb.com**	New York, NY	Provides quota reports, special bulletins, contract information, links to government, and shipping news for handbags and luggage
Luggage, Leathergoods, Handbags and Accessories Association of Canada (LLHAA) **www.llha.org**	Toronto, Ontario	Promotes the industries for vendors and retailers, and sponsors an annual trade show
National Fashion Accessory Association (NFAA) **www.accessoryweb.com**	New York, NY	Provides information to its manufacturer/importer members, fosters labor relations, and promotes and protects member interests
National Luggage Dealers Association **www.nlda.com**	Glenview, IL	Represents independent retailers nationwide as a collective buying organization
NPD Accessory Watch	Port Washington, NY	Tracks consumer purchases by brand, price point, and classification in up to 68% of all department stores and compiles data projections
Travel Goods Association (TGA) **www.travel-goods.org**	Princeton, NJ	Promotes the growth, profitability, and image of the travel goods industry

worn-out item, or to buy a handbag that coordinates with a specific outfit. Male shoppers are probably searching for a gift or a functional item as a replacement or first purchase. However, it is interesting to note that at most large department stores, handbags are located near main entrances on the ground level floors, which are prime locations for **impulse items** (items purchased with little or no prior consideration). Inexpensive novelty handbag items, such as seasonal totes, may be displayed on hanging fixtures on the aisles, while planned-purchase handbags (usually more expensive) are merchandised by brands in bays (similar to cosmetics).

Although not always possible in larger department stores, handbag departments in smaller department stores and specialty stores may be designed with a **total-look concept.** This means the handbags are displayed with related accessories, such as matching shoes, creating a one-stop shopping experience. According to the National Fashion Accessories Association, departments with a related merchandise display within viewing distance of the customer have a significantly greater chance of making **add-on sales,** or related merchandise sales. For example, a shoe

TABLE 8.4

Trade Publications for the Handbags, Small Personal Goods, Luggage, and Belts Industries

Trade Publication Name	Description
Accessories Magazine	Monthly trade publication covering most accessory classifications, including handbags, small personal goods, luggage, and belts.
BLLA News	Monthly news published by the British Luggage and Leathergoods Association.
Hong Kong Leather Goods and Bags	Published by the Hong Kong Trade Development Council and provides product information on leathergoods and bags.
Key Note Market Report: Hand Luggage & Leather Goods	A trade publication from England, available on CD-Rom and online.
Luggage, Leathergoods, and Accessories (LLA)	Created by the Retail Trade Group to cover the luggage and leathergoods trades.
Travelware	Business journal containing information on the luggage and leathergoods industries.
Women's Wear Daily – Monday	Trade newspaper, published daily by Fairchild. Features business and fashion information on handbags, small personal goods, baggage, and belt accessories.

department may position a display of leather handbags and attaché cases near leather pumps, or an apparel department may dress a mannequin in a suit and holding a coordinating handbag.

A department-wide theme is important for creating continuity and attracting customer interest, but it should be continually changing. **Handbag themes** may include color, the most attracting design element; texture, whether satiny-smooth or embossed; prints, such as plaids or animal prints; and lifestyle, whether career oriented or fashion forward. **Trend themes,** which

TABLE 8.5

Trade Shows for the Handbags, Small Personal Goods, Luggage, and Belts Industries

Trade Show	Location	Sponsor
AccessoriesTheShow	New York, NY	National Fashion Accessories Association
Hong Kong International Handbags and Leather Goods Fair	Central Hong Kong	Hong Kong Trade Development Council
International Travelgoods, Leather and Accessories Show	New Orleans, LA	Travel Goods Association
Luggage, Leathergoods, Handbags and Accessories Show (LLHA Show)	Toronto, Ontario	Luggage, Leathergoods, Handbags and Accessories Association of Canada
The Travel Goods Show	Las Vegas, NV	Travel Goods Association

TABLE 8.6

Percent of Handbag Sales by Store Classification for 1999

Store Classification	Percent of Total Sales
Department Stores	36%
Chain Stores	13%
Discount Stores	13%
Specialty Stores	11%
Miscellaneous	27%

Source: Retail Sales Hit New Highs. (Apr. 24, 2000). Advertising Supplement, *Women's Wear Daily,* p. 12. Courtesy of Fairchild Publications, Inc.

may encompass all of the above themes, are valuable for handbag departments. For example, if bamboo is the trend theme, handbags may feature bamboo handles and trim, be made of bamboo fibers, or be printed with bamboo patterns on the fashion fabric. Trend themes are found in the exciting and ever-changing fashion merchandise that offsets the less exciting inventory of staple handbags in neutral fabrics and leathers.

Travel Retail Stores

Many domestic handbag and small personal goods brands are expanding into overseas markets, often starting with duty-free shops in airports. Currently, South Korea, Japan, and China are some of the most sought-after markets by **travel retailers.** A natural outlet for small personal goods and luggage, airport retailers include small specialty shops and boutiques featuring limited lines of related carry-on goods.

A part of travel retailing includes catalogs (such as Sky Mall) located in the airline seat backs. These catalogs sell all kinds of gift and personal items, including small personal goods and luggage sets. Well-known catalog retailers, such as Lillian Vernon, can purchase a few pages of the catalog to show exclusive merchandise. For convenience, air travelers can telephone from the handsets on the plane, log on to a Web site, or take the catalogs with them.

Mulberry Leathergoods, known as "the Coach of the United Kingdom" is establishing a line of lightweight travel accessories, called Flight, targeted to the airport business traveler. Brands with international recognition have the greatest success at major international airports. LeSportsac, a United States company specializing in affordable nylon handbags luxuriously merchandised, has doubled annual sales each year for the past five years using travel retail channels.

Internet Retailing

Large handbag producers, such as Coach, Dooney and Burke, London Luggage Shop, and Wilsons Leather, have **branded Web sites** to market their men's and women's handbags and

---

Tech Talk: Mass Customization for Cybershoppers

Most business owners would agree that consumers deserve fashion options when shopping. Too often, shoppers are victims of standard products made for the masses. **Mass customization** (sometimes called **mass personalization**) is a merging of craftsmanship with mass production. Mass-marketed goods and services are individualized to satisfy specific customer needs or wants at affordable prices. Mass customization allows shoppers to control certain aspects of the product development process. The degree of control may be minimal, but usually consumers are allowed enough of a choice to clinch the e-sale. Jeans, shoes, swimsuits, fur coats, and handbags have been individualized. For example, first the Levi Strauss Personal Pair of classic five-pocket jeans, and later the Original Spin jeans were created to the customer's size specifications and shipped within two weeks. Store employees take the customer's measurements and enter them into the computer, which suggests existing sizes for a test fit. The measurements are sent via modem to a sewing factory where sewing operators construct the made-to-order jeans. Lands' End offers a build-your-own virtual model on its Web site that allows most clothing to be "tried on" before purchasing. Mass-customized clothing has become an important part of the Lands' End company's revenue. NikeiD offers numerous pairs of athletic shoes for customers to select the colors of the body, trim,

and sole of the shoe. Customers can have a personalized identification of up to eight letters inscribed on the shoe. The production and shipping total about three weeks.

Mass customization has expanded into the handbag industry with options that include fabric, color or pattern, and trim. One Web site, bgbags.com offers customers fabric and trim selection choices for handbags, totes, and small personal goods. Another handbag Web site offering mass-customized handbags was developed to be "fun" and "easy," making the shopping experience pleasurable for the customers.

Mass customization of apparel and accessories is a viable way for competitive brands to avoid the "sameness" of their merchandise assortment. It is a blurring of buying off-the-shelf goods and custom-made goods. The sheer competitiveness of the market is forcing some major brands to adopt mass-customization practices.

Custom-made apparel and accessories targeted at the mass audience have only been on the market for a few years. For some companies, the customization of goods is a long-term investment plan that may take years to be financially self-sustaining. If the demand for mass customization continues to grow, brands may choose domestic production over offshore production to reduce turn around times.

---

travel accessories products. A frequent feature of branded Web sites is a store-locator link for customers who prefer to make their purchases by visiting brick-and-mortar locations. Customers are provided with convenient options, such as returning Web site purchases to retail stores. The visual design of the Web site reflects the company's image and reinforces the positioning of the retail store.

Other Internet companies market handbags by style, with no mention of national or private-label brand names. One such company, Handbags Direct, allows customers to select styles, such as backpacks or tote bags, and then shows them several similar styles in a variety of colors and materials.

Catalog Retailing

In catalogs, handbags and related accessories are sold in conjunction with ready-to-wear. Handbags may be featured in a section of the catalog, but merchandisers are more likely to show a handbag as part of a total look featuring apparel, belt, shoes, and jewelry. This form of catalog merchandising has been proven to be successful in producing sales of multiple items.

SELLING HANDBAGS

In full-service retail environments, salespeople begin by showing customers moderately priced handbags, if no preference is mentioned. The salesperson should not assume what brands or styles a customer can afford based on the person's appearance. Astute salespeople listen carefully to customer opinions and preferences, concentrating on showing styles that reflect what they hear and pointing out hidden features and benefits that satisfy the customer's needs.

Price and Value

Handbag quality is evaluated on the rarity and type of materials used, manufacturing processes, workmanship, and detailing. The price points are reflective of these criteria but are also affected by the brand and retailer name. Buyers for retail stores should be aware that all of these criteria must be considered before determining a price point. For example, top-grain exotic leathers are usually more expensive than many cowhides because of their rarity. But factors such as brand name, manufacturing processes, and workmanship may cause a top-grain cowhide handbag to exceed the retail price of an exotic top-grain handbag. Workmanship is an important detail in evaluating handbags because the interior details, although hidden, should receive as much attention by the manufacturers as the visible exterior details.

In the United States and Europe, sales of lower- and higher-priced handbags are booming. Handbags priced over $100 accounted for 30 percent of dollar sales, while handbags priced in the $25 to $49.99 group accounted for 36 percent of the total handbag dollar volume.

Department store handbag departments realized 1999 sales increases of eight percent over 1998 sales. The increase is even more significant when the average retail price is factored into the picture. In 1998, the average retail price for department store handbags was $48.25, while the 1999 average retail price dropped to between $45.25 and $47.16. More than three-fourths of all handbags are priced at less than $50. Figure 8.4 shows the average price point distribution of department store handbags inventory in 2000.

Meeting Customer Needs

A trend in handbag accessories is toward multipurpose functions. Customers are more likely to buy an accessory that has options and flexibility. Most handbag manufacturers have developed their own lines of functional fashion bags to accommodate the prevalence of the cell phone by creating easily accessible pockets or compartments just for phones. Evening bags, typically small in size, are now constructed with enough room to enclose a cell phone as well as the

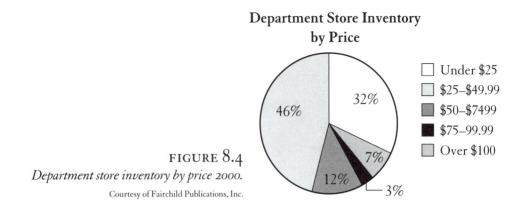

Department Store Inventory by Price

- ☐ Under $25
- ☐ $25–$49.99
- ▨ $50–$7499
- ■ $75–99.99
- ▨ Over $100

46%   32%   7%   12%   3%

FIGURE 8.4
Department store inventory by price 2000.
Courtesy of Fairchild Publications, Inc.

ever-present lipstick, keys, and cash. A unique multifunction capability was recently introduced in the form of backpacks that can be inflated to become impromptu portable stools.

Handbags with multipurpose functions are not new. A similar strategy was prevalent in the mid-1970s, when the handbag industry began capitalizing on the increasing number of working women and their need to be organized. Women also had concerns about safety and the ability to find their keys easily. "No more fumbling in dark hallways," stated one television advertising campaign. Key ring compartments were made for easy access. Variations of multi-pocketed and compartmental handbags were available at virtually every price point. As with all fashions, the organizer style became obsolete and eventually gave way to the drop-in style bag. Now the organizer may be on its way back in fashion.

After the customer has made a selection, salespeople should offer related items to increase selling in multiples. These include cleaning and maintenance products, smaller accessories that go with the purchase, or a second bag that may have been the customer's number two choice. Commissioned employees, or those with quota expectations, often take advantage of add-on sales as a means of increasing personal earnings. For the store, add-on sales are an important part of sales revenue and ultimately, customer satisfaction.

Often, merchandising methods facilitate self-selection, and no salesperson's assistance is needed. However, self-selection service should not translate into understaffed selling floors. Shoplifting problems increase if no employees are available to offer assistance. After closing the sale, salespeople should remove the paper stuffing from the handbags as a courtesy to honest customers and to check for hidden merchandise that shoplifters may have attempted to conceal.

SMALL PERSONAL GOODS

Small personal goods, sometimes called **personal leather goods** or **flat goods,** are small articles that may be hand carried, or carried in pockets or handbags. These goods include billfolds, wallets, key cases, daily planners, credit card cases, eyeglass cases, cell phone cases, cigarette cases, and portfolios. Many companies that began as handbag manufacturers have diversified into personal leather goods and luggage. This expansion into different markets has increased brand awareness among first-time brand buyers, while loyal customers, presold on the brand, appreciate the broadened selection of related goods. A company that plans strategically will retain its **core competency,** that is, continue to produce the products that made the company successful in the first place. For example, Coach Leather Company considers quality handbags as its primary business venture, but it is capitalizing on the success of the handbags and introducing a host of related products, including personal leather goods.

Basic Styles of Small Personal Goods

Following are some of the items categorized as small personal goods (see Figure 8.5):

Billfold Pocket- or purse-sized flat carrier for money bills, credit cards, or small photographs. May be a bi-fold (fold in half) or tri-fold (fold in thirds).

Cell phone case Rectangular shaped to carry a cellular phone. Holes on face of case allow ringing sound to be heard.

Cigarette case Usually ornamental, hard-sided, hinged-top case to hold cigarettes.

Change purse Small pouch with secure closure to hold loose coins.

Credit card case Rectangular, flat, fold-over carrier with multiple slots on each side to hold credit cards.

Document case Rectangular shape with rounded corners and a zipper on three sides, but no handle. Holds a pad of paper.

Eyeglass case Flat, soft-sided pouch into which eyeglasses are slid. May also describe a hard-sided and hinged case that prevents crushing of eyeglasses.

Folio Fold-over flat carrier with flap. May hold business cards, writing pad, and pen.

Key case Small case that secures keys inside a fold-over carrier with a snap. Designed so that only the key in use is outside the case.

Key ring Metal ring on which to hang keys. May have decorative piece or may be part of a key case.

Planner or organizer Similar to a folio, with calendar for daily appointment references.

Portfolio Flat, rectangular case with fold-over flap closure or zipper on three sides. Handles may be stationary or pull out. Portfolio is large in size to accommodate samples of work, such as artwork.

Wallet Another term for a man's billfold or a woman's combination billfold and change purse.

Materials

Small personal goods are often made exclusively of leather or leather combined with textiles or plastics. Popular textile fabrics for these items are usually made of the same fashion fabrics as the season's handbags. Plastic materials may take the form of leather-look vinyls or molded plastics. Some of these accessories may have zippers, snaps, or hooks made of metal or plastic.

FIGURE 8.5
Small personal goods.

Courtesy of Buzz by Jane Fox (cell phone case) and
Fairchild Publications, Inc.

cigarette case

wallet

MERCHANDISING TRENDS AND TECHNIQUES FOR SMALL PERSONAL GOODS

The outlook for the consumption of leather goods is expected to strengthen because of an increase in professional and white-collar employment segments associated with service industries and information systems. Employees of these industries may purchase more leather office supplies, business cases, computer cases, and luggage. Increasing numbers of professional women should stimulate the addition of fashion into these functional products.

Self-selection is frequently the merchandising method used for small personal goods at lower price points. The absence of a knowledgeable salesperson must be overcome by sufficient information provided at the point of sale. Hangtags, packaging, and clearly displayed signage are vital to successfully merchandising a self-selection department.

SELLING SMALL PERSONAL GOODS

Customers often visit the leather-accessories department to purchase a specific style of small personal goods. When purchasing a gift, a customer may have determined a price range, yet have no particular style in mind. A good salesperson asks leading questions to determine the customer's preference of price range, material, and use. Items purchased for the customer's own personal use may be selected on different criteria from those for gift selections. If the customer does not specify a price range, a salesperson should show goods in the medium price range. Based on the customer's reaction, the salesperson can move up or down the price range.

Stores usually lock more expensive small personal leather goods in cases. A salesperson should always be scheduled in or near these cases to ensure proper customer service. A salesperson should show only three items at one time to avoid overwhelming the customer.

As with handbags, much of the price of small personal goods is related to the materials and workmanship. Genuine leather products are usually more expensive, but salespeople should stress to customers that this purchase is an investment that will service the owner's need for several seasons. Some stores offer limited warranties for personal leather goods at higher price points. The warranty may guard against defective parts, such as handles, latches, or hinges.

LUGGAGE

Until the September 11, 2001, terrorist attacks in the United States luggage sales had been increasing each year because of an increased number of travelers. The terrorist attacks had a disproportionately negative impact on the luggage industry. In the aftermath of the attacks, one vendor reported its retail customers experienced a 16-percent sales decrease in September, an 11-percent decrease in October, and an 8- to 9-percent decrease in November. Samsonite Corporation reported a $14 million loss during its fourth quarter 2001 compared to a $6.9 million profit during the fourth quarter 2000.

In late September 2001, the Travel Goods Association launched Safer Travels-Safer World, a global campaign to encourage consumers to resume traveling and be safe travelers. To launch the campaign, the Travel Goods Association enlisted the help of travel goods retailers, manufacturers, distributors, suppliers, national travel organizations, and travel policy makers. Working together, these trade groups heavily promoted travel, including coining the term ***supportive tourists*** when referring to visitors to New York City in spite of concerns over additional terrorist attacks.

The trend in luggage has been toward lightweight, impact-resistant, soft-sided products on roller-blade wheels. The popular handbag fashions and fabrics influence colors and styles in the luggage industry.

Luggage Manufacturing

The outer covering of luggage may be manufactured on a steel frame, similar to handbags, or it may be attached to a heavy cardboard or fiberboard base, which is less durable. Lining materials are typically satin fabrics made of rayon or nylon because of their silk-like hand. Thin leather or suede may also be used to line luggage at higher price points.

Handles and other hardware are important features of luggage because of the abuse luggage suffers during transport. Durable leather and metal handles and trim may be used on pieces that are otherwise completely fabric or vinyl. The best handle hardware is polished brass or

Tech Talk: Rigorous Testing: American Tourister

In the 1970s, Denver-based Samsonite Corporation ran an advertising campaign depicting memorable but unrealistic treatment of luggage to show the durability of its American Tourister line. Television advertisements included a real gorilla manhandling a suitcase, a stick of dynamite exploding near a piece of luggage, luggage dropping out of an airborne plane, and a snow skier sledding down the slopes on luggage. Although these were simply marketing ploys, the truth was and is: Samsonite's American Tourister undergoes sophisticated testing at all stages of product development, calling itself "Worldproof."

Specialized laboratories around the world test the luggage components separately and as an entire system. For example, handles are raised and lowered repeatedly to ensure durability under heavy use. Wheels are tested with cases fully loaded to ensure wearability and impact resistance. Luggage cases are subject to three temperatures: freezing, ambient, and 150 degrees (to simulate the trunk of a car in the desert). Humidity rooms test the fabric and hardware durability under damp atmospheric conditions. The types of tests and the criteria have continually been updated as changes in technology have occurred.

Some of the best testing methods defy sophisticated technology, however. Taxicabs in Singapore have carried luggage in roomy rooftop enclosures, allowing the bags to slide back and forth, simulating an airline cargo hold. According to Bob Onysko of the Samsonite Corporation, "The most rigorous tests are performed by people, not technology." He cited examples in which fully loaded bags were wheeled back and forth through manufacturing plants, and employees were asked to take American Tourister luggage on business trips and travel vacations. Onysko further explained, "Consumers are even more abusive to luggage than machinery tests and airport baggage handlers." Rigorous product testing ensures that consumers can have confidence that each piece of luggage has been style- and end-use tested by real people, not just machinery.

Sources:

A Tough Case to Crack. (Jan 2000). *Advertising Age International,* p. 2.

Beirne, Mike. (Sep. 27, 1999). Samsonite's Strong Suit. *Brandweek,* 40(36), p. 20.

Onysko, Bob. (Sep. 21, 2000). Samsonite Corporation Telephone Interview.

stainless steel that is firmly riveted through the luggage material. Zippers should be heavy duty and have two-way or "self-mending" closings. Wheels must be firmly attached and slightly recessed so they will not be damaged during baggage handling.

Design

Designers are creating highly functional, ergonomic, practical luggage based on fashionable handbag styles. Wheels, retractable handles, padded shoulder straps, multiple compartments, and interior padding to protect electronic equipment are some new design features that accommodate the needs of today's customers. Many of these potential consumers are elderly, female, and business travelers who have higher disposable incomes and a greater likelihood to travel.

In addition to the obvious needs of gender and age, the increasing size of airports has created a need for upright, wheeled, and stackable luggage. Originally designed with ball-shaped wheels, the newer styles feature ball-bearing roller blade wheels with greater durability and less noise under pressure and friction. A four-wheel system, called "zero-weight" provides increased mobility and movement stability to luggage as it is pulled through airport terminals.

Satchels are often selected as carry-on luggage, and the contents may be quite heavy. Wider straps help distribute the weight. Some satchels are designed to sit directly on top of the wheeled, larger upright pieces, attached by snaps or by sliding over the handle of the upright.

Multiple compartments provide business travelers with built-in files. Expansion compartments may include mesh outer pockets for quick and easy access. Removable, padded inserts are used in business travel luggage, such as cases for laptop computers and printers. Once travelers reach their destinations, the padding can be removed, and the traveling case becomes a briefcase or tote.

Production

Consumers' desires for inexpensive luggage translate into overseas production, although the research and development frequently occurs in the United States. Luggage-company buyers often provide the overseas producers with product designs and specifications for luggage that best meet the needs of the company's target customers.

Materials

The trend in materials is to offer lightweight luggage in natural and synthetic fabrics that are inherently water-and-stain repellent or are coated to improve these qualities. Cotton canvas is covered with a vinyl coating for added durability. Other fabrics, like twill, brocade, and tapestry are durable weaves. High tenacity (strong) synthetic fabrics, such as ballistic nylon (used in wearable body armor), are used extensively as luggage materials.

CLASSIFICATIONS OF LUGGAGE

Luggage may be divided into three main categories—hardside, molded, and softside.

Hardside and **semi-hardside luggage** pieces are considered sturdy enough to withstand rough treatment by baggage handlers. Hardside luggage originally included trunks, and was made of leather or fabric over a basswood base. Today, expensive hardside luggage is made of leather and less expensive pieces are made of plastic.

Molded luggage is free of seams and is heat set into a permanent shape. It is more impact resistant than the other categories of luggage because there are no seams that might split.

Softside luggage is appealing to many value-conscious consumers because of its light weight and lower retail prices. It is less durable than hardside luggage, but the introduction of fashion fabrics into the luggage lines has encouraged more frequent purchases. New colors, new fabrics, and new styles at reasonable prices have created regular consumer buying cycles. Every few seasons the softside luggage wears out, but travelers may not object because of the desire to have the latest luggage fashions.

Basic Styles of Luggage

Luggage styles have decreased in size over the last several years. The luggage industry has developed condensed styles, in part to accommodate women and retired travelers. The basic styles, although generally smaller than a few decades ago, have changed more in materials and special features than in design. **Telescoping handles** or **loop strap handles,** wheels, and extra compartments are important features in contemporary luggage. Figure 8.6 shows some popular styles of luggage.

Backpack Compartmentalized carry-all pack, usually nylon. Secured on the back with two wide shoulder straps.

Bellows case Has an expandable, accordion-pleated top to accommodate additional purchases.

Carry-on Small satchel or upright suiter, required by airlines to fit under the passenger's seat or in the enclosed overhead compartment.

Duffle (duffel) bag Softsided and cylindrical or rectangular, with a drawstring or zipper top. May be wheeled or have a long shoulder strap.

Garment bag Softside luggage designed to carry hanging garments and to be hung in a closet by a top hook. May be folded to facilitate carrying by handle or detachable strap. May be wheeled.

Luggage cart Wheeled, collapsible, lightweight metal cart to which baggage is attached for transporting.

Overnight case Originally a small rectangular piece; now any style, usually for short trips.

backpack

duffle bag

garment bag

Pullman

tote

FIGURE 8.6
Popular luggage items.

Pullman, upright, suiter, or boarding case A larger version of the rectangular overnight case, length varying from 24″ to 30″, with inside compartments and often on wheels. The names are often used interchangeably, but a Pullman is usually wider than it is tall, while an upright is usually taller than it is wide.

Steamer trunk Originally for steamship travel, it stands upright with hang rods on one side and drawers on the opposite side. Often features secret hiding places, such as false bottoms or backs, for valuables.

Suiter May be an upright. Folds in half to resemble a suitcase, but is expanded to accommodate folded and hanging clothes; fits up to four suits.

Tote Soft-sided shoulder case, similar in appearance but larger than a tote purse.

Vanity, accessories, or cosmetic case Small, upright, compartmentalized case, often with mirror.

MERCHANDISING TRENDS AND TECHNIQUES FOR LUGGAGE

On the average, consumers buy luggage every seven years, often without having made specific travel plans. At George Washington University, a study of consumer motivations revealed that 70 percent of shoppers had yet to select where they wanted to go. This contradicted the previously held assumption that luggage purchases were made after travel reservations were finalized.

Luggage companies are teaming up with destination marketers to create travel and leisure environments inside stores. Rather than simply having luggage departments, stores are creating adventure-travel sections, complete with getaway promotions and props that simulate the vacation environment. Tropical trees, sailboats, nature soundtracks, and exotic souvenirs decorate the interiors.

Luggage pieces are designed to encourage multiple sales, although each piece may be purchased separately. If consumers don't purchase all the pieces they need at once, they run the risk of being unable to find another matching piece the next season. A typical set of nylon, softsided luggage includes carry-on satchel or tote, duffel, garment bag, small upright suiter on wheels, and large upright suiter on wheels. An added feature of luggage sets is the ability for smaller pieces to be stored inside larger pieces when not in use.

In most advertising, luggage on wheels is a primary feature of the merchandise and accounts for 60 percent of luggage sales. However, according to a *Wall Street Journal* article, the life cycle for wheeled luggage may be on the decline as carry-on-sized luggage becomes increasingly important. "The 'wheelie' has given way to duffels, totes and backpacks in bright colors and casual materials as America's top carry-on." ("Wheeled bags," 2000). The article cites the sales statistics of a leading luggage manufacturing company, Tumi, which reported that sales of soft, non-wheeled luggage showed a 30-percent increase over the previous year's sales, while wheeled luggage showed a 19-percent increase over the previous year's sales. Primary concerns about

---

Airline Carry-on Regulations

Each airline sets its own size limitations for carry-on luggage. Generally, if the outside dimensions of a bag are no greater than 14″ × 9″ × 22″ (including wheels, handles, corner protectors, and full pockets) the bag may be carried on most noncommuter, domestic airlines. Some airlines measure the size of the bag at the security conveyor (x-ray machine) belt, ensuring the carry-on bag fits through a sizing template. Sizer boxes may be located at the baggage check or the terminal gate. Before passengers board, airline personnel may perform a visual inspection of the bag. Carry-on bags in question will be measured for compliance. If a bag is too large, it must be checked.

---

wheeled luggage include the increasing size, which doesn't meet airport regulations, as well as the difficulty travelers have in controlling large, wheeled luggage in airport terminals.

In-Store Retailing

In moderately priced stores, most luggage pieces are softside, and made of fabrics, such as nylon and tapestry. Small-sized leather luggage pieces may be available in moderately priced stores, but larger pieces would be too expensive. More expensive leather luggage sets are carried in specialty stores and at airport stores.

Luggage is usually grouped by brand to encourage sales of multiple items. In some instances, specialty items such as garment bags or backpacks, might be grouped together regardless of the brand, so customers can comparison shop.

Because luggage is not considered an impulse item, it is located on upper floors or away from main entrances. For example, at Macy's 34th Street store in Manhattan, luggage sets and backpacks are located on the ninth floor, whereas handbags, small personal goods, and totes are located on the main floor.

Internet Retailing

Internet marketing is substantial in the luggage industry and offers many advantages over purchasing luggage at brick-and-mortar stores. Internet luggage buyers would need to know of a scheduled trip in advance, allowing enough time for the shipment of their order. The success of Internet retailing may be that Internet shoppers are typically more affluent and may travel more than noninternet users.

Affluence does not mean that consumers are willing to pay high prices for occasional-use luggage. Many of the Internet sites boast discounted prices or free shipping as ways to encourage online buying. An added incentive might be the absence of a state sales tax if the Internet company has no retail outlet in the customer's state of residence.

Price is not the only reason for buying online. Detailed descriptions, including sizes, special features, and enlarged visuals, allow potential customers to make educated decisions about purchasing luggage. Often the copy provided on the Web site is more detailed than a part-time luggage salesperson in a retail store could provide. In addition, all of the available colors are offered, some of which a retail store might not be able to accommodate due to the limited selling floor area.

Selling Luggage

Customers' motives for buying luggage vary. Some may desire fashion over durability, but still expect the luggage to withstand normal wear and tear during traveling. The methods for selling luggage are much the same as for handbags and personal leather goods.

Considerable price differences exist among grades of luggage. The **best-quality luggage** may be three to five times higher in price than luggage considered to be **better quality.** Durability is the primary factor on which luggage is graded, although fashion is also important. Some of the best-quality luggage brands available on the market are Hartmann, Tumi, and Andiamo.

A luggage buyer would benefit from comparing a best-quality bag with a better-quality bag. Both visible and hidden details should be evaluated. Some important quality components of durable luggage are:

- Durable outside covering, stain resistant
- Nylon-thread stitching
- Double-riveted lift points
- Bar tacking at all key stress points
- Retractable handle, rather than exposed strap handle

Consumers buy luggage for function and hassle-free traveling, rather than simply for show. Even the most fashionable luggage is a nightmare if the luggage wheels are dragging against the frame while being rolled through an airport terminal.

BELTS

When told "girdles are belts" and "braces are suspenders," today's student of fashion may wonder about the evolution of words. Both belts and braces serve similar purposes, which are primarily to keep clothing at the natural waistline. The items are not mutually exclusive each season, but an increase in the popularity of one item usually causes a decrease in the popularity of the other item. Belts tend to have had greater acceptance among wearers than suspenders.

Belt fashions are subordinate to ready-to-wear fashions. When nipped waists are popular, the waist becomes a focal point, and belts gain in popularity. A dropped- or raised-waistline fashion era may cause a significant decrease in belt sales for a few seasons. For the men's wear market, belts remain a fairly stable accessories item, while the popularity of belts in the children's wear industry follows women's fashion trends.

Belt Manufacturing

The men's wear industry offers a choice of belts or braces, while the women's wear industry manufactures primarily belts. Braces, or suspenders, are worn mostly by men who have trouble holding a belt at their natural waistline or by men interested in projecting their own personal style. Occasionally, the women's industry will introduce suspenders as a seasonal fashion accessory. The children's wear industry offers both belts and suspenders.

Belt manufacturers are said to be in the **cut-up trade** if they produce belts that are sold as part of an item of apparel, for example a self-belt made of the same fabric as a dress. Belts sold as separate accessories are produced in the **rack trade.**

Design

Belts styles range from narrow leather or chain-link belts to wide, corselet styles. Belts are designed to complement fashionable apparel or to be the focal point enhanced by apparel. They may be created to serve a functional or decorative need, and frequently they serve both.

Belt designs are sketched on paper or CAD (computer-aided design) systems and color, texture, and buckle materials are selected. Samples are made to ensure the design is workable. A line is created of the most marketable pieces from the selection of samples.

Production

Once a collection is identified, belt samples are taken to market and shown to accessories buyers. Orders are processed, and production begins. Some of the more basic belt styles may be reordered on an automatic-replenishment cycle, while fashion belts change seasonally, and re-orders may not be desirable.

Materials

Belts are made of the same materials found in footwear, but also of metal, plastic, wood, ribbon, or fashion fabric. Leathers of all kinds, most commonly cattle hide, but including reptile and exotic, are materials for the more expensive belts. Leather imitations, such as polyurethane and microfibers, are frequently produced into belts in the moderate- and lower-price zones.

Basic Styles of Belts

Belts are available in many styles to meet needs for fashion and function (see Figure 8.7).

Adjustable Sliding buckle or multiple buckle holes allow fitting to a variety of waist sizes.
Bandolier Worn diagonally across one shoulder and around the torso.

Belt bag, fanny pack, or **waist belt** Belt/pouch combination, zippered or snap closure. Adjustable belt straps to fit various waist sizes. Frequently made of nylon or canvas.

Boy Scout Sliding buckle on a durable fabric (such as twill).

Braid A variety of styles and materials with interwoven strips resembling a multiple strand braid.

Buckle Most often made of leather, the buckle belt may be braided, studded, tooled, or ornamented. Varied width, usually 1 to 3 inches. For men's wear, the most common width is 1 1/2 to 1 3/4 inches. The buckle fastener is often gold or silver tone, plastic, or leather covered. May have a belt loop through which the tail of the belt passes and is held in place.

Cartridge Originally to hold ammunition, such as bullets, now a decorative belt that features looped cylinders around the length of the belt.

Chain link More decorative than functional. Usually metal or plastic interlocking links, although other materials may be used.

Cinch Tight, restrictive belt that is supposed to give the appearance of a small waistline. May be elasticized for comfort.

Contour A belt that curves slightly upward, fitting closely above hips and around the natural waistline.

Corset or **corselet** A narrow version of the corset with laces or buckles to cinch the natural waistline creating the illusion of an hourglass figure shape. Sometimes called the "Merry Widow" corselet.

Cummerbund A horizontally pleated or flat-front fabric belt worn with formal wear, such as men's tuxedos. May be a contrasting color to the suit. Satin is the common fabric, but leather may also be used.

Fishscale Metallic belts (often stretch) with small gold, silver, or iridescent scales.

Obi A wide fabric sash with origins in Japan. Originally worn over a kimono, but has been adapted to western dress. The long sash (often over ten feet in length) is wrapped numerous times around the waist and arranged in bow-like folds in the back.

Polo Wider in front than sides and back, it is front-closed with one or two small straps inserted into small buckles.

Rope Corded yarns twisted to create a rope. The ends may be tied in a square knot, looped, or joined with a clasp.

Sash Often made of self-fabric or complementary colored ribbons; the sash is loosely tied in a square knot.

Self Made of the same fabric as the garment. Usually an inexpensive accessory offered by the apparel manufacturer. A good choice for those who want to camouflage their waist, as it does not call attention to the waistline. Fashion experts recommend that a leather belt replace the manufacturer's self belt. Customers should cut off the temporary thread belt loops on apparel and wear the belt at their natural waistline.

Skinny Less than 1/2 inch in width and made of leather or simulated leather or stretch metal.

Stretch An elasticized belt containing spandex, worn at the natural waistline. May be metallic fishscale design or simple knit.

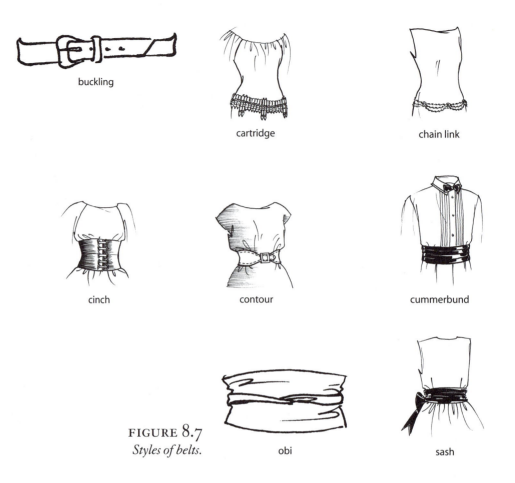

FIGURE 8.7
Styles of belts.

Suspender or **braces** Support straps that button (or clip) to the inside front waistband of the trousers and extend over the shoulders in a Y pattern, ending at the center back waistline. Upscale men's clothiers are disdainful of clip-on or elasticized suspenders, preferring rayon or silk fabric with leather fittings and adjustable brass levers.

Western or **cowboy** Tooled leather belt with ornamental buckle, often featuring a gold-and silver-toned rodeo sport, such as barrel racing or bull riding. The wearer's first name may be tooled across the center back of the belt.

Belt Sizes

Belts for men are usually sized according to the waist measurement. Women's belts may be sized by waist or classified by small, medium, large, or extra large. Some belts, especially stretch or adjustable, may be one-size-fits-all.

A man's small size is 30 to 32 inches, a medium is 34 to 36 inches, a large is 38 to 40 inches, and an extra large is 42 to 44 inches. Women's belt lengths span the 22- to 32-inch range or are sized to the garment if the manufacturer provides a matching belt with the apparel. A customer should choose a belt that can be fastened at the middle hole, or the end of the belt so that it fits just under the first belt loop.

Care of Belts

Belts should be rolled and stored flat in a drawer or hung on hangers. They should never be folded. If the belt is smooth leather or suede, proper leather care procedures should be followed, including polishing or buffing. A damp cloth should be used to wipe patent leather clean. Fabric belts should be hand washed or dry-cleaned. Fabric belts may get dingy, and customers may prefer to substitute a good-quality leather belt and discard the inexpensive self belt.

MERCHANDISING TRENDS AND TECHNIQUES FOR BELTS

Department stores dominate the handbag-market sales, but specialty stores account for the bulk of belt sales. Table 8.7 shows the percent of sales of women's belts by type of store for 1999. The greatest volume of women's belt sales occurs in specialty stores with 42 percent of total belt sales.

Department stores usually offer a large selection of women's belts on the main floor accessories department. The advantage of this merchandising technique is that customers can easily locate a complete assortment of belts from which to choose. Because color is the primary criterion on which a belt purchase is made, this advantage is valuable to the hurried, self-selection shopper.

Specialty stores may merchandise belts as a group or with related apparel for a total look. Shoppers may have to rely on a salesperson for assistance in locating belts if they are displayed throughout the store. The advantage to the store is the likelihood that customers will purchase an entire ensemble rather than making a single-item purchase.

Both types of merchandising are valuable and desired by today's customers. A store manager should have a thorough understanding of the target customers' preferences before deciding which merchandising method to use.

TABLE 8.7

Percent of Women's Belts Sales by Store Classification for 1999

Store Classification	Percent of Total Sales
Specialty Stores	42%
Department Stores	17%
Major Chains	11%
Discount Stores	11%
Other Stores	19%

Source: Retail Sales Hit New Highs. (Apr. 24, 2000). Advertising Supplement, *Women's Wear Daily,* p. 12. Courtesy of Fairchild Publications, Inc.

Adequate illumination is very important near a belt display fixture. The similarity between the navy and black colors makes color distinction difficult. Retailers should make efforts to affix color name labels to belts of questionable color. When using belts in apparel displays, stores should offer a selection of three belts cinched around the waist of the dress form or mannequin. This display technique makes a greater visual impact and satisfies a greater number of customers.

Selling Belts

Belts in women's wear are generally sold as self-selection items. In men's wear, salespeople often select two or three belts in appropriate colors from which customers can choose. Salespeople should ask customers whether they prefer gold- or silver-tone buckles. Customers should consider the jewelry color they will be wearing and match the metal buckle color to their jewelry. Consideration should be given to the width of the belt so it does not exceed the width of the belt loops.

Price and Value

The most common pricing factor is the materials used in the belt. Genuine-leather belts have the longest life span, especially if they are leather lined. Exotic leathers may be less durable, but they are more expensive because of their rarity. Some leather belts are lined with a cardboard-like backing, which eventually cracks and becomes unsightly, even though the leather face of the belt is still usable.

Most self-belts that are attached to apparel are inexpensive and should be replaced with a leather belt. A customer may prefer the self-belt because it does not draw attention to the waistline, but the life span of a manufacturer-provided belt is much shorter than the life of the garment. A customer should be encouraged to purchase a good-quality leather belt in a color that matches the dominant color scheme of the outfit.

The cost of the buckle may also significantly affect the price of a belt. Gold-plated buckles may lose the gold-tone color through rubbing and normal wear. A brass buckle is less likely to lose the gold metallic tone. In contrast, silver-tone metal buckles usually do not reveal a different color underneath as they show signs of wear.

SUMMARY

- Handbags account for 50 percent of all accessories sales. The fashion industry has responded to this demand by introducing a bag for almost every need. Handbags, backpacks, belt packs, luggage, and small personal goods are offered in several styles for a variety of end uses.

- Although handbags are used primarily by women, men are heavy users of backpacks, luggage, small personal goods, and belts.

- Function *and* fashion are important in this accessories category. Considered "pieces of equipment," these accessories must fit the lifestyle of the end user.

- Business professionals are a large group of purchasers of small personal goods; business professionals and retirees purchase luggage; and women of all ages purchase handbags.

- Handbags, luggage, and small personal goods may be manufactured with or without frames. The frames, linings, handles, closures, gussets, and trimmings should be durable for the life of the accessory.

- For smaller items, including belts, leather is the material of choice for outer coverings and linings; for larger items, plastics and fabrics are suitable substitutes and usually lighter in weight than most leathers.

- Many designers of ready-to-wear are offering handbag accessories as part of their collections. They have determined that related accessories, such as handbags, are an extension of women's fashions and serve to increase market shares.

- Designers and manufacturers of handbags at higher price points are plagued with a problem of knockoffs at lower price points. In the United States, as long as the registered trademarks are not copied, the actual style may legally be a line-for-line copy.

- Handbag production begins with a sample in muslin or felt. Outer coverings may be hand cut by individual layers or die, or laser cut in multiple layers. Some accessories may be molded from plastic or woven or knitted as pieces without cutting separate parts.

- The care procedures for handbags, luggage, leather goods, and belts are similar to those of shoes of the same materials.

- As with other accessories categories, much of the production of handbags, luggage, personal leather goods, and belts is performed offshore, especially in China. Manufacturers who choose domestic production do so because of the convenience and quicker production schedules.

- Handbags are sold in a variety of retail outlets. Department stores account for more than one third of handbags sales, while chain and discount stores combined account for 26 percent of the sales. Duty-free and specialty shops in airports offer prestigious handbag brands to international customers.

- Research has shown that handbags are not primarily an impulse-purchase item. Shoppers intentionally enter the accessories department with a specific purchase in mind. To attract the most attention, retailers should merchandise according to themes, such as colors, prints, lifestyles, or trends.

- Most catalog retailers offer handbags, small personal goods, and belts as part of a total shopping concept.

- For those brick-and-mortar retailers who have Internet shopping sites, the Web site should reflect the store image and the product positioning.

- The most common selling price range for handbags is between $25 and $50. The materials used determine much of the retail price. Workmanship is also an important factor in the pricing.
- Luggage categories include hardside, molded, and softside. The number of luggage styles being offered has increased, but the dimensions of luggage have decreased.
- Although no luggage is government approved, most domestic airlines have set maximum sizes for carry-on luggage.
- Consumers purchase luggage before finalizing travel plans. Retailers and travel agents are teaming up to create adventure travel promotions in stores.
- Consumers usually purchase multiple pieces of luggage from a set from a traditional retailer, but Internet Web sites are gaining popularity. Wheeled luggage is currently popular.
- Quality and prices vary significantly among brands of luggage; price, quality, fashion, or function may be a consumer's primary motivation.
- Belts and suspenders serve a functional purpose but may be decorative as well. Traditionally, belts have been significantly more popular than suspenders. Belt widths range from the narrow "skinny" belt to the wide "corselet" belt.
- Belts are produced much like other leather accessories and are made of many of the same materials as shoes and handbags. Leather is considered the best material.
- Belts are usually sized according to a person's waist measurement. They should be rolled for storage or hung on belt hangers.
- Care for belts is similar to the care of shoes and handbags.
- The majority of handbags are sold in department stores. Most belts are sold in specialty stores.
- In all retail settings, belts sell most successfully when they are merchandised as part of a "total look."
- Lighting levels must be high enough for customers to differentiate the colors of darker belts.

TERMS FOR REVIEW

add-on sales	better-quality luggage	cell phone case
adjustable belt	billfold	chain link belt
backpack	Boy Scout belt	change purse
bandolier belt	braid belt	cigarette case
barrel-top trunk	branded Web sites	cinch belt
bellows case	buckle belt	contour belt
belt bag (fanny pack,	budget bag	core competency
waist belt)	carry-on	corset (corselet) belt
best-quality luggage	cartridge belt	credit card case

cummerbund

cut-up trade

document and deed boxes

document case

duffle (duffel) bag

eyeglass case

fastener (closure)

fishscale belt

flat goods

folio

frame

garment bag

girdle

gusset

handbag themes

handles

hardside luggage

impulse items

investment handbags

key case

key ring

knockoff (copycat designing)

lining

loop strap handles

luggage cart

male bag

mass customization

mass personalization

molded luggage

obi belt

outer covering

overnight case

padding

Peacock Era

personal leather goods

planned purchases

planner (organizer)

pockets

polo belt

Pontova

portfolio

Pullman (upright, suiter, or
    boarding case)

rack trade

rope belt

sash belt

self belt

semi-hardside luggage

skinny belt

small personal goods

softside luggage

steamer trunk

stretch belt

suiter

supportive tourists

suspenders (braces)

telescoping handles

total look concept

tote

Toyo

travel retailers

trend themes

trimmings

underlining

vanity (accessories, cosmetic)
    case

wallet

western (cowboy)

REVIEW QUESTIONS

1. How have handbags evolved into status symbols?
2. In what ways do handbags reflect the lifestyle of their owners?
3. What are some popular handbag materials?
4. What are the components of a handbag?
5. When purchasing a handbag, what are some durability considerations?
6. Why are ready-to-wear designers branching into handbag and small personal goods?
7. What is meant by the merchandising concept "total look"?
8. What themes might a retailer use to merchandise a handbag and small personal goods department?
9. How do Internet Web sites selling handbags and luggage differ from traditional brick-and-mortar retail establishments?
10. What are some criteria that determine the retail prices of handbags, luggage, small personal goods, and belts?
11. In what ways have manufacturers made luggage more functional?
12. What are some luggage trends?

13. How are belt styles dependent on ready-to-wear fashions?

14. What are some important merchandising methods for selling belts, and when is each appropriate?

KNOWLEDGE APPLICATIONS

1. Sketch a design for a functional handbag that would fit the needs of a college student (or some other target customer). Design both the interior and exterior of the handbag. Describe the materials and hardware to be used.

2. Assume you are the manager of a handbag, luggage, small personal goods, or belt department that will be opening soon. Choose price points, season, styles, and fashion image. Locate a few magazine pictures of your merchandise category for visual aids. You want to find the best way to merchandise your inventory. With partners, develop a merchandise plan. What will be your merchandising theme? How will you subdivide the department? Describe how the walls and fixtures will look.

3. Participate in a field trip to a local department or specialty store and talk to the store manager about one or more of the accessories in this chapter.

4. Visit a handbag or luggage manufacturing company, or teleconference with a designer.

5. Visit a store with a handbag, personal leather goods, luggage, or belt department. Evaluate using the following criteria: price ranges, merchandising techniques (materials, colors, prints, or brands), and country of origin.

6. Using several mail-order catalogs or fashion magazines, cut out all handbags that are featured. Label and group according to style. Analyze your findings based on most/least popular styles, materials, colors, and handles. Calculate percentages and create pie charts on the computer depicting these percentages. Predict the fashion cycle emphasis for the season.

CHAPTER 9

SOCKS AND HOSIERY

Louis XVI, the French monarch was condemned to death by his country's revolutionary tribunal. On a cold and wet January 21, 1793, the king arose at 5:00 a.m. to prepare himself for his death sentence. "Give me another pair of stockings, these aren't suitable!" he said to his servant as he painstakingly dressed for his two-hour carriage ride to the guillotine. "These are for a formal reception…give me a more sober pair, this morning they honour me with a very solemn ceremony!"

—The History of Hosiery: a Secret and Sensual Accessory. Retrieved June 7, 2002, from
http://www.fast-italy.com

A BRIEF HISTORY OF SOCKS AND HOSIERY

LEG COVERINGS WERE PROBABLY FIRST WORN IN COOLER CLIMATES FOR WARMTH OR PROTECtion from the elements, rather than as a decorative accessory. One of the earliest types of legwear was strips of fur, leather, or cloth (probably cotton, wool, or linen) wound spirally around the lower leg and fastened under the knee. Greek and Roman soldiers called these strips of cloth **tibiales** and held them in place with leather straps and laces. Although rare in warmer climates, two ancient Egyptian and Assyrian relief carvings from approximately 1470 B.C. and 705 B.C. depict men wearing high quilted or knitted stockings. A pair of woven trousers, with attached foot, was discovered in the bogs of Germany dating from the first to third centuries A.D. Except for the belt loops, the trousers look crudely similar to a modern pair of tights. In some instances the hose were soled in leather, making them serve a dual purpose of a leg covering and a shoe.

Later, the footwear became more sock-like, but lacked the elasticized fit associated with contemporary socks. As fabric-making skills progressed, the fit of legwear improved. The introduction of knitting in the fourth century A.D. was a key to the success of close-fitting hosiery.

By the 11th century A.D., gartered hosiery was depicted in artwork in decorative and colorful patterns.

The introduction of armor for men required close-fitting undergarments to protect the knight from the sharp edges of the metal. Hosiery was cut to extend to a point at the front center of the thigh and was attached to long, fitted tunics called **pourpoints.** To hold up the hose, laces, or points were attached to the lower front edges of the pourpoint lining, and garters were worn below the knee to further secure the hose.

Women's legwear fashions are more difficult to chronicle because secondary sources like artwork rarely depict women's feet under their long skirts. However, documentation does show that for centuries women in cooler climates wore gartered stockings, paralleling the hosiery worn by men.

During the 14th century, the emphasis on nobility differentiation through heraldic devices and colors affected the legwear. Each noble had a unique coat of arms with a logo that would appear on all the regalia. A noble wife or daughter would adopt the symbol of her father and her husband, thus wearing costumes featuring both sets of patterns and colors. Hosiery was affected by this dual loyalty, and men and women adopted **parti-colored hose,** the left leg of one color and the right leg of a different color.

The Renaissance is important to legwear-fashion historians because hosiery was dyed in beautiful colors and elaborately embroidered. Many specialty fibers, including silk, rabbit's fur, angora, alpaca, and cashmere, were used to knit hosiery .

In the latter 18th through the early 20th centuries, embroidered designs decorated the upper foot and ankles of women's stockings. Better hosiery was made of knitted silk, while less expensive hosiery was made of cotton. Noblewomen wore elegant stockings with embroidery and lace that were held up with garters and garter belts. The French Empress Josephine set the fashion of wearing colored silk stockings in shades of red, white, and blue. However, usually stocking colors were basic, including black, off-white, and beige. The first fishnet stockings appeared around 1830.

The 1939 World's Fair in New York City featured the Du Pont pavilion with several glamorous models wearing nylon, the "synthetic wonder fiber," in the form of hosiery (see Figure 9.1). Women stood in long lines, three deep, to purchase these nylon stockings on the day of their debut in stores. By one o'clock, the supply of stockings, selling for $1.15 to $1.35 per pair, was exhausted.

The popularity of nylon stockings didn't wane, but the supply was short-lived. The need for nylon fibers during World Wart II soon exhausted the entire supply, making nylon stockings a precious commodity. Nylon production was devoted entirely to the war effort for parachutes, tents, tires, and cords. Some women, desperate for stockings, made do with leg makeup and an eyeliner pencil (for drawing the lengthwise seam up the back of the legs). One wartime survey of women showed the second-most sought after wartime item was a man, right behind the first place item—nylon stockings.

Socks were an important substitution during the absence of hosiery. The 1940s and 1950s are remembered for **bobby socks,** a turned-down anklet. Teenagers, especially, adopted this fashion that was worn with dresses, skirts, or pants.

A two-ton model of Marie Wilson's leg is unveiled by a Los Angeles hosiery shop. The actress is hoisted skyward for comparison. The modern fibre was for modern lifestyles. *Better Living*, 1950.

Hagley Museum and Library, Wilmington, Delaware

FIGURE 9.1
Display for Du Pont's nylon hosiery.
Courtesy of Du Pont.

Seamed stockings (seams up the center back of the legs) held up by garter belts continued to be in demand through the 1950s, until the invention of pantyhose in the 1960s. A gradual shortening of hemlines created a problem when the skirts became so short the garters were visible. The alternative, **pantyhose,** a combination of stockings and the panty, became a staple of every woman's wardrobe. By 1961, pantyhose were featured in the Sears & Roebuck mail-order catalog.

The women's movement of the 1970s made it acceptable for women to wear pants for work, for leisure, and even for church (a divisive battle). Legwear designers responded to women's changing needs by creating **knee-high hosiery,** which evolved into today's **trouser socks.** The women's movement also influenced women to discard restrictive undergarments, including girdles. Concern over tummy bulges did not die, however, and **spandex,** an elastic fiber already used in socks and hosiery tops, became the most important component of **control top hosiery.**

One marketing problem during the 1970s that continues today has been the customer's perception that few differences exist among brands. This makes price a critical factor in the success of brands. L'eggs brand hosiery created a unique selling proposition—inexpensive hosiery in an egg-shaped package. To date no other legwear manufacturer has matched the creative genius and success of the original L'eggs packaging.

INTRODUCTION TO SOCKS AND HOSIERY

Socks and hosiery are classified by the amount of leg coverage as well as unique characteristics, such as panty style, texture, fiber, and performance characteristics. Basic styles range from simple foot coverings to styles covering the entire leg. Because the socks and hosiery business is so competitive, many manufacturers attempt to build brand loyalty through national advertising and point-of-sale marketing. In 1999, *Women's Wear Daily* commissioned the NPD Group, an independent marketing research group, to conduct a survey of the 100 most recognizable women's brands. A cross section of 1,458 United States women responded with their opinions on which fashion brands were most recognizable. Three of the top four 100 most recognizable brands were legwear brands. Behind the number-one ranked Timex, were L'eggs, Hanes Hosiery, and Hanes Her Way (which included socks).

Socks and Hosiery Manufacturing

Manufacturers of socks and hosiery are as concerned with function as they are with fashion. Designs may be the fashion focal point, such as fishnet hosiery, or they may be subordinate to apparel, such as low-rise waistbands to accommodate hip hugger styles. Sock and hosiery designs, such as support hosiery or bacteria-controlling athletic socks, may also improve comfort for the wearer.

Sock and hosiery production is primarily an automated process, with very little hand labor required. Because it is not a labor-intensive industry, manufacturing can take place domestically. However, many developing countries with low labor costs produce cotton socks because about 80 percent of these countries also produce cotton commercially.

The materials used in sock and hosiery manufacturing depends on the end use. In addition to cotton, socks can be manufactured using synthetic fibers, such as acrylic, polyester, wool, or rayon. Imports of synthetic-fiber socks grew 22 percent in 2001, especially those from Taiwan. Hosiery is most often made of nylon and spandex, but other fibers like cotton, rayon, or silk are occasionally used.

Design

In recent years hosiery designers have been inspired by retro fashion trends. Designers and manufacturers agree there has been a return to women's legs as a fashion focal point (see Figure 9.2). Designers have offered patterned opaques, sheers, and fishnets hosiery to make fashion statements with the legs.

However, sales of legwear have not kept pace with sales of other accessory products. To many women, just the thought of donning a pair of pantyhose makes them opt for a pair of pants. With this consumer concern in mind, legwear manufacturers are turning to the cosmetic and skin-care industry for ideas. Words like *age defying, rejuvenating, anticellulite, body enhancing,* and *energizing* are making their way into the sock and hosiery industry. This concept is called **novelty wellness** and has become a new industry buzzword. Designers are creating antistress pantyhose enriched with plant extracts. Topical or digestible healing agents, such as aloe, ginkgo biloba, ginseng, and green tea are intended to relieve fatigue in legs. Floral, fruit-patterned, and scented socks have been introduced for the younger markets, and manufacturers

FIGURE 9.2
Du Pont's Tactel nylon hosiery advertisement.
Courtesy of Du Pont

are increasing the knee-sock offerings to meet a growing demand. Leg-softening aloe vera extract or rosemary and apricot moisturizers are being implanted into hosiery as tiny, scented, moisturizing beads. These are released through friction, as the tights move against the legs. To reinforce the moisturizing notion, the hosiery packaging includes the image of a moisturizing tube.

To boost sales in what is a tired, saturated legwear market, designers have offered innovative style designs. Thong-toed sheers, toeless sheers, and nonslip pantyhose are a few of the innovative designs in the sheer market. The nonslip sheers provide traction for sandals and slingback pumps. The soles are printed with transparent silicon dots to improve traction.

For men's socks, manufacturers are increasing their lines of casual dress socks, which are thinner than traditional casual socks, but not as silky as microfiber dress socks. The socks were designed to complement the increasingly dressy men's sportswear lines.

A slightly different technological approach to legwear has been the introduction of "power socks" by Adidas, a tight fitting, over-the-calf sock designed to compress leg muscles. The **graduated compression** reduces muscle oscillation during running and stimulates circulation. Fashionably similar to Britney Spears's music video knee socks, this accessory was designed to increase the runner's stamina (see Figure 9.3).

These socks were touted as a piece of equipment that improve performance and are part of Adidas's energy-maintenance concept, which involves studying the movements in various track and field events. Adidas did not invent compression hosiery, however. Graduated-compression

FIGURE 9.3
*British runner Paula Radcliffe
wearing Adidas power socks with
graduated compression.*
Courtesy of Fairchild Publications, Inc.

hosiery has been a feature of support hosiery marketed to aging women for many years. L'eggs Sheer Energy hosiery is actually a close relative of support hosiery, but it is marketed to a broader audience of women.

Retailers are open to novelty and innovation in legwear because basic collections have reached market saturation. With the technology available to chemically alter legwear, women can hope that one day hosiery manufacturers will create legwear fashions containing traces of depilatory products, so women can maintain the feel of smoothly shaven legs without using razors.

Production

Most hosiery is spirally knitted on a circular knitting machine that produces seamless legwear. **Full-fashioned hosiery** involves the dropping or adding of knit stitches during production to create a foot and leg shape. This hosiery is **boarded**—a permanent heat-setting operation on a metal leg form—producing hosiery that resembles a leg shape when removed from the package.

Two terms, *knitting gauge* and *denier,* are descriptive terms in hosiery production. **Knitting gauge** describes the distance between the needles on a knitting machine, referred to as 45- or 60-gauge knit. On a 60-gauge machine there are 60 needles to 1 1/2 inches, which is more closely knit than a 45-gauge knit. **Denier** refers to the ratio of weight-per-length of the yarn. Generally, hosiery with a lower denier contains lighter and finer yarns and is more sheer. Higher denier yarns often have more durability and are usually more opaque.

Materials

The widespread use of **microfibers** (very fine yarn filaments) in the hosiery industry has greatly improved the silky feel of hosiery. Microfibers lend themselves to very sheer looks, which have become increasingly popular for legwear fashions. Nylon microfibers are widely used in the making of lightweight, comfortable, and durable hosiery.

Hosiery manufacturers occasionally use absorbent fibers, such as cotton or rayon, to improve comfort. Cotton is often a part of the panty portion of the hosiery, and rayon can be manufactured into tights to allow the skin to breathe.

Fiber selection for socks is usually much broader than those used for hosiery. Fibers used alone or blended in socks include cotton, silk, wool, rayon, polyamide, acrylic, polyester, nylon, and spandex. Manufacturers hope consumers will perceive an added value from specialty and performance fibers. **Specialty fibers** include organic cotton, wool, and silk, while **performance fibers** include **antibacterial** (those that reduce bacteria and smelly socks) and wicking fibers. **Wicking** is a process in which perspiration travels along the length of the fiber away from the feet toward the surface of the sock where it evaporates, rather than being absorbed into the fibers. This is especially valuable in sports socks and is a characteristic of acrylic and some polyester fibers. Some manufactured fibers are hollow and absorb perspiration moisture into the center of the fiber. This fiber-construction method keeps the moisture away from the feet.

Manufacturers provide attractive and informative packaging for performance fiber socks to entice customers to buy. These socks may be priced as much as 50 percent higher than regular sport socks.

The Acrylic Council (www.fabriclink.com/acryliccouncil/SOCK/Home.html), which promotes the use of acrylic fibers in many consumer products, offers buying tips for selecting socks for specific sporting activities. Socks for aerobics, basketball, cycling, golf, hiking, running, skiing, tennis, and walking are described in relation to thickness and cushioning needed during these activities. A similar Web site maintained by The Hosiery Association (www.nahm.com) outlines appropriate sock choices based on style, fiber content, special finishes, and end uses.

Natural fibers, such wool and cotton, lack the elasticity of nylon but make a strong fashion statement to a select group of customers. Product developers have attempted to create the look of natural luxury fibers, but in a well-fitted and machine-washable product. One company, Ilux, offered cashmere, mohair, and merino wool socks with a special finish, which made them machine washable.

Metallic threads, such as Lurex®, are popular for evening legwear and the young teen or tween market. Additionally, texturized yarns and appliqués are ornamental materials used in the manufacture of tween legwear.

Classifications of Socks and Hosiery

Common styles of socks and hosiery include the following (see Figure 9.4):

Footies Socks or hosiery ending under the ankle, minimally visible at the shoe tops. Also labeled by specific sports, such as golf socks or tennis socks.

Anklets or socklets Socks with small, turned-down cuffs covering just the ankle.

Bobby socks Heavy cuffed anklet popular for girls in the 1940s and 1950s; periodic fashion revivals.

Crew Socks reaching mid-calf; usually a ribbed knit for elasticity.

Hiking Crew-style socks with thick ribs to protect lower legs from chafing under high-topped hiking boots.

Over-the-calf Common in men's wear; reaches almost to the knee so skin doesn't show when men are seated.

Tube socks Hosiery knit in the shape of a tube, without a knit-in heel. Primarily used as men's and boy's spectator athletic socks.

Knee-highs or trouser socks Usually women's socks or hosiery reaching up to the knee; worn with slacks. Colors range from sheer nude to solid colors and decorative patterns.

Over-the-knee socks Women's socks or hosiery covering the knee.

Leg warmers Originally worn by dancers to prevent leg cramps, this bulky, ankle-to-thigh knit tube became a fashion item during the 1980s. Recently reintroduced in a thinner fabric.

Thigh-highs An alternative to pantyhose reaching only to the mid-thigh. Lacy, elasticized band at top keeps the hose in position.

Leg-highs Slightly longer (two to three inches) than thigh highs, with microfiber bands rather than lace.

Stockings The original style from which most hosiery was adapted. Similar to thigh high hosiery, but without the elasticized top. Instead, elastic bands or **garters,** a clasp secured to lingerie, are attached to the upper stocking to hold it in place.

Pantyhose Stockings and panty knitted as a single unit. Popularized in the 1960s when skirt hemlines became shorter.

Tights Opaque filling-knit pantyhose worn for dance, exercise, or ready-to-wear in cold temperatures.

Body stocking Sold in hosiery and lingerie departments. Covers bust to toes; usually lace and sheer combinations.

Basic Terminology of Socks and Hosiery

An extensive vocabulary describes the practical and decorative features of socks and hosiery.

Demi-toe Reinforced toe and nude, sheer heel. Worn with open-backed shoes like slingback pumps.

footies

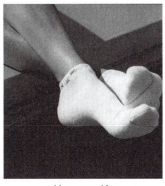

anklets or socklets

crew socks

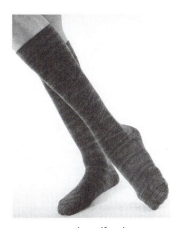

over-the-calf socks

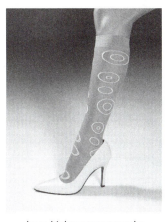

knee-highs or trouser socks

over-the-knee socks

thigh highs

tights

FIGURE 9.4
Basic styles of socks and hosiery.
Courtesy of Fairchild Publications, Inc.

Fishnet Characterized by a diamond net pattern created as a raschel knit, ranging from small to large.

Boy cut Panty portion drops slightly down on thighs, resembling a pair of short shorts.

French cut Panty portion is cut high on the sides of the thighs, giving the illusion of longer legs.

Maternity Expansive front panel for pregnant women and compression support to help circulation in the legs.

Opaque Heavier than sheer hosiery, but thinner than tights; usually worn in cooler seasons.

Reinforced toes or heels Heavier-gauge yarns in toes or heels to prevent punctures or holes forming in these high-stress areas.

Run-resistant or no-run Will not develop "runners" but may develop holes. Usually thicker and sturdier yarns.

Sandalfoot Sheer toe and heel; not reinforced. Also available with a two-part foot; a piece separates the big toe from the four smaller toes to accommodate a between-the-toes sandal.

Sheer Lightweight; of very fine, fragile yarns.

Sheer-to-waist Sheer fabric from toes to waistband; no reinforced areas.

Support Graduated compression helps prevent leg fatigue by gently massaging during movement; usually contains additional spandex.

Toe socks Decorative (often horizontal striped) socks with individual components for each toe, similar to gloves for the feet (see Figure 9.5).

Care of Socks and Hosiery

Most socks can and should be machine washed on the warmest water tolerated by the fiber content. Wool socks should not be washed in hot water because of the possibility of felting (irreversible shrinkage). However, washable woolens are available, and customers should closely

FIGURE 9.5
Toe socks.
Courtesy of Fairchild Publications, Inc.

follow care labels. Cotton, acrylic, nylon, and polyester socks can tolerate high temperatures that may be necessary for thorough cleaning. Chlorine bleaches damage spandex, the elastic fiber used in sock tops and hosiery. Nonchlorine bleaches are suitable for socks. Most socks, except woolens, can be dried in automatic clothes dryers.

Most hosiery products are more delicate than socks and require either warm water hand washing or delicate cycle machine washing. Open-weave net hosiery bags (or a tied pillowcase) are good choices for machine laundering to prevent snagging the fibers. Hosiery should be line dried.

THE GLOBAL SOCKS AND HOSIERY INDUSTRIES

Socks and hosiery are a $2.4 billion industry in the United States. Men's socks comprise about 47 percent of the total, while women's and children's socks and hosiery comprise the remainder. Overall, the sock and hosiery market has shown a continuous decline in shipments to retailers and distributors since 1998 as shown in Table 9.1.

Total hosiery imports grew 26 percent in 2000. Two thirds of these imports were socks that grew at a 34-percent faster rate than pantyhose, which had a 7-percent growth rate. Exports of socks and women's hosiery increased 13.92 percent and 1.00 percent respectively from 2000 to 2001. Socks are also exported to other countries, either for consumption or to be finished offshore (processing operations) before returning to the United States for sale. In spite of the increases in exports, imports exceeded exports by nearly two to one.

The average American buys approximately 12 pairs of hosiery products annually, with 70 percent of these purchases occurring during the fall and winter seasons. In 2001, sheer hosiery sales were 6.6 pairs per person, and sock sales were 9.1 pairs per person. Since 1995, the casual-legwear market has seen the greatest increase in sales, while the sheer-hosiery market has seen a decrease in sales. Overall, the legwear sales in 2001 were estimated at $3 billion.

At the end of 2000, there were 277 U.S. companies producing hosiery. The vast majority of these companies, 94 percent, produced socks, while the remainder produced sheer hosiery.

TABLE 9.1

Total Socks and Hosiery Shipments to Retailers and Distributors, 1998–2001

Year	(Dozens of Pairs in Thousands)	Percent Change
1998	335,202	−8.8%
1999	299,562	−10.7%
2000	295,941	−1.3%
2001	285,583	−3.5%

Source: Quarterly Statistics. The Hosiery Association. Retrieved June 5, 2002 from http://www.nahm.com

TABLE 9.2

The Ten Largest Distributors of Socks in the United States and Annual Sales in 2001

Company	Annual Sales
Kayser-Roth Corporation	387,100,000
Sara Lee Sock Company	296,000,000
Renfro Corporation	267,156,000
Kentucky Derby Hosiery Co., Inc.	170,994,038
V I Prewett & Son Inc.	150,000,000
Desoto Mills, Inc.	98,000,000
Charleston Hosiery	89,080,000
Clayson Knitting Co., Inc.	56,975,474
Neuville Industries, Inc.	56,544,168

Source: Duns Market Identifiers. (2002, August). SIC 2252.

However, the sheer-hosiery businesses were considerably larger in size, with an average employee number of 900, compared to an average employee number of 133 in sock companies. Tables 9.2 and 9.3 show the annual sales for 2001 for the top 10 sock and hosiery manufacturers in the United States.

Since 2000, European fashion legwear producers have increased their presence in the U.S. market because of an upswing of hosiery popularity. They have been successful because of their willingness to provide novelty lines in the U.S. market, already saturated with basic legwear. In

TABLE 9.3

The Ten Largest Distributors of Hosiery in the United States and Annual Sales in 2002

Company	Annual Sales
Americal Corporation	93,200,000
Kayser-Roth Corporation, Lumberton, NC	41,100,000
U.S. Textile Corporation	38,300,000
Highland Mills, Inc.	30,234,973
Phantom USA Inc.	27,600,000
Sara Lee Corporation, Winston-Salem, NC	27,500,000
Shogren Hosiery Manufacturing	26,000,000
Danskin, Inc.	24,000,000
Sara Lee Corporation, Yadkinville, NC	21,300,000
Wells Hosiery Mills, Inc.	20,938,509

Source: Duns Market Identifiers. (2003, August). SIC 2251.

TABLE 9.4

Socks and Hosiery Trade Organizations

Organization	Location	Objectives
The Hosiery Association (THA) www.nahm.com	Charlotte, NC	Represents more than 400 knitters, manufacturers, and suppliers; publishes magazines and statistical data books; and an online glossary of sock and hosiery terms (Spanish and English).
The Acrylic Council http://www.fabriclink.com/acryliccouncil/SOCK/Home.html	New York, NY	Builds awareness among consumers and retailers of the attributes of acrylic and enhances the marketability of acrylic products.

addition, European producers offer point-of-sale materials and visuals to entice retailers to carry their brands. These producers offer flexibility on minimum orders, convenient market times, and centrally located distribution centers—all of which appeal to U.S. retailers.

Charlotte, North Carolina, is the hub of the domestic-hosiery industry and Montichiari, Italy, is the hub of European-hosiery production. The United States and Italy offer global trade shows for the legwear industry. The countries have agreed to stagger the dates of the shows, so industry personnel can attend both important shows. Trade shows represent many accessories categories including legwear, and can specialize in every aspect of hosiery—from yarns to knitting machinery. Tables 9.4, 9.5 and 9.6 list the most common socks and hosiery trade organizations, publications, and shows.

TABLE 9.5

Trade Publications for the Socks and Hosiery Industries

Trade Publication Name	Description
Accessories Magazine	Monthly trade publication covering most accessory classifications, including socks and hosiery.
Directory of Hosiery Manufacturers, Distributors, and Suppliers	An alphabetical listing of industry segments. Also available in a CD-ROM version.
Hosiery News	A monthly publication of The Hosiery Association containing relevant legal and political issues, global trade and retail sales data, and personnel issues.
The Sheer Facts About Hosiery	Brochure published by The Hosiery Association.
Women's Wear Daily – Monday	Weekly issue of a trade newspaper published by Fairchild; features business and fashion information on socks and hosiery.

TABLE 9.6

Trade Shows for the Socks and Hosiery Industries

Trade Show	Location	Sponsor
Accessorie Circuit	New York, NY	ENK International
AccessoriesTheShow	New York, NY	Business Journals, Inc.
Fiber Yarns, Accessories, Services and Technology (FAST) Trade Show	Verona, Italy	Italian Association of Textile Apparel and Related Industries
International Hosiery Exposition	Charlotte, NC	The Hosiery Association
WWD Magic Show	Las Vegas, NV	Women's Wear Daily and Men's Apparel Guild in California

MERCHANDISING TRENDS AND TECHNIQUES

Generally speaking, socks and hosiery are considered impulse purchases. Because of this, they are available in virtually every type of retailing outlet. These include drugstores, supermarkets, convenience stores, discount and mass merchandise stores, sporting goods stores, upscale department and specialty stores, the Internet, mail order, catalogs, and even vending machines. Although other accessories are also sold through a variety of retailing channels, hosiery usually has greater visibility than other accessories, such as shoes, which would be stocked in a limited range of styles.

Store Retailing

Stores have traditionally taken two approaches to merchandising. They group socks and hosiery together in a legwear department and also include them with related items in other departments. This cross-merchandising concept also places socks and hosiery near checkout counters and on **end caps** (display units at the end of major aisles) to gain the greatest exposure to the customer. For example, a retailer may feature tennis socks near, or as part of, a display containing a tennis racket, tennis shoes, and sunscreen to encourage add-on sales.

The shrinking hosiery market has been plagued with high inventory levels and early markdowns. Several large retailers relocated their legwear departments from the main floor to less popular locations. To combat these problems at retail, large hosiery manufacturers ship their lines earlier in order to prolong the selling season and provide earlier opportunities for reorders. In addition, extensive advertising campaigns and updated packaging are designed to boost sales.

Some hosiery manufacturers and retailers have attempted to project a more fashion-forward image in their lines by introducing fancy labels, some with faux Italian names. For those retailers, such as H & M, the goal is to make shopping for legwear easy. A service-free environment is

FIGURE 9.6
7-Eleven's Heaven Sent hosiery.   Courtesy of Fairchild Publications, Inc.

a common concept touted by hosiery departments. Well-stocked shelves, orderly sizing, and detailed information on the packaging are integral to self-selection. Samples of hosiery colors and textures are often displayed on leg forms above the merchandise (see Figure 9.6).

The convenience store company 7-Eleven is using hosiery to lure potential female customers into the store. In 2000, women shoppers comprised about 30 percent of the company's customers. In an effort to build this clientele, 7-Eleven began offering their own private-label hosiery, Heaven Sent. Introduced quietly in May 2000, the sales of Heaven Sent hosiery rivaled those of 7-Eleven's national brand, L'eggs. The store's trend-sensitive brand was marketed with unique packaging—small, slender tubes, designed to fit easily in a glove compartment, purse, or briefcase.

The company's vision was to change what was typically an emergency purchase into a destination purchase. The print promotional campaign bore the tagline, "New York. Paris. Milan. 7-Eleven." The company's Web site offered a downloadable one-dollar coupon for a pair of Heaven Sent hosiery.

In the specialty athletic-sock market, merchandisers began using kiosk arrangements that grouped multiple styles of one brand of socks. Customers can differentiate among brands and price points as they move from one kiosk to the next.

Internet Retailing

Some of the larger legwear manufacturers have Web sites that range from online stores to public relations outlets. Retail giants like Bloomingdale's, JCPenney, and Nordstrom offer private-label hosiery as well as national brands. While both retailers' and manufacturers' Web sites feature merchandise for ordering, manufacturers' Web sites may also feature product information, chat rooms, recycling tips, links to philanthropic organizations, and opportunities to participate in product-testing panels.

Virtual Web sites may offer leg-care information as well as hosiery and related product sales. Leg-care information includes topics such as liposuction, varicose veins, and treatments for hair removal. One site even has physicians to answer online questions about health and wellness. Internet marketers may facilitate online ordering by offering a "never-run-out replenishment program." This allows customers to order merchandise on a preset schedule. Other creative marketing techniques include free shipping with a minimum order; gifts with purchase, such as a mesh hosiery bag; hosiery club cards—buy 12 get one free; and virtual models so customers can see how the merchandise looks on a model with a similar body shape and coloring.

Catalog Retailing

Hosiery and socks have always been popular offerings in mail-order catalogs. The ease of fit and basic colors simplify the purchase decision. Hanes Hosiery offers a print and electronic catalog called One Hanes Place, which features about 60 percent hosiery. The Hanes Web site also includes ready-to-wear links.

In some retail outlets, point-of-sale catalogs are offered to the consumer. Instead of spending large sums on postage, manufacturers offer attractive in-store promotional literature.

SELLING SOCKS AND HOSIERY

Most customers do not need a great deal of personalized attention when purchasing socks and hosiery. The merchandising must for a successful sock and hosiery department is to ensure that the merchandise is neatly organized and adequately stocked. Manufacturers realize that most hosiery departments are "service-free," so providing merchandise information to customers has become the responsibility of the manufacturer rather than the retailer. Careful labeling, clear illustrations, and nearby fabric samples are important product information needed by customers to make purchasing decisions.

Price and Value

The variable pricing of socks reflects the quality or durability of the merchandise, but the same is often not true of hosiery. The thickness of hosiery is a better indicator of its durability than price. For example, hosiery with a higher denier means greater durability, but sheer hosiery with low durability may command a higher price. Adequate labeling is required to convince the customer—sometimes in only a few seconds—of the improvement in performance that can be expected.

Many consumers consider socks a **commodity purchase,** which means consumers perceive few if any differences between sock brands. With commodity purchases, price is often the deciding factor. As a result, manufacturers are attempting to differentiate their products from run-of-the-mill brands by offering extra features unavailable in other sock and hosiery lines. These **value-adding features** might include wicking properties, graduated compression, antibacterial finishes, moisturizers, nonslip soles, and high-fashion colors. The inclusion of value-adding features allows manufacturers to command premium prices for their legwear. Socks that contain performance fibers and special finishes cost as much as 50 percent more than standard socks.

The brand image of legwear affects the selling price. Brand-name awareness simplifies the selection process for many consumers. For example, many men are loyal purchasers of Gold Toe socks, while women may be brand-loyal to Hanes hosiery. These consumers consider the national brands a good value and prefer not to spend time on the decision-making process. They simply select the appropriate color and size and make the purchase. They already know that the items will perform to their expectations.

The value image already associated with a brand name in ready-to-wear can be transferred to accessories offered under the same brand. By offering branded performance fabrics and finishes under recognizable names, retailers are able to command higher prices for socks and hosiery.

Sizing and Fitting

There is no universal sizing in the women's-hosiery industry, although most manufacturers offer similar size ranges. Men's and women's socks may be sold as **one-size-fits-all,** which ranges from a man's shoe size 10 to 13 and women's sizes 6 to 9. The problem with sock sizing has been that socks are sold by a sizing method different from shoe sizing. This tends to confuse the consumer. There are more shoe sizes than sock sizes because socks stretch, thereby fitting more than one shoe size.

Originally, hosiery was sized much like socks. Now, hosiery is sized based on height and weight. Depending on the manufacturer, sizes may be classified as small or petite; medium or average; large or tall; plus, queen, or king; or alpha letters (A, B, A/B, C, D, C/D, E, F, E/F, and Q). Most sizing charts are a combination of height and weight, although no two manufacturers size exactly the same. Customers whose sizes tend toward the upper ranges of a smaller size may opt to wear the next larger size for comfort or length.

One well-known brand, the Kayser-Roth Corporation's No Nonsense pantyhose, charted its small size as Size A. This hosiery wearer ranged from a height of 4′ 11″ to 5′ 7″ and a weight of 95 to 150 pounds. As the woman increased in the height range, the weight range decreased on the sizing chart. For example, a 4′ 11″ woman could weigh up to 150 pounds and wear Size A pantyhose. However, a 5′ 7″ woman could not exceed 110 pounds on the sizing chart if she was to wear the same Size A. Another major hosiery brand, Hanes, created a Size 1 and Size 2 chart for its Silk Reflections. It also produced the line in Petite and Plus sizes. Size 1 ranged from a height of 4′ 11″ to 5′ 7″ and a weight of 95 to 140 pounds. Size 2 ranged from a height of 5′ 4″ to 6′ and a weight of 120 to 165 pounds. Fortunately, most men and women have sufficient experience purchasing hosiery, so they can decipher unique sizing charts designed by individual manufacturers.

Meeting Customer Needs

Most manufacturers and retailers understand hosiery is a "here and now" category. Women don't want to buy hosiery ahead of or after the selling season. They want them in season, so retailers feature hosiery in their stores nearer the start of a selling season. Manufacturers have not always been finely attuned to this merchandising issue. Recently, Hanes Hosiery began offering "wear-now" merchandise every 13 weeks, rather than a collection once each season. Similarly, the Hot Sox Company realized that many stores look for merchandise changes every 30 to 60 days. To accommodate these retailers, the company offered several trends each season.

Close retailer-manufacturer partnerships encourage timely inventories. When manufacturers work more closely with retailers, they are better able to target prime-selling periods and key in on trends being spotlighted throughout the store.

When retailers buy closer to the selling season, customers are able to purchase socks and hosiery for immediate wear, rather than waiting until the season changes.

Corporate Casual

The adoption of casual dress in business caused a decline in sales of sheer hosiery, but it provided opportunities for potential increases in casual-legwear sales. Retailers concentrated on bold graphics and eye-catching displays of casual legwear. In 1999, Macy's East flagship department store relocated the sheer-hosiery department, moving it from the main floor to the mezzanine level and fifth floors. This move, signaling a possible nationwide trend away from sheers, alarmed sheer manufacturers. To compensate for declining sheer sales, manufacturing companies like L'eggs introduced additional styles of women's trouser, athletic, and casual socks. Hanes, a predominantly sheer-manufacturing company, offered a value-driven line of sheers at a slightly lower price point, hoping to attract young and price-conscious women. One Internet hosiery site offered cyber shoppers an opportunity to browse legwear merchandise grouped in a "Casual Friday" category.

The business casual trend in men's wear gave rise to an emerging sock classification called the **bridge sock,** or **Friday-wear sock,** which is a dressier casual sock. Under the influence of casual trends in the workplace, some men struggled with choosing appropriate attire, including socks. Should they wear the dressy and dark over-the-calf hosiery with khakis, or white athletic socks? The answer was to increase manufacturing and promotion of bridge socks, in argyles and small geometric patterns that blend fashionably with casual slacks.

Color

Color is a major selling tool in the sock and hosiery industry. Merchandisers often group socks and hosiery by color first, and brand name second. In spite of the color explosion in the legwear industry, basic hues—white, nude, and classic shades of black and navy—are must-haves in every collection.

A fashion-accessories industry trend is **head-to-toe dressing.** Customers select matching or complementing accessory items for each specific outfit. With this in mind, sock and hosiery manufacturers closely followed apparel fashions, offering the latest fashion prints and colors. For example, L'eggs began offering a line of hosiery, called In Season Silken Mist, which offered colors that perfectly matched fashionable ready-to-wear colors. Socks have become more colorful, and iconic prints have been popular. Both colors and designs of socks are related to ready-to-wear colors and prints. For example, E.G. Smith offered a tie-dyed sock in its collection (see Figure 9.7).

In 2002, shimmering hosiery generated a lot of interest at accessories markets, with many buyers opting for gold rather than silver metallic. After several seasons of popular silver tone, the trend toward gold appeared in legwear as well as jewelry accessories.

Another trend is offering a broader range of colors for the multicultural market. A skin-color palette has been in existence, but in limited hues. L'eggs brand pantyhose recently began offering a greater selection of skin-complementing darker tones, such as soft brown, mahogany, and coffee. To reach potential customers, L'eggs offered free samples and advertised in print media, such as *Essence magazine.*

FIGURE 9.7
E.G. Smith's tie-dye boot and anklet.
Courtesy of Fairchild Publications, Inc.

Profile Box: Rules are Made to Be Broken (If You Know How)

An increased emphasis on legwear means increased anxiety by fashion customers. Salespeople should have a fundamental understanding of traditional, aesthetically balanced, and pleasing combinations of apparel and accessories. Knowing the fashion basics offers opportunities to combine colors and textures in ways that create visual interest.

Like other accessories, a few fashion do's and don'ts are helpful to know when selecting hosiery. The following information offers some general fashion advice for frequently asked questions about socks and hosiery.

Hosiery Fashions FAQ's

■ Do I match my hosiery with my outfit or my shoes?

The customer should match (or intentionally contrast) the hosiery to the next largest surface area of color, generally the skirt. An exception might be if a woman wears slacks and contrasting colored shoes. For example, she could wear forest green slacks and black shoes. She has the option of wearing forest green trouser socks or black trouser socks. The closeness of color match may influence her decision. The customer is not limited to matching colors, however. Hosiery designers and manufacturers encourage experimentation with contrasting colors in legwear.

In men's wear, the socks/hosiery should be the same color or a shade darker than the slacks, but never lighter in color.

■ Can I wear dark hose with a light-colored outfit?

Not usually. Occasionally, fashion may allow for black or dark hose with a light skirt, but usually a safe color choice is one to match the skin tone.

■ Can I wear light hose with a dark-colored outfit?

Again, the answer is most often "no," because it visually cuts the wearer with horizontal lines, creating an illusion of being shorter in height. In times past, these fashion rules have been broken, but usually by tall and slender women, who have little concern for the perceived height reduction and weight increase. Men should not wear white athletic socks unless dressed in athletic apparel. They should never wear white socks with career clothing.

■ How can I create just the right hosiery look to complement an ensemble?

Avoid the pitfall of simply wearing nude-colored hosiery because of a fear of making the wrong selection. Closely peruse fashion magazines to see how designers feature legwear.

■ I work in a conservative office. What are my hosiery choices besides nude-colored sheers?

Even in the most traditional offices, females can select professional, yet durable styles, such as opaques and tights. Select a color that matches the skirt color for a taller, more conservative appearance.

The above answers are "safe" fashion advice. Once a customer finds her own style, she should be encouraged to experiment with unique combinations. The key to a successful ensemble is a "head to toe" look—not monochromatic, not parti-colored, but somewhere in between the two extremes.

Packaging

Because of the delicate nature of hosiery, the conservation concept of reduce, reuse, and recycle has been adopted only to a limited extent in the industry. Durable hosiery, sport socks, and trouser sock industries have been more effective in their recycling efforts, usually offering tiny plastic hangers and an adhesive label as the only disposable packaging. Some multipack socks are packaged in a lightweight plastic film.

Packaging is one of the most important selling tools for any manufacturer, since even in department stores salespeople may have limited knowledge about the products. For example, packaging has to tell if hose has a toner or a control top, a sewn or knitted waistband, or high- or boy-cut legs. Of course, manufacturers should not try to print everything on the package. The packaging should have simple, large type that does not overwhelm the shopper. Most manufacturers agree that a photograph or drawing provides customers with an important visual cue to what is in the package. Some of these images represent a lifestyle, while others are merely photographs of the product.

Typically, in mass merchandise, discount, and supermarket stores, the customer is greeted with an endless array of similar sock and hosiery styles in multipacks, with varying price points, and few perceived differences among these packages. Many of these consumers are price conscious with little concern for the brand name. But in spite of the prevalence of similar packaging styles across brands, there are opportunities for nationally branded companies to set their brands apart. Unique packaging, like Heaven Sent's slender tube or the original L'eggs egg, helps companies establish images that appeal to consumers looking for a premium product. Another company, Ridgeview, offered its Rêve Avoix leg highs and panties packaged together, with an option of purchasing replacement leg highs when needed. This combination of two products in one package and a replacement option made their brands stand out.

SUMMARY

- Originally, socks and hosiery served to protect the wearer from the elements and later evolved into a fashion accessory. As skirt hemlines rose above the ankles in the early 20th century, hosiery became decorative. Circular-knitted nylon stockings eventually replaced silk stockings. In the 1960s, pantyhose and knee-high hosiery virtually eliminated the desire for stockings.

- Socks have maintained a constant popularity for accessorizing casual clothing, especially for young people. The fitness trend created a need for sport-specific socks in performance fibers.

- Sock and hosiery manufacturing requires minimal hand labor and can be done inexpensively, even in the United States. North Carolina is an important knit-manufacturing state, and Italy is an important country for legwear production.

- In order to stimulate a stale legwear market, hosiery manufacturers are creating patterned legwear, inspired by popular ready-to-wear designs, patterns, and color trends.

- The concept of novelty wellness refers to the creation of legwear products that relieve stress during long periods of standing on the feet, or that enhance the skin through moisturizers and fragrances.

- Hosiery is produced in a variety of deniers and gauges. Microfibers have become key to the hosiery industry, providing a silky feel to manufactured fibers, such as nylon.

- Sock fibers are dependent upon the end use of the product. Acrylic and some polyester fibers are useful in socks because of the property of wicking. Cotton still remains a popular natural fiber for socks, while synthetic fiber socks is a growing category.

- Spandex is an important fiber for imparting stretch and providing holding power. Luxury fibers, like angora, have tactile aesthetic appeal.

- Numerous styles are available in legwear. Some are fashion forward, like fishnet hosiery or toe socks, while others are known for durability, like support hose or tights.

- Sizing of socks and hosiery is relatively simple, although the industry lacks standardization. Most customers have ample experience purchasing socks and hosiery and can easily identify their size based on the manufacturer's chart.

- It is best to hand wash hosiery or machine wash on the delicate cycle. Socks should be machine washed on the hottest appropriate water setting, unless the socks are wool or there is a concern over color fading.

- Foreign manufacturing companies have begun entering the U.S. market and have offered retailers enticements that are appealing and profitable. Product differentiation has become a marketing concern among domestic and foreign manufacturers.

- The popularity of legwear increased in the last few seasons, after an industry slump. Casual clothing has been blamed for some of the sales problems, but manufacturers have begun offering casual looks in legwear to boost sales.

- Packaging is important in the hosiery and sock industry. The L'eggs egg revolutionized hosiery packaging a few decades ago. More recently, 7-Eleven convenience stores creatively packaged hosiery to attract more female shoppers into the store.

- Customers typically purchase socks and hosiery on impulse. Retailers have begun merchandising these accessories with related goods to stimulate add-on sales and planned purchases.

- Hosiery is sold on the Internet and via direct-mail catalogs. Large manufacturers' Web sites and catalogs offer other products and services in addition to hosiery.

- Generally, consumers find it difficult to identify specific product characteristics that contribute to increased prices. Manufacturers must provide adequate product information at the point of sale to ensure customers understand the product and the price.

- Manufacturers work closely with retailers to offer the right product at the right time.

- Bridge socks in men's wear and additional styles of socks in women's wear are two merchandise classifications that have expanded as a result of the corporate casual trend.

- Retailers should emphasize color in their floor displays because color is a major selling tool. Head-to-toe dressing should also be considered when merchandising departments.

- Packaging information should be clear, concise, and visual; unique packaging is one way a manufacturer can set its brand apart from other brands.

TERMS FOR REVIEW

anklets (socklets)	body stocking	control top hosiery
antibacterial fibers	boy cut	crew socks
boarded	bridge (Friday-wear) sock	demi-toe
bobby socks	commodity purchase	denier

end caps

fishnet

footies

French cut

full-fashioned hosiery

garters

graduated compression

head-to-toe dressing

hiking socks

knee-high (trouser socks)

knee-high hosiery

knitting gauge

leg warmers

leg-highs

maternity

microfibers

novelty wellness

one-size-fits-all

opaque

over-the-calf socks

over-the-knee socks

pantyhose

parti-colored hose

performance fibers

pourpoints

reinforced toes or heels

run-resistant (no-run)

sandalfoot

seamed stockings

sheer

sheer-to-waist

spandex

specialty fibers

stockings

support

thigh highs

tibiales

tights

toe socks

trouser socks

tube socks

value-adding features

wicking

REVIEW QUESTIONS

1. What ready-to-wear fashion trends today influence fashions in the sock and hosiery industry?

2. What is meant by novelty wellness and graduated compression?

3. How does gauge differ from denier?

4. What fibers are used in the manufacture of socks, and why might customers choose different fibers depending on the end use?

5. What are the most recognizable brands in the hosiery industry?

6. What are some ways manufacturers and retailers can turn a commodity sock purchase or an emergency hosiery purchase into a fashion purchase?

7. Why have European manufacturers targeted the U.S. market for the introduction of leg-wear lines?

8. How do merchandisers use alternative forms of retailing, besides brick-and-mortar stores?

9. Explain the relationship of price and durability for socks and hosiery.

10. How can hosiery and socks be merchandised in a department to optimize sales?

KNOWLEDGE APPLICATIONS

1. Search through a collection of historic costume books looking for illustrations and additional information about the history of socks and hosiery. Be prepared to discuss and present your findings to the class.

2. Visit a historic costume museum and make notes about the hosiery and socks worn with period costumes.

3. Perform a fashion count of hosiery or sock advertisements in a recent fashion magazine Select and evaluate one variable, such as length, color, texture, unique selling proposition, or brand. Record your data in chart form and analyze your findings.

4. Find all the legwear advertisements in a current fashion magazine. List and group the marketing terms (such as *leg-softening* or *energizing*) used in each of the advertisements. Evaluate your findings for major themes or trends.

5. Visit the sock or hosiery departments of a discount store and a department or specialty store. Perform a comparative analysis of merchandising methods and evaluate the effectiveness of the methods. Base your evaluation on user friendliness, cleanliness, neatness, displays, and stock levels, and compare two similar brands on packaging, style and color offerings, display, and price. Present your findings to the class.

6. Visit a hosiery or sock-knitting mill or interview a legwear buyer to gain an understanding of career-related opportunities and challenges.

CHAPTER 10

SCARFS, TIES, AND HANDKERCHIEFS

Modern man is mindful of his seemingly useless strip of material: he rescues it from the toaster, yanks it from the elevator door, tightens it before the power lunch, fishes it from his seafood bisque, loosens it when the boss leaves and, with his last speck of adrenaline, rips it from his neck.

—Kaylin, L. (1987). The Semiotics of the Tie. *Gentleman's Quarterly, (57)* pp. 112, 115, 117.

A BRIEF HISTORY OF SCARFS, TIES, AND HANDKERCHIEFS

THE ROMAN ORATORS WHO WORE SCARFS AROUND THEIR NECKS TO WARM THEIR VOCAL chords may have donned the first documented neckwear. Credit for the invention of neckwear has also been given to the Chinese Qin Dynasty (3rd century B.C.), for the colorful neck cords worn by personal guards and soldiers of the emperor Shih Huang Ti to ensure the distinction of their elite corps.

An important neckwear innovation for men and women was the **ruff,** a starched collar made of many yards of narrow fabric stiffly set in a tight, wavy pattern. The ruff evolved in Europe over a period of decades, perhaps beginning in the 1540s as a mere ruffle and reaching its extreme size (supported by a wire framework) in the 1620s (see Figure 10.1).

During the Thirty Years' War, when Croatian horsemen arrived in Paris, France's King Louis XIV was impressed by their flamboyant, colorful neckerchiefs tied in a distinctive manner. The French adopted this fashion, called "a la Croate," believing it to be a symbol of elegance and cultivation. The neckerchief became the **cravat** (believed to be a derivative of the root word, *Croate*), a silk scarf worn by men, tucked inside the neck of their shirt.

The English soon adopted this fashion, and by 1800 English dandy Beau Brummell was setting standards for men's clothing, including starched cravats.

Eighteenth century **steinkirks,** loosely wrapped scarfs, began as men's wear fashions and were later adopted and adapted by women. The popularity of steinkirks soon gave way to stocks. **Stocks** were excessively stiff high collars that were worn by the French and German military. Made of pasteboard, bone, or other stiff materials, they could be recovered in silks, linens, or calicos when needed.

During the 19th and early 20th centuries, fashionable neckwear for American men was imported from England and France. **Bow ties** and **four-in-hand ties** were important to the well-dressed American man. Their minimal appearance supported the notion and importance of a strong work ethic. **Ascots,** pale gray patterned silks originating in England, were named after the formal Royal Ascot races. They became common in the late 19th and early 20th centuries in the United States.

Cowboys chose (and still choose) **bandana** neckerchiefs because of their many uses. Sun protection, dust protection, and washcloth were just a few of the practical uses of a cowboy's bandana. Bandanas also find their place in women's and teen's fashions from time to time. Another western neckwear accessory is the **bolo** or **string tie,** featuring a metal or stone ornament that slides (tightens and loosens) on leather strings.

Women often wore shaped shoulder scarfs called **pelerines** to cover a low **décolleté** (neckline) or smaller variations of the ruff, called the **Betsy,** which was seen until the 1840s. During the 20th century, women periodically adopted men's neckwear fashions, as well as created their own distinct scarf fashions. Rectangular scarfs appeared in the 1920s, knotted loosely at the neck. Girls and young women have worn small square neckerchiefs, rolled and knotted at the neck, in every decade of the 20th century. They continue to be offered in retail stores in the season's fashionable colors and prints.

The **Peacock Revolution** of the 1960s, a time of flamboyant men's fashions, took men's neckwear to extremes. Many men discarded ties because they were emblems of "the establishment." For those men who were required to wear ties at work, fashion worked in the extreme. Ties grew to excessive widths of five inches, matching the extreme widths of lapels and longer shirt collars.

The early 1970s **Annie Hall look** (inspired by the movie) created a neckwear fashion for women. Men's knitted or woven ties were worn by women with over-sized blouses and long skirts. In 2002, pop singer Avril Lavigne set a fashion trend of neckties for females after wearing one in her music video (see Figure 10.2).

The mid- to late 1970s was a time when silky bow ties were worn by aspiring career women as the equivalent to men's dress-for-success ties. Both genders selected a uniform of dark suits (skirts for women, pants for men), oxford cloth shirts, and appropriate ties and pocket squares for men, and silk scarfs for women.

Image consultant John Molloy, deemed a modern-day Beau Brummell, authored the infamous *Dress for Success* book for men in 1975 and later wrote one for women. For years Molloy's dress code became the standard for career clothing, and included very specific do's and don'ts for neckwear and other business accessories.

In the late 1970s and early 1980s, both men and women were wearing pocket squares with

FIGURE 10.2
Avril Lauigne, skate pop superstar, in necktie.
Courtesy of Fairchild Publications, Inc.

FIGURE 10.1
Fashionable ruff.

two- and three-piece suits. The 1980s was also a popular time for silk scarfs. Accessory departments offered continuously running videos on creative ways to wear scarfs, because many women appreciated the look of scarfs but didn't know how to wear them.

The **pashmina scarf** or **shawl,** so named because of pashmina fabric made of cashmere (or a silk and cashmere blend), became quite popular in the late 1990s. Pashmina fabric is the finest, softest, and warmest wool found in nature. It comes from the underbelly of the Capras goat in the remote regions of the Himalayas. The goats grow a thin, insulating layer of hair to protect them from the harsh winters. Each pashmina shawl requires the hair growth of three goats to provide enough fibers for manufacturing, making this a rather expensive accessory. But pashmina shawls are not new accessories. As early as the 18th century, French Emperor Napoléon gave Josephine a pashmina shawl.

During the late 20th century and into the 21st century, shawls of all fabrics continued to be a strong accessory item. Credit for their popularity was given to the apparel fashions of that time, which were bare-shouldered and spaghetti-strapped, even during cold seasons. Other interchangeable fashion terms used to describe shawls are the *stole,* the *shrug,* and the *wrap.* However, the term *shawl* tends to refer to fringed wraps.

Historic paintings often depict upper-class women holding lace-edged linen handkerchiefs as they sat for their portraits. The indispensable, always functional, and sometimes decorative handkerchiefs changed very little from century to century. Most often, the differences were in size and degree of sheerness. Since the development of disposable facial tissues, the popularity of handkerchiefs for women has greatly diminished, although sales are stable in the men's wear market.

AN INTRODUCTION TO SCARFS, TIES, AND HANDKERCHIEFS

Scarfs and ties are traditionally marks of allegiance, wealth, and belonging. They are still symbolic of the elite, telling others that the wearers of the neckpieces are the people who matter—the people who belong. Only as long as this image continues can neckwear designers and manufacturers command high prices for small pieces of fabric.

The basic style of neckwear remains the same, regardless of the price point. Therefore, designers and manufacturers must differentiate products through fabrics, workmanship, and the brand's image. Elegant fibers, unique patterns, and beautiful silk-screened or handwoven fabrics are manufactured into men's and women's neckwear. The degree and quality of hand workmanship affects the price of the neckwear. Men's neckties require more labor than scarfs, handkerchiefs, or pocket squares, all of which are basic rectangles.

The term *scarfs* may also be referred to as scarves. Industry representatives commonly use the term *scarfs*, while consumers often use the term *scarves*. Both are correct.

Scarfs, Ties, and Handkerchiefs Manufacturing

As with socks and sheer hosiery, many consumers are price sensitive to some scarfs, ties, and most handkerchiefs. To offer customers greater perceived value, manufacturers differentiate their products through fabrication and workmanship. Decorative weaves, such as jacquard, hand workmanship, stain-repellent coatings, slim silhouettes, and extra attention to details help customers distinguish among price points.

Design

Scarf, tie, and pocket square prints are inspired by many of the same sources that inspire ready-to-wear fabrics. Everything from vintage clothing to home fashions, nostalgic items, floral and animal prints and colors may be the basis for a scarf, tie, or pocket square fabric. Designers use computers to scan or draw a particular print. They can colorize it and print a sample piece of fabric on a fabric printer. Scarf designs may coordinate with popular colors for the season or the color may blend with the line's ready-to-wear colors. The selection of tie and pocket square colors is similar, but efforts are made to coordinate with popular shirt and suit colors. Sample scarfs and ties are produced, allowing sales representatives to show the line at market and take orders before mass production occurs. Pocket squares may be solid colors, or may match the prints of the ties.

Designers agree that an easy way to introduce color into men's wear is through neckwear. Men may be cautious about too much color in their apparel, but the small surface area of a tie or pocket square makes it easier for men to accept brighter colors and patterns.

No discussion of neckwear designing is complete until mention is made of Ralph Lauren, one of America's most famous designers. A rags-to-riches story, Lauren began his career selling, and later designing, men's wide ties when fashion trends were focused on narrow ties. His subsequent business success after his refusal to narrow the width or remove the polo player logo from his ties reflected his ability to correctly interpret the times.

Licensing

Licensing abounds in the scarf and neckwear industries. The popularity of a designer in one area, such as women's apparel, is a key to successful sales in accessories. Women, already purchasers of a designer's clothing for themselves, are likely to purchase ties from the same designer for their men.

Many apparel designers, including Mary McFadden and Nicole Miller, offer signature accessories through licensing agreements with scarf and neckwear manufacturers. Usually the fashion company or designer will enter into an agreement to have a silk-manufacturing company produce and distribute the neckwear under the fashion or designer label. A close working relationship between the two are vital for a licensing agreement to work. The product quality, price, and appearance must reflect the fashion company's or designer's image.

Production

Once the decision to mass-produce is made, fabric is selected. **Woven-silk** fabric has a woven-in design, while **printed silks** refer to a printed-on, or silk-screened, design. **Silk screening** is a method of creating a design on the fabric, one color at a time. Usually each color in the scarf or tie requires a separate screen. The number of colors used in the print affects the price of the item.

The necktie pattern is laid on the **bias** (diagonal) of the woven fabric. Handkerchiefs and scarfs may be cut on the **straight grain** (parallel to the selvage or tightly-woven edge) and sewn (hemmed), or they may be individually woven with fringed edges. Ties are usually cut and sewn with two or three pieces. In the case of knitted ties, they may be flat knitted and center-back seamed. The standard length for a man's necktie is 52 inches to 58 inches.

The manufacture of men's neckties uses only a small amount of fashion fabric, but the differences in quality are considerable. Better-quality ties are handmade, that is, cut by hand and handsewn. Ties may be made of two or three pieces of fashion fabric, joined with seams. Three-piece ties are generally considered better quality than two-piece ties. The tie may or may not be interlined with **buckram** or other stiffening agent to give the tie a firm hand. A lining fabric covers the interlining and provides extra body.

A necktie **shell** consists of the **front blade,** or **apron;** the **under blade,** or **tail;** and the connecting **neck gusset.** The **interlining,** or **lining,** gives the necktie body and shape. **Tipping,** or **facing,** refers to a method of finishing the blade ends to ensure coverage of hand workmanship. **Custom tipping** bears the signature of the designer. In addition, neckties have a **loop label, bar tack stitch,** and hidden **slip stitching** (see Figure 10.3).

Men's and women's scarfs, handkerchiefs, and pocket squares may have a machine hem or hand-rolled hem. In addition, scarfs may be fringed. A **machine hem** is usually sewn with

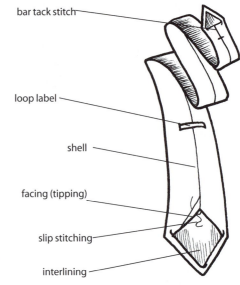

FIGURE 10.3
Parts of a necktie.

invisible (clear) thread and looks similar to a **hand-rolled hem,** although the latter is labor intensive and more costly. When scarfs are fringed, no hem is required, but an inconspicuous zigzag stitch may be used to prevent further raveling.

Materials

All-weather scarfs are made of lightweight woven fabrics, such as cotton, cotton/polyester blends, and wool. These scarf accessories tend to be worn for decoration rather than warmth. Winter scarf fabrics include lambswool or angora blended with wool or cashmere in higher-priced lines, or blended with acrylic in lower-priced lines. Synthetic fleeces, such as Polartec®, are popular fabrics for moderate- and lower-priced lines. The popularity of fur as an accessory material can be seen in the winter-scarf lines. Fur boas, collars, and shawls are offered either in the traditional-pelt styles or crocheted into lightweight fur fashions.

Necktie materials usually consist of silk or polyester microfibers. The excellent hand of polyester microfibers makes them very difficult to distinguish from pure silk. Other fibers may include nylon, wool, or cotton, such as in knitted ties.

Handkerchief fabric is usually cotton, because of the high absorbency of the fiber. Pocket squares (decorative, rather than functional handkerchiefs) may be crisp fabrics that crease well, such as linen or cotton, or fabrics such as silk or polyester microfibers, that drape well.

Scarfs, ties, and handkerchiefs may be solid colors or patterned in endless variations of colors and prints. With men's ties and pocket squares, more than with women's scarfs, an attempt to classify print patterns is somewhat manageable. The following list of traditional tie patterns is by no means comprehensive, but variations of these prints tend to recur in tie and pocket square fashions.

Traditional Tie Patterns

Tie patterns accessorize the dress shirt, complementing looks that range from whimsical and informal to conservative and formal. Traditional patterns include the following (see Figure 10.4):

- **Abstract** Semirealistic or indefinable image, no emerging pattern
- **Club** Print or pictures that represent an association, sport, or group
- **Conversational** An interesting or whimsical print that reflects the interests or likes of the wearer
- **Floral** Flower print
- **Foulard** Small geometric shapes, such as diamonds, on solid background
- **Novelty** Cartoons or other licensed products
- **Paisley** Large or small amoeba-shaped designs
- **Plaid** Lines or stripes crossing at 90-degree angles
- **Polka Dot/Pin Dot** Large (polka) or small (pin) circles on background color
- **Rep (repeating stripe)** Diagonal stripes with a pattern repeated at intervals
- **Solid** Uniform color, no printed pattern, but may have woven-in design like jacquard

abstract tie

floral

conversational

pin dot

solid

FIGURE 10.4
Traditional tie patterns.

The Four-in-Hand Knot and the Bow Tie Knot

The Four-in-Hand Knot

1. Drape the tie around your neck, the wide end on your left and touching the center of your belt. The narrow end should be shorter.
2. Cross the wide over the narrow and bring it through the loop.

3. Holding the narrow down, wrap the wide around the narrow by going over the right and under the narrow.
4. Wrap the wide across the narrow. Bring the wide under the narrow and up through the loop.
5. Slip the wide through the knot in the front. Tighten the knot up to the collar.

1st step 2nd step 3rd step 4th step 5th step *The Four-in-Hand Knot.*

The Bow Tie

1. Drape the tie around your neck. The right end should be 1–2 inches longer than the left end. Cross the longer end over the shorter end and bring up through the loop.
2. Fold the shorter end in half to form the front loop of the bow.

3. Hold the front loop in place. Drop the long end over the front loop.
4. With long end fold up to form back loop.
5. Poke back loop through center knot, even ends, and tighten.

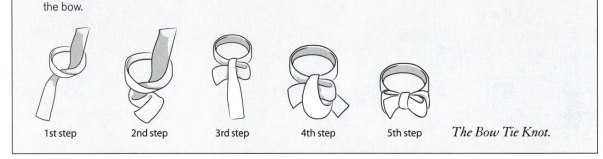

1st step 2nd step 3rd step 4th step 5th step *The Bow Tie Knot.*

Tying a Tie

An alternative to knotting a tie is to select a pre-tied clip-on tie, available in many boys' departments. With clip-on ties, there is no adjustment for length, but the simplicity is often desired by boys and infrequent tie wearers. Men who prefer to knot their own ties may choose one of three common knotting methods—the four-in-hand, the Windsor, and the half-Windsor. The **four-in-hand knot** is the most common, believed to have originated by coachmen driving a coach pulled by four horses. In order to prevent the wind from whipping the tie into his face while driving, he tied a tight knot.

The **Windsor** and **half-Windsor knots** were named for King Edward VIII of England, the Duke of Windsor, who popularized the knotted tie with a spread collar. Compared to four-in-hand knots, the Windsor and half-Windsor knots are larger in appearance. Regardless of the size of the knot, it should produce a small crease, or dimple, just below the knot. This forces the tie to billow and creates a fullness that lets its drape properly. Both blades of a tied tie should be equal in length or the back blade should be fractionally shorter.

Care of Scarfs, Ties, and Handkerchiefs

Care should be exercised when cleaning scarfs, ties, and handkerchiefs. Cleaning methods should be chosen according to the fabrics used. Most silk scarfs and ties should not be dry-cleaned because the luster of the silk may be dulled by repeated exposure to chemicals. Dry cleaning ties also may cause the lining to flatten and the tie will lose its body. Often, simply rubbing the silk fabric with the small blade of the tie will remove water stains. A spot remover, like carbon tetrachloride, removes many other types of stains. Handkerchiefs, if silk, are used for decoration, not function. They should be dry-cleaned only when needed. When cleaning pure silk scarfs is necessary, dry cleaning is preferable to wet cleaning (hand washing). Cotton or woolen, and some rayon, scarfs can be hand washed and laid flat to dry. Decorative cotton handkerchiefs may be machine washed on the delicate cycle, but color loss will occur with repeated washing. Functional white cotton handkerchiefs should be washed in hot water on the regular machine-washing cycle.

Ties should not be ironed. Creases from wearing should fall out when a woven tie is hung, knot untied. Severe creases may be removed by tightly rolling the tie for several hours. Knitted or crocheted ties should be laid flat or rolled rather than hung to prevent stretching.

THE GLOBAL SCARFS, TIES, AND HANDKERCHIEFS INDUSTRIES

The U.S. neckwear industry generated about $1.2 billion in sales at retail in 2000, $1.1 billion in 1999, and $1.5 billion in 1998. Table 10.1 shows the domestic companies with the greatest sales of boys' and men's neckwear in 2000.

Globally, Italy is probably the most influential country in silk-neckwear design and production. Slightly more than 53 percent of the world's value of silk neckwear is produced in Italy, compared to China's 22.31 percent share. However, China is the leading country in silk-fabric production. For more than 100 years, silk-textile mills in Italy have been producing imaginative prints and luxurious weaves for ties and scarfs. What began as family-run companies have turned into multimillion-dollar textile mills producing fabrics for the world's top designers.

TABLE 10.1

The Ten Largest U.S. Distributors of Men's and Boys' Neckwear and Annual Sales in 2000

Company	Annual Sales ($ millions)
Burma Bibas, Inc.	74.49
Mallory & Church Corp.	50.00
Superba	36.80
Robert Talbott, Inc.	30.00
MMG Corp.	24.14
Mulberry Thai Silks, Inc.	23.37
Stonehenge Ltd.	22.55
Mountain High Knitting, Inc.	16.70
Randa Corporation	15.10
Tuxacco, Inc.	15.00

Source: Dun's Market Identifiers. [Online]. Parsippany, NJ: Dun & Bradstreet.

China and South Korea have recently begun to erode the strong lead held by Italy. Italian ties, pocket squares, and women's scarfs were especially hard hit by less expensive Asian goods, as well as the casual trend, particularly in the United States, Germany, Italy, and Japan, which are major markets for these silk accessories. Italy's strength in luxury silks may erode over the next several years in the face of mid- and lower-priced silks from Asia. In particular, South Korea has been working with European and North American designers and textile manufacturers since the early 1990s in an attempt to gain silk-industry market shares. However, an emphasis on craftsmanship and tradition, and an investment in technology and innovative fabric production, are strategic ways to improve Italy's competitive edge.

China supplied more than half of the world's cotton handkerchiefs in 2001 followed by Pakistan, Korea, the Czech Republic, and India. The demand for cotton handkerchiefs almost doubled between 2000 and 2001, possibly due to the popularity of a more casual look in scarfs, such as bandanas and other neckerchiefs.

In the United States, only one specialized trade organization exists specifically for neckwear. The **Neckwear Association of America (NAA)** publishes newsletters and promotes international trade. Consumer brochures, such as "How To Tie a Tie", are produced by the NAA as well as by individual tie manufacturers. These pictorial steps are also available on several Internet sites. Trade publications usually cover these accessories as part of the larger accessories market. Scarfs, ties, and handkerchiefs are featured at general accessories and men's wear trade shows. Tables 10.2, 10.3, and 10.4 show important trade organizations, publications, and shows for the scarfs, ties, and handkerchiefs industries.

TABLE 10.2

Trade Organizations for the Scarfs, Ties, and Handkerchiefs Industries

Organization	Location	Objectives
Neckwear Association of America (NAA)	New York, NY	Offers member services including a resource directory, consumer brochures, merchandising ideas, and newsletters.
National Fashion Accessory Association (NFAA) and the Fashion Accessory Shippers Association (FASA) www.accessoryweb.com	New York, NY	Disseminates information to its manufacturer/ importer/shipper members, promotes high ethical standards, fosters labor relations in the international trade community, and protects the industry's best interests.

MERCHANDISING TRENDS AND TECHNIQUES

Scarfs, ties, handkerchiefs, and pocket squares are easily sold through all retailing channels because proper fit is not an issue. In addition, color matches do not have to be exact—a tie or scarf print is usually small and will blend with similar apparel colors.

In all channels of distribution, attractively presented merchandise is important. Compelling displays, complete with several options, show customers that these accessories are an important statement in fashion and in their own wardrobe.

TABLE 10.3

Trade Publications for the Scarfs, Ties, and Handkerchiefs Industries

Trade Publication Name	Description
Accessories Magazine	Monthly trade publication covering most accessories classifications, including scarfs.
Daily News Record	Fashion trade data, trends, and news; published by Fairchild.
Neckwear Industry Directory	Lists tie resources by geographic location and brand name; published by the NAA.
Neckwear News	Information on fashion trends and exporting opportunities in the neckwear industry; published by the NAA.
Tie Buyer's Handbook	Tips for retail store buyers on display and merchandising ties; published by the NAA.
Tie Scores	Consumer tips on knotting ties and integrating ties into a casual wardrobe; published by the NAA.
Washington Updates	Information on legislative action affecting the neckwear industry; published by the NAA.
Women's Wear Daily – Monday	Weekly issue of a trade newspaper; published by Fairchild. Features business and fashion information on scarfs as well as other accessories.

TABLE 10.4

Trade Shows for the Scarfs, Ties, and Handkerchiefs Industries

Trade Show	Location	Sponsor
Accessorie Circuit	New York, NY	ENK International
AccessoriesTheShow	New York, NY	Business Journals, Inc.
The Collective	Chicago, IL	The Chicago Men's Apparel Group
Miami Men's and Boy's Apparel Market	Miami, FL	Miami Merchandise Mart
National Association of Men's Sportswear Buyers (NAMSB)	New York, NY	National Association of Men's Sportswear Buyers
WWD Magic Show	Las Vegas, NV	Women's Wear Daily and Men's Apparel Guild in California

Store Retailing

Scarf retailers begin displaying cold-weather scarfs, along with hats and gloves, in the early fall before the temperature drops. By the time of the first real cold snap, retailers have mountains of these accessories to sell in the few short weeks before Christmas. Price is a major factor in consumer purchase decisions, so private labels rather than national brands dominate these offerings. A **private-label brand** is a store's exclusive brand, available only at that particular retailer. A **national brand** is available in many competing stores.

National-brand manufacturers attempt to gain market shares by diversifying into cold-weather accessories. Companies such as Nine West, Echo, and Anne Klein II license their company names to warm yet fashionable product lines in innovative yarns and fabrics. Cold-weather accessories are natural extensions of ready-to-wear product lines and therefore offer opportunities for licensing agreements.

Historically, price has been an important factor in determining selling success of all-weather scarfs. An important exception was the popularity of pashmina scarfs and shawls, retailing between $200 and $600. Success of these higher-priced items in a self-service environment was evidence that more expensive scarfs can be merchandised among other main floor accessories. For example, upscale specialty store Neiman-Marcus offered a variety of scarfs—pashminas, silks, silk blends, and specialty fibers, like piña cloth (sheer and lustrous fabric)—merchandised on hangers with lower-priced accessories on the main floor, rather than being featured within a perimeter boutique, as were the folded Hermès scarfs.

Discount stores may merchandise scarfs among other accessory products, often near the handbags. To facilitate self-service, neckerchiefs and scarfs are often looped through manufacturer-provided paper hangers and hung on peg fixtures. Fiber content, care, suggested wearing illustrations, and other product information are important on hangtags because salespeople are not available to assist customers.

Men's ties are merchandised by color, pattern, and brand name. Lower price points tend to be merchandised by color and pattern for convenience in selecting a coordinating tie. These ties are often displayed on tables or counters, or they may be hanging on countertop tie racks. The small size of the prints and importance of color coordination require placing ties in well-lit locations closer to the customers' eyes. Higher price points, such as designer ties are grouped by brand name. They may be located in glass cases requiring a salesperson's assistance. Adequate lighting inside the glass cases is important for accurate color perception.

A new tie and shirt are usually purchased when a man buys a suit. Therefore, the ties should be located near the dress shirts and suits to encourage add-on (multiple) sales. To assist men in maintaining the match between appropriate ties and suits once they leave the store, closet organizer accessories can also be merchandised near the ties. In addition, cotton handkerchiefs and pocket squares located near the register can be a source of impulse sales.

According to *Menswear Retailing* (July 2000) in 1999, popular retail price points varied between department and specialty stores. Generally, specialty stores sold ties at higher price points than department stores. Figures 10.5 and 10.6 represent the percentages of average selling prices for men's ties in department and specialty stores in 1999.

The dollar share has shifted in recent years away from department store domination of tie sales. In 1998, department stores' share of tie sales was 34 percent. By 2000, department stores' share had decreased to slightly more than 30 percent. Men's specialty stores' share of tie sales was almost 15 percent in 1998 but dropped to 9.6 percent in 2000. Discount stores and off-price retail stores both increased their shares during this time period. Consumers perceive tie quality to be similar at discount and off-price retail stores compared to department and specialty stores. Therefore, price competition has been the primary reason for the decline in sales at the higher-priced stores. As a result, in 2001 the average price of a tie dropped by 16 percent.

Department Stores 1999

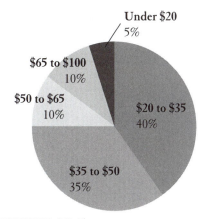

FIGURE 10.5
Average out-the-door retail prices for ties in department stores in 1999.

Courtesy of Fairchild Publications, Inc.

Specialty Stores 1999

FIGURE 10.6
Average out-the-door retail prices for ties in specialty stores in 1999.

Courtesy of Fairchild Publications, Inc.

In the women's scarfs, neckwear, and wraps market in 2000, department stores' share of scarf, neckwear, and wrap sales was 39 percent, followed by mass retailers and specialty chain stores. Table 10.5 shows a complete market share breakdown by U.S. retail outlet in 2000.

Internet Retailing

Scarfs, ties, and handkerchiefs are popular products for online retailers. This popularity can be attributed to their desirability as gifts and their universal sizing. Another reason for their popularity is that Web sites can feature more than just the items for sale. They feature related accessories items, such as cufflinks, tie bars and tacks, bow ties, and apparel; tips on how to fold pocket squares and scarfs, and knot ties; information on care and cleaning of these accessories; and a historical overview of these accessories. Customers that don't wish to order online can order by telephone using a toll-free number.

Companies that have had a brick-and-mortar presence in the retail industry for many years are offering services through the Internet. One such company, Tiecrafters in New York—boasting "Over 50 Years and 4 Million Ties Later"—offers cleaning and alteration services and custom-designed ties for corporations or special occasions. In 2001, the NASDAQ store in New York's Times Square teamed up with fashion designer Nicole Miller to offer online souvenirs and corporate gifts related to the stock market. Included in the collection were scarfs and ties bearing NASDAQ-inspired designs.

The Internet can be more than simply a "click-and-buy" selling tool. The potential for creating unique selling techniques is exciting. Web sites can offer customers the ability to scan in pictures of their existing wardrobe of dress shirts, in order to match ties. Virtual fashion assistants can help Internet shoppers narrow color selections. Mass customization can be promoted by allowing customers to personalize tie messages and prints. Made-to-order ties, scarfs, and shawls that appeal to luxury consumers can be promoted on Web sites. Offers of multiple

TABLE 10.5

U.S. Scarfs, Neckwear, and Wraps Market Share by Retail Outlet in 2000

	Percent of Total Retail Sales	$ Millions
Department Stores	39%	$252.3
Specialty Stores	10%	$70.5
Specialty Chain Stores	19%	$131.7
Mass Retailers	22%	$154.8
All Other	10%	$80.25
Total	100%	$689.5

Source: Scarves, neckwear & wraps census. (Jan. 2002). *Accessories Magazine, 103*(1), p. 38. Courtesy of Fairchild Publications, Inc.

purchase discounts, free shipping, and gift packaging entice consumers to purchase from the Internet.

Internet marketing is increasingly useful in the B2B neckwear industry. **B2B (business to business)** means businesses are selling to other businesses rather than to the ultimate consumers. A tie manufacturing company can show the neckwear line to retail store buyers and take orders via the Internet. Business to business companies believe the Internet is a primary selling tool, not just for convenient merchandise ordering, but also for showcasing the company's progressive image.

Catalog Retailing

Neckwear and scarfs are popular catalog items. A one-size-fits-all purchase, with light mailing weight and a long fashion life cycle make neckwear a profitable catalog classification. A traditional catalog is a good promotional selling tool for ties, especially if used in conjunction with a Web site. Customers can view small color and print samples of the ties online, and if interested, they can complete an online request for a print catalog.

SELLING SCARFS, TIES, AND HANDKERCHIEFS

As with other fashion accessories, the price points for scarfs, ties, and handkerchiefs range from just a few dollars to several hundred dollars. The value of these accessories depends on the customer's perception. Is the item prestigious? Does it reflect the customer's personality? Is it compatible with several items in the wardrobe? Does it meet his or her needs? Is it an image builder? A customer whose answer is affirmative to any of these questions is likely to perceive the item to be of value and to be willing to pay the retail price.

Price and Value

The prices of ties and scarfs are dependent upon several factors. These include the amount of hand workmanship, quality of workmanship, materials used, and brand name. Better-quality ties are three-part ties cut on the bias to prevent curling of the blades when the knot is tied. They should have an interlining that is an appropriate weight for the fashion fabric. Lightweight silk fabrics are paired with heavier woolen interlinings, while heavy silk fabrics require only a lightweight interlining. The **bar tack,** which holds the back flaps together, is a sign of a better-quality tie. It prevents the tie from twisting and becoming misshapen.

Hand-sewn ties can be identified by a single loop thread called a **slipstitch** visible on the back side of the tie. Hermès is an example of an expensive, hand-sewn brand that sells for several hundred dollars. The slipstitch thread gives added resilience to the tie. When the slipstitch is pulled on a quality handmade tie, the tie should gather.

Profile Box: Hermès Ties

For 164 years a powerful name in the leather fashion industry, Hermès, is even more powerful when it describes a silky, luxurious man's necktie. The first collection, begun in 1949, featured figures, geometric patterns, classic and neo-classic patterns, and **_trompe l'oeil_** (trick of the eye.) Currently, color themes are important classifications of Hermès ties, as are leaf patterns and elephant figures.

A Hermès tie is a collector's item. An average of seven silk screens are used per signature tie. Each season, Hermès offers about thirty designs, either in silk twill or heavier silk fabrics. This includes 25 new designs and five re-editions in different color schemes.

Unlike other competitors' three-piece ties, a Hermès tie consists of its trademark two pieces, both cut by hand. The lining of the tie is exactly matched to the dominant color of the tie. The craftsman who hand-finishes the Hermès tie initials it.

In New York City, the only place to purchase a Hermès tie is in the recently opened Hermès shop—a four-floor, 20,200-square-foot flagship store at 62nd Street and Madison Avenue. The 1928 building is a historic landmark in Manhattan and is four times larger than the previous store on East 57th Street. To commemorate the opening, the company offered a scarf print featuring Manhattan flora and fauna, an early city map, and a depiction of the Hermès mascot, a mounted soldier.

Once inside the Madison Avenue store, shoppers can easily locate the famous ties on the lower level, merchandised among shirts and related men's apparel. Leather decorates the store interior, and the tie hangers are actually a stylized stirrup. Women's scarfs are available on the main floor, alongside jewelry, small leather goods, bags, fragrances, and other accessories. To Laurent Mommeja-Hermès, president and CEO of Hermès, merchandise in the new Madison Avenue store is like pieces of art. "Products are like paintings. But if they're not in frames and hung, they're not complete. Hopefully they will find their frames in this house."[1]

Outside New York City, patrons can shop for exclusively distributed Hermès ties at Neiman-Marcus, Marshall Fields, and a few high-end specialty shops. In Neiman-Marcus, customers can find a boutique of many Hermès products, from ties and scarfs to bed linens. For a slightly lower price, duty-free shops at some airports, such as the Spata Airport near Athens, Greece, and the Charles de Gaulle Airport in France, offer the Paris-based delicacies.

Source:

[1]Palmieri, J. E. (2000, September 20). Hermès Opens Majestic Madison Avenue Store. *Daily News Record, 30*(111), p. 1. Courtesy of Fairchild Publications, Inc.

The Hermès flagship store in New York City.
Courtesy of Fairchild Publications, Inc.

Folding a Pocket Square

A man need not match his pocket square fabric and his tie fabric, although these are often sold as sets in retail stores. If a man chooses a patterned tie, the pocket square would be easiest to match (and look the best) as a solid color. Crisp white linen handkerchiefs are always a safe choice and always in fashion.

Several methods of folding pocket squares or handkerchiefs provide creative options and visual interest. These methods include the straight-edge fold, the single-point fold, the double-point fold, the quadruple-point fold, and the puff.

Straight-Edge Fold

1. Lay the handkerchief on a flat surface.
2. Fold the bottom half up to the top half, making a triangle.
3. Fold in the outside corners overlapping them.
4. Point down, tuck the pocket square into the jacket pocket, making sure the straight edge is visible by 1/2" to 3/4" above the pocket.

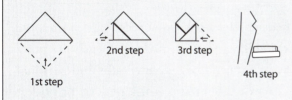

Single-Point Fold

1. Fold fabric to a 4 1/2" square.
2. Fold lower half of square up to make a triangle with points matching and facing upward.
3. Fold in remaining corners slightly smaller than pocket width.
4. Point up, tuck the pocket square into the jacket pocket.

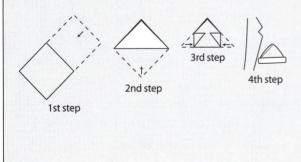

Double-Point Fold

1. Lay the handkerchief on a flat surface.
2. Fold fabric to a 4 1/2" square.
3. Fold in the side and bottom corners slightly smaller than pocket width.
4. Points up, tuck the pocket square into the jacket pocket.

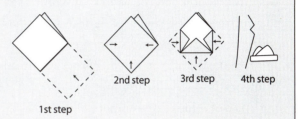

Quadruple-Point Fold

1. Lay the handkerchief on a flat surface.
2. Fold the bottom half up to the top half, but offset the top points, making a triangle with two peaks.
3. Fold up the remaining corners so their points reach across the center line, creating the 3rd and 4th peaks.
4. Slightly roll from the bottom until the pocket square slides into the pocket.

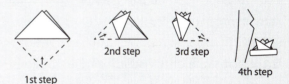

Puff

1. Lay the handkerchief on a flat surface.
2. Pinch it in the center and lift up.
3. With other hand, smooth down the hanging pocket square.
4. Fold the lower corners to the back and tuck the folded edge into the jacket pocket.

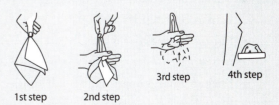

Meeting Customer Needs

Salespeople should explain the relationship between a tie's knot and the shirt collar. The knot shouldn't be too large, or it will cause the collar to spread, nor should it be too small in the space between the collar points. Bow ties should complement the facial shape and the collar spread as well. Generally, the bow tie ends should not extend beyond the width of the neck or farther than the points of the collar.

The men's neckwear industry has responded to the corporate casual trend with increased production of casual ties in the form of conversational, novelty, and large-scale prints. Often the designs are loose interpretations of women's ready-to-wear prints. Many customers prefer ties that reveal their personalities. The industry has been frustrated by the changing corporate dress codes, because many companies no longer require ties at all.

To make a profit in the men's necktie industry, some industry personnel believe the main challenge is to sell a tie to a man who doesn't necessarily need one. One answer is merchandising "the total look." Customers have less time, but there are far more color choices. Showing them three or four options that would look good with a particular shirt and suit can help close a sale.

Women's dressier (and heavier) pure silk scarfs have suffered a fate similar to the necktie industry, succumbing to the corporate casual trend. By contrast, cotton and rayon scarfs and neckerchiefs lend themselves to the casual trend.

As a group, scarfs and ties are relatively inexpensive wardrobe extenders. Scarfs also serve a practical function of preventing "ring around the collar." Shawls and larger scarfs are practical accessories when bare-shouldered eveningwear is fashionable. New looks and personal statements can be created by the addition of a scarf or the purchase of a new tie or pocket square. In order to remind customers of this easy updating option, stores should merchandise these items in highly visible locations and offer them as suggested add-on items. Manufacturers and retailers should offer a range of popular and classic looks that complement ready-to-wear fashions.

SUMMARY

- The origins of men's neckties can be traced back to ancient Rome and China. Cravats were first worn by the French and English.
- Variations of scarfs for women have been worn for decades and continue to be popular as wardrobe extenders.
- Fabric for neckties is usually silk or microfibers with a silk-like hand. Woven silks refer to a woven-in design, while printed silks refer to a printed or silk-screened design.
- Pocket squares are usually made of the same fabric as neckties, or of white linen.
- Handkerchiefs are usually cotton or linen.
- Fabrics for women's scarfs or neckerchiefs vary depending on the season, the end use, and the price point.

- Neckties may be handmade or machine made, with significant differences in prices. Men's necktie patterns may be classified as abstract, club, conversational, floral, foulard, novelty, paisley, plaid, polka dot/pin dot, rep, and solid.

- Necktie knots include the four-in-hand, Windsor, half-Windsor, and bow tie.

- Cleaning methods depend upon the fiber content and the product. Men's neckties are best left uncleaned except when absolutely necessary. Scarfs, neckerchiefs, and handkerchiefs should be cleaned according to the fiber content. Delicate-cycle washing or hand washing is recommended. Silk items should be dry-cleaned.

- The United States neckwear industry generates 1.3 billion dollars in retail sales. Specialty stores obtain higher retail prices and higher gross margins than department stores.

- Scarf and neckwear designers offer signature lines under licensing agreements with manufacturers. Designers seek manufacturing companies with the quality and image they desire to project.

- Cold-weather accessories represent a growing accessories classification for retailers. Manufacturers of fashion accessories have expanded into cold-weather accessories as a way to increase market share.

- Merchandising methods differ depending on the store type, brand name, and price point.

- The one-size-fits-all ease of neckwear makes it popular for gift, online, and catalog retailing. Unique designs, customization, virtual features, and free shipping are some of the merchandising techniques used.

- When purchasing neckwear, customers should be made aware that variances in workmanship and fabric quality, brand and design exclusiveness, and merchandising methods affect the retail price.

- Pocket square folds include the straight-edge fold, single-point fold, double-point fold, quadruple-point fold, and the puff.

TERMS FOR REVIEW

abstract	cravat	neck gusset
Annie Hall look	custom tipping	Neckwear Association of
ascot	décolleté	America (NAA)
B2B (business to business)	floral	novelty
bandana	foulard	paisley
bar tack	four-in-hand knot	pashmina scarf (shawl)
bar tack stitch	four-in-hand tie	Peacock Revolution
Betsy	front blade (apron)	pelerine
bias	half-Windsor knot	plaid pattern
bolo (string tie)	hand-rolled hem	polka dot (pin dot)
bow tie	interlining (lining)	printed silk
buckram	loop label	private-label brand
club	machine hem	rep (repeating stripe)
conversational	national brand	ruff

shell	steinkirk	under blade (tail)
shrug	stocks	Windsor knot
silk screening	stole	woven silk
slipstitch	straight grain	wrap
slip stitching	tipping (facing)	
solid	trompe l'oeil	

REVIEW QUESTIONS

1. What are some important neckwear fashions in history?
2. What are pashmina wraps, and why did they become an important fashion accessory of recent seasons?
3. How was the men's necktie industry affected by the casual dress code in business, and how did the industry adapt to consumer demands?
4. What are the major steps in tie production, and what are the three pieces comprising a necktie?
5. What are three methods of tying a tie?
6. What is a licensing agreement?
7. What are some indicators of quality in neckwear accessories?
8. What are some creative Web-based marketing techniques for neckwear?
9. Why are an increasing number of designers and manufacturers selling neckwear products via the Internet and through catalogs?
10. Why are neckwear accessories important sources of add-on sales?

KNOWLEDGE APPLICATIONS

1. Select a decade of the 20th century and research neckwear fashions of that decade, locating visual aids if possible. Write a brief history and make a presentation to the class.
2. With a partner, select two distinctly different stores to visit and do a study of the same section, either the women's scarfs or men's ties. Record brands, prices, styles, colors, prints, and display methods. Compare findings and develop a comparative analysis.
3. Collect catalogs featuring neckwear accessories. Classify the accessories according to the fabric's printed or woven design. What classifications are most common/least common? Why?
4. Bring scarfs, neckerchiefs, ties, and pocket squares to class. Practice necktie-tying techniques. Share scarf- and neckerchief-tying ideas with other class members. Practice folding pocket squares.
5. Perform a subject search of neckwear accessories on the Internet. What creative marketing techniques are used to sell neckwear through the Internet?
6. Talk to the buyer or manager of a men's or women's accessories department about scarf or tie merchandising. Request a "show and tell" explanation of neckwear construction.
7. Find a recent article from the Internet regarding the casual dress code in business and the role of men's neckties in a business wardrobe. Share the findings with the class.

CHAPTER II

❧

HATS, HAIR ACCESSORIES, WIGS, AND HAIRPIECES

Mad as a Hatter

Remember the Mad Hatter in Lewis Carroll's Alice's Adventures in Wonderland? *In the 1800s, makers of felt hats did indeed go mad as a result of mercury nitrate poisoning. Inhaling the mercury fumes during felt hat processing caused violent twitching and derangement, symptoms of a brain disorder. People often made fun of a hatter's "drunkenness" –impaired hearing, slurred speech, trembling, stumbling, and memory loss. Mercuric poisoning was sometimes called the mad hatter's syndrome, the hatter's shakes, or the Danbury shakes, because Danbury, Connecticut, was a U.S. hatmaking center.*

A BRIEF HISTORY OF HATS AND HAIR ACCESSORIES

THE TERM *MILLINERY* HAS BEEN DATED BACK TO 1529 WHEN POPULAR STRAWS FOR women's hats were imported from Italy, especially areas around Milan. The word *milliners* was also used to describe the **haberdasher shop** (men's furnishings) owners who imported these goods. Eventually, millinery became associated with the making of women's hats, not men's hats.

Historically, hat etiquette has been markedly different for men and women. Men were to remove their hats indoors and in the presence of all ladies, men of older age, or men of higher rank or status. Women were not expected to remove their hats because to remove and replace a hat required complicated and extensive adjustments, including the removal of hatpins. **Hatpins** are metal pins that are several inches in length and have a decorative end piece. They were used to secure veils and hats to upswept coiffures.

For centuries, hair accessories for girls have taken the form of ribbons and bows. While hat-wearing was often considered too "grown up," ribbons and bows were seen as acceptable hair ornaments and were often given as gifts.

Bonnets decorated with bows, flowers, feathers, and ruffles were extremely fashionable during the first half of the 19th century. Later in the century, bonnet popularity began to wane, while hats gradually increased in popularity and size.

Millinery was an important part of early haute couture houses in Paris. Hundreds of Paris milliners offered fashionable hats for social occasions in the late 19th and early 20th centuries.

The dawning of the 20th century brought extravagance and controversy. Women's hats had become enormous, both crowns and brims, to accommodate pompadour hairstyles and masses of feathers and flowers. Bird plumage, and even whole bodies of small birds and creatures were stuffed and mounted on spectacular hats. Angered by the cruelty to animals in the name of fashion, conservation societies organized to outlaw these fashions, or at the very least discourage the wearing of plumage.

Early 20th-century men's hats were the **boater,** a flat-topped, brimmed hat in Panama straw, and the silk top hat worn by fashionable gentlemen. The invention of the automobile created a need for close-fitting beret hats for men. However, women simply wore tightly tied veils over their voluminous hats while riding in motor coaches.

By the 1920s, the fashion pendulum for women's hats had swung to the **cloche hat,** a close-fitting and asymmetrical style covering closely cropped hair. Another popular head accessory was the **headache band,** a ribbon encircling the head and adorned with a plume or other ornament.

From the 1930s to the 1950s, decorative hats, netting, and veils were worn by women, and caps or fedoras were worn by men. New York City stores led the world in fashionable hat production. Many stores had their own millinery departments staffed with European immigrant milliners. Bergdorf Goodman, Henri Bendel, Macy's, and Saks Fifth Avenue created couture millinery in their own workrooms. Glamorous movie stars Greta Garbo and Joan Crawford popularized both brimless hats and brims that dipped on one side.

By the end of the 1950s and throughout the 1960s and 1970s, hats declined in popularity because of ever-increasing hairstyle volumes, a more casual society, and the negative implications surrounding hat wearing. Hats were considered "establishment" and restrictive, and long, loose hair was an outward expression of freedom for both males and females. Hats were considered fussy and unnecessary, except for a limited number of special occasions. Hat wearing was relegated to weddings, horse races, polo matches, and some religious services.

The late Diana, Princess of Wales was touted as a hat savior in the 1980s because of her enthusiasm for fashion and hats (see Figure 11.1). But even her worldwide popularity was not powerful enough to reverse the general population's decline in hat wearing. Couture designers featured hats on runway models, yet the fashions were not accepted by the masses.

Although hats have yet to make a comeback, hair accessories are simple enough to appeal to many females. Headbands and hair bows were popular for women of all ages during the 1990s. Former First Lady of the United States Hillary Rodham Clinton influenced the popularity of

FIGURE 11.1 *Diana, Princess of Wales renewed a popular interest in hat wearing.*
AP/Wide World Photos.

headbands during the 1992 presidential election. The television program, *Sex and the City,* which gained fashion industry exposure for fur apparel, also influenced the accessories industry with silk flowers as hat embellishments and hair ornaments. Actress Drew Barrymore has also been credited with popularizing the floral trend when she was seen wearing beaded and sequined floral hair ornaments.

AN INTRODUCTION
TO HATS AND HAIR ACCESSORIES

In the year 2000, caps and hats were two of the best-selling accessories for young men because they are a relatively inexpensive wardrobe builder. The resurgence of hat popularity began in the 1990s, thanks to young male consumers who wore casual ball caps featuring virtually any logo. The hat fashion was soon adopted by young female consumers, and "bad hair days" became a popular excuse for wearing hats. Ball cap styles in patterns and colors that coordinated with women's apparel soon saturated the market. From ball caps to **fishermen** or **bucket hats** (casual, with a soft crown and brim), the popular trend continues into the 21st century.

Other casual headwear styles include barrettes and clips, hair bows, headbands, and ponytail holders. Popular ready-to-wear prints and patterns usually surface in the fashion fabric of hair accessories. Hair accessories in popular fabrics saturate the market, but tend to have short life cycles.

In spite of the marginal market for fashion hats compared to earlier decades, special-occasion hat dressing is still an important concept. Usually fashion hats are selected for religious services. Weddings and Easter Sunday have traditionally been peak selling seasons for fashion hats. A recent trend toward feminine suits and ladylike fashions has sustained the market for dressier hats. The hat market, especially large and embellished hat silhouettes, for older and African-American women living in the Bible Belt in the United States has proved strong. (The Bible Belt is in the south central section of the United States.)

The consumer's increasing desire for sun protection has increased sales of hats and visors. Manufacturers offer wide-brimmed hats and extra-long visors, as much for sun protection as fashion appeal. The American Academy of Dermatology recommends a minimum of a four-inch brim on sun hats to protect from harmful ultraviolet sun rays. Packable or crushable hats, carried in satchels until needed for sun protection, are key items offered to meet consumers' traveling needs to resorts, beaches, and sunny geographic areas.

Knit hats and headbands as cold-weather accessories are small and close fitting to retain body heat. Not only are cold-weather hats popular for self-purchasers, they are equally important as gift items—especially in boxed sets with gloves and scarfs. When giving credit for the overall popularity of men's hats, Mother Nature still has more influence than any fashion trend. If winter weather is warm, hat sales are generally flat across the board.

Parts of a Hat

There are only a few basic parts of a hat, and these are merely options. The basic parts include the crown, brim, headband, and trim. A hat may have a crown, but no brim, or a brim, but no crown. Both the crown and brim are present in most hat styles and in innumerable combinations.

- **Crown** Top portion of the hat.
- **Brim** Projecting edge of a hat; may be upturned, downturned, or straight.
- **Headband** A strip of real or imitation leather or fabric on the inside of the hat, encircling the lower crown (usually just above the eyebrows).
- **Decorative trim** Ornamentation, including ribbons, feathers, flowers, netting, and any other suitable materials.

Hats and Hair Accessories Manufacturing

Hats and hair accessories may be hand crafted or mass-produced. Many small companies manufacture pricier, one-of-a-kind headwear. Large-scale manufacturers are important at all price points. To reach the greatest number of consumers, large hat manufacturers often produce hats in several price zones, both branded and private labels. For example, the 50-year-old Aldo Hat Corporation produces designer hats under several divisions including Mr. John Classic, Jack McConnell, Halston Millinery, and a catalog/private label division.

Design

Hat designers of the 20th century ranged from millinery specialists to couture designers, but all were influenced by societal forces, and the designers' styles reflected the mood of the people. Coco Chanel, famous as a couture designer, began her career as a milliner in the 1920s. Caroline Reboux and her apprentice, Lilly Daché, became famous for the 1920s cloche and turban hats. Daché was credited with designing the swagger hat worn by Hollywood star Marlene Dietrich. Designer Sally Victor began her career in Macy's millinery department and married a millinery wholesaler. She became popular designing hats for the general public. Hattie Carnegie also began her millinery career at Macy's at age fifteen. In just a few years, she built a successful hat and related accessories empire employing 1000 people. Roy Frowick Halston, another couture designer, was credited with designing Jackie Kennedy's inaugural pillbox hat in 1960 (see Figure 11.2.)

Milan, Italy, and Paris, France, continue to influence world millinery fashions. Runway designers show **millinery couture** (costly hat originals) that is interpreted by U.S. milliners. The design houses of Christian Dior and Philip Treacy, and European designers, Fredrick Fox,

FIGURE 11.2
First lady Jacqueline Kennedy wearing her trademark pillbox hat.
AP/Wide World Photos.

Peter Bettley, Cristianini, and Jacques Le Corre, all influence fabrics, trims, and colors. Hair accessories designers attend these showings, as well as fine jewelry shows, to gain inspiration for their lines.

Designers create hats and hair accessories by drawing a detailed sketch, complete with trim, from which a sample is made. Another design technique is to manufacture a **preproduction sample** (similar to a sample garment), which may be modified many times. Designers consider the appeal, wearability, proportion, and price point when creating hat and hair accessories designs. The complementary trim should add an interesting focal point but should not overwhelm the style or the wearer.

Hat designing encompasses the simple creation of new fabrications and trims for casual hats all the way to millinery couture (also called model millinery). In the face of a casual culture, a market of hat lovers who use hats to make a fashion statement still exists. Some hat designers with a willingness to hand stitch and hand sculpt hats have found a profitable niche. One such milliner is Jan Stanton of Los Angeles. Her handmade couture hats retail for more than $300. Her company, Heartfelt Hats, sells to specialty and department stores in the United States and meets the needs of a specific group of customers who want to be transformed into conspicuous consumers.

One of the important keys for success in designing saleable headwear is **market segmentation.** This means dividing the marketplace into demographic and psychographic segments. Design companies produce specialized colors, trim, embellishments, fabrics, and styles for homogeneous groups of customers. **Demographic segmentation** refers to classifying consumer groups by objective data, such as age, education level, geographic region, and annual income. **Psychographic segmentation** refers to classifying consumers by subjective data, such as lifestyle, degree of fashion interest, values, and opinions. For example, the basic style may not change in headwear, but designers may customize colors or materials based on consumers' demographic and psychographic variables. Certain colors may be accepted by **color-forward shoppers,** such as young people, African-American or Hispanic peoples, or high-income females. Other groups, such as conservative or older men, considered **color-prudents,** may resist the introduction of faddish or unusual colors.

Production

Hats may be woven, felted, knitted, or crocheted. **Buckram** (stiffened netting) may form the base of a fashion hat that will ultimately be covered in fashion fabric.

Hat linings are optional, but are usually present in more expensive hats. Lining fabrics are usually made of satin or satin-like fabrics, but may be of lightweight cotton in summer hats.

Both straw and felt hats are made with similar techniques. Both require **blocking** (the process that gives the hat its shape), either on **wooden block forms** or **aluminum pan forms.** The blocking process may be done by hand or machine. Before mass production of hats, most were blocked by hand with specialized tools and equipment. Another method, **hydraulic blocking,** may be used after the traditional hand-blocking method or the machine method. This method uses intense pressure to create a felt or straw hat that closely conforms to the shape of the pan.

Profile: Philip Treacy

"A good hat is like a cheaper form of cosmetic surgery."
- Philip Treacy

"Berets? Bah. The pillbox? Old hat." - People Weekly

For the first time in 60 years, the haute couture show in Paris was devoted exclusively to hats. Not since the 1920s have hats been important enough to warrant their own show. The invitation from the Fédération Française de la Couture was issued in an attempt to attract a younger group of customers to the couture showings. These customers enjoy looking at hats but may not feel compelled to buy or wear hats.

The invitation was extended to Philip Treacy (pronounced Trace-ee), a talented young designer from London who has created hat designs of fantastic proportions, from a sea anemone to a giant mimosa blossom. His shows have featured numerous styles of couture hats on models wearing couture clothing by Alexander McQueen, Chanel, Lacroix, Kenzo, Jean-Paul Gaultier, Louis Vuitton, Valentino, and many others. Treacy's couture hats are truly the icing on the cake.

Philip Treacy hat.

Courtesy of Fairchild Publications, Inc.

For his first professional fashion show in 1993, Treacy hired supermodels Christy Turlington, Kate Moss, and a topless Naomi Campbell. More recently, he hired celebrity Grace Jones to open and close his runway shows.

Fashion writer Peter Davis vividly described the audience reaction to the Treacy fashion show.

The Super Bowl-style applause and whooping cheers grew more deafening with each madcap hat that Helena [Christensen], Kate, Naomi et al. strutted out on the runway. By the end of Treacy's show, which was sponsored by Rolls Royce and *The New Yorker,* the jaded fashion flock had jumped to its feet for a thunderous standing ovation (*PAPERMAG: Philip Treacy,* n.d.).

Treacy sees himself as a craftsman, inspired by Picasso, sculpture, tribal art, and futuristic interpretations. The young designer explained, "I'm not a crazy designer, I just like to excite the eye of people about hats."[1] His successful launch of hats opened the door to his newer accessory lines: hair ornaments, scarves, gloves, and handbags.

Currently, his hats are available in nine countries: Australia, France, Germany, Ireland, Italy, Japan, Spain, the United Kingdom, and the United States. Domestic retailers are primarily located in New York, and include Bergdorf Goodman, Henri Bendel, and Saks Fifth Avenue. Neiman Marcus in Dallas, Texas, and the New Orleans Hat Shop in Louisiana also carry Treacy's hats.

So popular is Treacy, that he has been named the British Accessory Designer of the Year five times. Brits love his hats and are willing to pay between $100 and $1,000 for an original. The summer Royal Ascot races in England feature many Treacy hat wearers.

Philip Treacy.

Courtesy of Fairchild Publications, Inc.

Thirtysomething Treacy, born in Ireland, studied fashion at the National College of Art and Design in Dublin. He attended the Royal College of Art in London on a scholarship, graduating in 1990. Upon graduation, Treacy opened his London shop at 69 Elizabeth Street. An instant success, he began working with designer greats like Marc Bohan and Karl Lagerfeld for Chanel.

Treacy has designed couture hats for other houses, including Chanel, Versace, Valentino, and Givenchy. He is no stranger to runway shows in New York and London, having participated for several years. His impressive client list includes Jerry Hall, Sarah Ferguson (Fergie), Aretha Franklin, Tracey Ullman, Diana Ross, and Anjelica Huston.

Source:

1 Luscombe, B. (1999, March 1). Mad About Hats: Milliner Philip Treacy's fantastic creations are real head turners. *Time,* 153 (8), p. 73.

One disadvantage to hydraulic blocking is a diminished textural appearance of the straw because the pressure flattens the natural straw.

Straw Hat Production

China and South America are primary production countries for straw hats. The straw must be starched to create a workable strand for weaving. Straw hats are almost always made of hand-woven or **plaited** or **braided straw,** taking up to 25 hours for the weaving stage. Depending on the coarseness of the straw, weaving time varies. Finer straws require more time, while larger, coarse straws require shorter weaving times.

Straw is woven into one of three forms—capeline, cone, or braid. **Capeline weaving** is a one-piece woven crown and brim, usually for wide-brimmed hats. **Cone weaving** creates a conical-shaped, small-brimmed or brimless hat. Braided straws requires a slight overlapping of a narrow strip of braid beginning at the crown center and spiraling to create a crown and brim.

Once the **hood** (the section that will become the crown) is woven, the material is wetted and stretched over a crown shape and secured with string or pins at the base of the crown. Straw should be thoroughly dried and thinly coated with varnish to retain the hat's shape. The crown is blocked first and then the brim. Brim edges may be folded under and stitched or bound with **bias tape** or **petersham binding.** These are narrow woven fabrics that have some stretch and are folded and stitched around the raw edge. In the case of some expensive straws, the edge may be expertly woven into a tightly finished edge.

Felt Hat Production

Felt hats may be made of synthetic, wool, or fur fibers. A cone is created by **carding** (aligning) the fibers into a loose mass that is wound around a sized wooden cone. The cone is stretched over a frame, and a crown and brim are formed. After placing the hat on a sized hat block, pressure and ample steam heat are applied to shrink the hat to size. It is then stiffened with felt varnish and allowed to cool before being removed from the block. First the crown and then the brim are blocked. The hat is trimmed to a desired width and rolled by placing it on a heated projection or flange. Finally, it is allowed to dry before coating with varnish.

Felt-brim edges are finished similarly to straw hats. Finishing a felt brim may involve hand sewing millinery wire in an overcast stitch around the edge. Machine- or hand-sewn petersham ribbon is often used to finish the raw brim edge.

Materials

Hats and hair accessories are made of a wide variety of materials. Often headwear makers take cues from popular ready-to-wear materials. For example, leather and fur, popular materials in all fashion areas, are used to trim and embellish fashion hats or cover hair accessories, such as headbands and barrettes. Other popular materials for hats include fur fibers, felts, fashion

Tech Talk: Turning Heads

Those not involved with the creative end of headwear designing may think all ballcaps are basically the same. Not so! Ask any customer with dozens of caps in the closet, "What makes you want to buy another?" This is precisely the question being asked by market researchers. The responses aren't always the same, but a general theme emerges: a hat is an inexpensive fashion fix.

How do hat manufacturers continue to provide unique styles that are difficult for customers to resist? One answer is **textile technology,** fashion-futuristic textiles that all have a common thread—adaptability.

Consider the following hat innovations:

The consumers' **logomania** (obsession with cap logos) is encouraged by a solar active thread designed by the Robinson-Anton Textile Company®. This thread changes colors in ultraviolet light. Indoors, the decorative stitching on the front of the cap is white. Outdoors, the thread changes to a bright color.

The desire for built-in sunscreen is satisfied with a not-so-typical ball cap. This unique cap, manufactured in nylon and treated with a ceramic coating, is capable of reflecting ultraviolet rays. This Sunshield cap, created by Adams Fashion Headwear, also sports an extra long visor with a green undervisor.

A technological headwear fabric, called Outlast®, protects wearers from extended exposure to cold climates. Encapsulated in the fibers of the hats, Outlast absorbs, stores, and releases heat. The developer, Mental Headgear in Texas, has created temperature-regulating hats for consumers participating in winter outdoor exercises like running or skiing.

Gauging the consumer demand for wearable technology is probably more difficult than creating the technology. How technical do consumers want their clothing and accessories? How much are they willing to pay for the technology? Designers and manufacturers should ask themselves this important marketing question: "Is this just another clever invention, or is it really a product that empowers the consumer?"

fabrics, feathers, and straws. Usually spring/summer hats are made of straws and lightweight fabrics, while fall/winter hats are manufactured in leather, suede, furs, felts, pile, and heavyweight fabrics.

Hair accessories materials include horn, mother-of-pearl, tortoise, leather, suede, fur, feathers, fabric, metals, and jewels. As with hats, fashionable materials in apparel and related accessories can be interpreted into hair accessories. For example, gold chains and beading that may be featured on belts, handbags, or eveningwear can translate into materials for coordinated hair accessories.

The pervasiveness of any printed design, such as an animal print or floral pattern, can be determined by its appearance in accessories, as well as wearing apparel. For example, when floral patterns are popular in apparel fashions, accessories manufacturers offer silk flower hair accessories to coordinate with textile prints.

The types of straw used for hats are numerous. The most commonly used types are jute, palm fiber, Panama, parasisal, rush, seagrass, wheat, sisal and toyo paper. Straw types are defined in Chapter 3.

Basic Styles of Hats

Facial shape, head size, and hairstyle should determine which hat style a customer selects. Salespersons should know which types of hats may be worn at various angles to enhance a particular facial shape. Some hats may be worn perched atop the head, slanted forward or backward, or angled. Two general rules of thumb for wearing hats are—a hat style should contrast with the facial shape, and the hairstyle should be subordinate to the hat style. Hair should be pulled back or worn close to the head when a hat is the focal point. For example, a long, narrow face would look best with a low-crowned, wide-brimmed hat, such as a cartwheel hat style. A wide face would look best with a high-crowned, small-brimmed (or brimless) hat, such as a fedora or pillbox. People with small heads look best in wider brims, while people with large heads look best in narrower brims.

The following are some basic styles of hats (see Figure 11.3):

Beret A small brimless cap with a flat crown, worn on an angle at top of the head.

Boater Usually a man's straw hat with a low, oval crown, flat brim, and wide ribbon; originally worn for boating. The man's equivalent of a woman's sailor hat.

Bowler or **derby** Rounded crown and rolled brim, usually in a stiff felt material. First worn by men and later adapted by women. Named for the Earl of Derby in 19th-century England.

Breton Straw or felt with a flattened crown and evenly rolled brim all around the hat. Often worn toward the crown of the head.

Bumper A felt or cloth hat with a tightly rolled or tubular brim.

Cartwheel A close-fitting crown and a wide brim (beachbrim), often worn for sun protection. Openwork or lace cartwheel hats were popular as bridesmaids' hats in the 1970s.

Cloche A close-fitting crown and down-turned brim extending to cover the ear, popular 1920s fashion.

Coolie Peaked crown, slanting down in a shallow conical manner, forming a parasol-like sunshade. Made of straw, bamboo, or leaves with no definition between the crown and the brim. Worn by Chinese field workers known as Coolies.

Cowboy or **Western** High crown and wide brim, slightly angled up on the sides and down in the center front and back, a result of custom shaping. First worn by Mexican cowboys and later adapted by American cowboys. Also called a **ten-gallon hat** because the "gallon" was derived from the Spanish word *galón* meaning braid (braiding around the brim). Some believe the name was an exaggeration of the size of the crown—large enough to hold ten gallons of water! This became a fashion item in the 1980s, with the "urban cowboy" look.

Fedora Lengthwise center crease in crown and brim rolled upward on the sides. Sometimes called a homberg. Most popular 20th-century hat style for men. Occasionally adopted by women for brief fashion seasons.

Fez A tapered crown and no brim. Sometimes featured with a tassel, such as those worn by Shriners. Turkish origin.

Halo Sits on the crown of the head, with a large brim that encircles the face, giving the illusion of a halo.

Homberg Felt, with small, upturned brim and dented crown. Sometimes called a fedora.

Hood A draped head covering, often a detachable part of a coat.

beret   boater   derby   breton

bumper   cartwheel hat   cloche   cowboy hat

fedora   military   pillbox hat   pork-pie hat

slouch hat   tam   top hat   turban

FIGURE 11.3
Basic styles of hats.

Knit or **Stocking Cap** Close-fitting skullcap; may have long, tapering crown with tassel. Made of knitted yarns.

Military Small crown with folded-up brim; folds front to back for a creased effect in the center.

Mushroom Similar in appearance to a Coolie hat, but with rounded top that resembles a mushroom. May be felt or fabric, rather than straw.

Pillbox A small, round, brimless hat with flat crown. Made famous by First Lady Jacqueline Kennedy in the 1960s.

Pork Pie Low crown with a telescoped flat top originating in the 1930s. Straw, felt, or fabric materials.

Profile A hat with one side of the brim upturned and the other side downturned to show the wearer's profile.

Sailor Small, stiff crown with flat, low top and straight brim. Usually straw, worn with ribbon around the crown. The woman's equivalent of a boater.

Skimmer Similar to a sailor hat, but with a very low crown.

Skullcap, Calotte, or **Juliet Cap** Small, rounded cap that covers the crown of the head; dates back to the Renaissance time period.

Slouch Characterized by a flexible, drooping brim.

Sombrero Mexican word for "hat." Usually tall, flat crown and wide brim, encircled with decorative ribbon. May be felt or straw. Used to shade its wearer from sun.

Tam O' Shanter (Tam) Flexible and flattened crown extends over headband-style brim. Solid or plaid materials, originally wool; Scottish origin.

Top Hat or **Stovepipe Hat** High, cylindrical crown made in black silk with narrow brim; popularized by U.S. President Abraham Lincoln; used today as a magician's hat.

Turban High-crowned and brimless, with the appearance of a wrapped length of fabric wound around the head. Fabric ends may be invisibly tucked or decoratively tied in a small knot. Popular Middle Eastern style.

Visor or **Peak** Partial brim extending over the eyes to shade from the sun.

Basic Styles of Hair Accessories

Most hair accessories designs are variations on popular apparel or jewelry trends. For example, when leather and fur are popular in ready-to-wear, hair accessories are manufactured in leather and fur. In a typical season, clips and barrettes are similar to fashion jewelry designs.

A single hair accessories category, such as headbands, may be found at many price points, in a range of sizes, and made of a variety of materials suitable for the target market. Among basic styles of hair accessories are the following (see Figure 11.4):

Barrette Decorative metal or plastic bar backed with a clasp to hold the hair in place.

Butterfly and **Banana Clips** Decorative plastic or metal, spring-hinged claw that secures (closes

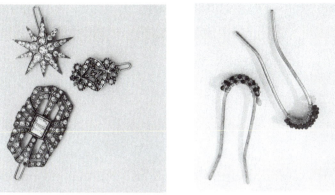

(a) hair jewelry (b) hairpin

(c) tiara

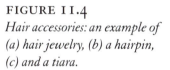

FIGURE 11.4
Hair accessories: an example of
(a) hair jewelry, (b) a hairpin,
(c) and a tiara.

around) a lock of hair. Sizes range from tiny butterfly clips for babies to large banana clips for thick hair.

Comb Hair ornament that slides into the hair on comb-like teeth. Decorations, such as flowers or ribbons, may be wired or glued to the comb.

Covered Rubber Band Elasticized band for securing ponytails and braid ends. Covered with yarn to protect hair and prevent tangling.

Earmuffs Partial headband with fur or napped fabric ear coverings for warmth.

Hair Extensions Synthetic hair attached with clips or other attachments to create the appearance of longer, fuller hair.

Hair Jewelry Any decorative hair accessory resembling fashion jewelry.

Hairpin Hair ornament without a clasp. Held in the hair on a bobby pin base or with a u-shaped metal piece.

Headband Circular-shaped band, may be full or partial. Made of plastic, metal, or stretch fabric. Usually worn above the forehead and under the nape of neck. May also be worn across the forehead, parallel to the eyebrows like the ancient Egyptians or early Native Americans.

Pony Cuff Decorative, semicircular ponytail covering with clasp that closes under the ponytail.

Scrunchies or **Ponies** Wide, elasticized bands, usually covered with a soft, fashionable material, such as leather, fur, fake hair, or fabric.

Switch Long hairpiece used to create hairstyle volume.

Tiara A delicate, crown-like headband bejeweled with diamonds or rhinestones.

Hat Sizing and Fitting

Most lower- and moderately priced hats today are one-size-fits-all for a head circumference of about 22 inches to 22 1/2 inches. Hat sizes range from 21 to 24 1/2 inches. Cowboy hats are usually sized based on head circumference. This is true at all price points. Knitted hats are not sized because they are expandable. They are often chosen as gifts because sizing is adjustable.

Hat size is usually measured level to the top of the head, just above the center of the forehead, where a hat would comfortably rest. Size should be recorded to the nearest 1/8 inch. A hat that is slightly large may be made to fit more snuggly by inserting foam tape or hat elastic inside the sweatband. A hat that is too small may be stretched by a dry cleaner on a heated hat stretcher.

Table 11.1 lists the approximate measurement of head circumference and related hat size in the United States. As in ready-to-wear, different manufacturers assign slightly different hat sizes to head circumferences. English hat sizes are usually 1/8 inch smaller than U.S. sizes (e.g. 7 1/4 U.S. hat size equals a 7 1/8 English hat size).

TABLE 11.1

Head Sizes and Hat Sizes

Head Size	Hat Size
20 1/2″	6 1/2
21 1/8″	6 3/4
21 1/2″	6 7/8
21 7/8″	7
22 1/4″	7 1/8
22 5/8″	7 1/4
23″	7 3/8
23 1/2″	7 1/2
23 7/8″	7 5/8
24 1/4″	7 3/4
24 5/8″	7 7/8
25″	8

Adapted from Black, B. (2000, December 30). *How to determine your hat size.* Retrieved Dec. 30, 2000, from http://www.brentblack.com/styles_size.htm

THE GLOBAL HAT INDUSTRY

The United States has about 389 hat manufacturers, with more than half employing fewer than twenty people. Although New York State has the greatest number of hat manufacturers, many of these facilities are quite small in relation to the number of employees. Missouri has more large facilities (employing more than 20 people) than any other state. Table 11.2 shows a 1997 ranking of states with the greatest number of hat manufacturing facilities.

The United States Census Bureau classifies domestically produced hats under three headings—cloth hats and caps, hats and hat bodies, and millinery. Cloth hats and caps represent the largest segment of hat manufacturing. Between 1992 and 1997, cloth hat and cap production increased by 8.4 percent. Hats and hat bodies included most men's and junior boys' hats, such as straws, furs, and wool felts. The production of this classification decreased by 2.3 percent. The third classification, millinery, included most women's and children's hats. Millinery production in the United States decreased by 4.6 percent between 1992 and 1997.

Production continually moves offshore, especially to Asia. China, Bangladesh, Korea, Hong Kong, and Taiwan are significant producers of headwear. An ample supply of workers and low labor costs encourage manufacturers to produce hats and hat materials in these countries. Statistics show that China, Hong Kong, Korea, and Taiwan combined produce about 42 percent of the world's total hats.

Trade organizations may have broad or narrow representation. Some trade organizations specifically promote and represent businesses associated with the domestic hat industry. Others represent all accessories designers, wholesalers, manufacturers, and retailers, including those associated with the hats, hair accessories, wigs, and hairpieces industries. Tables 11.3, 11.4, and 11.5 show the various trade organizations, publications, and shows associated with the headwear industries. Specialty hats, such as outdoor wear, active sportswear, western hats, bridal headpieces, and leather and fur, are featured at specialty trade shows with related product lines. Each of these industries has its own publications and trade shows.

TABLE 11.2

State Rankings by Number of Hat Manufacturing Facilities in 1997

New York	86
California	53
Missouri	37
Texas	27
Pennsylvania	17

U.S. Census Bureau. (1999, June 19). 1997 Economic Census, Products Statistics: 1997 and 1992, Manufacturing-Industry Series, NAICS 315991. Retrieved January 16, 2001, from http://www.census.gov/products/ec97/97m3159a.pdf

TABLE 11.3

Trade Organizations for the Hats, Hair Accessories, Wigs, and Hairpieces Industries

Organization	Location	Objectives
British Hat Guild	Luton, Bedfordshire, UK	Provides information about hat manufacturing in the United Kingdom.
Fur Information Council of America http://www.fur.org	New York, NY	Monitors legislation, research and development, and promotes fur fashions.
Headwear Information Bureau http://www.hatsny.com/HIB/	New York, NY	Represents the men's and women's headwear designers, manufacturers, and suppliers through national public relations and promotional activities.
Millinery Arts Alliance http://www.millinaryartsalliance.com	Chicago, IL	Promotes the art of couture millinery and hosts special events.
National Fashion Accessory Association and the Fashion Accessory Shippers Association (NFAA/FASA) http://www.accessoryweb.com	New York, NY	Represents all accessory categories, including millinery and hats.

TABLE 11.4

Trade Publications for the Hats, Hair Accessories, Wigs, and Hairpieces Industries

Trade Publication Name	Description
Accessories Magazine	Monthly trade publication covering most accessory classifications, including hats and headwear.
Daily News Record	Men's wear fashion trade data, trends, and news; published by Fairchild.
Hat Life Directory	Assists companies locating suppliers, manufacturers, and wholesalers; published by Hat Life.
Hat Life Online	Electronic newsletter featuring hat fashion trends and sales and marketing advice; published by Hat Life.
The HAT Magazine	Quarterly magazine promoting the making and wearing of hats; published by Carole and Nigel Denford in London, England.
Women's Wear Daily – Monday	Weekly issue of a trade newspaper; published by Fairchild. Features business and fashion information on hats and headwear as well as other accessories.
WWD Accessory Supplement	Fairchild special edition featuring fashion information on all accessories, including hats and headwear.

TABLE 11.5

Trade Shows for the Hats, Hair Accessories, Wigs, and Hairpieces Industries

Trade Show	Location	Sponsor
Accessorie Circuit	New York, NY	ENK International
AccessoriesTheShow	New York, NY	Business Journals, Inc.
Femme	New York, NY	Men's Apparel Guild In California (MAGIC)
The International Fashion Accessory Trade Show	Paris, France	French Women's Wear Association
Prêt à Porter: Atmosphere and Première Classe	Paris, France	SODES, a subsidiary of the French Women's Wear Association

MERCHANDISING TRENDS AND TECHNIQUES

Popular accessories trends move aggressively and must be identified early. Retailers have learned from experience that a popular accessory trend, like those involving fashion hats and hair accessories, requires immediate action. The business is intensely trend driven, and when a hot item presents itself, retailers need to react very quickly or risk missing a lucrative opportunity. Buying hair accessories monthly ensures retailers a steady influx of new accessory items and keeps them abreast of rapidly changing consumer tastes.

Within the headwear industry, the rise in popularity of one style may signal a decline in the popularity of another style. Even within a single merchandise category, such as hair ponies, the materials may change from metallic fabrics to furs and leathers. Trendspotting becomes the key to a prolonged, successful season.

Store Retailing

Women's and men's fashion hats and headwear are usually merchandised on the main floor accessories departments. To optimize sales in department stores, headwear and hair accessories should complement other store goods, and department displays should be cross-merchandised. Children's hats are usually located within the children's departments, near coordinating apparel. In smaller and specialty stores, hats and other accessories are prominently grouped near the main checkout because customers are more likely to purchase these items on impulse. In discount stores, women's fashion hats are located in the accessory department. Hair accessories are primarily merchandised in the health and beauty aids section, near hairbrushes.

To sell a unisex casual hat, such as a ball cap, the location is critical. Often, casual hats are placed in more than one location in the store to reach a variety of customers. Or, the casual hats are located on the perimeter of the men's and boy's departments. Women are frequent purchasers of ball caps, and they are comfortable purchasing them in men's and boy's departments.

In most stores, the selection of hats is limited, and the selling area is small. If a hat department exists, it is most likely merchandised by occasion or materials. For example, in a large hat department the formal and church hats are grouped in one area; the casual hats, such as cloth or ball caps, are clustered; and sun straws are grouped together. During optimal selling seasons, such as pre-Easter, hats can be placed near the front of the department or relocated near related apparel sections to encourage impulse buying. Cold-weather hats, such as knits, are placed near the front of the department in the weeks prior to Christmas because of their potential for gift sales.

Hat and headwear departments should be neatly stocked with several styles. Most customers prefer to try on several styles before making a purchase decision. Displays should be straightened and easily accessible. Many hats lack shelf appeal, so hat trees and forms are valuable selling tools. A large mirror should be close at hand, and a second mirror to present the back view should be available.

Internet Retailing

In today's climate of a casual market, the demand for specialty and fashion hats is relatively small. Designers and retailers have found the Internet to be a more cost-efficient channel than catalog retailing for marketing this type of headwear. Many designers retail unique or one-of-a-kind headwear creations for the more affluent or fashion-forward customers. Options, such as hand-painted, aromatherapy-enhanced, vintage recreations, and others, are available online. Through online channels, specialty headwear designers can reach potential customers directly, without going through wholesalers or retail stores.

Other Internet retailers prefer to offer a collection of related merchandise, which includes inexpensive hats in many styles and colors. Cyber shoppers can choose hats for a specific lifestyle category, such as sports enthusiast and the casual athlete.

Catalog Retailing

Hats are sold through specialty catalog retailing devoted to headwear alone, or they may be featured as part of an ensemble in apparel catalogs. Most apparel catalogs feature a small selection of hats to complement apparel (see Figure 11.5).

FIGURE 11.5
A hat may serve as the finishing touch of an ensemble.

SELLING HATS AND HAIR ACCESSORIES

Price and fashion are two of the most important selling points for hats. Workmanship and materials are of lesser importance, except when selling western hats, couture millinery, fur hats, and some men's straw hats. These accessories carry a higher price tag and require salespeople to have extensive product knowledge so they can justify the higher prices. High-quality handiwork, brand names, and rare materials often justify a higher selling price.

Price and Value

Hat prices are dependent upon the amount of hand workmanship, the materials and trim, the quantity produced, and the brand. The degree of hand stitching affects the price of a hat. Hand-stitched hats require many hours of labor, thus increasing the selling price. Less expensive hats generally are machine stitched and have glued components.

With straw hats, the finer and smoother the weave, the better the hat. A **finely woven hat** means that the individual straws used to weave the hat are **fine** (thin). As the width of the straw is reduced by half, the labor time is quadrupled. Therefore, a hat twice as fine takes four times as long to weave and significantly increases the cost of the hat. A **smoothly** or **well-woven hat** is also important for judging the quality of a straw hat. A hat might be finely woven, but it must also be smoothly woven. Ideally, every straw should be the same width, or fineness, and each row should be straight and even. The rows should all fit together with no gaps, bumps, and knots.

The materials used affect the price of hats. With straw hats, there are varying qualities of straws available. Straw quality is evaluated from fine to coarse, and each straw is assigned a grade. Knitted-fabric hats are manufactured on circular knitting machines that greatly reduce production costs and selling prices. Felt hats may be made of wool or fur fibers (such as beaver) or man-made fibers that simulate wool, such as acrylic or modacrylic. Usually, more expensive hats are made of natural fibers, while less expensive hats are of man-made fibers.

Western or cowboy hats are quality-graded with Xs. With each X, the grade and cost improves. For example, a 2X hat (wool) retails for about $50, while a 100X hat (cashmere) retails for about $1200.

Bridal headpieces should have combs that are securely fastened, and extra hairpin loops should be supplied for stability. In lower-price headpieces, the netting tiers are initially stacked, then machine gathered with one line of stitching. In better-quality (and more costly) headpieces, each layer of netting is gathered separately by hand, then attached to the headpiece.

Factory hats are mass-produced hats and sell at mid- to lower-price points. They are sold in hat shops, department stores, mass merchandise stores, and discount stores. Customers may opt for factory hats when a special occasion calls for a hat. This customer is price conscious and can justify a limited number of wearings only if the price is low.

Couture or **model millinery** represents one-of-a-kind hats, usually handmade and more expensive. A customer buying model millinery usually wears the hat frequently and can justify the higher price.

A final component in the price/quality relationship is the brand. Not always, but frequently, the brand name on a hat is an indicator of the level of quality. Brand name gives customers a starting place to begin judging, but by no means is it the only indicator of quality.

Hair accessories prices are dependent upon characteristics similar to hats, but especially those related to materials and trim. For example, real horn, mother-of-pearl, or tortoise are much more costly than plastic simulations, and these headwear pieces will be priced to reflect the rarity of the materials.

Care of Hats

Some hats are not made to be cleaned, because they are inexpensive and can be disposed of instead. More expensive hats require a professional steam cleaning and need reblocking. Cloth caps or hats may be machine or hand washable. Customers should carefully follow the care label. All hats should be stored clean, especially woolens, to prevent insect (e.g. moths) attraction during the warm season.

Hats that have been bent or slightly misshapen may be professionally steamed into the correct shape. For small areas, a clothes steamer can soften felt or straw fibers just enough to allow reshaping of the damaged area.

Water-saturated hats require slow drying. Fast-dry techniques, like hairdryers, will cause wrinkling and shrinkage. Creases and dents should be gently pushed out to round out the crown. Once the hat is dry, gently reform the crease.

To clean straw hats, a cloth dipped in warm suds should be gently rubbed on the soiled areas. Then a clean, damp cloth should be used to removed the soap suds. Excessive water should be wrung out of the cloths before touching the hat because shrinkage occurs when straws absorb too much water.

To clean felt hats, dust daily with a soft-bristled brush called a **hatter's brush.** Dark-colored brushes are used for dark hats, and light-colored brushes are used for light hats. If preferred, a terrycloth washcloth can also be used to remove dust. Gently rub the cloth in a circular counterclockwise motion over the surface to quickly remove dust. An art-gum eraser can be used for stubborn spots and should be rubbed counterclockwise to the grain. For deeper stains, fine sandpaper rubbed counterclockwise against the spot may be required, but only the tiniest layer of felt should be removed. Oily stains, such as heavy perspiration stains, require professional hat cleaning or the purchase of a professional-strength hat cleaner available at drug stores and hat retailers.

Meeting Customer Needs

Many customers lack confidence in their choice of hats, even though they may be very confident when purchasing apparel. They should be encouraged to try on all of the hats they like to find the one that best suits the occasion and that they will feel relaxed about wearing. They may try on many hats or bring a friend a few days later. Salespeople should be diplomatic, encouraging, and willing to model hats for the customer.

Good lighting and a large three-way mirror are important to meeting customer needs. Customers need to clearly evaluate how the hats will look on their heads. Not all hats have shelf appeal, especially cloth or soft hats. Putting a hat on a head allows the hat to "come alive" and the customer can see the hat from a different perspective.

When selling specialty hats, like bridal headpieces, the customer should be encouraged to wear a neckline that resembles the color and line of her wedding dress. Astute retailers can provide white and candlelight white drapes or bodices simulating a variety of necklines to make visualizing easier for the customer.

A BRIEF HISTORY OF WIGS AND HAIRPIECES

Wigs and hairpieces have been worn to denote occupations or authority, cover hair loss, and simply for adornment. Sometimes wigs are associated with occupations. For example, British barristers (lawyers) have been identified by their gray wigs and Japanese Geisha girls were known to wear elaborate, lacquered black wigs. In Europe, law enforcement branches, such as the army, navy, or police, each had its own distinctive style of wig.

The term wig is derived from the French word *periwig*. The ancient Egyptians are credited with inventing the wig. Their cleanliness and fastidiousness often resulted in shaving of heads to prevent infestation of head lice. The ancient Egyptians might go bareheaded at home, but don wigs for public appearances. The Cleopatra image that comes to mind is a good example of ancient Egyptian wigs. Braided and curled wigs were made of palm and wood fibers, animal or human hair, and affixed to the head by beeswax. Egyptions thought thick hair was best and so they used hair extensions and wigs. They wore colored wigs in blues, greens, blondes, and golds. Gold and silver hair accessories helped identify the rank or status of the wearer. Scented wax cones were sometimes worn on the top of the head, to melt over the wig during the hot evenings, coating the wearer with perfumed oil.

From the ancient Egyptian times until the 1600s, wigs were worn by both genders, but wigs for women were most common. During the 16th and 17th centuries, elaborate coifs and wigs were popular for women, eventually becoming acceptable for men. In 1624, Louis XIII of France popularized the white, curly periwig as a fashion to cover his baldness. His courtiers soon adopted the fashion. For decades afterward, this wig style was worn in Europe and the American colonies. Heavily powdered and large curls reaching almost to a man's waist became fashionable in the latter part of the century. The increase in wig proportions necessitated the carrying of the hat in hand rather than atop the head. Women's wigs also became extravagant and were flour coated in the 18th century. The big wigs for men and women disappeared during the American and French revolutions when such blatant symbols of social rank became unfashionable and life threatening.

After the revolutions, men continued to wear powdered wigs, but they were generally smaller and lighter. Some wigs were tied back into a **queue** (low ponytail) encased in a black silk bag, and others were braided.

By the 18th century, hairdressers and wigmakers had formed a profession dominated by men. The famous French hairdresser Legros de Rumigny served the royal court. He later published a book, *Art de la Coiffure Des Dames* (1765), and opened a hairdressing school in 1769.

During the late 19th century, wealthy European women occasionally wore elaborately coifed wigs in fashion colors, including blues and greens. For men, natural hair was popular, so they went to great lengths to achieve fullness, including the application of heavy greases, oils, tonics, and false hair. Crocheted and embroidered antimacassars on the backs of parlor furniture served a fashionable and a functional purpose—to prevent the hair tonics from staining the upholstery!

The 1960s showed a small increase in wigs and hairpieces because of the availability of natural-looking hairpieces in the form of full wigs, half wigs, falls, and switches. **Falls** and switches are hanks of false hair worn by women for extra volume in their natural hair. The variety of price ranges made wigs affordable for woman who wanted to own one or more hairpieces. For men, **toupees,** or hairpieces, became more acceptable, as the youthful trend continued to influence all ages of people.

During the latter 1990s and early 2000s, elaborate and beautiful hair extensions were woven into natural hair and became fashionable for African-American women. Pony cuffs (ponytail holders) of synthetic hair were fashion items for teens.

WIGS, HAIRPIECES, AND TOUPEES

Wigs and hairpieces appeal to a small customer base, usually to those men and women who have experienced hair loss. The poor comfort factor of artificial hair discourages widespread popularity. Wigs and hairpieces may be made of human hair or synthetic fibers (often nylon or acrylic) sewn into silk or lace foundations. Brand names for women's wigs and hairpieces include Eva Gabor, Dolly Parton, Raquel Welch, Cheryl Tiegs, Adolfo, and Zury. Hair extensions, 3/4 falls, or hair weaving accessories may be used with the natural hair to create a longer length for women (see Figure 11.6).

Most men who wear toupees put them on during the daytime and remove them at night. These hairpieces are attached by gluing or taping the hairpiece to the head, or finely braiding the edge of the toupee to a man's existing hair, a more permanent solution.

Merchandising Trends

Most major cities have specialty-store wig shops. Larger department stores with hair salons may offer hairpieces as aesthetic accessories. They may sell wigs and hairpieces exclusively or offer these items as a service for their hat-buying customer base. Many are located near hospitals or cancer treatment clinics because of the hair loss caused by chemotherapy. These retailers have

FIGURE 11.6
Hair extensions may appear to be a natural part of a hairstyle or may be obviously artificial.
Courtesy of Fairchild Publications, Inc.

large special-order businesses. Others are located in cities with high Jewish populations because among some Orthodox Jews, married women cover their hair as a sign of modesty while in the presence of men other than their husbands.

Some wig and hairpiece shops have expanded into online services. One of the largest brick-and-mortar and Internet specialty retailers of men's and women's wigs and hairpieces is Wilshire Wigs & Accessories, with 30 years of large-scale retailing experience in Los Angeles, California. The company's Web site allows customers to narrow their search by brand name, style or length of hair, or materials (human hair or synthetic). In addition to hairpieces, the Web site features a variety of wig accessories, including wig stands, cleaners and shampoos, and boxes. Because purchasing wigs appeals to a relatively small market and requires detailed fitting, many of the larger department stores' Web sites do not offer wigs for sale.

Price and Value

Moderately priced synthetic women's wigs range from $35 to $75 at retail, with an average price of $45 to $55. Human hair wigs for women range in price from $45 to $250, with an average retail price of $100 to $150. There is a small market for expensive wigs for women, but most of the wigs sold are moderately priced.

Retail prices for men's toupees range from $100 to $4,000, depending on the materials and the method of application. The most expensive toupees have as many as 20,000 human hairs inset in a nylon mesh base that is braided into the perimeter of the surviving hairline. This toupee requires regular adjustments as the natural hair grows.

Care of Wigs and Hairpieces

The care of wigs and hairpieces depends primarily on whether human or synthetic hairs are used. Synthetic hairs are more durable, but heat must be avoided. Curling iron, blow dryers, and steam or electric curlers will damage heat-sensitive synthetic fibers. Special shampoos, conditioners, and hair sprays are available where wigs are sold. Customers should be encouraged to treat wigs and hairpieces in the same way they would treat a fine cashmere sweater or scarf. Clean them only when needed and use care when cleaning. The following steps are recommended for synthetic hair wigs:

1. Add a small amount of mild shampoo to a basin of lukewarm water. A teaspoon of baking soda may be added to help remove smoke or other strong odors.
2. Swish wig gently for 30 to 60 seconds.
3. Rinse wig thoroughly in cool water.
4. Gently shake wig out and allow to drip dry. Do not brush the wig when wet.
5. No setting is necessary; the curls will snap back into position when the wig is completely dry.

Meeting Customer Needs

Most customers have little if any expertise in selecting wigs, hairpieces, and toupees. Poorly fitting hairpieces have long been the topic of jokes. In some instances, hairpieces are not shipped ready-to-wear. They must be cut and styled by a barber or stylist to ensure a natural fit with the wearer's existing hair.

Salespeople should be empathetic and tactful when assisting customers. Whether for cosmetic or medical reasons, the customers should be encouraged to select their hairpieces based on several important criteria. The hairpieces should:

- Be lightweight and of the proper thickness
- Have natural or resilient fibers that are easy to style
- Complement the facial shape
- Fit the head shape properly
- Have an undetectable hairline

A person's hair symbolizes beauty and greatly affects a person's self-esteem. Most people do not opt to wear a hairpiece for strictly fashion reasons. They usually are suffering from hair loss and may be desperate to reverse the problem. Confidential, personalized service and a quality product are valued by customers seeking wigs and toupees.

SUMMARY

- Millinery, or women's hats, has origins from the 16th century, although the wearing of hats dates as far back as recorded history. Both men's and women's hat were equally ornate, until the 19th century, when men began to adopt functional headwear, with the exception of evening attire.

- Over the centuries, the sizes of women's hats have evolved from wide to high, and small to large. The turn of the 20th century boasted elaborate and large hats for women. An influx of European immigrants skilled in the millinery trades created a hat empire among department stores in New York City during the first half of the 20th century.

- Hats gradually declined in popularity during the 20th century, but the latter decades saw a noticeable increase in hat wearing, particularly baseball-cap styles. Hats continued to be worn for special occasions, such as Easter and weddings, and by pockets of consumers in certain ethnic groups, usually to religious services.

- Paris, France, and Milan, Italy, are major contributors to headwear fashions. American companies interpret foreign designs, creating hats that reflect the preferences of domestic customers.

- Hat designers should consider the degree of appeal, wearability and comfort, proportion and enhancement, and selling price. Couture hat designers create "model millinery," while other designers simply select new fabrication and trim for existing styles.

- Many small and large hat manufacturing companies are located in the United States, particularly in New York, California, Missouri, Texas, and Pennsylvania.

- The four major parts of a hat are the crown, brim, headband, and trim. These four components can be combined into a multitude of hat styles.

- Materials for hats include many types of woven straws, felted woolens, fur fibers or manufactured fibers, knitted and crocheted yarns, woven fabrics, and covered buckrams. Materials used for other types of headwear, such as headbands, combs, barrettes, butterfly and banana clips, and ponytail holders, are varied. Materials include leather and fur, horn, mother-of-pearl, tortoise, feathers, fabric, metals, and jewels.

- Felt and straw hat production techniques include shaping cones and blocking the material into desired shapes. Often a stiffening agent is applied to ensure the retention of the hat shape.

- Most hats are one-size-fits-all, although more expensive hats may be sized to the circumference of the head, just above the eyebrows.

- If hats require cleaning, some fabrics may be machine washed. Felt hats should be steam cleaned by a professional. Other hats, especially straws, are not made to be cleaned. The fragile nature of straw may result in only one season of wearing.

- The headwear industry changes rapidly, so buyers need to be aware of emerging trends and willing to quickly modify assortment plans.

- Internet retailing is an important channel for the headwear industry. Specialty hat designers often market their products on Web sites. Specialty and department stores offer hats at their brick-and-mortar locations, but also through catalogs and the Internet.

- The trend toward casual dressing means fewer dress-and special-occasion hats are being sold, but the casual trend has improved the sales of casual cloth hats and caps. The desire for sun protection has bolstered the sales of straw hats.

- To effectively sell hats in a retail store, the hats should be attractively displayed, easy to try on and view, and available in a variety of styles. The lack of customer confidence in selecting a hat style lends itself to personalized service.

- Price is affected by the amount of hand workmanship, materials, trim, quantity produced, and brand name.

- The development of wigs was credited to the ancient Egyptians, although the term is derived from the French word *periwig*. In the past, wigs were designed to look artificial and fanciful, unlike wigs today, which resemble natural hair.

- Toupees are hairpieces for men that sell for less than $100 to several thousand dollars. The price variation may be attributed to degree of "naturalness" of the appearance. Some toupees are removable, while others are painstakingly braided into the natural hairline.

- Wigs, hairpieces, and toupees may be synthetic or real hair. The synthetic hairpieces can be cleaned at home but should not be subjected to heat. Natural hairpieces have a shorter life span, but can be cared for in much the same way as natural hair.

- Salespeople should be sensitive to the concerns of people who experience hair loss. Informative and well-trained salespeople are highly desired.

TERMS FOR REVIEW

aluminum pan forms	carding	decorative trim
barrette	cartwheel	demographic segmentation
beret	cloche	earmuffs
bias tape	cloche hat	factory hats
blocking	color-forward shoppers	falls
boater	color-prudents	fedora
bowler (derby)	comb	fez
Breton	cone weaving	fine
brim	coolie	finely woven hat
buckram	couture (model millinery)	fishermen (bucket hats)
bumper	covered rubber band	galón
butterfly/banana clips	cowboy (Western)	haberdasher shop
capeline weaving	crown	hair extensions

hair jewelry	millinery	skimmer
hairpin	millinery couture	skullcap (Calotte or Juliet cap)
halo	mushroom	slouch
hatpins	periwig	smoothly (well-)woven hat
hatter's brush	petersham binding	sombrero
headache band	pillbox	switch
headband	plaited (braided straw)	Tam O' Shanter (Tam)
homberg	pony cuffs	ten-gallon hat
hood	pork pie	textile technology
hydraulic blocking	preproduction sample	tiara
knit (stocking) cap	profile	top hat (stovepipe hat)
logomania	psychographic segmentation	toupees
market segmentation	queue	turban
military	sailor	visor (peak)
milliners	scrunchies (ponies)	wooden block forms

REVIEW QUESTIONS

1. How is the decline in the popularity of hats related to the increase in a casual culture and lifestyle?
2. What are the crown and brim of a hat?
3. What is meant by the term *blocking?*
4. What is meant by model millinery?
5. What are some popular warm-weather hat materials?
6. What are some popular cold-weather hat materials?
7. How are hats sized?
8. What are some important merchandising trends in the hat and millinery industry?
9. What are some basic styles of hair accessories?
10. What are the important considerations when a customer purchases a wig, toupee, or hairpiece?

KNOWLEDGE APPLICATIONS

1. Standing a few inches away from a large mirror, draw your facial shape onto the mirror with a dark crayon. Press a sheet of white paper to transfer the facial shape image. With a partner, identify your facial shape (oval, round, heart, square, etc.) and select hat styles that a) complement, and b) emphasize the facial shape. Share your findings with other class members.
2. Using mail-order catalogs, compare and contrast hats on the following: style, color, materials, and trim. Compile the class findings, then identify and analyze important trends.

3. Visit a retail store carrying a wide selection of hats or headwear. Identify the merchandising methods used. Where and how are hats merchandised? What are some unique merchandising techniques used? Write an analysis of your findings.

4. Visit a retailer and identify the price range of a selected group of headwear accessories. What is the lowest price point? the highest price point? the average price point? How many price points are available in one headwear classification? Write an analysis of your findings.

5. Visit two Web sites specializing in similar products, either hats, headwear, or hairpieces. Compare the two sites on prices, materials, workmanship, services, assortments, and ease of navigation through the Web site.

6. Develop a list of interview questions for a millinery or headwear accessories buyer. Find out how the buyer reacts to changes in fashion trends.

7. Research a millinery designer of your choice. Write a paper summarizing his or her design philosophy.

8. Identify some celebrities today who have been influential in millinery fashions.

9. Visit one of the millinery trade association Web sites. What type of information is available?

CHAPTER 12

❧

GLOVES, UMBRELLAS, AND EYEWEAR

Dear Anxious:

For formal functions greet your escort completely attired and ready to depart. Your gloves should be donned in the privacy of your boudoir and of course worn during the entire evening. This observance is correct for less formal afternoon teas and so forth. However, afternoon gloves are short and can, on occasion, be put on in the presence of your escort since the shortness of the glove deprives the act of the immodest intimacy connected with formal, longer gloves.

—*Mrs. Hale, in* Lady's Magazine, *circa 1880s.*
Source: Collins, C. C. (1945). *Love of a Glove*. NY: Fairchild.

CHAPTER 12 COVERS THREE FASHION ACCESSORIES CATEGORIES—GLOVES, UMBRELLAS, AND eyewear. Because of the unique nature of the three categories, they are each discussed separately in the chapter. The general focus is on fashion gloves, umbrellas, and eyewear. However, work gloves, patio umbrellas, and prescription eyewear are briefly mentioned as they are also (to a lesser degree) influenced by fashion.

A BRIEF HISTORY OF GLOVES

Early civilizations probably used some form of fur covering to protect their hands from the cold. Originally, animal skins may have been wrapped around the hands or fashioned into a mitten. By the time of the ancient Egyptians, the craft of glove making had been refined. Pieces of leather gloves dating to 1300 B.C. have been discovered in Egypt, and well-shaped gloves have been found in Egyptian tombs of the pharaohs, including King Tutankhamen. Gloves are also mentioned in the Old Testament of the Bible when Rebecca made kidskin gloves for her son

Jacob. Ancient gloves were manufactured with numerous pieces, as many as 150 in some instances, compared with today's gloves of fewer than ten pieces.

The symbolism associated with gloves was important to the civilized world. Women began to wear gloves in the 11th century. Men and women often sat for portraits wearing one glove and holding the other. Gloves made of the softest leather and permanently perfumed were an important part of the wardrobe. A knight clad in iron gauntlets wore his lady's glove into battle, tying it to his arm for good luck. To assure the legality of a contract, gloves were given as a pledge of good faith in business transactions. A slap across the face with a man's gauntlet, a long glove, meant a challenge to a duel. For certain rituals the church and state required the wearing of gloves, representing the purity of hands needed to perform duties of the position.

Glove-making grew in importance, especially in areas with access to sheep and goat skins. In Perth, Scotland, as early as the 12th century, glovers incorporated as craftsmen. Perth became a prominent glove-manufacturing hub, eventually giving way in later centuries to English glove-making centers—London, Worcester, York, Oxford, Chester, Newcastle, Yeovil, and Hull.

Excessiveness of fashion was evident during the 13th century, when gloves became extremely wide and long, preventing the wearer from performing any work at all. Buttons became excessive; sometimes as many as 24 were sewn onto a long glove. Gold and pearl buttons signaled the conspicuous wealth of the wearer, as did jewel encrusting.

Gloves can be seen in 14th-century paintings and illustrations. A fashion article for the wealthy, gloves were governed by **sumptuary laws** (clothing regulations based on moral or religious grounds) in an attempt to restrict the wearing of fingered gloves to the upper classes. Although laws of this type were almost impossible to enforce, the artwork of the period features most working-class people either bare-handed or in fingerless gloves.

Sixteenth-century gloves of leather or silk were worn by fashionable men and women. Short cuffs evolved into longer, decorated cuffs with metallic and silk embroidery. Slashing, a fashion decoration in apparel, found its way into glove fingers, exposing numerous rings. This was a technique of cutting decorative parallel slashes in the outer garment fabric so the undergarment was visible.

By the 17th century, mittens and gloves were made of leather from deer, kids, goats, lambs, and sheep. Kidskin gloves, made by the French, were prized because of their natural elasticity and close fit. Additionally, bias-cut woven fabrics and knitted fabrics were popular. Gloves were designed with very deep, embroidered cuffs edged in lace, fringe, stones, tassels, or ribbons. Wide-flaring gauntlets matching the apparel were worn by fashionable gentlemen (see Figure 12.1). The end of the 17th century saw elbow-length, close-fitting gloves sleekly fitted to the wearer.

In 1760, Sir William Johnson obtained land from English King George III in North America, in what is now New York State. Perth glovers were among those who first settled there and gave rise to the adjoining towns of Gloversville and Johnston. These two towns became the established center of the glove-making industry in the States.

FIGURE 12.1
Charles I of England in gauntlet gloves.
Painting by Daniel Mytens, c. 1629.
Source: Courtesy of the National Portrait Gallery.

During the 18th and 19th centuries, women's gloves were often closely matched to shoes. Gloves were important to 19th-century women of good breeding. They were worn indoors and removed only when eating. A wealthy woman might buy a dozen pairs of gloves to get her through the season. Short-sleeved women's apparel of the period required long gloves for formal occasions, ranging from elbow-length to shoulder-length. Long-sleeved dresses required short gloves.

For 18th- and 19th-century well-bred gentlemen, social etiquette dictated wearing gloves when outdoors and for formal occasions. Plain gauntlets were fashionable for riding, while elegant yet businesslike gloves were worn for more formal occasions.

The 20th century's trend toward informality was evidenced in the decline of the glove. As early as the 1920s, B. Eldrid Ellis noted in his book, *Gloves and the Glove Trade,* that dress gloves were no longer social requirements for men at dinner and dances. Gloves were only required at court or state functions. Twentieth-century men valued the notion of a strong work ethic, and gloves did not support this notion (except as a necessity for protection from the elements).

The evolution of controlled climates indoors reduced the necessity of gloves for comfort, but in spite of the relatively comfortable indoor temperature during winters, 20th-century women continued the wearing of gloves. For women, the purpose of gloves was to enhance apparel fashions. A common glove for fashionable women was the **opera glove,** a full-length glove that continued in popularity for the early decades of the 20th century.

World War II rationing included glove materials, and women simply "made do" with pre-war gloves already in their wardrobes. Gloves available during the war were simple and functional. After the war, it became socially acceptable to be bare-handed in public, and women chose not to continue the inconvenient fashion. For church and special occasions, **bracelet length** and **shortie gloves** (ending above and below the wrist, respectively) were fashionable in the 1950s and 1960s (see Figure 12.2). From the1970s through the remainder of the century, gloves became used primarily as sports apparel or outdoor winter wear. The fingernail art of the 1990s created a fingertip focal point, further driving the fashion emphasis away from gloves.

AN INTRODUCTION TO GLOVES

Today, the wearing of fashion gloves is not dependent upon the social elite to set the glove fashion; it is dependent upon the weather. Glovemakers view cold, dry winters as vital to a profitable glove accessories season. During warm, wet winters and warmer spring and summer seasons, gloves are really a non-item in popular fashions. The marketing of gloves tends to be focused on sports and special occasions.

Fashion glove makers encourage women to wear gloves to flatter the appearance of their apparel. The simplest to the most-expensive dress can be enhanced and enriched when accessorized with beautiful gloves. A woman uses her hands to emphasize her conversation and express her personality, and gloves can be the fashion focal point of her ensemble.

FIGURE 12.2
Hansen's ad showing the 1960s bracelet-length glove look.

Parts of Gloves

Most gloves have fewer than ten parts, which are relatively easy to identify. Usually, the more pieces in a glove, the closer the fit. However, the addition of stretch fibers, such as spandex and knitted yarns, can create a close fit with minimal glove parts. The following terms describe the major components of a glove.

Trank The rectangle of fabric from which the main pieces of the glove (front and back) are cut to the correct size.

Fourchettes Narrow, oblong strips inset along the inside lengths of the finger, providing extra space and a fitted shape. Also called a **gusset** or **sidewall.** *Fourchette* is a French glove term referring to the fingers.

Quirks Triangular or irregular diamond-shaped fourchettes fitted at the base of the fingers and thumb to allow for flexibility and expansion.

Thumb Separate piece attached to the hole in the trank.

English or Bolton Thumb The thumb quirk is cut in one piece with the trank, which allows for superior movement of the thumb.

Set-in Thumb Entire thumb piece is sewn into an oval hole in the trank.

French or Quirk Thumb Thumb and thumb quirk are sewn together, then inserted into hole in trank.

Novelty Thumb Thumb piece extends to the cuff.

Cuff Extension of fabric beyond the palm, protecting the wrist or forearm. May be knitted for a close fit, slit for ease of removal, or extra long to protect forearm.

Linings Fabric sewn inside the glove to increase warmth and allow for ease of wearing. Should be secured inside, so it doesn't invert when gloves are removed.

Domes Snaps that fasten the glove at the wrist.

Hearts or **Stays** Reinforcing sections on the palm of the glove.

Binding Tape edging at the wrist that is both decorative and functional (finishes the upper edge and protects the stitching).

Gore A triangle-shaped inset on the cuff, causing a flare.

Pointing Three rows of decorative stitching on the back of the glove; also called silking.

Buttons Unit of measurement. One button equals approximately one inch in arm length from the wrist upwards.

Glove Manufacturing

Because of the few structural parts of gloves and the functional need for maximum dexterity, the basic processes change very little from year to year. Many work-and dress-glove companies boast of their traditional manufacturing processes and labor-intensive production. Active sportswear-glove manufacturers take a more technologically advanced approach, using high-performance fabrics and finishes and producing gloves with low bulk but high-warmth factors. Novelty knitted-glove manufacturers emphasize fashion at reasonable prices.

Design

Domestic manufacturing is comprised of 90 percent work gloves and 10 percent fashion gloves. In order to boost production in a commodity market (meaning price is the primary purchase consideration), U.S. companies are creating fashion appeal in the work-glove category. New styles and extensive label information are encouraging increased sales in work gloves. Other techniques that increase sales are the addition of bright colors; floral and contemporary pattern designs; matching parent-child sets; and more special-use gloves, such as gauntlets for rose gardening or special grips for working in damp gardens.

In spite of the relatively small fashion-glove market, some designers, such as Shaneen Huxham and Carolina Amato, continue to produce fashion gloves to complement their ready-to-wear lines. Customization and personalization have helped these glove designers survive in a mass-production climate. Bridal gloves are an important part of this market, and Amato offers custom dyeing of bridesmaids' gloves to ensure a perfect match. Other designers, such as those at Sullivan Glove Company, work with their customers to create customized gloves that meet special needs and demands. As an added selling feature, Sullivan will embroider and emboss leather products to personalize the merchandise.

Production

The production of sized and leather gloves is an exacting process. Many of the steps are carefully hand guided to ensure precision. One-size-fits-all gloves are fully automated and do not require hand workmanship. Most of the steps described below refer to gloves requiring cutting and sewing to achieve a careful fit.

The pattern used for leather-glove production may be a **clute-cut pattern** or a **gunn-cut pattern.** A clute cut is a full, one-piece palm shape, with the fingers cut in one piece with the palm. There is no seam across the palm, which is very comfortable for the wearer. A gunn cut is useful for heavier leather gloves and requires the fingers to be cut separately from the palm.

Leather gloves are cut with a steel die cutter that resembles a four-finger-shaped cookie cutter. This process, called **clicking,** requires the metal die to be sharp enough to cut through leather or layers of fabric. A hydraulic press causes the dies to cut through the leather layer.

Because knitted gloves are constructed in only one piece, they are faster to produce and usually retail at lower price points. **Full fashioning** is a knitting term referring to dropping and adding stitches to produce gussets between the fingers during the manufacturing of the glove. This is less expensive than a separate sewing step to insert the gussets.

Specialized sewing machines, using a lock stitch, are used to manufacture gloves. Seam-construction types, from least to most expensive, include inseaming, outseaming, overseaming, and

Tech-Talk: Gore-Tex: Guaranteed to Keep You Dry

Waterproof and breathable (WP/B) gloves translate into no more damp, cold fingers and no more sweaty palms. Gore-Tex performance fabrics keep moisture droplets from penetrating the outer fabric covering, yet allow moisture vapor (perspiration) to pass through its microscopic pores, away from the wearer's hands.

W.L. Gore and Associates pioneered this nonstick, (polytetrafluoroethylene) Teflon membrane that bars water, dust, mold spores, bacteria, and smoke. Gore-Tex has become a household word, synonymous with "keeping dry while out-of-doors."

Recently, the company has developed a SOFT insert that is so lightweight and thin, it is virtually invisible. Applications for the SOFT insert include close-fitting athletic gloves in which high dexterity and pliability are needed. Athletes are able to adjust boots and close zippers without taking off the lightly insulated, flexible gloves.

The dependability of a pair of Gore-Tex gloves is only as good as the construction and care techniques used. Seams must be sealed to prevent water from penetrating the needle holes. Tears or rips in the outer fabric may cause moisture leakage. W.L. Gore recommends launder-ing the gloves in cold water and powdered detergents rather than liquid detergents because of residual surfac-tants (surface chemicals) from liquid detergents.

How the Gore-Tex membrane works.
Photo courtesy of W.L. Gore & Associates.

---

piqué or half-piqué seaming. **Inseaming** involves sewing the back and front pieces with right sides together. **Outseaming** means sewing the back and front pieces with wrong sides together, which creates an exposed seam on the face of the gloves. A **Davey tip** is a leather covering that may be sewn on the outseam that protects the exposed stitching. **Overseaming** is similar to out-seaming, except an overlock stitch covers the exposed seam, and the appearance is somewhat ca-sual. **Piqué seams** are created by sewing one edge of the glove piece over the other edge of the matching glove piece, exposing only one raw edge. **Half piqué** means only the seams on the glove back are sewn with a piqué technique, while the seams on the glove front use one of the less-expensive seaming methods.

Materials

Supple leather in cowhide, lambskin, and pigskin is the preferred material for dress gloves. Other durable and pliable leather sources include cabretta and capeskin (both from sheep), deerskin, buckskin, doeskin, kidskin, and goatskin. For work gloves, horsehide or suede may be used alone or in combination with a durable cotton twill fabric. Winter materials include nylon, polyester fleece, acrylic, wool, cotton, and vinyl. Teflon® coating or membranes, such as Gore-Tex®, may be applied to base fabrics for extra protection against wind, cold, and moisture. Thinsulate® by 3M and Polartec® performance materials are used to increase insulative properties of gloves. Gloves may be lined with flannel, fleece, velvet, or other pile fabrics, and fake or real fur. If a filling is used between the lining and the outer fashion fabric, it is usually fiberfill or down feathers.

BASIC STYLES OF GLOVES

Sleeve length determines the correct style of glove to complement apparel (see Figure 12.3). Bare-shouldered clothing looks best with above-the-elbow length gloves. Long sleeves require shortie gloves, generally not extending beyond the hem or cuff of the sleeve

Biarritz Short, slip-on glove, with no vent.

Driving Short, flexible gloves, leather or knitted fabric, with steering-wheel palm grips. May be vented on the back of the hand.

Fingerless or Waif Fingers end just below the center joint, exposing the fingertips. Uses include sports activities and an accessory fad adapted from the street urchin look. Originally a glove for peasants.

Gauntlet Glove extending up the wrist, protecting the forearm with a flared cuff.

driving

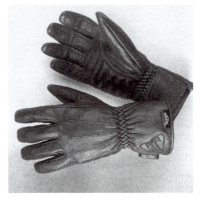

gauntlet

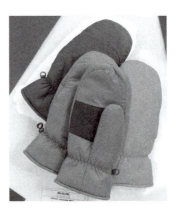

mitten

mousquetaire

work gloves

FIGURE 12.3
Five basic styles of gloves: (a) driving, (b) gauntlet, (c) mitten © Lands' End Inc.
used with permission, *(d) mousquetaire* Courtesy of Fairchild Publications, Inc.,
and (e) work.

Glove liners Nylon or silk undergloves used to absorb perspiration and prevent skin rashes under irritating glove materials. May be worn under latex and rubber gloves or as added protection from the cold weather.

Kid Soft, supple leather, originally used for almost all leather gloves. "To handle with kid gloves" means to take extreme caution.

Lace Open-work fabric, usually white, for special occasions in spring and summer.

Mitt or **Mitten** Glove with one thumb and a single section to house the four fingers.

Mousquetaire (French)/Opera (English) (moos-ke-tare) Long-cuffed glove, extending several inches up the forearm and sometimes to the shoulder. Length varies from eight buttons (to the middle of the arm) to sixteen buttons (to the shoulder). A close fit requires a vertical slit to allow for expansion during removal.

Novelty Any glove featuring an unusual ornamentation, such as fabrication or trim.

Work Protective gloves for industrial and health/safety occupations. Includes latex, leather, and high-performance fabrics.

Glove Fitting and Sizes

Many gloves are sized as small, medium, and large, or one-size-fits-all (especially knitted fabric gloves in women's and children's wear). Leather gloves require a more accurate fit than do most fabric gloves because the leather has less elasticity. Some types of men's gloves, such as work gloves, are offered with the medium size as the smallest size available. The standard procedure for measuring the correct size is to place a tape measure around the knuckles of the dominant, open hand. Make a fist while the tape measure in still in place; the circumference equals the glove size (see Figure 12.4.) Somewhat rarer is the method of glove sizing that entails measuring from the bottom of the palm to the tip of the longest finger.

Adult gloves are manufactured with size variations every one-half inch in fabric gloves and every one-quarter inch in leather gloves (for a smooth fit). The trend in sizing gloves is toward fewer sizes. Small, medium, and large, or one-size-fits-all predominate the market offerings.

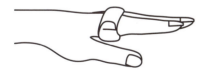

Step 1

Extend hand flat and loop measuring tape around the circumference at the knuckles.

Step 2

Keeping tape around knuckles, make a fist. Record the circumference measurement in inches and compare to sizing table.

FIGURE 12.4
How to determine your glove size.

Children's glove sizes range from zero to seven and are usually equal to half the child's age. For example, a six-year-old would wear a size three glove. Tables 12.1 and 12.2 represent a composite of the standard size ranges and corresponding dimensions for men's, women's, and children's gloves. Sizes may vary depending on the manufacturer.

Care of Gloves

Care is required during the wearing, removal, cleaning, and storage of gloves. One of the biggest problems with the wearing of gloves is the amount of dirt collected on the palm side of the glove. Gloves that are prone to show dirt should be selected for occasional use rather than daily wear. When removing gloves, the wearer should gently pull each fingertip, gradually sliding the glove off the hand.

As with other accessories categories, consumers prefer gloves that require little care. Many of the soft leathers used in gloves are not water resistant or washable due to tanning procedures. Exposure to moisture may result in a hardening of the leather that cannot be reversed. Even

TABLE 12.1

Men's and Women's Standard Glove Sizes

Size	Men's	Women's
Extra Small	7	5 1/2
Small	7 1/2–8	6
Medium	8 1/2–9	6 1/2
Large	9 1/2–10	7
X Large	10 1/2–11	7 1/2
XX Large	11 1/2–12	8

TABLE 12.2

Children's Standard Glove Sizes by Age

Size	Age
0	1
1	2
2	4
3	6
4	8
5	10
6	12
7	14

with washable leathers, once wet, the leather may feel stiff. The application of a moisturizing leather balm will soften the hand (feel of the leather). Gloves that have both fabric and leather should be cared for according to leather-cleaning methods.

Fabric gloves, whether knitted or woven, lined or unlined, and filled or quilted, are usually machine or hand washable. Consumers should carefully follow the instructions on the care label before cleaning the gloves. To hand wash gloves, fill a basin with warm sudsy water. Submerge the gloves and allow the water to penetrate the materials. Rinse thoroughly, then lay flat to air dry, away from heat sources. Some of the more durable gloves may be worn on the hand and washed.

Some manufacturers caution against alternating machine washing and dry cleaning. Streaks may appear on gloves that have been washed at home in washing machines and then sent to a professional dry cleaner. They recommend selecting one cleaning method and using it repeatedly.

THE GLOBAL GLOVE INDUSTRY

Historically in the United States, gloves were manufactured in areas where tanneries were located. One such area was Gloversville in Fulton County, New York. A 19th-century historian recounts, "In those portions of the city occupied by the leather mills, one can see acres of lamb, sheep, calf, hog, goat, deer, kangaroo, and dog skins hung upon racks to dry. Cart loads of skins in every process of dressing are met on every street and alley, and every thoroughfare contains its share of glove shops." (Gloversville history. (2000, October 25), *Masonic Lodge* 429.)

Today, much of the manufacturing of leather goods occurs in off-shore facilities, including China, with 73 percent of the production, and to a lesser extent, the Philippines, with five percent of the production. Domestic companies producing fashion gloves include totes>>>Isotoner®, which manufactures leather and driving gloves; Grandoe, a Gloversville, New York manufacturer of high-performance hand wear, including snow skiing, outdoor, biking, casual, and dress gloves for men and women; and La Crasia, a New York manufacturer of fashion gloves. La Crasia manufactures about 60,000 pairs of gloves annually for customers all around the world. Some companies, such as Shalimar Accessories in New York, manufacture private label accessories, including gloves, hats, and scarves.

The United States also exports unassembled gloves to Canada and glove parts to China, Mexico, and Hong Kong. The glove parts are assembled in these countries and reenter the United States for sale and consumption. The North American Free Trade Agreement (NAFTA) allows Mexico to export gloves to the United States duty-free. According to the U.S. Industry and Trade Outlook 2000, a 20-percent increase in exports of leather gloves and mittens brought the United States' glove export value to $8.6 million in 2000.

The United States, European Union countries, and Japan are key producers of sports gloves because of the requirement of high-performance, high-priced leathers. Baseball and golf gloves fall in this category. Golf gloves are coordinated with the fashion apparel for the sport.

Trade Organizations, Publications, and Shows

Several glove-specific trade organizations exist for safety, health, sports, work, and hobbies, but none are currently specific to the fashion industry. Likewise, the umbrella industry is represented by general accessories trade organizations. Gloves and umbrellas are featured in general accessories publications and at trade shows. Tables 12.3, 12.4, and 12.5 list some of the more important trade organizations, publications, and shows that represent these industries.

TABLE 12.3

Trade Organizations for the Gloves and Umbrellas Industries

Organization	Location	Objectives
British Glove Association (BGA) www.gloveassociation.org	Kent, UK	To represent British glove trade businesses to the government, other national organizations, and related trades.
National Industrial Glove Distributors Association (NIGDA) www.nigda.org	Philadelphia, PA	To improve distribution methods for industrial gloves, to influence legislation, and to foster trade relationships.
National Sporting Good Association (NSGA) www.nsga.org	Mt. Prospect, IL	To represent retailers, dealers, wholesalers, manufacturers, and sales agents in the sporting goods industry.
National Fashion Accessory Association and the Fashion Accessory Shippers Association (NFAA/FASA) www.accessoryweb.com	New York, NY	To represent all accessories categories, including gloves and umbrellas.
Sporting Goods Manufacturers Association (SGMA) www.sgma.com	Miami, FL	To represent the sports-products industry; dedicated to growing the business of sports and fitness.

TABLE 12.4

Trade Publications for the Gloves and Umbrellas Industries

Trade Publication Name	Description
Accessories Magazine	Monthly trade publication covering most accessories classifications, including gloves and umbrellas.
Bridal Apparel News	Provides apparel trade information to retailers and manufacturers about bridal accessories, including gloves.
Women's Wear Daily—Monday	Weekly issue of a trade newspaper, published by Fairchild. Features business and fashion information on gloves and umbrellas, as well as other accessories.
WWD Accessory Supplement	Fairchild special edition featuring fashion information on all accessories, including gloves.

TABLE 12.5

Trade Shows for the Gloves and Umbrellas Industries

Trade Show	Location	Sponsor
Accessorie Circuit	New York, NY	ENK International
AccessoriesTheShow	New York, NY	Business Journals, Inc.
China Textile and Apparel Trade Show	New York, NY	Specialty Trade Shows, Inc., and the China Council for the Promotion of International Trade
The Super Show	Las Vegas, NV	Sporting Goods Manufacturers Association

MERCHANDISING TRENDS AND TECHNIQUES

Fashion gloves are often impulse and gift purchases. The merchandise should be highly visible and easily accessible to optimize sales. Offering similar gloves in at least two distinct sections of a retail outlet ensures greater visibility and maximizes sales.

One of the most successful merchandising philosophies is to cater to the target customer's lifestyle. Creating a **lifestyle story** means providing the appropriate merchandise, visual displays, décor, and ambiance (atmosphere) to reflect the customer's mode of dressing. For example, retailers might create a dressy story, a career story, or a fun, active story to sell gloves and related accessories.

Store Retailing

Fashion gloves and mittens are sold in many types of retail stores, but the largest percentage of sales is in department and discount stores, each with 24 percent of sales. Specialty stores account for 16 percent of sales, and major chains, such as JCPenney, Kohl's, and Sears, account for 15 percent of sales.

In all types of stores, fashion gloves are usually located in the accessories department, near hats, scarves, and handbags. Knitted winter gloves may be sold as a set with muffler scarves and knitted winter caps. These may be moved to aisle end caps during the holiday season because of the potential for gift sales.

Boutique- and better-priced store merchandisers locate gloves in display cases that require a salesperson's assistance. These gloves will carry fairly high price points, starting at $50 per pair for a name brand. Designer gloves may be much higher in price and presented in locked display cases.

In discount stores or mass-merchandise stores, fashion gloves may be labeled with a store price tag, but carry no manufacturers' brand names. The store may carry a variety of styles

❧

Profile: totes>>Isotoner

Isotoner is a common word used to describe a classic pair of close-fitting, stretchable, knit driving gloves with palm grips. The gloves have been around since 1969. However, the totes>>Isotoner Corporation makes much more than just these basic gloves. Their accessories list includes a full line of gloves, slippers, rain gear, cold-weather accessories, and of course, umbrellas.

In 1923, the SoLo Marx Company began manufacturing rubber boots that could easily slip over shoes, protecting them from wet weather. These rubber overshoes, called totes (because they were easily transported), were the first in a line of outdoor accessories designed to protect the wearer from the weather.

The Isotoner company began in 1910, when brothers Arthur, Robert, and Irwin Stanton created ARIS (name acronym) gloves for the fashionable woman. Declining sales during the 1960s caused the brothers to rethink their fashion strategy and offer functional gloves, in keeping with customers' wants. Their classic 1960s glove, the ARIS Isotoner, continued to be a top selling holiday item for gift giving. The two companies, totes and ARIS Isotoner, finally merged and were renamed the totes>>Isotoner Corporation.

Currently, totes>>Isotoner produces a range of gloves, from the IsoFlex smooth leather or suede gloves, with cashmere lining and spandex insets, to the classic nylon gloves with Lycra® spandex, leather or vinyl palm grips, and a 3M lining fabric called Thinsulate.

In addition to gloves, the totes company produces umbrellas under the totes line, and lower-price lines called Chromatics and Watercolors, which are sold in mass-market retail stores. In Fall 2000, totes introduced the Pocket Wonder, a collapsible umbrella the size of a cellular telephone.

Isotoner has become aggressive in manufacturing specialty fabrics and styles. The company developed an insulating lining fabric, IsoLoft, with a brushed nap, making the lining soft and able to retain body warmth. IsoSport gloves is a style that combines an athletic glove with a leisure glove, called an **athleisure style.** The close-fitting style is made from performance fabrics that resist moisture and allow the skin to breathe.

In Spring 2001, totes>>Isotoner and Warner Brothers Consumer Products introduced a line of licensed umbrellas and raincoats for children and adults, associated with the best-selling book series, *Harry Potter,* by J.K. Rowling. The initial offerings of the licensed products were featured in department and specialty stores. Previously, totes and Fisher-Price® joined in a licensing venture to produce raincoats and umbrellas for children up to age six. Children aged 7 to 12 were targeted for a flashlight-handled umbrella called Splash Flash.

Today, totes>>Isotoner is a $500 million dollar company headquartered in Cincinnati, Ohio, and is owned by Bain Capital of Boston. The company continues to thrive by producing value-oriented products carefully marketed to its loyal customers. So well known is the totes name, that it was ranked 43rd in the Fairchild 100 list of most recognized brands.

at the same price point, with the merchandising emphasis on wide assortments of styles at one low price. Work gloves and sports gloves are located near the tools and equipment that require their use.

Internet Retailing

Internet sales are predominantly limited to sporting gloves, work gloves, and some special occasion gloves. The largest Internet market is sporting gear, such as skiing and other snow sports, mountain climbing, bicycling, shooting, and driving. In addition to active sports, Internet offerings include glove liners, functional and work gloves, safety gloves, health-industry latex gloves, traditional white gloves for parades and funerals, and satin gloves for formal occasions and weddings.

Catalog Retailing

Gloves are usually sold by apparel and accessories-catalog retailers along with related outerwear products. Cabela's, L.L.Bean, Lands' End, JC Penney, and many other catalog retailers feature gloves for fashion and protection.

SELLING GLOVES

Retailers should have an adequate selection of gloves so gift givers and self-purchasers can choose a style appropriate for their needs. An adequate selection includes multiple price points and a variety of materials, colors, and styles. Some gloves are seen as a commodity purchase, and consumers are very price-conscious. When selling fashion gloves, the name brand is less important than the overall fashion look. When selling functional gloves, the name brand is often the selling point that clinches the sale.

Price and Value

The price of gloves is heavily dependent upon the materials (including linings) used, the name brand, the degree of hand workmanship, and the decorative details. Certain types of leather, whether top grain versus split leather or soft and rare leather, such as kidskin, are more expensive to purchase. Lining materials, such as cashmere versus a polyester fleece lining, affect the price. The name-brand recognition of some gloves allows retailers to command higher prices. Name brands can be an indicator of quality, but some private-label gloves may be equal in quality but cheaper in price. Workmanship and details that affect the selling price of gloves include specialized tanning methods, the amount of hand stitching, and special trims.

For example, a wide range of price points is offered for similar styles of leather gloves. Among leather gloves on the market, a pair of Hermès lambskin gloves may retail for $355, Celine gold-chained gloves for $325, Malo cashmere-lined gloves for $290, Kate Spade gloves decorated with stitched flowers for $165 or bows for $155, Fownes leather gloves at J.C. Penney for $34, and Gloves International, Inc., leather driving gloves for $19.99. Retail stores carry gloves at price points acceptable to the target customers, with a variety of materials and colors offered to maximize sales.

Meeting Customer Needs

The glove-manufacturing industry has responded astutely to customer needs in the active-sportswear industry. The rise in sports participation by casual athletes has created a market for high-performance outerwear gloves at high prices for many different sporting activities, from golf to snowboarding.

A surge in driving-glove sales has caused department stores to increase their offerings of designer- and national-brand gloves, and accessories companies not traditionally associated with the manufacture of gloves are meeting customers' demands by offering their own version of the driving glove. Customers often give these one-size-fits-all gloves as a gift during the holidays.

Discount and mass-merchandise store buyers know their customers desire fashion gloves made of fabrics and trims that are popular in the ready-to-wear lines. Low prices and trendy fashions may be the two biggest motivating factors behind customers' purchases.

A BRIEF HISTORY OF UMBRELLAS

The modern **umbrella** serves multiple purposes—to protect from weather and the elements, for prestige and status, and as a symbol for religious ceremonies. The word *umbrella* is derived from the Latin word *umbra,* which means shade or shadow. **Parasols** or **sunshades** are used for sun protection.

The umbrella, probably Chinese in origin, dates back more than 4,000 years. Several countries, including Egypt, Assyria, Greece, and China have visual evidence of ancient umbrellas and parasols. Mesopotamian King Ashurbanipal is featured in a relief carving dated to 625 B.C. riding in a ceremonial chariot and protected from the elements by a curtained, decoratively woven parasol (see Figure 12.5).

The ancient Greeks and Romans may have copied their numerous parasol fashions from the Near East, using them for rituals and protection from the sun. Ancient Chinese produced silk parasols on bamboo frames and are credited with the first waterproofing techniques, by covering their paper parasols with wax and lacquer.

In 16th-century Europe, the wet climate encouraged the use of umbrellas by women and, later, by men. Parasols and gloves were fashionable apparel accessories during the latter part of the 17th century and into the 18th.

Women's fashions of the 19th century popularized lightweight parasols that resembled a cane when closed. This fashion continued until the early 20th century, when women discarded the sun-shielding parasols (and several other impractical fashions) in favor of the tanned look.

Samuel Fox, founder of the English Steel Company, is credited with the invention of the steel-ribbed umbrella in 1852. His invention was one of many during a time in which umbrella frame weights were being reduced from a ten-pound whalebone frame to a one-and-a-half-pound steel frame. William C. Carter, an African-American inventor, registered his 1885 patent for an umbrella stand.

With the exception of a few sun-sensitive individuals who carry parasols or umbrellas, modern Americans carry umbrellas almost exclusively for protection from the rain. The Japanese use paper umbrellas for protection from the sun and for traditional ceremonies.

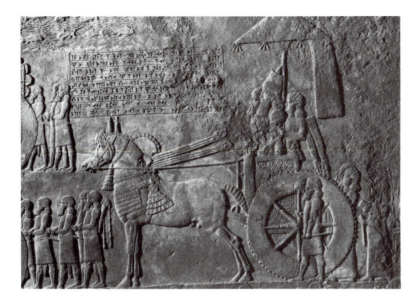

FIGURE 12.5
King Ashurbanipal in his war chariot.
© Copyright The British Museum.

UMBRELLA MANUFACTURING

The overall trend in umbrella preferences is to have umbrellas that are more compact or collapsible, lightweight, and decorative. The sun-shading parasol or the rain-repellant umbrella must be durable. In the United States, different regions have their own color and canopy preferences. Large cities, such as New York City, tend to prefer smaller, black or dark-colored umbrellas, while midsouth regions trend toward colorful and larger umbrellas.

Design

Designers continually introduce new aesthetic and functional features for umbrellas to encourage replacement sales. These new features include canopy-fabric designs and technical features that increase durability.

During the 1990s, designers introduced screen-printed umbrellas featuring reproductions from great artists, such as Van Gogh and Raphael. Many museums license art from their collection or offer their own private-label umbrellas at museum stores and through mail-order catalogs. Top designer names like Pierre Cardin have made fortunes in licensing agreements for items like umbrellas, and other designers come up with new twists regularly.

Although the canopy-fashion fabric might look the same, the durability of the umbrellas might be very different. High-end umbrella designs usually have a longer life span than low-end designs. One key factor is an umbrella's ability to withstand wind gusts. Creative designers and production engineers develop unique designs to prevent damage from umbrellas inverting. Tests up to 50 miles per hour in wind tunnels are part of the stringent design-testing process.

Parts of the Umbrella

Each part of the umbrella has a practical or decorative function or both (see Figure 12.6).

Frame The metal form that gives the umbrella its shape. Frames may be aluminum or steel and may be coated with brass or chrome. Parasol frames may be bamboo.

Ribs Metal supports to which the canopy is attached. Usually between 7 and 16 ribs.

Canopy or **cover** The fabric covering the metal ribs and frame. Made of triangular sections of fabric sewn together in a pie shape. **Canopy size** may be small, medium, large, or, for sports, extra large.

Tip End of each rib attached to the seams of the canopy.

Shaft The central pole or axis. Most umbrellas for adults have a shaft about two feet long.

Handle Holds the rib tips when closed. May be crooked, carved, or hollowed. Materials include wood, plastic, leather, cane, metal, and horn.

Ferrule/Finial The decorative top piece.

Stretchers or **spreaders** Metal rods that connect the ribs to the sliding sleeve over the shaft. The spreaders slide upward or downward into place with a spring mechanism inside the shaft that runs from the handle to the ferrule or finial.

Band/tape A tab that secures the canopy close to the frame and handle with a snap or Velcro when closed.

Sleeve A fabric tube to hold the umbrella closed. Some umbrellas sleeves have shoulder straps to free the carrier's hands when the umbrella is not needed.

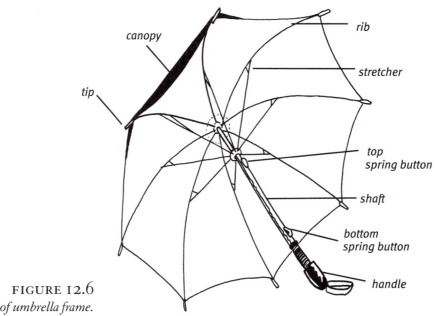

FIGURE 12.6
Illustration of umbrella frame.

Production

Umbrellas are typically constructed in two different ways. The first construction method is **solid construction,** which means the handle and shaft are part of a single continuous piece. **Two-piece construction** means the handle and shaft are separate components.

Canopies vary in size, but an average size range is 60 to 62 inches. Small adult umbrellas usually have diameters of 42 to 43 inches. Golf umbrellas may be larger, up to 68 inches in size.

Materials

The most common material for umbrella canopies is nylon. The tightly woven fabric and its inherent resistance to moisture make nylon ideal. Some manufacturers use polyester or cotton materials treated with a water-repellent finish. Vinyl canopies are waterproof and suitable for umbrellas.

Umbrella frames are usually made of fiberglass or tempered steel because of the strength needed to resist wind gusts. For lightweight umbrellas, the frame may be made of aluminum. Lightning-proof umbrellas, such as those used on golf courses, are made of nonmetal materials and have rubber handles. Quality tips to hold the canopy in place are made of lacquered metal and are hand-sewn onto the ribs; less-expensive tips may be plastic or clip-on metal.

Basic Styles of Umbrellas

Some basic styles of umbrellas follow (see Figure 12.7):

Automatic Shaft extends to full height and canopy opens with the push of a button on the handle.

Ballerina A bell-shaped canopy with a small ruffle around the circumference.

Bubble A dome-shaped canopy that extends to the carrier's shoulders. Particularly fashionable in the 1960s in clear vinyl.

Cocktail Smaller canopy, more decorative in appearance.

Folding or **Collapsible** Hinged ribs to reduce by one half the radius of the collapsed canopy. Shaft may telescope to reduce its length when closed.

Golf Large canopy, usually white and a color; held by a caddy over the head of the golfer. Popular for general use.

Oversize A larger-than-average canopy diameter.

Parasol A lightweight-fabric canopy carried to prevent overexposure to the sun.

Stick Folds into a narrow tube.

Telescoping Refers to the collapsible nature of the shaft.

Windproof Holds up under strong wind gusts, designed to prevent the canopy from inverting.

bubble umbrella

collapsible umbrella

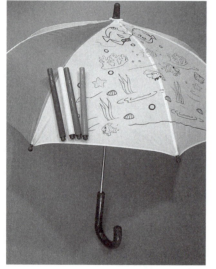

stick umbrella

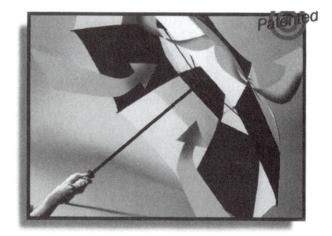

windproof umbrella

FIGURE 12.7 *Basic styles of umbrellas.*

THE GLOBAL UMBRELLA INDUSTRY

Most umbrellas and related components are mass-produced in Asia, particularly China, where labor costs are lower than in the United States. Tables 12.6 and 12.7 show a comparison between U.S. imports and exports in 2002.

In 2000, the New York City-based Uncle Sam Umbrellas, an umbrella manufacturer and repair company, closed its business due to declining sales revenues. One of the last of its kind, it was well known for creating custom umbrellas and repairing umbrellas.

TABLE 12.6

U.S. Imports of Umbrellas and Umbrella Frames in 2002

Country	Dollar Value of Umbrella Imports	Dollar Value of Frame Imports
China	50,037,000	420,000
Hong Kong	2,857,000	83,000
Taiwan	1,174,000	41,000
Thailand	2,926,000	—
United Kingdom	399,000	15,000

U.S. trade quick-reference tables: December 2002 imports: 660191.and 6603.20.3000. (2002, December). Retrieved June 27, 2003, from http://www.ita.doc.gov/td/industry/otea/Trade-Detail/Latest-December/Imports/66/660191.html

Companies with headquarters in the United States engage in overseas production in order to take advantage of lower labor costs. Peerless Umbrella, a full-service manufacturer, has a union shop in Harrison, New Jersey, but boasts that it is one of the largest umbrella importers in the United States. If a retailer needs a shipment of umbrellas quickly, Peerless can domestically produce special orders; otherwise it manufactures the goods in developing countries and passes on the labor savings to the retailer.

MERCHANDISING TRENDS AND TECHNIQUES

Manufacturers and retailers offer varying qualities and price points of umbrellas. Some customers prefer inexpensive umbrellas, often purchased in desperation during a rainstorm, while others plan their purchases for more expensive and durable umbrellas.

TABLE 12.7

U.S. Exports of Umbrellas and Umbrella Frames in 2002

Country	Dollar Value of Umbrella Exports	Dollar Value of Umbrella Frame Exports
Bermuda	—	37,000
Canada	23,000	68,000
Costa Rica	—	37,000
Japan	20,000	95,000
Mexico	262,000	240,000
Netherlands Antilles	10,000	—
Switzerland	—	45,000

U.S. trade quick-reference tables: December 2002 exports: 660191. and 6603.20.3000. (2002, December). Retrieved June 27, 2003, from http://www.ita.doc.gov/td/industry/otea/

During rainstorms in New York City, street-smart umbrella hawkers sell inexpensive black umbrellas to rain-pelted customers for five dollars (negotiable to three or four dollars). Convenience stores lay several inexpensive umbrellas on the checkout counter for impulse purchases. Retail stores relocate umbrella displays near the front entrance on rainy days. It seems that many people don't think to buy umbrellas until they get wet.

Store Retailing

Prior to the peak seasons, retailers may want to create a shop concept, or a destination point in the stores, by offering related categories of merchandise, such as rainwear and other water-resistant accessories. Merchandising in this manner creates a bigger visual impact, makes shopping more interesting for consumers, and affords the retailers opportunities for add-on sales from impulse shoppers.

Merchants should carry complete assortments during peak seasons. Once the selling season is underway, manufacturers are advised to allow retailers to "cherry pick" reorder assortments according to what the store buyers know will sell, rather than force stores to reorder manufacturers' prepackaged assortments.

Customers may not be well educated in technical characteristics of umbrellas, but they want to know features and benefits of the umbrellas before selecting a particular brand. Manufacturers and retailers include some of the following marketing terms in their advertisements: wind-defying, wind-proof, wind-resistant, wind-tunnel tested, aerodynamically designed infrastructure, and inversion-proof.

Internet Retailing

Most umbrella Web sites sell directly to customers, bypassing traditional retail establishments. They offer a variety of products, including novelty-print umbrellas, golf umbrellas, and patio umbrellas. This method of retailing does not emphasize name brands.

Name-brand umbrellas are more likely to be promoted rather than actually sold on manufacturer-sponsored Web sites. Through this pull-marketing technique, shoppers are encouraged to visit their favorite retail store and ask for the brand.

Catalog Retailing

Most catalog merchants offer specialty umbrellas to go with other accessories products, as they do with gloves. For example, a catalog page featuring an all-weather coat may also feature a decorative-canopy umbrella, reminding customers that a new raincoat doesn't go well with a worn-out umbrella. If the umbrella is at the right price and unique in appearance, the customer will be more inclined to order the related accessory.

SELLING UMBRELLAS

Marketers of umbrellas should view them as both impulse items and planned purchases. During rainy-weather seasons, lower-priced umbrellas become impulse items and should be highly visible in the store. During dry-weather seasons and gift-giving seasons (June and December), higher-priced umbrellas should be attractively merchandised with related accessories to create strong fashion presentations.

Price and Value

Name-brand umbrella manufacturers spend large sums on their advertising budgets to capture customer awareness. The most recognizable brand, totes>>Isotoner, uses both print and television advertising to maintain their dominant market share. Catering to a different target customer, Brigg umbrellas are priced much higher (retailing for as high as $350) with such noteworthy extras as a concealed cigarette lighter.

For customers preferring brand names, the concept of value must be presented to justify the higher price tags associated with them. This isn't necessary with customers who prefer the lowest prices, with little thought devoted to technical features.

Patio umbrellas and accompanying stands range in retail price from $150 to $1,000. Their value is determined by the ability to remain upright in windy conditions and the degree of protection from harmful ultraviolet sunrays. Ability to withstand exposure to wet weather is also a factor. Iron bases are considered important to prevent wind gusts from tipping canopies, while an enameled base retards rusting. Unfortunately these bases may weigh nearly fifty pounds. Sun protection is measured by canopy size or span, which is another value factor. Canopy spans usually range from 8 1/2 to 10 feet in diameter. Canopy materials may be stain- and moisture-resistant acrylic or polyester-canvas fabric, or Teflon-coated cotton canvas. All outdoor canopies should have some type of finish to resist aging caused by nature's elements.

Hardwood frames are considered more durable than aluminum; those that allow for canopy tilt are preferred by customers. Poles may be sectioned for ease of assembly, but the pieces should fit snugly when assembled. Poles range from 1 1/4 to 2 inches in diameter.

Meeting Customer Needs

Umbrella manufacturers strive to offer customers new and enticing options. Mini folding umbrellas, golf-sized umbrellas that fold into compact sizes, rain-repellent umbrellas with special UV coating for sunny days, and umbrellas with shoulder straps are examples of the ongoing innovations that motivate customers to purchase replacement umbrellas.

Care of Umbrellas

Retail sales associates should advise their customers on the care of their purchase. Umbrellas should be thoroughly air-dried before being closed. Avoid wiping the canopy with a towel because the water-repellent finish may be removed. Seasonally, spray a saturating water-repellent coating, such as Scotchguard®, on opened fabric canopies and allow them to dry.

A BRIEF HISTORY OF EYEWEAR

The ancient Chinese first used spectacles about 2,000 years ago to protect their eyes from evil forces. In Rome in about 4 B.C., the tragedian Seneca was said to have read many books by looking through a water-filled glass globe. The Italians developed a **reading stone**—a glass sphere laid against written documents to magnify the letters. The reading stone was later improved by mounting it in front of the eyes.

Reading spectacles were made in the late 13th century, although the inventor is unknown. Written references to, and painted frescoes of, spectacles date the invention between 1268 and 1289. Concave lenses, made for the nearsighted were invented in the 16th century. Pope Leo X claimed he could see better than his hunting companions when wearing concave spectacles. Quartz lenses in bone, metal, or leather frames were riveted in an inverted V-shape and carefully perched on the bridge of the nose.

In England in 1629, the Spectacle Makers Company was formed with the motto: "A blessing to the aged." By 1730, the English had perfected the rigid sidepieces to hold the spectacles on the face most effectively. In 1752, eyeglass designer James Ayscough invented a pair of spectacles with double-hinged sidepieces and two sets of lenses—clear and tinted in blues and greens.

The cost of spectacles was high (as much as $200 in the early 1700s), restricting the wearing of glasses to the affluent. American statesman and bifocal inventor Benjamin Franklin is said to have tired of changing between his near- and farsighted spectacles. Franklin later wrote he "had the glasses cut and a half of each kind associated in the same circle" (Drewry, 2001) (see Figure 12.8). Spectacles were continuously improved over the next two centuries, and by the 20th century the use of bifocals in silver, steel, and hard rubber frames (manufactured by J.J. Bausch) had greatly increased.

The monocle, lorgnette, scissor glasses, and pince-nez (pinch nose) were 18th and 19th century adaptations of eyewear. **Monocles,** or eye rings, were developed in Germany in the 1700s and introduced in London in 1800. Worn by socially elite men, particularly the German military, the monocle became unfashionable after World War I (see Figure 12.9).

Lorgnettes were framed lenses held in place with a single long handle. These replaced the **scissor glasses** with handles that were connected under the nose, appearing as though they were about to cut it off. **Pince-nez glasses** had no handles or earpieces and were conveniently secured to a ribbon or chain worn around the neck or pinned to the lapel.

FIGURE 12.8
Benjamin Franklin is often depicted
in his wire-framed bifocal spectacles.

FIGURE 12.9
Monocle.

During the 1930s, advertisements began to emerge for tinted-lens **sunglasses,** the most fashion-forward addition in eyewear. Sam Foster began selling his Foster Grants® sunglasses in fashion colors at the Woolworth store in Atlantic City.

The demand for sunglasses continued to grow steadily because sunglasses were an inexpensive way to accessorize outfits. Note the amusing excerpt from a thirty-year-old fashion textbook about the emerging classification of fashion sunglasses. "One of the most important fashion accessories items to be found in the Notions Department is inexpensive, fashionable eyeglasses for wearing in the sun. One manufacturer has made sunglasses available with five sets of different fashion-colored lenses that let you coordinate your glasses with your costume. These are a complete fashion sunglass wardrobe for sun-fun, fashion-wise gals" (Tolman, 1973).

AN INTRODUCTION TO EYEWEAR

The eyewear industry is comprised of relatively few manufacturing companies, compared with the number of manufacturers in other accessories categories, such as footwear. Huge eyewear-manufacturing companies own smaller companies and frequently work together in joint ventures. The largest player in eyewear production is Luxottica, with sales over $2 billion in 2000. Designers tied to Luxottica include Giorgio Armani, Byblos, Chanel, Bulgari, Ferragamo, Moschino, and Genny. Following Luxottica are Safilo, De Rigo, Marcolin, and Italocremona. Although a few powerhouses control the bulk of the sales, thousands of small producers, like artisans with technical acumen, produce fashion eyewear.

Much of the designing and production occurs at Italian manufacturing firms, although most customers are unaware of this. There is a plethora of licensed eyewear brands, but most can be traced back to just a few giant Italian firms. Two giant non-Italian manufacturing firms are Kaneko Optical Company of Japan and Brendel of Germany.

Most of the large Italian companies create eyewear for very recognizable brand names. Ray-Ban, a subsidiary of Bausch & Lomb, as well as Sunglass Hut and LensCrafters, are owned by Luxottica. Safilo Group manufactures Gianfranco Ferre, Burberry, Yves St. Laurent, Nine

West, Diesel, Kate Spade, Gucci, Valentino, and Polo Ralph Lauren. De Rigo manufactures eyewear for Sting, Fila, Police, Celine (under the guidance of Michael Kors), Fendi, Etro, La Perla, Loewe, and Prada. In 2000, Prada and De Rigo entered into a joint venture called the Eyewear International Distribution that manufactures several lines, including Jill Sander, Prada Optical, Helmut Lang, and Miu Miu. Chloe eyewear is manufactured by Marcolin and Versace eyewear is manufactured by Italocremona.

Parts of Eyewear

Eyeglasses and sunglasses have the following parts (see Figure 12.10):

Lens The clear or tinted piece through which the wearer sees.
Frame Holds the lens in position.
Templepiece Located at the face temple, connects the frame to the earpiece.
Earpiece Part of the frame that fits snuggly above the ears and may curve down behind the ears.
Bridgepiece Part of the frame that crosses the bridge of the nose acting as a support for the frame.

Styles of Eyewear

The following styles give eyewear its fashion appeal (See Figure 12.11):

Aviator glasses Style popularized by WWII airmen.
Cat Eyes or **Kitty Cat glasses** Narrowing and upturning of frames at temples.
Gradated lens Lighter on the bottom and darker on the top.
Bi-gradient lens Two colors that blend into each other in the lens.
Goggles Close fitting (airtight or watertight) around the eyes. For sporting or working activities.
Rimless A floating effect for the frame, minimizes the visibility of the frame shape.

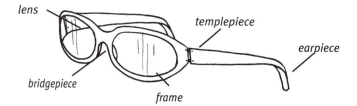

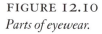

FIGURE 12.10
Parts of eyewear.

Aviator

Goggles

rimless

wrap

FIGURE 12.11 *Basic Styles of Eyewear.*
Courtesy of Foster Grant, Inc. and Fairchild Publications, Inc

Readers Nonprescription eyewear with varying magnification levels such as $+1$, $+1$ $1/2$, or $+2$.

Wrap glasses Sporty frame that curves or wraps around the face and temples, rather than a straight front with two templepieces.

Eyewear Manufacturing

Technology has been an important factor in the design and production of eyewear. Important innovations include lightweight frame materials, such as titanium or magnesium, and lenses that reduce glare and eliminate harmful ultraviolet lights. Traditional materials, such as silver and gold metals, tortoiseshell, or marbled wood, are usually merged with ultraviolet ray-screening, polarized lenses.

Design

Designers often look to the past for historic frame shapes and meld these with modern features. For example, designers have enlarged the size and modernized the bridge and temple treatments of the classic aviator frame (see Figure 12.12).

Designers rely on innovative frame and lens colors to encourage multiple purchases, creating an eyewear wardrobe. As colors are selected for ready-to-wear, eyewear designers create coordinating eyewear. Customers who already own a few frames desire more up-to-date colored frames and tinted lenses.

Many of the sunglasses are unisex in appearance. This design strategy allows manufacturers to offer more lens/frame color combinations.

Licensing

Licensing eyewear is a large part of the eyewear business. Licensing agreements offer eyewear manufacturers an opportunity to link with prestigious trademarks or brands with high recognition in a target market. The close ties with apparel companies provide opportunities for eyewear fashions to be in sync with apparel fashions. For example, recognizable names, such as Wrangler® and Nascar® are licensed to Gargoyles, a manufacturer of eyewear. Esprit, known for colorful sportswear, has also branched into a line of colorful and trendy sunglasses (see Figure 12.13).

Apparel brands Mossimo and Paris Blues (denim and knitwear) have also signed licensing agreements for eyewear manufacturers to produced eyewear collections under the apparel brand names.

Production

Frames are designed using a CAD (computer-aided design) drawing system. Once the design is selected and a printed version of the frame is altered and approved, the CAD system generates multiple frame sizes. A flat sample of the frame is cut for further approval.

The production of eyewear frames requires the use of several unique pieces of machinery including a hydraulic production press and digital cutting machine, an eye-rim-forming machine, and a heat-treatment machine. Frame soldering and surface finishing of lenses are done by skilled, experienced technicians.

Prescription frames have three standardized-size measurements to help manufacturers and optical personnel fit them for consumers. For example, a frame might bear the numbers 48-19-140. The number 48 represents the size of the lenses; 19 is the bridge size, which ensures that the

FIGURE 12.12 *Gucci eyewear.*
Courtesy of Fairchild Publications, Inc.

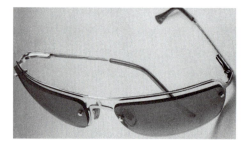

FIGURE 12.13 *Esprit eyewear.*
Courtesy of Fairchild Publications, Inc.

frame fits the nose; and 140 is the templepiece length (templepieces are the parts that extend to the ears). Frames vary by their shapes and sizes, so there is no set of numbers that would apply to one person for all frames. Each frame must be fitted individually.

Materials

Eyewear frame materials range from natural substances to plastics or metals, and combinations of these materials. In some seasons fashion dictates that natural materials, or at least natural looks, dominate the eyewear market. This includes tortoiseshell, mother-of-pearl, wood, or other materials that simulate nature. Other fashion seasons emphasize the high-tech look. Acetate, nylon, carbon, plastics, and lightweight metals such as aluminum, nickel, stainless steel, titanium, and magnesium, dominate the eyewear offerings.

Lens materials may be glass, acrylic, or polycarbonate, which is stronger and safer than acrylic lenses. Nonscratch and antireflective or nonglare coatings may be applied to the lens, but this usually increases the consumer prices.

Popular embellishments that adorn apparel and other fashion accessories are also used on eyewear. For example, when glitter, crystals, or rhinestones are featured in other accessories products, eyewear manufacturers will adorn frames and lens with similar materials.

THE GLOBAL EYEWEAR INDUSTRY

The Benullo Valley in Italy has traditionally been viewed as an eyewear mecca. Italy has been credited with the production of one fourth of the world's total manufactured eyewear, and it had a 71-percent market share of all high-end eyewear. France (25 percent) and the United States (14 percent) also produced high-end eyewear. Since 1990, Italian eyewear exports have increased 400 percent. The United States represents over 40 percent of Italy's exports.

Sunglasses sales are the most important type of eyewear for fashion retailers. In 2001, more than 96 million pairs of sunglasses were sold in the United States. Tables 12.8 and 12.9 show the top values of U.S. imports and exports. China and Italy produce the greatest values of sunglasses imported into the United States. The U.S. primarily exports eyewear to France, Canada, the United Kingdom, Australia, and Mexico.

Concerns exist in the eyewear industry over the rampant importation of low-priced eyewear that are imitations of high-end branded products. The black market associated with the practice was valued at $69 million in 2001. Although it is difficult to combat the sale of illegal goods, authorities have imposed strict standards and closely monitor Asian exports.

Another concern of U.S. eyewear companies is a trade disagreement between the United States and the countries in the European Union. In response to a 2002 decision by the U.S. government to impose tariffs on imported steel, the European Union threatened to impose stiff duties of up to a 100-percent tariff on American sunglasses as well as 300 other American products. This tariff would double the wholesale cost of American sunglasses sold in Europe.

TABLE 12.8

U.S. Imports of Sunglasses in 2002

Country	Dollar Value of Sunglass Imports
China	258,026,000
Italy	213,077,000
Taiwan	46,659,000
Japan	36,971,000
France	25,330,000
Hong Kong	21,948,000

U.S. trade quick-reference tables: December 2002 imports: 9004.10.000. (2002, December). Retrieved June 27, 2003, from
http://www.ita.doc.gov/td/industry/otea/Trade-Detail/

Although the concern is very real, analysts suggest the tariff impact would be softened because there are ways to ship American goods made outside of the U.S. to the European Union countries without invoking the tariff. In addition, most of the manufacturing of sunglasses is done outside the United States.

The global eyewear industry is made up of highly specialized trade organizations and publications. Trade shows exist exclusively for eyewear, unlike other accessories trade shows that often represent several accessories categories. Tables 12.10, 12.11, and 12.12 show some of the more important eyewear trade organizations, publications, and shows.

TABLE 12.9

U.S. Exports of Sunglasses in 2002

Dollar Value of	Dollar Value of Sunglass Exports
France	26,687,000
Canada	18,005,000
United Kingdom	14,352,000
Australia	12,775,000
Mexico	7,418,000

U.S. trade quick-reference tables: December 2002 exports: 9004.10.000. (2002, December). Retrieved June 27, 2003, from
http://www.ita.doc.gov/td/industry/otea/

TABLE I 2.I 0

Trade Organizations for the Eyewear Industry

Organization	Location	Objectives
Optical Goods Manufacturers' National Association (ANFAO)	Italy	To represent eyewear manufacturers
European Sunglass Association	France	To perform market research for members, protect the industry against unnecessary regulations, and promote the sunglass industry to consumers
Sunglass Association of America (SAA) www.sunglassassociation.com	Norwalk, CT	To issue market research reports on trade and sales data, monitor industry regulations, and promote the sunglass industry to consumers
Vision Council of America (VCA) www.visionsite.org	Alexandria, VA	To educate consumers about quality eyewear —a nonprofit optical association

MERCHANDISING TRENDS AND TECHNIQUES

Retailers choosing display locations and assortment plans should note some important facts about eyewear merchandise. Two thirds of nonprescription eyewear is fashion sunglasses, while about one third is sports sunglasses. Sunglass eyewear has a high sales-per-square-foot potential volume for retailers. With the bulk of eyewear selling between $50 and $150, and the ability to merchandise many pairs in a small space, retailers can realize high sales. In-store customers try on an average of eleven pairs of glasses before making a purchase decision. A balanced assort-

TABLE I 2.I I

Trade Publications for the Eyewear Industry

Trade Publication Name	Description
Accessories Magazine	Monthly trade publication covering most accessories classifications, including eyewear
EyeMagine	Online eyewear information from the Accessories Council (www.accessoriescouncil.org)
Training Guide 2002	Provides professionals a comprehensive understanding of sunglasses and the role they play as protective devices; published by the European Sunglass Association
Women's Wear Daily – Monday	Weekly issue of a trade newspaper, published by Fairchild; features business and fashion information on eyewear, as well as other accessories
WWD Accessory Supplement	Fairchild special edition featuring fashion information on all accessories, including eyewear

TABLE 12.12

Trade Shows for the Eyewear Industry

Trade Show	Location	Sponsor
Accessorie Circuit	New York, NY	ENK International
AccessoriesTheShow	New York, NY	Business Journals, Inc.
Eyequest	Rosemont, IL	Vision Council of America/Reed Exhibitions
International Vision Expo East	New York, NY	Vision Council of America/Reed Exhibitions
International Vision Expo West	Las Vegas, NV	Vision Council of America/Reed Exhibitions
MAGIC International	Las Vegas, NV	Men's Apparel Guild in California
MIDO	Milan, Italy	Optical and Eyecare Fair Agency (EFOP)

ment of prices and styles is needed to ensure having adequate stock levels of most popular selling styles and enough of a selection to provide customers with several styles.

Display and merchandising methods depend on the type of retailer, brand name, and price points of the eyewear. Glass showcases, tabletops, wall shelves, countertop or floor rotating fixtures, and mall kiosks are common fixtures for eyewear. Mirrors should be located with all eyewear fixtures. It is common for upper-end eyewear manufacturers to provide stores with customized display units.

Because of the ease of accessibility, eyewear retailers must constantly be vigilant against theft. Shoplifting is a significant problem with all accessories, and sunglasses are easily concealed or worn out of the store.

Store Retailing

Nonprescription eyewear is considered an impulse item and should be featured prominently in stores. Retailers also strategically locate eyewear outposts near ready-to-wear or related product areas.

Department stores usually offer a large selection of sunglasses and may offer a small rack of fashionable nonprescription reading glasses. The sunglasses are often grouped by brand names on customized fixtures provided by the manufacturers.

Specialty stores, such as optical retailers, offer a higher level of personalized service than most other retailers. Merchandising methods do not necessarily lend themselves to self-selection because opticians are usually available. Lower- and moderately priced frames are often grouped together with little brand-name distinction. Higher-priced frames are grouped by brand name on manufacturer-provided display units (see Figure 12.15). Fashion specialty stores featuring apparel and accessories usually locate eyewear display units near the registers and as part of in-store displays.

FIGURE 12.15
Eyewear displays in a retail store. Courtesy of Fairchild Publications, Inc.

Sunglass Hut, a specialty niche retailer, offers brand-name eyewear to shoppers in high-traffic areas and tourist destinations. In Fall 2002, the company enticed gift-buying consumers with point-of-purchase promotions. These included two styles of Ray-Ban sunglasses featured in the Columbia TriStar movie, *Men in Black II.*

Discount retailers are expected to stock eyewear in several key locations throughout the store for eyewear. In a typical discount store a large sunglass kiosk is located at the front entrance to the store and a smaller rotating rack of sunglasses is located in the accessories department, near the costume jewelry, wallets, and watches. A smaller rack of children's sunglasses is located in the children's department, atop a round rack. The health and beauty aids department has a rack of magnification reading glasses. The sporting goods department houses a rack of reflective aviator-style sunglasses for shoppers purchasing hunting or fishing gear. The possibilities are numerous, and creative merchandising is the key to add-on sales.

In large discount and low-end stores, such as drug stores, eyewear merchandising is often the responsibility of the manufacturer. This concept of maintaining the inventory is called **category management.** Duties include display maintenance, stock replenishment, **SKU** (stock-keeping units or individual styles) selection, promotions, and other merchandising responsibilities performed by manufacturers' representatives who regularly visit the stores. Because fashion-eyewear sales are steadily increasing, store personnel are getting more involved with style selection and in-store promotions.

Internet Retailing

The rising costs of frames through traditional retail outlets have improved the market for Internet retailing. Customers are encouraged to purchase online for price savings. Sophisticated Web sites allow a customer to upload a photograph and virtually try on any frames.

Some Internet retailers believe the success of their Web site is related to the success of their brick-and-mortar stores. Stores that support Web sites are called **click-and-mortar stores.** Consumers like the idea of buying from a trusted retailer that supports its Web site through its retail shops, with services like repairs, exchanges, and information. One click-and-mortar retailer, Sunglass Hut, believes the widespread recognition of its stores has improved the success of its Web site.

Although in-store customers prefer trying on several pairs of eyewear before making a purchase, retailers have been surprised to find that sunglass customers do not necessarily need to try on the merchandise before they buy it. Online marketers have had success selling $100+ sunglasses via the Web. Other customers use the Internet to obtain complete information about styles and brands. Rather than purchasing online, they prefer actually trying on the eyewear to find the most flattering style.

Catalog Retailing

The popularity of sunglasses as a fashion statement has created a profitable marketing opportunity for catalog retailers. As the popularity of sunglasses increases, with customers purchasing multiple pairs each season, catalog offerings should keep pace. Because many customers prefer to try on a pair of frames before buying, catalog retailers should offer best-selling frame styles to minimize the possibility of returns.

SELLING EYEWEAR

Customers should be encouraged to purchase fashion eyewear that *complements* (not *repeats*) their facial shape, rather than simply purchasing what is "in fashion." Salespeople should have customers try on several frames before selecting a pair (or two!). Three key selling points are as follows: the frame shape should contrast with the face shape, the frame size should be in scale with the face size, eyewear should repeat the customer's personal best feature (such as a blue frame to match blue eyes).

Price and Value

Price is often an indicator of quality. The price of eyewear is related to design, workmanship, materials, and brand image. A good-quality pair of eyewear is mechanically sound, including well-secured hinges and sturdy solder points at the bridgepiece, nose pad, and templepiece areas. Materials should not discolor and should be corrosion and heat resistant. Silicone nose pads and spring coils reduce slippage and prevent pinching. Spring hinges provide exceptional alignment and reduce the need for adjustments. Flexible frames will bend and twist and return to their original shape.

The brand image of licenses may also require an inflated price. Some manufacturers have refused to sell to retailers not selling at certain price points. In spite of these artificial pricing factors and the degree of ornamentation, the quality of the product still depends on the frame and lens materials.

Meeting Customer Needs

Several reasons have been given for the popularity of eyewear. These include the failing eyesight of the aging baby boomer population, the increased awareness of the sun's harmful effects resulting in wrinkles and cataracts, the casual athlete trend, and the widely accepted notion that eyewear can be fashionable.

The aging demographics of America have been recognized as an important eyewear opportunity. Reading glasses and **sun-reader glasses** (sunglasses with magnification) sales will be key items for the next decade. Additionally, comfort (lightweight) and casual are important concepts for the aging eyewear consumers. Lightweight frames are especially important to consumers who need eyewear for improved vision.

Eyewear has become important for sun protection, just like the increase in the sales of hats as a sun-protection accessory. Once just worn to reduce glare, now eyewear is frequently tinted to protect from the sun's harmful ultraviolet lights, blamed for causing cataracts.

Although women have always been heavy purchasers of fashion eyewear, sales to men are steadily increasing. Street-fashion looks, weekend wear, sportswear, and the sport influence contributed to the popularity of casual eyewear. Multiple pairs of sunglasses have become a vital part of a man's sportswear wardrobe and are considered the final layer on work and weekend fashions.

Basic Facial Shapes for Eyewear

Retail sales associates can help customers select flattering styles of eyewear by taking into account the shape of the wearer's face.

- *Round face* Select narrow, angular eyewear that plays down the roundness. Deep colors, such as black or tortoise, also minimize fullness.
- *Square face* Frames should be slightly curved, rather than angular. Templepieces extending beyond the face will help soften the straight lines of the face.
- *Inverted triangular face* Frames with a thin rim and vertical lines help balance the narrower part of the lower face. Frames should sit slightly lower on the face. Avoid large frames, heavy nose bridges, bold colors , and square shapes.
- *Oblong face* The length is minimized on long narrow faces when wide, deep frames cover as much of the center of the face as possible. Frames will minimize the length of the face if they have no up-curve.
- *Oval face* A variety of frames can be worn on oval faces, as long as the frame size is in proportion to the face size.

Eyewear Dos and Don'ts

- **Do** choose frames that follow slightly under the curve of the natural eyebrow, enhance the cheekbones, and allow the wearer's true beauty to be visible.
- **Do** update frame styles with the fashions.
- **Do** choose frames slightly upturned at the templepiece to create an upswept eye appearance, something like the plastic-surgery technique.
- **Do** choose lens and frame colors that blend with or complement hair highlights or eye color.
- **Do** ensure the eye is in the center of the lens.
- **Do** be aware that not all eyewear is made the same. Just as a poor-quality window or mirror distorts views, so can poor-quality lenses.
- **Do** choose antireflective coatings for lenses to minimize glare.
- **Don't** try to make a "statement" with eyewear. Generally, the eyeglasses should not be the first thing noticed about a person, except under special circumstances.
- **Don't** choose invisible, "barely there" glasses. These may create a bland look and de-emphasize facial features.
- **Don't** be overly distracted by comparing UV performance claims. Most sunglasses have adequate levels of UV blockage.
- **Don't** choose lined bifocals. Request no-line, progressive lenses.

SUMMARY

- Gloves originated as functional accessories and evolved into fashion accessories. They have been associated with symbolism, wealth, love and devotion, legalism, religion, and battle. Gloves continued to be essential parts of every fashionable person's wardrobe until the early 20th century when fashion took a backseat to function.

- Materials, quality of workmanship, and brand names affect the retail price of gloves. With fewer than ten parts, glove manufacturing can be easily automated and priced inexpensively. However, despite the relatively few seams, gloves may be entirely handmade as a craft and sold for a few hundred dollars per pair.

- In addition to soft and supple leathers, gloves may be knitted or manufactured in high-performance fabrics that repel moisture.

- Most gloves made in the United States are work gloves. Specialty subcategories are being developed to encourage sales of work gloves.

- Glove styles and lengths are coordinated to apparel fashions. Long sleeves require short gloves, while short sleeves allow for long gloves.

- The trend in fitting gloves is toward fewer sizes with greater stretch capabilities. Most knitted gloves are one-size-fits-all, or small, medium, and large. Leather gloves require a more accurate fit and may have a greater range of sizes.

- If gloves are hand washable, care should be taken to ensure the gloves are not stretched out of shape. Some leather gloves must be professionally dry cleaned by a leather expert.

- China is a leader in fashion-glove production, although a few domestic manufacturing companies do exist.

- Department stores and discount stores sell almost one half of all fashion gloves purchased in the United States. Fashion gloves are merchandised with handbags, hats, and scarves. Work gloves may be merchandised with related work tools. Sporting gloves and special-occasion gloves are merchandised with other items of apparel related to a particular activity.

- Umbrellas or parasols probably originated in Asia. They were first used for sun protection, and later the canopies were waterproofed for damp weather. As the tanned look became popular in the 20th century, sun-shading parasols lost their importance, and rain umbrellas became the mainstay.

- Umbrellas have evolved into compact, collapsible, lightweight, and decorative accessories. Convenience is an important purchasing motivation for lower-priced umbrellas. Durability, in the form of wind resistance, is a key purchasing motivation for higher-priced umbrellas.

- Canopy sizes range from 40 to 68 inches in diameter. Many canopies are tightly woven nylon or polyester fabrics, which are inherently water repellent. However, most umbrella canopies are treated with a water-resistant finish, regardless of the fiber content. Canopies should be left open to dry to prevent mold or mildew.

- China is the chief producing country for umbrellas because labor costs are low. Some domestic companies manufacture umbrellas in the United States to ensure a quick response to reorders.

- Because umbrellas are emergency accessories, retailers try to make them easy to locate on rainy days, such as near the front entrance, for impulse buyers. Umbrellas are best merchandised with related merchandise items, such as raincoats, boots, and matching totes.

- Umbrellas are available for sale on the Internet and in direct-mail catalogs. On Web sites, golf umbrellas are heavily featured at higher price points; novelty-print and patio umbrellas are also featured. Most mail-order catalog merchants offer specialty umbrellas on the same page as other accessories products.

- When selling umbrellas, retailers and manufacturers must ensure that customers understand the value. Knowledgeable salespeople or descriptive hangtags should explain the special features of brand names.

- Eyewear, although relatively new as a fashion accessory, has become very popular in the last several decades.

- Customers purchase multiple frames for their fashion wardrobe.

- Retailers offer eyewear in various accessories outposts throughout the store as well as through nontraditional retail outlets.

- Innovative materials, especially lightweight metals and plastics, continue to be popular for eyewear, as are materials that protect the wearer from harmful ultraviolet rays and glares.

- Italy is well known for the manufacturing and design of high fashion eyewear.

- Most eyewear is produced by a few companies under licensing agreements with successful retail brand names.

- The main parts of eyewear are the lens, frame, templepiece, earpiece, and bridgepiece.

- Designs involve both fashion and function.

- Although many customers prefer to try on several frames before selecting one, many customers are willing to purchase (without fitting) moderately priced fashion eyewear through the Internet and via catalogs.

- Sunglass eyewear has high sales-per-square-foot of retail selling space. Most sunglasses sell between $50 and $150 per pair.

- Many factors affect the retail price of eyewear including design, workmanship, materials and brand image.

- The popularity of eyewear has been attributed to the aging population of American consumers, the customers' desire to protect their eyes from the harmful rays of the sun, and the trend toward casual dressing.

- Just as clothing may look different on each customer, eyewear can as well. Eyewear should be tried on and evaluated by the consumer.

TERMS FOR REVIEW

athleisure style	biarritz gloves	bubble umbrella
automatic umbrella	bi-gradient lens	buttons
aviator glasses	binding	canopy (cover)
ballerina umbrella	bracelet-length gloves	canopy size
band/tape	bridgepiece	cat eyes (kitty cat glasses)

category management

click-and-mortar stores

clicking

clute-cut pattern

cocktail umbrella

cuff

davey tip

domes

driving gloves

earpiece

ferrule/finial

fingerless (waif) gloves

folding (collapsible) umbrella

fourchettes

frame (umbrella)

frame (eyewear)

full fashioning

gauntlet gloves

glove liners

goggles

golf umbrella

gore

gradated lens

gunn-cut pattern

gusset

half-piqué

handle

hearts (stays)

inseaming

kid gloves

lace gloves

lens

lifestyle story

linings

lorgnettes

mitt (mitten)

monocles

mousquetaire gloves

novelty gloves

opera gloves

outseaming

overseaming

oversize umbrella

parasol umbrella

pince-nez glasses

piqué seams

pointing

quirks

readers

reading stone

ribs

rimless

scissor glasses

shaft

shortie gloves

sidewall

SKU

sleeve

solid construction

stick umbrella

stretchers (spreaders)

sumptuary laws

sun-reader glasses

sunglasses

sunshades

telescoping umbrella

templepiece

thumb

tip

trank

two-piece construction

umbrella

windproof umbrella

work gloves

wrap glasses

REVIEW QUESTIONS

1. What are some reasons fashion gloves and parasols were replaced by functional gloves and umbrellas in the 20th century?

2. What are the basic parts of a glove? an umbrella? eyewear?

3. Identify recent technological innovations in fabrics and fabrications for gloves and umbrellas. How has the eyewear industry changed its fabrication processes through the years?

4. Under what circumstances would manufacturers desire to produce gloves or umbrellas in the United States? in China?

5. What are the basic steps in glove production?

6. What are some primary differences between gloves, umbrellas, or eyewear retailing at high and low price points? How do you account for the price difference? Is there a relationship between price and value?

7. How have manufacturers created "fashion" in work gloves? in umbrellas? in eyewear?

8. What are some merchandising methods used by umbrella retailers?
9. What factors have contributed to the popularity of eyewear?
10. When selecting eyeglass frames, what are some consumer considerations?

KNOWLEDGE APPLICATIONS

1. Visit a portrait museum and view the gloves and parasols worn or held by the subjects. Make a timeline or table showing portrait dates, materials, styles, and colors. Analyze your findings.

2. Select a retail store and develop a data chart to record the following: glove styles, materials, linings, price points, and store merchandising methods. Compare your findings with the class.

3. Visit several Web sites selling gloves, umbrellas, or fashion eyewear. Describe the trends that you see in evidence.

4. Look up U.S. testing standards for umbrellas. How does a manufacturer relay information to the consumer regarding its compliance with the standards?

5. Bring an umbrella to class and label its various parts.

6. Compare the quality of two umbrellas or pairs of sunglasses at distinctly different price points. Evaluate which of the two is the better value.

7. On a rainy day, perform a fashion count of the colors and patterns of umbrella canopies. Analyze your findings. What do these findings say about merchandising umbrellas in your area?

8. Visit a department store, mass-merchandise store, or discount store. Locate the umbrellas and evaluate the merchandising strategy used. Is the store using the shop or destination-point concept by offering related categories of merchandise?

9. Discreetly watch the sunglasses section in a retail store. Observe several customers in an allotted time period as they try on sunglasses. Record the number of sunglasses tried on by each customer. Calculate the average number of eyeglasses tried on by males and females. Compare the data from the two groups. Obtain permission from the store management before performing the count.

CHAPTER 13

FINE JEWELRY

"A woman needs ropes and ropes of pearls."

—Coco Chanel

A BRIEF HISTORY OF FINE JEWELRY

FINE JEWELRY IS USUALLY MADE FROM INORGANIC MATERIALS, SOME OF WHICH ARE billions of years old. Because of the durability of the components, some jewelry has survived in burial mounds, tombs, buried cities, and other dwellings of civilizations. The fate of much of the ancient jewelry was to be melted down and recast after the fashions had changed.

The ancient Egyptians were well known for their love of fine jewelry. Many drawings and statues portray men and women in the famous large gold collars, girdles (belts), and aprons. Collar necklaces were often so heavy that they required a **counterpoise** (counter weight) to be worn down the center back, preventing the necklace from dropping in front. The discovery of King Tutankhamen's (King Tut's) tomb in 1922 was an incredible archaeological find. The fact that the tomb had not been plundered by thieves allowed museum visitors to imagine the magnitude of the wealth of an Egyptian pharaoh.

The jewelry of the ancient Sumerians of Mesopotamia (the Fertile Crescent, which lies between the Tigris and Euphrates Rivers) is closely tied to a discovery in the Royal Tombs of Ur. Beads of alabaster, rock crystals, and carnelian were discovered in the Royal Tombs, as were miniature gold animal pendants, similar to contemporary charm bracelets. Necklaces of gold and semiprecious stones, like lapis lazuli mounted in gold settings, were forms of adornment worn by wealthy Sumerians. Their jewelry was made into unusual symbols that became the basis for the zodiac signs.

Jewelry was not limited to women's wear. Men chose heavy armlets and bracelets or earrings that harmonized with more muscular, masculine forms. Archaeological evidence from many of the early civilizations shows the males as heavily adorned as the females. If the presence of decorated weapons is included, the males could be considered even more adorned.

Throughout history, royal **diadems** (crowns) have been subjects of great interest. Usually made of gold, these elaborate pieces of jewelry contained many rare and beautiful gems.

The ancient Greeks were lovers of gold jewelry, colored using an enameling technique. Greek women wore earrings, diadems, bracelets, and armlets. Gods, goddesses, and animals were common themes in jewelry decorations. Gemstones were carved using **cameo** (which means raised design) and **intaglio** (pronounced in 'tal yo, which means recessed design) techniques. The men of ancient Greece were adorned with naturalistic gold wreaths for headbands, necklaces, armlets, and bracelets. Signet rings (replacing cylinder-seals), engraved with the owner's name or symbol, were frequently worn by men of importance, especially in ancient Rome.

Like their male Greek counterparts, Roman men traditionally wore functional jewelry, like the fibula and signet ring. The **signet ring** had an engraved seal that could be pressed into warm wax. It was used for sealing documents to ensure they were not opened and read by any party other than the intended. Spiral bracelets were commonly worn by women and occasionally by men of rank. The Romans began to use gold coins as pendant jewelry, a fashion feature that continues to recur periodically.

From about the 5th to the 15th centuries, the Far East had a great influence on jewelry. The art of **cloisonné,** which referred to fine gold wires looped into a design and filled with an enamel substance, was developed. Jewelry became more decorative and fanciful, such as multiple strands of jeweled beads and jewel-encrusted and emblazoned clothing. Diadems and hair ornaments were important in women's clothing. Elaborately crafted jewelry made of Chinese jade found its way into fine jewelry.

The Middle Ages was a time for religious and mystical jewelry. For wealthy women, large jeweled girdles, brooches, and buttons of precious metals were important fashions. Gemstones may have been chosen on the basis of their supposed supernatural powers.

The Renaissance began with the 15th century and continued into the 16th century. Costly brooches were often pinned to hats, belts, capes, and bodices. Men and women of status and rank wore rounded pendants (center stone surrounded by smaller, round stones) on thick chains. Matching pendant necklaces and headbands (headache bands) are visible in paintings of leisure class women of the era. Beaded pearl choker-style necklaces became fashionable for women in the later Renaissance period. By the time of the 16th century, men's and women's thick rope-style or large-beaded necklaces had lengthened, making way for the expansive ruffs. Figure 13.1 shows England's Queen Elizabeth bedecked in jewels, literally from head to toe.

In the 17th century, collars and ascots chiefly replaced men's jewelry. Pearls continued to be a strong fashion for women and were usually worn at the jewel neckline or as a choker. Pendants (especially crosses) maintained their popularity during this century. Enameling and gem cutting were improved, adorning nonjewelry items like sword hilts.

FIGURE I3.I *Engraving, Queen Elizabeth, 1603.* ©Bettmann/CORBIS

Eighteenth-century fashions included watches and **chatelaines** (chains suspended from belts), which were useful for attaching mirrors, watches, and signet seals. Low décolletages of the latter part of the 18th century warranted strands of pearls or other beads to display against or disappear within creamy bosoms. Earrings, either drops or hoops, were mentioned in fashion literature of the time.

By the 19th century, men's jewelry had been reduced to functional items, such as watches or seals. An occasional conservative lapel pin was worn above a white linen handkerchief. Women's jewelry of this century was relatively inconspicuous, including dangling drop earrings, delicate bracelet pairs, and simple beaded necklaces, sometimes in multiple strands.

Artisans of the 19th and early 20th centuries created beautiful jewelry designs. Among these famous designers was Carl Fabergé, royal designer for the Russian czar. Fabergé is best known for his **Fabergé eggs** encrusted with jewels and precious metals and given as Easter gifts by the czar to his wife, beginning in 1884. René Lalique (1860–1945) of France, known for his sleek art nouveau and art deco crystal designs, created beautiful jewelry with glass and gemstones.

Tiffany & Company, whose flagship store is in New York City, opened in 1837 as Tiffany and Young. Selling stationery and fancy goods, Tiffany eventually gained a reputation as *the place* to buy fine jewelry. The **Tiffany setting** is a six-prong ring design still popular today. Three 20th-century designers became famous creating Tiffany jewelry—Jean Schlumberger, Elsa Peretti, and Paloma Picasso.

A study of 19th- and 20th-century fine jewelry is not complete without reference to the royal jewels of the queens of England. Leslie Field has compiled a thorough and colorful book of the priceless jewels of the royal family called *The Jewels of Queen Elizabeth II: Her Personal Collection.* Defending the need for such a mass of wealth, Field explained, "Jewels are an important part of the royal image and on State occasions the Queen has a duty to be regal, for these events are part of the national heritage and there is splendour and glory in their observance. Pageantry is an indispensable part of royalty. . . . The royal jewels are above fashion and beyond price."

The late 1960s showed an increase in size and scope of fine jewelry. Slave bracelets (ring chained to a bracelet), large brooches and disc-shaped pendants, multiple bangle bracelets, and enormous hanging earrings were fashionable.

As the 1970s progressed into the early 1980s, men's jewelry was primarily functional. The "Dress for Success" look mandated that jewelry be simple and tasteful (read "expensive-looking"). Expensive jewelry items, such as Rolex® watches, were considered the epitome of good taste. Expensive but not functional gold rings and chain necklaces for men became fashionable for after-business hours.

AN INTRODUCTION TO FINE JEWELRY

Jewelry has been a form of self-expression and adornment since the beginning of social history. Even in civilizations in which people wore very little clothing, they wore some forms of adornment, such as shells, animal teeth, beans, or beads. Blanche Payne, in her book, *History of Costume,* aptly explained adornment. "The desire to possess an object of beauty and to have it within sight is compelling and can account for much that we wear." However, the wearing of jewelry represents more than strictly adornment. Before the advent of coinage, jewelry served an economic function. It was capital for the owner or was used as currency. Additional reasons for the wearing of jewelry are listed below.

- *Adornment* earrings and brooches
- *Function* watches, clasps, and signet rings
- *Hiding Places* locket necklaces and poison rings
- *Symbols* wedding and engagement rings
- *Religious Meanings* cross pendants or Star of David charms
- *Magic* pendant necklaces and rings used for mystical rites
- *Membership* fraternal orders and athletic team championship and school rings
- *Motherhood* mother's rings of children's birthstones
- *Status* expensive brands of watches or large precious stones in precious-metal settings

Jewelry is categorized as fine jewelry, bridge jewelry, and costume (or fashion) jewelry. **Fine jewelry** is made of the precious metals, gold and the platinum group, and precious or semiprecious gems. Fine jewelry carries a much higher price than bridge or costume jewelry. **Bridge jewelry** refers to jewelry at prices lower than fine jewelry. Sterling silver, vermeil (gold-plated sterling silver, pronounced "ver-may"), and 10-karat gold are used in bridge jewelry. In some instances 14-karat or 18-karat gold are used, but usually in small quantities mixed with larger quantities of sterling silver. Rhodium may be electroplated on sterling silver to prevent it from tarnishing. The stones in bridge jewelry are usually semiprecious, but may also be crystals or cut glass. Amethysts, opals, freshwater and cultured pearls, carnelian, turquoise, and coral are frequently used in bridge jewelry. **Costume** or **fashion jewelry** is sold at the lowest price points and is made of other materials, such as wood, plastic, glass, shells, and inexpensive metals.

In the *Women's Wear Daily* survey of the top 100 luxury brands in fashion, 25 percent of the brands listed were fine jewelry and watches in 2001. Table 13.1 shows the survey results of the most recognizable fine jewelry companies.

Vintage and Estate Jewelry

Vintage, estate, antique, period, and **heirloom** all describe the collectible fine jewelry from past decades and centuries. A piece of jewelry just a few years out of fashion may seem ugly or tacky. But the same piece after a few decades seems quaint or beautiful. There have been a number of books published by vintage jewelry collectors that contain information on dating and valuing pieces. Factors contributing to the value of a vintage piece include the condition, materials, rarity of design, designer, and whether the piece is signed or unsigned. Auction houses, estate sales, jewelry collectors, and Internet sites offer an enormous array of vintage fine jewelry pieces.

TABLE 13.1

Fine Jewelry Companies Ranked in the 2001 WWD *Luxury Top 100 Companies*

Company Name	Ranking in the Top 100
Tiffany & Company	2
Cartier	3
Van Cleef & Arpels	15
Harry Winston	26
Piaget	35
Bulgari	43
Mikimoto	49
Boucheron	52
David Yurman	67
Chopard	70
Fred Joaillier	76
Fred Leighton	87
Asprey & Garrard	96

WWD Luxury: Top 100. (2001, February). *Women's Wear Daily.* Courtesy of Fairchild Publications, Inc.

Descriptions of some of the more popular jewelry styles from specific periods are:

- *Georgian period (1714 to 1837)* Large, gaudy stones in elaborate but symmetrical settings.
- *Victorian era (1837 to 1901)* Realistic shapes, rich colors; romantic, grand, and aesthetic styles; flora and fauna motifs; inspired by ancient Greek and Egyptian jewelry.
- *Art Nouveau period (circa 1895 to 1910)* Natural sinuous forms; fanciful, swirling lines known as whiplash; unusual materials and subtle colors; dream-like blending of nature and fantasy; female faces and figures; nature motifs.
- *Edwardian period (circa 1901 to 1915)* Filigree and lace-like creations with sparkling diamonds and white pearls; platinum and gold; delicate and romantic feathers, tassels, ribbons, swags, garlands, and laurels.
- *Art Deco period (1910 to 1935)* bold geometric shapes; stylized figures; black and white infused with striking, vibrant colors; long pendants, dangling earrings, bangle bracelets, and cocktail rings; diamonds in unusual cuts—baguette, pear, marquis.
- *Art Retro period (circa 1940 to 1950s)* Wavy or hexagonal lines; chunky, sculptured, and 3-D; ballerina, bows, and large-link chain motifs; colored golds like rose and green; large stones like diamonds and peridots.

Vintage jewelry has become popular with the twenty-something consumers, particularly those in the Hollywood set. Many celebrities attending the various award galas choose authentic or reproductions of vintage jewelry to complement their elaborate dresses (see Figure 13.2).

FIGURE 13.2 *Necklace worn by Mae West.*
Courtesy of Fairchild Publications, Inc.

Contemporary designers rework antique jewelry pieces or design modern jewelry to resemble vintage pieces in shapes that were popular decades ago, such as cameos, fans, bows, butterflies, and combinations of black velvet and diamonds.

MANUFACTURING FINE JEWELRY

Fine jewelry making is an art, but it is not immune from the improvements of technology. Computer-aided design (CAD) and computer-aided manufacturing (CAM) have significantly changed the traditional jewelry-making methods. **Computer-aided design** refers to the use of computers to draw and draft models of jewelry pieces for mass production. Once working diagrams are established for basic components, they can be used repeatedly. **Computer-aided manufacturing** refers to the use of computers to actually create **prototypes** or **models** (first samples) of jewelry that will eventually be mass-produced. Computers provide efficiency and exactness in model designs that were once hand created by **model makers.** Three-dimensional (3D) prototypes can be made with CAM. Lasers can create fine jewelry casts in plastic or in wax, more precisely than traditional jewelry-making methods. Once the models are created, it takes a trained metalsmith to pour the molten metal into the mold and enrich the resulting piece until it is a refined piece of jewelry. **Goldsmiths** are often trained to work with a variety of metals including silver and platinum. However, there are also **silversmiths** and **platinumsmiths.**

Most goldsmiths and jewelry manufacturers stamp the karat quality in gold jewelry. According to the Federal Trade Commission, this is not required by law but it is recommended. Beside the karat stamp, the manufacturer's registered trademark is required by law to be stamped.

Design

Like other accessories designers, fine-jewelry designers have obtained their inspiration from history, different cultures around the world, costume jewelry, nature, art, technology, and many other people, places, and things. One of the more unusual pieces of jewelry was featured on the front cover of *Women's Wear Daily* in 1997. The gold piece was Givenchy's 1997 runway necklace, almost identical to some featured in a 1979 *National Geographic* magazine in the photo spread of women of the Padaung tribe in Burma (now Myanmar). They wore close-fitting brass rings around their necks, and over time, these rings pushed down their clavicles (collarbones) giving the illusion of giraffe-like necklaces.

More recently, fine jewelry designers have gained inspiration from technology. The results are minimal and sleek in silver-toned metals, such as platinum and palladium. Stones and settings that resemble satellites, asteroids, and meteorites are reflective of society's fascination with space (see Figure 13.3).

Most fine jewelry trends originate in Europe, New York, and California. European trends

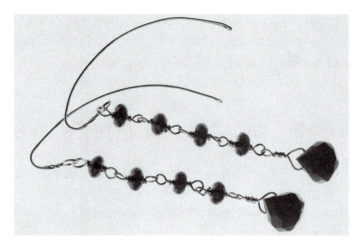

FIGURE 13.3 *Favero earrings.*
Courtesy of Fairchild Publications, Inc.

may take more than a year to trickle over to the United States. U.S. buyers visit foreign markets, like Italy, to gather information on trends that will eventually hit the domestic market. For example, colored stones set in yellow gold became fashionable in the United States two or three years after the trend began in Europe.

The fashion trend away from silver-toned metals toward yellow-toned metals has been slow moving. Costly fine jewelry is not easily replaced for most people, so a fundamental change takes time as people adjust their fine jewelry wardrobes to the new look. To accommodate this changing tonal trend, designers mixed both colors, such as in reversible jewelry or combination-metal designs. The general consensus among fine-jewelry experts is that diamonds look best in white precious metals, while yellow gold is better mixed with colored gemstones.

Materials

Fine jewelry is comprised of precious metals and precious or semiprecious gems. The precious metals include yellow gold, white gold, and the platinum family metals, which includes palladium. Occasionally, silver is included in the fine-jewelry classification, but more often it is classified as bridge or fashion jewelry, especially when combined with semiprecious stones, like turquoise. Precious gems include diamonds, sapphires, rubies, emeralds, and pearls. Semiprecious gems are sometimes used in fine jewelry, but they are set in precious metals. The costs of fine jewelry are relatively high.

Production

When creating individual pieces rather than mass-produced jewelry, the original design of the piece starts with a sketch that is approved by the customer. A prototype is carved in wax and ultimately encased in a hard substance like plaster or ceramic. Called the **lost wax casting** technique, the encased wax is fired in a furnace for several hours, causing the wax to vaporize.

The empty space (cavity) resulting from the burned-out wax is filled with molten (hot liquid) metal. When cooled, the metal model perfectly reproduces the hand-carved wax model. Rubber or plastic molds are made from the metal models to make single or multiple replicas of the piece.

Preparing Stone Settings

During the production of fine jewelry, **stonesetters** use a variety of techniques to create special visual effects shown in the designers' sketches. Precious and semiprecious stones are set into fine jewelry by one of the methods listed below (see Figure 13.4). The setting is chosen based on the type and delicacy of the stone, the amount of wear the jewelry item will receive, the preference of the wearer when pieces are made to order, and fashion.

Buttercup Setting Gemstones are placed in metal scalloped prongs shaped like flower petals.
Channel Setting Tiny beads of a precious metal are pressed up against small gems to hold them in place.
Cluster Setting Several smaller stones are grouped together or surround a large stone to create a visual impact.
Flush or **Bezel Setting** A narrow band of precious metal encircles the gemstone to hold it in place.
Illusion Setting Similar to a bezel setting, but the precious metal surrounding the stone is usually decorative and intended to make the stone appear larger than actual size.
Inlay Gemstones are placed in a recession in the precious metal so that the surface is not raised.
Paste Setting In this inexpensive setting, glues are used to hold the stones in place.
Pavé Gemstones are closely set, so little or no metal shows between them.
Prong or **Tiffany Setting** Four or six raised metal prongs hold the stone in position and prominently in view.
Tension-Mount Setting This setting has no prongs, but still allows a significant amount of the stone to show.

Buttercup   Channel   Tiffany

FIGURE 13.4 *Stone settings.* Courtesy of Fairchild Publications, Inc.

Preparing Metals for Fine Jewelry

As discussed in Chapter 6, "Metals and Stones," sterling silver and platinum jewelry are usually more pure than gold jewelry. That is, they have a greater concentration of the actual metal. Platinum jewelry, comprised of 90 to 95 percent pure platinum, is usually polished to a mirror-like finish.

Gold can still be called karat gold and be comprised of as little as 10 of 24 parts (41.67 percent) actual gold. Most often, copper, nickel, or silver alloys are added to karat gold to give it durability and unique colors. Copper gives gold a reddish cast, nickel gives it a whitish appearance, and silver gives gold a greenish cast. After the metal is cooled, the surface of the jewelry can be treated by a depletion method to remove the nongold alloy metals. Called **coloring the gold,** the purpose is to give the impression the metal is a higher-karat gold than it is. It takes a trained goldsmith to refine fine jewelry using one of the surface techniques described below.

Antiquing Creating a patinaed or darkened finish on the metal, giving it an heirloom or antique look.

Casting To pour molten metal into a plaster, sand, lost wax, or other mold, where the metal cools and solidifies.

Chasing Tapping designs into precious metals with a hammer and a punch; similar to engraving.

Engraving Cutting tiny grooves into metal to create a design.

Etching Applying acid to eat away some of the surface areas of the metal, thereby creating recesses in it.

Florentining Cutting minute scratches that cover the surface of the metal.

Hammering Beating metal with a small hammerhead creating dents on the surface.

Repoussé Hammering thin sheets of metal into a three-dimensional shape.

Soldering Melting metal (such as silver) between two pieces of jewelry. The silver solder fuses the two pieces of precious metal together or holds the ornamentation onto the backing.

Wax Mold A carved, three-dimensional design, such as for a ring, that will become the shape for the ceramic mold.

JEWELRY STYLES

It is difficult, if not impossible, to describe every jewelry style that has ever been created. However, it is possible to group and categorize many of the pieces. Selected terms have been chosen based on their current fashion application and historic importance.

Necklaces

An important variation in necklaces is the length, ranging from tightly fastened around the neck to hanging down to the waistline.

Necklace Lengths

The following terms describe necklace lengths:

- *Choker* 14–15 inches, fits snugly around the neck
- *Jewel* Hangs at the base of the throat on the collarbone
- *Chains* Measured in two-inch increments, from 16 to 24 inches
- *Matinee* 30–35 inches
- *Opera* 48–120 inches

Necklace Styles

Following are some popular necklace styles (see Figure 13.5):

Bib Necklace or **Collarette** A short necklace with dangling- or flowing-front ornaments.

Diamonds by the Yard Introduced in 1974 at Tiffany's in New York. Strands of diamonds (or any other precious stone) purchased for use as a necklace, bracelet, or belt.

Dog-Collar Choker A tight-fitting, studded necklace resembling a dog's collar. Popularized by Princess Alexandra of England in the 19th century.

Graduated Pearl Necklace Of varying lengths, the pearls are smaller on either side of the clasp and gradually increase in size, with the largest pearl at the center front of the necklace.

Lariat Necklace Cylindrical chain resembling a cord that has been looped many times around the neck.

Pendant, Lavaliere, or **Drop Necklace** Any necklace from which a drop ornament, such as a precious stone or a locket, is hung. A drop necklace has a small ornament suspended on a delicate chain.

Rope Necklace Extra long strands of beads, such as pearls, wrapped multiple times at different lengths, around the throat, neck, and chest. In the 1920s, rope necklaces were knotted once and worn hanging freely in one strand.

Chain Necklace Especially popular in layered multiples during the late 1970s and early 1980s (think Mr. T of *The A-Team*). Chains may be classified according to a variety of link styles—box, Byzantine, herringbone, hollow rope, rope, and serpentine or snake.

Slide, Zipper, or **Y-Necklace** Popular in the late 1990s, these created the illusion of the letter Y by featuring the chains hanging below the pendant.

Earrings

Earrings are worn primarily by women, but from ancient times to the present, men's earrings have periodically been a common fashion accessory. Today, while it is not unusual for men to wear earrings, they are not a part of a conservative man's jewelry collection and are considered

Bib

Dog-Collar-Choker

Pendant

Y

Rope

FIGURE 13.5 *Necklace styles.*
Courtesy of Fairchild Publications, Inc.

inappropriate with business attire in traditional organizations with formal dress codes. Earrings are usually worn in matched pairs, but unmatched pairs, single earrings, or multiple earrings on one ear are other options favored by those who want to accessorize a hip-hop or avant-garde look.

Earring Fastenings

Earring fastenings are designed for pierced or unpierced ears. The following fastenings may be used:

- *Pierced* Requires a hole in the ear through which a post or wire is inserted; removable back attaches to the post preventing it from slipping out of the earlobe. Pierced earring posts should be made of gold or surgical stainless steel, not a plated metal, to prevent infection.
- *French clip* Posts inserted through the piercings have spring hinges to hold them in place.
- *Clip-on or clip-back* Does not require pierced ears; attached with a spring hinge that clamps on the lobe.
- *Screw-back* Does not require pierced ears; placed over the lobes while the backs are screwed tightly enough to hold the earrings in place.
- *Magnetic* Magnetized backs hold the earring front in place; no spring hinges or pierced holes are needed.

Earring Styles

Following are some common styles of earrings (see Figure 13.6):

Button Small, round, and flat or ball-shaped, resembling a button; may be of precious metals or pearls.

Chandelier Made to look like dangling chandelier crystals; comes in various shapes.

Changeable or **Earring Jacket** An outer disc made to surround a button-style earring; often a precious-metal circlet worn around a diamond stud.

Drop Usually a button-style post and a dangling bead, ball, charm, jewel, or pendant.

Ear Cuff A spliced, circular band of metal, similar to a miniature wedding band; clamps over the upper back edge of the ear. May also be a pierced earring in the same shape.

Hoop or **Gypsy** Circular wire of varying diameters that goes through the pierced hole or is attached to a button-style post. The hoop may have a dangling charm or bead that swings freely on the wire.

Stud Usually the first pair of pierced earrings, inserted with a piercing gun. Characterized by a precious-metal ball or a gemstone that sits against the earlobe and does not dangle; similar to a button earring.

Button

Chandelier

Drop

Ear cuff

FIGURE 13.6 *Earring styles.*
Courtesy of Fairchild Publications, Inc.

Hoop

Bracelets

This classification includes any decorative bands that encircle the wrists, arms, or ankles. The word *bracelet* was derived from the Latin word, *bracchium,* meaning arm. An **armlet** or **arm-band** refers to a band that encircles the upper arm. An **ankle bracelet** encircles the ankle and is sometimes referred to as an **anklet.**

Common bracelet styles include the following (see Figure 13.7):

Bangle or **Hoop** Narrow, rigid bracelets worn in multiples, often so numerous they reach from wrist to forearm. Ancient Egyptian origins.

Charm A sturdy chain-link bracelet from which tiny commemorative, sentimental, or symbolic items are suspended. Usually the charms are of materials similar to the bracelet links (such as gold or silver) but may be precious or semiprecious stones.

Cuff A wide, rigid bracelet in an elliptical shape. A back opening allows the wrist to slide into the bracelet. Most are plain, but the wide face of the bracelet allows for a gemstone or watch face to be inset.

Tennis or **Diamond** A narrow row of precious-metal settings that accommodate small, faceted diamonds (or other gemstones). This bracelet was so-named because during the 1987 U.S. Open tennis tournament, Chris Evert, the top-ranked player, accidentally dropped her diamond bracelet on the tennis courts. National television cameras presented the viewers with a close-up view of her diamond bracelet lying on the court. Jewelers across the United States capitalized on the event and sold enormous quantities of "tennis bracelets," which are still very popular.

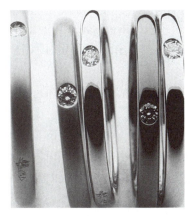

Bangle

Charm

Cuff

Slave

FIGURE 13.7 *Bracelet styles.*

Courtesy of Fairchild Publications, Inc.

Slave ring, or **Bracelet Ring** This is a combination of ring and bracelet, connected on the back of the hand by a chain or medallion. May also include a toe-ankle bracelet, which is a toe ring connected across the top of the foot to an ankle bracelet.

Brooches, Pins, and Clips

These fine jewelry items usually have pin backings to hold them in place. They can be worn on a hat or scarf, or on apparel—commonly at the neckline, shoulder, or waistline. A few have hinged clips to hold them in place, but pins are usually more secure. Styles of brooches, pins, and clips include the following (see Figure 13.8):

Bar Pin A rectangular brooch.

Brooch or **Broach** An ornamental piece of jewelry with a pin backing, usually worn at the center of the neckline.

Hatpin A nine- to twelve-inch pin with an ornamental head and small end piece. The pin is inserted into the side crown of the hat, is woven through the hair, and emerges several inches toward the back of the crown. The end piece is fastened on the sharp end to hold the hatpin and the hat in place. Hatpins were popular functional accessory items in decades past, when hats were more important fashion accessories.

Lapel Pin A small version of a brooch, worn on the lapel of a jacket. Can have a safety-pin-style closure or a single sharp prong that pokes through the fabric and has a removable back, similar to a pierced earring back.

Scarf Clip A functional brooch backed with dual rings through which scarf ends can be threaded and held secure.

Stickpin A small ornament (such as a set diamond) attached at the top of a vertical pin about three inches long. The pin is woven through the lapel fabric and capped with an end piece. Similar to a hatpin, but much smaller.

Brooch

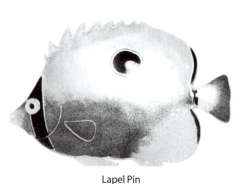

Lapel Pin

FIGURE 13.8 *Brooch and pin styles*

Courtesy of Fairchild Publications, Inc.

Rings

The following descriptions of rings include particular forms as well as meanings associated with rings (see Figure 13.9).

Birthstone A precious- or semiprecious-stone set in a precious metal to symbolize the birth month of the wearer.

Bridal set Matching engagement and wedding band set.

Class Signifies graduation from high school or college. Usually has the school name and graduation date engraved and may have a diamond or a colored stone that represents the school colors.

Championship Signifies a winning team of tournament or playoff sports competition. Especially common in football; similar in appearance to a class ring.

Cocktail or **dinner** Cluster of gemstones piled or swirled into a showy design.

Engagement Usually a diamond, any cut, given to a future bride as a pledge to be married by the future groom. It is worn on the left hand, third finger from the thumb.

Eternity Band encircled with gemstones, given as a token of love.

Filigree Thin wire shaped and twisted into an attractive design; filled with enamel. The design is called *cloisonné*.

Fraternal Symbolizes an organization, such as Eastern Star or Greek college fraternities. May be engraved with the organization's emblem and may have a stone, such as a black onyx or other gem, that is symbolic.

Mother's Created in the early 1900s to symbolize motherhood. Settings hold the birthstone of each child.

Nugget Often made of melted gold from sentimental odds and ends jewelry in the owner's jewelry box. Irregularly shaped (like a chunk of gold ore), may be inset with diamonds from the owner's collection.

Poison Large and elaborate hinged face with a top that opens. Inside is a hiding place for suicidal poison, in case of capture by an enemy. Also might be used as a means for committing murder.

Signet Large ring bearing the initials or crest of the wearer. Used to imprint warm wax on the seal of a letter to ensure the letter remains unopened until the appropriate time.

Spinning A fashion ring, popular in the 1990s, with a moving-wire circlet that "spins" when the wearer moves her hand.

Spoon A sterling-silver baby spoon handle bent into a circular shape. The relative bulk of this ring made it popular for the larger fingers of young men. For smaller fingers of young women, the rings were worn on the thumbs. Popular in the 1970s.

Toe An adjustable band, usually worn on the second toe, although sometimes it has been popular to wear it on the big toe.

Class

Cocktail and Eternity

Wedding and Engagement

FIGURE 13.9 *Ring styles.*

Courtesy of Fairchild Publications, Inc.

Wedding band Given as a symbol of unity on the wedding day. Usually a simple design; may be matching for husband and wife. Many brides have the wedding band and engagement ring soldered together to prevent abrasion.

Headpieces

The terms *circlet, coronet, crown, diadem,* and *tiara* all refer to variations of a jeweled headpiece; circlets and coronets are usually smaller than crowns. Delicate tiara designs usually focus more on the gemstones than the precious metals.

THE GLOBAL FINE JEWELRY INDUSTRY

Fine jewelry is one of the "necessary indulgences" that has built the luxury fashion category into a powerful economic contributor for many countries. Italy exports up to one third of its manufactured fine jewelry to the United States, for whom it is the chief supplier. Table 13.2 shows

TABLE 13.2

Top U.S. Import Sources of Precious-Metal Jewelry in 2002 by Country

Country	$ Import Value (In thousands)
Italy	1,508,744
India	875,938
Thailand	684,921
China	560,218
Hong Kong	515,123

U.S. trade quick-reference tables: 2002 imports: 3911. *International Trade Administration.* Retrieved June 24, 2003, from http://www.ita.doc.gov/td/ocg/imp3911.htm

TABLE 13.3

Top U.S. Export Values and Destinations for Precious-Metal Jewelry in 2002

Country	$ Export Value (In Thousands)
Japan	253,777
Switzerland	212,321
Netherlands	191,019
Mexico	184,410
Hong Kong	138,746

U.S. trade quick-reference tables: 2001 exports: 3911. International Trade Administration. Retrieved July 17, 2002, from http://www.ita.doc.gov/td/ocg/exp3911.htm

the value of imports from the top five countries supplying the United States with precious-metal jewelry in 2002.

The United States exports significant amounts of precious-metal jewelry to more than 25 countries worldwide. In 2002 U.S. exports totaled were more than $1.8 billion. Table 13.3 shows the U.S. precious-metal jewelry export values to the top five countries in 2002.

Trade Organizations, Publications, and Shows

Several trade organizations service the fine-jewelry industry. Table 13.4 shows the most popular trade organizations. Some of these are also listed in Chapter 6, "Metals and Stones." Important fine-jewelry trade publications and shows are listed in Tables 13.5 and 13.6.

MERCHANDISING TRENDS AND TECHNIQUES

According to the American Gem Society, about one half of their member stores posted sales increases of at least 20 percent during 1999. The end-of-the-century sales were the largest fine-jewelry sales in more than a decade. Sales were expected to continue increasing through 2010, with a cumulative growth rate of 197 percent during the first decade of the century.

Several factors have contributed to the increase in sales. These include an aging population, nationwide economic growth, a shifting of expenditures from home to person, working women with higher incomes, a trend toward more feminine fashions, and a greater promotion of jewelry accessories by fashion designers.

The baby-boomer population was estimated at 77 million people who were expected to reach their peak earning years in this decade. With an empty-nest household on the horizon, this population group would have greater opportunities to afford fine jewelry. Milestones, such as anniversaries and birthdays, may be celebrated with luxury gifts. In addition, the highest numbers

TABLE 13.4

Trade Organizations for the Fine-Jewelry Industry

Organization	Location	Objectives
American Society of Jewelry Historians www.jewelryhistorians.com	New Rochelle, NY	Publishes newsletter and sponsors lectures. An offshoot of the British Society of Jewelry Historians.
Estate Jewelers Association of America www.ejaa.net	New York, NY	Sponsors a trade show.
International Watch and Jewelry Guild (IWJG) www.iwjg.com	Houston, TX	Hosts trade shows.
Jewelers of America (JA) www.jewelers.org	New York, NY	Serves the retail jewelry and watch industry by conducting research, providing educational assistance, and publishing manuals.
Jewelry Information Center (JIC) www.jewelryinfo.org	New York, NY	Provides public relations and consumer advocacy for the fine-jewelry industry.
Manufacturing Jewelers & Suppliers of America (MJSA) http://mjsa.polygon.net/	Providence, RI	Sponsors trade shows, industry research, publishes the AJM magazine, monitors monitors government affairs, and promotes and markets members.
National Cufflink Society www.cufflink.com	Prospect Heights, IL	Offers a quarterly publication, locator service, and hosts an annual convention.
National Fashion Accessory Association (NFAA) and the Fashion Accessory Shippers Association (FASA) www.accessoryweb.com	New York, NY	Represents all accessory categories, including fine jewelry.
Professional Jeweler www.professionaljeweler.com	Philadelphia, PA	Sponsors trade show and magazine.
World Gold Council www.gold.org	London, England	Promotes the wearing of gold jewelry and provides data on the gold indusry.

of children of the baby boomers (baby busters) are expected to marry in 2003, creating a significant market for wedding-set jewelry.

The increase in economic prosperity in the late 1990s, especially with regard to stock market investments, created a generation of wealthy investors. Early 2000s downslides in the stock market may require a readjustment of anticipated fine-jewelry sales. According to the World Gold Council, an economic slowdown may result in consumers purchasing precious-metal jewelry designed without the costly gemstones.

The last decade of the 20th century was a time for buying ornaments for the home. A shift to buying ornaments for the person bodes well for fashion and accessories, including fine jewelry. Retailers may want to combine home fashions and fine jewelry in lifestyle displays. For exam-

TABLE 13.5

Trade Publications for the Fine-Jewelry Industry

Trade Publication Name	Description
Accessories Magazine	Monthly trade publication; covers most accessory classifications, including fine jewelry.
American Jewelry Manufacturers Magazine (AJM)	Print and online magazine for jewelry manufacturers; published by the MJSA.
InfoSource	Promotes growth among jewelry manufacturers and designers.
International Jeweler	Focuses on jewelry influences, inspirations, and trends; published by VNU Business Publications.
National Jeweler	Bi-monthly publication for the jewelry industry, with print, face-to-face, and online information; published by VNU Business Publications.
Professional Jeweler Magazine	Provides information about the latest selling techniques, key products, store-management techniques, and employee education; published by Professional Jeweler.
Women's Wear Daily – Monday	Weekly issue of a trade newspaper, published by Fairchild; features business and fashion information on fine jewelry, as well as other accessories.
WWD Accessory Supplement	Fairchild special edition featuring fashion information on all accessories, including fine jewelry.

TABLE 13.6

Trade Shows for the Fine-Jewelry Industry

Trade Show	Location	Sponsor
Accessorie Circuit	New York, NY	ENK International
AccessoriesTheShow	New York, NY	Business Journals, Inc.
Antique Jewelry Show	Miami, FL	
Basel World Watch and Jewelry Show	Basel, Switzerland	MCH Basel Global Exhibitions, Ltd.
Couture Jewelry Collection and Conference (CCC)	Scottsdale, AZ	VNU Expositions, Inc.
Dallas Fine Jewelry Show	Dallas, TX	M.I.D.A.S.
GemFair	Tucson, AZ	American Gem Trade Association
International Watch and Jewelry Guild Shows	Cities across the U.S. (New Orleans, New York, Detroit, Dallas, Miami, Orlando, Las Vegas)	International Watch and Jewelry Guild
JA International Jewelry Show	New York, NY	Jewelers of America and VNU Expositions, Inc.
Jewelers' Circular Keystone Show (JCK)	Las Vegas, NV	JCK
Las Vegas Estate Jewelry Show	Las Vegas, NV	Estate Jewelers' Association of America
MJSA Expo	New York, NY	Manufacturing Jewelers & Suppliers of America
The Professional Jeweler Show	Las Vegas, NV	Bond Communication
Vicenzaoro Trade Fair	Vicenza, Italy	Fiera Di Vicenza

ple, a gift department may display several fine-jewelry or crystal-collectors' pieces under the crystal goblets in an elegant table setting.

As more women ascend in the corporate workplace, they continue to increase their spending on luxury purchases. Traditionally, men have been the largest purchasers of fine jewelry for women, but this trend may be reversing. The importance of the female self-purchase market (regardless of her income) continues to expand. At Zale Corporation, women purchasers accounted for 60 percent of sales in 1999. In response to the increasingly affluent female market, fashion houses like Escada, Dior, and Chanel are offering their own lines of fine jewelry because they have discovered it is a profitable source of revenue (see Figure 13.10). Even the home fashion company Waterford Wedgwood began offering fine jewelry as part of its national lifestyle-accessories expansion that caters to affluent women.

Female customers are more likely to purchase fine jewelry if retailers offer environmental enhancements and improved merchandising methods. Fine jewelry retailers should consider the following methods:

- Move jewelry displays closer to the customer's eye, so she does not have to bend over.
- Make counters wheelchair accessible.
- Make jewelry cases more user friendly, on the same concept as sunglass kiosks, with less of a physical barrier between the salesperson and the customer.
- Create a "fantasy" for women, allowing them to imagine the piece of jewelry being owned and worn to a special occasion.
- Add fine-jewelry departments in stores not traditionally expected to have fine jewelry, but with a similar target customer.
- Adapt retail designs to reflect the nuances of the location, such as urban or mall.
- Add dressing rooms so customers can wear the outfit and match the jewelry.
- Offer lighting options for daylight, office, nightclub, and restaurant.
- Offer fabric drapes for customers to put over clothing while considering and trying on pieces of jewelry.

FIGURE 13.10 *Escada jewelry.*
Courtesy of Fairchild Publications, Inc.

- Provide adequate seating for friends.
- Provide a play area for children.
- Use the store for a variety of special events pertaining to women's organizations, and build relationships with these organizations.

Recent-sales history and growth potential in the men's fine-jewelry sector has caused a few designers to shift their focus from women's to men's jewelry. Reasons for the upswing in men's jewelry purchases include a greater acceptance by men of the wearing of jewelry, a broadening of wealth, and the popularity of affordable sterling-silver jewelry. In spite of the willingness of men to wear jewelry, women still account for about 90 percent of men's jewelry purchases. The percent of male self-purchasers is expected to increase over the next few years.

Store Retailing

Fine-jewelry sales have made significant inroads in the mass market. According to the World Gold Council, consumers have become more confident buying 10k and 14k gold and gemstone jewelry from respected mass merchants and discounters, like Ames, Kmart, Sears, ShopKo, Venture, and Wal-Mart. Fine-jewelry products can be marked up by 60 percent, an incentive for discount stores to stock it. Sales increased an impressive 23 percent from 1995 to 1996, and a comparable increase occurred the previous year. These stores responded to the momentum by expanding, updating, and relocating their fine-jewelry departments.

In Sears stores, the fine-jewelry departments were renovated to improve the department ambiance. In addition, they were relocated on the selling floor to spaces adjacent to the main aisles. This exposure ultimately helped shoppers remember Sears as a purchase destination when shopping for fine jewelry. The Sears merchandising philosophy was based on the theory that women look for the size and sparkle of jewelry at a retailer they already trust.

Another mass merchandiser, Venture, expanded its fine-jewelry departments to help reposition the chain as a mid-tier department-store retailer. Venture's assortment includes fine-jewelry pieces that resemble those carried by upscale department and specialty stores. The line substitutes 10k gold and semiprecious stones to keep price points in line with the store's target customers' preferences. Like Sears, Venture's aim is to give customers more size for their money.

Specialized training for buyers and salespeople has created success in these departments. Store internships and vendor-sponsored workshops increase the knowledge of the selling staff and support personnel, including targeted problem areas like loss prevention.

Upscale fine-jewelry retailers also saw a significant increase in their **open-to-buy** (amount of money buyers are allotted to spend at market) in the late 1990s. With budgets increased by as much as 25 percent, these retailers opted for some one-of-a-kind designs, as well as Italian designs, especially in platinum metals.

TABLE 13.7

2000 Ranking of Distribution Channels for U.S. Gold-Jewelry Sales in Thousands of Dollars ($000)

Distribution Channel	$ Sales (In Thousands)
Jewelry Stores	7,508,647
Discount/Catalog	3,402,599
Department Stores	3,070,475
Nonstore Retail	1,319,316
Total	15,301,037

Audits and surveys worldwide. (2000). U.S. Sales of Primary Value Gold Jewelry. World Gold Council, New York.

Table 13.7 shows the variety of retailing channels in which gold jewelry is sold. In 2000, chain jewelers lead in total sales, followed by discount stores/catalog showrooms. Department stores and nonstore retailing were third and fourth in the ranking.

Internet Retailing

A large number of Internet retailers sell lower- and moderately priced fine-jewelry on Web sites. Online product offerings are usually limited to a popular-style selection of fine jewelry ranging from inexpensive to $1,000 items. Some high-end companies provide custom-order jewelry designed to the shopper's specifications. Others use e-commerce to sell fine jewelry containing certified diamonds. Established brick-and-mortar retailers like Tiffany & Company offer diamond jewelry backed by a certificate guaranteeing the stone. The store's reputation provides customers with the confidence to trust their Internet purchase. Just as brick-and-mortar retailers maintain Web sites to advertise the store, Internet retailers can use traditional advertising media to promote their Web sites.

Some independent jewelers pay Internet companies to link their store name to an online catalog. Internet shoppers can visit each retailer's independent Web site and products. One site boasts as many as 40,000 jewelry items online and in stock, claiming to be the world's largest online catalog, although the individual stores actually own the inventory.

Catalog Retailing

Some fine-jewelry retailers publish store circulars as advertising supplements, especially around the peak fine-jewelry-selling holidays like Valentine's Day and Mother's Day. The fourth-quarter holiday season is also especially profitable, with 40 percent of sales occurring between Thanksgiving and Christmas. Most of these retailers have traditional brick-and-mortar locations. Gemstone pieces are more difficult to sell "sight unseen" than solid precious-metal pieces, which need only list the precious metal content. Like Internet retailers, catalog retailers can offer diamond jewelry backed by a certificate of guarantee.

SELLING FINE JEWELRY

Fine-jewelry salespeople need specialized training to provide the best possible service to customers. Some jewelry vendors send manufacturer's representatives into the stores for sales training. Some trade associations and fine-jewelry institutes offer distance education courses. From the most exclusive retailer to discount stores, customers require some degree of personalized service in the fine-jewelry department, and they expect the salesperson to have a reasonable knowledge of fine jewelry. A common mistake made by many is to pronounce jewelry as "jewlery"—a transposition of two letters. Salespeople should practice the correct pronunciations of related words, such as unusual gemstone names. Because it is impossible to know everything about fine jewelry, salespeople should have resource materials (books, brochures, and videos) available in the department to study or refer to when necessary.

Purchasers of fine jewelry must have confidence that what they buy is authentic and of true value. Successful retailers are those with an established reputation for honesty, often through word-of-mouth advertising. The Federal Trade Commission recommends several issues that should be addressed before a sale is transacted. Retailers benefit from the following customer relations suggestions offered in the Federal Trade Commission publication, *All That Glitters…How to Buy Jewelry:*

- Have a reasonable and documented return policy.
- Make sure all jewelry has appropriate karat quality and registered trademark markings.
- Explain fundamental differences in product quality, as between natural, cultured, or imitation pearls; or between natural, synthetic, or imitation gems.
- Truthfully disclose stone treatments—visible or invisible, temporary or permanent. Let the consumer understand how these affect the price.
- Provide written documentation of the gem's weight, size, or other determinants on the original sales receipt.
- Provide gem-grading reports from a gemological laboratory.

If consumers are not satisfied with their purchase, retailers should make every attempt to resolve the problem fairly. If a consumer still does not believe the problem has been corrected, he or she may contact the Jewelers Vigilance Committee (www.jvclegal.org) in New York City. This is a nonprofit group whose purpose is to ensure ethical practices in the jewelry industry. It publishes the *Retailers Legal Handbook* for jewelry stores.

Tech-Talk: Gemstone Enhancement

Any method used to create a more beautiful stone, whether cutting or polishing or more sophisticated and controversial methods, is considered a **gemstone enhancement.** Most reputable jewelers agree enhancements meant to improve the beauty (color and clarity) and durability of the stone are acceptable. Enhancements meant to repair damaged places in the stone or increase the carat weight are unacceptable to most jewelers. Any of these treatments may lower the value of the stone. Experts estimate an altered diamond is worth 10 to 30 percent less than a similar, unaltered diamond, depending on the enhancements used. The practices of enhancing gemstones can be traced back 4,000 years to the ancient Egyptians. They were known to soak emeralds in colorless oils to create a more lustrous and beautiful gem. At a recent state fair, jewelry-booth owners hawked six ounces of a special "cleaning solution" for a "low price of $29.95." The product was simply colorless oil, creating an iridescent bluish cast to the diamond. The effect was beautiful, but temporary.

According to the Tiffany & Company Web site, Marco Polo was reputed to have observed the heating of rubies in Ceylon and carried the practice back to Europe. **Heating** is still a common practice among miners and lapidaries. This means a gemstone is heated to lighten, darken, or completely change the color and clarity. General Electric developed a high heat and pressure treatment for whitening diamonds.

Other commonly used enhancements include the following:

- **Bleaching** Uses chemicals to create a uniform surface color or lighten/whiten some gems, jade, or pearls.
- **Dyeing** Alters the gem's color or improves color uniformity.
- **Infusion** A filling process using wax, resin, or glass, which may be clear or colored, to improve the appearance of the gemstone.
- **Coating** or **Impregnating** Wax, resin, or colorless oil applied to the surface of a porous stone to improve durability, surface uniformity, clarity, and appearance.
- **Diffusion** Adds color to the gem's surface.
- **Irradiation** A radiation treatment for improving color in diamonds, gemstones, or pearls; may be combined with the heating enhancement.

Other enhancements are less accepted (some say unethical), but difficult to detect, even with the most sophisticated of equipment. According to Tiffany & Company, this has led to complex debates concerning what is acceptable in the gemstone community. The two most debated enhancements are fracture filling and lasering.

According to the Federal Trade Commission, **fracture filling** is when a colorless plastic or glass substance is injected into a crack (feathered inclusion) to improve clarity. Fracture-filled stones may also be referred to as **clarity-enhanced stones.** Usually, a fracture-filled stone has inclusions visible to the naked eye. By filling them, the inclusions become invisible. The filling may be identified as a neon color when the stone is viewed face-down under a scope.

The Federal Trade Commission describes **lasering** as a method of clarifying diamonds that have black carbon spots or inclusions. A tiny laser beam is aimed at the inclusion, drilling a hole to the inclusion. Acid is forced through the tunnel to make the inclusion colorless. The permanent tunnel remains, but is not usually visible looking down upon the face of the diamond. These diamonds do not require special care.

Are fracture filling and lasering illegal? No. Unethical? Only if undisclosed to the buyer. *Caveat emptor* (let the buyer beware).

Price and Value

The retail price of jewelry depends on several factors, but most importantly on the materials used. Precious metals and gemstones are commodity products, and prices are based on what the market will bear (usually high.) Other factors that affect the retail price are the target customer, retail store policies and desired markup, and brand or store name. Discount stores and specialty stores often cater to very different customer bases. Each store should offer jewelry at price points its customers are willing to pay. Each type of store has a markup percent based on store policies that it strives to achieve. Stores with greater buying power ("a bigger pencil") are able to negotiate for lower prices because of quantity purchases. These savings are often passed on to the customers. The brand of the jewelry and the store name where jewelry is purchased are becoming increasingly important to consumers. Recognizable brands and names create a positive image with consumers. Many consumers lack the confidence in their own knowledge, and are quite willing to transfer the status of a familiar brand or store to the purchase of fine-jewelry products.

Care of Fine Jewelry

Fine jewelry is made to be durable enough to last for many years. Consumers do not have to worry about "the finish" wearing off of fine jewelry. Jewelry should be cleaned according to the delicacy of the materials. As mentioned in Chapter 6, ultrasonic cleaners should not be used on the more delicate stones. Harsh chemicals, such as chlorine bleach, may pock some precious metals and are unnecessary to maintain a shine. A very diluted solution of household ammonia and water can be used to carefully clean diamonds. Jewelry should be stored without touching other pieces, rather than "heaping" it in a jewelry box. Some stones and metals are harder than others and may scratch the more delicate materials. Pearl jewelry should be kept away from hair sprays, perfumes, or other toiletries that may cause discoloration. Pearls may be wiped with a damp cloth after wearing. If worn often, pearls should be restrung annually.

Gemstones may become cloudy, or precious metals may gradually exhibit dull surfaces. Over time, prongs may weaken or wear down, resulting in a loss of the stone. Clasps can break, and jewelry can be lost. Regular inspections and cleaning by jewelry professionals can preserve and protect fine-jewelry investments.

Meeting Customer Needs

Many customers, regardless of income level, prefer jewelry with lasting power. One reason frequently cited for the purchase of fine jewelry is its ability to outlast the quick fashion changes and still be beautiful several years later. Trends do exist in the fine-jewelry market, with metal trends lasting longer than gemstone trends. Consumers have traditionally viewed fine jewelry as a planned purchase and investment.

In the past, retailers have found customers less interested in the name brand of the stone set in the jewelry than in other factors, such as store name (like Tiffany's), size, jewelry brand, or price. All kinds of retailers, whether discount stores, mass merchandisers, or exclusive specialty stores, can profitably offer one or more of the purchase criteria to their target customer.

Diamond suppliers, aware of the lack of gemstone brand-name awareness, are hoping to add

Profile: Tiffany & Company

Mr. Tiffany and Mr. Young congratulated each other on their store's opening day sales: a whopping $4.98! On September 18, 1837, Charles Lewis Tiffany and John B. Young opened Tiffany & Young, a stationery and fancy goods emporium at 259 Broadway in New York City. The rest is history . . . in a blue box . . . Tiffany Blue.

In 1853, Charles Tiffany renamed the store Tiffany & Company. Some of the more important landmark events included the 1886 introduction of the still-famous, six-prong Tiffany setting for rings; a 1940 store move to 727 Fifth Avenue; Truman Capote's *Breakfast at Tiffany's,* published in 1950 and filmed with actress Audrey Hepburn in 1961; and a 1967 creation of the first National Football League's Super Bowl trophy. Tiffany introduced its own square-cut Lucida diamond in 1999.

Tiffany has been associated with three famous designers: Jean Schlumberger (1956), Elsa Peretti (1974), and Paloma Picasso (1980). Schlumberger was known for his eclectic designs and mixing colored stones in yellow gold. Peretti, who gets her inspiration from nature, is known for her sensuous and sculptured sterling silver forms. Picasso's designs are whimsical and use unique color combinations.

In spite of the elegant (and pricey) reputation Tiffany & Company has earned over the last 160+ years, Tiffany advertises ring prices on its Web site that begin at $970. Tiffany & Company is aware that it must woo the customers aspiring to become affluent, as well as those who already have luxury goods purchasing power. Believing in market share growth opportunities, Tiffany & Company is working toward offering merchandise geared to a younger crowd, as well as products for shoppers (mostly women) who buy for themselves.

Tiffany & Company began offering an online wedding gift registry in 2000 in conjunction with another Internet

branded diamonds as one more purchase criteria. Through strategic and cooperative advertising, eventually consumers may consider the brand of stones when purchasing fine-jewelry.

Branding a product means creating a lifestyle concept. Successful jewelry-advertising campaigns assure the consumers the company understands who they are. The advertisements have graphic imagery and evoke emotions with a visual setting that creates a sense of history, a mood, and a lifestyle. In the past, many fine-jewelry advertisements focused on a close-up image of a piece of jewelry against a dark background. With so many of these look-alike photos in magazines, the jewelry was not memorable or distinguishable from other advertised pieces. More recently, fine-jewelry advertisements feature more realistic settings with an emphasis on the target customer's lifestyle rather than a still shot of the jewelry or a close up of a glamorous model wearing the jewelry.

Profile: Tiffany & Company *(continued)*

company called WeddingChannel. Tiffany & Company benefits from this joint venture because of WeddingChannel's far reach. An estimate of the number of WeddingChannel Web site visitors was approximately 20 percent of brides per year in the United States.

Engaged couples may visit any Tiffany store to register for the online service. Couples can access the Web site's "Create a Table Setting" option, which allows them to pair china and flatware patterns. Cybershopping gift-givers can access the couple's selections, by name of the bride or groom, or allow the store to make gift suggestions appropriate for engagements, showers, and weddings. Other services offered on the Tiffany & Company Web site include educational links, such as "How to Buy a Diamond," and an informational booklet, "About Your Tiffany Gemstone & Pearl Jewelry."

Tiffany & Company has stores in five European countries, numerous Asia-Pacific locations, and all three countries in North America. In spite of the dozens of stores worldwide, the flagship store in Manhattan still generates about 13 percent of total annual sales for the company. In 2001 company sales were over $1.6 billion, showing a four percent decrease in sales under the previous year.

The tragic events of September 11, 2001, adversely affected Tiffany's retail activity, especially in the Manhattan flagship store. The restrained customer spending in 2001 was tied to difficult conditions in the economy and the financial markets, as well as the impact on store traffic following the terrorist attacks in the United States. However, Tiffany's nonstore (Internet/catalog) U.S. sales showed a strong growth in 2001.

In the February 2001 *Women's Wear Daily* survey of most recognizable luxury brands, Tiffany & Company was rated number two behind Rolex. The distinctive blue Tiffany Box has been described as an "American icon of style and sophistication."

Sources:

About your Tiffany gemstone & pearl jewelry. (1998). *Tiffany & Company.* Retrieved June 1, 2001, from www.tiffany.com

Braunstein, P. (2000, August 9). Tiffany wedding registry online. *Women's Wear Daily, 180*(26), p. 2.

Curan, C. (1999, October 18–24). Multifaceted success. *Crain's New York Business, XV*(42), 1, 89.

Hessen, W. (2000, November 21). Tiffany to renovate Fifth Avenue store. *Women's Wear Daily, 180*(97), p. 14.

How to buy a diamond. (2000). *Tiffany & Company.* Retrieved June 1, 2001, from www.tiffany.com

Robertson, R. (2001, February 5). De Beers homes in on diamond retail market. *Northern Miner, 86*(50), 1.

The 100. (2001, February). *Women's Wear Daily Special Report: WWD Luxury.*

Tiffany annual report. (2001). *Tiffany & Company.* Retrieved July 18, 2002, from www.tiffany.com

SUMMARY

▪ The wearing of fine jewelry has always been a form of self-expression and adornment. More specific reasons for the wearing of jewelry include function, hiding places, symbols, religious meanings, magic, organization membership, graduation, motherhood, and status.

▪ Jewelry is classified as fine jewelry, costume jewelry, and bridge jewelry, which span the price range between fine and costume jewelry. The higher-priced fine jewelry is usually made of precious metals combined with precious or semiprecious gems.

▪ Many ancient civilizations contributed their own unique fine-jewelry materials and styles. Egyptians left a wealth of gold artifacts inlaid with precious and semiprecious stones. Mesopotamian cultures supplied us with the original zodiac symbols.

- *Cloisonné* techniques were fine-tuned by the far eastern civilizations. Jade was (and still is) an important stone of the Chinese. European cultures created elaborate brooches, girdles (belts), and pendants.

- Fine-jewelry designers' inspiration sources include historical artifacts, different cultures, costume jewelry, nature, art, and technology. Design trends often originate in Europe, New York, and California. It may take several seasons for these to become popular with the masses. Two current trends in designing jewelry are versatility and mixing metal tones.

- Fine jewelry is manufactured using a variety of techniques. Many pieces are handcrafted and one-of-a-kind; these carry a higher price point.

- A setting is designed to show a stone to its best advantage. Settings include inlay, pavé, buttercup, channel, cluster, flush or bezel, illusion, paste, prong or Tiffany, and tension-mount.

- Precious metals may receive special treatments, such as antiquing, engraving, etching, florentining, and hammering.

- Most fine jewelry can be classified as necklaces, earrings, bracelets, brooches, pins, clips, rings, and crowns. Within each classification numerous styles exist and are continuously being developed.

- Care procedures vary depending on the precious metal and the stone. Abrasive surfaces, harsh chemicals, perfumes, and extreme temperature changes should be avoided when wearing all fine jewelry. Jewelry may scratch if pieces rub against one another. Proper storage minimizes this risk. As with all "investment" accessories, cleaning and repairs should be regular and performed by professionals.

- U.S. consumers purchase more than $15 billion in gold jewelry annually.

- Fine jewelry was once primarily sold by prestigious jewelers who still lead the channel of distribution. More recently, jewelry stores have been losing market shares because of a trend toward mass-market fine jewelry, which offers more affordable items to a wider range of customers.

- Discount stores and mass-merchandise stores have increased fine-jewelry department size and offerings to take advantage of sales opportunities. Success has been built on the consumers' perception of a trustworthy retailer.

- The late 1990s and early 2000s proved to be a healthy economic climate, conducive to sales of fine jewelry. Industry analysts predicted the trend to continue through the first decade of the new century. Factors attributed to improved sales included baby boomers celebrating milestone events, nationwide economic growth, a shifting of expenditures from home to person, working women with higher incomes, a trend toward femininity, and increased promotion at the production channels.

- Internet retailing is available at all price points, but is more common at lower and moderate prices. Certificates of authenticity may accompany diamond jewelry at higher values.

- Catalog retailers may also offer certificates of purchase. Catalogs are most likely to be delivered to consumers during the peak fine-jewelry selling events—Valentine's Day, Mother's Day, and the fourth-quarter holiday season.

- Vintage and estate jewelry have become a popular category of fine jewelry. This includes reproduced and refurbished jewelry that dates back several decades.

- The Federal Trade Commission recommends retailers offer documentation to buyers regarding store policies, jewelry grading, and all stone enhancements. Retailers should consider offering services to build a strong and lasting relationship with potential customers.

- Fine jewelry is considered an investment. Consumers differ on their purchase motives, but common preferences include jewelry with lasting power, versatility, quality, and a strong visual impact.

- Advertising has begun to focus on creating emotional responses in consumers. A successful advertisement is one that assures the consumers the company understands who they are. It shows the company is willing to meet their needs with a brand befitting their lifestyle.

TERMS FOR REVIEW

ankle bracelet (anklet)	chasing	engagement ring
antiquing	chatelaine	engraving
armlet (armband)	clarity-enhanced stones	etching
bangle (hoop) bracelet	class ring	eternity ring
bar pin	*cloisonné*	Fabergé eggs
bib necklace (collarette)	cluster setting	filigree ring
birthstone ring	coating (impregnating)	fine jewelry
bleaching	cocktail (dinner) ring	florentining
bracelet	coloring the gold	flush (bezel) setting
bridal set ring	computer-aided design	fracture filling
bridge jewelry	(CAD)	fraternal ring
brooch (broach)	computer-aided manufactur-	gemstone enhancement
buttercup setting	ing (CAM)	goldsmiths
button earring	costume (fashion) jewelry	graduated pearl necklace
cameo	counterpoise	hammering
casting	cuff bracelet	hatpin
chain necklace	diadem	heating
championship ring	diamonds by the yard	hoop (gypsy) earring
chandelier earring	diffusion	illusion setting
changeable (earring jacket)	dog-collar choker	infusion
earring	drop earring	inlay
channel setting	dyeing	intaglio
charm bracelet	ear cuff earring	irradiation

lapel pin

lariat necklace

lasering

lost wax casting

model makers

mother's ring

nugget ring

open-to-buy

paste setting

pavé

pendant (lavaliere or drop) necklace

platinumsmiths

poison ring

prong (Tiffany) setting

prototypes (models)

repoussé

rope necklace

scarf clip

signet ring

silversmiths

slave-ring (bracelet-ring) bracelet

slide (zipper or Y-) necklace

soldering

spinning ring

spoon ring

stickpin

stonesetters

stud earring

tennis (diamond) bracelet

tension-mount setting

Tiffany setting

toe ring

vintage (estate, antique, period, or heirloom) jewelry

wax mold

wedding band ring

REVIEW QUESTIONS

1. What are the reasons people wear jewelry, and which do you consider the most important?

2. What materials are used for fine jewelry?

3. What are some of the more common stone settings used in the manufacture of fine jewelry?

4. What are some of the precious-metal finishes used in the manufacture of fine jewelry?

5. What are the categories of fine jewelry?

6. What is the importance of the United States' role in the worldwide fine-jewelry market?

7. What factors have improved fine-jewelry sales in the United States, specifically in the discount and mass markets?

8. Which factors have a significant bearing on the retail price of fine jewelry?

9. How should fine-jewelry be cared for?

10. How might fine-jewelry businesses effectively meet customer needs?

KNOWLEDGE APPLICATIONS

1. Interview five to ten students and ask them to consider why they wear their favorite piece of fine jewelry. Using the reasons described in the introduction, classify each response. Assimilate class findings and analyze the results.

2. Visit a museum whose holdings include fine-jewelry displays; photograph a piece from a personal collection or locate an illustration in an historic book. Research the era, and in a written paper, explain how the item reflects the time in which it was worn.

3. Locate and remove all of the fine-jewelry advertisements from a fashion magazine. Classify the jewelry according to style. Also analyze the type of advertisement. Is it a product advertisement or a lifestyle advertisement?

4. Write a short essay on the validity of the statement in this chapter that, "Most fine jewelry trends originate in Europe, New York, and California." Find evidence to support or refute this statement and include it in your paper and bibliography.

5. Develop a list of five questions regarding fine jewelry. Visit a fine-jewelry store and make an appointment to interview the manager or a knowledgeable salesperson. Write a paper about your findings.

6. Visit two Web sites selling fine jewelry. Compare and contrast the sites and services.

7. Using the Monday issues of *Women's Wear Daily* (available through your library search engines), locate and summarize an article on fine jewelry. Be sure to include a bibliographic citation or a printed copy of the article.

8. Obtain a Sunday issue of a newspaper with a large circulation. Analyze all of the fine-jewelry advertisements based on advertisement size, featured products, location, target customer, store image and services, retail prices, and any other relevant criteria. Make a one-page chart for your findings that allows you to record and compare a variety of advertisements.

CHAPTER 14

COSTUME JEWELRY

The Democratization of Fashion in Ancient Egypt: So Faux!

Did the ancient Egyptians have similar value distinctions between fine and costume jewelry that we do today? Evidence suggests they regarded their newly invented faux gemstones not only as clever creations, but often as costly jewels. Historians suggest the primary purpose of glass imitation stones was to discourage tomb raiders. By creating worthless reproductions of precious jewelry, the deceased pharaohs might lie undisturbed. However, a counter argument suggests that ancient Egyptians considered glass to be of the same value as precious gems and metals. Did they believe the process of creating glass and faience stimulated special and priceless magical fertility powers? Is this the real reason faience and glass are combined with precious stones and metals in many pieces of tomb jewelry? Famous King Tut's tomb contained an intricately detailed necklace with red and blue glass beads in a solid gold setting. To us, "a great imitation ultimately remains an imitation, a forgery. Did the Egyptians share this perception or did they perceive each material as distinct, valuable in its own right for its own specific properties?"

Illes, J. (2001, August 1). Beauty secrets of ancient Egypt: Glass beads, "fabulous fakes" and the birth of costume jewelry. Tour Egypt monthly: An online magazine, II(8). Retrieved December 18, 2002, from *http://www.egyptmonth.com/mag4.htm*.

A BRIEF HISTORY OF COSTUME JEWELRY

THE ANCIENT EGYPTIANS MAY HAVE INVENTED COSTUME JEWELRY USING THE ART OF *alchemy,* a precursor to modern chemistry. The Egyptian custom of burying the dead with their belongings attracted tomb robbers, so the Egyptians created imitation jewelry with less expensive metals and alloys and fake stones to place beside the deceased. The Egyptian working classes adopted this costume jewelry for everyday fashions. Decorative materials included glazed pottery beads called *faience* and glass beads or **inlay.**

While the Western civilizations chose to adorn the person, the ancient Chinese chose to use jewelry to adorn long-sleeved and high-collared costumes. Showy necklaces, bracelets, and earrings of the West were comparatively rare in the East. Instead, ornate hooks and buckles, and strings of beads decorated the elaborately embroidered costumes. The clothing itself provided the distinction of rank and wealth, and jewelry was often dispensed with altogether.

Artistic movements, such as Art Nouveau and Art Deco, influenced costume jewelry. Highly stylized designs characterized **avant-garde jewelry** (outlandish or high fashion). Stones were used primarily as color accents, with the choice of stones less important than the colors they contributed. Synthetic substances that replaced celluloid and hard rubber, such as Bakelite® (circa 1909 and named for its inventor, L.H. Baekeland), became popular for fashion jewelry during the decades prior to World War II.

Couture designer Coco Chanel has been credited with the modern popularization of all kinds of costume jewelry during the 1920s fashion revolution. Her love of pearl ropes, knotted or worn in multiple strands, became a fashion must-have for women of all socio-economic classes (see Figure 14.1). Those who could not afford the real thing were encouraged to purchase faux or imitation pearls and wear them flamboyantly. Breast-binding became a fad to ensure the proper hang of the pearl ropes.

FIGURE 14.1 *Coco Chanel popularized costume jewelry and faux pearls in the 1920s.* Courtesy of Fairchild Publications, Inc.

Costume jewelry continued to be a fashion staple throughout the remaining decades of the 20th century. The Great Depression of the 1930s created a market for inexpensive wardrobe extenders. With World War II patriotism riding high in the 1940s, jewelry manufacturers experienced a shortage of some metals, especially precious metals. Inexpensive substitute materials were used in costume jewelry, affordably priced for the newly created class of working women. Costume-jewelry pins and brooches were mainstays of the 1950s in painted metals, enamels, and rhinestones.

The 1960s fashions introduced a costume-jewelry explosion, which continued well into the 1970s. Stainless steel POW (prisoner of war) bracelets, imprinted with the name, rank, and serial number of prisoners of the Vietnam War were patriotic costume jewelry during this era. High-tech plastics, like Lucite® and Plexiglas® were used for chunky bangle bracelets, large, colorful earrings and rings, and pendants on leather laces.

The popularity of jewelry for men reached a modern high during the 1960s social revolution. The clothing manifestation of the social upheaval was deemed the Peacock Revolution—the origins of which have been credited to Pierre Cardin's colorful European looks. Some unisex jewelry made antiestablishment (antiwar) statements, such as choker-style love beads (tiny, colorful glass beads) and peace-symbol jewelry (see Figure 14.2). Other popular men's jewelry of the 1960s and 1970s included identification bracelets; wide tie holders, such as tie bars, pins, and tacks; and lapel ornaments (for the wide lapels).

FIGURE 14.2 *Love beads were part of the "flower child"*
look popular among young adults in the late 1960s.

As the 1970s progressed into the early 1980s, the dress-for-success era created a need for expensive-looking costume jewelry. The dress-for-success look mandated that jewelry be simple and tasteful for working hours. After hours, gold rings and chain necklaces were popular for men and women. Gold-toned, classic-jewelry pieces were available at popular price points.

The American male's 20th-century final crossover into women's jewelry was the wearing of pierced earrings. In spite of a great deal of social resistance, young men chose pierced studs as earrings, first for one ear, and later both ears. To make a more powerful fashion statement, some young men adopted body piercing, while others chose a permanent body adornment, tattooing.

Semiprecious stones and bridge jewelry became important classifications in the 1990s (refer to Chapter 13 for a detailed explanation of bridge jewelry). Many consumers began to choose jewelry based on lasting power, rather than to satisfy one season's fashion look. In addition, the long-lasting casual trend elevated the status of casual-bridge jewelry in sterling silver and semiprecious stones. By the end of the 20th century, most types of retail stores offered a bridge-jewelry department because of the increase in demand and the potential for significant departmental profits.

Matched sets became important at all jewelry price points, such as earrings and necklace ensembles. Many fads occurred in the 1990s jewelry market; among them were power beads, *Titanic's* "Heart of the Ocean" necklace design, spinner rings, Y-necklaces, tattoo jewelry, and silk-flower pins.

AN INTRODUCTION TO COSTUME AND BRIDGE JEWELRY

As discussed in Chapter 13, a single fashion look may be available as fine, bridge, or costume (sometimes called fashion) jewelry. The term *fashion jewelry* encompasses all jewelry that is not fine jewelry, including bridge and costume jewelry. For distinction, bridge and costume jewelry will be discussed separately throughout the chapter. The main difference between fine, bridge, and costume jewelry is the costs of materials and labor. **Bridge jewelry** bridges the price between inexpensive costume jewelry and costly fine jewelry. **Vintage jewelry** refers only to the era, not the price. **Junk** or **fun jewelry** is cheap costume jewelry, such as Mardi Gras beads and children's play jewelry. It includes plastic, unplated metal, and wood materials. Usually junk jewelry has a short life cycle because of the breakage of poorly constructed components.

Manufacturing Costume Jewelry

A few large manufacturing companies produce most of the costume jewelry. One company, Victoria & Company, acquired by Jones Apparel Group in July 2000, was estimated to produce between 20 percent and 45 percent of all costume-jewelry brands found in mass-merchandiser and moderate department stores. Some of the licenses Victoria & Company holds are Nine West

Jewelry, Givenchy, and Tommy Hilfiger. Napier and Richelieu are two of Victoria & Company's own brands.

Victoria & Company also manufactures private-label costume jewelry for many other companies. This includes the private labels Jaclyn Smith for Kmart and Worthington for JCPenney. Private-label costume jewelry provides retailers with opportunities for profit-margin enhancements as well as a way to differentiate the store from its competitors.

Manufacturers are finding men's bridge jewelry a small but increasingly important accessories classification. Men's sterling-silver jewelry has been a growth area during the last few years. This growth has been attributed to a resurgence of formal or sharp dressing, including cuff links, studs, bracelets, and pocket watches. The growth potential in this classification has caused a few manufacturers to shift their focus from women's to men's jewelry. Reasons for the upswing in men's jewelry purchases include a greater acceptance by men of the wearing of jewelry, a broadening of wealth, and the popularity of affordable sterling-silver jewelry.

In spite of the willingness of men to wear jewelry, women still account for about 90 percent of men's jewelry purchases. The percent of male self-purchasers is expected to increase over the next few years.

Design

Designers of bridge and costume jewelry should possess technical drawing skills, such as Computer-Aided Design (CAD). They must have the ability to translate fashion and product trends to jewelry. Jewelry-product developers take the design one step further. They determine the most efficient means of production for the designer's models. They negotiate prices and deadlines and obtain jewelry parts from sources all over the world, many of which are in the Far East.

Costume-jewelry designers must possess an awareness of prevailing ready-to-wear trends and reflect these trends in their designs. Customers choose jewelry that complements their apparel styles. Costume- and bridge-jewelry designers work closely with apparel designers for runway shows, because of the potential for international exposure. A top fashion designer's runway clothing is scrutinized for every detail, including accessories. Costume-jewelry designers hope to link their product name with the credibility of the fashion designer's name.

The pieces designed for runways are usually larger than the commercial pieces because they have to stand out enough to be seen at a distance. Designers may choose to mass-produce the larger sizes used for runways if they anticipate their customers will prefer the greater visibility that comes with larger jewelry.

Some ready-to-wear designers branching into costume-jewelry design have targeted the junior market. Michael Kors and Miuccia Prada recently studied a sophisticated fashion group of juniors dubbed the Park Avenue princesses, the daughters of New York City's top business tycoons and socialites. Ladylike jewelry, such as colored faux-pearl strands, and brightly colored rhinestone bracelets, necklaces, and pins were created for this trendy set of young women, heavily influenced by the media.

Several key jewelry trends in the junior market are:

- Preppy, English influence
- Necklaces of all types
- Early eighties chic
- Colored stones
- Large links
- Stackable rings
- Multiple bangle and cuff bracelets
- Insect motifs (butterflies, ladybugs, and dragonflies)
- Colored pearls and colorful crystals
- Black and white
- Patriotic

Some costume jewelry is attractively packaged to simplify and encourage purchasing. Some designers believe the packaging is as important as the product to customers, particularly when several competing companies produce a similar product. The packaging can be used as the Unique Selling Proposition (USP) to entice customers to purchase one brand over another, rather than simply going with the lowest price. When items are given as gifts, the packaging becomes even more important. For example, the Nine West Company created a special clear-plastic tube as a package for an ordinary pink rhinestone tennis bracelet.

Ethnic Jewelry

Inspiration for designing ethnic jewelry often comes from historic origins. Nature, art, native costumes, rituals, and religion are sources of inspiration. The American Indian's heavy use of sterling silver can be traced to Spanish traders who introduced the craft of silversmithing. Initially, Native Americans hammered out and shaped Mexican silver pesos and American silver dollars. Later, they began to melt these coins to create cast designs. Native Americans use turquoise, onyx, denim lapis, coral, hematite, malachite, opals, and pink shells.

Famous designs, like Kokopelli (a mythical dancer) and the squash blossom design, are important in Indian jewelry for their historically rooted significance. Several tribes (mostly in the Southwestern United States) are famous for their unique jewelry. These include the Navajo, Zuni, Hopi, Santo Domingo, and Acoma Indians. The popularity of Native-American jewelry may be partly due to the accessibility of the crafters. Tourists can actually visit the craft centers, located on domestic soil, usually in the Southwestern states, including New Mexico, Colorado, and Arizona (see Figure 14.3).

Somewhat less pervasive than Native-American jewelry is African-American jewelry, inspired by traditional designs and materials from the African continent. The use of animal prints and images, leather and carved wood materials, and deep, warm colors can be traced to African ancestry.

One designer, Coreen Simpson, owner of The Black Cameo, became famous not for her African jewelry, but for her creative genius filling a void in the marketplace for traditional cameo jewelry featuring the profile of a black woman.

Novelty Jewelry

The costume-jewelry industry abounds with novelty jewelry. Each season, manufacturers and retailers attempt to attract customers with **novelty jewelry**—faddish items that may last no longer than one season. Recent examples include toe rings, power beads, tattoo necklaces and bracelets, and illusion necklaces. Other novelty jewelry includes specialty items, such as jewelry coins and bezels, antique typewriter keys, chatelaines, and body decorations, such as piercing jewelry.

Coin-art jewelry is created for a small market of customers. The coin's key features may be embellished, or the coin may be mounted in a bezel (an outer rim that holds the coin). Bezels may be set with small stones encircling the coin, or they may be strictly functional and lack ornamentation. U.S. laws prevent the defacing of circulating currency, but it is not against the law to alter U.S. currency no longer in circulation (see Figure 14.4).

Antique typewriter keys can be creatively made into jewelry, such as bracelets, earrings, and watchbands. Each key is set in sterling silver and forms one of the links in the bracelet or watchband. Single typewriter keys can be worn as drop earrings.

FIGURE 14.4
Coin jewelry in bezel rim.

FIGURE 14.3 *Native America influenced jewelry.*

Courtesy of Fairchild Publications, Inc.

Profile: The Black Cameo

Coreen Simpson: photographer, writer, world traveler, sculptor, and jewelry designer. She is a unique artist devoted to her African heritage. A lifetime New Yorker, Simpson attended the Fashion Institute of Technology and Parsons School of Design. Her career as a writer and photographer took her all over the world on assignments, including coverage of the European fashion collections.

In 1982, to supplement her income, she designed and manufactured the type of jewelry she wanted to wear but was unable to find. Combining stones in unique ways, her necklaces were labeled "power necklaces." In 1983, designer Carolina Herrera purchased eleven of Simpson's designs for her resort collection saying, "each piece is more magnificent than the last."

A few years later, one of her clients requested a cameo of a woman of color. Simpson was unable to find any contemporary manufacturer of black cameos, so in 1990, she began to manufacture her own Black Cameo in both fine-jewelry materials and as affordable costume jewelry. Simpson was not the first to design a black cameo, however. In 1850, a British company manufactured a *blackamoor* (very dark person) *cameo habillé* (clever cameo—described as a cameo figure wearing a necklace or earrings, often with an embedded gemstone). But these cameos are rare and costly antiques.

The Black Cameo is reflective of Simpson's African heritage. Her design is a cameo of a contemporary woman of color, in the traditional relief style. Her large and dominant cameos were again referred to as "power pins." For costume jewelry, the affordable cameos are manufactured in polymer and set in gold-plated or silver-plated pewter.

Coreen Simpson has a long history of awards and honors. Her contributions to the visual arts are well recognized. In 1992, she was honored for her design contributions by the Smithsonian Museum in Washington, D.C., and in 1994 she received the Evvy Fashion Award. In 1994, Simpson signed a three-year licensing agreement with Avon. She designed exclusive costume jewelry for the company's African American customers under the label, The Coreen Simpson Regal Beauty Collection. Pieces of Simpson's work are featured in museums throughout the world and are owned in private collections by notable women, including actress Diahann Carroll and opera diva Kathleen Battle.

Coreen Simpson has always been interested in photographing the way people decorate themselves. Her Web site features photographs of "The Black Cameo sightings" on powerful women in the world. What began as filling a void in the jewelry industry has become a popular symbol for women of color.

Chatelaines are functional or decorative ornaments suspended from chains. Many of the chatelaines available on the auction block, such as eBay, the most popular Internet auction site, are Victorian-era chatelaines. A recent perusal of eBay located ornate chatelaines functioning as nail files, scissors, tape measures, pin cushions, needle cases, button hooks, magnifying glasses, perfume vials, flirtation mirrors, pill boxes, and match boxes (see Figure 14.5).

The increasing popularity of body piercing and tattoo-like decorations has created a profitable accessories niche for the industry. Consumers can choose from a wide variety of titanium, surgical stainless steel, 14- or 18-karat gold, and niobium-pierced jewelry in the form of nose studs, banana bells, and retainers (for piercing navels, eyebrows, tongues, etc.). For those wanting the look without actually piercing the body, magnetic jewelry and clips are available in many of these styles. Web sites offer pierced jewelry at many price points, extensive information on care after piercing, piercing options, and a glossary of terms.

The rhinestone trend in costume jewelry has expanded into body decorations with less permanence. Stick-on tattoos have been particularly popular with preteens. Bead or crystal decals in heart shapes or spelling out "kiss" or "love" have been popular temporary body decorations.

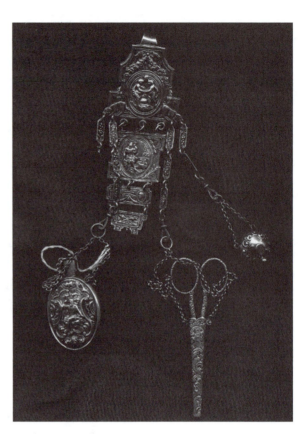

FIGURE 14.5
Chatelaine hanging ornaments.

Materials

At first glance, costume jewelry and bridge jewelry may look similar. Usually, costume jewelry is made of materials other than silver, gold, or other precious metals. Stainless steel, anodized aluminum, and brass are used in place of precious metals. Inexpensive metals, such as copper, nickel, brass, cadmium, chromium, pewter, and zinc, may be lightly coated in silver or gold, such as gold-filled, gold overlay, and rolled gold plate. Costume jewelry may also be manufactured in nonmetal materials, such as plastics, with mineral flecks embedded in the jewelry. Other materials include enamel (a fused glass), ceramic, specialty woods, such as rosewood, leather, hemp, seeds, and shells.

Findings are mass-produced component pieces of jewelry and mechanical fittings used to fasten the piece of jewelry to the person or clothing. Findings include eternity-ring settings with holes drilled ready for a choice of stones, earring backs, pin closures for brooches, and catches for bracelets and necklaces. All jewelry, whether fine, bridge, costume, or junk, require findings, but the primary difference is the type of metal used to manufacture the findings.

The stones in costume jewelry may be inexpensive stones, plastic, or brilliant, heavy glass, called *stras* (after the French inventor, George Frederic Stras). **Stras** is a highly refractive glass paste used for artificial gemstones. Foil backings are sometimes used on the artificial stones to create more brilliance and sparkle. **Doublets** and **triplets** are manufactured gems made of two or three pieces of smaller or inferior gemstones or glass. They may be glued in place or mounted with metal prongs and settings fashioned similar to fine jewelry.

Cubic-zirconia stones (faux diamonds) set in 10-karat gold are also considered bridge jewelry because of the gold content, not because of the stone type. Another faux diamond is a heat-treated zircon stone, called a *matara* (or *matura*). This is a naturally occurring zircon stone heated to make it colorless and diamond-like. Austrian crystals resemble diamonds, as do *Diamonique®* and *Diamonaire®*, two registered trade names for faux or fake diamonds.

MEN'S JEWELRY STYLES

Men's jewelry styles are fewer than those for women, and many are merely heavier versions of similar styles. Depending on which materials are used for manufacturing, the jewelry is classified as fine, bridge, or costume jewelry. The following is a description of common men's jewelry (see Figure 14.6).

Cuff link or **cuff button** Worn in place of regular buttons on French cuffs (double cuffs) of shirts. Designed as two buttons joined together by a short chain link. May be inset with gemstones or engraved with a monogram.

Stud Used on a formal shirtfront, the neckband, and cuffs. Designed as ornamental and removable buttons attached to a small post with a smaller button on the back.

Tie tack Holds the top and bottom blade of the tie together. Designed as a decorative button mounted on a post that is inserted through the center of the tie.

Tie clip or **clasp** Worn in place of the tie tack to hold the tie blades to the shirt front. A metal bar, bent double, similar to a hairpin, slides over both blades of the tie and the shirt front placket.

Collar pin Holds the spread collar points together. The pin is placed through the collar point eyelets, under the tie knot, slightly lifting the knot away from the neck button on the shirt.

Money clip Used to hold folded money bills, rather than in a billfold.

THE GLOBAL COSTUME JEWELRY INDUSTRY

The United States imports considerably more costume and bridge jewelry than it exports. This is especially true with regard to low-end costume jewelry. The World Trade Organization (WTO) initiative has negotiated lower United States tariffs on imported costume jewelry, from about 11 to 5 percent. This means developing countries may be encouraged to export more costume jewelry to the United States. **Duty-free status** is available under the North American Free Trade Agreement (NAFTA) for Mexico and Canada and for most developing countries under the Generalized System of Preferences (GSP). This means a participating country can export to

cuff buttons

FIGURE 14.6

Common men's jewelry.

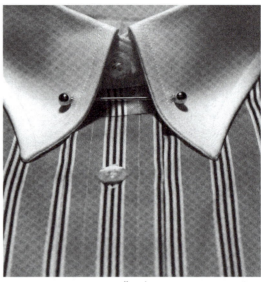

collar pin

another participating country without being charged a protective tariff or tax. The GSP does not include China, South Korea, Taiwan, and Hong Kong.

Table 14.1 shows the top five countries supplying the United States with costume jewelry in 2002. During the 1990s, the number of imports from China increased significantly, while the number of imports from the other countries fluctuated. In 1996, China supplied only about 33 percent of the United States' costume jewelry. By 2002, the supply from China was nearly 64 percent.

The primary states producing costume jewelry are New York and Rhode Island. Combined, these two states produce about two thirds of costume-jewelry shipments. Attleboro, Massachusetts, an historic town noted for jewelry making, has also been an important source of employment. In 1999, the industry consisted of many small companies, totaling about 900 manufacturers and 12,200 employees.

TABLE 14.1

Top U.S. Import Sources of Costume Jewelry in 2002 by Country

Country	$ Import Value
China	492,372,000
Korea	85,733,000
India	26,863,000
Thailand	26,756,000
Hong Kong	22,933,000

U.S. trade quick-reference tables: 2002 imports: 3961. *International Trade Administration.* Retrieved June 26, 2003, from http://www.ita.doc.gov/td/ocg/imp3961.htm

TABLE I4.2

Top U.S. Export Values and Destinations for Costume Jewelry in 2002

Country	$ Export Value
Canada	21,611,000
Japan	15,360,000
Mexico	9,805,000
Austria	9,010,000
Dominican Republic	8,072,000

U.S. trade quick-reference tables: 2002 exports: 3961. *International Trade Administration.* Retrieved June 26, 2003, from http://www.ita.doc.gov/td/ocg/exp3961.htm

The United States exports costume jewelry to several countries. Table 14.2 shows the top 5 export markets for costume jewelry products in the United States in 2002.

Exports from the United States are expected to decrease annually because of the low labor costs of developing countries, especially China. Labor-intensive jewelry manufacturing that cannot be economically automated or otherwise improved may move to foreign-labor markets for production. As production moves overseas, surviving costume-jewelry companies may be forced to produce high-end or bridge categories of costume jewelry with better materials, or they may have to shift their focus from domestic production to domestic marketing and styling.

Most of the same organizations and publications for fine jewelry also offer their services to manufacturers of bridge jewelry. Trade shows may combine bridge and fine jewelry or bridge and costume jewelry. However, fine and costume jewelry are usually shown at separate trade shows. Tables 14.3, 14.4, and 14.5 show some of the more important trade organizations, publications, and shows.

TABLE I4.3

Trade Organizations for the Costume-Jewelry Industry

Organization	Location	Objectives
American Gem Trade Association (AGTA)	Dallas, TX	To serve the North American natural-colored gemstone and cultured-pearl industries. To provide educational programs and materials, publicity, and government and industry relations.
American Opal Society	Garden Grove, CA	To promote interest and knowledge of opals.
Jewelry Manufacturers Association	Providence, RI	To support the jewelry-manufacturing trades and hosts trade shows.
National Fashion Accessories Association, Inc. (NFAA) and the Fashion Accessory Shippers' Association, Inc. (FASA)	New York, NY	To represent all accessories categories, including fine jewelry.

TABLE 14.4

Trade Publications for the Costume-Jewelry Industry

Trade Publication Name	Description
Accessories Magazine	Monthly trade publication; covers most accessories classifications, including bridge and costume jewelry.
International Jeweler	Focuses on jewelry influences, inspirations, and trends; published by VNU Business Publications.
National Jeweler	Bimonthly publication for the jewelry industry with print, face-to-face, and online information; published by VNU Business Publications.
Women's Wear Daily – Monday	Weekly issue of a trade newspaper, published by Fairchild; features business and fashion information on costume jewelry, as well as other accessories.
WWD Accessory Supplement	Fairchild special edition featuring fashion information on all accessories, including costume jewelry.

TABLE 14.5

Trade Shows for the Costume-Jewelry Industry

Trade Show	Location	Sponsor
AccessorieCircuit	New York, NY	ENK International
AccessoriesTheShow	New York, NY	Business Journals, Inc.
Australian Jewellery Fair	Sydney, Australia	Expertise Events
GemFair	Tucson, AZ	American Gem Trade Association
Intermezzo Collection	New York, NY	ENK International
Jewelry Manufacturers Association Trade Show	Providence, RI	Jewelry Manufacturers Association
MJSA Expo	New York, NY	Manufacturing Jewelers & Suppliers of America
Mirage Jewelry Show	Las Vegas, NV	Associated Surplus Dealers and Associated Merchandise Dealers (ASD/AMD)
Vicenzaoro Trade Fair	Vicenza, Italy	Fiera Di Vicenza
WWD/MAGIC Show	Las Vegas, NV	Women's Wear Daily and Men's Apparel Guild in California
International Fashion Jewelry Show in New York	New York, NY	International Fashion Jewelry and Accessory Group (IFJAG) Accessory Show

MERCHANDISING TRENDS AND TECHNIQUES

Costume jewelry is an important accessories classification among the consumer groups consisting of baby boomers (born between 1946 and 1964), Generation X (born between 1965 and 1979), and Generation Y (born between 1980 and 1994). The average price spent on costume jewelry was $20.73 reported by *Women's Wear Daily* in 2000. Older baby boomer women spend the most on jewelry, with a per person average of $209 annually. According to the NPD Group and the Accessories Council, the three consumer groups ranked the purchase of costume jewelry either second or third behind other accessories competing for their dollars (see Chapter 1 for a complete ranking).

The NPD Group reported the top brands purchased by Generation Y in 2000 as follows:

1. Claire's
2. Afterthoughts
3. Old Navy

The top brands purchased by Generation X and baby boomer consumers in 2000 were:
1. Monet
2. The Limited
3. Old Navy
4. Napier

Store Retailing

Costume jewelry needs to command attention when displayed in a store. Because of the relatively small sizes of jewelry, customers can easily bypass the items. Merchandisers may choose to group related small items to make a strong visual impact or display single pieces surrounded by open space to focus the attention on the item (see Figure 14.7).

FIGURE 14.7
This ad shows a single item against a black background for maximum visual impact.

Bridge jewelry is often prominently featured in a section of fine-jewelry departments in guarded but highly visible locations. The impulse purchase nature of the lower price points helps fine-jewelry retailers improve profit margins. Bridge jewelry may also be located in gift shops and as extensions in better department and specialty-store jewelry sections.

Costume jewelry is often displayed on revolving circular racks, easily accessed by customers, and usually not under lock and key. Because of the increased potential for shoplifting, the initial markups on these items may be higher than many other accessories areas.

Vendors suggest stores focus on adequately representing a limited number of key bridge- and costume-jewelry resources rather than carrying small quantities of several lines. This type of merchandising makes a stronger impression. Stores need to have enough pieces to make a statement to the consumer.

Internet and Television Retailing

Jewelry of all kinds, whether fine, bridge, or costume, is prevalent on the Internet, accounting for an estimated six percent of United States spending. The relatively high markup of jewelry has created a lucrative e-commerce business. Manufacturers of jewelry have begun to offer their own Web sites, bypassing traditional retail stores. It remains to be seen if this competition will create a lowering of profit margins for store retailers by requiring that they undercut their prices to compete for limited consumer dollars. Most of the Web sites refer to costume jewelry as fashion jewelry. The term *bridge jewelry* is not widely used by Web site developers. Instead, Web sites may subcategorize jewelry using terms such as semiprecious, sterling silver, or baby jewelry (jewelry for infants, such as tiny rings).

For those customers who do not have leisure time access to the Internet, television shopping represents an important retailing medium. Television shopping channels are important avenues for bridge and costume jewelry. However, Web sites offer opportunities to comparison shop easily across several suppliers, whereas television channels (and brick-and-mortar stores) offer limited selections.

Television-shopping channels and mass-merchandising stores are finding they have similar customer bases. For example, Sarah Coventry Company, a well-known home-party-plan from 1949 to the early 1980s, relaunched the dormant jewelry line in 2003. The jewelry is sold on television-shopping channels and mass merchandisers. Additionally, a partnership was formed between QVC home-shopping television channel and Target stores in 2001. Jewelry, QVC's biggest-selling category, is being sold in all Target stores. Initially, 22 stock-keeping units of Diamonique jewelry were placed in the stores, ranging in price from $20 to $200. With QVC's reach into 77 million U.S. homes, Target saw the initiative as an opportunity for two great retailers to fuel each other's growth.

In an example of celebrity endorsements, daytime television actress Susan Lucci (Erica Kane on the soap opera *All My Children*) began offering a line of costume jewelry on the Home Shopping Network. The 40-piece line, called the Susan Lucci Jewelry Collection, retails at between $24.50 and $95. The line was inspired by her personal collection and includes a reproduction of a gold bracelet that was a wedding gift from her husband.

Catalog Retailing

Fashion and bridge jewelry is an important part of catalog retailing. Proper fit is rarely a problem with these items, so purchase returns are lower than those for apparel. Customers are more likely to purchase ensembles (apparel and related accessories) if the jewelry is photographed with the apparel or featured on the same page.

The JCPenney retail chain offers a minimal amount of costume jewelry in their semiannual Big Book catalogs. Instead, the company prints a separate specialty-jewelry catalog, which includes merchandise also available online. Consumers may visit the JCPenney Web site and sign up to receive the publication.

SELLING COSTUME AND BRIDGE JEWELRY

Most costume jewelry is packaged as a self-selection product. Fashion and bridge jewelry at higher price points may require a salesperson's assistance because of restricted access. The availability of attentive salespeople acts as a deterrent to shoplifting and provides assistance for buying customers.

Stores offering sales assistance should provide adequate training and materials for the associates. A manual (or this textbook) that includes a list of birthstone gems, gemstone-care charts, a glossary of terms, and other pertinent information should be readily available to help answer customers' questions. Even part-time or floating associates should have access to information about frequently asked questions.

Consumers have a wealth of knowledge available before making a purchase of costume or bridge jewelry. They can access any number of Web sites selling fashion and bridge jewelry. Many of these sites also offer definitions and descriptions that inform and educate consumers. A successful costume-jewelry department needs to be staffed with knowledgeable salespeople who have also done their homework.

Price and Value

Prices of costume and bridge jewelry are dependent upon the materials used, target customer, and brand name. As discussed in Chapter 6, "Other Materials," the variance in retail prices may be a result of rarity of the materials. Some semiprecious stones are as expensive as some precious stones and therefore may be classified as fine jewelry rather than bridge jewelry. Plastics, wood, and glass usually do not retail for high prices, unless combined with sterling silver or semiprecious stones.

The target customer and brand image affect the retail price of the jewelry. For example, two Victoria & Company licensed brands, Nine West and Tommy Hilfiger, cater to different target markets. The price points reflect the prices the target customer is willing to pay. Nine West jewelry retails between $12 and $80, while Tommy Hilfiger offers the junior market a beginning price point of $11 and goes up to $125 for the women's market. Similarly, Liz Claiborne's LCI Jewelry Group, which acquired the venerable Monet brand of costume jewelry, differentiates product lines by target customers. The two lines may be adjacent in a costume-jewelry department, but the Liz Claiborne line targets a more casual customer, while the Monet line, retailing from $18 to $260, targets the classic and modern customer.

Sizing

Most costume jewelry is created in styles similar to fine jewelry. Styles may be categorized as necklaces, earrings, bracelets, brooches, pins and clips, and rings. For a detailed description of jewelry styles, see Chapter 13.

Rings are popular fashion- and bridge-jewelry accessories requiring proper sizing, unless they have an adjustable band. Table 14.6 shows the U.S. standard for the more common ring sizes and the corresponding diameters in inches.

Care of Costume and Bridge Jewelry

The care of bridge jewelry is similar to that of fine jewelry and is discussed in detail in Chapter 13, "Fine Jewelry." Fashion or costume jewelry has a short life cycle, often only one season, and

TABLE 14.6

United States Ring Size Chart and Diameter in Inches

Standard Size	Diameter in Inches
4	.585
5	.618
5 1/2	.634
6	.650
6 1/2	.666
7	.683
7 1/2	.699
8	.716
8 1/2	.732
9	.748
9 1/2	.764
10	.781

The International Gem Society. Ring Size Comparison Chart. (n.d.). International Gem Society. Retrieved May 27, 2003, from http://www.gemsociety.org/info/chrings.htm

excessive cleaning should be avoided. Many of the plated metals have only a thin layer of gold or silver and are susceptible to wearing away. If necessary, costume jewelry may be wiped with a damp cloth to remove dirt.

Meeting Customer Needs

Bridge jewelry offers gift-seeking customers higher price points from which to choose and offers self-purchasers better-quality and more lasting jewelry compared to costume jewelry. Salespeople should recommend spending at least $20 for a gift.

Fashion or costume jewelry offers customers the look of better jewelry without paying the higher prices required of bridge lines. Costume jewelry is an inexpensive way to complete a look or update a wardrobe. Fashions are short-lived, and trends change quickly in the jewelry industry. Designers, manufacturers, and retailers must anticipate customers needs and wants in order to have the right merchandise at the right time, in the right quantities, and at prices consumers are willing to pay.

SUMMARY

- Costume jewelry may have originated in ancient Egyptian times to imitate the costlier jewels of the ruling class. The ancient Chinese used beads and semiprecious stones, like jade, to adorn their costumes.

- Couture designer Coco Chanel encouraged women to wear faux jewels, and she is considered the 20th-century advocate of costume jewelry. Her contribution of fake pearls has a legendary status in fashion history.

- Improvements in inexpensive materials and the development of synthetic materials improved the availability and popularity of fashion or costume jewelry.

- Bridge jewelry evolved during the 1990s, paralleling the casual trend. By the 21st century, bridge jewelry was an important classification and significant source of profit for most jewelry departments. Discounters, mass merchandisers, gift shops, specialty, and department stores all offered bridge jewelry lines to women who appreciated fine jewelry but preferred the lower price points.

- Costume and bridge jewelry are heavily promoted to the junior and young women's markets. Interesting packaging, celebrity endorsements, media exposure, and ready-to-wear runway shows are tools used by jewelry manufacturers to reach and appeal to these consumers.

- Ethnic jewelry is available in many price zones. Southwestern Native-American jewelry is often manufactured in sterling silver and turquoise stones. African-American jewelry may be interpretations of animal prints and images, worked in leather or carved in wood.

- Novelty jewelry is a category for nontraditional jewelry. It includes coins, typewriter keys, chatelaines, body-piercing jewelry, and body decorations.

- Costume or fashion jewelry is made of any substance other than precious or semiprecious metals or stones. This includes plastics, leather, wood, glass, paste, ceramic, enamel, inexpensive stones, seeds, and shells. Most costume jewelry rarely lasts more than a fashion season or two. Junk or fun jewelry is very cheap costume jewelry.

- Bridge jewelry *bridges* the price between inexpensive costume jewelry and costly fine jewelry.

- Findings are mass-produced components for all jewelry. These include premanufactured settings, clasps, hinges, backs, and other mechanical devices.

- Most costume jewelry is manufactured by a small number of large companies. Many of these companies are located overseas, especially in China.

- Care depends on the type of jewelry and the materials used. Most fashion or costume jewelry requires little care beyond wiping with a clean, damp cloth. Bridge jewelry should be cared for like fine jewelry.

- In the United States, New York and Rhode Island are important costume jewelry manufacturing centers.

- China is the largest supplier of costume jewelry to the United States.

- Costume jewelry is an important purchase classification among the baby boomers, Generation X, and Generation Y market segments. The average price per purchase of costume jewelry in 2000 was $20.73. The baby boomer group purchased the greatest amount of costume jewelry, averaging $209 annually.

- Display techniques should include showing groupings of small pieces of jewelry, usually within manufacturers' lines, and displaying important single items surrounded by open space. Retailers should take advantage of the impulse-purchase potential of costume jewelry and offer displays in highly visible and accessible locations. Most manufacturers recommend offering substantial lines of a particular brand in order to make a statement.

- Internet, television, and catalog retailing are important sources of costume- and bridge-jewelry retailing.

- Catalog retailing offers a variety of merchandise, including fine, bridge, and costume jewelry. Some companies offer the same merchandise through online and print catalogs.

- Costume jewelry is often merchandised as self-selection because of the lower price points. Bridge jewelry is frequently featured under lock and key because of the higher price points.

- Prices are affected by the materials used, the target customer, and the brand name. Many of the mass-produced costume-jewelry brands are priced according to the brand image and target customer, with the cost of materials quite nominal.

TERMS FOR REVIEW

avant-garde jewelry	cuff link (cuff button)	faience
bridge jewelry	doublets	fashion jewelry
collar pin	duty-free status	findings

inlay

junk (fun) jewelry

matara (matura)

money clip

novelty jewelry

stras

stud

tie clip (clasp)

tie tack

triplets

vintage jewelry

REVIEW QUESTIONS

1. What are some considerations of a costume-jewelry designer when developing a line?
2. How has the casual-lifestyle trend influenced bridge- and costume-jewelry offerings?
3. What are differences between bridge jewelry and costume jewelry?
4. How is bridge jewelry similar to and different from fine jewelry?
5. What are findings?
6. How does novelty jewelry differ from costume jewelry, and what are some specific examples?
7. To which countries does the United States export costume jewelry?
8. From which countries does the United States import costume jewelry?
9. What are some recommended merchandising and retailing methods for bridge and costume jewelry?
10. How has electronic commerce changed the retailing of jewelry?

KNOWLEDGE APPLICATIONS

1. As a class, make a list of memorable jewelry fads. Discuss how these were completely appropriate for the time in which they were fashionable in terms of social, political, and economic happenings.
2. Refer to the list of key jewelry trends identified for juniors presented in the chapter. As a class, brainstorm and make a list of other trends evident in the costume-jewelry industry.
3. Visit some Web sites featuring Native-American jewelry. Identify key themes, important materials, and the historical significance of the designs.
4. Refer to the lists of popular brands preferred by the baby boomers, Generation X, and Generation Y. Using your own experiences with the jewelry brands listed, what marketing appeals are these brands using to attract the target customers?
5. Bring a collection of related jewelry items and props to class. Set up a mini display during class.
6. Visit a retail store and analyze its method of merchandising fashion or bridge jewelry. Critique the merchandising method in a two-page paper. One page should discuss positive comments, and the second page should discuss your recommended improvements.

CHAPTER 15

WATCHES

The Perfected American Watch

A good watch is a necessity of civilization. Many a man has lived to a ripe old age without taking closer note of time than he could from the sun's advance or the recurrence of his desire for food. So many have dwelt within the sound of the locomotive without ever having traveled by railroad train. Such persons are as milestones by which the surrounding community marks its progress.

Everyone may not always feel the need of a good watch. The same may be said of bread or meat: but there often comes the moment when a reliable watch is master of the situation. That is the necessity; and the point is the possession not only of a pocket timepiece, but of a good one. With a good watch one need never be late nor hurried. A poor watch is worse than none.

—The Waltham Watch Company, 1907

A BRIEF HISTORY OF WATCHES

Horology is the art and science of time, timekeeping, and timekeepers (clocks and watches). Horology's origins are prehistoric; the human race has always had a fascination with the movement of the sun.

The invention of portable timepieces can be traced back about five centuries, although availability was limited until the mid-1800s. Some of the earliest watches were manufactured in Nürnberg, Germany, at the beginning of the 16th century. Intricately decorated and unusually shaped—into drums, balls, pears, skulls, or crosses—these portable timepieces were fashioned with latticework to protect the rock-crystal watch faces. Many were suspended from *chatelaines,* or chains, and attached to belts.

As the centuries progressed, watches became increasingly complex, and by the 18th century, they were designed with minute and second hands under protective polished rock crystals, with real jewels as pivotal point bearings.

European crafters organized guilds to ensure quality standards and protection of the art of clock making. The Paris Guild of Clockmakers (1544) and the London Clockmakers Company (1630) were two such guilds. Other countries, like the Netherlands, Germany, and Switzerland, organized their own clock-making guilds. Switzerland, well known for fine watches, centered the cottage industry of watchmaking in the Jura Mountains. Families would manufacture watch parts at home, and then sell them to a master watchmaker who would assemble the watches and sell them around the world.

Thomas Harland of Connecticut began U.S. production of watches in the early 1800s with his 200-units-per-year watch factory. The process was painstaking, and watches were individually hand made, piece-by-piece. In 1836, the Pitkin brothers of East Hartford, Connecticut, produced an American design containing a machine-made part.

In 1850, machine-made parts began replacing some previously handcrafted watch parts, decreasing the cost of watches and increasing the precision of timekeeping. Two competing American horologists improved on watch designs and the machinery used for mass production. Edward Howard started the E. Howard Watch Company that is still in existence today as a unit of the Keystone Watch Case Company. The other American was Aaron Dennison, who established the Waltham Improvement Company in 1854, later changing the name to the Waltham Watch Company. The company helped pioneer assembly-line-manufacturing techniques. The concept of interchangeable watch works parts became the basis for mass production in other industries. Lasting for over 100 years with several name changes (it closed in 1957), the American Waltham Watch Company produced forty million jeweled watches and other precision instruments (see Figure 15.1).

FIGURE 15.1 *Waltham pocket watch.*

As pocket watches became mass-produced and affordable, prices dropped to just a few dollars, and pocket watches became common personal possessions. One famous American watch brand, Waterbury, sold for a mere four dollars because the mechanism was machine stamped. The term **dollar watches** referred to later versions of inexpensive watches, such as Ingersol and Ingraham watches.

The first documented wristwatches sold in the United States were advertised in 1906 as bracelet watches. These were primarily for women—men believed them to be too effeminate. However, during World War I, officers adopted the convenient wristwatches over the standard issue pocket watches. Mechanical wristwatches became widely available and popular for both genders after World War I.

During the 20th century, technology surpassed expectations. Electric wristwatches were introduced in 1957, and within two years, electronic watches hit the market. Illumination techniques, such as the **LED (light-emitting diode)** and the **LCD (liquid crystal display)** were scientific advancements of the 1960s and 1970s. Quartz watches were introduced in the early 1970s, and by the 1980s quartz movements dominated the watch industry. Fine Swiss watchmakers initially balked at the new quartz movements. Failing to adopt the new movements quickly enough, the Swiss watchmakers' share of the watch market dropped from 30 percent to 9 percent between 1974 and 1984. Helping the Swiss make a comeback in 1982 was the famous Swatch® watch, manufactured by Asuag-SSIH. More recent developments in the watch industry include dust and moisture-resistant seals; Braille watches for the blind; alarm clock and calendar watches; and solar-, body heat-, and atomic-energy-powered watches.

AN INTRODUCTION TO WATCHES

The watch industry is an increasingly important accessories classification. Customers typically purchase multiple watches for a variety of looks rather than owning only one all-purpose watch. Known as **watch wardrobing,** this trend has helped drive watch sales in the United States and Europe (see Figure 15.2).

European manufacturers are wooing the American market, encouraging them to purchase several watches for a variety of moods and occasions, such as specific sports, dressy, casual, or youth oriented. Men have always purchased multiple ties, belts, and other accessories, and manufacturers are helping them realize they can do the same with watches to coordinate them with different outfits.

Not only are customers buying multiple watches, they are spending more for them. According to a 1999 survey funded by the Jewelers' Circular Keystone, 16.1 million American adults purchased watches retailing over $100, with men comprising 49 percent and women the remaining 51 percent of the watch buyers.

Brand-name recognition is important in the watch industry. A ranking of watch company brands was performed by the Fairchild 100 survey. The most recognized fashion brand in the United States was Timex Corporation. The 50-year-old memorable Timex watch slogan, "It

FIGURE I5.2
A watch can complete a sporty, dressy, or casual look.
Courtesy of Fairchild Publications, Inc.

takes a lickin' and keeps on tickin'," and Timex's worldwide distribution helped propel the brand to first place in the survey.

The 10 most recognized watch brands according to the survey respondents are listed below.

1. Timex
2. Seiko
3. Rolex
4. Citizen
5. Casio
6. Swiss Army
7. Swatch
8. Monet
9. Nine West
10. Tiffany

The Fairchild 100: Watches/Jewelry. (2000, January). *Women's Wear Daily Special Report,* pp. 114, 116.

By contrast, a smaller survey performed for the Jewelers' Circular Keystone in 1999 asked respondents to volunteer the name of a watch brand. The ranking of the study's four most recognized watch brands sold in jewelry stores is presented below.

1. Rolex (see Figure 15.3)
2. Seiko
3. Bulova
4. Citizen

What motivates Americans to buy jewelry and watches: Part 4 of 4. (1999, November). *Jewelers' Circular Keystone, CLXX* (11), 112.

Fairchild also ranked the top 100 recognizable and perceived luxury brands, regardless of the category. Watches, jewelry, handbags, and clothing were some of the luxury brands included in the ranking. Rolex, with annual U.S. sales of more than $450 million, held the number one spot in the Top 100. Tiffany & Company and Cartier, both of which manufacture watches and fine jewelry, ranked second and third. Table 15.1 lists the top 10 recognized luxury-watch manufacturers and their ranking by affluent women in Fairchild's Top 100 Luxury Brands.

Parts of a Watch

Watches have the following parts (see Figure 15.4):

Watchcase Holds the watch mechanisms.
Dial The face of the watch.

FIGURE 15.3
Rolex is the most recognized brand of watch sold in jewelry stores, according to one survey.
Courtesy of Fairchild Publications, Inc.

TABLE 15.1
Fairchild's Top 100 Luxury Brands Ranking in 2000

Brand Name	Ranking in the Top 100
Rolex	1
Tiffany	2
Cartier	3
Van Cleef & Arpels	15
Montblanc	18
Patek Philippe SA	24
Movado	25
Piaget	25
Baume & Mercier	39
TAG Heuer	40

WWD Luxury: The 100. (2001, February). *Women's Wear Daily Special Report*, 8, 10–15. Courtesy of Fairchild Publications, Inc.

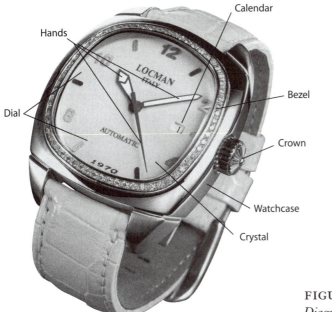

Hands
Calendar
Dial
Bezel
Crown
Watchcase
Crystal

FIGURE 15.4
Diagram of watch details for an analog wristwatch.

Crystal The transparent covering over the dial. (Sapphire crystals are the most scratch resistant.)

Bezel The rim around the dial, especially on sports watches.

Hands The moving pointers that record hours, minutes, and seconds.

Crown or Stem The winding stem on the side of a watchcase used to wind the mainspring and move the hands.

Mainspring The driving spring (makes the watch tick), contained in the watchcase.

Functions of a Watch

Terms that explain how a watch functions include the following:

Analog Moving hands on the dial to show the time.

Digital Numeric time-display on the dial.

Automatic A self-winding mechanism, such as the movement of the wearer's wrist. As the wrist moves, the mainspring is wound. Does not use a battery.

Mechanical A watch movement in gear-driven analog watches that requires winding of a mainspring, which slowly uncoils. Does not use a battery.

Quartz A battery-powered watch movement. An extremely accurate timekeeping method in which a quartz (or synthetic sapphire) crystal oscillates thousands of times per second.

Jewel Usually seventeen synthetic ruby jewels (sometimes real gems, such as rubies, sapphires, and garnets) are used as bearings to reduce friction at pivotal points in the mechanical watch movement, helping it run more smoothly and accurately.

Chronograph A stopwatch (can be started and stopped) to record elapsed time.

Tachymeter A stopwatch feature that records speed over a certain distance.

Watch Manufacturing

Mass-produced quartz watches are usually made in Asia. Hong Kong, China, South Korea, and Taiwan are important manufacturing locations.

Switzerland is an important manufacturing center for handcrafted mechanical watches and is considered the capital of fine watchmaking. To become a master crafter, watchmakers begin as apprentices, serving several years in various positions of repairs and service. In Switzerland, high-end watchmakers choose to follow the demanding Geneva Seal standards. To be awarded a **Geneva Seal** means the Swiss watch has been inspected and approved by an exclusive horological bureau that examines and certifies the best mechanical watches.

A watch legally labeled "Swiss made" provides consumers with a guarantee that the watch was assembled and tested in Switzerland, and that most of the movement components are from Switzerland.

Design

Large companies offer customers several distinct styles each season. A company's design team creates a collection of watch-product brands that has its own target market, design concept, and marketing program. Part of the marketing program includes advertising campaigns that can contribute to sizable sales increases for watch companies.

Promotions designed to attract new targets occur in the fine-watch industry. Many costly advertising campaigns are geared toward women, who are increasingly sought after by marketers of luxury and fashion accessories.

Companies like Megeve and Patek Philippe that have mainly catered to men's watches have begun to target the affluent, female self-purchasers. After discovering that women were buying men's watches for themselves, the companies began to design feminine watches to appeal to the female market rather than offering downsized men's styles (see Figures 15.5 and 15.6). Timex

FIGURE 15.5
A Megeve women's watch.
Courtesy of Charriol. Charriol Megeve Watch
(800) 872-0172.

FIGURE 15.6
Patek Philipe's T-150 watch.
Courtesy of Fairchild Publications, Inc.

Profile: Fossil®

Fossil, Inc., of Richardson, Texas, was founded in 1984 on the notions of fun, fashion, humor, and nostalgic value—1950s Americana. In the early 1980s, watches were generally more of a functional accessory than a fashion accessory, but Fossil, under the direction of president and CEO Kosta Kartsotis, sought to change this notion.

The complete line of Fossil accessories includes hundreds of watch styles (many retailing between $55 and $75), sunglasses, key chains, wallets, belts, small leather goods, backpacks, and casual wear and jeans apparel. Gift givers can purchase Fossil gift certificates creatively packaged in collectible tins. Fossil's Web site offers for sale a complete watch and accessories collection, product searches, company and employment information, financial information, and live audio Web casts of quarterly meetings.

Fossil, Inc., manufactures watches under the Relic and Avia brands (sold in the United Kingdom), and has a licensing agreement with Emporio Armani, DKNY (Donna Karan New York), and Diesel. In addition to branded merchandise, Fossil produces private-label watches and related merchandise for corporations, such as national retailers, entertainment companies, and theme restaurants. The software giant Microsoft Corporation announced plans to provide its employees with incentives, such as Fossil watches when they reported other employees giving away company secrets.

To gain exposure among teenagers, Fossil has entered into contracts with the television star and members of the band, O-Town, to promote the Fossil brand. Fossil outfitted the entertainers in a full wardrobe of Fossil clothing and accessories and sponsored guest appearances in Fossil stores worldwide, including London, Philadelphia, and Atlanta.

stores in 85 countries including Australia, Canada, Japan, Italy, the United Kingdom, regions of Asia, the Caribbean, Europe, Central and South America, and the Middle East. The Japanese market has been a lucrative watch market for Fossil. In June 2001, Fossil sold half its stake in Fossil Japan to Seiko, creating a joint venture called SFJ, Inc.

In addition to traditional retail formats, Fossil watches may be purchased at airport kiosks and on cruise ships. Discontinued Fossil merchandise is sold in Fossil outlet stores across the United States.

With an emphasis on global expansion, Fossil continues to increase net sales annually. The table below shows Fossil's net sales from 1996 through 2001.

Fossil, Inc. Net Sales from 1996 through 2001

Year	Dollar Sales
2001	545,541,000
2000	504,285,000
1999	418,762,000
1998	304,743,000
1997	244,798,000
1996	205,899,000

Fossil company information. (2002). Retrieved July 7, 2002, from http://www.fossil.com/CompanyInfo

The outlook for Fossil continues to be strong, with first quarter sales in 2002 showing an 18.6 percent increase over the first quarter sales in 2001. As the company continues to emphasize **brand building** (increasing consumer awareness of the brand) through promotional efforts, the affordably priced watches should maintain a favorable status as "collectibles."

Fossil was privately owned until its initial public offering in 1993 (NASDAQ symbol: FOSL). Fossil merchandise is sold in department stores and upscale specialty

Corporation spent approximately $19 million on advertising in 1999, especially targeting the younger, female consumers.

Watch designs closely follow jewelry designs. For example, an increase in yellow gold and colored diamonds in the manufacture of fine jewelry translates into a similar increase in watches.

Most fashion-watch designers try to create trendy designs that will last a couple of seasons and cater to the widest markets, particularly females in the 15 to 35 age range. This group comprises the biggest slice of the market for fashion watches. These consumers are most likely to follow the latest trend in fashion and are more open to new watch designs.

The general themes in watch designing are to make the product versatile and highly visible on the wrist. This currently includes interchangeable parts, colorful dials, and oversized faces. Interchangeable parts allow consumers to create watch wardrobes without purchasing multiple watches. Some manufacturers offer three or four bezel options in colors to match clothing, or gold, silver, or mixed tones; and removable watchbands in nylon, plastic and leather. Color-changing dials, at the push of a button, are another way to stretch the color coordination of a watch. As designers create watches with multiple functions, watch faces continue to get larger to accommodate the extra dials and displays.

Licensing

Watch brands are numerous, but large-scale manufacturing is done by a limited number of formidable giants. Licensing is prevalent among these large companies, such as Swatch, Richemont, Movado, and LVMH. The Movado Group, manufacturer of bridge and fine watches, has entered into licensing agreements with apparel and accessories companies, such as Tommy Hilfiger and Coach. Movado also manufactures watches under its own name, as well as the Concord and ESQ watch brands (see Figure 15.7).

FIGURE 15.7
Tommy Hilfiger watches are licensed to Movado.
Courtesy of Fairchild Publications, Inc.

Tech–Talk: Wrist Technology: GPS, EDI, PC, TV, and VCR

But will it keep time?

"High-tech sports watches are the SUVs of timepieces: Excessive, expensive, loaded with features that will never be put to the test—and very hot." [1]

Casio, Inc., well known in the consumer world for its electronic musical instruments, offers some sophisticated wrist-data devices, also known as men's and women's watches. Notably, Casio was the first company in the world to offer the Satellite Navi PAT-2GP watch with a global positioning system (GPS) receiver. By 2002, several watch manufacturers offered similar versions. These navigation watches import data from orbiting satellites. Hiking enthusiasts can plot their location, route, and destination on a computer and transfer the data to their watches using special software. Once on the trail, the watch pinpoints the exact latitude, longitude, and altitude measurements anywhere in the world. Runners can calculate their speed and distance as well. Data retrieval is literally at the fingertips. Timex offers a similar wristwatch with global-positioning satellite options that retails for $175 plus a $10 monthly service fee.

For those customers who are not quite outdoor enthusiasts, but who enjoy the secret-agent lifestyle, several watch manufacturers including Motorola and Samsung now offer consumers high-tech watches. One style is reminiscent of the two-way wrist radio worn by crime solver Dick Tracy in the comic strip started in 1946. These prototype digital-phone watches were featured at the Consumer Electronics Show in Las Vegas, Nevada, in 2000. Casio created a camera watch, capable of recording up to 80 compressed digital images that can be transferred in color to a personal computer. Users can preview the shots on a black and white screen. Casio also offers a wristwatch product featuring a tiny TV/VCR watch face, a **telememo watch** that stores up to 30 pages of documents, and a wristwatch that plays audio files.

Wrist devices continue to gain popularity for all kinds of data management because of the convenience and location, location, location. In addition, the shrinking sizes of technological devices enable them to be worn on the person. Wristbands become necessities to prevent miniature devices from getting lost.

The excitement of having all the bells and whistles on a wristwatch isn't a substitute for accurate timekeeping. **Thermic watches,** like Seiko Instrument's Ruputer watch, are powered by the wearer's body heat. When removed, the watch reverts to a power-saver mode, while maintaining accurate timekeeping. The Eco-Drive watches by Citizen contain rechargeable batteries powered by artificial or natural daylight. So powerful is the storage capability, these watches can remain functional for up to five years in total darkness. Extremely accurate timekeeping, also known as **atomic precision** timekeeping, was defined (tongue-in-cheek) by Peter Lewis of the New York Times. "Atomic precision these days means the watch will neither gain nor lose a second in some 20 million years, which more than covers the probable warranty period." [2] For less than $200, a consumer can get SUV-like wristwatches *and* atomic precision timekeeping.

[1] Meadows, S. (2001, June 25). For the wrist that has everything. *Newsweek, 137*(26), 80.

[2] Lewis, P. (2000, January 20). Look out! New wrist devices on the loose. *New York Times, Late Edition,* Section G Circuits, p. 1.

Children's watches are driven by fun features and licensed names, such as McDonald's McKids™ and Mattel's Barbie™. Timex Corporation, in an effort to capture the pre-teen market, created a Barbie and a TMX® watch. The $24.95 analog Barbie watches feature one of six fashion Barbies on the dial in a pink heart-or petal-shaped bezel. The watches are equipped with screen-saver modes that generate fourteen random mystery responses (like the popular Magic Eight Ball), such as "sure," "no way," and "hazy." The oval cases and bands are in bright shades of purple, blue, green, or red.

Production

Watches can be entirely handmade by master crafters, or they can be mass-produced by machinery on an assembly line. Watch production begins with a first sketch that is translated into a computer design or an initial blueprint. Lathes, boring, grinding, and polishing machines are used in watch manufacturing. Many watchmakers have also studied jewelry making because some of the metalworking is similar. Electronic watches are computers rather than mechanical devices and can be sold inexpensively, unless they are equipped with "extras" like global positioning satellite technology.

Materials

Watches, like jewelry, are classified as fashion, bridge, and fine. The workmanship and cost of materials are important in determining the classification. Fashion watches are usually made of inexpensive metals or plastic and are usually inexpensive. Bridge watches literally "bridge" the price points between fashion and fine watches. Materials include stainless steel, titanium, sterling silver, and plated gold. Bridge watches may retail for hundreds of dollars. Watches made of precious and rare metals, including gold or platinum, are used in fine watches. These watches may cost thousands or even hundreds of thousands of dollars.

Titanium metal is one of the lightest weight watch materials. Its steel-like strength makes it ideal for sports watches. White metallic titanium rivals yellow 18-karat gold as the choice among choices for watchcases. One company, TAG Heuer, took the titanium watch a notch higher when it created a watch from an alloy of elements used in the aerospace industry—titanium, aluminum, and vanadium—for its Kirium Ti5 watch.

Another watch, the Rado Vision 1, has a case made of 4,000 ground diamonds. Sterling silver coated with tarnish-resistant rhodium, another element, is a popular and affordable choice for watchcases.

Moderately priced fashion watches may be manufactured in a base metal of brass and plated with gold or steel. Aluminum watches are lightweight, and stainless-steel watches are popular in bridge and higher price points because of the excellent wear and tarnish resistance. According to the Federation of the Swiss Watch Industry, stainless-steel watches account for 40 percent of Swiss exports destined for the United States.

Watchstraps and bracelets may be made of the same materials as the watchcase, or leather, vinyl, rubber, plastic, or nylon. The choice of watchband materials depends on the intended end use. Leather bands are often found on casual or dressy watches designed for minimal wear and tear. Leather is a breathable and comfortable choice, but excessive perspiration or exposure to water may discolor the leather. Fashion and inexpensive watches often have vinyl watch bands; some have interchangeable colors. Unlike leather, vinyl does not "breathe" and may become uncomfortable if worn outside in the heat. Nylon watch bands are excellent choices for active sports because they require little care; are extremely strong, durable, abrasion-resistant; and do not discolor with perspiration. In addition, submersion in water has no ill effects on nylon.

Styles of Watches

Watch styles are similar for men and women, with the primary difference being size. Watches are categorized by how or where they are worn, such as pocket, wrist, bracelet, necklace, ring, and watch fobs.

Pocket watch Suspended on a **watch chain** and carried inside a vest or jacket pocket. Chain is threaded through a buttonhole to ensure the watch is not lost or dropped (see Figure 15.8).

Wristwatch Worn securely at the wrist, either buckled in place or worn on an elasticized band. A few wristwatches are adhesive backed and do not require a band.

Bracelet watch Also worn near the wrist, but does not fit securely. Instead, it hangs loosely like a bracelet.

Necklace watch Worn on a chain or ribbon around the neck.

Ring watch Tiny watch face and mechanisms on a finger ring.

Watch fob Short chain or ribbon to which a pocket watch is attached. Precious-metal fobs may be monogrammed.

Shapes of Watchcases

Several popular shapes of watchcases are available for consumers. These include round, oval, octagonal, flared, square, and rectangular. Figure 15.9 shows case design variations.

THE GLOBAL WATCH INDUSTRY

Watches are produced in a variety of countries, depending on the type of power used in the movements. For example, Switzerland produces most self-winding watches and jeweled mechanical watches. Asia produces the greatest number of battery-powered watch movements, especially Japan and China. Switzerland and Italy are well known for quality watchcases, while low-end watchcases are produced in Asia. Japan, China, and Thailand produce most of the world's watch batteries.

FIGURE 15.8
Pocket watch.

rectangular watch face

square watch face

round watch face

FIGURE 15.9
Shapes of watchcases.
Courtesy of Fairchild Publications, Inc.

The United States exports a limited number of low- and high-end watches to other countries. Table 15.2 shows a comparison of countries to which the United States exports watches, in either lower- to mid-priced base metal cases or high-end precious-metals cases.

TABLE 15.2
*Value Ranking of U.S. Exports of Low- to Mid-priced and High-end
Wristwatches in 2002 by Country*

Ranking	Countries Buying Low- to Mid-priced Watches	Countries Buying High-end Watches
1	Mexico	Switzerland
2	Japan	Hong Kong
3	Canada	Mexico
4	United Arab Emirates	Canada
5	Hong Kong	United Kingdom

U.S. trade quick-reference tables: Dec. 2002 exports: 9101 and 9102. *International Trade Administration.* Retrieved June 28, 2003, from http://www.ita.doc.gov/td/industry/otea/
Trade-Detail/Latest-December/Exports/91/910219.html

A growing number of counterfeit-luxury watches being smuggled into the United States has frustrated many luxury-watch manufacturers and retailers. It is estimated that fake watches are the fourth most commonly counterfeited merchandise. In June 2001, U.S. customs officials seized 40,000 counterfeit watches and watch parts shipped from Hong Kong to Los Angeles. Counterfeited trade names included Cartier, Bulgari, Armani/Fossil, Technomarine, TAG Heuer, Omega, Movado, and Rolex. It has been difficult, if not impossible, for consumers to know the difference between authentic- and fake-luxury watches, especially when packaged in authentic-looking boxes and carrying false certificates of authenticity. Many fake watches are being sold via the Internet, some for thousands of dollars, including a fake Rolex watch that sold for $44,000!

Trade Organizations, Publications, and Shows

In some instances, watches are combined with jewelry trade organizations and publications. Some south Asian regions that manufacture significant quantities of parts for watches have their own manufacturers' trade associations, including Taiwan, Hong Kong, and Singapore. Fine-jewelry or fashion-jewelry trade shows almost always include comparable watches as part of the show's offerings.

Tables 15.3, 15.4, and 15.5 show some of the more important trade organizations, publications, and shows.

MERCHANDISING TRENDS AND TECHNIQUES

Lower-priced watches are frequently impulse buys, while mid- and upper-priced watches are often planned purchases. In addition, watches are commonly given as gifts, so attractive packaging is important.

Watches are displayed in a variety of ways. However, they are generally merchandised by brand name first and lifestyle category second.

Uniquely packaged watches are especially attractive to younger consumers and to gift-giving consumers. One company, Aigner Group, redesigned its packaging, graphics, and fixtures in a strategy aimed to sell their products to holiday gift buyers. Men's key chains and wallets were encased in uniquely shaped burgundy gift boxes that could be interlocked to create an in-store display. Another master packager is the Fossil Company with its Americana-themed tins that are often consumer collectibles.

Manufacturers have engaged in creative publicity tactics to promote their watch lines. An "official watch" status of particular high-profile events can help promote company goodwill as well as sell watches. For example, Omega Watches were designated as the official timekeeper of the PGA (Professional Golfers' Association) tour, while Technomarine watches were the official timekeepers of the ESPY Awards (sponsored by sports news network ESPN). The Summer 2001 blockbuster movie *Pearl Harbor,* by Touchstone Pictures, outfitted the actors and actresses in Hamilton watches. Hamilton Watch Company was a chief supplier

TABLE 15.3

Trade Organizations for the Watch Industry

Organization	Location	Objectives
American Watch Association (AWA)	Washington, D.C.	To provide services to importers, assemblers, manufacturers, and suppliers of clock and watch movements.
American Watchmakers-Clockmakers Institute (AWI) http://www.awi-net.org/	Harrison, OH	To support workmanship in the horological crafts and set quality standards for restoration and repair practices.
British Horological Institute http://www.bhi.co.uk/	Upton Hall, Notts, UK	To perform research, sponsor education, and publish a technical journal.
British Watch and Clock Collectors Association http://www.ubr.com/clocks/bwcca/bwcca.html	Truro, Cornwall, UK	To bring together watch collectors with similar interests.
Federation of the Swiss Watch Industry (FH) http://www.fhusa.com/	Bienne, Switzerland	To represent Swiss watchmakers, publish data, and educate consumers.
International Watch and Jewelry Guild (IWJG) http://www.iwjg.com/	Houston, TX	To host trade shows.
Jewelers of America (JA) www.jewelers.org	New York, NY	To serve the retail jewelry and watch industry by conducting research, providing educational assistance, and publishing manuals.
National Association of Watch and Clock Collectors (NAWCC) www.nawcc.org	Columbia, PA	To serve as a nonprofit educational and cultural resource for members and the public.
National Fashion Accessory Association (NFAA) and the Fashion Accessory Shippers Association (FASA) www.accessoryweb.com	New York, NY	To represent all accessories categories, including watches.

of World War II timepieces and chronometers. To commemorate the 50th anniversary of the attack on Pearl Harbor and the release of the film, Hamilton launched a Hack watch, in a style similar to the original 1940s watch.

Store Retailing

Merchandisers realize the power of numbers and location when trying to make a brand impact in the stores. Usually, watches are merchandised by brands rather than by function, materials, or price points. Within each brand, the watches may be subdivided by function, such as sport, casual, and dressy. Watch brands with the best sell-through are often featured near a main

TABLE 15.4

Trade Publications for the Watch Industry

Trade Publication Name	Description
Accessories Magazine	Monthly trade publication; covers most accessory classifications, including watches.
American Time	Monthly trade publication; covers current events at the manufacturing and retail level.
Clocks Magazine	Monthly publication for collectors and restorers of watches and clocks.
Horological Times	Monthly trade publication published by the AWI; contains manufacturing and technical trade information.
Illustrated Professional Dictionary of Horology/Berner Watch Dictionary	Contains thousands of horological terms in four languages.
International Wrist Watch	Offers newsworthy current events and trade information on higher-end watches.
Women's Wear Daily – Monday	Weekly issue of a trade newspaper, published by Fairchild; features business and fashion information on watches, as well as other accessories.
WWD Accessory Supplement	Fairchild special edition featuring fashion information on all accessories, including watches.

entrance and in other 100-percent traffic areas. At the Bloomingdale's store in Manhattan, a fashion-watch bay is located at one of the street-level entrances.

Manufacturers of moderate- and lower-priced watches may offer retailers freestanding kiosks made especially to house, stock, and display the watches. These in-store merchandising displays,

TABLE 15.5

Trade Shows for the Watch Industry

Trade Show	Location	Sponsor
Accessorie Circuit	New York, NY	ENK International
AccessoriesTheShow	New York, NY	Business Journals, Inc.
Annual Clock and Watch Show	UK	British Horological Institute
Baselworld—The Watch and Jewellery Show	Basel, Switzerland	MCH Basel Global Exhibitions, Ltd.
International Watch and Jewelry Guild Shows	Cities across the U.S. (New Orleans, New York, Detroit, Dallas, Miami, Orlando, Las Vegas)	International Watch and Jewelry Guild
Salon International de la Haute Horlogerie (SIHH)	Geneva, Switzerland	Comité International de la Haute Horlogerie

called **point-of-purchase (POP)** display fixtures, have eye-catching graphics to stop passers by and encourage a closer look at the product. Manufacturer-provided point-of-purchase displays encourage customers to make an impulse purchase and encourage retail store buyers to write larger orders, since inventory management is simplified for the store personnel.

The opening of watch-specialty chains is another factor contributing to increased sales of watches. Stores such as Movado, Fossil, Swatch, Watch Station and Watch World (both divisions of Sunglass Hut), and Tourneau offer a wide selection of timepieces for all occasions. Tiffany & Company made the decision to stop selling the brand through independent jewelry stores, instead selling exclusively through their Internet web site and their own Tiffany & Company retail outlets.

Internet Retailing

Many brands of watches are easily purchased online. The NPD Group reported in November 2000 that Internet sales accounted for less than five percent of all accessories sales, and most of the purchasers were baby boomers.

The downside to this method of retailing is the difficulty consumers have obtaining repairs should any mechanical defects occur during the warranty period. In anticipation of this hindrance to Internet sales, companies are forming alliances with brick-and-mortar retailers. Some Internet watch companies form partnerships with independent watch retailers, calling them **affiliate retailers.** These jewelers are authorized to make repairs, clean, and appraise the Internet purchase. The potential for buyer's regret is minimized because consumers can obtain face-to-face help if needed.

Brand building is an important Internet trend among watch companies. A few of the top manufacturers, such as Seiko, Rolex, and Citizen have created informational Web sites showcasing their brands, but refrain from selling them. However, more than half of Fairchild's Top Ten most recognized watch brands sell from their Internet Web sites. Brick-and-mortar retailers are concerned that manufacturers may find Internet selling too appealing and directly compete with the stores.

Some watch companies fear their brand image may be suffering because of the Internet, while other companies feel Internet sales are boosting their brand identity. A trade magazine, *Travel Retailer International,* contacted several luxury brand manufacturers, including Breitling, Cartier, Raymond Weil, Rolex, Gucci, and Chopard. These companies were concerned about product sales by unauthorized online dealers. They felt the level of service and the clarity of online visuals were not satisfactory. These companies did not authorize any selling of their brands through the Internet, even though some unauthorized retailers have been identified as selling the luxury brands on the Internet.

Although a photograph may never equal holding a watch in the hands, the visual component of the Internet is rapidly improving. Patek Philippe's Web site allows customers to rotate and open the Star Caliber 2000 watch by accessing a series of still photograph frames in rapid succession. Fossil's Web site offers cybershoppers 3-D technology to help them view the merchandise more easily. Consumers can enlarge items on the Web site, activate the movements of the timepiece, or work the wristwatch clasp.

Some manufacturers believe Internet sales will help boost brand identity of moderately priced watches, but not necessarily of the higher-priced styles. The more sophisticated styles are sold at brick-and-mortar stores. Face-to-face interaction for selling higher-priced watches is considered an important part of the selling process that cannot be replaced by technology.

Catalog Retailing

Fashion watches may be featured in catalogs because of the impulse-purchase qualities of lower- and middle-priced accessories. Usually, because of space constraints, only a few styles are available through catalogs. The featured styles may be adaptations of proven sellers. It is common for catalog retailers to show the same watch multiple times throughout the catalog as accessories on the clothing models.

Sunglass Hut, Watch World, and Watch Station customers received 2001 catalogs featuring watches. An estimated 8 to 10 million current customers received at least one issue in the mail during the year. About one million copies of each of 10 to 12 catalogs were printed and mailed to customers. The purpose of the catalogs was two-fold—to sell via direct mail and to encourage catalog recipients to visit their nearest retail stores.

SELLING WATCHES

Watch retailers should have the customer try on several watches before making a selection. Most customers have some idea of the type of watch they are considering, even before they go shopping. Important considerations include brand preference, budget, lifestyle, fashion taste, and body size.

When giving watches as gifts, buyers often prefer popular brands because they may lack confidence in selecting a style for the wearer. Although purchasers cannot always be exactly sure what style will look best on the wearers, they can at least feel confident in their brand selection. Because watches can be quite costly, retailers should direct customers to watches that are in an acceptable price range for the buyers. A common selling technique is to show mid-range prices first, and then let the customer direct the salesperson to higher or lower price ranges.

Price and Value

According to the 1995 and 1996 *Gentlemen's Quarterly* jewelry and watch surveys of the magazine's subscribers, a major trend in men's accessories has been an increase in the number of male self-purchase shoppers. Respondents to the study were generally more style-savvy and affluent; they owned an average of five watches. When purchasing watches for themselves, these men ranked prestige and image of the watch company as more important than the price of the watch. They also ranked watch style/design, quality/craftsmanship, and value as important when purchasing any watch or jewelry. Less important purchase criteria were family's/friends' recommendations, magazine articles and advertising, and salespeople recommendations.

A 1999 study asked respondents to divide their watch purchases (over $100) by price range. The following ranges were used to group the responses: $100–$299, $300–$499, $500–$999, and $1000+. Table 15.6 shows the data from the survey, with most respondents spending in the $100–$299 price range. Interestingly, one third of the consumers surveyed spent over $500 for their watches.

Care of Watches

Mechanical and automatic watches should be cleaned and serviced every three years. Replace batteries in automatic watches as needed. Foreign objects, such as dirt particles, may enter the watchcase, causing watches to stop timekeeping. Because of the working movements, water and sudden impacts may damage watches. Manufacturers have created water-resistant and shock-resistant watches, especially in their sports lines. Manufacturers make screw-down bezels for watches that will be subjected to excessive perspiration, showering, and swimming to ensure a watertight watch.

Divers' watches should be water resistant to a minimum depth of 330 feet. Water-resistant seals should be changed annually and the depth resistance checked using the manufacturer's pressure equipment.

Watch manufacturers use metals that do not rust and can be wiped clean with a damp cloth as needed. Sterling silver will tarnish unless coated with a layer of a nontarnishing metal, such as iridium. Karat-gold watches employ a relatively soft metal that may scratch during physical activity. Gold is usually reserved for dressier watches and pocket watches that are not subject to excessive wear and tear. Although many metals are resistant to chemicals, regular exposure to chemicals, such as chlorine or seawater, may damage straps and plated cases.

TABLE 15.6

Consumer Spending on Watches over $100 in 1999

Price Range	Percent of Consumers
$100–$299	45%
$300–$499	22%
$500–$999	18%
$1000+	15%

What motivates Americans to buy jewelry and watches: Part 3 of 4. (1999, November). *Jewelers' Circular Keystone, CLXX* (11), 108.

Meeting Customer Needs

Like athletic shoes, the functional watch is quite diverse and able to meet the very specialized needs of the user. In addition to function, the purchase motives of customers include durability, adaptability, fashion, and status.

Many consumers engage in active sports and desire watches that can withstand physical abuse and exposure to the elements. These consumers prefer metal watchbands that won't absorb perspiration or water. Titanium-metal watches are extremely lightweight and will not corrode in salt water. Watches that can withstand water to a depth of several hundred feet are suitable for showering, swimming, and diving. Chronograph functions allow athletes to rate their speed.

Watchmakers are using technology to create multifunctional wristwatch products for data management, making life less (or more?) complicated. Built-in microprocessors, cameras, global positioners, time-zone indicators, calendars, alarms, lighted dials, and beepers are available for techno-savvy consumers.

Some consumers prefer fashion over function and are satisfied with attractive watch faces, bezels, and bands. Manufacturers provide these markets with colorful dials and bands, gem-encrusted or decorative bezels, and bracelet bands. In the 1980s, Swatch began an enormously successful marketing campaign to sell youthful and colorful plastic fashion watches with interchangeable components.

Status-conscious consumers may desire function and fashion, but they also prefer recognizable name brands like Bulgari, Cartier, Gucci, and Rolex. Like other buyers of luxury goods, purchasers of status watches appreciate being recognized for their elevated taste level, and admiration of technical perfection and material integrity, not to mention their, *sizable expenditure* for the watch (see Figure 15.10).

FIGURE 15.10
A Cartier watch.
Courtesy of Fairchild Publications, Inc.

SUMMARY

- Horology is the study of time, timekeeping, and timekeepers.
- Portable timepieces evolved during the 15th century in Europe.
- Crafters' guilds developed in Europe to support clockmakers and ensure quality standards.
- Many of the early manufacturers were cottage industries.
- In the United States, watch factories were established on the East Coast.
- Machine-made, interchangeable parts assembled on production lines helped decrease the cost of watches.
- Finely crafted mechanical watches were believed to be the ultimate timekeeping devices, until quartz watches were introduced in the 1970s.
- Swiss manufacturers, who failed to buy into the quartz concept, lost significant market share.
- The last decades of the 20th century resulted in extremely high-tech watches.
- Watches may be classified as fashion, bridge, and fine.
- Watch parts include a case, dial, crystal, bezel, hands, crown or stem, and mainspring.
- Watch functions include analog, digital, automatic, mechanical, quartz, jewels, chronograph, and tachymeter.
- Watch materials include the popular stainless-steel and the lightweight titanium and aluminum elements, as well as karat gold or plated gold and sterling silver.
- Watchbands are made of the aforementioned metals, or leather, vinyl, rubber, plastic, or nylon.
- Large manufacturing companies produce many of the watch brands under licensing agreements or as joint ventures between two companies.
- Children's watches are often theme related, featuring licensed characters, that appeal to children.
- High-end watch producers once catered primarily to male purchasers, but this trend is changing. Companies are finding the female self-purchaser an important target customer.
- Most watches should be cleaned and serviced by professionals. Water-resistant watches require regular seal replacements and pressure checks. Many popular watch materials are rust and tarnish resistant, like stainless steel.
- The trend in watch buying is to buy multiple watches, creating a watch wardrobe.
- Watch purchases range from just a few dollars to thousands of dollars. Consumers are willing to spend significant amounts of money on their watches.
- Important and recognizable watch brands include Timex, Rolex, Seiko, and Citizen watches. A source of problems for many of the popular and luxury-brand manufacturers

is counterfeited merchandise that has been imported into the United States. Many of these fake brands are virtually impossible to distinguish from the authentic watches.

■ Watches may be an impulse purchase or a planned purchase.

■ Watches are usually merchandised first by brand and second by lifestyle.

■ The Internet is a popular retail outlet for watches and men's jewelry. Companies use their Web sites for brand building or to compete with brick-and-mortar stores.

■ Viewing of fine details and access to repair services are two things lacking on Web sites.

■ Catalog retailing is a well-used medium for selling watches and men's jewelry. Like the Internet, catalogs may be used to sell these accessories, or they may be used to refer interested shoppers to the nearest store.

■ Advertising campaigns are designed to reinforce the brand image or reach new target markets.

■ Limited-line specialty stores have become important avenues for retailing watches. Movado, Fossil, Swatch, Tourneau, Watch Station, and Watch World are company-owned stores selling watches.

■ To some consumers, watch-purchase decisions are based on criteria other than price. These include the company image and prestige, watch style and design, quality and craftsmanship, value, durability, and adaptability. Consumers who are price-conscious prefer visible price tags in retail stores.

■ Active-sports enthusiasts require lightweight and moisture-resistant watches. Multi-function watches may be designed with chronographs, data-management capabilities, alarms, calendars, cameras, telephones, and other technological devices.

■ Fashion enthusiasts may prefer colorful and interchangeable watch faces, bezels, and bands. Status-conscious consumers may choose expensive metals and gemstones, as well as recognizable brands.

TERMS FOR REVIEW

affiliate retailers	digital	point of purchase (POP)
analog	dollar watches	quartz
atomic precision	Geneva Seal	ring watch
automatic	hands	tachymeter
bezel	horology	telememo watch
bracelet watch	jewel	thermic watch
brand building	LCD (liquid crystal display)	watch chain
chatelaine	LED (light-emitting diode)	watch fob
chronograph	mainspring	watch wardrobing
crown (stem)	mechanical	watchcase
crystal	necklace watch	wristwatch
dial	pocket watch	

REVIEW QUESTIONS

1. What are some of the major developments in the watch industry?
2. In 19th- and 20th-century America, men have worn primarily functional jewelry. Why is this so, and what social changes have improved men's acceptance of wearing jewelry?
3. What are the main parts of a watch? What is the difference between analog and digital watches?
4. What are some of the movements used in watches?
5. What factors might affect a consumer's choice of watch and watchband materials? Why?
6. Explain the terms *watch wardrobing* and *brand building*.
7. Besides price, what are some consumer purchase motivations when buying watches?
8. How are watch manufacturers building brand awareness?
9. What are some marketing and merchandising tactics used by stores to improve the sales of watches and men's jewelry?
10. What are some of the advantages and disadvantages of the Internet and catalog retailing as selling tools?

KNOWLEDGE APPLICATIONS

1. Take a virtual tour of the National Watch and Clock Museum in Columbia, Pennsylvania, at *www.nawcc.org/Library/library.htm*.
2. Locate at least three watch advertisements in a fashion magazine. Evaluate the advertisements on the following criteria: target customer, fashion image, estimated price range, watch features, and material used. Compare your findings with other students in the class.
3. Arrange an interview with a watch buyer. Develop a list of ten questions in advance of the visit regarding merchandising issues, such as display techniques, pricing and markup, promotions, and fashion trends. Type a summary and critique of the interview.
4. Choose a particular manufacturer of watches. Research the company/designer (past, present, and future issues) and report your findings. You may want to develop a pictorial timeline and other creative visual aids.
5. As a class, design a mini research project involving students on campus. Poll at least 200 watch wearers to determine important brands and purchase motivations. Conduct the survey, compile the data, record the results, and develop the conclusions.

BIBLIOGRAPHY

A to Z dictionary. (2001). *Infoplease.com*. Retrieved June 20, 2001, from http://www.infoplease.com/ipd/

About Enjewel. (1999–2000). Enjewel. Retrieved October 13, 2000, from http://www.enjewel.com

About Indian jewelry. (2000). *Rocking Horse Ranch*. Retrieved June 20, 2001, from http://www. indianjewelry.com/aboutindianjewelry.cfm

About Pashmina. (n.d.) Retrieved April 1, 2001, from http://www.spencerspashmina.com/ aboutpashmina.html

About your Tiffany gemstone & pearl jewelry. (1998). *Tiffany & Company*. Retrieved June 1, 2001, from www.tiffany.com

Accessory Report: Coventry's Comeback. (2002, July 15). *Women's Wear Daily, 184*(10), p. 17.

Agins, T. (1999, November 23). Forget the clothes– fashion fortunes turn on heels and purses. *Wall Street Journal*, p. A1, A14.

All about gems. (n.d.). Arnold J. Silverberg (AJS) Gems. Retrieved May 3, 2001, from http://www.ajsgems.com/about-gems.htm

All about jewels: Illustrated dictionary of jewelry. (1999). *All about jewels glossary*. Retrieved November 3, 1999, from http://www.allaboutjewels. com/jewel/glossary

All that glitters: How to buy jewelry. (2001, March). *Federal Trade Commission*. Retrieved May 15, 2001, from http://www.ftc.gov/bcp/conline/pubs/ products/jewelry.htm

Allison, L. (n.d.). *Making Ties*. Retrieved April 17, 2001, from http://www.leeallison.com

American Airlines announces restrictions on baggage size. (1999, November 17). *Dallas Morning News*.

Anderson, J. F. (2000, January 30). *The best road to success*. Retrieved December 17, 2002, from http://www.thegavel.net/Maylead2.html

Arney, E. B. (2001, January). Gold. *U.S. Geological Survey, Mineral Commodity Summaries, 49–52, 71*. Retrieved May 7, 2001, from http://minerals.usgs. gov/minerals/pubs/commodity/gold/300798.pdf

Askin, E. (2001, January 5). Neckwear weathers a bumpy ride. *Daily News Record, 31*(3), p. 4.

Askin E. (2001, January 14). Nursing neckwear. *Daily News Record, 32*(2), p. 20.

Askin, E. (2001, June 4). Wanna buy a tie? *Daily News Record, 31*(60), p. 18.

Athens hints at further branded fashion areas. (2001, March 1). *Duty-Free News International, 15*(4), p. 11.

Atmore, M. (ed.). (1999). *FN Century: 100 Years of Footwear*. New York, NY: Fairchild.

Atmore, M. (1999, February 4). Connecting the dot-coms. *Footwear News, 56*(6), 14.

Attleboro. (2001). *Encyclopedia Britannica online*. Retrieved June 19, 2001, from http://www. britannica.com/eb/print?eu=11309

Audits and surveys worldwide. (2000). *U.S. sales of primary value gold jewelry*. World Gold Council. Email correspondence, May 25, 2001, John Calnon, World Gold Council, New York.

Bannerot, R. (n.d.). Gold fashioned girls. *World Gold Council*. Retrieved May 24, 2001, from http://www.gold.org/Gra/Pr/GFGirlsCam.htm

Barkow, A. (1998, April 30). Double-canopy umbrella has aversion to inversion. *The New York Times, 147*, p. C5(L), col. 3.

Barth, B. (2000, April 26). Head to toe customization on the Web. *Women's Wear Daily, 179*(81), p. 12.

Before this century: Great moments in shoe history. (2000). Retrieved April 28, 2000, from http://www.centuryinshoes.com/before/before.html

Beirne, M. (1999, September 27). Samsonite's strong suit. *Brandweek, 40* (36), 20.

Bernard, S. (1999, February 4).Webbed feet. *Footwear News, 56*(6) 34.

Behind the seams events. (n.d.). *Sewn Products Equipment & Suppliers of the Americas.* Retrieved September 4, 2001, from http://www.behind-the-seams.com/events.htm

Bio: Manolo Blahnik-the master. (1999). *Focus on fashion.* Retrieved November 12, 1999, from http://www.focusonfashion.com/footwear/blahnik.html

Birthstone chart. (n.d.). *International Gem Society.* Retrieved April 20, 2001, from http://www.gemsociety.org/info/chbstones.htm

Bittar, C. (2000, October 16). Waterford goes lux in leather, jewelry, per "lifestyle" push. *Brandweek XLI*(40), 13.

The Black Cameo. (n.d.). *The Black Cameo.* Retrieved June 20, 2001, from http://www.theblackcameo.com

Boehlert, B. Sole trained. (1999). *World of Style,* Hearst Corporation. Retrieved December 15, 2000, from Homearts.com/depts/style

Bold, K. (1996, October 31). The Cachet's in the bag. *Los Angeles Times, Orange County Edition,* p. 1.

Braunstein, P. (2001, January 22). Weaving a net of gems. *Women's Wear Daily, 181*(14), p. 32.

Brockman, E. S. (2000, March 5). A woman's power tool: High heels. *The New York Times.* p. 2.

Brodsky, R. (2000, February 11). New York men's shows take it to the neck. *Daily News Record,* p. 82.

Brodsky, R. (2000, March 3). Bright days ahead for new sunwear brands. *Daily News Record, 30*(2), p. 5.

Brodsky, R. (2000, March 3). Hermès ties: hard to resist, now harder to find. *Accessories for Men Supplement, Daily News Record, 30*(2), p. 4.

Brooks, D. (2001, April 29). The machine age: High-end watches. *New York Times on the Web.* Retrieved May 1, 2001, from http://www.nytimes.com

Bukowski, E. (1999, May 7). Under palm trees, sunny skies, the fur flies. *The Wall Street Journal,* p. W15.

Bruns, R. (1988, December). Of miracles and molecules: the story of nylon. *American History Illustrated, 23*(8), 24-29, 48.

Bruton, E. (1982). *The history of clocks and watches.* New York, NY: Crescent Books.

Buss, D. (1999, November). Teen nation. *Brandmarketing, VI*(1), 16, 18, 21.

Buying gold and gemstone jewelry: The heart of the matter. (2001, January). *Federal Trade Commission.* Retrieved May 15, 2001, from http://www.ftc.gov/bcp/conline/pubs/alerts/goldalrt.htm

Buying guide to sport specific socks. (1997). Acrylic Council, Inc. Retrieved November 15 2002, from http://www.fabriclink.com/acryliccouncil/SOCK/Home.html

Byron, J. (2000). Footwear, leather, and leather products. *U.S. industry and trade outlook 2000.* U.S. Department of Commerce/International Trade Administration. Washington D.C.: McGraw-Hill.

Calasibetta, C. & Tortora, P. (2003). *The Fairchild dictionary of fashion.* New York, NY: Fairchild.

Can gold polish up its tarnished image? (2000, December 12). *Marketing Week,* 15. Retrieved May 7, 2001, from http://newfirstsearch.oclc.org/WebZ/FSP...8523-cmglmikc-5mwo82:entitypagenum=33:0

Canedy, D. (1999, September 7). Advertising. *The New York Times,* p. C11.

Carmichael, C. (1999, July 19). Ticking away. *Footwear News, 55*(29), 25.

Carr, D. (1999, July 19). Get smart. *Footwear News, 55*(29), pp. 18–19.

Carr, D. (2000, February 4). Salt Lake City outdoor show mirrors all-season growth. *Footwear News 56*(6), p.4.

Carr, K. (2000, October). Showing off. *Women's Wear Daily Accessories Supplement,* 6.

Charting the stars. (2000, October). *Women's Wear Daily Accessories Supplement,* 40, 42.

Chen, J. (2000, August). Bag lady. *Women's Wear Daily Accessories Supplement,* 6.

Chen, J. (2000, August 14). Classic action. *Women's Wear Daily, 180*(29), p. 6.

Choosing fur: A consumer's guide to selecting and caring for a new fur. (n.d.). *Fur Council of Canada and Fur Information Council of America.*

Claire's creates teen center. (2000, August 14). *Drug Store News, 22*(11), 48.

Clark, D. (n.d.). Gem cutting terms. *International Gem Society*. Retrieved April 20, 2001, from http://www.gemsociety.org/info/igem6.htm

Clark, D. (n.d.). Hardness and wearability. *International Gem Society*. Retrieved April 20, 2001, from http://www.gemsociety.org/info/igem6.htm

Clark, D. (n.d.). What is a gem? *International Gem Society*. Retrieved April 20, 2001, from http://www.gemsociety.org/info/igem2.htm

Clocks and watches. (2001). *Microsoft Encarta Online Encyclopedia*. Retrieved July 18, 2001, from http://www.encarta.com

Clutton, C. & Daniels, G. (1979). *Watches: A complete history*. Totowa, NJ: P. Wilson.

Collier, B., & Tortora, P. (2001). *Understanding textiles*. Upper Saddle River, NJ: Prentice-Hall.

Collins, C. C. (1945). *Love of a glove*. New York, NY: Fairchild.

Colored gemstones. (1999). *Gleim Jewelers*. Retrieved May 3, 2001, from http://www.gleimjewelers.com/glmgems.htm

The colors of 2000: Forecasters predict a blue year. (1999, March 1). *Catalog Age, 16*(3), 10.

Colavita, C. (2000, December 11). New ideas at hosiery workshop. *Women's Wear Daily, 180*(109), p. 9

Colavita, C. & Seckler, V. (2001, January 23). Sunglass Hut Web site to sell Armani watches. *Women's Wear Daily, 181*(15), p. 2.

Company in the *Muskogee Phoenix & Times Democrat,* p. C-2.

Conaway, F. (2000, January 31). The right fit. *Footwear News, 56*(5), p. 100.

Cooper, N. (1999, August). Index early word. *Vogue,* 189, 266.

Cory, N. (2000, August). Erin Brockovich and chromium. *Leather Industries of America*. Retrieved Dec 15, 2000, from www.leather-usa.com/LABA5.html

Cotton Incorporated Spring/Summer 2002 color card. (n.d.). *Cotton Incorporated,* New York, NY.

Cross merchandising: What to buy, how to dress. (2000, April 24). *Women's Wear Daily Advertising Supplement, Accessor-Ease,* p. 34.

Cumming, V. (1982). *Gloves*. London, England: B.T. Batsford.

Curan, C. (1999, August 9). Retail gets dolled up. *Crain's New York Business,* p. 3.

Current highlights. (1999). *ShoeStats*. Footwear Industries of America. Retrieved April 30, 1999, from www.fia.org

Dang, K. (1995, June 26). CCC fine jewelry show debuts with by-invitation attendance. *Women's Wear Daily, 169*(122), p. 6.

Daniel, A. (1945, January 21). Inside story of a handbag. *The New York Times*.

Daswani, K. (2001, August 27). The new new thing. *Women's Wear Daily, 182*(40), p. 20.

Davenport, M. (1948). *The book of costume*. New York, NY: Crown Publishers.

Debnam, B. (1999, July 26). Gems and minerals. The Mini Page Publishing.

Del Franco, M. (2001, March 15). Sunglass Hut watches its catalog business. *Catalog Age, 18*(4), 6.

Determine your glove size. (2000, October 31). *Sullivan Glove*. Retrieved June 22, 2000, from www.sullivanglove.com

Dewan, S. (2000, April 4). Last of a dying breed folds up shop. *The New York Times,* p. A18(N), B3(L), col. 2.

Diamond, J. & Diamond, E. (1994). *Fashion apparel and accessories*. Albany, NY: Delmar.

Diamond, J. S. (1999, November). What motivates Americans to buy jewelry and watches: Part 1 of 4. *Jewelers' Circular Keystone, CLXX* (11), 98.

Diamonds: Facts and fallacies. (1991). *The American Gem Society*. Los Angeles, CA.

Dickerson, K. (1995). *Textiles and apparel in the global economy*. Englewood Cliffs, NJ: Prentice-Hall.

Did you know Croats invented neck ties? (n.d.). *Neck Ties*. Retrieved February 21, 1997 from http://www.middlebury.edu/~otisg/Croatia/ties.html

DiMartino, C. (2001, August). Winning strategies: Danner aims high with systems integration. *Bobbin Magazine*. Retrieved September 4, 2001, from http://www.bobbin.com/BOBBINGROUP/BOBBINMAG/aug01/winning0801

Dodd, A. (2000, April 7). Clothing consultation addresses the variable dress code. *Daily News Record, 30*(42), p. 16.

Doublet, D. (1991, December). Australia's magnificent pearls. *National Geographic, 180*(6), 108–123.

Dressier casual socks sell. (2002, September 23). *DSN Retailing Today, 41*(18), p. A14.

Dressing for sock-cess. (1996). *MBA Style.* Retrieved February 9, 2001, from http://members.aol.com/mbastyle/web/socks.html

Drewry, R. D. (2001). What man devised that he might see. *History of eyeglasses.* Retrieved June 22, 2002, from http://www.eye.utmem.edu/history/glass.html

Dun's market identifiers online. (1999, December 27). Dun and Bradstreet.

Dun's market identifiers, SIC 3171. (2000, August 18). Dun and Bradstreet.

e-diamonds.com. (2000, October 6). *Wall Street Journal, CCXXXVI*(68), p. A2.

Ellis, B. E. (1921). *Gloves and the glove trade.* London, England: Pitman & Sons.

Ellis, K. (2000, April 24). Partners Prada, De Rigo, launch sunglass line. *Women's Wear Daily, 179*(79), p. 11.

Ellis, K. (2001, February 13). Gargoyles retools executive team. *Women's Wear Daily, 181*(30), p. 23.

Enjewel advisor glossary of terms. (1999–2000). Enjewel. Retrieved October 13, 2000, from http://www.enjewel.com

Ewing, E. (1981). *Fur in dress.* London, England: B.T. Batsford.

Eye on Paris. (2000, July 24). *Women's Wear Daily, 180*(14), p. 8.

Fabric University. (2000). FabricLink. Retrieved August 31, 2000, from www.fabriclink.com

Facts about fur. (2000, July 6). *Fur Commission USA.* Retrieved December 15, 2000, from http://www.furcommission.com/resource/FAF.html

The Fairchild 100: Watches/jewelry. (2000, January). *Women's Wear Daily Special Report, 114,* 116.

Findings. (2001, July 16). *Women's Wear Daily, 182*(10), p. 7.

Findings: Potter mania. (2000, August 7). *Women's Wear Daily, 180*(24), p. 17.

Fallon, J. (2001, January 17). Diamonds: LVMH's new best friend. *Women's Wear Daily, 181*(11), p. 14.

Fashion traction. (2002, February 24). *The New York Times,* p. 3., Section 9.

Fashion vs. fine. (1994, October 17). *Discount Store News, 33*(20), A30.

FAST at Verona. (2000, March 14). Retrieved February 9, 2001, from http://fast-italy.com/eng/stampa/maroo.html

FAST Fair. (1999, March 3). Retrieved February 9, 2001, from http://fast-italy.com/eng/stampa/maroo.html

Feitelberg, R. (2000, January). An industry reinvents itself: The Fairchild 100. Legwear *Women's Wear Daily,* 98, 100.

Feitelberg, R. (2000, February 14 a). Ridgeview readies reve avoix leg-highs. *Women's Wear Daily, 179*(30), p. 18.

Feitelberg, R. (2000. February14 b). Gazelle.com: All about legs. *Women's Wear Daily, 179*(30), p. 19.

Feitelberg, R. (2000, May 15 a). New lines liven market. *Women's Wear Daily, 179*(94), p. 22.

Feitelberg, R. (2000, May 15 b). Longstockings' encore. *Women's Wear Daily, 179*(94), p. 23.

Feitelberg, R. (2000, June 19). It's about time, say makers. *Women's Wear Daily, 179*(118), p. 17.

Feitelberg, R. (2000, July 10). Vendors ready for Fall turnaround time. *Women's Wear Daily, 180*(4), pp. 15, 27.

Feitelberg, R. (2000, July 17). Giving socks power. *Women's Wear Daily, 180*(9), p. 10.

Feitelberg, R. & Karimzadeh, M. (2000, August 7 a). Brights and 'burbs light up spring. *Women's Wear Daily, 180*(24), p. 18.

Feitelberg, R. & Karimzadeh, M. (2000, August 7 b). Bold prints and colors brighten spring. *Women's Wear Daily, 180*(24), p. 20.

Field, L. (1992). *The jewels of Queen Elizabeth II: Her personal collection.* New York, NY: Harry N. Abrams.

First offering of nylon hosiery sold out. (1939, October 25). *The New York Times,* p. 1.

Flusser, A. (n.d.). Neckwear. Retrieved Mar. 22, 2001 from http://www.fashionmall.com/flusser_book/doc/ch4.htm

Flusser, A. (1985). *Clothes and the man.* New York, NY: Villard Books.

Flusser, A. (1996). *Style and the man.* New York, NY: HarperStyle.

Foiled again. (2000, July 24). *Women's Wear Daily, 180*(14), pp. 6–7.

Foley, B. (2000, June 22). Tom gets ready. *Women's Wear Daily, 179*(121), p. 6+.

Fossil quarterly report for the first quarter 2002. U.S. Securities and Exchange Commission Form 10-Q. Retrieved July 7, 2002, from www.fossil.com/CompanyInfo/Financials

Fossil acquires the Avia Watch Company. (2001, May 21). New York, NY: PR Newswire wirefeed. UMI Article Re. No: PRN-3477-448.

Fossil and Seiko Instruments announce joint venture in Japan. (2001, June 28). New York, NY: PR Newswire wirefeed. UMI Article Re. No: PRN-3515-380.

Fossil company information. (2000). Retrieved July 28, 2001, from http://www.fossil.com/CompanyInfo

Fossil, Inc. notice of specialty retail conference Webcast. (2001, July 5.) New York, NY: PR Newswire wirefeed. UMI Article Re. No: PRN-3522-135.

Fossil partners with teen sensation, O-Town. (2001, April 12). New York, NY: PR Newswire wirefeed. UMI Article Re. No: PRN-3438-40

Foster, V. (1985). *Bags and purses.* New York, NY: Drama Books.

Framing America: Eyewear dos and don'ts. *Vision Council of America.* Retrieved Feb. 9, 2001, from http://www.visionsite.org/frame/dodont.htm

Frings, G. (1999). *Fashion: From concept to consumer.* Upper Saddle River, NJ: Prentice Hall.

FT900 report (CB-99-202). (1999, August). Bureau of the Census, Foreign Trade Division. Retrieved September 5, 1999, from www.census.gov/foreign-trade/Press-Release/current_press_release/exh15.txt

Fur care. (2000, February 25). *Fur Information Council of America.* Retrieved December 15, 2000, from http://www.fur.org/retcare.html

Fur facts. (2000, February 25). *Fur Information Council of America.* Retrieved December 15, 2000, from http://www.fur.org/edmat.html

Fur farming in North America. (n.d.). *Fur Farm Animal Welfare Coalition, Ltd.,* St. Paul, MN.

The fur industry history. (2000, July 12). *Fur Council of Canada.* Retrieved December 15, 2000, from www.furcouncil.ca.

Fur industry in America. (1998, April 2). *Fur Information Council of America.* Retrieved December 15, 2000, from http://www/fur.org/furind.html

GQ reveals truth: Men shop too. (1997, April). *Jewelers' Circular Keystone,* 37.

Gardening gloves. (1999, July 26). *Discount Store News, 38*(14), p. 47+.

Gault, Y. (1990, July 30). Tying into a market: new entrants expand neckwear. *Crain's New York Business, 6*(31), p. 1.

Gem care and handling. (1996). *International Colored Gemstone Association (ICA).* Retrieved March 19, 1997, from http://www.gemstone.org/care.html

Gems for Evert. (1995, July 24). *Women's Wear Daily, 170*(14), p. 16.

Gems of the rich and famous. (n.d.). International Colored Gemstone Association (ICA). Retrieved May 3, 2001, from http://gemstone.org/gem-o-rama/_famous.html

Glossary of terms. (n.d.). Majesty gloves. Retrieved October 31, 2000, from www.majglove.com/glossary_index.htm

Glossary of terms. (2001). Federation of the Swiss Watch Industry FH. Retrieved July 16, 2001, from http://www.fhs.ch

Glove glossary. (2000). *Sullivan glove.* Retrieved October 31, 2000, from www.Sullivanglove.com

Glove talk. (2000). *Gates gloves.* Retrieved October 26, 2000 from www.gatesgloves.com

Gloversville history. (2000). *Masonic Lodge #429.* Retrieved October 26, 2000, from www.telenet.net/commercial/masonic/Glover.html

Gloves add dimension to weather protection. (1999, August 16). *Chain Drug Review, 21*(13), p. 80.

Gold, A. (1975). *75 Years of Fashion.* New York, NY: Fairchild.

Gold recovers in '99. (1999, October 21). *Monthly investment review in standard & poors industry surveys, Vol. 3, M-Z,* 1, 8.

Goldberg, D. (1998). Crazy about comfort. *Footwear+*. The Landau Group. Retrieved December 15, 1999, from www.shoesonthenet.com/septftwr+/upfront.html

Good Microsoft. Now heel; Thursday's appellate court ruling does nothing to lessen the need for controls on the software giant's unfair business practices. Editorial. (2001, June 29). *Los Angeles Times*, p. B16.

Gore-Tex: Guaranteed to keep you dry. (1990). *User's guide by W.L. Gore & Associates*. Elkton, MD.

Green, P. L. (1997, May 5). Footwear imports were flat in 1996. *The Journal of Commerce*, 6A–7A.

Greenwood, K. & Murphy, M. (1978). *Fashion innovation and marketing*. New York, NY: Macmillan.

Grossman, A. (1998, October 5). Retailer participation, fashion grow eyewear sales. *Drug Store News*, p. 30.

Guide to the fur industry: Fact vs. fiction. (1993). *Fur Information Council of America*.

Guides for select leather and imitation leather products. (n.d.). 16 C.F.R., Section 24. *Federal Trade Commission*, Retrieved August 31, 2001, from http://www.ftc.gov/os/statutes/textile/gd-leath.htm#24.0

Haber, H. (2000, October). Full color. *Women's Wear Daily Accessories Supplement*, 54.

Hackney, K. and Edkins, D. (2000). *People and pearls: The magic endures*. New York, NY: Harper Collins.

Hamilton co-stars in Touchstone Picture's Pearl Harbor. (2001). *International Wrist Watch*, (47), 10.

Handbag wisdom. (2000, February). *Accessories Magazine*. 30.

Harris, J. (1999, August). Other consumer durables: Jewelry. *U.S. industry & trade outlook 2000*. U.S. Department of Commerce/International Trade Administration. Washington, D.C.: McGraw-Hill.

Held in a tangled web. (2001, May). *Travel Retailer International*, 91.

Hernadez, D. (2001, June 23). Los Angeles: Keeping watch on watches pays off. *Los Angeles Times*, p. B5.

Hessen, W. (1994, August 22). Selling under the sun. *Women's Wear Daily, 168*(38), p. S7.

Hessen, W. (1995, April 24). The new rain dance. *Women's Wear Daily, 169*(78), p. S12.

Hessen, W. (1999, September 7). Eyewear firms shift focus. *Women's Wear Daily, 178*(47), p. 22.

Hessen, W. (1999). Coach has a new game plan. *Women's Wear Daily, 178*(65), p. 18.

Hessen, W. (2000, February 14). Repeat performance. *Women's Wear Daily, WWD/Magic, Section II*, p. 14.

Hessen, W. (2000, April 10). Rosy times continue for watches. *Women's Wear Daily*, pp. 14–15.

Hessen, W. (2000, July 10). Keeping a strong cycle going. *Women's Wear Daily, 180*(4), p. 14.

Hessen, W. (2000, September 18). Special recognition for the best accessorized television program. *Women's Wear Daily, 180*(53), p. 31.

Hessen, W. (2000, October 3). Enjewel to launch Web site. *Women's Wear Daily, 180*(64), p. 19.

Hessen, W. (2000, November 6). Tommy's two-tier take on time. *Women's Wear Daily, 180*(87), p. 17.

Hessen, W. (2001, January). No worries. *WWD/MAGIC Supplement*, 30.

Hessen, W. (2001, February 21). Fine jewelry and watches. *Women's Wear Daily Special Report: WWD Luxury*, p. 31.

Hessen, W. (2001, March 15). Tiffany's to refurbish flagship. *Women's Wear Daily, 181*(51), p. 3.

Hessen, W. (2001, May). What women want. *Women's Wear Daily Jewelry and Watches Fall 2001 Supplement*, pp. 14, 52.

Hessen, W. & Karimzadeh, M. (2000, November 6). Presentation lacks punch in hosiery. *Women's Wear Daily, 180*(87), p. 6.

Hessen, W. & Kletter, M. (2000, March 13). Scarfs, handbags get early fall focus. *Women's Wear Daily*, p. 17.

Hessen, W. & Ozzard, J. (2000, February 7). The status-bag game: U.S. designers still playing catch-up. *Women's Wear Daily, 179*(25), p. 1+.

Hessen, W. (2001, January 2). Let it snow, let it snow, let it snow. *Women's Wear Daily*, p. 22.

Hilliard, H. E. (n.d.). Platinum-group metals. *U.S. geological survey, mineral commodity summaries*, 99–108. Retrieved May 7, 2001, from http://minerals.usgs.gov/minerals/pubs/commodity/platinum/550798.pdf

Hilliard, H.E.. (n.d.). Silver. *U.S. geological survey, mineral commodity summaries,* 99–108. Retrieved May 7, 2001, from http://minerals.usgs.gov/ minerals/pubs/commodity/silver/880798.pdf

Hinchliffe, M.B. (2000, September). *Accessories Magazine,* 52.

History of the handbag. (1997). *National Fashion Accessory Association.* Retrieved September 9, 2000, from http://accessoryweb.com/history.html

The history of hosiery: a secret and sensual accessory. Retrieved June 7, 2002, from http://www. fast-italy.com

History of jewelry design. (2001). *Encyclopedia Britannica online.* Retrieved June 19, 2001, from http://www.britannica.com/eb/ article?eu=108954&tocid=14095

History of ties. (n.d.). Hermès- Ties. Retrieved March 20, 2001 from http://www.fpl.com/products/ hermes/ties_history.html.

Holiner, R. (1987). *Antique purses: A history, identification and value guide.* Paducah, KY: Collector Books.

Hollen, N., Saddler, J., Langford, A., & Kadolph, S. (1988). *Textiles.* New York, NY: Macmillan.

Holt, N. D. (1999, August 6). A place out of the sun. *The Wall Street Journal,* p. W4(W), W4(E), col.3.

Hong Kong travel goods and handbags industry. (2000). *Hong Kong Trade Development Council.* Retrieved September 9, 2000, from www.tdctrade.com

How big is the accessory market? (1999, April 19). *Women's Wear Daily Main Floor Magic Supplement,* p. 8.

How to buy a watch. (1999–2001). Blue Nile. Retrieved June 14, 2001, from http://www.bluenile.com/ watch_guide.asp?track'58

How to fold pocket squares. (2001). Retrieved March 22, 2001, from http://www.ties.net/foldinginfo.htm

How to sell accessories. (1991). *National Fashion Accessories Association, Inc.* New York, NY.

Hoyos, C. (2001, March 8). World news: Liberian diamonds embargo by UN. *Financial Times London Edition Financial Times,* p. 39.

If the shoe fits-online tour. (1999). De Young Museum, Fine Arts Museums of San Francisco. Retrieved December 15, 1999, from www.thinker. org/deyoung/exhibitions/shoe/index.html

Ilari, A. (2000, February). Look sharp. *Women's Wear Daily Italy Supplement,* p. 116.

Ilari, A. (2000, October 16). Notebook from Milan. *Women's Wear Daily, 180*(72), p. 18.

Ilari, A. (2002, June 3). Mido fair gives bright outlook for sunglasses. *Women's Wear Daily, 183*(109), p. 116.

Illes, J. (2001, August 1). Beauty secrets of ancient Egypt: Glass beads, "fabulous fakes" and the birth of costume jewelry. *Tour Egypt monthly: An online magazine, II*(8). Retrieved December 18, 2002, from http://www.egyptmonth.com/mag4.htm

In the loupe: Advertising diamonds, gemstones and pearls. (2000, January). *Federal Trade Commission.* Retrieved May 15, 2001, from http://www.ftc.gov/bcp/conline/pubs/buspubs/ loupe.htm

International Gem Society. (n.d.). Retrieved May 9, 2001, from http://gemsociety.org/info/info.htm

Isotoner history. (n.d.). Retrieved October 26, 2000, from www.isotoner.com

Isotoner materials guide. (n.d.). Retrieved October 27, 2000, from www.isotoner.com

Italian exports to China. (2002, April 6). *Textile & apparel: News from Italy.* Retrieved June 30, 2002, from http://www.fukui-iic.or.jp.kokusa/milano/ T&ANews/T&A7(E).htm

Ito, R. (1999, October). Lassie, go home. *Los Angeles, 44*(10), 28.

It's about time. (2000, July). *Magazine of Menswear Retailing, 11*(7), 102.

It's all in the accessories. (2000, July). *Magazine of Menswear Retailing, 11*(7), 96.

Iverson, A. (1997, July). Manolo Blahnik. *Harper's Bazaar,* 110.

Jack, J. (2000, November 6). Accessories go bold and beautiful. *WWD Advertising Supplement: The accessory industry speaks,* pp. 4–6, 8.

Jarnow, J. & Dickerson, K. (1997). *Inside the fashion business.* Upper Saddle River, NJ: Merrill.

Jewelry and gems. (1998). *Compton's on-line encyclopedia.* Retrieved May 3, 2001, from http://www.comptons.com/encyclopedia/ ARTICLES/0075/00962816_A.html

Johnson, M. & Moore, E. (2001). *Apparel product development.* Upper Saddle River, NJ: Prentice Hall.

Jones, R. A. (2000, August). Stone love. *Women's Wear Daily Accessories Supplement,* p. 44.

Joseph, M. (1988). *Essentials of textiles.* New York, NY: Holt, Rinehart & Winston.

Kapner, S. (2001, April 26). Oppenheimer family and partners raise offer for De Beers. *The New York Times.* Retrieved May 1, 2001, from www.nytimes.com

Karimzadeh, M. (2000, August). Growing pains. *Women's Wear Daily Accessories Supplement,* 20, 22.

Karimzadeh, M. (2000, August 28). In the bag. *Women's Wear Daily, 180*(39), pp. 48, 50.

Karimzadeh, M. (2000, September 11). FAE adopts a new name. *Women's Wear Daily,* p. 32.

Karimzadeh, M. (2000, September 18). Ace is high. *Women's Wear Daily, 180*(53), p. 30.

Karimzadeh, M. (2000, September 18). Growing the Euro niche. *Women's Wear Daily, 180*(53), p. 22.

Karimzadeh, M. (2000, October 30). Scarfs and bags boost Paris shows. *Women's Wear Daily,* p. 16.

Karimzadeh, M. (2000, November 6). Legwear made easy at H & M. *Women's Wear Daily, 180*(87), p. 7.

Karimzadeh, M. (2001, January). From Coco to cowgirl. *WWD/MAGIC Supplement,* 22, 29.

Karimzadeh, M. (2001, April 27). Jones Apparel Group acquires Judith Jack. *Women's Wear Daily, 181*(84), p. 2.

Karimzadeh, M. (2001, May). Shiny, happy people. *Women's Wear Daily Jewelry and Watches Fall 2001 Supplement,* p. 34.

Karimzadeh, M. (2001, June 4). Susan Lucci launches jewelry line on HSN. *Women's Wear Daily, 181*(111), p. 9.

Karimzadeh, M. (2002, June 3). Wolford's next step: individual nature. *Women's Wear Daily, 183*(109), p. 8.

Karimzadeh, M., & Kletter, M. (2002, July 15). Taking innovative steps for Fall. *Women's Wear Daily, 184*(10), p. 16.

Kaylin, L. (1987, July). The semiotics of the tie. *Gentleman's Quarterly, 57*(7), pp. 112, 115, 117.

Kazanjian, D. (1997, November). That touch of mink. *Vogue, 187,* 352–355.

Keshishian, J. M. (1979, June). Anatomy of a Burmese beauty secret. *National Geographic, 155*(6), 798–801.

King, S. (1999, December 11). Sisyphus of the sneaker makers. *The New York Times,* pp. C1, C4.

Kleeberg, I. C. (1975). *Butterick fabric handbook.* New York, NY: Butterick Publishing.

Kletter, M. (2000, January). A tale of time. *Women's Wear Daily Special Report: The Fairchild 100,* 114, 116.

Kletter, M. (2000, January). Bracelets, beads and brights. *Women's Wear Daily, WWD/Magic Supplement,* 26–27.

Kletter, M. (2000, February 14). Busting out. *Women's Wear Daily, WWDMagic/Junior Accessories,* p. 26.

Kletter, M. (2000, April 17). New views for eyewear. *Women's Wear Daily,* p. 13.

Kletter, M. (2001, October 4). Teen market shows red, white & blue. *Women's Wear Daily, 182*(65), p. 12.

Kletter, M. (2002, May 6). Makers putting on the glitz. *Women's Wear Daily, 183*(90), p. 18.

Knot Bad Choices. (1996). *MBA Style.* Retrieved Feb. 21, 1997, from http://members.aol.com/mbastyle/web/ties.html

Krall, S. (2000, December 1). The case for jewelry. *Gifts & Decorative Accessories, 101*(12), 179.

LVMH buys stake in De Rigo. (2000, December 28). *Women's Wear Daily, 180*(121), p. 2.

Lady avenger. (1997). *Women's Wear Daily, 174*(14), p. 1.

Latest gold news. (2001, April 20). *Kitco.* Retrieved April 20, 2001, from www.kitco.com.

Leather Apparel Association—about us. (2000, August 11). *Leather Apparel Association.* Retrieved December 15, 2000, from http://www.leatherassociation.com

Leather facts. (1994). Peabody, MA: New England Tanners Club.

Legwear report: Legbeat. (2000, August 28). *Women's Wear Daily, 180*(39), p. 23.

Lettich, J. (1993, November 1). Chains strike gold with fine jewelry. *Discount Store News, 32*(21), 34.

Light work. (1987). *Coreen Simpson.* Retrieved June 20, 2001, from http://www.lightwork.org/residency/simpson.html

Lockwood, L. (2001, April 17). Harry Winston taps new marketing firm. *Women's Wear Daily, 181*(76), p. 8.

Lombardy, D. (ed). (2000). *Ulrich's international period- icals directory 2000.* New Providence, NJ: R.R. Bowker.

Lorusso, M. (2000, March 6). New Cole Haan lifestyle line injected with Nike technology. *Footwear News, 56* (10), pp. 2, 31.

Major shippers report: cotton handkerchiefs. (2002, May 16). Office of Textiles and Apparel, U.S. Department of Commerce. Retrieved June 16, 2002 , from http://otexa.ita.doc.gov/msr/cat330.htm

Major shippers report: silk neckwear. (2002, May 16). Office of Textiles and Apparel, U.S. Department of Commerce. Retrieved June 16, 2002, from http://otexa.ita.doc.gov/msr/cat758.htm

Malone, S. (1999, July 27). Making strides in mass cus- tomization. *Women's Wear Daily, 178*(18), p. 12.

Marcinek, L. (2000, July 8). What's hot? *Fur Age.* Retrieved December 15, 2000, from http://www.fur.com/FUR/FurAge136.html

Marquardt, K. (1998, April 2). *Putting People First.* Internet correspondence. Retrieved December 15, 2000, from http://www.thewild.com/ppf

Mason, A. (1974). *An illustrated dictionary of jewellery.* New York, NY: Harper & Row.

Mass market rings up strong jewelry sales. (1996, August 19). *Discount Store News, 35*(16), A42.

Matched sets. (2000, June 12). *Women's Wear Daily, 179*(113), p. 6.

Matlins, A. L. (1998). *Jewelry and gems: The buyer's guide.* Gem Stone Press.

McCants, L. (2000, May 16). Indies take to fashion furs. *Women's Wear Daily,* 179(95), pp. 8–9.

McCants, L. (2000, June 13). Fur week's 'sex' appeal. *Women's Wear Daily,* 179(114), p. 8.

McKinney, M. (1999, March 19). Women's designer Mary McFadden to do first-ever neckwear collec- tion. *Daily News Record,* 29(33), p. 2.

Meadows, S. (2001, June 25). For the wrist that has everything. *Newsweek, 137*(26), 80.

Meadus, A. (1995, January 17). Market week perks. *Women's Wear Daily, 169*(10), p. 14.

Meadus, A. (1995, October 16). Safety meets style. *Accessories Magazine, 170*(71), p. S16.

Medina, M. (2001, January 8). New best friends. *Women's Wear Daily, 181*(5), p. 18.

Medina, M. (2001, January 8). A new shine for vintage jewelry. *Women's Wear Daily, 181*(5), p. 14.

Meilach, D. (1971). *Contemporary leather: Art and acces- sories, tools and techniques.* Chicago, IL: Regnery.

Mendoza, D. (2000, August 28). It's in the bag. *Women's Wear Daily, 180*(39), pp. 58–59.

Menkes, S. (1998, December). What a pair. *Town & Country Monthly, 218.*

Men's colonial shoes. (1999). Fugawee Corporation. Re- trieved December 15, 1999, from www.fugawee. com

Meyer, M. (2000, October 7). Wearable technology is the latest fashion revolution. *St. Louis Post- Dispatch, p. 32.*

Midwest Expo gets new home. (2000, June). *Jewelers' Circular Keystone, 171*(6), 416.

Mills, B. (1985). *Calico chronicle.* Lubbock, TX: Texas Tech Press.

Mineral production. (1998). *International marketing data and statistics 1998.* London, England: EURO- MONITOR Plc.

Minerals yearbook: Metals and minerals 1998, Vol. 1. (2000). U.S. Department of the Interior, U.S. Geological Survey. Washington, D.C.: United States Government Printing Office.

Mink national agricultural statistics service. (1999, May 4). Washington, D.C.: USDA. Retrieved December 15, 2000, from http://jan.mannlib. cornell.edu/reports/nassr/other/zmi-bb/ mink_07.23.98

Moin, D. (2001, March 26). QVC will distribute Diamonique to Target. *Women's Wear Daily, 181*(58), p. 2.

Mossimo eyes. (1999, July 26). *Women's Wear Daily, 178*(17), p. 14.

Murphy, R. (2000, June 26). Escada licenses scarf, lingerie lines. *Women's Wear Daily, 179*(123), p. 10.

NAICS 315: Apparel manufacturing. (1997). 1997 Eco- nomic Census. Retrieved April 9, 2001, from http://www.census.gov/epcd/ed97brdg/E97B1315. HTM

Neckwear Association of America, Inc. (1995). Apparel Net, Inc. Retrieved April 10, 2001 from http://apparel.net/naa/naa-news.html

Nelson, S. (2000, January). New technologies improve shoe store efficiency. *Stores Magazine, 82* (1), 68, 70, 83.

Wide Width and Narrow Shoes. (2000). New Balance. Retrieved Dec 1, 2000, from www. newbalancewebexpress.com/width_sizing.htm

New soft insert for Gore-Tex gloves offers better feel, greater flexibility. (2000, January 29). *Gore(TM) fabrics: 2000.* Available: www.gorefabrics. com or www.gore-tex.com

Newman, J. (2000, August). Victoria's Secret. *Women's Wear Daily Accessories Supplement,* 8, 10.

News. (2001). *International Wrist Watch,* (47), 6.

News about Lezanova. (2000, August). Osaka, Japan: Daikin Industries, Ltd.

North American Fur and Fashion Exposition (NAF-FEM) press release. (2000, July, 6). *The Canadian Fur Trade Development Institute.* Retrieved December 15, 2000, from http://www.naffem.com

Of men and money. (1995, April). *Jewelers' Circular Keystone, CLXVI*(4), 40.

O'Neil, P. (1983). *Planet Earth: Gemstones.* Chicago, IL: Time Life Books.

Open your store. (2000). Shoenet1. Retrieved January 18, 2000, from www.shoenet1.com/yourstore.asp

Ozzard, J. (2000, September 19). Hermes's Paris accent spreads in NY with newest, largest store. *Women's Wear Daily, 180*(54), p. 1.

Palmeri, C. (1999, November 15). Filling big shoes. *Forbes, 164* (12), 170, 172.

Palmieri, J. E. (2000, September 20). Hermes opens majestic Madison Avenue store. *Daily News Record, 30*(111), p.1.

Passy, C. (2000, October 13). Blown away. *The Wall Street Journal,* p. W14.

Payne, B., Winakor, G., & Farrell-Beck, J. (1992). *The history of costume. New York,* NY: HarperCollins.

Peerless umbrella history. (n.d.). *Peerless Umbrella Company.* Retrieved November 1, 2000, from www.PeerlessUmbrella.com

Peltz, L. (1986). *Fashion accessories.* Mission Hills, CA: Glencoe.

People of the fur trade: The auction. (2000, July 8). *The Fur Institute of Canada.* Retrieved December 15, 2000, from http://www.fur.ca/people/auction.html

Platinum-group metals statistics and information. (n.d.). *U.S. geological survey, mineral commodity summaries,* 99–108. Retrieved May 8, 2001, from http://minerals.usgs.gov/minerals/pubs/ commodity/platinum.

Point of information systems begins with Broadway generation. (1999). Gemmar Systems International, Inc. Retrieved September 15, 1999, from www.gsi.ca/press_details.asp?PressID=22

Power, D. (2000, March 8). Fossil's new dimensions online and in the stores. *Women's Wear Daily,* p. 15.

The precious world of platinum. (n.d.). *Platinum Guild International.* Retrieved May 3, 2001, from http://www.ags.org

Precision points. (2001, February 5). *Women's Wear Daily, 181*(24), p. 4–5.

Productivity: The DSN annual productivity report. (1999, August 9). *Drug Store News, 38*(15), p. 69.

Redecker, C. (1999, May 10). Buyers scope shows for newness and flair. *Women's Wear Daily.* p. 14(1).

Redecker, C. (2000, January). Brands capitalize on the lifestyle image. *The Fairchild 100 Supplement Women's Wear Daily,* 78–80.

Reebok shoes get kids moving. (1999, December 13). *Footwear News 55*(50), p. 6.

Retail sales hit new highs. (2000, April 24). *Women's Wear Daily Accessories Supplement,* 12.

Revolution: The bracelet watch. (1996, September). *Jewelers' Circular Keystone,* 290.

Reynolds, V. (2001, February 27). Platinum group metals prices expected to remain strong. *American Metal Market, 109*(39), n. p.

Ring size comparison chart. (n.d.). *International Gem Society.* Retrieved Apr. 20, 2001, from http://www.gemsociety.org/info/chrings.htm

Robertson, R. (2001, February 5). De Beers homes in on diamond retail market. *The Northern Miner, 86*(50), 1+.

Rossi, W. (2000, January 31). Selling floor: Future shock. *Footwear News, 56* (5), pp. 130–131.

Rossi, W. & Tennant, R. (1993). *Professional shoe fitting.* New York, NY: National Shoe Retailers Association.

Samsonite reports fourth quarter results. (2002, March 19). *CBS MarketWatch.* Retrieved May 24, 2002, from wysiwyg://31/http://cbs.marketwatch.com

Scarves, neckwear & wraps census. (2002, January). *Accessories Magazine, 103*(1), p. 38.

Schachter, R. (ed.). (1983). *The art and science of footwear manufacturing.* Philadelphia, PA: Footwear Industries of America, Inc.

Schneider-Levy, B. (2000, January 31). Interior motives. *Footwear News. 56*(5), pp. 34, 36, 38, 40.

Schneider-Levy, B. (2000, February 4). Zeroing in. *Footwear News, 56* (6), p. 98.

Schneiderman, I. P. (1999, November 29). Extra, extra. *Footwear News, 55*(48), p. 13+.

Schneiderman, I. (2000, January). The Fairchild 100. *Women's Wear Daily,* 10, 12.

Schwartz, J. & Urman, E. (2001, March 11). Gem-dandies jewelry trends sparkle aplenty. *Denver Rocky Mountain News,* p. 28.

Screen test. (2000, August). *Accessories supplement, Women's Wear Daily,* pp. 38, 40.

The sheer facts about hosiery. (2000). *National Association of Hosiery Manufacturers.*

Sheets, T. (Ed.). (2000). *Encyclopedia of Associations, Vol. 1, 36th Edition.* Farmington Hills, MI: The Gale Group.

Sherwood, J. (1999, October 23). How to spend it: Wild things. *London Financial Times,* p. 10.

The Shoe Museum (1999). *Temple University School of Podiatric Medicine.* Retrieved December 1, 1999, from www.pcpm.edu/shoemus.htm

Shoe history. (2000). *Shoeinfonet.* Retrieved January 11, 2000, from www.shoeinfonet.com/history/usm/hi_shoes.htm

Show news. (n.d.). Retrieved November 3, 2000, from http://www.busjour.com/fae/news_content.html

Shuster, W.G. (2001, April). Record sales in Europe for 2000. *Jewelers' Circular Keystone, 172*(4), 74.

Shuster, W. G. (2000, July). Real men do wear silver. *Jewelers' Circular Keystone, CLXXI* (7), 106+.

Silver. (2001). *Navajo Shopping Center.* Retrieved June 20, 2001, from http://www.navajoshop.com

Sims, C. (1999, November 26). Be tall and chic as you wobble to the orthopedist. *The New York Times International,* p. A4.

Siu, T. (2000, January 31). Interior motives. *Footwear News. 56* (5), pp. 34, 36, 38, 40.

Sizing. (n.d.). *Gloves-online.* Retrieved October 24, 3000, from www.gloves-online.com

Solemates: The century in shoes. (2000). Retrieved January 17, 2000, from www.centuryinshoes.com/intro.html

Solnik, C. (1999, April). Taking inventory. *FN Century,* 58, 60, 62, 64.

Solnik, C. (2000, June 5). The sacred cow. *Women's Wear Daily, 179* (27), p.16.

SPESA news release. (2001, August). *Sewn Products Equipment & Suppliers of the Americas.* Retrieved September 4, 2001, from http://www.spesa.org/news_releases.htm

Soucy, C. (2001, March). Escada joins fine jewelry brigade. *Jewelers' Circular Keystone, 172*(3).

Spat, W. J. (n.d.). A loosening of ties. Retrieved Apr. 10, 2001, from http://fly.hiwaay.net/~jimes/necktie/spatHistory.html

Specter, M. (2000, March 20). High heel heaven. *The New Yorker,* pp. 102–111.

Spevack, R. (1997, October 10). Accessories a key link in the golfwear game. *Daily News Record, 27*(122), p. 17.

Stankevich, D. (1997, April a). The sock hop. *Discount Merchandiser, 37*(4), 84–87.

Stankevich, D. (1997, April b). Who left their socks here? *Discount Merchandiser, 37*(4), 88–89.

Stankevich, D. (1999, May). Keeping the sparkle. *Discount Merchandiser, 39*(5), 113–115.

Stanton, J. (2001). Jan Stanton hat designer. Retrieved April 26, 2003, from http://www.heartfeltbyjanstanton.com

Steele, V. (1999). Shoes: *A lexicon of style.* New York, NY: Rizzoli.

Stocks and ... scarfs? (2001, January). *On Wall Street, 11,* p. 16.

Stoecker, D. L. (ed.) (2000). Leather and fur industries. *38th edition: Ulrich's International Periodicals Directory 2000.* New Providence, NJ: R.R. Bowker.

Stohr, K. (2000, May 15). Vision quest. *In Style, 1*(2), p. 146+.

Stone, E. (1999). *The dynamics of fashion.* New York, NY: Fairchild.

Store display. (1997). National Fashion Accessory Association. Retrieved August 31, 2002, from http://www.accessoryweb.com.

Storm, P. (1987). *Functions of dress: Tools of culture and the individual.* Englewood Cliffs, NJ: Prentice-Hall.

Sun glasses. (n.d.). Retrieved March 6, 2001, from http://www.eyeglasses-site.com/sun_glasses.htm

THA major publications. (n.d.) *The Hosiery Association.* Retrieved February 27, 2001, from http://www.nahm.com/majorpubs.html

Tait, H. (Ed.). (1986). *Jewelry: 7000 years.* New York, NY: Harry N. Abrams.

Takamura, Z. (1993). *Fashion with style.* Tokyo, Japan: Graphic-sha Publishing Company.

The 100. (2001, February). *Women's Wear Daily Special Report: WWD Luxury.*

The top 100. (2000, January). *Women's Wear Daily Special Report: The Fairchild 100.* 15, 20.

Tie me, try me. (2000, February 25). *Daily News Record, 30*(24), p. c3.

Tie, tie again. (2000, July). *Men's Wear Retailing,* p. 110.

Titanium gets trendy. (2000, May 15). *Review of Optometry, 137*(5), p. 122.

Tolman, R. (1973). *Guide to fashion merchandise knowledge, Volume I.* Bronx, New York, NY: Milady Publishing.

Tolman, Ruth. (1982). *Selling Men's Fashion,* New York, NY: Fairchild.

Tortora, P. & Collier, B. (1997). *Understanding textiles (5th ed.).* Upper Saddle River, NJ: Prentice Hall.

Tortora, P. & Eubank, K. (1989). *A survey of historic costume.* New York, NY: Fairchild.

Trade show USA calendar. (2001, June 27). *Women's Wear Daily, 181*(128), pp. 10–11.

Trim Pickings. (Oct. 2, 2001). *Women's Wear Daily, 182*(63), p. 10.

Tully, S. (1984, August 26). The Swiss put the glitz in cheap quartz watches. *Fortune,* 102.

U.S. branded athletic footwear market. (2000). *Sporting Goods Intelligence News.* Retrieved June 23, 2000, from www.sginews.com

U.S. slowdown tells upon gems and jewellery exports. (2001, April 21). *Economic Times,* n.p.

U.S. trade quick-reference tables: December 2001 imports and exports: 6601.91, 6603.20.3000, and 9004.10. (2001, December). Retrieved June 27, 2002, from http://www.ita.doc.gov/td/industry/otea/

U.S. trade quick-reference tables: Dec. 2001 exports: 9101 and 9102. (2001, December). International Trade Administration. Retrieved July 11, 2002, from http://www.ita.doc.gov/td/industry/otea/Trade-Detail/Latest-December/Exports/91/910219.html

Ultimate diamond information site. (1998). *Good old gold.* Retrieved June 4, 2001, from http://www.goodoldgold.com/clarity2.htm

United to limit size of carry-on luggage. (1998, October 15). *Houston Chronicle,* n. p.

United States Watch Company. (n.d.). Retrieved July 19, 2001, from http://www.oldwatch.com

Vexed generation bags victory. (2000, June 23). *Design Week,* 5.

Vierhile, T. (2001, August 17). Personal correspondence.

Vierhile, T. (2000, July). The new "hemp": It's not what you think. *Health Products Business, 46*(7), 50.

Vogel, M. (2000, July). Beauty care suppliers look to teens to drive business. *Chain Drug Review, 22*(12), 6.

Von Neumann, R. (1972). *The design and creation of jewelry.* Radnor, PA: Chilton Book Company.

Waltham Watch Company. (1907, 1976). *The perfected American watch.* Kansas City, MO: Heart of America Press.

Waltham Watch Company FAQs. (n.d.). Retrieved July 19, 2001, from www.waltham-community.com

Ward, F. (1979, January). The incredible crystal diamonds. *National Geographic, 155*(1), 84–113.

Ward, F. (1990, July). Emeralds. *National Geographic, 178*(1), 38–69.

Warner, B. (1999). Just do it online. *The Industry Standar, 1999.* Retrieved January 22, 1999, from www.idg.net/crd_online_65562.html

Watch. (2000). The Columbia electronic encyclopedia. Columbia University Press. Retrieved July 18, 2001, from http://www.infoplease.com/ce6/sci/A0851562.htm

Waterhouse, V. (2001, January 29). Italian jewelry shines, but with less luster. *Women's Wear Daily, 181*(19), p. 12–13.

Watson, T. (1998, November 12). Terror on the beasts' behalf. *USA Today,* p. 3.

Weber, L. (2001, April 8). The diamond game, shedding its mystery. *The New York Times, 150*(51, 717), pp. 1, 11.

Weir, J. & Wolfe, D. (1999). *The Weir/Wolfe Report, 1,* (10). The Doneger Group, HDA Productions, Inc.

What motivates Americans to buy jewelry and watches: Part 2 of 4. (1999, November). *Jewelers' Circular Keystone, CLXX* (11), p. 106+.

What motivates Americans to buy jewelry and watches: Part 3 of 4. (1999, November). *Jewelers' Circular Keystone, CLXX* (11), p. 108+.

Wheeled bags roll out of style. (2000, July 14). *Wall Street Journal-3 Star, Eastern Edition.* pp. W1+.

Where to get more information on gemology and gemcutting. (n.d.). Retrieved May 3, 2001, from http://phya.yonsei.ac.kr/~maskmanx/jewelry/moreinfo.html

Whitaker, B. (1999, December 19). Diamond buyers wonder: Is it real or treated? And does it matter? *The New York Times, Sunday,* p. 16.

White, P. (1974, January). The eternal treasure gold. *National Geographic, 145*(1), 1–51.

Who invented the umbrella? (2003). *Inventors with Mary Bellis.* Retrieved November 10, 2000, from http://inventors.about.com

Why we love platinum. (n.d.). *Precious platinum.* Retrieved May 3, 2001, from http://www.preciousplatinum.com/about_history.asp

Williamson, R. (2000, August 28). The late night hosiery spot. *Women's Wear Daily, 180*(39), pp. 22.

Wilson, C. (2000, April 24). Council's Web site is link to the industry. *Women's Wear Daily Advertising Supplement, Accessor-Ease,* p. 26.

Wilson, E. (1999, May 25). Furs cut from a different cloth. *Women's Wear Daily, 77*(100), p. 8.

Wilson, E. (2000, May 2). Cassin's second act shapes up. *Women's Wear Daily, 179*(85), p. 11.

Wilsons leather. (2000). The Wilsons for women executive collection. Retrieved September 9, 2000, from www.wilsonsleather.com

Winning stripes. (2000, August 28). *Women's Wear Daily, 180*(39), p. 20.

Women's handbag and purse manufacturing. (1997). *Economic Census.* U.S. Census Bureau. U.S. Department of Commerce. Retrieved September 9, 2000, from www.uscensus.gov

World demand soars for leathergoods and accessories. (2000, March 1). *Duty-Free News International, 14*(4), p. 33+.

World Gold Council seventh international symposium dedicated to gold jewellry technology. (n.d.). *World Gold Council.* Retrieved May 9, 2001, from http://www.gold.org/Wgc/Gfl/Gf001108.htm

World leather markets. (1998, October). *Leather,* p. 29.

Yaukey, J. (2000, November 14). Computers to wear. *Muskogee Daily Phoenix,* p. 1–2C.

Year of the handbag; new fabrications and status brands propel handbags into the fashion forefront. (2000). *Accessories Magazine 101*(4), 44+.

Your guide to diamonds: Nature's most precious gift. (n.d.). Moody's Jewelry, Tulsa, OK.

Zargani, L. (2000, June 16). Baldoria ties into the Internet. *Women's Wear Daily,* p. 12.

SUBJECT INDEX

Abalone, 135
Abstract tie patterns, 245
Acetate, 48
Adamas, 117
Add-on sales, 191
Adjustable belts, 206
Advertising in leather industry,
    78
Affiliate retailers, 396
Affordable luxury, 133
African Americans
    and hair extensions, 280
    and hats, 262, 264
    jewelry, 365, 366, 367
Agents in leather tanning, 70
Agricultural societies, 45
Airline carry-on regulations,
    204
Akoya saltwater cultured pearls,
    133
Alabaster, 327
Alarm clock watches, 382
Alchemy, 360
Alligator skin, 74
Alligators, 77
Aluminum, 135
Aluminum pan forms for hats,
    264
Amber, 131
Amethyst, 118
Analog watches, 385
Ancient Egyptians' fine jewelry,
    327, 360
Ancient Hebrews and Egyptians
    tanning leather, 68
Angora rabbits, 48
Aniline dye, 72
Aniline finish, 73
Animal preservation, 77–78
Animal skins, 67
    see also Leather
Animal-rights activists, 92,
    101
Ankle bracelets, 340
Anklets (bracelets), 340
Anklets or socklets, 222

Annie Hall look, 240
Antibacterial fibers, 221
Antimacassars, 280
Antique jewelry, 331
Antique typewriter keys,
    366
Antiquing, 336
Antistress pantyhose, 218
Apparel industry and fashion
    accessories industry,
    10
Apron of necktie, 243
Arch supports, 141
Area sales managers, 20
Armbands, 340
Armlets, 340
Art deco period in jewelry, 332,
    361
Art nouveau period in jewelry,
    332, 361
Art retro period in jewelry,
    332
Artificial flowers, 57
Artificial silk, 48
Artisans, 329
Ascots, 240
Assembly-line-manufacturing
    techniques, 381
Assistant accessories buyers,
    20–21
Assistant designers, 18
Athletic shoe stores, 166
Athletic shoes, 156, 158
Athletic socks, 218, 229
Atomic precision timekeeping,
    289
Atomic-energy-powered
    watches, 382
Attaché cases, 180
Au natural look, 58
Automatic self-winding watches,
    385
Automatic umbrellas, 305
Automobile interiors, 86
Avant-garde jewelry, 361
Aviator glasses, 312

B2B (business to business), 253
Baby boomers, 151, 321, 345,
    346, 372
Backpacks, 183, 202
Bacteria-controlling athletic
    socks, 218
"Bad hair days," 261
Bakelite, 361
Ball caps, 261, 267, 275
Ballerina umbrellas, 305
Bamboo, 53
Band/tape of umbrella, 304
Bandanas, 240
Bandolier belts, 206
Bangle bracelets, 341
Bar pins, 342
Bar tack stitch on neckties, 243,
    253
Baroque pearls, 132
Barrel-top trunks, 181
Barrettes and clips, 261, 270
Base soles, 152
Baseball gloves, 297
Bating hides, 71
Bear's paw shoe style, 148
Beef industry, 74
Belleseime, 76
Bellows cases, 202
Belt bag, 207
Belts, 54, 205–210
    care tips for, 209
    global markets, 189
    history, 180–182
    manufacturing, 206
    selling, 210
    sizes of, 208
    styles of, 206–208
    trade organizations, 191
    trade publications, 192
    trade shows, 192
    women's belt sales by store
        classifications, 209
Berets, 268
Best-quality luggage, 205
Betsy (variation of the ruff), 240
Better-quality luggage, 204

Bezel settings, 335
Bezel of a watch, 385
Bi-gradient lens, 312
Biarritz gloves, 294
Bias cut, 243
Bias tape for hats, 266
Bib necklaces or collarettes, 337
Bible, 287
Bifocals, 310, 311, 322
Billfolds, 197
Binding of feet, 157
Binding of a glove, 291
Bird plumage, 260
Birthstone rings, 343
Birthstones, 134, 330, 375
Black Cameo, 367
Blackamoor cameo, 367
Bleaching furs, 95
Bleaching gemstones, 352
Bleaching hides, 73
Blocking of hats, 264
"Blood" diamonds, 136
Boarded hosiery, 220
Boarding hides, 73
Boaters (hats), 260, 268
Bobbin lace, 52
Bobbinet lace, 52
Bobby socks, 216, 222
Body heat-powered watches, 382
Body piercing, 367
Body stockings, 222
Bolo ties, 240
Bonnets, 260
Boots, 148, 155, 158, 159, 160
    see also Footwear
Bottoming process in shoes, 154
Bouclé yarn, 49
Bovine leather, 73, 74
Bow tie knot, 246
Bow ties, 240
Bowlers, 268
Bows, 56, 260, 261
Box stores, 165
Boy cut hosiery, 218, 224
Boy Scout belt, 207
Bracelet length gloves, 290
Bracelet watches, 391
Bracelets, 340–342
Braces, 205, 208
Braid belts, 207
Braided straw, 266
Braids, 55

Braille watches, 282
Brand building, 387
Brand loyalty, 218, 231, 235
Brand-name recognition in watches, 382–384
Branded Web sites, 193–194
Brannock Device, 172, 173
Breast-binding, 361
Breton hat, 268
Brick-and-mortar stores, 320
Bridal gloves, 292
Bridal set rings, 343
Bridge jewelry, 330–331, 363, 374
    see also Costume jewelry
Bridge socks, 232
Bridge watches, 390
Bridgepieces in eyeglasses, 312
Briefcases, 180, 183
Brilliant cut, 126
Brilliants, 133
Brim of a hat, 262
British barristers, 279
Brooches, pins, and clips, 342
Brush-dyeing hides, 73
Bubble umbrellas, 305
Bucket hats, 261
Buckle belts, 207
Buckles, 55
Buckram, 243, 264
Budget bags, 180
Budget footwear, 155
Buffing of hides, 72
Bumper hat, 268
Businesses in fashion accessories, 4–5
Buttercup settings, 335
Butterfly or banana clips, 270
Button earrings, 339
Buttons, 54
Buttons (measurement unit with gloves), 291

CAD. *See* Computer-aided design (CAD) systems
Calendar watches, 382
Calotte caps, 270
Cameos, 328
Cancer treatment, 280
Canopy or cover of umbrella, 304, 305
Capeline weaving, 266
Capras goats, 47

Caps, 261
    see also Hats and hair accessories
Carat, 125–126
Carding fibers, 266
Care tips
    belts, 209
    costume jewelry, 376–377
    fine jewelry, 353
    footwear, 160–161
    fur products, 104–105
    gloves, 296–297
    handbags, 187
    hats, 278
    leather products, 80–83
    metals and stones, 134–136
    scarfs, ties, and handkerchiefs, 247
    socks and hosiery, 224–225
    umbrellas, 310
    watches, 398
    wigs and hairpieces, 282
Career opportunities in fashion accessories industry, 17–22, 23
Carnelian, 327
Carry-on luggage, 201, 202, 204
Cartwheel hat, 268
Casting, 336
Casual dress in business, 232
Casual fitness, 158
Cat eyes glasses, 312
Catalog retailing
    costume jewelry, 375
    eyewear, 320
    fine jewelry, 350–351
    footwear, 168
    gloves, 301
    handbags, 194–195
    hats and hair accessories, 276
    scarfs, ties, and handkerchiefs, 253
    socks and hosiery, 230
    umbrellas, 308
    watches, 397
Categories of accessories, 5
Category management, 319
Cattle industry, 73
Cell phone cases, 197
Cellulose fibers, 46–47
Chain link belts, 207
Chain necklaces, 337
Chain stores, 165
Championship rings, 343

Chandelier earrings, 339
Change purses, 197
Changeable earrings, 339
Channel settings, 335
Charm bracelets, 341
Chasing, 336
Chastity belts, 180
Chatelaines, 329, 367, 368, 380
Chemical tannins, 70
Chemotherapy, 280
Chenille, 49
Children's shoes, 174
Children's watches, 389
Chinchilla, 97, 103
Chinese lily foot, 157
Choker necklaces, 337
Chopines, 148
Chrome tanning, 71
Chromium mineral salts for
    tanning, 68
Chromium pollutants, 77
Chronographs, 385
Cigarette cases, 197
Cinch belts, 207
Circlet headpieces, 344
Clarity in gemstones, 127, 128
Clarity-enhanced stones, 352
Class rings, 343
Clay, 135
Clean Water Act, 77
Click-and-mortar stores, 320
Clicking with gloves, 292
Clip-on or clip back earrings,
    339
Clip-on ties, 246
Cloche hats, 260, 263, 268
Cloisonné, 328
Club tie patterns, 245
Cluster settings, 335
Clute-cut glove pattern, 292
Coated fabrics, 51
Coating gemstones, 352
Cocktail rings, 343
Cocktail umbrellas, 305
Coin-art jewelry, 366
Coinage, 330
Cold-weather accessories, 250
Cold-weather protection from
    hats and headbands, 262,
    276
Collar pins, 369
Color in gemstones, 128
Color selection, 30–32
Color in socks and hosiery, 233
Color-forward shoppers, 264

Color-prudent shoppers, 264
Coloring the gold, 336
Coloring hides, 71, 72
Combs, 271
Comfort technologies, 158, 160
Commodity purchases, 231, 292
Complex yarns, 49
Computer chips in shoes
    to measure athletic
    performance, 159
Computer imaging in footwear,
    172
Computer-aided design (CAD)
    systems, 206, 314, 333,
    364
Computer-aided manufacturing,
    333
Conditioning of hides, 72
Cone weaving, 266
"Conflict" diamonds, 136
Consignment selling of furs,
    112
Content, labeling, and
    advertising in leather
    industry, 78
Continuing education, 60
Contour belts, 207
Control top hosiery, 217
Controversy in furs, 101
Conversational tie patterns, 245
Coolie hat, 268
Copper, 336
Copycat designing, 185
Copywriters, 21
Coquille, 57
Coral, 132
Corduroy-grooved furs, 95, 96
Core competency, 197
Coronet headpieces, 344
Corporate casual, 158
Corset belts, 207
Cossacks (boots), 148
Costume jewelry, 331, 360–379
    definitions, 363
    global markets, 369–371
    history, 360–363
    junior market trends, 365
    manufacturing, 363–369
        design, 364–365
        ethnic jewelry, 365–366
        materials, 368–369
        novelty jewelry, 366–367
    men's jewelry styles, 369, 370
    merchandising trends and
        techniques, 372–375

    catalog retailing, 375
    Internet retailing, 367, 374
    store retailing, 373–374
    television retailing, 374–375
    selling, 375–377
        care tips, 376–377
        customer needs, 377
        price and value, 375–376
        sizing, 376
    trade organizations, 371
    trade publications, 372
    trade shows, 372
    see also Fine jewelry
Cottage industries, 45
Cotton, 45, 46
Cotton gins, 46
Counterfeit luxury watches, 393
Counterfeited trade names, 393
Counterpoise, 327
Counters, 152
Couture millinery, 264, 277
Covered rubber bands, 271
Cowboy belts, 208
Cowboy boots, 148
Cowboy hats, 268
Crackowe, 147
Cravats, 239
Credit card cases, 197
Crew socks, 222
Crochet, 53
Crocodiles, 77
Cross trainer athletic shoes, 158
Cross-merchandising, 228
Crown of a hat, 262
Crown headpieces, 344
Crown or stem of a watch, 385
Cruelty to animals, 260
Crystal of a watch, 385
Cubic zirconia, 133
Cubic-zirconia stones, 369
Cuff bracelets, 341
Cuff of a glove, 291
Cuff links or buttons for men,
    369
Cultured pearls, 132, 133
Cummerbund belts, 207
Curing of leather, 70
Cushioned insoles, 141
Custom tipping on neckties, 243
Customer needs
    costume jewelry, 377
    eyewear, 321
    fine jewelry, 353–354
    gloves, 301–302
    handbags, 195–196

hats, 278–279
scarfs, ties, and handkerchiefs, 256
socks and hosiery, 232
umbrellas, 309
watches, 399
wigs and hairpieces, 282–283
Cut of gemstones, 126–127
Cut-up trade in belts, 206
Cutters in fur construction, 96
Cutting process in shoes, 154
Cyberbranding, 167–168
Cylinder-seals, 328

Danbury shakes, 259
Davey tip on gloves, 293
Décolleté, 240
Decorative trim of a hat, 262
Deed boxes, 180
Deliming hides, 71
Demi-toe hosiery, 222
Demographic segmentation, 264
Denier, 220–221, 230
Department managers, 19–20
Department stores, 165
belts, 209
handbags, 190–193, 196
ties, 251
Depilatory products, 220
Derby hat, 268
Design
belts, 206
costume jewelry, 364–365
eyewear, 313–314
fine jewelry, 333–334
footwear, 155–160
furs, 102–103, 114
gloves, 292
handbags, 184–185
hats and hair accessories, 263–264
leather products, 78, 80
line and collection, 28–34
luggage, 200–201
scarfs, ties, and handkerchiefs, 242–243
shoes, 153
socks and hosiery, 218–220
umbrellas, 303
watches, 386–388
Designing, 29–30
distribution channels, 15–16
Developing countries, 60

Diadems (crowns), 328, 344
Dial of a watch, 384
Diamonaire, 369
Diamond boycotts, 136
Diamond bracelets, 341
Diamond centers worldwide, 136
Diamond mines, 136, 140
Diamond pipeline, 137
Diamonds, 117, 118, 125–128, 334
Diamonds by the yard, 337
Diamonique, 369
Diffusion of gemstones, 352
Digital watches, 385
Dinner rings, 343
Dip-dying hides, 73
Discount stores, 235, 250, 319, 352
Distressed leather, 80
Distribution channels, 15–17
Divers' watches, 398
Document boxes, 180
Document cases, 197
Dog-collar choker, 337
Dollar watches, 382
Domes of a glove, 291
Domestic fur farming, 94
Domestic production, 39
Double face furs, 95
Doublets, 134
Doublets (gems), 368
Drawstrings, 54
Dressing down at work, 158, 232
Dressing furs, 95
Driving gloves, 294
Drop earrings, 339
Drop necklaces, 337
Dry cleaning of leather, 80
Dry milling of hides, 72
Dry operations for leather processing, 72–73
Drying of hides, 72
Duckbill shoe style, 148
Duffle bags, 202
Duty-free, 297
Dyeing furs, 95
Dyeing gemstones, 352
Dyeing hides, 73

E-commerce sites, 167
Ear cuff earrings, 339
Earmuffs, 271

Earpieces in eyeglasses, 312
Earrings, 337, 339–340
Easter Sunday, and hats, 262
eBay, 367
Economic function of jewelry, 330
EDI. *See* Electronic data interchange
Edwardian period in jewelry, 332
Elasticity, 51
Electric wristwatches, 382
Electronic data interchange (EDI), 63, 166
Electronic watches, 389, 390
Elephant skin, 74
Embossing hides, 73
Emeralds, 118, 128–129
Employment assistance, 60
End caps, 228
Endangered Species Act, 77, 78, 97, 100
Engagement rings, 343
English or bolton thumb, 291
Engraving, 336
Environmental issues
fur industry, 97
leather industry, 77
Estate jewelry, 331–333
Etching, 336
Eternity rings, 343
Ethnic jewelry, 365–366
Ethnic minorities, 46
European immigrant milliners, 260
European Union, 297, 315
External manufacturing, 39
Eyeglass cases, 197
Eyewear, 310–322
global markets, 315–316
history, 310–311
manufacturing, 313–315
design, 313–314
licensing, 314
materials, 315
production, 314–315
merchandising trends and techniques, 317–320
catalog retailing, 320
Internet retailing, 320
store retailing, 318–320
parts of eyewear, 312

selling, 320–322
  customer needs, 321
  do's and don'ts, 322
  facial shapes for eyewear, 321–322
  price and value, 321
  styles of eyewear, 312–313
  trade organizations, 317
  trade publications, 317
  trade shows, 318

Fabergé eggs, 329
Fabrications, 50
Facets, 126
Facial shapes for eyewear, 321–322
Facile, 76
Facing on neckties, 243
Factory hats, 277
Factory system, 46
Fads in jewelry, 363, 366–367
Faience, 361
Fairchild's top 100 luxury watch brands in 2000, 384
Fake cloth fur category, 103
Fake watches, 393
Falls (hairpieces), 280
Fanny packs, 207
FAQs. *See* Frequently asked questions (FAQs) in hosiery, 234
Fashion accessories industry, 3–27
  background and definition, 3–6
    businesses, 4–5
    categories of accessories, 5
    reasons for studying accessories, 5–6
  career opportunities, 17–22
  area sales managers, 20
  assistant accessories buyers, 20–21
  assistant designers, 18
  copywriters, 21
  department managers, 19–20
  junior sales representatives, 19
  production specialists, 19
  store planners, 21–22
  visual merchandisers, 21
  channels of distribution, 15–17

designing, 15–16
manufacturing, 16–17
retailing, 17
wholesaling, 17
fashion life cycle, 8–9
  culmination or peak stage, 9
  decline stage, 9
  introduction stage, 8–9
  obsolescence stage, 9
  rise stage, 9
influences on accessories, 6–8
  pragmatic fashion accessories theory, 7–8
  trickle-down, trickle-up, and trickle-across theories, 6
marketing and merchandising, 11–15
relationship to apparel industry, 10
salaries for fashion accessories careers, 22, 23
trade organizations, publications, and shows, 22–24
Fashion do's and don'ts in hosiery, 234
Fashion footwear, 171
Fashion jewelry, 331, 363
  see also Costume jewelry; Fine jewelry
Fashion life cycle, 8–9
"Fashion victim" in shoes, 157
Fashion-watch designers, 388
Fasteners or closures of handbags, 183
Fatliquoring hides, 71, 72
Faux diamonds, 369
Faux (fake) fur, 104
Faux gemstones, 133–134, 360
Faux pearls, 361
Feathers, 57, 58
Fedoras, 268
Felt, 51
Felt hat processing, 259
Felt hat production, 266
Ferrule/finial of umbrella, 304
Fezes (hats), 268
Fibulae (sharp pins), 54
Filigree rings, 343
Filled metals, 123–124
Final costing, 37
Findings in jewelry, 368

Fine jewelry, 359–327
  definitions, 330–331
  global markets, 344–345
  history, 327–330
  manufacturing, 333–336
    design, 333–334
    materials, 334
    production, 334–335
  merchandising trends and techniques, 345–351
    catalog retailing, 350–351
    Internet retailing, 350
    store retailing, 349–350
  metals for, 336
  reasons for wearing, 330
  selling, 351–355
    care tips, 353
    customer needs, 353–354
    price and value, 352–353
  stone settings, 336
  styles, 336–344
    bracelets, 340–342
    brooches, pins, and clips, 342
    earrings, 337, 339–340
    headpieces, 344
    necklaces, 336–337, 338
    rings, 343–344
  trade organizations, 346
  trade publications, 347
  trade shows, 347
  vintage and estate jewelry, 331–333
  see also Costume jewelry
Fine weave straws, 277
Finely woven hats, 277
Fingerless gloves, 294
Finishing hides, 72
Finishing process in shoes, 154
Finishing treatments for leather, 73
Fishermen hats, 261
Fishnet hosiery, 218, 224
Fishscale belts, 207
Fitting process in shoes, 154
Flat goods. *See* Small personal goods
Floral tie patterns, 245
Florentining, 336
"Flower child" look, 362
Flush settings, 335
Folding or collapsible umbrellas, 305
Folding pocket squares, 255
Folios, 197
Footies, 222

Footwear, 147–178
  care of, 160–161
  classifications of, 155, 156
  design of, 155–160
  global markets, 161–163
    distributors in the U.S., 163
    production, 161–162
  history of, 147–150
  manufacturing of footwear,
    153–155
  materials for, 155
  merchandising trends and
    techniques, 165–168
    catalog retailing, 168
    in-store retailing, 165–166
    Internet retailing, 167–168
    leased departments, 166
    merchandising techniques,
      168, 169, 170
    POI systems, 167
    stock control, 166
    vertical marketing, 167
  parts of footwear, 151–152
  selling footwear, 168–173
    customer needs, 173
    price and value, 171
    sizing and fitting, 171–173,
      174
  standard footwear
    measurement, 154
  trade organizations, 163, 164
  trade publications, 164
  trade shows, 163, 165
"Form follows function," 153
Foulard tie patterns, 245
Four-in-hand knot, 246
Four-in-hand ties, 240
Fourchettes of a glove, 291
Fracture filling in gemstones,
  352
Frame of umbrella, 304
Frames in eyeglasses, 312
Frames of handbags, 183
Fraternal rings, 343
French clip earrings, 339
French cut hosiery, 218, 224
French or quirk thumb, 291
Frequently asked questions
  (FAQs) in hosiery, 234
Freshwater cultured pearls, 133
Friday-wear socks, 232
Front blade of necktie, 243
Full fashioned gloves, 292
Full or top grain of skins or
  hides, 69

Full-fashioned hosiery, 220
Full-service shoe salon, 168
Fun jewelry, 363
Fur, 48, 92–116
  classifications of fur, 97,
    98–99
  construction of fur products,
    96–97
  definition, 95
  durability of furs, 97, 100
  fashion industry, 101–105
    care of fur products,
      104–105
    design, 102–103, 114
    faux (fake) fur, 104
  fur controversy, 101
  fur dressing and processing,
    95
  fur treatments, 95–96
  global markets, 105–107
    fur auctions, 106–107
    top producing countries for
      fur pelts, 106
    U.S. fur sales, 106
    U.S. markets, 107
  history of, 92–94
  and the media, 103
  merchandising trends and
    techniques, 109–112
    home fashion accessories,
      109–110
    Internet retailing, 110–111
    leased departments, 109
    previously owned furs,
      111–112
  regulations for fur industry, 97,
    100–101
    Endangered Species Act
      (1973, 1988), 100
    fur farming regulations,
      100–101
    Fur Products Labeling Act
      (FPLA), 97, 100
  selling furs, 112–114
    price and value, 113–114
    restyling furs, 113
  top U.S. fur farming states, 94
    trade organizations,
      107–108
    trade publications, 108
    trade shows, 107
Fur boas, 244
Fur collars, 244
Fur farming regulations,
  100–101

Fur farming states, 94
Fur fibers, 48, 51
Fur on fur, 95
Fur Products Labeling Act
  (FPLA), 97, 100
Fur shawls, 244
Fur trapping, 93, 94

Galón, 268
Garment bags, 202
Garters, 222
Gauntlet gloves, 289, 294
Gemstone enhancement, 352
Generalized System of
  Preferences (GSP),
  369–370
Generation X, 372, 373
Generation Y, 372, 373
Geneva Seal, 386
"Genuine leather," 78
Georgian period in jewelry, 332
Girdles, 180, 205
Glass, 135
Glass beads, 361
Glass imitation stones, 360
Glasses. *See* Eyewear
Glazing hides, 73
Global markets
  belts, 189
  costume jewelry, 369–371
  eyewear, 315–316
  fine jewelry, 344–345
  footwear, 161–163
  fur, 105–107
  gloves, 297
  handbags, 189–190
  hats and hair accessories, 273
  leather, 69, 83–85
  luggage, 189
  metals and stones, 136–137
  scarfs, ties, and handkerchiefs,
    247–248
  small personal goods, 189
  socks and hosiery, 225–228
  textiles and trims, 60
  umbrellas, 306–307
  watches, 391–393
Global positioning system (GPS)
  in watches, 389, 390
Glove liners, 295
Gloves, 287–302
  care tips for, 296–297
  fitting and sizes, 295–296
  global markets, 297
  history, 287–290

manufacturing, 291–294
  design, 292
  materials, 293–294
  production, 292–293
merchandising trends and
    techniques, 299–301
  catalog retailing, 301
  Internet retailing, 300–301
  store retailing, 299–300
parts of gloves, 291
selling, 301–302
  customer needs, 301–302
  price and value, 301
  styles of gloves, 294–295
  trade organizations, 298
  trade publications, 298
  trade shows, 299
Go-go boots, 159
Goat skin, 74
Goggles, 312
Gold, 119–121, 137, 331, 336
Gold filled, 124
Gold flashed, 124
Gold overlay, 124
Gold plate, 124
Gold Rush (1849), 119
Gold washed, 124
Gold-toned metals, 118
Goldsmiths, 333
Golf gloves, 297
Golf umbrellas, 305
Gore of a glove, 291
Gore-Tex, 82, 155, 293
Grading leather, 73
Graduated compression, 219,
    220
Graduated lens, 312
Graduated pearl necklaces, 337
Grain of the skin, 69
Great Depression, 362
Grommets, 55
Grosgrain ribbon, 56
GSP. *See* Generalized System
    of Preferences
Guard hairs on furs, 95
Gunn-cut glove pattern, 292
Gusset of a glove, 291
Gussets of handbags, 183
Gypsy earrings, 339

Haberdasher shops, 259
Hair accessories. *See* Hats and
    hair accessories
Hair extensions, 271, 280
Hair jewelry, 271

Hair loss, 280, 282–283
Hair weaving, 280
Hairpin, 271
Half-piqué seams on gloves,
    293
Half-Windsor tie knot, 246,
    247
Halo hats, 268
Hammering, 336
Hand knitting, 46
Hand (tactile qualities), 59
Hand-me-down shoes, 174
Hand-rolled hems, 244
Handbag themes, 192
Handbags, 182–188
  care tips for, 187
  contents of, 179–180
  global markets, 189–190
  handle styles, 184
  history of, 180–182
  manufacturing of, 183–187
    design, 184–185
    materials, 185–187
    production, 185
  merchandising trends and
      techniques, 190–195
    catalog retailing, 194–195
    department stores, 190–193
    handbag sales by store
        classification, 193
    Internet retailing, 182–183,
        193–194
    mass customization, 194
    travel retail stores, 193
  parts of, 183
  selling handbags, 195–196
    customer needs, 195–196
    departmemt store inventory
        by price, 196
    price and value, 195
  styles of, 187, 188
  top producers of handbags in
      U.S., 190
  trade organizations, 191
  trade publications, 192
  trade shows, 192
Handkerchiefs. *See* Scarfs, ties,
    and handkerchiefs
Handles of handbags, 183
Handles of umbrellas, 304
Hands of a watch, 385
Hardside luggage, 201
Hat etiquette, 259
Hat linings, 264
Hatpins, 259, 342

Hats and hair accessories, 46,
    259–279
  global markets, 273
  hair accessories, 260,
      261–262, 264, 267,
      270–272
  hat sizing and fitting, 272
  history of, 259–261
  manufacturing, 262–267
    design, 263–264
    felt hat production, 266
    materials, 266–267
    production, 264, 266
    straw hat production, 266
  merchandising trends and
      techniques, 275–276
    catalog retailing, 276
    Internet retailing, 276
    store retailing, 275–276
  parts of a hat, 262
  selling, 277–279
    care tips for hats, 278
    customer needs, 278–279
    price and value, 277–278
    styles of hair accessories,
        270–272
    styles of hats, 267–270
  technological headwear, 267
  trade organizations, 274
  trade publications, 274
  trade shows, 275
Hatter's brush, 278
Hatter's shakes, 259
Haute couture, 151
Hazardous chemical effluents,
    77
Head-to-toe dressing, 233
Headache bands, 260
Headband of a hat, 262
Headbands, 260–261, 271
Headpieces, 344
"Heart of the Ocean" necklace
    design, 363
Hearts or stays of a glove, 291
Heating gemstones, 352
Heel lifts, 152
Heel pads, 141
Heels, 142
Heirloom jewelry, 331
Hemp, 46, 47
Hemp controversy, 47
Hessians (boots), 148
Hides, 69
High heels, 157
High-button shoes, 149

Hiking socks, 222
Hispanics, 264
Hombergs, 268
Home accessories in leather, 86
Home fashion accessories in
    furs, 109–110
Home-based industries, 45
Hood of a hat, 266
Hoods, 268
Hoop bracelets, 341
Hoop or gypsy earrings, 339
Hope diamond, 129
Horn, 135
Horology, 380
    see also Watches
Hosiery. See Socks and hosiery
House slippers, 155, 160
Hydraulic blocking for hats, 264,
    266

Illegally mined diamonds, 136
Illusion settings, 335
Imitation pearls, 134, 361
Imitation or simulated leather,
    69, 76, 78
Imitation stone, 133
Immigrants, 46
Impregnating gemstones, 352
Impulse purchases, 191, 228,
    308
Industrial Revolution, 45
Industrial zippers, 54
Information dissemination, 60,
    63
Infusion of gemstones, 352
Inlay, 361
Inlay settings, 335
Inseaming on gloves, 293
Insoles, 152
Intaglio, 328
Integrated technology, 63
Interlining of necktie, 243
Internal manufacturing, 38
International airports, 193
Internet, 63
    costume jewelry, 367, 374
    eyewear, 320
    fine jewelry, 350
    footwear, 167–168
    fur, 110–111
    gloves, 300–301
    handbags, 182–183, 193–194
    hats and hair accessories, 276
    leather, 87–88
    luggage, 204–205

scarfs, ties, and handkerchiefs,
    242–253
socks and hosiery, 229–230
umbrellas, 308
watches, 393, 396–397
    see also Web sites
Investment handbags, 187
Invisible zippers, 54
Irradiation of gemstones, 352
Ivory, 135

Jardin in emeralds, 129
Jeffersons (brogans), 148
Jet, 132
Jewel necklaces, 337
Jewel watches, 385
Jewelry industry, 119
    see also Costume jewelry;
        Fine jewelry
Juliet caps, 270
Junk jewelry, 363
Jute, 46, 47

Key cases, 197
Key rings, 197
Khaki casual, 158
Kickers for fur processing, 95
Kid gloves, 294
Kimberlite, 118
Kiosk arrangements, 229, 319
Kitty cat glasses, 312
Knee-high hosiery, 217
Knee-highs or trouser socks,
    222
Knit hats, 270
Knits, 46, 50–51
Knitting, 50–51
Knitting furs, 95
Knitting gauges, 220
Knockoffs, 184
Koh-i-noor diamond, 129

Label pins, 342
Labeling in leather industry, 78
Lace gloves, 295
Lace making, 46
Laced leather, 56
Land animals used for leather,
    75
Lapidaries, 126, 352
Lapis lazuli, 327
Lariat necklaces, 337
Laser drilling, 136
Lasering diamonds, 352
Lasting process in shoes, 154

Lasts for shoes, 153
Lavaliere necklaces, 337
LCD (liquid crystal display),
    382
Leased departments
    footwear, 166
    in fur retailing, 109
Leather, 48, 67–91
    classifictions of leather, 73–76
        land animals used for
            leather, 75
        water animals used for
            leather, 76
    definition, 69
    fashion industry in leather,
        78–83
        care of leather products,
            80–83
        design of leather products,
            78, 80
    finishing treatments, 73
    global markets, 69, 83–85
        foreign suppliers of leather
            to the U.S., 84
        top four countries by bovine
            population, 85
        U.S. leather exports, 85
        U.S. leather goods imports,
            83
    high-performance leather
        (Lezanova), 77
    history of, 67–69
    imitation or simulated leather,
        69, 76, 78
    manufacturing process,
        70–73
        dry operations, 72–73
        wet operations, 70–72
    merchandising trends and
        techniques, 85–88
    regulations for industry,
        77–78
        animal preservation,
            77–78
        content, labeling, and
            advertising, 78
        environment, 77
        for shoes, 155, 161
    trade organizations, 86
    trade publications, 87
    trade shows, 88
Leather balm and conditioners,
    81, 83
Leather scraps, 48
Leather textures, 74

Leather-bag making, 180
Leatherette, 76
Leathering in fur construction, 96
LED (light-emitting diode), 382
Leg coverings. See Socks and hosiery
Leg makeup, 216
Leg warmers, 222
Leg-care information, 230
Leg-high stockings, 222
Legislative actions, 60
Lens in eyeglasses, 312
Letting out in fur construction, 96
Lezanova, 77, 81, 82
Licensing
  eyewear, 314
  scarfs, ties, and handkerchiefs, 243
  watches, 388–389
Lifestyle story of customers, 299
Light refraction, 126
Lightning-proof umbrellas, 305
Line and collection design, 28–34
Line plan, 30
Line sheets, 34–35
Linen (flax), 45, 46, 47
Lining
  of gloves, 291
  of handbags, 183
  of necktie, 243
Liquid Leather, 76
Lizard skin, 74
Lizards, 77
Lobbying, 60
Logomania, 267
Loop label on neckties, 243
Loop strap handles, 202
Lorgnettes, 310
Lost wax casting, 334
Loupe, 127
Love beads, 362
Lowers in shoes, 152
Lucite, 362
Luggage, 199–205
  airline carry-on regulations, 204
  classifications of, 201
  design, 200–201
  global markets, 189
  history, 180–182

  manufacturing, 199–200
  materials, 201
  merchandising trends and techniques, 203–205
    in-store retailing, 204
    Internet retailing, 204–205
  production, 201
  selling, 205
  styles of, 202–203
  testing for durability, 200
  trade organizations, 192
  trade publications, 192
  trade shows, 192
Luggage carts, 202
Lurex, 56, 221

Machine hems, 243–244
Macramé, 52
Mad hatter's syndrome, 259
Made-to-order ties, scarfs, and shawls, 252
Magnetic earrings, 339
Mail bags, 180
Mainspring of a watch, 385
Male bags, 180
Mallorca pearls, 134
Manufactured fibers, 48–49
Manufacturing
  belts, 206
  considerations in, 38–40
  costume jewelry, 363–369
  distribution channels, 16–17
  eyewear, 313–315
  fine jewelry, 333–336
  footwear, 153–155
  gloves, 291–294
  handbags, 183–187
  hats and hair accessories, 262–267
  leather, 70–73
  luggage, 199–200
  process of, 34–38
  scarfs, ties, and handkerchiefs, 242–244
  socks and hosiery, 218–220, 218–221
  textiles, 49–53
  umbrellas, 303–305
  watches, 386–391
Marabou feathers, 57
Market segmentation, 264
Marketing, 11–15
Markings in top grain, 69

Mass customization or personalization, 194, 252, 292
Mass merchandising, 235, 349
Mass production
  of shoes, 153
  of textiles, 46
  of watches, 386
Matara or matura, 369
Materials
  belts, 206
  costume jewelry, 368–369
  eyewear, 315
  fine jewelry, 334
  footwear, 155
  gloves, 293–294
  handbags, 185–187
  hats and hair accessories, 266–267
  luggage, 201
  scarfs, ties, and handkerchiefs, 244
  selection of, 33
  small personal goods, 197
  socks and hosiery, 221
  watches, 390
Maternity hosiery, 218, 224
Matinee necklaces, 337
Measuring hides, 73
Mechanical watches, 385
Media and furs, 103
Men's jewelry, 328, 329, 362, 363, 369, 370
Men's small accessories in leather, 86
Men's socks, 219
Merchandising, 11–15
Merchandising trends and techniques
  costume jewelry, 372–375
  eyewear, 317–320
  fine jewelry, 345–351
  footwear, 165–168
  fur, 109–112
  gloves, 299–301
  handbags, 190–195
  hats and hair accessories, 275–276
  leather, 85–88
  luggage, 203–205
  metals and stones, 137–140
  scarfs, ties, and handkerchiefs, 249–253
  small personal goods, 198
  socks and hosiery, 228–230

textiles and trims, 63
umbrellas, 307–308
watches, 393–397
wigs and hairpieces, 280–281
Mercury nitrate poisoning, 259
Mesopotamia, 327
Metallic threads, 56
Metals for fine jewelry, 336
Metals and stones, 117–143
   care of metals and stones,
      134–136
   faux stones and gems,
      133–134
   gemstone industry regulations,
      136
   global markets, 136–137
   history, 117–119
   merchandising trends,
      137–140
   other accessories materials,
      135
   other gems, 131–133
     amber, 131
     coral, 132
     jet, 132
     real pearls, 129, 132–133
   plated and filled metals,
      123–124
   precious metals, 119–123
     gold, 119–121
     palladium, 123
     platinum, 121–123
     price comparisons, 119
     silver, 121, 122
   precious stones, 125–129
     diamonds, 125–128
     emeralds, 128–129
     real pearls, 129, 132–133
     rubies, 128
     sapphires, 128
   semiprecious stones, 130
   trade organizations, 138
   trade publications, 139
   trade shows, 139
Microfibers, 48–49, 52, 221
Military hats, 270
Millinery, 259
   see also Hats and hairpieces
Millinery couture, 263, 264
Minerals in leather tanning, 79
Mink, 114
Mittens, 295
Moccasins, 148
Modacrylic fiber, 51
Model millinery, 264, 277

Models (first samples), 333
Mohs scale of hardness, 124,
     125, 136
Molded luggage, 201
Money clips, 369
Monocles, 310
Mother-of-pearl, 135
Mother's rings, 343
Mousquetaire (French)/opera
     (English) gloves, 295
Multicultural markets, 233
Museum stores and private-label
     umbrellas, 303
Mushroom hats, 270
Mutation in furs, 95

NAFTA. See North American
     Free Trade Agreement
Napoleons (boots), 148
Napping hides, 73
Nacre, 132
National brands, 250
Native Americans
   furs, 92, 93
   jewelry, 365, 366
   leather tanning, 68
   moccasins, 148
Natural materials, 58
Natural pelts, 95
Naugahyde, 76
Neck gusset of necktie, 243
Necklace watches, 391
Necklaces, 336–337, 338
Neckware. *See* Scarfs, ties, and
     handkerchiefs
Needlepoint, 46
Needlepoint lace, 52
Netting, 52
Nonprescription eyewear, 318
Nonputrescible material, 71
Nonwovens, 51–52
North American Free Trade
     Agreement (NAFTA), 297,
     369
Notions and trims, 54–58
Novelty gloves, 295
Novelty jewelry, 366–367
Novelty thumb, 291
Novelty tie patterns, 245
Novelty wellness, 218
Novelty yarns, 49
Nubuck, 73
Nugget rings, 343
Nylon, 48, 50, 155, 216, 221
Nylon hosiery, 217, 218

Obi belts, 207
Off-price stores, 251
Off-shore facilities, 297
Oil tannins, 70
One-size-fits-all, 231
One-size-fits-all gloves, 292,
     295
Opals, 135
Opaque gemstones, 124
Opaque hosiery, 218, 224
Open-to-buy, 349
Opera gloves, 289, 295
Opera necklaces, 337
Organizers, 197
Orthodox Jews and wigs, 281
Orthotics, 141
Ostrich skin, 74
Outdoor footwear, 155
Outer covering of handbags,
     183
Outlast, 267
Outseaming on gloves, 293
Outsoles, 152
Over-the-calf socks, 222
Over-the-knee socks, 222
Overnight cases, 202
Overseaming on gloves, 293
Oversize umbrellas, 305

Padding of handbags, 183
Paisley tie patterns, 245
Palladium, 123, 333
Pantyhose, 217, 222
Parasols, 302, 305
Parti-colored hose, 216
Pashmina, 47–48
Pashmina scarf or shawl, 241
Paste settings, 335
Patent leathers, 73, 81
Patina in leather, 80
Patio umbrellas, 287
Pattens, 148
Pattern making for shoes, 153
Pavé settings, 335
Peacock Era, 182, 240, 362
Pearls, 129, 132–133, 328, 353
Pedorthists, 174
Pelerines, 240
Pelts, 95
Pendant necklaces, 337
Performance fibers, 221
Period jewelry, 331
Periwig, 279
Personal leather goods. *See*
     Small personal goods

Petersham binding for hats, 266
Phallic symbols, 147
Pickling hides, 71
Pierced earrings, 339, 363
Pigment or paint for hides, 73
Pillbox hats, 263, 270
Pillow lace, 52
Pin dot tie patterns, 245
Pince-nez glasses, 310
Piqué seams on gloves, 293
Plaid tie patterns, 245
Plaited straw, 266
Planned purchases, 190
Planners, 197
Planograms, 168, 169, 170
Plastic, 135
Plated and filled metals, 123–124
Platform shoes, 150, 157
Platina, 121
Plating hides, 72
Platinum, 121–123, 333
Platinumsmiths, 333
Pleather, 76
Plexiglas, 362
Plucking furs, 96
Pocket squares, 249–250, 255
Pocket watches, 381, 382, 391
  see also Watches
Pockets, 180
POI systems, 167
Point-of-purchase (POP), 396
Pointed-toe shoes, 147
Pointing furs, 96
Pointing of a glove, 291
Points, 126
Poison rings, 343
Polartec, 244
Polished rock crystals, 381
Polka dot tie patterns, 245
Pollution in leather tanning, 77
Polo belts, 207
Polyester, 48, 49
Polyvinyl chloride (PVC), 51, 76
Pontova, 186
Pony cuffs, 272, 280
Ponytail holders, 261, 271
POP. *See* Point-of-purchase
Pork pie hats, 270
Portable timepieces, 380
  see also Watches
Portfolios, 183, 197
Poulaine, 147
Pourpoints, 216

Power beads, 363, 366
Power necklaces, 367
Power socks, 219
Pragmatic fashion accessories theory, 7–8, 155
Precious metals, 119–123
Precious stones, 125–129
Precosting, 35–36
Preproduction samples, 264
Prescription eyewear, 287, 314
Previously owned furs, 111–112
Pricing, 37–38
Printed silks, 243
Prisoner of war (POW) bracelets, 362
Private labels
  of brands, 250
  in costume jewelry, 364
  in hosiery, 229
  in shoes, 167
  of umbrellas at museum stores, 303
Product development, 28–42
  line and collection design, 28–34
    color selection, 30–32
    line plan, 30
    material selection, 33
    shape selection, 33–34
    styling and designing, 29–30
  manufacturing considerations, 38–40
    domestic production, 39
    external manufacturing, 39
    internal manufacturing, 38
  manufacturing process, 34–38
    final costing, 37
    precosting, 35–36
    pricing, 37–38
    production schedules, 37
    production stages, 36–37
    prototypes and line sheets, 34–35
    specifications, 36
Production
  belts, 206
  eyewear, 314–315
  fine jewelry, 334–335
  gloves, 292–293
  handbags, 185
  hats and hair accessories, 264, 266
  luggage, 201

  scarfs, ties, and handkerchiefs, 243–244
  socks and hosiery, 220–221
  umbrellas, 305
  watches, 390
Production schedules, 37
Production specialists, 19
Production stages, 36–37
Profile hats, 270
Prong settings, 335
Protein fibers, 47–48
Prototypes, 34–35, 333, 334
Psychographic segmentation, 264
Public relations, 60
Pullman, upright, suiter, or boarding cases, 203
PVC. *See* Polyvinyl chloride

Quarters, 152
Quartz watches, 385
Queue (low ponytail), 280
Quick response, 166
Quirks of a glove, 291

Rack trade in belts, 206
Ranched fur, 94
Rayon, 48
Reading glasses, 313, 319, 321
Reading spectacles, 310
Reading stone, 310
Receiving and storing hides, 70
Regulations
  for fur industry, 97, 100–101
  for gemstone industry, 136
  for leather industry, 77–78
Reinforced toe or heel hosiery, 218, 224
Religious services and hats, 262
Rep tie patterns, 245
Repoussé, 336
Research, 60
Resource Conservation and Recovery Act, 77
Restyling furs, 113
Retailing distribution channels, 17
Retanning, 71, 72
Reversible furs, 95
Rhinestones, 133, 134, 367
Rhodium, 331
Ribbons, 45, 260
Ribs of umbrella, 304

Rice pearls, 133
Rimless glasses, 312
Ring watches, 391
Rings, 343–344
Ritz Stick, 172
Rock crystals, 327
Rolled gold, 124
Rolled gold plate, 124
Rope belts, 207
Rope necklaces, 337
Round ideal cut, 126
Royal Tombs of Ur, 327
Rubies, 128
Ruffs, 239, 241
Run-resistant or no-run hosiery,
        218, 224
Russian braid, 55
Rybuck, 73

Sable, 114
Saddle soap, 81
Saddles, 152
Sailor hats, 270
Salaries for fashion accessories
        careers, 22, 23
Sales representatives, 19
Sandalfoot hosiery, 218, 224
Sapphires, 118, 128
Sash belts, 207
Satchels, 201
Satin ribbon, 56
Scarf clips, 342
Scarfs, ties, and handkerchiefs,
        239–258
    care tips, 247
    folding pocket squares,
            255
    global markets, 247–248
    history, 239–241
    manufacturing, 242–244
        design, 242–243
        licensing, 243
        materials, 244
        production, 243–244
    merchandizing trends and
            techniques, 249–253
        catalog retailing, 253
        Internet retailing, 242–253
        store retailing, 250–252
    selling, 253–256
        customer needs, 256
        value and price, 253
    trade organizations, 249
    trade publications, 249
    trade shows, 250

traditional tie patterns, 245
    tying a tie, 246–247
Scarves versus scarfs (spelling),
        242
Scissor glasses, 310
Scotchguard, 82
Screw-back earrings, 339
Scrimshaw, 135
Scrunchies or ponies, 272
Sea lions, 77
Seamed stockings, 217
Self belts, 207
Self-selection departments, 198,
        210, 250
Self-service shoe departments,
        171
Self-winding watches, 385
Selling
    belts, 210
    costume jewelry, 375–377
    eyewear, 320–322
    fine jewelry, 351–355
    footwear, 168–173
    furs, 112–114
    gloves, 301–302
    handbags, 195–196
    hats and hair accessories,
            277–279
    luggage, 205
    scarfs, ties, and handkerchiefs,
            253–256
    small personal goods,
            198–199
    socks and hosiery, 230–235
    umbrellas, 309–310
    watches, 397–399
Semi letting out in fur
        construction, 96
Semi-hardside luggage, 201
Semiprecious stones, 130
September 11, 2001, terrorist
        attacks, 199
Sericulture, 45
Service-free environment,
        228–229, 230
Set-in thumb, 291
Setting out of hides, 72
Shaft of umbrella, 304
Shanks, 152
Shape selection, 33–34
Shark skin, 74
Shearing furs, 96
Sheer hosiery, 218, 224
Sheer-to-waist hosiery, 224
Shell of necktie, 243

Shells and stones, 58
Shock-diffusion inserts, 141
Shoe department planogram,
        169
Shoe pouches, 160
Shoe stockroom planogram, 170
Shoe therapists, 174
Shoe trees, 160
Shoe widths and descriptions,
        154
Shoehorns, 160
Shoes, 155
    see also Footwear
Shoplifting, 318
Shoppertainment, 166
Shortie gloves, 290
Shrugs, 241
Sidewall of a glove, 291
Sightholders in diamond industry,
        137
Signet rings, 328, 330, 343
Silicon sprays, 82
Silk, 45, 46, 48, 49
Silk screening, 243
Silk-flower pins, 363
Silver, 121, 122
Silver-toned metals, 118
Silversmiths, 333
Simple yarns, 49
Simulated leather, 69, 76, 78
Simulated stone, 133
Sizing and fitting of footwear,
        171–173, 174
Skimmer hats, 270
Skin-on-skin in fur construction,
        96
Skinny belts, 207
Skins, 69
Skullcaps, 270
SKUs. See Stock-keeping units
Slashing, 288
Slave ring bracelets, 330, 341,
        342
Slavery, 46
Sleeve of umbrella, 304
Slide, zipper, or Y-necklaces,
        337
Slip stiching on neckties, 243
Slouch hats, 270
Small personal goods, 196–199
    global markets, 189
    history, 180–182
    materials for, 197
    merchandising trends and
            techniques, 198

selling, 198–199
styles of, 197, 198
trade organizations, 191
trade publications, 192
trade shows, 192
"Smart" shoes, 159
Smooth-surfaced leathers, 81
Smoothly or well-woven hats,
277
Snake skin, 74
Snakes, 78
Snaps, 54–55
Sneakers, 156, 158
Soaking hides, 70
Sock linings, 152
Socks and hosiery, 215–238
care tips for, 224–225
classification of, 222, 223
global markets, 225–228
history, 215–217
manufacturing, 218–221
design, 218–220
materials, 221
production, 220–221
merchandising trends and
techniques, 228–230
catalog retailing, 230
Internet retailing, 229–230
store retailing, 228–229
selling, 230–235
casual dress in business,
232
color, 233
customer needs, 232
fashion do's and don'ts,
234
packaging, 234–235
price and value, 230–231
sizing and fitting,
231–232
terminology of, 222, 224
trade organizations, 227
trade publicatons, 227
trade shows, 228
Softside luggage, 201
Solar active thread, 267
Solar watches, 382
Soldering, 336
Solid construction of umbrella,
305
Solid tie style, 245
Sombrero hats, 270
Soutache braid, 55
South Sea pearls, 132
Spandex, 48, 50, 217, 218

Special-ordering shoes, 173
Specialty fibers, 221
Specifications in manufacturing,
36
Spectacles, 310
see also Eyewear
Spinning mills, 46
Spinning rings, 343, 363
Splits of a hide, 72
Splits in leather, 69
Splitting machine, 68
Splitting and shaving hides, 71
Spoon rings, 343
Sport bags, 183
Sports gloves, 297
Sports watches, 389
Stain-resistant leather, 77
Staking of hides, 72
Standard footwear
measurement, 154
"Standard Measurement of
Lasts, The," 154
Star rubies, 128
Star sapphires, 128
Status handbags, 182
Steamer trunks, 203
Steel, 135
Steinkirks, 240
Stenciling furs, 96
Sterling silver, 121, 330
Stick umbrellas, 305
Stick-on tattoos, 367
Stickpins, 342
Stiletto heels, 149, 175
Stock-keeping units (SKUs), 63,
319–320
Stocking caps, 270
Stockings, 222
Stocks, 240
Stoles, 241
Stone settings, 336
Stones, 58
see also Metals and stones
Stonesetters, 335
Stopwatches, 385
Store planners, 21–22
Store retailing
costume jewelry, 373–374
eyewear, 318–320
fine jewelry, 349–350
footwear, 165–166
gloves, 299–300
hats and hair accessories,
275–276
luggage, 204

scarfs, ties, and handkerchiefs,
250–252
socks and hosiery, 228–229
umbrellas, 308
watches, 394–396
Stovepipe hats, 270
Straight grain cut, 243
Stras in jewelry, 368
Straw hat production, 266
Straw for hats, 267
Straws and bamboo, 53
Stretch belts, 207
Stretch wovens, 50
Stretchers or spreaders of
umbrella, 304
String ties, 240
Stringing materials, 135
Stud earrings, 339
Studs, 369
Styling, 29–30
Subdivisions of a full hide, 71
Suede cloth, 52
Suede leather, 48
Suede-finished leathers, 81
Sueding hides, 73
Suiter cases, 203
Sumptuary laws, 288
Sun protection with hats, 262
Sun protection with umbrellas,
302
Sun-reader glasses, 321
Sunglasses, 311, 319
see also Eyewear
Sun's movement, 380
Sunscreen in hats, 267
Sunshades, 302
Super-suede, 76
Supermarkets, 235
Supermodels and furs, 103
Supernatural powers of
gemstones, 328
Support hosiery, 220
Supportive tourists, 199
Suspenders, 205, 208
Swiss watchmakers, 382, 386
Switch (hairpiece), 272, 280
Symbolism of gloves, 288
Synthetic fibers, 218
Synthetic hair wigs, 280, 282
Synthetic stones, 133

Tachymeters, 385
Tactel nylon hosiery, 219
Tahitian pearl, 132
Tail of necktie, 243

Tam O'Shanter, 270
Tanning leather, 68, 70, 71
    hazardous chemical effluents
        in, 77
Tariffs, 315, 316
Tattoo jewelry, 363, 366
Tattoo-like decorations, 367
Technology
    in gemstone enhancement,
        352
    integrated, 63
    textile, 267
    in watches, 389, 399
Teflon, 49, 82, 155, 293
Telememo watches, 389
Telescoping handles, 202
Telescoping umbrellas, 305
Television retailing of costume
        jewelry, 374–375
Templepieces in eyeglasses,
        312
Ten-gallon hat, 268
Tennis bracelets, 341, 365
Tensile strength in hides, 72
Tension-mount settings, 335
Termic watches, 389
Terrorists attacks of September
        11, 2001, 199
Textile fabrics for shoes, 155
Textile fibers, 46–49
Textile mills, 46
Textile technology, 267
Textiles and trims, 45–66
    fabrics, colors, and prints,
        59
    global industries, 60
    the hemp controversy, 47
    history of, 45–46
    merchandising trends and
        techniques, 63
    notions and trims, 54–58
        artificial flowers, 57
        braids, 55
        buttons, 54
        feathers, 57, 58
        shells and stones, 58
        snaps, grommets, Velcro, and
            buckles, 54–55
        threads, lacing, ribbons, and
            bows, 55–56
        zippers and pulls, 54
    textile fibers, 46–49
        cellulose fibers, 46–47
        manufactured fibers, 48–49
        protein fibers, 47–48

textile manufacturing process,
        49–53
    crochet, 53
    fabrications, 50
    knits, 50–51
    lace, 52
    macramé, 52
    nonwovens, 51–52
    straws and bamboo, 53
    wovens, 50
    yarns, 49
textures of textiles, 59
trade organizations, 60–61
trade publications, 62
trade shows, 62
Textures of textiles, 59
Thigh-high stockings, 222
Thinsulate, 155
Threads, 55–56
Thumb of a glove, 291
Tiaras, 271, 272, 344
Tibiales, 215
Tie clasps or clips, 369
Tie tacks, 369
Ties. *See* Scarfs, ties, and
        handkerchiefs
Tiffany settings, 329, 335
Tights, 222
Timekeepers, 380
    see also Watches
Tip dyeing furs, 96
Tipping furs, 96
Tipping on neckties, 243
Tips of umbrella, 304
Titanium, 135
Toe caps, 152
Toe rings, 343, 366
Toe socks, 224
Tomb raiders, 360
Tongues, 152
Top fine jewelry companies,
        331
Top footwear-producing
        countries in 2001, 162
Top hats, 260, 270
Top producers of handbags in
        U.S., 190
Top producing countries for fur
        pelts, 106
Top U.S. distributers of hosiery in
        2001, 226
Top U.S. distributers of socks in
        2001, 226
Top U.S. distributors of footwear,
        163

Top U.S. distributors of men's
        and boys' neckwear, 248
Topgrain leathers, 74
Tortoiseshell, 135
Total carat weight, 126
Total-look concept, 191
Tote bags, 183
Totes, 203
Toupees, 280, 282
Toyo, 186
Trade names in leather, 78
Trade organizations, 22–24
    belts, 191
    costume jewelry, 371
    eyewear, 317
    fine jewelry, 346
    footwear, 163, 164
    fur, 107–108
    gloves, 298
    handbags, 191
    hats and hair accessories, 274
    leather, 86
    luggage, 192
    metals and stones, 138
    scarfs, ties, and handkerchiefs,
        249
    small personal goods, 191
    socks and hosiery, 227
    textiles and trims, 60–61
    watches, 394
Trade publications, 22–24
    belts, 192
    costume jewelry, 372
    eyewear, 317
    fine jewelry, 347
    footwear, 164
    fur, 108
    gloves, 298
    handbags, 192
    hats and hair accessories, 274
    leather, 87
    luggage, 192
    metals and stones, 139
    scarfs, ties, and handkerchiefs,
        249
    small personal goods, 192
    socks and hosiery, 227
    textiles and trims, 62
    watches, 395
Trade shows, 22–24
    belts, 192
    costume jewelry, 372
    eyewear, 318
    fine jewelry, 347
    footwear, 163, 165

fur, 107
gloves, 299
handbags, 192
hats and hair accessories, 275
leather, 88
luggage, 192
metals and stones, 139
scarfs, ties, and handkerchiefs, 250
small personal goods, 192
socks and hosiery, 228
textiles and trims, 62
watches, 395
Trademark infringement, 185
Trading posts, 93–94
Traditional tie patterns, 245
Tramping machine for fur processing, 95
Trank of a glove, 291
Translucent gemstones, 124
Transparent gemstones, 124
Trapping animals, 93, 94
Travel boxes, 180
Travel retail stores, 193
Trend themes, 192
Triacetate, 48
Trickle-down, trickle-up, and trickle-across theories, 6, 185
Trimming and siding hides, 71
Trimmings of handbags, 183
Trims, 54–58
 see also Textiles and trims
Triplets (gems), 368
Trompe l'oeil, 254
Trouser socks, 217
Trunks, 181
Tube socks, 222
Turban hats, 263, 270
Turquoise, 131, 135
Two-piece construction of umbrella, 305
Two-way wrist radios, 389
Tying a tie, 246–247

Ultrasonic cleaners, 135
Ultrasuede, 48, 52, 76
Umbrellas, 300, 302–310
 basic styles, 305–306
 global markets, 306–307
 history, 302–303
 manufacturing, 303–305
  design, 303
  materials, 305
  parts of umbrella, 304

production, 305
 merchandising trends and techniques, 307–308
  catalog retailing, 308
  Internet retailing, 308
  store retailing, 308
 selling, 309–310
  care tips for, 310
  customer needs, 309
  price and value, 309
Under blade of necktie, 243
Underfur, 95
Underlining of handbags, 183
Unhairing hides, 70
Unique Selling Proposition (USP), 365
Unisex casual hats, 275
Universal product codes (UPC), 166
UPCs. See Universal product codes
Upholstered furniture in leather, 86
Uppers in shoes, 152
U.S. fur markets, 107
U.S. fur sales, 106
USP. *See* Unique Selling Proposition
UV blockage in sunglasses, 322

Value-adding features, 231
Vamps, 152
Vanity, accessories, or cosmetic cases, 203
Vegetable matter (bark) as tanning agent, 68, 70
Velcro, 55
Vellum, 68
Vena amoris, 117
Vermeil, 330–331
Vertical marketing of footwear, 167
Victorian period in jewelry, 332
Vintage and estate jewelry, 331–333, 363
Vinyl, 51, 76
Visor or peak, 270
Visual merchandisers, 21

Waif gloves, 294
Waist belt, 207
Wallets, 197
Washable leathers, 77, 81, 82–83
Watch chains, 391

Watch fobs, 391
Watch wardrobing, 382
Watchbands, 399
Watchcase, 384
Watches, 329, 380–402
 brand-name recognition, 382–384
 Fairchild's top 100 luxury watch brands in 2000, 384
 functions of a watch, 385
 global markets, 391–393
 history, 380–382
 manufacturing, 386–391
  design, 386–388
  licensing, 388–389
  materials, 390
  production, 390
  technology in watches, 389, 399
 merchandising trends and techniques, 393–397
  catalog retailing, 397
  Internet retailing, 393, 396–397
  store retailing, 394–396
 parts of a watch, 384–385
 selling, 397–399
  care of watches, 398
  customer needs, 399
  price and value, 397–398
 shapes of watches, 391, 392
 styles of watches, 391
 trade organizations, 394
 trade publications, 395
 trade shows, 395
Water animals used for leather, 76
Water-repellent leathers, 81–82
Waterproof and breathable (WP/B) gloves, 293
Waterproof leather, 77, 81–82
Wax molds, 336
Wearable technology, 267
Weaving, 50
Web sites
 branded, 193–194
 for footwear, 167–168
 on gemstones, 131
 handbags, 194
 retailing of leather, 87–88
 scarfs and ties, 252
 socks and hosiery, 229
 see also Internet
Wedding bands, 344

Weddings and hats, 262
Wellingtons (boots), 148
Welts, 152
Western belts, 208
Western hats, 268
"Wet blue" leathers, 71, 84
Wet operations for leather
    processing, 70–72
Wheeled luggage, 204
White ermine, 93
Wholesaling distribution
    channels, 17
Wicking, 221
Wig accessories, 281

Wigs and hairpieces, 279–283
    care tips, 282
    customer needs, 282–283
    history of, 279–280
    merchandising trends,
        280–281
    price and value, 281–282
Windproof umbrellas, 305
Windsor tie knot, 246, 247
Wood, 135
Wooden block forms for hats,
    264
Wool, 45, 46, 48, 51, 155
Work gloves, 287, 292, 295

Woven-silk fabric, 243
Wovens, 50
Wrap glasses, 313
Wraps, 241
Wringing and sorting hides,
    71
Wristwatches, 391
    see also Watches

Y-necklaces, 363
Yarns, 49

Zippers and pulls, 54
Zodiac signs, 327

NAME INDEX

AAFA. *See* American Apparel & Footwear Association
Accessorie Circuit, 12, 24, 228, 250, 275, 299, 318, 347, 372, 395
Accessories Council, 9, 13, 16, 22, 24, 373
Accessories Magazine, 24, 192, 227, 249, 274, 298, 317, 347, 372, 395
Accessories (trade magazine), 15
AccessoriesTheShow, 12, 13, 15, 24, 192, 228, 250, 275, 299, 318, 347, 372, 395
ACID. See Anti-Copying in Design
Acoma Indians, 365
Acrylic Council, 221, 227
Adams Fashion Headwear, 267
Adidas, 47, 151, 156, 158, 219, 220
Adolfo, 280
Afterthoughts, 373
AGS International Conclave, 139
Aigner Group, 393
ALDA. *See* American Luggage Dealers Association
Aldo Hat Corporation, 263
ALF. See Animal Liberation Front
All China Leather Exhibition, 88
All My Children, 374
AMA. *See* American Watch Association
Amato, Carolina, 292
Americal Corporation, 225
American Academy of Dermatology, 262
American Apparel & Footwear Association (AAFA), 61, 164
American Gem Society, 138, 345
American Gem Trade Association, 138, 371

American Jewelry Manufacturers Magazine, 347
American Leather Chemists Association Journal, 87
American Luggage Dealers Association (ALDA), 191
American Opal Society, 371
American Orthopaedic Foot and Ankle Society, 157
American Society of Jewelry Historians, 346
American Time, 395
American Tourister, 200
American Trapper, 108
American Veterinary Medical Association, 101
American Watch Association (AWA), 394
American Watchmakers-Clockmakers Institute (AWI), 394
AmericasMart (Atlanta), 12
Ames, 349
Andiamo, 205
ANFAO. *See* Optical Goods Manufacturers' National Association
Animal Liberation Front (ALF), 101
Anne Klein II, 250
Annual Clock and Watch Show, 395
Anti-Copying in Design (ACID), 185
Antique Jewelry Show, 347
ARIS Isotoner, 300
Armani, Giorgio, 47, 311, 393
Arnault, Bernard, 111
Art de la Coiffure Des Dames (de Rumigny), 280
Art of Science of Footwear Manufacturing, The, 164
Ashurbanipal (king of Mesopotamia), 302, 303
Asia Pacific Leather Fair, 88
Asprey & Garrard, 331
Asuag-SSIH, 282
Atelier, 12

Athlete's Foot (company), 165
Australian Jewellery Fair, 372
Avon, 367
AWI. *See* American Watchmakers-Clockmakers Institute
Ayscough, James, 310

Badge Sales, 185
Baekeland, L.H., 361
Bain Capital, 300
Bakelite, 361
Baker Furniture, 79
Barbie, 389
Barrymore, Drew, 261
Barse, 131
Basel World Watch and Jewelry Show, 347
Baselworld-The Watch and Jewellery Show, 395
Battle, Kathleen, 367
Baume & Mercier, 384
Bausch & Lomb, 311
Behind the Seams, 62
Belleseime, 76
Bergdorf Goodman, 260, 265
Bergen, Candice, 79
Berner Watch Dictionary, 395
Bertelli, Patrizio, 111
"Best Accessorized Television Program, The," 9
Bettley, Peter, 264
B.F. Goodrich Company, 54
BGA. *See* British Glove Association
Bible, 287
Birger Christensen, 109
Black Cameo, 366, 367
Black, John, 79
Blahnik, Evangeline, 176
Blahnik, Manolo, 10, 175–176
BLC Journal, 87
BLLA News, 192
BLLA. *See* British Luggage and Leathergoods Association
Bloomingdale's, 81, 109, 111, 229
Blue Book of Farming, 108
Bobbin Buyers Guide, 62

Bobbin Group, The, 61
Bobbin Magazine, 62
Bobbin Mexico, 62
Bobbin World, 62
Bohan, Marc, 365
Boucheron, 331
Boyle, Robert, 118
Bradshaw, Carrie, 8
Brannock Device, 172, 173
Brannock Device Company, Inc., 173
Breakfast at Tiffany's (book and movie), 354
Breitling, 396
Brendel of Germany, 311
Bridal Apparel News, 298
Brighton, 18
British Fur Trade Association, 108
British Glove Association (BGA), 298
British Hat Guild, 274
British Horological Institute, 394
British Luggage and Leathergoods Association (BLLA), 191
British Watch and Clock Collectors Association, 394
Brummell, Beau, 239, 240
Bulgari, 311, 331, 393, 399
Bulova, 384
Burberry, 311
Burdine's, 81
Burma Bibis, Inc., 248
Business Ration Plus: Leather Manufacturers & Processors, 87
Byblos, 311

Cabela's, 301
California Mart (Los Angeles), 12
Campbell, Naomi, 103, 265
Canada Fox Breeders Association, 101
Canada Mink Breeders Association, 101
Cardin, Pierre, 303, 362
Carnegie, Hattie, 263
Carroll, Diahann, 367
Carroll, Lewis, 259
Carson Pirie Scott, 109
Carter, William C., 302
Cartier, 331, 384, 393, 396, 399
Cartier, Pierre, 129
Casio, 383, 389
CAUS News, 32

CAUS. *See* Color Association of the United States
CCC. *See* Couture Jewelry Collection and Conference
Celine, 312
Celine gloves, 301
Chanel, Coco, 57, 182, 184, 185, 188, 263, 265, 311, 327, 348, 361
Charles de Gaulle Airport, 254
Charles I (king of England), 289
Charleston Hosiery, 226
Cher, 175
Chicago Apparel Center, 12, 13
Chicago Daily Hide and Tallow Bulletin, 87
Chicago Merchandise Mart, 12
China Textile and Apparel Trade Show, 299
Chloe, 312
Chopard, 331, 396
Christenen, Helena, 265
Citizen, 383, 384, 389, 396
Claiborne, Liz, 53, 76, 376
Claire's, 373
Clayson Knitting Co., Inc., 226
Cleopatra, 279
Clinton, Hillary Rodham, 260
Clocks Magazine, 395
Coach Leather, 79, 86, 193, 197, 388
Cole-Haan, 158
Collective, The, 250
Color Association of the United States (CAUS), 10, 30, 32
Color Box, 31
Colour Matters, 18
Columbia TriStar, 319
Combs, Sean (P. Diddy), 103
Concord, 388
Consumer Electronics Show, 389
Copote, Truman, 354
Coreen Simpson Regal Beauty Collection, 367
Cotton Board, 61
Cotton Council International, 61
Cotton, Incorporated, 61
Council for Leather Exports, 86
Couture Jewelry Collection and Conference (CCC), 347
Cox, Elyce, 186
Crafted with Pride in the USA Council, 39
Crawford, Joan, 260
Cristianini, 264
Cultured Pearl Information Center, 138

D3 Doneger, 31
Daché, Lilly, 263
Daikin Industries, 77, 81, 82
Daily News Record, 249, 274
Dallas Chapter of The Fashion Group International, 28
Dallas Fine Jewelry Show, 347
Dallas Market Center, 12, 14
Danskin, Inc., 226
David Yurman, 331
Dayton's, 109
De la Renta, Oscar, 103, 114
De Rigo, 311, 312
De Rumigny, Legros, 280
DeBeers Consolidated Mines, 118, 137, 139, 140
DeBeers, Diedrich, 140
DeBeers, Johannes, 140
Deep E, 47
Denver Merchandise Mart, 12
Design Intelligence, 31
Desoto Mills, Inc., 226
Diamonaire, 369
Diamond Trade and Precious Stone Association of America, Inc., 138
Diamonique, 369
Diana (Princess of Wales), 182, 260, 261
Diaz, Cameron, 182
Diego, Shannon, 45
Diesel, 312, 387
Dietrich, Marlene, 263
Dillard's, 81
Dior, Christian, 175, 263, 348
Directory of Hosiery Manufacturers, Distributors, and Suppliers, 227
DKNY, 387
Dooney and Bourke PR, Inc., 185, 190, 193
Dr. ("Doc") Martens, 151
Dress for Success (Molloy), 240
Du Pont, 216, 217, 219
Duke of Windsor, 247

E. Howard Watch Company, 381
Echo, 250
Eco-Drive watches, 389
Eddie Bauer, 79
Edward II (king of England), 171
Edward III (king of England), 93
Edward VIII (king of England), 247
efurs.com, 112
E.G. Smith Company, 47, 233

Elizabeth (queen of England), 328, 329
Ellis, B. Eldrid, 289
Embroidery Trade Association, 61
Emporio Armani, 387
English Steel Company, 293
Environmental Protection Agency (EPA), 77, 97
Escada, 137, 348
ESPN, 393
Esprit, 314
ESPY Awards, 393
ESQ watch brands, 388
Essence (magazine), 233
Estate Jewelers Association of America, 346
Estée Lauder, 186
Etro, 312
European Sunglass Association, 317
Evert, Chris, 341
Excel, 18, 19
Excel Handbags Co., Inc., 190
Export Promotion Council for Finished Leather and Leather Manufacturers, 86
EyeMagazine, 317
Eyequest, 318
Eyewear International Distribution, 312

Fabergé, Carl, 329
Facile, 76
Fairbanks, Douglas, 3
Fairchild 100 list of most recognized brands, 300
Fairchild's top 100 luxury watch brands in 2000, 384
FAME. *See* Fashion Avenue Market Expo
FASA. *See* Fashion Accessory Shippers Association
Fashion Accessory Shippers Association (FASA), 13, 22, 24, 191, 249, 274, 298, 346, 371, 394
Fashion Association, The (TFA), 61
Fashion Avenue Market Expo (FAME), 12
Fashion Coterie, 24
Fashion Footwear Association of New York, 22, 164
Fashion Group International, The, 28
Fashion Institute of Technology, 367

Favero earrings, 334
FCUSA. *See* Fur Commission USA
Federal Trade Commission (FTC), 136, 333, 351, 352
Fédération Française de la Couture, 265
Federation of the Swiss Watch Industry, 390, 394
Femme, 12, 275
Fendi, 312
Fendi, Adele, 110
Fendi, Alda, 110
Fendi, Anna, 110
Fendi, Carla, 110
Fendi, Franca, 110
Fendi, Paola, 110
Fendi, Silvia, 111
Fendi Sisters, 103, 110–111
Fenidssime collection, 111
Ferguson, Sarah, 175, 265
Ferragamo, 311
Ferragamo clutch purse, 182
Fiber Yarns, Accessories, Services and Technology (FAST) Trade Show, 228
Field, Leslie, 330
Field, Paricia, 9
Field, Rebecca, 9
Fila, 312
Filene's Basement, 109
Fisher-Price, 300
Flight, 193
FOCUS: An Economic Impact Profile of the Apparel and Footwear Industries Footwear Market Monitor, 164
Foot Locker, 165
Footwear Distributors and Retailers of America, 164
Footwear News, 164
Fossil, Inc., 387, 393, 396, 397
Foster Grants, 311
Foster, Sam, 311
Fownes gloves, 301
Fox, Fredrick, 263
Fox, Samuel, 302
Franklin, Aretha, 265
Franklin, Benjamin, 310, 311
Fred Joaillier, 331
Fred Leighton, 331
FTC. See Federal Trade Commission
Fur Age, 108
Fur Commission USA (FCUSA), 108

Fur Council of Canada, 107, 108
Fur Farm Animal Welfare Coalition, 100, 101
Fur Fashion Week, 103
Fur Information Council of America, 22, 108, 274
Fur Information Council Newsletter, 108
Fur Institute of Canada, 108
Fur Taker Magazine, 108

Gabor, Eva, 280
Galliano, John, 30, 175
Garbo, Greta, 260
Gargoyles, 314
Gaudin, Marc, 133
Gaultier, Jean-Paul, 265
GemFair, 347, 372
Gemmar Systems International (GSI), 167
Gemological Institute of America (GIA), 138
Gems and Gemology, 139
Genny, 311
Gentlemen's Quarterly, 239, 397
George III (king of England), 288
George Washington University, 203
Gerber Technology, 31
GIA. See Gemological Institute of America
Giacca, 104
Gianfranco Ferre, 311
Givenchy, 103, 265, 333, 364
Global Sources, 62
Gloves and the Glove Trade (Ellis), 289
Gloves International, Inc., 301
Gold, 139
Gold Toe socks, 231
Goldin, Anne Dee, 103
Goldsmith's, 109
Gore, W.L., 155, 293
Gore-Tex, 81, 82, 155, 293
Grandoe, 297
GSI. *See* Gemmar Systems International
Gucci, 312, 314, 396, 399
Guess?, 190
Guinness, Lulu, 51

H & M, 228
Hack watch, 394
Hall, Jerry, 175, 265
Halston Millinery, 263
Halston, Roy, 114, 263

Hamilton Watch Company, 393, 394
Handbags Direct, 194
Hanes Her Way, 218
Hanes Hosiery, 218, 230, 231, 232
Hansen, 290
Harland, Thomas, 381
Harry Potter (Rowling), 300
Harry Winston, 331
Hartmann, 205
Hat Life Directory, 274
Hat Life Online, 274
HAT Magazine, The, 274
HBO, 8, 103, 176
Headwear Information Bureau, 274
Heartfelt Hats, 264
Heaven Sent hosiery, 229, 235
Helmut Lang, 312
Hemp for Victory (film), 47
Henri Bendel, 260, 265
Hermès bag, 182
Hermès gloves, 301
Hermès ties, 253, 254
Herrera, Carolina, 175, 367
Hide and Leather Bulletin, 87
Highland Mills, Inc., 226
Hoisiery Association, 221
Home Shopping Network, 374
Hong Kong International Handbags and Leather Goods Fair, 192
Hong Kong Leather Goods and Bags, 87, 192
Hope Diamond, 129
Hope, Henry Philip, 129
Hopi Indians, 365
Horological Times, 395
Hosiery Association, The (THA), 227
Hosiery News, 227
Hot Sox Company, 232
Howard, Edward, 381
Howe, Elias, 153
Hudson's, 109
Huepoint, 31
Huston, Anjelica, 265
Huxham, Shaneen, 292

ICA. *See* International Color Authority
Illustrated Professional Dictionary of Horology, 395
Illustrator, 18
Ilux, 221
In Season Silken Mist, 233

Indian Leather, 87
Indian Leather Technolgists' Association, 86
InfoSource, 347
Ingersol watches, 382
Ingraham watches, 382
Intermezzo Collection, 24, 372
International Color Authority (ICA), 31
International Colored Gemstone Association, 138
International Fashion Accessory Trade Show, 275
International Fashion Fabric Exhibition, 62
International Fashion Jewelry Show in New York, 372
International Fur Trade Federation, 108
International Gem Society, 131, 138
International Gemological Institute, 138
International Hosiery Exposotion, 228
International Jeweler, 347, 372
International Leather Guide, 87
International Sewn Products Expo, 62
International Textile Manufacturers Association Exhibition, 62
International Travelgoods, Leather and Accessories Show, 192
International Vision Expo East, 318
International Vision Expo West, 318
International Watch and Jewelry Guild (IWJG), 346, 394
International Watch and Jewelry Guild Shows, 347, 395
International Wrist Watch, 395
Intertextile, 62
inViso, 7
Isotoner, 300
Italocremona, 311, 312
IWJG. *See* International Watch and Jewelry Guild

JA International Jewelry Show, 347
JA. *See* Jewelers of America
Jack McConnell, 263
Jaclyn, Inc., 190
Jaclyn Smith, 364

Jacob Javits Convention Center, 15
Jacobs, Marc, 175
Jagger, Bianca, 175
Japan Consumer Information Center, 157
Japan Pearl Exporters Association, 137
Japanese Association of Leather Technology, 86
JCK. *See* Jewelers' Circular Keystone Show
JCPenney, 21, 168, 229, 299, 301, 364, 375
Jewelers of America (JA), 346, 394
Jewelers' Circular Keystone, 382, 384
Jewelers' Circular Keystone Show (JCK), 347
Jewelers Vigilance Committee, 351
Jewelry Information Center (JIC), 346
Jewelry Manufacturers Association, 371
Jewelry Manufacturers Association Trade Show, 372
Jewels of Queen Elizabeth II, The: Personal Collection, 330
JIC. *See* Jewelry Information Center
Jill Sander, 312
J.J. Bausch, 310
J.L.N., Inc., 190
Johnson, Sir William, 288
Jones Apparel Group, 363
Jones, Grace, 265
Josephine (Empress of France), 216, 241

Kaneko Optical Company of Japan, 311
Karan, Donna, 186
Kartsotis, Kosta, 387
Kate Spade gloves, 301
Kate Spade LLC, 190, 312
Kaylin, L., 239
Kayser-Roth Corporation, 226, 231
KC Accessories, 186
Keds, 9, 151
Kelly bag, 182
Kelly, Grace (Princess Grace of Monaco), 182
Kennedy, Jacqueline, 263

Kent, Claire, 140
Kentucky Derby Hosiery Co.,
    Inc., 226
Kenzo, 265
*Key Note Market Report: Hand
    Luggage & Leather
    Goods,* 87, 192
Keystone Watch Case Company,
    381
Kimberley Diamond Mine, 140
King, Charles W., 6
Kirium Ti5 watch, 390
KISS performers, 150
Kiwi, 82
Klein, Calvin, 47, 76, 81
Kletter, Melanie, 3
Kmart, 349, 364
Koh-i-noor Diamond, 129
Kohl's, 299
Kokopelli, 365
Kors, Michael, 175, 185, 312,
    364
Krakoff, Reed, 79
Kunstler, Mort, 69
Kwiat Diamonds, 139

La Crasia, 297
La Perla, 312
Lacroix, 265
Lady Dior bag, 182
Lady's Magazine, 287
Lagerfeld, Karl, 110, 111, 114,
    265
Lalique, René, 329
Lands' End, 194, 301
Las Vegas Estate Jewelry Show,
    347
Lauren, Ralph, 79, 242–243
Lavigne, Avril, 240, 241
Lazarus, 109
LCI Jewelry Group, 376
Le Corre, Jacques, 264
Le Marier, 57
Leady, L.S.B., 67
Leather, 87
Leather Apparel Association, 86
Leather Conservation News, 87
*Leather, Hides, Skins, Footwear
    Report,* 87
Leather Industries of America, 86
*Leather Industries of America
    Membership Directory
    and Buyer's Guide,* 87
*Leather Industries of America
    Technical Bulletin,* 87
Leather Manufacturer, 87
Leather Markets, 87
Leathers, 87

Leavers, John, 46
Lee, William, 46
L'eggs, 217, 218, 220, 229, 232,
    233, 235
LensCrafters, 311
Leo X, Pope, 310
LeSportsac, 193
Levers, John, 52
Levi Strauss, 194
Lewis, Julie, 47
Lewis, Peter, 389
Lezanova, 77, 81, 82
Life Magazine, 182
Lil' Kim, 103
Lillian Vernon, 193
Limited, The, 373
Lincoln, Abraham, 270
Liquid Leather, 76
L.L. Bean, 301
LLHAA. *See* Luggage,
    Leathergoods, Handbags
    and Accessories
    Association of Canada
Loewe, 312
London Clockmakers Company,
    381
London Luggage Shop, 193
Louis XIII (king of France), 279
Louis XIV (king of France), 129,
    239
Louis XVI (king of France), 215
Lucci, Susan, 374
Lucida diamond, 354
Lucite, 362
*Luggage, Leather Goods, and
    Accessories,* 87
Luggage, Leathergoods,
    Handbags and
    Accessories Association of
    Canada (LLHAA), 191
Luggage, Leathergoods,
    Handbags and
    Accessories Show, 192
Lurex, 221
Luxottica, 311
LVMH Moet Hennessy Louis
    Vuitton, 140, 388
Lycra spandex, 300

McFadden, Mary, 243
McKids, 389
McLean, Evalyn Walsh, 129
MacPherson, Elle, 175
McQueen, Alexander, 265
Macy's, 81, 109, 204, 232, 260,
    263
Madonna, 103, 175
Magic Eight Ball, 389

MAGIC Interntional, 318
Malkemus, George, III, 176
Mallet, Laurie, 47
Mallory & Church Corp., 248
Malo gloves, 301
Manufacturing Jewelers &
    Suppliers of America
    (MJSA), 346
Marcolin, 311, 312
Marino, Robin, 186
Marquardt, Kathleen, 101
Marshall Fields, 109, 254
Mary of Burgundy, 117
Material World Miami Beach, 62
Mattel, 389
Maximilian, Archduke of Austria,
    117
Megeve, 386
Meltonian, 82
Men in Black II, 319
Menswear Retailing, 251
Mental Headgear, 267
Miami Men's and Boy's Apparel
    Market, 250
Microsoft Corporation, 387
Microsoft Word, 19
MIDO, 318
Mikimoto, 331
Miller, Nicole, 243, 252
Millinery Arts Alliance, 274
Mirage Jewelry Show, 372
Miranda, Carmen, 150
Mischka, Badgley, 175
Miu Miu, 312
MJSA Expo, 347, 372
MJSA. *See* Manufacturing
    Jewelers & Suppliers of
    America
MMG Corp., 248
Mohs, Frederick, 124
Molloy, John, 240
Mommeja, Laurent, 254
Monet, 373, 376, 383
Monet Group, The, Inc., 190
Montana Denim, 131
Montblanc, 384
Moore, Julianne, 79
Moschino, 311
Moss, Kate, 175, 265
Mossimo, 314
Motorola, 389
Mountain High Knitting, Inc., 248
Movado, 50, 79, 384, 388, 393,
    396
Mr. John Classic, 263
Mulberry Leathergoods, 193
Mulberry Thai Silks, Inc., 248
Munsell Color Theory, 31, 32

Museum of Bags and Purses, Amstelveen, the Netherlands, 181

NAA. *See* Neckwear Association of America
NAFFEM. *See* North American Fur and Fashion Exposition in Montreal
NAMSB. *See* National Association of Men's Sportswear Buyers
Napier, 364, 373
Napoleon (Emperor of France), 241
Nascar, 314
NASDAQ store, 252
National Association of Men's Sportswear Buyers (NAMSB), 250
National Association of Watch and Clock Collectors (NAWCC), 394
National Chinchilla Breeders of Canada Bulletin, 108
National College of Art and Design in Dublin, 265
National Cotton Council of America, 61
National Cufflink Society, 346
National Fashion Accessory Association (NFAA), 12, 22, 24, 190, 191, 274, 298, 346, 371, 394
National Football League's Super Bowl trophy, 354
National Gem Collection, National Museum of Natural History, 129
National Geographic, 333
National Industrial Glove Distributors Association (NIGDA), 298
National Jeweler, 347, 372
National Luggage Dealers Association, 191
National Marine Fisheries Service, 77
National Museum of Natural History, National Gem Collection, 129
National Network of Embroidery Professionals, 61
National Shoe Retailer Association, 164
National Sporting Good Association (NSGA), 298

National Trappers Association, 108
Natori, Josie, 56
Naugahyde, 76
Navajo Indians, 365
NAWCC. See National Association of Watch and Clock Collectors
Neckwear Association of America (NAA), 248, 249
Neckwear Industry Directory, 249
Neckwear News, 249
Neiman-Marcus, 186, 250, 254, 265
Network, 62
Neuville Industries, Inc., 226
New Balance, 158
New Orleans Hat Shop, 265
New York Diamonds, 139
New York Times, 136, 389
New Yorker, The, 265
Newton, Sir Isaac, 126
NFAA. See National Fashion Accessory Association
NIGDA. See National Industrial Glove Distributors Association
Nike, 151, 156, 158
NikeiD, 194
Nine West, 250, 312, 363–364, 365, 376, 383
No Nonsense pantyhose, 231
Nordstrom, 229
North American Fur Association, 107
North American Fur and Fashion Exposition in Montreal (NAFFEM), 107, 109
Nouveau Collection, 12
NPD Accessory Watch, 186, 191, 218
NPD American Shoppers Panel, 4
NPD Group, 373, 396
NSGA. See National Sporting Good Association

O-Town (band), 387
Occupational Safety and Health Administration (OSHA), 97
Old Navy, 373
Omega, 393
One Hanes Place, 230
O'Neil, Paul, 117
Onysko, Bob, 200
Oppenheimer, Nicky, 140

Optical Goods Manufacturers' National Association (ANFAO), 317
OSHA. *See* Occupational Safety and Health Administration
Outlast, 267

Padaung tribe in Burma (now Myanmar), 333
Pakistan Society of Leather Technologists, 86
Paltrow, Gwyneth, 103, 182
Panamerican Leather Fair, 88
PANTONE, 31
Paris Blues, 314
Paris Guild of Clockmakers, 381
Parker, Samuel, 68
Parker, Sarah Jessica, 8, 103, 175
Parsons School of Design, 367
Parton, Dolly, 280
Patek Philippe SA, 384, 386, 396
Payless Shoe Source, 171
Pearl Harbor (movie), 393
Pedorthic Footwear Association, 164
Peerless Umbrella, 307
People for the Ethical Treatment of Animals (PETA), 78, 101, 103
People Weekly, 265
Peretti, Elsa, 329, 354
Pernoud, Règine, 180
PETA. *See* People for the Ethical Treatment of Animals
PGA. *See* Professional Golfers' Association
Phantom USA Inc., 226
Photoshop, 18
Piaget, 331, 384
Picasso, 265
Picasso, Paloma, 329, 354
Pinchbeck, Christopher, 118
Pinchbeck Gold, 118
Pitkin brothers, 381
Platinum Guild International, 138, 139
Plexiglas, 362
Pluczenik Group, 137
Polartec, 244, 293
Police, 312
Polo, Marco, 45, 352
Polo Ralph Lauren, 312
P.P.F. *See* Putting People First
Prada, Miuccia, 185, 312, 364

Prada Optical, 312
Première Classe, 28–29
Prêt à Porter: Atmosphere and Première Classe, 275
Professional Golfers' Association (PGA), 393
Professional Jeweler, 346
Professional Jeweler Magazine, 347
Professional Jeweler Show, The, 347
Professional Shoe Fitting, 174
Putting People First (P.P.F.), 101

QVC, 374

Radcliff, Paula, 220
Rado Vision I watch, 390
Rainbow Feather Dyeing Company, 60
Ralph Lauren/Polo Sport, 190
Randa Corporation, 248
Rangila, Muhammad Shah, 129
Raphael, 303
Ray-Ban, 311, 319
Raymond Weil, 396
Reboux, Caroline, 263
Reebok, 156, 158
Renfro Corporation, 226
Retailers Legal Handbook, 351
Rêve Avoix, 235
Rey, Felix, 56
Rhodes, Cecil, 118, 140
Richelieu, 364
Richemont, 388
Rich's, 109
Ridgeview, 235
Ritz Stick, 172
Rivers, Joan, 175
Robert Talbott, Inc., 248
Robinson-Anton Textile Company, 267
Rolex watches, 330, 355, 383, 384, 393, 396, 399
Rolls Royce, 265
Ross, Diana, 265
Rossi, William, 173, 174
Rowling, J.K., 300
Royal Ascot races, 265
Royal College of Art in London, 265
Royal Tombs of Ur, 327
Ruputer watches, 389
Ryder, Winona, 175

SAA. *See* Sunglass Association of America
Safer Travels-Safer World, 199
Safilo, 311
Sak Elliott Lucca, 20
Saks Fifth Avenue, 109, 260, 265
Salon International de la Haute Horologerie (SIHH), 395
Samsonite Corporation, 200
Samsung, 389
Samuel Aaron International, 20
Sandy Parker Reports, 108
Sandy Parker's Fur World, 108
Santo Domingo Indians, 365
Sara Corporation, Winston-Salem, NC, 226
Sara Lee Corp., 190
Sara Lee Corporation, Yadkinville, NC, 226
Sara Lee Sock Company, 226
Sarah Coventry Company, 374
Satellite Navi PAT-2GP watch, 389
SATRA. *See* Shoe and Allied Trade Research Association
Schlumberger, Jean, 329, 354
Scotchguard, 81, 310
Sears & Roebuck, 217, 299, 349
Seiko, 383, 384, 387, 389, 396
Semaine du Cuir, 88
Seneca, 310
7-Eleven, 229
Sewn Products Equipment & Suppliers of the Americas (SPESA), 61
Sex and the City, 8, 103, 176, 261
SFJ, Inc., 387
SGMA. See Sporting Goods Manufacturers Association
Shah, Nadir, 129
Shalimar Accessories, 297
Sheer Facts About Hosiery, The, 227
Shih Huang Ti, 239
Shoe and Allied Trade Research Association (SATRA), 164
Shoe and Sport Talk (SST), 166
Shoe Stats, 164
Shoesonthenet.com, 164
Shoeworld.com, 164
Shogren Hosiery Manufacturing, 226
ShopKo, 349
Signature Eyewear, 79

SIHH. *See* Salon International de la Haute Horologerie
Silk Reflections, 232
Simpson, Coreen, 366, 367
Simpson, Edwin B., 172
Skinner Division of Spring Mills, 52
Slater, Samuel, 46
Smith, RaeLeann, 78
Smithsonian Museum, 367
Society of Lether Technologists and Chemists, 86
Sole Source, 164
SoLo Marx Company, 300
Spade, Andy, 186
Spade, Kate, 29, 186
Spata Airport, 254
Spears, Britney, 219
Spectacle Makers Company, 310
SPESA. *See* Sewn Products Equipment & Suppliers of the Americas
Spice Girls, 150
Sporting Goods Manufacturers Association (SGMA), 298
Spring Mills, Skinner Division, 52
SST. *See* Shoe and Sport Talk
Stall-Meadows, Celia, 92
Stanton, Arthur, 300
Stanton, Irwin, 300
Stanton, Jan, 264
Stanton, Robert, 300
Star Caliber 2000 watch, 396
Sting, 312
Stone, Sharon, 103
Stonehenge Ltd., 248
Stras, George Frederic, 368
Sumerians of Mesopotamia, 327
Sunglass Association of America (SAA), 317
Sunglass Hut, 311, 319, 320, 396, 397
Sunshield cap, 267
Super Show, The, 299
Super-suede, 76
Superba, 248
Support Plus, 172
Susan Lucci Jewelry Collection, 374
Swatch, 382, 383, 388, 396, 399
Swiss Army, 383

TAG Heuer, 384, 390, 393
Talon Company, 54

Tavernier, Jean-Baptiste, 129
TCCA. *See* Textile Color Card Association
Tech-U-Wear, 7
Technomarine, 393
Teflon, 49, 81, 155, 293
Tennant, Ross, 173, 174
Terners of Miami Corp., 190
Textile Color Card Association (TCCA), 32
TFA. *See* Fashion Association, The
TGA. *See* Travel Goods Association
THA. *See* Hosiery Association, The
Thinking Materials, 7
Thinsulate, 155, 293
3M, 82, 293
Tie Buyer's Handbook, 249
Tie Scores, 249
Tiecrafters, 252
Tiegs, Cheryl, 280
Tiffany & Company, 133, 329, 331, 335, 337, 350, 352, 354–355, 383, 384, 396
Tiffany, Charles Lewis, 354
Time Products, 190
Timex Corporation, 218, 382, 383, 389
TMX watches, 389
Tolkowsky, Marcel, 126
Tommy Hilfiger, 364, 376, 388
Tote Le Monde, 53
totes>>Isotoner Corporation, 300
Touchstone Pictures, 393
Tourneau, 396
Training Guide 2002, 317
Trapper and Predator Caller, 108
Travel Goods Association (TGA), 191, 199
Travel Goods Show, 192
Travel Retailer International, 396
Travelware, 192
Traxtar, 159
Treacy, Philip, 10, 57, 58, 263, 265
Tucson Gem Show, 139
Tumi, 203, 205
Turlington, Christy, 265

Tutankhamen, King, 287, 327, 360
Tuxacco, Inc., 248

Ullman, Myron, 140
Ullman, Tracey, 265
Ultrasuede, 52, 76
Umbrella stands, 302
Uncle Sam Umbrellas, 306
United Nations Security Council, 136
United States Department of Treasury, 121
United States Fish and Wildlife Service, 77, 78, 108
United States Trade and Industry Outlook 2000, 77
Uomo line from Fendi, 111
U.S. Leather Industries Statistics, 87
U.S. Open tennis tournament (1987), 341
U.S. Textile Corporation, 226

V I Prewett & Son Inc., 226
Valentino, 265, 312
Van Cleef & Arpels, 331, 384
Van Gogh, 303
VCA. *See* Vision Council of America
Velcro, 185
Venture, 349
Verneuil, Auguste, 133
Versace, Donatella, 175, 265, 312
Vexed Generation, 185
VG Leather, 186
Via Spiga, 30
Vicenzaoro Trade Fair, 347, 372
Victor, Sally, 263
Victoria & Company, 363, 364, 376
Vision Council of America (VCA), 317
Vogue, 103
Vuitton, Louis, 185, 265

Wakely, John, 140
Wal-Mart, 136, 349
Wall Street Journal, 203
Waltham Watch Company, 380, 381
Warner Brothers Consumers Products, 300
Washington Updates, 249

Watch Station, 396, 397
Watch World, 396, 397
Waterford Wedgwood, 348
WeddingChannel, 355
Week of Gold Technology, 139
Weekly International Fur News, 108
Weitzman, Stuart, 139
Welch, Raquel, 280
Wells Hosiery Mills, Inc., 226
West, Mae, 332
Whitney, Eli, 46
Wilshire Wigs & Accessories, 281
Wilsons Leather, 182, 193
Winston, Harry, 129
Women's Wear Daily Accessory Supplement, 24, 274, 298, 317, 347, 372, 395
Women's Wear Daily (Monday), 14, 164, 185, 192, 218, 227, 249, 274, 298, 317, 331, 333, 347, 355, 372, 395
Woolworths, 311
World Diamond Congress, 139
World Diamond Council, 138
World Footwear Markets, 164
World Footwear Materials Exposition, 62
World Gold Council, 138, 139, 346, 349
World Leather, 87
World Trade Organization (WTO), 369
World's Fair (1939), 48, 216
Worldwide Intercolor, 30
Worthington, 264
Wrangler, 314
WTO. *See* World Trade Organization
WWD/MAGIC Show, 24, 228, 250, 372

Young, John B., 354
Yves St. laurent, 311

Zale Corporation, 348
Zuki, 102
Zuni Indians, 365
Zury, 280